PETER APPLEBOME

Scout's Honor

A Father's Unlikely Foray Into the Woods

HARCOURT, INC.

Orlando   Austin   New York   San Diego   Toronto   London

www.HarcourtBooks.com

Excerpt from "Does My Son Have to Quit the Boy Scouts?" by Susan Brenna,
Salon, July 7, 2000. Reprinted by permission of Susan Brenna.

Excerpt from "Demerit Badge" of Randy Cohen's *The Ethicist*,
the *New York Times Magazine*, July 23, 2000, Section 6, Page 19.
Reprinted by permission of Randy Cohen.

Library of Congress Cataloging-in-Publication Data
Applebome, Peter.
Scout's honor: a father's unlikely foray into the woods/
Peter Applebome.—1st ed.
p.   cm.
ISBN 0-15-100592-3 (alk. paper)
1. Boy Scouts. 2. Father and child—United States—Case studies.
3. Boy Scouts of America.   I. Title.
HS3313.A66   2003
369.43'092—dc21   2002155933

Text set in Fairfield Light
Designed by Linda Lockowitz

Printed in the United States of America
First edition
A C E G I K J H F D B

For Ben, who showed the way

Contents

Year III

Acknowledgments

One of the greatest pleasures of doing a book is getting a chance at the end to thank the people who helped along the way. Thanking them all might double the size of the book, so these are just some of them.

First and foremost were the grownups and kids of Troop 1—and your guess which was which is as good as mine. As noted elsewhere, most of the names have been changed to protect everyone's privacy, but the troop is the result of an extraordinary amount of work by both the adult leaders—the dads who helped out and the moms who did much of the organizational work—and the Scouts themselves. I owe a debt to each and every one of them.

As with my last book, I owe a special debt to Steve Harrigan, Eagle Scout and Alamo-ologist extraordinaire. He served as the world's best sounding board via our daily e-mail, and somehow took the time to read the first draft of every chapter, no matter how lame, I sent his way. Also invaluable readers and critics were Matt Purdy, Dan Pedersen, Bruce Feiler, Dave Watson, Bill Flank, and my brother, Edward Applebome.

At the *New York Times,* I'm particularly indebted to Jon Landman, once described as the greatest leader since Moses, or some such thing, who generously cut me a few weeks' slack at the beginning and end of this process, first to prime the pump, then to have some time to see the book whole. Without his support, I would never have been able to make this work. Of my many friends and colleagues on the *Times*'s Metro Desk, Susan Edgerley, Joe Sexton, Gerry Mullany, Kate Phillips, Mary Ann Giordano, Joan Nassivera, Jeanne Pinder, Bill Goss, Anne Cronin, Tony Marcano, Wendell Jamison, and others, I owe particular thanks to Patrick Farrell, who was always there to step in whenever needed and helped make it possible to somehow get this done during the most excruciating year of newspapering any of us expect to live through.

My agent, Esther Newberg, though not exactly the Boy Scout type, was a diligent, efficient, and even enthusiastic advocate for the book. At Harcourt, I owe particular thanks to André Bernard, who was a great supporter of my last book and from the start saw the potential in this one. I was extraordinarily lucky to have as my editor Andrea Schulz, who was as helpful and enthusiastic as an editor can be and was unfailingly, almost annoyingly, accurate in seeing what needed pruning or elaborating. If something goes on too long, you can assume I ignored her counsel.

My parents, Jerome and Sydel Applebome, were, as always, an enormous, irreplaceable source of support, especially during my time off when I used a bedroom of their house as my writing cottage.

At home, I would be remiss if I did not put in a heartfelt word for Wally, the world's most loyal dog, who stayed up with me every single late night I worked on this book. My daughter, Emma, was, as always, a source of joy and support. I am, of course, indebted in countless ways to my wife, Mary Catherine, who deserves most of the credit for the fact that both of our kids turned out to be such jewels.

And without Ben's humor, patience, wisdom, and grace there would be no book. Thanks, Ben, for letting me come along.

Truth in Advertising

This is the true story of the author's belated introduction to the world of Boy Scouts. All the events played out as described here—with discreet deletions and amendments for taste and tact. The three leaders of Troop 1, Bill Flank, Marc Toonkel, and Chuck Johnson, are identified by their real names, as are figures from the troop's past. All the Scouts are identified by pseudonyms to protect their privacy. Most of the Scout characters are based on real kids in Troop 1. A few of the Scout characters are composites, using the attributes and experiences of more than one kid. And the names of most of the other adults, both in Troop 1 and elsewhere, as well as the names of some of the other troops, have been changed as well. For parents or their agents trying to determine the identities of the more mischievous characters here, a simple rule should suffice: If there's anything remotely, possibly, conceivably less than perfect expressed or implied about any character here, it's not your kid.

Introduction: My Unexpected Detour

In the final year of the last tired old millennium, the year I turned fifty, I found myself doing something I hadn't quite planned on. I joined the Boy Scouts.

If we want to get technical here, I was almost four decades too old to officially join Chappaqua Troop 1, which was founded in 1913, three years after Scouting began in America. And as a committed indoorsman, whose camping experience consisted of one night sleeping in a borrowed tent with my son Ben's Cub Scout pack in a backyard in Atlanta, where we had lived before moving north, I'm not sure the troop would have taken me anyway. I'm all for sensible aerobic pursuits like tennis or running, and had a fair jump shot and first step to hoop in my basketball prime hundreds of years ago. But Grizzly Adams I am not. I can barely swim, having never quite figured out the breathing part of doing the crawl. I cannot tie a knot more complicated than the one it takes to tie your shoelaces and couldn't tell a floor lashing from a shear lashing if the fate of the universe depended on it. I've never made a fire in anything other than a gas grill. The allure of sleeping in some cold, wet, mosquito-infested tent, with bears, lethal deer ticks, coyotes, rabid skunks, beavers, snakes, muskrats, jaguars, cougars, and bears lurking around, when you could be safely at home watching a ball game, an old movie, or the Countdown of the 100 Best Songs of All Time on television—or even just sleeping in your own bed—remains one of life's enduring mysteries.

But the troop had taken Ben, and for various reasons—love, guilt, terror at how fast he was growing up, curiosity—I decided to come along for the ride. And before long I found myself poring over the Boy Scout Handbook pondering the mysteries of the square knot, tautline hitch, and clove hitch, and learning the manly art of one-pot cookcraft, the tenets of no-trace camping, and the moral code of the Scout Law. Before I knew it, I was joining Ben and his troop on countless hikes, camporees, trekorees, canoe trips, nature walks, camp-outs, bird-cage cleaning expeditions, Christmas tree sales, the annual Klondike Derby, and three week-long sojourns at beautiful Camp Waubeeka at the Curtis S. Read Scout Reservation in upstate New York.

It would be hard to overstate how unlikely all this was. I was hardly unaware of the primal role Scouting played in the lives of many boys and the mythic, Norman Rockwell way it served as a repository of enduring American values. I have since been regaled by many friends' stories—glorious and awful—of how Scouting helped define their youth. I've heard of their memories of majestic sunsets on West Texas camp-outs, being tormented by sadistic Eagle Scouts, guzzling cherry vodka smuggled into their Scout canteens, having girls laugh at their Scout uniform, smoking pieces of grapevine, and finding themselves in a canoe with an angry cottonmouth. I've heard them go on and on about their Scoutmasters—some distinctly creepy, others revered mentors and surrogate fathers, of learning skills they still use forty years later, of blowing up tents with propane stoves, of learning how to be a leader, of learning an admirable code of conduct, and of learning how to fart in Spanish, fill a fellow Scout's backpack with rocks, or score a six-pack of beer.

But as a child in suburban New York, Boy Scouting was about as much a part of my childhood as castrating calves. I vaguely remember visiting my cousin Ricky in the Bronx and going to some Cub Scout event in what seemed like a dingy urban school. I remember the odd-looking uniforms, particularly his yellow neckerchief, an item of apparel as unlikely and vestigial as pantaloons. I sat with my Aunt Hannah in old wooden auditorium seats as the Scouts were awarded mysterious badges and awards and swore abstruse oaths. It all seemed as arcane, musty, old-fashioned, and inscrutable as a Masonic initiation rite.

No one I knew in the town on Long Island where I grew up was interested in Scouting. Why would you be? On our block, in the Cretaceous Era of the 1950s and '60s, every day was game day. Everyone sentimentalizes his youth, but when I think back to my childhood on Tanners Road what strikes me most is the sense of freedom that I took for granted and that my own kids have never known. Every day after school, we all gathered at our suburban cul-de-sac for whatever sport was in season— baseball at the high school intramural field behind our house or the big lot at the bottom of the hill, football in the street with the goal lines from the Mohrs' driveway to the Zalks' tree, basketball in the Biblowitzes' driveway. (It was so long ago that today's two essential suburban sports, soccer and computer games, had not yet been invented.) We came up with our own customized local variations of certain sports—a whiffle-ball golf game played in the plantings around the birches and shrubs at the Bretts' next door, an indoor game with no rules called wrist muscles that consisted of hitting a basketball with a baseball bat into a bunch of cushions, a two-person baseball game without a bat called Giants and Dodgers, a winter basketball game in the snow that devolved into a contest to see who could throw the most snowballs into the open window of my parents' bedroom (that proved very much a one-time experience). It was all pack-like, unplanned, and innocent (well, maybe not the snowballs), and it never crossed our minds—or our parents'—that anyone needed to keep an eye on us or worry about our safety.

If I thought about Scouting at all, it was with an instinctive, dismissive snort of disapproval. The drab, hopelessly uncool uniforms! The borderline fascist marching! The hilariously goofy grownups in those ridiculous shorts, neckerchiefs, and high socks! And the world around us had the same low-level disdain. Not for nothing did the author Paul Fussell note the contempt with which "the right sort of people" view Scouting. After all, he wrote, "a general, the scourge of the Boers invented it; Kipling admired it, the Hitlerjugend (and the Soviet Pioneers) aped it. If its insistence that there is a God has not sufficed to alienate the enlightened, its khaki uniforms, lanyards, salutes, badges and flag worship have seemed to argue incipient militarism, if not outright fascism. . . . Then there are the leers and giggles triggered by the very word scoutmaster, which in knowing circles is alone sufficient to promise comic pederastic narrative."

Back then we weren't privy to that particular narrative, and truth to tell, it wasn't really the faux fascism of Scouting that turned us off; it was the dorky superfluity of it. Why put on those silly uniforms and go hiking with someone's father when we could wander off by ourselves into the woods behind our house, have crab-apple fights to our heart's content, or rocket—helmetless, of course—down Cardiac Hill on our bikes? Why join a pack when we already had one?

Still, Scouting seemed a quaint and harmless enough diversion when Ben ventured first into Tiger Cubs in first grade, then into Den 4, Pack 370, in Atlanta, the first steps in the progression from Tiger Cubs to Cub Scouts to Webelos to full-fledged Boy Scouts. Actually, Ben's initiation into Scouting passed me

by: My wife signed him up with a bunch of his friends. But I realize now that when he made us purchase a flag and flagpole
and fly the flag on patriotic holidays, when he passed a Red
Cross first-aid class in fourth grade, when he delivered impromptu lectures on how to crawl on your belly out of a burning
house or what to do on the occasion of a fall through ice—not a
huge problem in Georgia, but you can never be too prepared—
it was all part of the journey down the Bobcat Trail, which lays
out the skills Cub Scouts have to master to advance in Scouting.
Every now and then I dutifully participated. I went with Ben to
the Pinewood Derby, where kids make little racing cars from a
kit and then see which ones roll downhill the fastest. Unlike the
dads who had fancy sets of Craftsman tools and a knowledge of
how to use them, I was little help, and our rickety car with its
wobbly wheels invariably brought up the rear. For our troubles,
we got a blue Cub Scout ribbon reading I DID MY BEST and the
booby-prize designation: BEST OLD-FASHIONED. I picked Ben up
after the pack meetings at the Peachtree Presbyterian Church. I
scribbled my name a few times to show he'd completed activities in his manual, the Big Bear Cub Scout Book, a Cub Scout
version of the Boy Scout Handbook ("Tell what to do in case of
a school bus accident"), and went to the annual pack dinner. It
all seemed harmless enough. And in a world defined by play
dates—a concept my neighborhood friends would have found
as alien as Kurdish poetry—it did seem to offer broader social
interaction than his usual activities. But it all seemed like a trifling
sideshow to my parenting life, something like the Teenage Mu-
tant Ninja Turtles or the Mighty Morphin Power Rangers, that
would have its brief day and then drift into the past.

My heart was in the Darwinian competition of soccer and
basketball, and, most of all, the green pageant of Little League—
keeping score, hits and misses. I loved every moment of batting
practice or playing catch on the front lawn. When Ben evolved

from fumbling rookie to an equal partner, I was usually the one trying to drag things out before going back inside. Helping out with all his teams from second grade to fifth—the triumphal march of the invincible Braves, the Oedipal drama of the tormented Astros, the Zenlike amity of the Giants, our one moonlighting expedition into fall baseball with the scrappy River Dogs—was to me the essence of dad-dom. My travel schedule as a journalist covering stories across the South made it hard to be the main coach—my highest rank was co-coach of the River Dogs. But just bringing my antique Rawlings Ken Boyer Trapeze glove out of retirement felt like a kind of rebirth, and every time a kid called me "Coach" I got a tiny, surreptitious jolt of pleasure. So whether hitting fungoes to the outfielders, warming up the relievers, serving as first-base coach, or yelling encouragement from the dugout, I felt so right in Little League I could even put up with the over-the-top dads who were already pushing their kids toward their dates with destiny in the bigs.

One year, when I'd been traveling too much, I was invited to a cultural event—something on the order of a celebration of American poetry—at the White House on a day when Ben had a big play-off game. Half out of guilt, half out desire (hell, I really didn't want to hear a night of poetry anyway), I chose the game. Ben wasn't the star, and I wasn't really essential personnel, but I just wanted to be there. He thought I was completely crazy at the time, but was more pleased than baffled by my choice. Ben still calls it the Gold Standard of Good Dad-dom, though I did it as much for me as for him.

Ben loved Little League too, but more with a sense of enjoying the camaraderie, the uniforms, and the postgame Gatorade than with a manic passion to win every game or become a star. All his friends were Braves fans, so he became one too in a casual way, but he never studied box scores and sports-page agate the way I had when I was a kid and never suffered unduly when they lost. I thought we had bonded on my terms forever when Ben was five and danced around with me like my little soulmate during perhaps my ultimate ecstatic experience as a fan, Christian Laettner's miracle last-second shot that allowed Duke to beat Kentucky in the 1992 NCAA Basketball Tournament. But, in fact, the moment came and went in his life without leaving a trace.

Instead, it turned out, he really loved Scouting. He'd pore over the Wolf Cub Scout Book, the Big Bear Cub Scout Book, and the Webelos Scout Book: handbooks filled with a heady mix of Kipling and Indian lore, the practical (knot tying, fire safety, first aid), and the principled (patriotism, religion, respect for nature) with the requisite paranoia—even for eight-year-olds!—about drugs and child abuse. In the summer after fifth grade, I drove Ben up to Scout camp in the foothills of the North Georgia mountains. He and his friends seemed tiny and utterly innocent next to the pimply and vaguely thuggish middle school Boy Scouts who drove up with us, the screeching guitars and THUMP THUMP THUMP of Dr. Dre, Nirvana, and Puff Daddy leaking out from the headphones of their Discmans like premonitions of the dark mysteries of teenagerdom to come. The rudimentary, military green army surplus tents on their wooden pallets seemed an invitation to a horrid week of heat stroke and poodle-sized Georgia mosquitoes. Two men in Scout uniforms were spending the week there as Cubmasters or packmasters or whatever they were called. I couldn't tell if they were saints or lunatics, but whatever my outer limit of good daddom was, it sure as heck didn't stretch that far. Ben came back glowing with tales of wondrous rafting trips on perilous rapids, fabulous all-protein and carbohydrate dinners, and amazing experiments in minimalist personal hygiene.

So when we moved to New York when he was eleven, one way to ease his transition seemed to be to join the local Scout troop. And I had particular reason to see that the transition worked. There is a dreaded moral abyss to which all modern men are in danger of descending—the fallen state of being a bad dad. Some dads are indeed failures as fathers and as humans—bigamists, family deserters, wife beaters, Type A jerks who never stop barking into their cell phones at Little League games. But caught between hellish demands at work and a vague ideal of the nurturing New Age Man, many men feel like they're guilty no matter what they do. And moving one's family, with its potential to wreak grievous and irreparable psychic harm to frail juvenile psyches, can be seen as prima facie proof of bad dad-dom. So I was thrilled to find a new Scout troop for Ben, and even willing to participate a bit to ease the transition. I was excited to sign him up for his new Little League, but he had only a year left to play. So if the main event was going to be Scouting, I figured I'd give it a try too. Better the dorkiness and potential social ostracism of Scouting than the eternal damnation of being consigned to the circle of hell reserved for substandard dads.

In that spirit, after my wife had done some investigative reporting on the two Scout troops in town, I found myself one September evening at our town hall attending Troop 1's annual organizational meeting. It reminded me of nothing so much as my cousin Ricky's inscrutable pack meeting. A handful of dads and moms were gathered in the tan upholstered chairs in a meeting room. As I walked in they were poring over the proposed schedule for the upcoming year, checking every date against the school calendar, discussing the order of camp-outs and camporees and hikes with Jesuitical precision and seriousness of purpose. At the front of the room was a man who looked to be in his midsixties with a bristling white beard and steel-rimmed glasses, wearing a Boy Scouts of America T-shirt, a red Boy Scouts windbreaker, and olive pants with a tooled leather

Boy Scouts belt. There were long discussions about whether the Clear Lake camp-out would conflict with Young Writers Day or whether the canoe camp-out could be held on the same weekend as the eighth-grade social. The man at the front of the room pondered each scheduling dilemma with an aggressively professorial mien. He'd cock his head, check his legal pad, and posit solutions ("What if we held the Court of Honor on the twelfth and move the overnight canoe trip to the weekend of the fifteenth?") like a general plotting strategy for a winter offensive. After much animated discussion, they'd go on to the next event. I did my best not to nod off and scurried out when the meeting finally ran its course. If passing up the White House for Little League was largely for me, this was definitely for Ben.

What happened over the next year was not at all what I was expecting when I left that meeting room. But, to my utter surprise, I soon found myself sucked in to Scouting. I liked the way it brought kids and dads together in a totally noncompetitive way. I liked the skills and values—well, most of them—that it taught. I liked being in a group that, in the end, wasn't about whose kid was going to be treated like royalty because he had the best fastball and whose was just tolerated because he wasn't a star. I loved the hiking on the Appalachian Trail or in the myriad forests just up the Taconic Parkway, and I came to tolerate— sometimes—the camping that came with it. And before too long I found myself wanting to know more about Scouting, the boys in it, and how its retrograde rituals fit into the hyperactive, jaded lives kids live in contemporary suburbia. Scouting could not recreate for my son what I liked about my childhood. But in some ways it offered a different version of the same experience, one so many kids lose out on now as they shuttle between music lessons, soccer games, religious school, SAT tutoring, and whatever else they start doing by middle school to make their résumés look good for the Ivy League.

And once I got involved, the venture seemed to offer a lot. A way to learn about the too-rich-for-my-blood town to which I had moved, a place that soon became semi-famous as the residence of the Clintons, those plucky avatars of timeless values. A way to grab hold of my son as he plummeted way too fast toward the terrifying maw of teenagerdom and the real separation not far beyond that. A window onto something that seemed at once a defining slice of Americana—square and traditional in the best sense—and a lunkheaded anachronism intent on rendering itself totally irrelevant.

And finally, it seemed an oddly appealing way to contemplate my diminishing place in the cosmos. Barreling toward the big Five-O, and facing the predictable demon of self-doubt and the specter of closing doors, Scouting seemed an intriguing vehicle for taking stock as I navigated the shoals of midlife angst. Rather than get divorced, quit my job, move to Montana, buy a cherry-red Porsche, study Buddhism, or take up the flute, I decided to hike into the woods with a bunch of kids and try to figure out what Lord Robert S. S. Baden-Powell was up to when he founded Scouting in 1907. I'm not saying this was the smartest choice in the world. I'm not even saying it seemed like such a great idea at the time. I'm just saying it's what I decided to do.

"Adventure, learning, challenge, responsibility—the promise of Scouting is all this and more," my Boy Scout Handbook read, following the greeting from Chief Scout Executive Jere B. Ratcliffe, who beamed out at us with a beefy air of congenial affability. "Are you ready for the adventure to begin?" Well, as things turned out, I wasn't ready at all. Not for the latrines at Camp Waubeeka. Not for the Scouts' gourmet Beefaroni/ramen noodle/mystery meat/oatmeal campfire stews. And certainly not for the Scouts' proclivity for kicking up ugly controversies and ill will by choosing to expel gays and atheists—even if they had achieved Scouting's top rank as Eagle Scouts. Having finally bought in to the virtues of Scouting, I was immediately forced to confront its vices and to wonder whether Scouting was destined to become just another cultural battleground in American life, charged turf in which you had to take sides for or against them.

And that turned out to be one more thing that I wasn't ready for. Because having grown up a card-carrying member of the Scouting-averse constituency, and disagreeing with their expulsions of gays and atheists, it should have been easy to know which side I came down on. It was not. Scouting may be an anachronism, a holdover from Edwardian England and the dying days of the American frontier that's rapidly losing out in the vast new suburban marketplace of kid-oriented events and attractions. But if it's a throwback, it's still a resonant one that over the years has enrolled more than 100 million American boys, evolved into a global movement that now includes 25 million boys in 217 countries and territories, and become so much a mirror of the way Americans see themselves that many people are amazed that Scouting began in Britain, not the United States.

Scouting has always been a conservative organization, and in the past several years those conservative instincts have seemed to be driving the organization off a cliff. Still, the more time I spent around Troop 1, the more I came to feel that if the corporate bureaucrats who run Scouting from their bunker in Irving, Texas, have a lot to learn, the members of the liberal thought police who managed to turn Scouting into a hate crime do too. And, to my surprise, in the end what was admirable and worthy about Scouting seemed far more important than what was stupid and narrow about it.

But all that came later. First I had to figure out how to tie the damn knots.

Year I

1: Canoeing at Jerry's

Since 1976, Troop 1 has been coming to Jerry's Three River Canoes and Campground on the Delaware River between New York and Pennsylvania for the 13.5-mile canoe trip from Pond Eddy, New York, to Matamoros, Pennsylvania, that begins the Scouting calendar each September. It was easy to see why.

When the Delaware was discovered—at least by white guys—by Henry Hudson in 1609, he described it, a bit redundantly, as "one of the finest, best and pleasantest rivers in the world." And from the time the Lenni-Lenape Indians first began plying it in hollowed chestnut logs, its 330 miles, and particularly the 73.4 miles of the Upper Delaware, have been viewed as some of the most scenic stretches of navigable river in the Northeast. Once polluted, the river is now full of brown and rainbow trout, smallmouth and striped bass, walleye, pickerel, panfish, carp, catfish, and white suckers, and the Upper Delaware, which is burrowed into the Appalachian Plateau, has become the most popular canoeing river in the Northeast. The river begins near Hancock, New York, at the edge of the Catskills, and meanders down past tiny riverside hamlets like Buckingham and Lordville, Kellams and Callicoon, which had their heyday in the era of the Erie Canal. It makes its way in artful twists and turns past spectacular shale and sandstone cliffs rising several hundred feet in the air and finally empties into the Atlantic Ocean at the mouth of Delaware Bay.

Ben and I joined the assembled masses of Troop 1 on a crisp September morning at the troop's traditional meeting place at Roaring Brook Elementary School. We caravaned up the Taconic Parkway, across the Bear Mountain Bridge, through the desultory town of Port Jervis. As we arrived at the river, I had two conflicting thoughts.

The first thought was that, all things considered, this didn't seem too bad. Ben had been to one of the troop's weekly Wednesday-night meetings and seemed almost instantly at home there. One father I knew in Atlanta had referred quite proudly to his bratty kid, who found something to whine about at every birthday party, Little League game, or school trip, as "oppositional"—as if his kid's fits, snits, and tantrums bespoke some glorious inner reserve of independence and creativity. Ben was not oppositional. He tended to assume that the natural order of things was benign, not malignant, and that other kids were likely to be benign too. So while he didn't really know anyone in the troop, he was immediately a part of it, happy to plop down on the floor with the other kids intently listening to the Troop 1 Scoutmaster, Dr. Flank, the white-haired gentleman from my introductory session, give pretrip instructions on gear, garb, and canoeing technique. And truth to tell, what was there not to like in spending a gorgeous fall day canoeing down the Delaware River? Even for me, who was maybe a tad oppositional, this trip felt like a felicitous, wholesome introduction to our new life as rugged venturers into the great outdoors, especially since it was not likely to entail sleeping outside, forgoing indoor plumbing, or coping with animals better viewed at the zoo or in wildlife videos than in the wild. The trees were showing the first reds, yellows, and golds of fall. Our fellow Scouts and Scout dads, in their Timberland, Columbia, and Patagonia outdoors gear, seemed full of virtuous vigor and good cheer. Jerry's World Headquarters, a ramshackle wood frame cabin with a Direct TV satellite dish on top and canoeing safety instructions and photographs of visiting bears on the walls, had a pleasantly behind-the-times quality that seemed worlds away from our immaculately manicured little slice of suburbia in Westchester County. Two golden Labs and one black Lab jumped in and out of the water nearby and a crew of beefy young men took your money, carried canoes on their head, and transported adventurers in vans old enough to have survived Vietnam. And it was either this or rendering myself inept at some household chore, so it wasn't like I had a better alternative.

The second thought was that maybe I should have paid more attention to the waiver I had signed from the Three Rivers Canoe Corporation. I had absentmindedly skimmed the legalese acknowledging that I was fully aware that canoeing down the Delaware River carried inherent risks, dangers, and hazards that might result in "injury or illness including, but not limited to, bodily harm, disease, fractures, partial and/or total paralysis" and other things that I was disinclined to experience. The waiver added that there was, of course, the danger that the guide might misjudge terrain, weather, and water level; and the risk of unforeseen events like falling out of my canoe and drowning. (At one time, an average of ten people a year drowned in the Delaware, a number that has declined to two or three a year since the National Park Service took over management of the upper part of the river in 1978.)

As Dr. Flank, a retired chemistry professor, stood in the tall grass down the hill from Jerry's World Headquarters building, waving his paddle above him like Crazy Horse brandishing his rifle as he prepared to attack the cavalry, a third disquieting thought began to nag at me: I didn't have the slightest idea how to paddle a canoe, especially down the rapids clearly marked on the mimeographed map we had been given. And the more Dr. Flank went on, the more I found myself thinking about the helpful hand-lettered sign next to the pay phone: "Any serious life threatening or medical emergencies 911 in effect in this area."

True, Ben and I were lined up next to perhaps twenty kids, some brawny high school kids, most scrawny little twerps barely out of elementary school, and if they could do it, I guessed I could. Of course, like all good Boy Scouts, we were prepared. We had our balers, made by keeping the handle and bottom but cutting the top off one-gallon plastic milk jugs with our Swiss army knives. We had tied the baler to the seat of the canoe using some knot or another that the kids knew even if I didn't. We had on our bright orange personal flotation devices. We had our spare clothes, extra pair of wool socks, and bag lunch all tucked into the hermetically sealed waterproof bag Ben and I had purchased at great expense earlier in the week. Most of us had compasses just in case. I'm not sure in case of what—my guess was you were going to paddle downstream whether it was E-SE or E-NW—but we had them anyway. We had our first-aid kits with assorted bandages, creams, poultices, scissors, and tweezers. We were led by Dr. Flank, who at sixty-seven had only done this about a thousand times. He was aided by his able assistants: Mr. Johnson, a middle school science teacher; Mr. Toonkel, who owns a business that sells plumbing and heating supplies; and our Dudley Do-Right, all-star Scout, Senior Patrol Leader Todd Davis, who was only in tenth grade but gave off an air of imperial confidence as he walked around checking kids' life vests and conferring with Jerry's minions.

But the more Dr. Flank went on, the more I started wondering if this was such a great idea, especially since, as Dr. Flank helpfully reminded us, a drowning is eight times more likely in a canoe than in any other form of aquatic conveyance.

"Listen up!" shouted Dr. Flank, glaring at the kids like some kind of Old Testament prophet on a bad hair day. Dr. Flank had various forms of address, I came to learn, and this was his full-throated "YOU-BETTER-LISTEN-VERY-CAREFULLY-TO-EVERY-WORD-OR-YOU'LL-PROBABLY-DIE" mode. First, he told us that the water temperature was about 50 degrees and went on and on about how fast hypothermia, which can be fatal, would set in if we found ourselves under water for any length of time. The body loses heat 240 times faster in water than in air, and a person capsized into water below 55 degrees Fahrenheit can face hypothermia, which causes disorientation, drowsiness, and lack of coordination, within fifteen minutes or so. I wasn't all that happy to jump into a cold swimming pool on a hot summer day, much less face death by frigid dopiness like one of the first hapless city slickers to die in a wilderness horror movie, stumbling through the forest in a dull, chilly haze until falling nose first to the ground stone dead, too addled even to check his stocks before dying.

Then he ran through the proper technique for the J stroke, which allowed the person in the rear of the boat—me—to use the paddle as a rudder to steer the boat as we moved downstream. The idea, as any idiot who has ever paddled a canoe knows, is to begin with a forceful stroke, propelling the canoe forward, then to bring the paddle around behind the canoe as if forming a J. We all mimicked the J stroke, our paddles whooshing through the air on cue. I stroked dutifully, hoping the mere motion would turn me into an accomplished canoeist.

"Follow the black snake," Dr. Flank went on, meaning the clear ribbon of water indicating there were no rocks underneath. "If you see an inverted V, it means there's a rock straight ahead. You want to steer away from the rocks. If you don't, if you find yourself stuck on a rock, this is what you do. First thing," he said. Then he repeated it louder in case any of the kids were already drifting off into other frequencies. "FIRST THING! You need to lean hard on the downstream gunwale to raise the other end of the boat above the waterline. It takes four to six seconds to fill a boat with a half ton of water. That happens today, you're in big trouble. Then, when you're stable, use the grip of the paddle, not the tip, to push yourself off the rocks and back into the water. If you do tip over, let the boat go first. You don't want the boat behind you ramming into you from behind, especially when it could slam you into a boulder. A boat full of water can squash you flatter than a pancake. You can literally be crushed to death. And then float down feet first, with your feet as high as you can get them. You don't want to get your feet caught on a rock and get pulled under. And when you go through the rapids, get off the seat and kneel down on the bottom of the canoe to bring down your center of gravity and keep the canoe stable. Leave about twenty yards between one another, and be sure to go where it's smoothest. Don't try to be a hero or you'll be a wet hero."

Ben seemed oddly oblivious to the potential disasters at hand, but my head was swimming, which was more than I could probably do if I ended up in the water. I briefly considered suggesting that he go with a more experienced partner, but then I realized that half the adults looked as spooked as I felt. *They didn't get it either!* Forget the lawyer's language about partial and/or total paralysis, which seemed terrifying but rather abstract. As we pushed the canoe into the water, getting dangerously wet and cold suddenly seemed almost inevitable.

We clambered in, Ben in front, me in back, and shoved off from the muddy banks of the river, at which point it became clear my incipient panic was not misplaced. I still had no idea how to do the J stroke. I felt like a duck with Alzheimer's—what exactly was I supposed to do?

Ben was in the front earnestly paddling away under the assumption that I knew what I was doing as our navigator. But despite my ineffectual efforts at J stroking, the boat seemed to be going where it wanted to. Maybe the better thing was to paddle on the right when I wanted to go left and paddle on the left when I wanted to go right. That's how the Indians did it in every movie I had ever seen, and if it was good enough for them, it was surely good enough for me. We tried that and splashed around for perhaps ten seconds. Other Scouts and dads, no matter how befuddled they had seemed on land, were sailing merrily down the stream, with the lads, no doubt, comforted by the assured competence of their old man. Mr. Toonkel, who was wearing a black wet suit and paddling around imperiously in a bullet-shaped kayak as he looked out for the stragglers at the rear of the flotilla, watched us from a distance, obviously sizing us up as the class dunces.

After paddling, stroking, splashing, and floundering around for another few seconds, I heard an unmistakable metallic grinding sound. Then I felt a dull, ominous thud. Then we ground to a dead stop. I didn't know much about canoeing, but, though my mind raced frantically for alternative possibilities (We'd dropped anchor? I'd accidentally activated a braking system no one had told me about? We'd been attacked by river sharks?), I quickly realized what had just happened. In my first fifteen seconds of sanctioned Boy Scout activity, I had managed to land the canoe on a rock, almost certainly setting in motion one of the cataclysmic scenarios Dr. Flank had so grimly outlined for us. Hypothermia? Flattened against jagged rocks by a runaway half-ton canoe? Drowning as our feet were being crushed under subaqueous boulders? Our old standby of partial and/or total paralysis? It was bad enough to put myself at risk, without imperiling my son as well, and the thought passed fleetingly through my brain that if I managed to drown us in our first fifteen seconds, I'd almost certainly go down in history as the single worst Scout who ever lived.

Ben shot me a look that bespoke mild annoyance, a distinct

lack of confidence in my canoeing abilities, and/or tempered amusement, rather than serious concern for life and limb. He apparently didn't realize the gravity of our peril. "We're on a rock, Dad," he said helpfully.

"Thank you for sharing," I replied, trying but failing to affect an air of blithe, I've-got-it-all-under-control unconcern. "I'm well aware of that."

"Do you know how to get us off?"

"Of course I do," I lied.

My first concern was for the risk of our boat being swamped by that half ton of water Dr. Flank had told us about. But before we could adjust our weight toward the downstream gunwale, whatever that was, something surprising happened: Nothing. The canoe did not fill up with water. We were not pitched perilously into the swirling river. We did not have to worry about floating downstream with our feet in front of us or slipping into a fatal hypothermic torpor.

Dr. Flank had made it all sound so dire and perilous back on land. But now that I had almost instantaneously put us in harm's way, it was quite clear that short of panicking and standing up in the canoe, it was going to be pretty hard to sink it. Despite the water rushing by, we seemed fairly secure in our temporary roosting place on the rock. So first we kind of shimmied the canoe off its resting place. And then, with a minimum of pushing with the paddle handle, we were able to slide off the rock, into the water, and back to our ineffectual floundering around. I had learned a little about canoeing, but a lot about Scouting. Indeed, my first Scouting epiphany was: IT'S GOOD TO BE PREPARED, BUT, IN TRUTH, THINGS ALMOST NEVER TURN OUT AS BAD AS YOU FEAR THEY WILL.

I resumed our journey with a new sense of vigor and purpose, having proved that my son was safe, after all, under my command. Ben continued paddling away. Mr. Toonkel, looking like a mustachioed mallard in his kayak, shouted out a little encouragement about proper J-strokemanship, and I gave it another go. Let's see, paddle forcefully, bring the paddle behind in a J, then straighten it out like a rudder to steer. Push it toward the left and the canoe goes to the right. Push it to the right and the canoe goes to the left. It wasn't nuclear physics. Sure enough, this time it made sense, and almost instantly I became the master of my canoe-bound domain. Before long, we were seriously hauling butt in an effort to catch up with everyone else. Within a few minutes we were in the thick of our armada. This turned out to be a pretty varied group. Two canoes held boys and their moms, which we were told was a first-ever female incursion into Troop 1's little male world. In one canoe a man with blond hair seemed to be arguing nonstop with his son. You could hear them all the way to Port Jervis.

"PADDLE, KENNETH," the man hollered.

"I AM PADDLING, DAD. MY ARMS ARE TIRED," the kid hollered back.

"THIS IS THE LAST TIME WE'RE DOING THIS, KENNETH."

"GOOD, DAD. IT WAS YOUR IDEA ANYWAY."

Several canoes were captained by older Scouts, high school kids in muscle shirts and do rags. Todd was with one of the smaller kids and Dr. Flank was with another. We were all spread out across perhaps a 150-yard stretch of river in a haphazard flotilla, joined by an occasional raft, tube, or canoe full of college kids from Pennsylvania, Hasidic Jews on an outing from communities in Rockland County, or nurses celebrating a birthday.

Once I had mastered the J stroke, our trip turned, with amazing dispatch, into a thing of quiet, surprising bliss. By midmorning the temperature was in the low 60s. The sun was bright. The sky was a vivid, cloudless blue. There was no wind and no humidity. It was a perfect day for canoeing. We paddled along, sometimes pushing the tempo to pass another canoe, sometimes trawling at a leisurely pace. The river was relatively high, which meant it didn't take much work to keep up with the group, and the canoe slithered effortlessly over most of the rocks beneath us. The air was thick with wildlife, here a turkey vulture, there a hawk. We spotted a bald eagle within the first hour and watched the Canadian geese squawking overhead.

Before long, we passed our first rapids, which turned out to be a blink-and-you-miss-them affair known as Staircase Rift. It presented us with pleasingly churning water that felt like a very mild version of the wave machines at landlocked water parks. So much for the horrific rapids. (See Epiphany #1 above.)

Before long, it was time for lunch. We paddled our canoes to the shore and pulled them out of the water at a brushy gravel bar called Mongaup Island. Ben and I found a commodious rock to sit on, opened up our waterproof bag, which looked like a small body bag, and pulled out our lunch—two peanut-butter-and-jelly and two turkey sandwiches, a bag of sesame sticks, chocolate-chip granola bars, carrot sticks, and, the *pièce de résistance,* a Snickers bar for each of us.

The big kids largely hung out together under a big pin oak tree, the two women and their sons ate under another, and everyone happily unveiled a profusion of modest delights— giddy bags of brightly colored M&Ms; gaudy deli sandwiches of turkey, pastrami, and ham; coveted containers of Pringles; plastic bags full of pretzel rods; one kid's famous homemade teriyaki beef jerky; assorted trail mixes or "gorp" of peanuts, walnuts, Craisins, raisins, dates, apricots, Rice Chex, Cheerios, chocolate drops, and Lord knows what else; Cokes and big plastic Nalgene jugs of water and Arizona Iced Tea and drink boxes of toxic but irresistible Yoo-Hoos.

We all pretty much ate what we brought, but the snacks like the trail mix and pretzels got passed around. When we got ready to get back in the canoes, Mr. Toonkel walked through the group with a big bag full of red, green, purple, and orange Tootsie Roll Pops, which he gave out to grownups and kids alike. Fortified and sucking happily away, we packed up our bags, wrappers, and debris, emptied it all into garbage bags stowed in our waterproof bags, climbed back into the canoes, and shoved off.

The rest of the way was even better. The rapids past Mongaup Island and Butler Falls were more challenging, and after the river bent sharply to the right about three-quarters of the way through our route, we turned into the most spectacular scenery of the trip—250-foot sheer cliffs rising from the left banks of the river, which made us feel like agreeably inconsequential bit players at the bottom of a sublime aquatic canyon. We waved jauntily to the onlookers up on the bluffs. It was by now hot enough for everyone to take off their jackets and fleeces and make the trip in T-shirts, many of which soon got very wet. I'm not sure who fired the first splash, probably some of the younger kids trying to aggravate the older ones, but as we sailed under the cliffs about half the boats started splashing each other, a use of the paddle that Dr. Flank had not mentioned in our initial briefing but now seemed to tolerate as acceptable youthful exuberance.

Ben would have been perfectly happy to be a combatant, but I opted for a safe, dry distance from the hostilities. Instead, we got ourselves wet in the exhilarating final plunge down Sawmill Rift, where you were supposed to hug the right side of the stream while avoiding a bunch of massive boulders strewn casually around in the middle. We bounced on through, not exactly candidates for some PBS white-water rafting epic, but feeling we'd got our money's worth nonetheless. Then we exited the canoes—Jerry's minions were on hand to turn them over, dump the water out, and affix them to the top of the ancient, rusted-out vans. We'd been on the river, counting lunch, for about five hours.

We'd made the trip largely as a solitary pair, sharing a canoe and sharing a lunch, so it felt more like a father-son outing than a Scout outing. But once we all hit land, we became a group, like returning explorers who now had our perilous journey in common. We all helped Jerry's men lift the canoes and compared notes about this or that rapid or rock. Todd Davis came over to us to see how we did. Todd had a way of walking that made him look like he was bouncing off the soles of his feet and a gift for talking to younger kids as if they were his equals instead of the awed squirts they felt like.

"This your first time canoeing?" he asked Ben, who nodded. "You guys did good then," Todd said. "And you were smart enough to stay pretty dry." Then Dr. Flank came over, checked on our progress, and told us he was glad we had joined the group. We all milled around, then piled into the vans in anticipation of being repatriated to mere civilization and bounced and rocked our way merrily back to Jerry's. From there, we recovered our gear, threw it in the car, and stopping only to worship at the shrine of the Golden Arches, headed for home. Despite myself, I'd liked every part of it—the trip to a place I'd never been, the physical exertion of the canoeing and the meditative bliss of floating down the river, and the sense of being a part, however tenuously, of this armada of dads and kids. I loved the idea of Mr. Toonkel handing out the Tootsie Roll Pops to the kids and dads—who pampers dads in this world? And what I liked best was doing it with Ben, and on his turf, not on mine.

2: Trustworthy, Loyal, Helpful

"Guys. Guys. Keep it down. Guys. Guys. Pay attention, OK?"

There were many things that could be said about Bob Heller, most of them having to do with his remarkable ability to stay asleep. He was legendary in the troop for the four alarm clocks he used to wake up each morning, the three beepers he needed to rouse him for nighttime calls from the Volunteer Ambulance Corps, the way he could be blissfully snoring away in his tent at nine in the morning as all around him younger Scouts who had been up since seven were brewing up some dubious concoction for breakfast, loudly debating the fine points of Starcraft, the favored computer game, or yelling about just who was to blame for bringing to camp the seven-inch butterfly knife Mr. Toonkel had just confiscated. But though he was a high school junior overseeing a bunch of middle school kids, one thing you could not say was that he had any ability at all to keep the others quiet or to get them to pay any attention to him as he was trying to impart various essential truths of Scouting wisdom.

The troop met every Wednesday evening from 7:30 to 8:45 at the Roaring Brook Elementary School. And it took only a few meetings to get a sense of the cast of characters and the way each meeting was a delicate balancing act between the forces of chaos and the forces of light. There had been some semblance of order at the beginning of this week's meeting, held three weeks after we returned from canoeing. The dramatis personae waltzed in, affecting the odd mix of adolescent bravado and pallid ghetto style ("Yo!" "What's happenin?" "'Sup dude?") that has become the mark of the suburban teenager. A few shot baskets in the gym with its eight-foot-high hoops. One threw a rubber ball against the wall. A few sat down and leafed through their Scout Handbooks.

After a while, Dr. Flank barked out, "All right, let's get going," and the kids lined up in three rows. These represented the three patrols, the basic unit of troop organization. At the top of the troop pecking order was the Senior Patrol Leader—Todd Davis, of course. Below him were Bob Heller and Jack Larson, the two assistant Senior Patrol Leaders. All of them were high school juniors. Each patrol had a Patrol Leader, usually an eighth or ninth grader. The patrols were filled out by the rest of the kids in the troop, most of them in sixth and seventh grades. The meeting began with a reasonably earnest recitation of the Pledge of Allegiance. That was followed by an equally respectable version of the Scout Oath ("On my honor, I will do my best / To do my duty to God and my country / and to obey the Scout Law / To help other people at all times / To keep myself physically strong, mentally awake and morally straight") and the Scout Law ("A Scout is trustworthy, loyal, helpful, friendly, courteous, kind, obedient, cheerful, thrifty, brave, clean and reverent"). Neither, of course, is to be confused with the Scout Motto ("Be Prepared") or the Scout Slogan ("Do a Good Turn Daily").

But within a few minutes, all that sense of civility and order was forgotten in the face of a series of unspeakable disasters that had apparently afflicted the troop. Soon Scouts were strewn like wreckage from an accident across the wooden floor, each one facing a peril more dire than the next. There was Louis, lying on his back, his right arm apparently immobilized by some fall from a tree, errant axe blade, marauding bear, portage mishap, spelunking dunking, rock-climbing fall, wild-dog mauling, unexpected blow from an improperly lashed tree limb, or any other rogue catastrophe. The rest of his patrol gathered around. Their task was to make a sling out of a Scout kerchief, an item none of them had ever been known to wear or carry, which may have explained why, even in this desperate hour of need, Louis was clearly fighting off the urge to break out laughing.

"Guys. You tie an overhand knot in the largest angle of the triangle," Bob said, reading from the newest version of the venerable Scout Handbook. "Now place the sling over the chest with the knot at the elbow of the injured limb and one end over the opposite shoulder. Guys. Pay attention. Guys? Guys. Guys!"

"I did not have sex with that woman, Miss Lewinsky," said Louis, his eyes closed, apparently delirious from his injuries. "She was only there to deliver the pizza."

"Guys. Be serious. OK. OK. It's cold out. He's turning blue. What do you do?"

"One of the inaugurated presidents died of hypothermia from a cold Inauguration Day."

"No he didn't, you idiot. He died of pneumonia."

"Guys, cut it out. We're doing first aid. Not presidents."

"McKinley."

"Not McKinley. He was shot."

"At his inauguration?"

"No, not at his inauguration. Years later."

"Guys. Guys. Cut it out."

"So who got pneumonia at his inauguration?"

"Garfield."

"The cat?"

"No, not the cat. James A. Garfield. The president."

"No, he was shot too."

"Guys. Guys. Guys."

And so it went, with no one ever paying appropriate tribute to the memory of William Henry Harrison, who at the age of sixty-seven delivered an endless 8,500-word inaugural address hatless and coatless in a frigid drizzle, caught cold, and died of pneumonia thirty-one days after entering the White House in 1841 as the ninth president. Had the Boy Scout Handbook been around at the time ("Getting chilled during an outing can be miserable and sometimes dangerous . . . you should always be equipped for a surprise storm or cool evening winds"), he might have had a happier and lengthier term in office.

But we digress. As did most of the other Scouts around the room, where similar scenes of potentially fatal carnage were also playing out. The theme for the meeting was first aid, as opposed to nights reserved for canoeing or Jeff Gottlieb, the suburban frontiersman who came every year and showed the Scouts his deerskin moccasins, skins from roadkill, and homemade stone tools. All around the room, in clumps of five or six kids, Scouts were preparing splints for lower-leg and thigh fractures and treatments for hypothermia, frostbite, and heatstroke. They were practicing the walking assist, one-person carry, four-handed seat carry, and two-person carry, all of which enabled Scouts to transport their fellows around with no gear necessary. They used wooden poles (though of course strong saplings, tool handles, oars, and tent poles would have done in a pinch) to fashion a stretcher out of a blanket (a tent fly or a sleeping bag with the bottom corner seams opened would also have sufficed). Oddly, no mention was made of the fallback position of lashing together three metal pack frames. Amid the general chaos, Scouts were responding to shouted questions about treatments for burns, bleeding, poisoning, snake bites, bee stings, jellyfish stings, heat exhaustion, frostbite, blisters, sprained ankles, and fish hooks stuck in your skin.

"How do you tell a third-degree burn?"

"Charred flesh! Skin may be burned away!"

"Do you remove clothing?"

"Yes!"

"No! It might be sticking to the flesh."

"Right!"

"Do you apply creams or medicine?"

"No! Wrap him in a blanket and get him to the hospital!"

"Yes. Good."

"Now, bites and puncture wounds..."

Troop 1 membership in recent years had gone up and down between about fifteen active Scouts to about forty. At the moment the figure was near the higher end. It was not exactly a spit-and-polish assemblage. At the first meeting of the year in early September, Dr. Flank had given a stern lecture about coming to the meetings appropriately dressed. As it turned out, he gave the same lecture every year, to only modest effect. For Troop 1, "appropriately dressed" did not mean, say, coming with your Scout neckerchief properly held in place with a slide. It did not mean any kind of headgear—whether a mesh cap or a broad-brim number—or Scout socks or belt. It basically meant showing up looking reasonably neat wearing the traditional field uniform shirt and khaki pants, which these days usually meant cargo pants with many hundreds of pockets large and small.

Troop 1 was a somewhat motley assemblage in other ways as well. The constant factor was the adult leadership. Dr. Flank, Mr. Toonkel, and Mr. Johnson all had kids who had graduated from the troop years ago. Dr. Flank had a long commitment to Scouting; he had been active ever since he was a Scout in Philadelphia in the 1940s. Mr. Johnson, whose title was Troop

Committee Chairman, and Mr. Toonkel, the Assistant Scoutmaster, were both former Scouts who had drifted into it as volunteer leaders when their kids were in Troop 1 and then stayed.
Dr. Flank had a Ph.D. in chemistry and a fierce, bristling quality that inspired respect and a bit of fear from the kids. Mr.
Johnson was laid-back and laconic, more likely to roll his eyes at
the kids than to bark at them. And Mr. Toonkel, who sported a
bushy mustache he sometimes waxed up for an amiably villain-
ous quality, was a study in perpetual motion who always seemed
to have some project he wanted the kids to tackle. The three
men were like old fishing buddies, who knew each others' favorite recipes and quirks so well that they ran the troop with a
sort of telepathic empathy. The other dads, like me, who showed
up at the weekly meetings, mostly just hung around and
watched, or chatted quietly among themselves, until it was time
to take their kid home.

The troop composition varied from year to year depending
on how many new kids were recruited and how many older ones
stayed around, but it was usually structured like a pyramid, with
a sparse crop of senior boys at the top and larger classes of
younger kids at the bottom. Most kids joined at eleven or twelve
and dropped out by sixteen or seventeen, as Scouting was replaced by high school sports and social activities or squeezed
out by the crush of schoolwork. So the goal was to keep at least
two or three older high school kids around to keep the younger
kids quiet at the meetings, share the teaching, and serve as role
models. Next came the younger high school kids and older
middle school ones, peach fuzz beginning to crop up on upper
lips, who had been around the troop long enough to attain the
status of veterans. This meant either that they (A) knew a little
and shared it, or, more commonly, (B) conferred on themselves
the status of aspiring wise guys and shared that too. At the bottom were the younger middle school kids like Ben, new to the

troop and often to each other, who mostly watched in awed, cowed, respectful silence. The older kids had often achieved the coveted rank of Eagle Scout. The younger ones were dutifully collecting their merit badges and working on advancement from Tenderfoot, to Second Class, to First Class, to Star, to Life. It all had the quality of an adolescent anthill, at once chaotic and quite rigorously organized.

A casual inventory of the cast of conspicuous characters would have begun with Todd, the third Davis brother to make Eagle, whose blond good looks, trim build, consummate Scout skills, and air of energetic self-confidence stood in sharp distinction to the awkward and unsure younger kids still trying to find their way. It's yet another indicator of Scouting's diminished status in American life that the term Eagle Scout is as likely to evoke suspect inferences (goody two-shoes, repressed straight arrow) as glowing ones (high-achieving, All-American kid). But it was hard to find much not to like in Todd Davis. At various times he was on the varsity soccer, swimming, and track teams. His house was full of musical instruments—piano, vibraphone, cellos, clarinets, saxophones—and he was an ace trombonist who played or sang in six different musical assemblages ranging from all-state and county jazz bands to rock garage bands to the high school a cappela group called the Acafellas. He was photo editor of the student yearbook and an accomplished photographer on top of being a master of sundry Scouting skills. It was not clear when he slept and, indeed, he often had the slightly bleary look of someone trying to cram twenty-four hours of activity into seventeen or eighteen hours of day.

Becoming a Scout was an easy choice for Todd. The middle Davis brother, Jeff, a senior, was an Eagle Scout, and the oldest sibling, their brother Robert, is still a troop legend: He earned an astounding fifty-one merit badges (it takes twenty-one to make Eagle), more than any boy in memory and almost certainly more than anyone in the history of the troop. Todd's thirty-eight may well have been second. When the Scoutmasters sized up kids for their outdoors skills, Todd was the standard they judged against. You did not have to attend many meetings to start hearing Todd Davis stories. When he cooked, the Scoutmasters were quick to remind newcomers and the other Scouts, it wasn't some pedestrian one-pot stew. He liked to cook dishes with Spanish rice, or elaborate pizzas, or apple pies for dessert. For breakfast, he brought vanilla frosted cinammon rolls that baked in an Outback Oven, sort of a Mylar dome perched on top of a Coleman stove, or pancakes or a cheese omelet he'd bring in a plastic bag and then cook. He'd bring a hunk of sausage and cut the meat in neat slices and then cook it up in a skillet, while the younger kids waited like supplicants to get a slice. He did too many things to be fixated on Scouting, but it was an important part of his life. He wasn't self-conscious about Scouting the way some kids were. If people didn't appreciate it, he figured that was their problem. He worried where Scouting was headed and took his role in the troop seriously. He was aware that for some kids Scouting counted mostly as a credential, like those kids who made Eagle—one more item for their college résumés— and then more or less disappeared. It offended his sense of what Scouting was supposed to be. But, that aside, he had liked being a little Scout, and he also liked being a big one, helping the kids set up their tents or learn to cook on their Coleman stoves, giving a hard time to the wise guys, watching the new kids come into the group. Trustworthy. Loyal. Helpful. Friendly. Courteous. Kind. Obedient. Cheerful. Thrifty. Brave. Clean. Reverent. I had no way of knowing how he stacked up on all the twelve elements of the Scout Law, but as far as I could tell, he was doing pretty well.

If Todd Davis was one version of contemporary boyhood, the Polo Boy was another. The image of the Polo Boy had stuck with me ever since I first saw him staring out with a glazed expression of cool disdain from an advertising poster in the Boy's Department of Bloomingdale's in White Plains. He's got the exquisite, sexually ambiguous WASP features of the Polo cosmology and wears a Ralph Lauren Polo for Boys denim shirt ($37) over a white T-shirt, the two top buttons on the shirt and the two buttons on the collar unbuttoned. He has long dirty-blond hair cascading down over his shirt collar, one strand of which tumbles over his face obscuring his right eye. He's holding an old brown wooden baseball bat with frayed black tape on the handle. It's a ridiculous art director's conceit. Kids use metal bats and have for twenty years. And if they occasionally use wooden ones, they're sleek Louisville Sluggers or something comparable. No kid has used a bat vaguely resembling this one since 1972.

Still, if the image doesn't reflect reality, it does ooze attitude. Polo Boy's eyes are narrowed into little slits, his lips pursed. Who knows what he's so mad about? Maybe he had a learning disability or severe attention-deficit disorder. Maybe he can't read. He killed his investment-banker father. He's a runaway from a sadistic Parisian boarding school. He's a brilliant computer geek whose brain processes information at too high a level to allow him to talk to anyone. His mom's a movie star with a drinking problem who left him with a bored Danish nanny, who does her nails and talks to her friends on the phone all day. Or maybe he's just mad that he's supposed to bat and all he has is this ridiculous wooden antique. Who knows? Something's definitely awry. But the point is not that he's a mess, but that he's so cool, *it doesn't matter!* He's not a cautionary figure, but a study in style, Madison Avenue's idea of a hip contemporary kid, and he's as likely to be a Boy Scout as he is to have Glenn Miller or Benny Goodman CDs in his Discman.

As I hung around the troop I began to see Todd Davis and the Polo Boy as two poles of contemporary boyhood. It wasn't quite like the old comic stock image of the angel in white with halo on one shoulder and the devil in red with pitchfork on the other. Todd was not without a bit of attitude himself, and both types have their place in the psychic makeup of adolescent boys. But the media are full of celebrations of gifted-but-screwy variations on the Polo Boy—surly athletes, profane rappers, druggy actors, bored scions of famous families. All the positive images we have of Scouting are as antique as the Polo Boy's ridiculous prop of a bat. Try to come up with an advertising campaign or contemporary pop culture image that makes use of Scouts in a nonironic context. It can't be done. Even when Madison Avenue wants to portray an all-American scene, it might be a kid and his floppy-eared dog or a soccer mom and her happy brood or Little Leaguers or almost anything other than a Scout in his uniform. Now when Scouting shows up in popular culture it's often as an arch or campy effort in mockery, like the February 2000 issue of *Out* magazine, which features on the cover a too-pretty Scout with thick lips and a pink sleeveless Scout shirt and inside features a fashion spread ("Snap to it, boys. Scout camp's in full swing, and your old beige uniform just won't cut it anymore.") of Scouts in $128 khaki industrial poplin shirts and $115 pale rose short-sleeve sweatshirts.

So if Todd was at one end of the scale and the Polo Boy at the other, the sixth, seventh, and eighth graders who formed the heart of the troop seemed like an intriguing laboratory of unchanneled adolescent possibility, all floating barely formed somewhere between the two. Halo or pitchfork? Todd or Polo? Trustworthy, loyal, helpful or cool, detached, ironic?

For now, the great middling masses of Troop 1 defied easy categorization. The youngest ones, just out of elementary school, were too cowed to affect much more than an air of respectful solicitude. The older ones included samples of almost whatever Boy Scout stereotype you wanted—nerd, straight arrow, misfit, jock, all-American kid, unpretentious average Joe.

Some of the kids came in matched sets. Hal and Herb were identical twin eleven-year-olds with identical braces and identical T-shirts showing a TV remote control and the words "IT'S A MAN THING. YOU WOULDN'T UNDERSTAND." They were in constant motion, usually either conspiring with or sniping at each other, and no one ever had the slightest idea which twin was which. Sam 'n Eric, who only seemed like twins, were SUV-sized football players and world-class hams who liked to play at being the class clowns. Knowing that they were guaranteed an amused and appreciative reception from their peers, they'd be the ones to ask, in mock bewilderment, what *Russian Water* was when Dr. Flank was talking about canoeing down *rushing water.* Though only a year older than Hal and Herb, they seemed ready for high school and were partial to metal music, dirt bikes, acting tougher than they were, and acting totally shocked, baffled, and hurt whenever any of the adults called them on their behavior. Barrett, Jonah, and Mark, the Three Amigos, were pint-sized motormouths who had been in the same Cub Scout pack since third grade. Left to their own devices, they tended to rattle on about an amazing mix of subjects—meteorology (Barrett's specialty), computer drives, the Simpsons, rocketry, James Bond, fighter jets. Les and Rick were clearly visitors from another planet, dropped off at the meetings or driven to camp by well-meaning parents, but totally uninterested in Scouting. They spent the meetings huddled together like refugees, watching from a distance and occasionally glancing at their watches to see how soon they could go home. The only question about them was how long they would last before dropping out.

Others were very much one of a kind. Elliot, who had brought the homemade beef jerky to the canoe trip, was a science and math whiz who never seemed to go anyplace, summer or winter, without a heavy fleece, and whose measured air of bespectacled gravity always reminded me for some reason of the older of the two Darling boys in *Peter Pan*. Bernie mixed an utterly cherubic mien and a fondness for technology with a blithe disregard for anything the Scoutmasters ever said. If he wasn't showing off a forbidden weapon in his best Homer Simpson voice, he was climbing a tree while the Scoutmasters were trying to keep the troop organized. Doug had the most advanced case of computer lust in the group. He always seemed a bit lost and forlorn offline, rattling on and on about strategy for Terrans, Zergs, and Protoss in Starcraft like an emigré pining for the plugged-in Old Country. Allen, a blend of Chef Emeril and Napster, wore Teva sandals with wool socks summer and winter, rain or shine. He was usually either cooking up a respectable quiche or breaking into the kind of show tunes or early Beatles songs no kids listen to anymore. George was a blur of stray ions, unable to slow down or sit still, who drove even the other kids a bit crazy with his air of perpetual puppy-dog excitement. Louis was small and serious with round glasses, and looked and acted like Harry Potter. Jimmy was the biggest seventh grader on the planet, a hulking football player with an intense, serious air and a wry, cutting wit. Tommy, even at twelve, seemed ready to outgrow the whole thing, as if the only test he really worried about was the one for his driver's license. There were sons of lawyers and sons of doctors, sons of auto repair shop owners and sons of teachers. There were Jews, Catholics, Baptists, and Methodists, but only a smattering of Asian kids and, as was pretty much true of the town as a whole, no blacks, though years ago Milt Williams, a local trumpet teacher and the father of the singer Vanessa Williams, had had a son go through the troop and was Scoutmaster or assistant Scoutmaster for many years. There was a grandson of Woody Guthrie, who attended meetings in his Scout shirt and black seaman's cap.

And then there was my son. We like to think of our kids as extensions of ourselves, but already at eleven Ben was getting to be his own person. His best quality, I thought, was an impeccable inner compass. He seemed strikingly detached from most of the world's social currents, oblivious to rap and pop music, uninterested for the most part in pro sports, sort of agreeably square. He'd go from one interest to another—space travel, the Civil War, an endless profusion of books, favorite films we watched together like *The Godfather I* and *II, Airplane,* and, a little later, *Dr. Strangelove*—at his own pace, not all that concerned about whether it was fashionable or cool or on anyone else's radar screen. Which, no doubt, was one reason he liked Scouting. For all the kids in the troop, it took a certain degree of self-assurance to do something that didn't bring much social reinforcement. But Ben loved the outdoors, and he was far more cooperative than competitive. Scouting fit his temperment. I sometimes asked him who was the smartest or the best athlete or particularly popular among the kids he knew, but he just shrugged. He didn't seem to think in terms of comparisons. Even his biased father knew he wasn't perfect. He was an average athlete—he did fine at soccer and baseball—but didn't have a passion to compete; and at eleven he had a modest ring of baby fat and needed to be in much better shape. If I worried about anything about him, I worried a little he'd end up a wuss. And, though no father should say this, I wished he had just a small bit of Polo Boy's ironic, knowing cool in him sometime. I loved all kinds of music, particularly jazz and the more ragged varieties of country. He'd pick up on a song I played every now and then, usually something with a sense of humor. But while his sister knew every pop group out there, he seemed mostly oblivious to music. It was a place, like sports, where I was looking for a connection between us that wasn't there. And sometimes I worried that Ben was too nice for his own good. Every father wants to shelter his kid, and I was glad he was eleven going on twelve, not sixteen. But I also know it's a competitive world out there, probably more so where we lived than most places. I watched him sometimes and worried that he needed just a little bit more of a jagged edge. At the same time, I was thankful to have found this amicable oasis for him to attach himself to after our move.

The meeting was coming to an end. We began with a calm pageant of ceremony and tradition and devolved predictably into adolescent disorder and mass confusion; the trick was to bring the meeting back to an even keel before it broke up. This was not an easy thing. By then the energies of the evening had often reached a manic peak. There were jokes to be continued. Alliances to be nurtured. Rivalries to be picked at. Fun still to be had. But between Dr. Flank's fish-eyed stare, Mr. Toonkel's no-nonsense traffic management, and some firm words from Todd Davis, it usually got done.

So at 8:35, after the splints and dressings had been peeled off, the first-aid equipment had been stowed, and the Scout Manuals closed for the day, Dr. Flank looked around, checked his watch, and commenced to bring order to the chaos.

"All right, make a circle. C'mon, it's time to finish up," Dr. Flank barked, in the same stern tones that got the meeting going. He put up his right hand in the Scout sign, the three middle fingers upright, the thumb folded over the pinky, and barked, "Signs up," in the Scout's fairly civilized signal for silence. Most of the kids did the same. Sam 'n Eric and Hal and Herb continued chattering away for a moment, but after Todd walked over in front of them and shot them the evil eye they quieted down too. The whole group dutifully formed a circle and joined hands, their arms crossed right over left, each Scout clasping the hand of the Scout or Scoutmaster on either side of him.

"I think we learned a lot tonight—at least I hope so," Dr. Flank began. "You should have learned something both about how to do first aid and how to take it seriously, because when you need it, it's very serious business indeed."

There were a few more announcements—about an upcoming merit badge seminar, the date of the next camp-out, an older Scout needing help on his Eagle Project. They all said together: "May the Great Master of All Scouts be with us until we meet again." They shook their linked arms, like a chain bouncing up and down. Then they let go. It was time to go home to homework, to familial amity or familial dysfunction, to the Yankees or Mets on television, to the Internet, to Harry Potter or Tom Clancy, to the real world, to sleep.

3: Troop 1 and Other Chappaquacks

When asked how kids had changed over his half century in Scouting, Dr. Flank invariably shrugged his shoulders and said, "Boys are boys. There's not much difference." But whether or not the kids had changed, Scouting certainly had. Troop 1's story is a microcosm of that change.

Chappaqua, the largest hamlet and main population center of the Town of New Castle, lies thirty-five miles north of Times Square in Westchester County. The name, pronounced CHAP-a-kwa, comes from the town's earliest denizens, the Indians of the Wappinger Confederacy, part of the Algonquin language group of the Mohicans. As best as anyone can tell, Chappaqua derives from *Shapeqwa,* an Algonquin word translated—depending on who's translating—as "running water," "boundary," "place of separation," "laurel swamp," or, most lyrically, "place where the wind rustles through the leaves."

The descriptions are not idle verbiage. When the land around the town and most of Westchester County was purchased by an Englishman named Colonel Caleb Heathcote for one hundred pounds from the Indians' Chief Wampus in 1696, it was described as "gardens, orchards, arable lands, pastures, feeding woods, underwoods, meadows, marshes, lakes, ponds, rivers, rivulets, mines and minerals." Its first white settlers were

Quakers, drawn from Long Island in the 1720s by the abundance of water, and the Meeting House built in 1752 still stands on Quaker Road. Even today, the town looks impossibly green and pastoral—like a place where the wind rustles through the leaves. If you look past the suburban bustle and harried lawyers pacing back and forth as they bark into their cell phones at the railroad platform in the morning, it can take your breath away.

The village grew hardly at all, existing as an obscure farming outpost of less than 1,500 people, until 1846, when the New York and Harlem Railroad came to town. Suddenly farmers could get their wares to New York by train rather than horse-drawn stagecoach and people from New York, for better or worse, could get to the town. Chappaqua's first commuter and most famous pre-Clinton resident was the crusading newspaper editor Horace Greeley, who bought his dream house and farm there in 1854. He came up from New York almost every weekend back when the train ride took two hours and eighteen minutes each way. He farmed, shot the breeze with the guys hanging out on Main Street, and gave Chappaqua its first taste of fame when he ran for president against Ulysses S. Grant in 1872. His opponents called his supporters Chappaquacks, and Greeley's race was a disaster. He won only six of thirty-seven states and died a few weeks after the election. Best known for proclaiming, "Go West, young man," his last words had the same tightly edited, aphoristic quality: "It is done. I have fought the good fight. I know that my Redeemer liveth." His statue now stands forlornly by the access road to the Saw Mill River Parkway, which split the town in half when it was built in 1934.

Thanks to the new railroad, the town of New Castle, the governmental unit that includes Chappaqua and the much smaller village of Millwood, grew from 2,401 in 1900 to 3,573 in 1910 and 5,176 in 1920. But it wasn't until the great suburban boom of the 1950s, when the town mushroomed from 8,802 in

1950 to 14,338 in 1960—it's about 18,000 now—that Chappaqua changed fundamentally from an isolated village in northern Westchester to an upscale suburb. And today it's like much of suburbia only more so, with more SUVs, bigger and more expensive houses, and one nail salon per female resident. The current wisdom is that Chappaqua is really the Indian word meaning "high taxes." It has terrific schools that residents continually obsess about, eight million organized activities for kids, and an air of competitive bustle that's in dramatic distinction to its genuinely lovely stone walls, verdant greenery, rushing streams, placid ponds, and country serenity. I had never heard of it before we moved there. But after the arrival of the Clintons in 1999, Chappaqua became well enough known that most people around New York, at least, have learned to put the accent on the first syllable instead of pronouncing it cha-PA-kwa, and most realize it's not the place where Teddy Kennedy drove his car off that bridge. In recent years, we've even come up with enough of our own misbehavior to put the town on the map. One school year ended with a furor over a little black book assessing the sexual habits of high school girls that was circulated on the Internet by high school boys. The next began with a preseason party for the high school football team for which some really thoughtful parents had hired a stripper to entertain. It's a nice place to live, but, to tell you the truth, it could probably use a bit more of the Scout Law somewhere in its collective suburban unconscious.

The village now shares geography and little else with the community that existed in 1913 when the first group of boys in town put on khaki uniforms and campaign hats and called themselves Boy Scouts, three years after the Boy Scouts of America was incorporated. There were ox-drawn carts, animal droppings, and simple frame buildings where ninety years later suburbanites would buy Tuscan cannellini beans, walnut raisin biscotti, and Key lime tarts at the Chappaqua Village Market. And Scouting's evocation of community, service, nature, and faith, which now can seem quaint and dated, hit the town like a bracing summer squall.

The Scouts' philosophy and organization was a blend, and as we shall see not always a natural one, of the work of Lord Robert Baden-Powell, the British war hero, author, and youth leader, and Ernest Thompson Seton and Daniel Carter Beard, two American naturalists and prosyletizers for the virtues of the outdoor life. Seton and Beard, it turned out, had Chappaqua ties. Both were members of the Camp Fire Club, a pioneering group of naturalists and outdoorsmen that included Teddy Roosevelt, Buffalo Bill Cody, and Gifford Pinchot, the father of the U.S. Forest Service. The Club purchased the land on which it built its permanent home in Chappaqua in 1917, which meant Seton and Beard were regulars in town at the time Scouting was beginning in the United States.

During Troop 1's first few years, nearly every boy in town between the ages of twelve and seventeen belonged. The Reverend Otis T. Barnes was the first Scoutmaster, and the First Congregational Church, which had recently seceded from the Society of Friends, was the first sponsor. Meetings were held in Carleton Quinby's father's five-room barn. The activities were more for fun and public service than for advancement—no one had the time to work on merit badges or imagine going for Eagle. But the troop grew enough by 1930 that a second troop was formed, beginning a process in which Troop 2s formed and folded over time. In December 1941, the troop rented the one-room schoolhouse built in 1914 at the top of Old Roaring Brook Road and christened it the Scout Hut. The boys raised money to fix the floor, redo the roof, install lights, and purchase an oil burner. Families donated old furniture. And before long, the Scouts had something that's hard to imagine today—a home of their own, sitting on what today is some of the priciest residential real estate in Westchester County.

It was perhaps the peak of Scouting in town. The troop was so popular it had to set up a waiting list. There were well over one hundred kids in troops 1 and 2, and there was talk of starting a third troop. The local newspaper regularly gave spirited reports of each hike and the citations the troops won at each camporee. "Under a cold sky lit by a full moon," the *New Castle Tribune* reported on January 14, 1955, "the scouts of Troop 1 Chappaqua on Saturday January 8 held an all-night campout in temperatures that went to 16 degrees above." The Scoutmaster, George Kron, known as Jerry, owned a four-hundred-acre slice of wilderness on a mountain in Vermont, known as Beaver Valley, and the troop went there for the camp-out that began the Scout year then the way the canoe trip on the Delaware begins it now. The kids hiked; the dads and Jerry's fellow Scoutmaster, Rick Barns, hung around Jerry's cabin playing cards.

Kron retired in 1961. Barns stayed until 1967 and developed the policy that still stands—that the boys, not the adults, should plan the activities and run the meetings. In 1970, a man named Don Vanderbilt took over the troop. Vanderbilt is still Troop 1's most enduring link between the past and the present. And he's a reminder that for all the high-minded Scout rhetoric about selfless Scoutmasters and all the cheap, wink-wink, nudge-nudge insinuations about their real motives, sometimes the interactions between men and boys that form the heart of Scouting remain mysterious and unknowable.

You could not dream up a character like Donald Maxwell Vanderbilt Jr. He was a squat, never-married man who lived with his mother, worked as a mortician (in the pre-euphemism era, he listed his occupation in troop records simply as "undertaker") at a funeral home in Queens, and brought the funeral-home pillows along on camp-outs for kids who needed them. He smoked four packs of Benson and Hedges a day, quietly sharing them at times with the older kids who were already smokers. Perhaps five feet, six inches tall and weighing about 260 pounds, he was balding and drove a tiny yellow Alfa Romeo. Vanderbilt could barely squeeze his bulky body behind the wheel, and when he finally got in the whole car tilted to the side like a boat in danger of sinking. He also had a dark green Cadillac with the license plate "Scout 1," which he drove to camp-outs or when anyone else had to ride along. The kids never called him anything other than "Don," and he made it clear to any overly respectful new Scouts that was the way he wanted it.

Vanderbilt, who when asked claimed a distant relationship to the swells of the same name, grew up in Greenwich, Connecticut, and was a Scout as a kid, making it all the way to Eagle. But in Troop 1 he was not much for hiking, climbing, or any of the more strenuous elements of Scouting. Instead, he was like a combination of mother hen, favorite uncle, and the character who ran the chuckwagon in a Western movie. He loved to bake bread and cook, and a culinary highlight of every year was the full turkey dinner he'd prepare for the annual winter cabin camping trip. At the other hikes, while the kids trooped off, he'd be back cooking up a huge pot of stew. He was a connoisseur of fine cheeses—Stilton, Brie, and the choice Goudas that Bill Flank brought back from business trips to Holland. His wines tended to be good Burgundies and Bordeaux. His Scotch was Chivas Regal. This was well before anorexia became a fashion statement, and if Vanderbilt, a diabetic, felt his belly was something to be ashamed of, he never let on. Instead, he could talk about food for hours, happily proclaiming, "I'd eat shit if it had cheese on it."

He viewed Scouting as both fun and serious business, and he expected the Scouts to behave that way too. A September 1976 report from the Troop Committee read, "Our experience shows that the morale of the troop is boosted if all boys wear a complete Scout uniform." Vanderbilt expected each boy to show up in a Scout shirt, pants, neckerchief, and cap with visor. Though the kids were expected to dress in uniform, Vanderbilt never ran the troop entirely by the book. He was not above turning profane every now and then, particularly with the older kids. When he got mad enough, like the time one of the kids set a tree on fire at camp, he would end his disquisition with the words "you stupid fuck," which only managed to send the kids into spasms of glee. But he was also a great listener, with an instinctive sense of fairness and respect for kids and for how they differed and what they needed.

For almost two decades Vanderbilt went to Scout camp in the Adirondacks, taking the kids in leadership positions out to an expensive steak dinner in Lake George before camp began. Then, the kids carried his voluminous gear—bed, desk, fly net, etc.—to the campsite while he looked on like a pasha. He loved all kinds of music, and each summer brought a collection of tapes ranging from Bach and Vivaldi to ABBA. He had one of the best collections of Scout patches in the country back before collecting patches caught on in a big way, and he also collected stamps, coffee mugs, knives, and black powder rifles. He always had a short Japanese knife like a little samurai sword, and he always gave a special knife to each departing Senior Patrol Leader. Vanderbilt liked to do fancy rope splicings, where you weave the ends of two ropes together or one rope back into itself. When he was in the mood he'd sometimes teach the simple ones to the kids, who would usually gather around his tent to hang out in the evenings. When he was in a different mood, he would remove his dentures and shine a flashlight up his face, turning himself into something like a deranged, toothless pumpkin, which particularly horrified the new kids who thought his teeth were real. You didn't need Jason or *Friday the 13th* to get scared at night when you had Don Vanderbilt.

One summer, some kids found a racy magazine in his tent. No one remembers just what it was—hard core, soft core, boys, or girls—but people remember kids laughing and whispering as they passed on the news and Vanderbilt sitting on something on his bed looking very embarrassed and refusing to budge until the kids left him alone. Sometimes, when the kids milled around his tent, he would secretly record their conversations, and sometimes he would play old tapes for the troop as a way almost to summon up kids who had long since gone off to college. To the contemporary mind, the combination of single man, Scoutmaster, and anything suggestive adds up to something obviously suspicious. Once one of the older boys, John Rescigno, now a neurologist in Connecticut, asked Vanderbilt if he had ever been to a gay bar. He said he had. But, without exception, the Scouts of the 1970s and '80s said he never did and never would do anything inappropriate. He dated—women—every now and then, but admitted to friends he knew he didn't cut the world's most dashing figure.

In truth, Vanderbilt didn't have any romantic life. His life was his job at the mortuary, his home with his mother, and his extended family with Troop 1. If it wasn't suburban life by the textbook, it was a full life nonetheless, and Vanderbilt lived it his own way, handling the troop's voluminous paperwork at the funeral home while waiting for the Grim Reaper to deliver up the next cold body.

But it wasn't the 1950s anymore, and Vanderbilt was entirely aware of Scouting as a depreciating asset in American life. Scouting had became so uncool that the Scouts in the 1970s adopted a self-conscious slogan: "Scouting today's a lot more than you think." Vanderbilt would grouse about the ever-expanding panoply of organized activities for kids. "I remember when there was nothing but fishing and Scouting," he'd complain. But throughout the 1970s and '80s he still took his duties as seriously as Otis Barnes, George Kron, or Richard Barns did, showing up at a kid's doorstep, for example, if he missed three or four meetings. He sent each kid a birthday card each year. When boys left the troop, they or their parents wrote him neat, regretful letters thanking him for his help and explaining why they were dropping out.

Still, if Scouting was losing favor in the world at large, within the troop life at the Hut moved along by its comfortable old rhythms. The Hut was a squat white stucco building, one story high, with a display of the troop's Eagles and its Scoutmasters beginning with Reverend Barnes in the front foyer. There was a large main meeting room, a quartermaster room where the troop kept its camping gear, a senior patrol room (which was really more of a closet), and a staff lounge, where the adults and older kids usually hung out during meetings. Underneath was a dark, spooky basement with a dirt floor and stone walls, where the troop stored sleds and gear. The Hut was technically only open for meetings, but all the senior kids had keys, and they would sometimes hang out there after school or on weekends. The Hut was a rat's nest, but it was their rat's nest.

Troop 1 and Don Vanderbilt may have been dinosaurs, but they were taking on a mildly imperial quality, with a home that had lasted almost a half century and a leader who had been in place for two decades. But, of course, nothing lasts forever, including Don Vanderbilt. On September 25, 1990, at his dinner table at home, he suffered a heart attack so massive that he was dead before his big body hit the floor. He was fifty-one years old. A huge crowd showed up for his funeral in nearby Pleasantville, where he was decked out in an open casket, wearing an Eagle badge that the other troop leaders permanently borrowed from one of the kids in the troop.

Seen in the light of prevailing suburban fashions, it's hard not to see him as a somewhat comic figure—a rotund, balding bachelor in a Scoutmaster uniform driving that little yellow Alfa Romeo or big green Cadillac. But Vanderbilt was, at heart, serious in the best sense. Once he gave a copy of Baden-Powell's *Scouting for Boys* to Rick Barns. "To Rick," the inscription read. "My 'father' in Scouting. To he who inspires Reaps everything." And when his former Scouts talk about him today, there's a palpable sense of Don Vanderbilt as a friend, teacher, mentor, and, in his own way, an inspiration as well. Doug Rohde, a Scout who researched Troop 1's history for his Eagle project, had to add an addendum to mark Don's death: "Troop 1 can never be the same, but one can only hope that the memory of Don's optimism and devotion will inspire the troop to continue to forge ahead. Once when asked if he ever regretted not having a family of his own, Don remarked that he had the greatest family a man could want, the Scouts of Troop 1. We have truly lost a great father and a great friend."

4: Gathering of the Tribes

Our first camp-out was no mere routine expedition where the troop camped alone. Instead, it was the Paul Bunyan Camporee, a gathering of troops for which Scouts came from across West-chester County—from Ossining and Tarrytown, from Hawthorne and Yonkers, from mighty Scarsdale, New York's wealthy *Ur* Suburb—to muck through the woods, camp out in the chilly autumn air, and hone their Scouting skills.

The good news was that our Boy Scout Handbook had many pages of helpful information on how to prepare for a camp-out. "Pull on your Scout shirt and lace up your hiking boots. Grab your grub and gear. You're a Scout now, and that means you're going camping!" it began. Subsequent pages reported on where to camp and how many of us should come along. Will there be water? Are campfires allowed? There was a long checklist on the Scout outdoor essentials—pocketknife, first-aid kit, extra clothing, rain gear, canteen or water bottle, flashlight, trail food, matches and fire starters, sun protection, map and compass.

The bad news was that I had not read our Boy Scout Hand-book. And despite observing a month or so of Wednesday night meetings where kids worked on their knots and learned what to take and what not to take on a hike, my Scouting skills had not progressed at what anyone would term a dramatic rate. So while Ben had done a reasonable job of packing for himself, I woke up on a distressingly cool and cloudy October morning to realize that the wool socks, extra pair of underwear, fleece, shaving kit, and other necessities I had hurriedly thrown into my bag, a modest external-frame backpack that was a hand-me-down from Ben, were not all that would be necessary.

First, I had forgotten to purchase his cans of Sprite, the sine qua non of outdoor activity in our house. We were, amazingly, almost out of toilet paper, an item that seemed likely to come in handy during twenty-four hours in the great outdoors. And, when I belatedly checked our pack of AA batteries, it turned out we didn't have enough for one flashlight, Maglite, Mini Maglite, or whatever we were bringing along, let alone two.

It was 7:45—*just 45 minutes before we were supposed to meet the troop in the Roaring Brook parking lot!!*—and I had just finished slapping together the requisite peanut-butter-and-jelly and turkey sandwiches when the depths of our lack of preparation caught up with me. So I put the sandwiches aside, tore out of the house, jumped in the car, raced to the nearest A&P, scooped up the Sprites, double-ply toilet paper, and a four-pack of AA batteries, and frantically thrust my money at the sleepy-eyed checkout person. Then, no doubt looking like an insomniac terrorist with a colon problem or a Sprite addiction, I ran to the car and sped back home. Precious seconds were ticking away, and I'd never hear the end of it—*more bad dad points!!*—if I caused us to miss our first camp-out. I finished the lunch and feverishly threw more gear in my backpack. Fat Nalgene jars of water? Check. Insect repellent? Check. Charleston River Dogs baseball cap? Check. We'd been advised that the expedition was leaving at 8:30 sharp, so we hurriedly threw our packs into the back of the station wagon, slammed the doors, and roared off to Roaring Brook Elementary School.

Luckily, we arrived at the parking lot at 8:28. *Two minutes to spare!* Or maybe not. Because, as the seconds ticked toward the time when we would presumably synchronize our watches and head out, it was clear we were no more likely to leave at 8:30 than we were to take the Concorde to the Clear Lake Scout Reservation on the east side of the Hudson Highlands. At 8:30 cars were still pulling up, and the gathering felt more like a pre-game tailgate party than a tightly wound commando operation. In fact, as we soon learned, our schedule operated on Troop 1 time, in which 8:30 meant maybe 8:40, perhaps 8:45 or so. Men ambled across the lot in hiking boots, camouflage pants, fancy North Face shells, and old flannel shirts to discuss hiking and camping gear, favored fishing locales, and the weather. Kids jumped out of their parents' cars, vans, and SUVs and started climbing on top of the boulders just off the lot or comparing Magic cards.

Least hurried of all was our ringmaster, Dr. Flank, who had formed half of an odd couple with Don Vanderbilt during Don's tenure as Scoutmaster and then taken over after he died. A Supreme Being with a sense of humor must have picked Dr. Flank to follow Vanderbilt. During Vanderbilt's tenure, Flank had been Mr. Outdoors to Vanderbilt's more sedentary role. At sixty-seven, Flank still got excited about every hike and led the annual High Adventure trip, on which a handful of dads and older, more accomplished kids took off for a week of canoeing in the wilderness of northern Canada. Where Vanderbilt was slow and heavy, Flank was edgy and wiry, about five foot nine with a slender build, an erratically trimmed white beard, and a fringe of white hair surrounding not much on top. Vanderbilt was a political conservative, who supported the war in Vietnam; Flank was a liberal who opposed it. Vanderbilt was a connoisseur of guns and a member of the National Rifle Association; Flank didn't like *axes* let alone guns. Instead of Vanderbilt's sporty Alfa

Romeo or boxy Cadillac, Flank drove a sensible blue Volvo with a "BLAME GE" sticker on the back windshield, in reference to a decades-long controversy about the pollution of the Hudson by PCB contamination from General Electric plants along the river. While Vanderbilt's swearing was a subject of troop lore, no one could remember ever hearing a blue note issue from Flank's mouth. On the other hand, the kids feared and respected him much the way they did Vanderbilt. When angry, he could emit a glare so cold and withering it would turn even the most macho fourteen-year-old into a contrite, apologetic penitent responding with humble "yes sirs" and "no sirs" that must have been summoned up from somewhere deep in his unconscious. And though he had a wife and two grown kids, Flank viewed Troop 1 as a family in much the way Vanderbilt did.

Flank was born in Akron, Ohio, in January 1932. His parents moved to Philadelphia before he was three, then separated, and his father died soon after of what was termed blood poisoning—Flank assumes it was tetanus. Flank grew up taking care of himself by day while his mother worked. He loved the city's enormous Fairmount Park and often played hooky and hung out in the woods all day, figuring he could learn more there than in class. He'd build a fire and cook a meal, observe animals, trees, and plants, then scurry off to the library to figure out what he'd seen. And when his friends joined the Boy Scouts he did too; it struck him as a way to camp and hike and do what he enjoyed doing.

Back then troops were often huge—sixty kids or more—and led by military veterans who inclined toward more marching and drill than he would have liked. But even as an urban Jewish kid, Flank found himself taken both by the outdoors activity and by the—how to put it?—moral code of Scouting. He couldn't claim to be wholly expert in living his life in accordance with the Scout Law. Obedience in particular was never a strong point. But like Vanderbilt, he saw Scouting as something serious and worthy as well as just fun. Flank continued through school, studying chemistry and eventually getting his doctorate after doing his dissertation on "The Geometric Factor in Ethylene Oxidation Over Gold-Silver Alloy Catalysts," but he stayed active in Scouting. In Philadelphia, he helped develop a groundbreaking experiment in Block Scouting, recruiting inner-city residents, often women, to develop troops based around city blocks as a way to avoid conflicts over gang turf. He scouted out sites for troop meetings, showing up with his chemistry set and putting on a magic show to get the kids excited. And when he moved to Chappaqua in 1971 after being hired to work for Union Carbide in Tarrytown, he immediately hooked up with Scouting, first with the district, the administrative office that oversees the local troops, then with his son's Cub Scout pack, and finally with Troop 1. His personal quirks and habits—the maple walking stick he brought on camp-outs, the signature campfire tales of Lenni-Lenape Indian lore, the spectacularly bad collection of Scout couture—was not, perhaps, as eccentric as Vanderbilt's. But when Vanderbilt died, there was no question that Dr. Flank would step in. There was one speed bump about a year after he took over: The School District finally condemned the Scout Hut, which had been deteriorating for years and was deemed an accident waiting to happen. The troop printed up T-shirts and hats with the Hut in the middle of the troop seal, hauled out all its gear, and took to meeting across the street at the school instead.

Now, after ten years as Scoutmaster, Flank had made Troop 1 as undeniably his as it had been Vanderbilt's. This entailed a reverence for nature and the outdoors that bordered on the doctrinal. It reflected an ability to be stern and fear-inducing that was balanced by what some parents saw as a tendency to be overly forgiving of malefactors. Dr. Flank was as likely to help the kids with their chemistry or calculus as with their knots, and when Todd Davis had to do a photography and writing project for school, he did an artful photo essay of Dr. Flank at home and a long verbatim transcript of his wisdom on fishing, Scouting, ethics, and philosophy. Dr. Flank's influence showed up in the troop's studied disregard for many of the traditional trappings and conventions of Scouting, hence the hit-or-miss uniforms. And he clearly cared more about some elements of the Scout Law (trustworthiness and loyalty, for example) than others (obedience and reverence). "This is what happens when an aging peacenik takes over a Boy Scout troop," one of the dads once said—much more approvingly than not, but not 100 percent approvingly either.

So as we milled around, everyone knew what time we would leave—whatever time Dr. Flank wanted us to leave. Finally, he called everyone over and made sure the twenty or so kids had a ride with one of the eight dads making the trip. I ended up driving the Amigos, Barrett, Mark, and Jonah. This seemed like a stroke of luck to me, since the Amigos seemed more like Ben than the football players, would-be weapons specialists, or high school kids, and the forty-minute drive might be a chance for Ben to make some new friends.

The Amigos took the backseat. Ben and I were up front. But instead of mingling, the trio in the backseat immediately launched into a mile-a-minute barrage of Amigo talk. As in the old joke about the comedians' convention where everyone knew the material so well they just yelled out the numbers for the jokes, almost all the talk seemed to flow from previous agenda items in Amigo-land.

So first came much rapturous yakking about the SR-71, an alleged spy plane that apparently flies on the edge of the atmosphere. Then a stretch on whether test pilots still throw up after being whirled around in vomit-inducing machinery once they've done it a few times already. And which amusement park rides are most likely to produce the same result. Then Seinfeld: who would be worse to have as a neighbor, George or Kramer? Then a discussion of the "Like a Rock" song on the Chevy truck commercials ("Now let me get this straight. We're supposed to believe that driving a rock is a good thing?" asked Mark), which segued into the nature of tectonic plates, how fast they can shift and whether we could ever have an earthquake in West-chester County. Other topics included the eternal question: Which is better, Florida or California? And the tragic death of Princess Diana, which remained surprisingly disquieting and sad to them more than two years after it happened—and par-ticularly interesting because it turned out she was the friend of a friend of someone's dad. Jackie Kennedy—Why did they call it Camelot? And did you know her husband was part of the Mafia? Finally, they broke into an impromptu oldies medley— "Lollypop, Lollypop, Oh Lolly Lolly Pop," "Hound Dog," "Bar-bara Ann."

It was all precociously charming in its way, but I sat there thinking, "Hey, wise guys, what about Scouts being friendly, courteous, and whatever it is they're supposed to be to new kids?" Part of my agenda was to see that Ben made new friends, so I spent the drive wrapped up in paternal paranoia about whether he was feeling left out and pining for his old Amigos, Sam and Michael, from Atlanta. In truth, the only one fretting was me. While I was worrying, he was looking forward to the trip, thinking about gear like the borrowed tent we were bring-ing along, and enjoying the rapid-fire repartee emanating from the backseat. He was already at home in the troop, even if he wasn't yet friends with the other kids.

But I found that out only later, and as we drove up, the Ami-gos chattering away like magpies, I began to think about my friend Dan. Even though I had never been a Scout and never wanted to be one, I had a sense of the alleged wonderfulness of Scouting—making friends, learning skills, helping old ladies across busy intersections, knowing which fingers to put up in the Scout sign. This, I was perfectly willing to concede, was a good thing. It just wasn't my thing. Indeed, I was more than willing to see my lifelong Scout-a-phobia as more a failing than a virtue—part of the arrogance of the out-of-touch, northeastern chattering classes, who could never figure out why the country kept electing conservative Republican presidents.

But as I checked around and asked about friends' Scouting experiences, it became clear that though many had fond memories of Scouting, others viewed their days in uniform through a much darker lens. There were those who attended a meeting or two, then got away as soon as their parents said they could. Dan had a more noxious experience, however, and he made it clear that any consideration of the topic should include an acknowledgment of THE DARK SIDE OF SCOUTING. By this, he did not mean the depraved, child-abusing Scoutmasters who periodically popped up in newspaper stories. Instead, he meant the routine jerkiness and cruelty that some kids choose to inflict on others, an experience that formed the heart of his own dismal Scouting career.

"A bit of autobiography is in order here," Dan had said. "Unlike you, I grew up in Nebraska—Scouting's heartland if ever there were one. After a pleasant enough time in Cub Scouts and an apprenticeship in Webelos, I was ready to experience the real thing. I lasted six months as a Tenderfoot. The reason: three Eagle Scouts named Keith, Fred, and Fulgie—out-and-out sadists. Most Boy Scouts, to my knowledge, have a tradition of initiations for new Scouts on the first camp-out—some twisted inheritance from Native American culture, I'm sure. I had to eat garbage that we'd buried in the earth after dinner a few hours earlier, then swallow a bottle of Tabasco sauce.

"The problem was Keith, Fred, and Fulgie were utterly bored after climbing Scouting's last mountain to Eaglehood. They instituted a new practice of initiating each Tenderfoot not just on his first camp-out, but on his first visit to each new campground. Since Nebraska and Iowa have loads of campgrounds, at least a dozen initiations loomed before me. I made it to the third one, which I think entailed pulling down my pants and having my naked bottom stuck with various types of thorns. Appealing to a higher court was not an option. The Scoutmaster believed that K, F, and F could do no wrong. After all, they were Eagles! I decided to pack it in, and have been a left-wing Democrat ever since. But I don't think I'm out of touch—at least with my own past—when I say that fascism, whiffs of the *Hitlerjugend,* and serious psychiatric disorders all need to be addressed in any honest look at Scouting."

Well, the *Hitlerjugend* seemed to be taking things a little too far. But I began to remember that even Ben's sunny foray to Scout camp in Georgia had not been without its moments of modest hazing in the form of towel whipping and illegal wrestling holds inflicted by the big kids on the little ones in their troop. And while the Three Amigos of Troop 1 did not seem to have anything in common with the Three Sadists of the Prairie, this was Ben's first camp-out with Troop 1, so I figured I should be alert for untoward incidents and made a mental note to myself to keep an eye on the hulking high school kids.

Before long, we arrived at the Clear Lake Scout Reservation, a 1,400-acre preserve that used to be the property of a world-famous authority on glaciers named Dr. William B. Osgood Field Jr. We passed a park rangers' house with a great, big wood carving of a bear out front and turned onto a rutted, narrow road now jammed with Dodge vans, rusted-out Chevys, and fancy new Ford Explorers. Compared to Chappaqua, it was relatively light on fancy Acuras and Lexuses and more weighted toward meat-and-potatoes American models with bumper stickers reading "SUPPORT YOUR LOCAL POLICE" or "I'M PROUD OF MY EAGLE SCOUT." We bumped and rattled and bounced our way for a mile or so until we came to a big, open field being used as a parking lot by perhaps sixty cars.

The scene unfolding before us had a manic, tribal quality, one part *Braveheart* and one part *Lord of the Flies*. All it lacked was kids wearing headgear made out of animal hides with antlers and horns sticking out. There were a few pristinely out-fitted troops in Scout shirts, pants, hats, and neckerchiefs. But since the weather at night figured to dip near freezing, most kids wore the insignia and coat of arms not of their town or troop but of the booming universe of fashionable outdoors outfitters, of REI and EMS, Eddie Bauer and L.L. Bean, Columbia and Lands' End, Patagonia and, most of all, The North Face, whose overpriced fleeces, coats, jackets, and shells had suddenly become the first items of clothing that Ben expressed a consuming interest in owning. The kids, perhaps 250 in all, spilled into the unpaved parking lot in a great inchoate rush of adolescent testosterone. High school football players with buffed-up chests were throwing a football. Skinny little eleven-year-olds were struggling on rubbery legs with packs as big as they were. There were kids with fresh buzz cuts, kids with great scruffy manes, kids wearing the garb of every sports team ever to play, but particularly those who played anywhere near New York—Yankees and Mets, Giants and Jets, Knicks and Nets, Rangers, Devils and Islanders. Getting out of the car next to us was a creature I did not know existed, a truly radical Scout dude with a shiny nose ring and a half dozen visible body piercings and God knows how many in places I didn't even want to think about. Like a fourth dimension, this was a concept I had trouble wrapping my mind around—*a punk rock Boy Scout!*—as if a mad scientist had tried to cross two utterly dissimilar forms of life, say a zebra and a radish, just to see what kind of unnatural life form he could create.

"Everyone get their packs," Dr. Flank barked. "Make sure you have your lunches and everything you're planning to take with you, because we're not coming back until tomorrow. If you need it, be sure to bring it now."

Ben and I dutifully checked our packs.

"Uh, Dad," Ben said. "Where are the sandwiches?"

"They're in there."

"Where?"

"Somewhere," I said, a bit grumpily. What's the use of having a son to comfort you in your middle age when he can't even find the sandwiches? "Maybe they're in mine."

But, as a few moments of casual rummaging followed by five minutes of frantic digging indisputably proved, they were not in his pack. They were not in my pack. They were not in the car. They were nowhere near the Clear Lake Scout Reservation. They were at home. On the kitchen counter. Where I had left them. As I soon figured out in a doleful accounting of what had transpired when I hurriedly threw our stuff together after making the mad dash to the A&P, I had forgotten the sandwiches. I had remembered the Sprites. I had remembered the four-pack of AA batteries. I had forgotten the double-ply toilet paper. Don't ask how; I just did. All this to dash out in a fevered haste to get there before 8:30 for a trip that did not begin until 8:50 or so. Which was a reminder of Scout Rule #2: AT ALL TIMES, IN ALL ACTIVITIES, NEVER PLAY A GAME UNTIL YOU UNDERSTAND THE RULES.

The whole sequence of events—bratty kids, possible sadistic hazing, pierced-up dude Scouts, incipient food deprivation—was not the optimal beginning for our outing. But, remembering that we had survived our brush with hypothermic death during the canoe trip, I figured we were probably not in imminent peril of starving. And I had skimmed enough of my Scout Manual to at least get a whiff of the can-do positivism we Scouts were supposed to exemplify. We did have various snacks, packed in case we were stranded by a sudden blizzard or lost for days on the trail, so we wouldn't starve. And Scouts had coped with worse disasters, so we pulled on our packs—mine a Camptrails Scout External Frame Pack, Ben's a more elaborate EMS Long Trail ST internal frame pack—and began hiking with the troop toward the campsite about a mile away.

We fell in behind Todd Davis in a clump that included the Amigos, some dads I didn't know, Sam 'n Eric, and a few others. Before long the scuffing of hiking boots on the dirt trail, the gentle clanking of canteens or pots rubbing against packs, and the fraternal greetings to and from other Scouts became rather soothing. As my mood brightened a bit, it did occur to me that I had nothing against hiking, which seemed aerobic and medi-tative enough to qualify in my mind as a worthwhile activity. It was the camping that I could do without.

Our destination turned out to be a clearing in a forest of white and red oak, ash and maple. There was a ring of stones in the middle for a campfire. There were plenty of flat areas in the campsite proper that were suitable for pitching a tent, and everyone set up shop there except for Todd, who was wearing a jaunty shell and an Indiana Jones–style fedora. He took his one-man tent to the farthest reaches of the site and set it up alone, one of the privileges of being a senior Scout and a way to squeeze every sliver of authenticity out of the hike.

Ben and I found a spot and began putting together our tent. This turned out to be harder than expected. We, of course, did not own a tent, an item I had never needed, wanted, or given so much as a passing thought to in my previous forty-eight years on the planet. But it was clear that a tent would come in handy for this particular outing, so I borrowed my friend Jill's trusty REI four-person dome tent. As a noncamper, I thought of tents as old canvas Neanderthal-level shelters on the order of the ones soldiers used, so like a caveman contemplating fire I was quite taken with hers, which was made out of some lightweight synthetic fiber with flexible poles in segments linked by a bungee-like cord in the middle. She had shown us how to put it together, and we had repeated the procedure in our living room at home just to be sure we knew how. But here in the wild, our skills suddenly left us. As the dad, I felt it was my job to be able to do this, but I found myself flummoxed. Which way did the big poles go and which way the small ones? What was the deal with the rain fly anyway, and did we really need it? Was there a ground tarp in there, or were we supposed to bring our own? I was prepared to dispense with the rain fly, the covering on top of the tent that keeps moisture away from the tent proper, until Mr. Johnson walked over and, apprehending the depth of our ignorance, set up the whole tent for us. It took him about two minutes.

"It's a borrowed tent," I said in a lame attempt to convey the idea that we were not total incompetents, only temporarily stymied by this unfamiliar tent. "We haven't used this one before." He gave me a sympathetic but condescending look, making it clear I hadn't fooled anyone.

"You got your bear bag?" Mr. Johnson asked.

"Our WHAT?" I blurted out, in a voice that no doubt betrayed more concern than I wanted to express at that moment.

"Your BEAR BAG," he said twice as loud, the way Americans do in foreign countries when they assume the ignorant locals will understand their English if they just say it loud enough.

"Holy shit," I thought. Now, *this* was serious. I was not unmindful of my lessons from the canoe trip about the relationship between possible peril and the chances of it ever actually transpiring. But even if there was just a small chance of a bear wan-

dering into the campsite, no one had told us anything about trapping him (or her) in a bag. Questions began racing through my mind. What kind of bag could it possibly be? Where did you get one? Did you sneak up behind him and slip the bag over him? Or did you set a trap—presumably with a honey jar—and wait for the bear to wander into the bear bag? What if the bear didn't fit in the bear bag? Shouldn't we have had some bear-bag instruction rather than on-the-job training with one thousand pounds of very hacked-off bear? What if he (or she) got out? What if he (or she) *didn't* get out? Where could you possibly take a bear bag loaded, as it were, for bear? What did loaded for bear mean anyway? Which was the really mean one, the brown bear or the black bear? And would it matter much if you had an angry bear already in your bear bag? Wouldn't either be mean enough?

"You hang it from a tree, Dad," said Ben patiently, realizing the nature if not the extent of my confusion. "You put your food in a bag and hang it from a tree, so the bears can't get it. Bears have a great sense of smell, so you don't want any food in your tent. It's very unlikely there's a bear around, but you do it just in case."

Oh. *That* bear bag. As Emily Litella used to say, "Never mind."

By this point everyone had got their tents up, and it was time for lunch. Of course, we didn't have a real lunch that normal people or children with a responsible parent might eat. But we did have the bag of snacks—Snicker's, sesame-seed sticks, chocolate-chip granola bars—plus our precious Sprites. It had the look of a meal prepared when the inmates were running if not the whole asylum, at least the asylum's kitchen, but we made the best of it as the others broke out their turkey subs, bologna-and-cheese, and tuna on rye. Ben and I ate together, but we were not alone; the outing had already, as if by some form of wilderness osmosis, taken on a comfortable packlike quality reminiscent of our happy armada floating down the Delaware.

Before long the Scouts wandered off to do freelance Scout stuff, which basically meant playing with knives and matches in the woods. Aside from the obvious ones like Todd Davis or Sam 'n Eric, I was still having trouble remembering which Scout was which. The dads, on the other hand, came instantly and rather reassuringly into focus. In fact, as we sat around drinking coffee and waiting for the afternoon's activities to begin, I had the feeling of being in an updated version of a World War II movie, with its assortment of recognizable stock characters updated for contemporary suburbia. So we had our moon-faced Southern Baptist, Dennis, who did market research. We had a Verdi Italian, Vince, who was burly and gregarious and ran an auto repair shop in blue-collar Fleetwood, and a Vivaldi Italian, Robert, who was quiet and precise and taught Italian and Spanish in a middle school in White Plains. We had a divorced dad, Larry, who traveled around the country for one of those high-powered consulting firms and did his best to fly in from Atlanta to attend every camp-out with his son Doug, the video game and computer whiz. Harry, an earnest public relations executive, had grown up in Brooklyn the son of Holocaust survivors. And, of course, we had Dr. Flank, Mr. Toonkel, and Mr. Johnson.

There aren't many places where suburban parents, particularly men, find themselves sitting around with nothing much to do but get to know each other. I guess women do it at the nail salon, the only possible way to explain why anyone would pay perfectly good money to sit around while someone paints your nails the color of a Tootsie Roll Pop. So it felt almost illicit to be sitting around in the middle of the day, with no work and no errands, no fix-it jobs to flub, no garbage to take out or kids to drive or finances to ponder or dog to walk, no light bulbs or hamburger meat or school supplies to buy. I fell in with Vince, whose son was the first half of Sam 'n Eric. Vince had an unaffected, heavy-duty Bronx accent and a funny, laconic manner. He had been born in Muro Lucano, a hill town in south central Italy that dates back to the ninth century, and had come to America—to the Bronx's version of Little Italy around Arthur Avenue—when he was eight. He had moved his family to Chappaqua in 1991 and often wondered if he had made the right decision—the big shot, big-head syndrome in town being a bit much for his tastes. "A friend of mine who lives in Goldens Bridge always says to me, 'What kind of a town you living in, Vince?'" he said. "'When the train stops in Chappaqua, you see them get on like they own the damn thing. The atmosphere changes as soon as they get on, all tense and acting like they're entitled to everything. What are you doing there?' And to tell you the truth, sometimes I'm not sure."

It would have been nice to continue to drift off into our suburban version of *Sergeant York,* but soon Dr. Flank started rounding up the boys for the main focus of the trip, a marathon day of Scouting activities. Each patrol was given a name—Scorpions, Pathfinders, Rebels, Seals, Wolverines, Flaming Arrows, Kings, Road Runners, Eagles—and a list of seventeen stations of the cross we were supposed to visit to witness or perform some Scouting skill. Dr. Flank stressed that each patrol would be judged on how well it did and the scores added up at the end of the day.

"What do we get if we win?" asked Sam hopefully.

"You get a ribbon or patch," Dr. Flank said.

Sam looked disappointed, but even I knew that the only way to get anything better than a ribbon or a patch was to save someone's life, in which case you got the gold Honor Medal, a round medal hanging from a blood-red field. For almost everything else, you got a ribbon or a patch. If you passed basket weaving, famous as the easiest merit badge, you got one. If you mastered snorkeling or completed the mile swim, you got one. If you obeyed the tenets of no-trace camping, if you camped outdoors in below-freezing temperatures, if you showed organ donor awareness, or if you just showed up for the Paul Bunyan Camporee, you got one.

We divided up into our patrols and headed back down the dirt road to the staging area. The first station we reached was manned by a burly man in full Scout regalia. Arrayed around him, ominously, were dozens of tough strands of rope. He looked at the kids with a skeptical appraising eye. "Who knows how to do the timber hitch?" he asked. Right out of the box, we had come to the quintessential test of our Scouting skills—knot tying. As knots go, the timber hitch was pretty elementary. Not so elementary, of course, that I had any idea how to do it, but elementary enough that Scouts past the level of Second Class—the step past Tenderfoot—probably did.

Todd Davis, of course, stepped forward.

"OK," the man asked. "What do we use a timber hitch for?"

"To drag a log across the ground," Todd replied.

"And what does a hitch do?"

"It's a knot that ties a rope to an object."

"Can you show us how to do it?"

In about five seconds Todd had passed the end of the rope around the log and looped the short end around the standing part of the rope. He wrapped the end around itself three or four more times and tightened the hitch against the log. Then he manfully dragged the log ten or fifteen feet to show that it worked. The others, or at least the ones who knew how to do it, stepped forward and repeated Todd's feat.

Next, showing that the Paul Bunyan business was not just for effect, came the two-person saw, in which two kids sawing together cut their way through a log. Next, a dad talked about his cameras and lenses and showed off photos. There was a

Civil War reenactor, a guy in a tattered Union uniform heating up his coffee out of a vintage Civil War–era kettle, showing off his Enfield rifle, and passing around his .58-caliber lead mini balls. What exactly he had to do with Scouting wasn't completely clear, but he rattled on in the present tense like a happy psychotic, allowing how General Sheridan was doing this and General Hood was doing that, and the Rebels weren't going to be able to hold on much longer. He had a supply of hardtack, which he offered to the kids. It wasn't much, but it was better than our lunch had been. Next was archery, where each kid got to shoot five arrows in the vague direction of the target, and then the inevitable compass course, with much incomprehensible talk about true north, magnetic north, and declination.

Then came the all-important flapjack flip. A beefy guy with a beard and a red flannel shirt—he'd obviously taken this Paul Bunyan stuff to heart—greeted us with a suspiciously cheery "Hi, guys." The kids responded with a wary "Yo." On a long wooden table were two thick copper skillets and a stack of pancakes that appeared to be the consistency of hockey pucks.

"How many of you have ever flipped flapjacks?" he asked, in a tone of voice that suggested a query more on the order of "How many of you would like to ride dirtbikes down the Grand Canyon?"

There were a few halfhearted grunts.

"Well," he said, oblivious to the lukewarm responses, "that's what we're going to do today." He picked up his skillet and plopped one of the ossified pancakes in the pan, where it landed like a lead ball on a concrete floor. It would have made the hardtack taste like filet mignon. With a graceful flip of the wrist, he sent the pancake gently skyward, where it turned over twice and landed with a metallic thud flat in the pan. Cirque de Soleil it was not, but the kids each took their turn trying to prove their flapjack competence. It struck me as just about the dopiest exercise in perfecting useless skills I had ever witnessed. Indeed, the whole thing had a good-hearted but makeshift quality. That, I was coming to realize, was Scouting. We increasingly fork over cash for our kids' pleasures—video games, rented movies, Game Boys. Or we pay professionals to do things for them. If they're fat, they get personal trainers. If they're promising athletes, they get their own coach. If they're problematic students, they get a tutor. There are people in Westchester County who are paid to teach your kid how to ride his bicycle. Scouting, by comparison, is largely run by volunteers who do it for various benign, charitable, inscrutable, or suspect reasons. Sometimes it seems admirable, sometimes it seems half-assed. But more often than not it feels like something from another time.

We dutifully finished the last few events: another log pull, a relay race, and an exhibition of chain-saw wizardry—the last definitely a look-but-don't-touch affair. But by this point, we were all ready to trudge back to the campsite. Dr. Flank had a fire going, and we wasted no time getting ready for dinner. Outdoors cooking can be quite an art, and Dr. Flank's voluminous files contained recipes for sweet-and-sour spareribs, chicken, blueberry cobbler, fried rice, and tomato pepper steak. His personal favorite was eggplant in hoisin sauce. But, of course, it can be pretty elemental too, as in the traditional Scout one-pot stew, which exemplified the main cooking style for the evening.

This was a patrol cooking affair, which meant each patrol brought what it needed to cook for its six or eight Scouts and whatever dads needed to be fed as well. Ben's group played it pretty straight. They boiled their water, then put in two three-ounce packages of America's Choice Oriental Style Ramen Noodle Soup. When that softened and turned noodlelike, they dropped in ample chunks of precooked chicken and a package of Birds Eye frozen vegetables. The scene had a slightly Macbethean quality, with the Scouts, wooden ladles in hand, plopping ingredients into the murky brew, but the concoction itself seemed more innocent than not. The same could not be said for the meal made by the patrol cooking nearby. They began with the water and the Ramen noodles and some ground beef, which seemed enough for a respectable stew. But sometimes it's important to go the extra mile, so they added some oatmeal to give it a little texture, then some Craisins to give it that indefinable wilderness *je ne sais quoi*. A little beef stock. Some of Elliot's beef jerky to give it a little flavor. Some salt. Some pepper. A bay leaf. Some tomato sauce. A few garlic breadcrumbs. Finally it was deemed to be ready, and they ladled it out onto plastic plates. It had the mottled look of something meant to be served in another form—freeze dried for astronaut food or ground up and hardened like a vitamin pill. Tom, the one who was twelve going on sixteen, took the first taste and not surprisingly pronounced it "awesome." Like a Greek chorus, the other diners pronounced themselves equally pleased. We all ate like happy cavemen. After dinner there was coffee for the grownups and Chips Ahoy! and other cookies for the whole crew.

We had one more activity, the campfire, where all the troops would gather in one grand, pan-Westchester affair. We hiked toward the site, flashlights beaming bouncing darts of light through the darkness. Scouts seemed to pop out of every hill and gully, in groups of two or three or whole tribes marching through the night, like a gallant boy army gathering for some virtuous crusade. (Of course, it could have been a dubious gang of boy thugs bent on mayhem, but they were Scouts, so I was willing to give them the benefit of the doubt.) We reached an amphitheater carved into a clearing with a semicircle of logs used as seats. They were filled with Scouts facing a huge unlit pyre of thoroughly combustible matter—layers of kindling twigs on the bottom, then modest branches and tree limbs, then big, stout logs, all stacked in a neat pyramid at least four feet high. Everyone was quiet and orderly until all the seats filled up.

Then the chant began—"Light the fire. Light the fire. Light the fire."—first a few kids, then, it seemed, everyone, louder and louder. Now we were really getting to *Lord of the Flies* terrain. Could "Kill the pig, cut his throat, spill his blood" be too far behind? Luckily, two older Scouts finally stepped forward and did the deed. Within minutes, the scene was lit by an enormous bonfire that lit up the sky like a blazing torch. A great plume of yellow flame crackled into the night and above that burning embers climbed upward into the black sky like fiery bugs, the last ones rising fifteen feet above the fire until they finally died out. We all watched the dancing flame and swirling embers in total silence for five or ten minutes, until one of the senior Scouts who had lit the bonfire stepped in front of it. He leaned forward from the waist, hands on both knees.

"You having a good time?" he hollered.

"Yeah," we hollered back.

"I CAN'T HEAR YOU!" he yelled in the inevitable attack of hearing impairment that has accompanied every such oration in history. "YOU HAVING A GOOD TIME?"

"YEAH," we yelled a little louder.

"Awright, that's more like it. We all had a great day. I saw a lot of great Scout spirit out there. Now we've got a great campfire planned, so let's get going."

Once upon a time, this might have meant an old-fashioned sing-along. Scout songbooks from the 1960s included 150 sing-along favorites divided into Opening Songs ("Hail, Hail the Gang's All Here," "How Do You Do?"), Scouting Spirit ("I'm Happy When I'm Hiking," "There's Something About a Boy Scout,"), Patriotic Songs, Action Songs, Quiet Songs, Worship Songs (from "Onward Christian Soldiers" to "Sholom A'ley-chem"), and Closing Songs ("Auld Lang Syne," "Taps"). Today's songbook isn't that much different, but it's hard to imagine too many fourteen-year-olds who want to sit around the campfire singing "If You're Happy and You Know It Clap Your Hands," "Waltzing Matilda," or "Sweetly Sings the Donkey."

Still, the program that ensued did have a remarkably time-less quality. There were skits, most having to do with familiar body odors that follow an imperfectly digested meal, unsightly females, or misunderstandings involving a pickle. Lucky Scouts were recruited to the bonfire to tackle tongue-twisting and memory tricks, the main one requiring the Scout to remember and recite a list of ten items of increasing obscurity and length. I got about as far as "one fat hen, a couple of ducks, and three frigidy frogs" and then lost track.

One skit called for a bunch of kids to act out the parts of a story—a nervous woman, a concerned cop, and a chimpanzee. One kid, a boy of about twelve or thirteen with short dark hair, wearing a dark blue fleece and blue jeans, stood out. His job was to play a chimpanzee. Each time his cue came up, the boy dashed around the fire, the mammoth bonfire serving as a crack-ling, flickering backdrop. He scurried around making snuffling chimplike sounds, swinging his arms just so, head hunched down, chest out, legs taking clumsy, bow-legged, brisk chimp-like strides. The other boys played their parts with a hammy kind of enthusiasm, but this kid stood out to the point I looked forward to his recurring role to see if he could keep up the same primeval level of energy and authenticity, which he invariably did. I wasn't sure what was so striking about the kid until I thought back to the Polo Boy. Who knows? Maybe this kid went home and sat slack-jawed by the television listening to Marilyn Manson on headphones and watching *South Park* all night. But, for this moment at least, he was the un–Polo Boy. There was not a sliver of attitude, no ironic distance, no sense of superior cool, just primal, unadulterated boyhood energy. He seemed everything the Polo Boy's contrived, antique bat was supposed to denote but wasn't—like a kid who had never seen a computer or a video game or a mall and was working from a pre-Microsoft, pre-Napster, pre-Britney, pre-*Simpsons* operating system. I tried to think of a group other than Boy Scouts whose goal was to teach that kid the same kind of values. I couldn't think of any.

The campfire was winding down. We sang a song or two, then stood and linked arms as a kid with a bugle played "Taps." We—or at least the Scouts who knew them—sang the words:

> Day is done, gone the sun;
> From the lake, from the hills, from the sky;
> All is well, safely rest,
> God is nigh.

> Fading light dims the sight;
> And a star gems the sky,
> Gleaming bright;
> From afar, drawing nigh,
> Falls the night.

Somehow my own ironic distance was whittled away as well. We all walked quiet as mice back to our campsites. Ben and I found our tent, opened our sleeping bags, and crawled in. Lying on the plastic mat underneath the sleeping bag wasn't much different from sleeping on cement, and the sweaters I fluffed up under my head to serve as a pillow didn't help. Outside the temperature was dipping below 40. The night was thick with alien noises: hooting owls, kids conspiring in hushed tones, the crackle and crunch of unknown footsteps on dry leaves. It was, in short, all the discomfort and senseless deprivation I had expected. But, that said, inside the tent things were warm and pleasantly cocoonlike. It was a comfortable, intimate thing to be alone, just the two of us, in this strange tent in the woods. Ben took out his flashlight and started to read a Tom Clancy book he'd already read three times, part of his ritual before going to sleep.

"Not too long, OK?" I said. "It's getting late."

"Ten minutes," he replied.

"OK. Ten minutes max."

Maybe it was ten or maybe it was twenty or maybe it was an hour or two. You couldn't have known by me. Long before he finished, I was out like a block of cement, snoring the sleep of the weary dead blissfully into the night.

5: The Hero of Mafeking

Our band of merry adventurers had many fathers, both the troop leaders of the past and the men who almost a century ago gave rise to what has become the biggest voluntary youth movement in history. But the most important figure in Scouting's history was an astoundingly complex man—self-knowing and self-deceiving, ruggedly masculine and sexually ambiguous, a hero of war who saw himself as a man of peace, an imperialist and a universalist—who was one of the most celebrated figures of his time and now is all but forgotten outside of Great Britain.

Born in 1857, Lord Robert Baden-Powell became one of Britain's most admired heroes when his badly outnumbered garrison held off a much larger army of Boers for seven months at Mafeking in South Africa from October 1899 to May 1900. The siege, relentlessly chronicled in the British press, made him a national celebrity. Out of that celebrity he was able to fashion a movement to train boys in outdoor skills and traditional values that swept the nation, and swiftly spread to America and most of the rest of the world.

But rather than a clear-cut exemplar of Edwardian virtue, Baden-Powell was a figure of tantalizing eccentricities and contradictions. While one of the most famous men in Britain, he headed the Boy Scouts for three decades for no pay other than expenses. He rose at five each morning after sleeping alone on his balcony, did five minutes of exercise, peeled himself an apple, did two hours of writing, and at 7:30 took a cold bath, always drying himself with a stiff, partially starched towel. He much preferred what he called "the religion of the woods" to any organized variety, which made him very unpopular with many churchmen. He was called "the inspired mystic of Scouting," and saw himself more as a moral leader than a military one. He was Knight Commander of the Order of the Bath, recipient of the Jubilee Medal and some thirty-seven other medals, decorations, and orders and six honorary doctorates, founder of the Boy Scouts, and Chief Scout of the World.

He also spent most of his life obsessed by a younger soldier he invariably called "the Boy." The two lived together in shared bungalows and exchanged presents and ardent letters when they were apart. When the Boy was held prisoner during the siege of Mafeking, Baden-Powell sent him under flags of truce cocoa, wine, a soft mattress, hairbrushes, books, mosquito curtains, cologne, soup, lemonade, stamps, stationery, and money. Baden-Powell was a talented actor who loved playing women's roles and making his own dresses, and he designed embroidery patterns for regimental wives. Even in the veldt, he insisted on bathing every day with scented soap. Whenever possible, he sought out the local executioner when he traveled. He loved visiting battlefields of all kinds and recording bizarre forms of death, ranging, as one biographer put it, "from a novel form of strangulation in Tunisia, to the fate of a workman who fell down one of the steep metal water-collecting slopes on Gibraltar and burst into flames with the friction." He credited all his success to his mother.

Baden-Powell married in 1912 at the age of fifty-five, and after dispensing with the messy unpleasantness of sex achieved a warm, comradely union with the woman who became his partner in Scouting. Describing in his autobiography the importance of picking the right guide for a Scouting expedition in hostile territory, he wrote: "The selection is one that cannot be lightly made. It is as bad as choosing a horse—or a wife. There is a lot depending on it."

A lot of what people think of the Boy Scouts depends on how they read Baden-Powell, who either sums up the glories of a truly inspired movement for human betterment or reflects its shallowness and hypocrisy. It's not hard to find both views. One worshipful biography, published at the peak of Baden-Powell's fame in 1924, begins:

> In a quiet street, on the north side of Hyde Park, that blessed breathing space of London babies and London birds, was born on the 22nd of February 1857, a baby whose future career was destined to have perhaps more widely reaching effect than that of any man since the Founder of Christianity. No "star of the east" heralded his coming. There was nothing miraculous about his birth and babyhood; yet there are literally millions of people in the world today who are the better for Robert Baden-Powell having been born.

At the other extreme is a 1984 biography by a Columbia University professor, Michael Rosenthal, which casts Baden-Powell as little more than a reflection of the evils of British imperialism. Baden-Powell, Rosenthal stresses, served a crown that subjected "more than 345 million people to the will of Her Majesty's government by threat of force, justified through the moral imperative to bring the blessings of peace and justice to people in need of guidance." And his biggest service to the crown, Rosenthal concludes, was to hatch "an obedience-engendering scheme" whose aim was to "produce efficient recruits for the empire for generations to come." In Rosenthal's eyes, Baden-Powell was a racist and anti-Semite, soft on fascism, who created a cold "character factory" while others tried to build more genuinely humanistic youth movements. One can feel cool derision on every page.

Robert Stephenson Smyth Powell, or Stephe for short, was the eighth of ten children born to Henrietta Grace Powell and the Reverend Baden-Powell, Savilian Professor of Geometry at Oxford. Before his birth his mother had lost three children, which left seven years between Robert and the next youngest sibling. And three years after his birth, his father died suddenly. The result was an extraordinary bond between mother and son. He wrote her two thousand letters over the course of his life, kept elaborate illustrated diaries and notebooks to share with her, and turned motherhood into almost an object of worship. And as he developed into a precocious, imaginative child, a natural actor and a talented artist, a complicated dynamic began to play out. On the one hand, he was utterly devoted to and obsessed with pleasing his mother. On the other, he was struggling to develop a male identity without any father to emulate. The two drives coalesced into his life's work: Baden-Powell became one of the most celebrated and admired men in England by forming an organization built around teaching boys how to become men.

In 1870 he was sent off on a scholarship to Charterhouse, one of the elite English public schools that produced England's leaders. He proved an indifferent student. In 1876 he failed the examination for a university education at Balliol and then at Christ Church. Instead, he did what many others of his class did: He joined the British Army in search of adventure.

At the time, the glory days of Empire, the military was a natural route to advancement, and Baden-Powell took to it with gusto, entertaining his fellow soldiers with plays from his Charterhouse days. He spent two years in India and Afghanistan, came back to England, then returned to Afghanistan, where he perfected the odd balance of jocular stagecraft and imperial gravity that he maintained throughout his military career. On the one hand were mayhem, hangings, and floggings of recalcitrant Indians and Afghans; on the other was the thirteen Hussars mounting a production of *The Pirates of Penzance,* with swords planted in the dirt to mark off the stage and revolvers loaded just in case.

In Afghanistan, Baden-Powell threw himself into two things. The first was the theater—he organized four plays in two months. The second was a friendship with a twenty-year-old officer named Kenneth McLaren, who cut such a striking figure as the female lead in two productions that one subordinate noted: "One of our fellows made a very pretty girl." Their regiment moved to Muttra, where Baden-Powell and McLaren took a bungalow together and where for three years, Baden-Powell's letters home were dominated by one or another diverting snippet about "the Boy." He would praise his friend's fit body and recount a trip to the palace of the Maharaj of Deng, where the two shared a magnificent room and the Boy read a novel to him as they lazed in bed until breakfast time. When the Boy went on leave to Kashmir, Baden-Powell's sunny mood turned to "beastly melancholy," and he wrote home asking his mother to purchase "a nice little present for the Boy—I think a pair of ivory brushes—good ones with M. McL. on the back would be rather nailing." For more than twenty years, they continued a relationship that led Baden-Powell to call McLaren "my best friend in the world."

It is, of course, dangerous to impose one era's values and standards of conduct on another. Intense, even passionate, relationships between men were often celebrated in the nineteenth century, with no sense that the relationship was homosexual. And despite much scholarly picking and digging, there is no real evidence that the relationship between Baden-Powell and

McLaren was ever a physical one. But Tim Jeal, the British biographer whose *The Boy-Man: The Life of Lord Baden-Powell* is the best Baden-Powell biography to date, says that the older man's passionate relationship with McLaren was certainly consistent with the predilections he expressed in his life. He delighted in male nudity, while he found female nudity distasteful and recoiled at overtly sexual women. He enjoyed looking at pictures of naked boys with a friend from Charterhouse. When he finally married late in life, he began to experience agonizing headaches, which disappeared when he took to sleeping outside on the balcony instead of with his wife. It was a different time, with different strictures, but even Jeal, who is inclined to champion Baden-Powell, concludes that the evidence points "inexorably" to the conclusion he was a repressed homosexual.

Baden-Powell's unit did not see any combat until 1896 in Africa. And his military training left him enamored less with warfare itself than with the more cerebral life of the scouts, the wily outriders who became the eyes and ears of the army. Through them, he became a student of what he called "the science of woodcraft"—how to move invisibly through enemy territory, learning the tracks of animals; how to live off the land and read the small details of the natural life of the veldt. And over time, the self-taught virtues of the African tribesmen, the teamwork of the army, the ability to adapt to harsh terrains, and the character-building attributes of the outdoor life began to come together in his mind as something between a discipline and a faith.

Baden-Powell had had some success thus far—at forty, he had become the youngest colonel in the British Army. Still, his career was moving along in a rather conventional path until a combination of fate, guile, pluck, and chance made him a national hero. In 1899 he was sent to South Africa, where relations were deteriorating by the day between the modest British forces stationed there and the Boer farmers hoping to win their independence in a land with the world's richest gold reefs. Baden-Powell was dispatched with the imprecise mission of diverting and engaging some five thousand to six thousand Boers until more British armies could arrive.

His command took him to the small tin-roofed trading town of Mafeking—the name means "Place of Stones"—on a sun-baked rise surrounded by a treeless veldt about 650 miles north of Cape Town. There his force of about two thousand men, most of them untrained, was soon besieged by some six thousand Boers, who were superior fighters and horsemen. It's a measure of how charged Baden-Powell's legacy is that historians are still battling over most elements of the siege, including whether Baden-Powell was there out of necessity or thanks to a tactical error or a carefully staged show of heroism. What is clear is that Baden-Powell, the most theatrical of soldiers, turned Mafeking into a dramatic tour de force, and at the end of 217 days of siege, from October 13, 1899, to May 17, 1900, when relief arrived and the Boers skulked away, he had emerged as one of Britain's greatest war heroes.

Baden-Powell's critics ascribe his sudden elevation to national celebrity to his shrewd instinct for showmanship and, as Rosenthal put it, "a supporting cast of stolid, rather immobile Boers reluctant to take much initiative." His supporters say he survived a truly perilous situation by craft and cunning, and that his fame reflected the perfect match between a romantic military victory and a nation that was ripe for a stirring victory and new hero. But whatever the case, Baden-Powell performed like a man determined to turn his big moment into a Gilbert and Sullivan operetta. He'd sit calmly dictating messages in the market square, like the embodiment of British pluck, as enemy shells exploded around him. "Four hours bombardment; one dog killed," went one published in British newspapers. He went on nocturnal scouting missions behind enemy lines on his own. And, as the siege dragged on, he sponsored regular entertainments of concerts and plays, from Hottentot dances to what he called his "World Wide Show" of singing and dancing and playing the fool. Transmitted by reporters and his own messages sent through enemy lines, every triumph, show of moxie, and display of comic drollery was played up in the papers back home and made his exploits a national sensation.

One aspect of his performance that was not much mentioned was his treatment of the Africans in Mafeking and under his command. Beginning with Thomas Pakenham in 1979, some historians have argued that Baden-Powell's rationing of food so egregiously favored whites over blacks that it amounted to something close to mass murder. It is a complicated discussion, based on different accounts of just what food was available at what time to which African populations, some under his control, some not. Jeal is persuasive in arguing that while Baden-Powell clearly favored whites over blacks in food distribution, the most critical accounts mischaracterized the food available to blacks and distorted the reports made at the time. Still, neither side portrays Baden-Powell in a favorable light, and even Jeal said he was scandalously ungenerous and deceptive in not giving credit to African soldiers and officers in the defense of Mafeking.

It is still a raw issue. In 1999 just before South Africa was scheduled to host the World Scout Conference, which brings together about one thousand delegates from more than 150 countries and territories, African tribal leaders filed a $5.9 million petition with the British government. The Baralong-Boora-Tshidi Tribal Authority said that black Africans were entitled to compensation for damages and for promises Baden-Powell made but never kept. And if many saw a hero, others, even at the time, were not so sure: "He seems to close every argument with a snap," wrote Angus Hamilton of the *Times* of London, "as though the steel manacles of his ambition, had checkmated the emotion of the man in the instincts of the soldier."

Baden-Powell partly benefited from an accident of timing: Britain had just undergone a string of imperial reversals around the world, and news of the undermanned garrison holding out against superior forces played perfectly to the popular mood. It set off a celebration so raucous that the word *maffick* entered the language as a verb, defined by Webster's as "to celebrate with boisterous rejoicing and hilarious behavior." At least nineteen musical pieces were composed in his honor, with titles like "The Baden-Powell Schottische" and "The Hero of Mafeking Valse."

There was a final element of Mafeking that came to loom large in Baden-Powell's life. It did not seem important at the time; he did not even make mention of it in his reports on the siege. But during the siege, the defenders of Mafeking at times enlisted the services of the youths of the town. The boys in question were part of the local cadet corps, something of a military auxiliary. Baden-Powell later said they were trained in scouting, which was apparently not true. They were under the command of two other officers, not him. But in a garrison that never had enough men to do all the jobs they had come in handy, carrying messages, doing odd jobs, and thus freeing the adults to serve as riflemen in the trenches. And when Baden-Powell in 1908 published *Scouting for Boys,* his first tale was of the boy scouts of Mafeking, some of whom rode bicycles under enemy bombardment to deliver letters to distant forts in a town five miles away. He asked his young readers if they would be able to be as heroic. "I am sure you would—although probably you wouldn't much like doing it," he wrote. And then he ended his Camp Fire Yarn No. 1 with the following thought: "But you need not have a war in order to be useful as a scout. As a peace scout there is lots for you to do—any day, wherever you may be."

Of course, one of the perils of heroism and celebrity is coming up with a second act. In March 1903 Baden-Powell returned to England as Inspector General of the Cavalry. His job was to inspect cavalry regiments around the world and rethink the role of the cavalry in the future. It was a perfectly respectable post and one consistent with a successful life as a military officer. But for the thirty-seven years since he had left for India as a nineteen-year-old, he had spent almost all his time abroad in far-flung, adventurous locales. Now, the hero of Mafeking was taking a desk job and moving back in with his mother. It turned out to be something of a comedown. His tour was not viewed as a great success, and his mother was pressuring him to finally find a bride, something he attempted without great enthusiasm.

But he did find something else to get enthusiastic about. As a result of his celebrity, Baden-Powell was often asked to inspect cadet corps and organizations involved with the training of youths. It was the right time: Military reversals in the nineteenth century had set in motion a national hysteria about Britain's incipient decline and industrialization, and the movement of boys from the countryside to the city exacerbated the fears. Anxiety about national decline and the deterioration of the nation's youth is a common note in modern life. But in England, a tiny island of forty million people in 1900 trying to control an empire of 11.5 million square miles and 345 million people, the anxiety had particular sociopolitical throw weight. Baden-Powell, too, worried about the deterioration of the nation's moral fiber and the spread of "loafers and wasters," typically working-class lads who hung out on street corners, drank and smoked, gambled and watched sports instead of playing them, and grew thin and pale. He was also suspicious of public schoolboys, who spent all their time buried in books rather than out in the fresh air. Slowly, Baden-Powell came to see a new challenge—a national crusade to inspire, seduce, and invigorate the boys of Britain.

At that time there was a modest movement of Boys' Brigades, quasi-military units that mixed Christianity, military drill, and social uplift into a rather dour form of character training. Asked in April 1904 to review the brigades, Baden-Powell offered muted praise. The boys looked impressive and seemed proud of what they were doing, he said. But, he added, the movement would have grown faster "if the work really appealed to the boys." And how to make that work more appealing? He suggested scouting, the discipline of nature, woodcraft, military intelligence, and the understanding of the outdoors. He had written about this discipline already in a book entitled *Aids to Scouting for N.C.O.'s and Men,* which he published in 1898. After Mafeking, it became an enormous bestseller.

Baden-Powell wasn't quite sure how to create what he came to call his "Boy Scout Scheme." But he took the first serious step in 1907, when he (with the help of the Boy and two other associates) held a camp for twenty-two boys of all social classes on Brownsea Island off England. Baden-Powell taught the boys camping and scouting skills and regaled them around the campfire with tales of battling Zulus and tracking wild lions. "Eeengonyama—gonyama," the Great Man would sing around the campfire. "Invooboo. Yah bo. Invooboo," they would sing back. It meant, more or less, "He is a lion! Yes! He is better than that; he is a hippopotamus." The boys were organized into patrols, roused each morning by a koodoo horn that Baden-Powell had captured in Africa, and spent their days tracking animals, playing games in the woods, and cooking their own food. In the days before radio, when an adventure might be a picnic in the country or a frolic in a grimy urban park, to camp on an island with the Hero of Mafeking must have been exciting beyond belief.

At the same time, prodded by the newspaper tycoon and promoter C. Arthur Pearson, Baden-Powell was working to adapt his *Aids to Scouting* for boys. The result, *Scouting for Boys,* was a sensation. Pearson, who made most of the money on it, sent Baden-Powell on an extended lecture tour, helped come up with the name "Boy Scouts" (wisely rejecting Baden-Powell's own suggestion of "Imperial Scouts"), and cooked up a weekly newsletter, "The Scout." Unofficial patrols began sprouting immediately.

Pearson, with the instincts of a shark, saw a gold mine in the making. When he realized how many patrols had formed on their own, he helped Baden-Powell put together a formal Scouting organization. Pearson earned nearly all the profits from the book and newsletter; all Baden-Powell got was a one-room office and Pearson's help in getting the organization going, the ability to use "The Scout" to communicate with his boys, and a modest share of royalties, all of which went to getting the Boy Scouts organization off the ground. As a businessman, the Hero of Mafeking was either uninterested or clueless.

Still, if the plan could not have been worse for him financially, it made Scouting an instant sensation. Almost on its own, the movement spread across England, and in 1910 Baden-Powell quit the army to work full time on Scouting. By the end of the year, there were more than 100,000 Scouts in Great Britain.

Exactly what kind of an organization he wanted to create is still the subject of much debate. When he viewed the Boys' Brigades back in 1904, Baden-Powell wrote to recommend Scout training, saying it would help the boys develop their minds by becoming more observant. And he concluded: "The results would not only sharpen the wits of the Boy, but would also make him quick to read character and feelings, and thus help him to be a better sympathiser with his fellow-men."

It was Baden-Powell's first reference to Scout training in boys, and in some ways it got to the heart of an argument that still rages. Was he advocating Scouting as part of a quasi-military scheme, which was devoted to maintaining Britain's social status quo? Or were the humanistic, benign themes of his remarks proof that Scouting was really about helping boys, not just helping to train them to defend the Empire?

Rosenthal, not surprisingly, sees Scouting as thoroughly about the former. As exhibit A, he cites a passage in Baden-Powell's writing entitled "Be a Brick":

> This means you should remember that being one fellow among many others, you are like one brick among many others in the wall of a home. If you are discontented with your place or with your neighbours or if you are a rotten brick, you are no good to the wall. We are all Britons, and it is our duty each to play in his place and help his neighbours. Then we shall remain strong and united, and then there will be no fear of the whole building—namely our great Empire—falling down because of rotten bricks in the wall.

There are other exhibits, particularly a letter Baden-Powell published December 22, 1906, in the *Eton College Chronicle*. Citing the military threats to England, it quite explicitly lays out a plan to form clumps of boys who would be taught patriotism and honor; be trained to scout, aim and shoot miniature rifles, drill, and skirmish; and be prepared to defend England, if necessary.

But Baden-Powell also wrote, "A boy should take his own line rather than be carried along by herd persuasion." In his view, the outdoor life created not just self-sufficient boys, but generous and chivalrous ones—boys who became "gentle men" because of their love of the outdoors. And, as Jeal noted, in many of his lists of the elements that make up an admirable character, intelligence and individuality precede loyalty and self-discipline. Maria Montessori, the advocate of creative education, said Scouting freed children "from the narrow limits to which they had been confined."

Commenting on the Scout uniform, Baden-Powell took pains to say it was an amalgam of practical elements he had observed in his years in the wild and designed to be something that all boys could wear on an equal basis. "There was nothing military about it," he wrote. "It was designed to be the most practical, cheap and comfortable dress for camping and hiking and in no way copied from a soldier's kit." He had little or no use for marching and formal parades, and when a great rally was scheduled in 1911 to show off Baden-Powell's new organization to King George V, the grand moment was not a show of crisp military marching and drill but an inspired bit of boy theater. Baden-Powell, mounted on a great black horse, blew his whistle, and suddenly thirty thousand roaring boys began running toward the king's reviewing area. As one witness described it: "The thirty thousand closed in on the King as a great foaming wave, and it seemed that nothing would stop it; the spectators trembled lest the King should be enveloped. But, at a line, which none but the Scouts knew, the wave stopped dead, as if suddenly frozen—the shouting and the tumult died, and then—silence."

John Hargrave, one of Baden-Powell's most charismatic lieutenants, saw him not as a dour, obedience-engendering bricklayer, but the opposite—a Huck Finn, a backwoods urchin, a "Boy-Poltergeist" allowing thousands of boys to make their escape from "a dreary, half-dead commercialized and deadly dull civilization."

And rather than a cold, quasi-military document, Baden-Powell's *Scouting for Boys* is a rich stew of whimsy and practical advice, patriotism and positive thinking, full of alluring tales from Kipling and Zulu tribesmen, from the Matabele War in

Africa and Scott's last expedition to the South Pole. It begins with the Scout Promise ("On my honour I promise that I will do my best—To do my duty to God, and to Queen, To help other people at all times, To obey the Scout Law") and an early version of the Scout Law, ten items phrased in terms of what a Scout should do, instead of what he should not:

A Scout's honour is to be trusted.
A Scout is loyal to the Queen, his country, his parents, his
    employers and those under him.
A Scout's duty is to be useful and to help others.
A Scout is a friend to all and a brother to every other Scout.
A Scout is courteous.
A Scout is a friend to animals.
A Scout obeys orders of his parents, Patrol Leader, or
    Scoutmaster without question.
A Scout smiles and whistles under all difficulties.
A Scout is thrifty.
A Scout is clean in thought, word and deed.

It has short, concise lessons on knot tying, axe handling, and latrine digging, as well as on honor, politeness, and humility. It teaches the right way to breathe (through the nose), cut your nails (square across the top, not rounded), squat (put a piece of wood or sloping stone under your heels), and stalk an animal (always downwind). It tells boys what they should do—smile, be chivalrous to women, be thrifty but generous—and what they should not—accept tips, drink alcohol or smoke cigarettes, masturbate. "Want of laughter means want of health," Baden-Powell tells his charges. "Laugh as much as you can. It does you good."

In fact, it does not take much time reading anything by Baden-Powell to realize how much of the early success of Scouting is a result of the appeal of Baden-Powell himself. On every page of every book, he conveys the jaunty air of an adventurer offering up tales of battlefield derring-do, an analysis of the mountaineering skills of the Ghurkas of northern India, or a tale of woodcraft deduction worthy of Sherlock Holmes. At times, he's a stern lecturer on manly skills: "It is a disgrace to a Scout if, when he is with other people, they see anything big or little, near or far, high or low, that he has not already seen for himself." At others he's just the soul of eccentric Edwardian bloviation, full of charming nonsense from around the globe:

> Montenegro is a small country high up in the mountains on the east side of the Adriatic. The men are splendid great fellows and very patriotic, fond of their country, and although not real soldiers, they all dress in the same uniform, practice rifle shooting, and always go about fully armed with rifle, knives and pistols. Yet they are the most peaceful people, and are the only people I know of who do not know how to steal.

It would be hopelessly naive to think Scouting was simply an exercise in woodcraft fun and games that was divorced from the military and political needs of the British Empire. But to see *Scouting for Boys* and the Boy Scouts as simply a calculated scheme to create loyal, patriotic drones for the Empire, you need to buy a simple, didactic view of Baden-Powell that's wholly at odds with the rich, complicated, conflicted figure he was. And in lots of ways, *Scouting for Boys* is a paradigm for Scouting not in terms of providing one message or one agenda, but in providing many different ones.

So Scouting became a sensation, first in Great Britain, then in the United States, and eventually around much of the world. But it was not wholly admired. Some upper-class types saw Baden-Powell's criticism of snobbery and social caste as almost revolutionary. Some lower-class ones saw the movement as effete and sissified, and a jeer reported during the time went:

"Here come the Brussel Sprouts, The stinking, blinking louts." A 1912 pamphlet entitled "The Boy Scout Bubble" saw the movement as trivial and escapist, encouraging boys to engage in silly, useless adventures. It read in part:

> I refuse to believe that character will ever be built by un-settling the minds of the young, by turning their thoughts from practical everyday life and the best way to live it, to dreams and vision of a life that not one in a hundred will ever be called upon to live. So strong is the imagination of the youngster that it may be several months before he be-gins to ask himself what earthly use the knowledge of how to light a damp fire with one match will be to him when he answers the advertisement for a junior clerk.

Baden-Powell's Boy Scouts was not his era's only approach to boy training, only the most successful. In America, the natu-ralist Ernest Thompson Seton based a movement, the Wood-craft Indians, on an almost mystical attachment to the outdoors and the values and skills of the American Indians. Daniel Carter Beard's Sons of Daniel Boone was built on the experience of the American explorers and woodsmen. In England, on the right, William Smith's Boys' Brigades flourished in forms as diverse and unlikely as the Anglican Church Lads' Brigades and the Jewish Lads' Brigade. Cadet Corps, many tied to public schools, were even more explicit in serving as training grounds for the military. Perhaps the oddest and the most direct challenge to the Boy Scouts came from a group founded by John Hargrave, an early Boy Scout leader who for a time was thought to be a likely successor to Baden-Powell. Hargrave yearned for a transforming wilderness experience, one that would keep "knowledge and physical training hand in hand and try to breed a race of Intel-lectual Savages." He came to see the Boy Scouts as infected by militarism and British imperialism and went on to launch the

Kibbo Kift Kindred, an eccentric blend of woodcraft, utopian economics, and global politics. It espoused outdoors training for boys and girls and an esoteric agenda of economic reform to be disseminated by infiltrating banking and finance, the cinema, the universities, and the other power points of Britain. Boys were to dress in shorts, jerkin, and cowl, accessorizing with a rough ash staff and rucksack. Girls were to wear a one-piece dress to the knee with leather belt and headdress. "The costume of the Kin," Hargrave proclaimed, sounding like the clueless captain of a ship about to hit an iceberg, "releases efficiency, calls for conscious unity of purpose and proclaims a dynamic difference in impressive silence."

Prospective leaders of mass movements will probably not be using Hargrave, whose group finally morphed into an inscrutable organization bent on economic reform called the Green Shirt Movement for Social Credit, for rallying the faithful. Instead, the definitive text for organizations for boys—and the inspiration for the Girl Scouts as well—remains the one Baden-Powell cooked up. Part of Baden-Powell's genius was to steal from everyone, to put together a movement that was nature and militarism, world peace and national preparedness, fun and serious, left and right, an alluring mix of disparate elements—British explorers and Zulu tribesmen, the garish triumphs of Empire and the quiet glories of the woods.

Of course, an organization that can be many things to many people runs the risk of being caught in the middle if different factions or constituencies disagree vehemently on what it should be or how it should evolve. That's probably particularly true for a group dealing with something as emotionally charged as the training of a nation's youths. But it's worth remembering that Baden-Powell succeeded where others failed by building an organization that was inclusive in the broadest sense. It was certainly too regimented for the true wilderness mystics and too frivolous for those intent on training future soldiers. But, in the beginning and for most of its life span, Scouting has prospered by building the broadest possible tent. And it's not hard to draw the conclusion that if the Scouts come to be seen as part of a particular ideology or faction, they do so at their own peril.

6: A Winter Hike on the A.T.

Having survived the raging rivers of the canoe trip and the raging testosterone of the camporee, it was probably time for me to return to what passed for my normal life. I had gone on the first two outings partly to do due diligence—making sure the troop wasn't a cabal of depraved child abusers—and partly to perform some vaguely perceived duty to help Ben integrate into the troop. I'd already done that. Like an unexpected detour off the highway, it was fine for what it was. I was truly grateful that it wasn't worse. But it wasn't a place I expected to hang around.

Still, the next event was something that genuinely sounded like fun—a Troop 1 hike along the Appalachian Trail near the lovely town of Kent, Connecticut, in the foothills of the Berkshires. Ben, of course, was planning to go. It was late fall, getting on winter. There wasn't much on my schedule for the weekend, and I figured I could use the exercise, so I decided to come along on this one too.

Like most Scout activities, it loomed as a mixed experience. My policy was still Hiking = Good, Camping = Bad. This was to be five miles of hiking followed by a night of cabin camping, an interesting compromise. Instead of sleeping in the too-cold, or too-hot, or too-insect-ridden, or too-wet or too-bear-friendly outdoors, we would sleep in the cabins at the Siwanoy Boy

Scout camp nearby. Not the Pierre, but not bleak, freezing wilderness either. It figured to be cold, but not completely miserable. I didn't have hiking boots, but I could always get some. As far as life's challenges went, it seemed manageable.

At the meeting the Wednesday before, Dr. Flank ran through what the kids needed, beginning with a stern lecture on the virtue of wool socks. This was not unexpected. No one had ever found a little red book entitled *The Teachings of Chairman Flank*, but one could imagine a modest volume with Dr. Flank's lectures on the J stroke and the moral virtue of no-trace camping, on the proper way to build a fire and the peril and utter uselessness of the axe. And, if such a volume existed, it is absolutely certain that it would begin with a meditation on wool socks.

"What goes inside your boots?" he asked in his stern, rapid-fire, this-is-a-test classroom voice.

"Wool socks," answered the older kids wearily, like POWs who've been subjected to an interminable indoctrination campaign.

"Right," said Dr. Flank with a look of pleasure far out of proportion to the information being imparted. "Nothing will keep your feet warmer and drier than good, wool socks. And nothing will keep you more comfortable than warm, dry feet. Actually since you'll be hiking, you'll need something else as well. You need a pair of thin liner socks, polypropylene or polyester liner socks. You use them to transfer moisture to the outer layer of socks, so your feet won't get damp and clammy. Then you put the wool socks over that. You want a poncho or rain jacket. You want something for your head, a hat or cap, because the body loses half its heat through the head. You need a good pair of gloves. And you want to dress in layers, so you can peel some off if you get overheated. You, of course, need your hiking boots."

Mr. Toonkel stepped forward brandishing a trail guide that described the hike. "You cross a swampy area on a log here," he said. "You cross the stream by walking across rocks here. You cross a shallow stream to get to the dirt road here. So you should get the idea; it's not going to be a dry trip. If it's cold enough, some of it will be frozen. If it's warm enough, there might be a lot of mud. So what did Dr. Flank tell you? I don't want to see anyone without hiking boots, and I don't want to see anyone who didn't think about what to put over his feet. Do you need a tent? No. We're sleeping inside. You need to bring a lunch, but we'll be cooking the rest. You'll need a mess kit, a cup, dish, bowl, fork, and spoon. I'm not bringing cups for you. You need canteens filled with water. Don't get up there with an empty water bottle and ask where you can fill it. Everything you bring should be in your pack. As far as the hike, you'll need a small day pack to carry your water and any extra clothes, a jacket or sweater you're not going to be wearing when we leave. The guidebook or maps we'll supply. You'll need your compass, canteen, flashlight. You might bring a couple of Band-Aids. I trust you'll all be prepared, gentlemen."

I, of course, wasn't remotely prepared, having no wool socks, no hiking boots, and not much of the rest. So I ventured out to my own bargain-basement version of an outdoors outfitter, a discount emporium on Ninth Avenue in the Garment District in Manhattan where all the employees were Indians, half the signs were in Spanish ("*Se Venta Hoy!*"), and most of the customers were Asian or black. It specialized in huge piles of heavily discounted Levi's, most of them with big waists and small legs or odd-lot dimensions that only fit the characters on *The Simpsons*.

"Fit you good," one of the salesclerks said as he picked up a pair of jeans that two of me could have fit inside.

"No thanks," I replied amiably. "I already have a tent."

He nodded agreeably, apparently satisfied that was the appropriate response, but hovered around expectantly as I moved on to the boot section. I soon spied a sturdy-looking pair of brown Gore-Tex hiking boots marked down to $59.99. Gore-Tex, of course, is the hiker and camper's material of choice for almost anything and a material that costs the same per ounce as platinum. My guess was this was the boot world's answer to the $15 Rolexes that enterprising merchants sold to unwary tourists in Times Square, but they fit just fine, and I figured even if it was faux or semifaux Gore-Tex, that was probably OK for me.

"These any good?" I asked stupidly. Having tried to sell me jeans ample enough to house me and Ben together, the sales-clerk was going to tell me to go to Florsheim's for a pair of boots?

He could have just laughed at the idiocy of the question, but instead considered my question gravely and then picked up the right boot and held it up to the light, apparently thinking one evaluated Gore-Tex boots the way one evaluated a bottle of Cabernet. At least he didn't look for the cork and try to smell it.

"Oh, yes," he said, in a lilting Indian accent. "Very good. Very good. You do very fine hiking in those hiking boots."

I figured I might as well let myself feel vaguely comforted by his seal of approval, since these were the only $59.99, more-or-less-Gore-Tex hiking boots I was likely to find. So I took the plunge and found some grayish wool socks to throw in as well. I figured I could make do with what I had for the rest.

On the morning of the outing I threw the usual haphazard collection of couture—jeans, extra socks, extra underwear, fleece, sweater, hideous-looking red sleep shirt—into my back-pack, packed up our lunch, and drove off to the usual meeting place. We dithered along at the customary pace, until Mr. John-son took a look at his watch and then at Dr. Flank.

"Professor, we about ready to roll?"

"Can't see why not. All right, gentlemen," Dr. Flank said. "Let's head out."

The highlight of the drive up came when we passed the group of dank red brick buildings that were the largely deserted remains of the Harlem Valley State Hospital, a state mental institution that loomed off the roadway with memorable, brooding menace. About fifteen minutes later, near the town of New Milford, Connecticut, we pulled off the road and drove over a single-lane covered bridge into a dusty parking lot full of cars and SUVs with kayaks on top and perhaps a half dozen healthy-looking hikers milling outside. We divided into three patrols, studied our contour maps, checked our compasses, and waited for last-minute instructions from Dr. Flank.

It was an awfully big group to be hiking, about twenty kids and six dads. But on Dr. Flank's signal, we began trekking resolutely into the woods like a crack commando force embarking on a precision military operation. We veered away from the river into a dense thicket, past the ruins of an old cottage that had burned down forty years earlier. This was more rustic and obscure than I had expected. Who knew the fabled Appalachian Trail was so dense and wooded and the trail itself so elusive? I tried to imagine walking to Georgia this way. It seemed impossible. Pretty soon there was hardly any trail at all. Like frontier woodsmen, we doggedly pushed on for a minute or so. Before we went too much farther, though, the leaders stopped and huddled together.

"Uh, Bill, what color is the A.T. blaze supposed to be?" asked Mr. Johnson, referring to the tree markings that denote the trail.

"Uh, I don't think it's supposed to be blue," responded Dr. Flank.

Indeed, the A.T.'s characteristic blaze was white, a marking nowhere to be seen. We stopped, and the Big Three hurriedly reviewed our bearings on the hieroglyphiclike topographic map we had brought along. Sure enough, we had begun our hike by charging determinedly in the general direction of downtown Waterbury.

Undeterred, we retraced our steps to the parking lot, where we picked up the white blaze and began our march across a rugged rocky trail winding along the west bank of the Housatonic River. About a half mile later we passed through a gap in a stone wall and then crossed over a 120-foot bridge over the river. We continued along the south bank of Ten Mile River, with the trail unfolding in a gorgeous series of woodland tableaux of mostly bare winter trees, rocky streams, gentle rises, and steep slopes. A little more than a mile into the hike we began an ascent, which varied from moderate to—by my standards, anyway—pretty damn serious, toward the top of Ten Mile Hill, with an elevation of one thousand feet. It left most of us winded and the king-sized kids like Sam 'n Eric gasping for breath and complaining at every incline.

"How far have we gone?" Sam asked about a tenth of a mile into the climb.

"We've just started," said Mr. Toonkel. "Don't start asking how far we've gone."

"How far have we gone?" Sam asked five minutes later.

"I told you not to ask me that," Mr. Toonkel said. "If you're getting tired we'll just leave you here, so the birds will have something to eat."

Sam was quiet for another five minutes, then tried a different approach.

"How much farther do we have to go?" he asked.

Mr. Toonkel was not amused.

"That won't work either. Just keep walking. When we stop it means we're there. If we're still hiking, we're not there yet. Is that clear enough?"

Sam remained quiet as he huffed and puffed for a few more minutes. Then he moved on to more fundamental issues.

"What's the point of the hiking?" he asked when we were ready for our first break. In Scouting, this was one of those ontological questions that got to the nature of reality, like "Is there a God?"

"To hike," said Mr. Toonkel, in a voice as devoid of affect as he could manage. "It's good exercise."

"You hike to hike? That's pretty dumb. What's the point if you're not going anywhere?"

"That's for you to find out," Mr. Toonkel said with finality.

Mr. Toonkel did his best to withdraw from the dialogue, but the thread led to an ongoing discussion between Sam 'n Eric on the pointlessness of the day's events, the unseemly weight of their day packs, the length of the outing, the kind of music they'd rather be listening to, the kind of dirt bikes that would make this trek tolerable, the specific teachers they wished were doing this in their stead, and, most important, how long it was until lunch.

"I call your lunch, in case you die," Tom announced.

"That's not funny," Sam replied.

In fact, Sam lived until lunch, which we ate when we reached the top of the hill, about two miles into the hike. It overlooked a gorgeous vista of wooded glen, above which we perched on rocks like eagles catching the midafternoon sun. Ben and I sat together sharing our sandwiches, Goldfish, granola bars, and sesame sticks. He had a habit of asking me questions I was invariably unable to answer. Do pigs sweat? If you were as rich as Bill Gates, could you buy a fighter plane? Would you rather die painfully without knowing you were going to die or painlessly and slowly but you knowing you were dying? What would life be like if the power source were static electricity? Do things happen to dogs seven times faster because a dog's year equals seven of ours? But sitting here in the wild, neither of us felt much need to talk. And we mostly ate in silence, appreciating the tranquil scene below.

When we resumed our trek, the hardest part was already over. The rest of the hike, which covered 5.4 miles from start to finish, was largely downhill. By the time we got to the cabin it was about three in the afternoon.

Camp Siwanoy turned out to be a seventy-five-year-old, 659-acre preserve that had seen better days. The camp was one of four properties owned by the Westchester–Putnam Council, the local Scouting umbrella group. Unfortunately, the council had the resources for only three, and Siwanoy, which was up for sale, had the frayed and forlorn feel of a place in the process of being abandoned.

Our abode was a rough-hewn cabin sitting on cement blocks with bare pine floors, a pitched roof, a modest front porch, and two main rooms—a living room with a big fireplace and a dormitory-style bedroom with a wood-burning stove and wooden bunks that had the look of the accommodations in prisoner-of-war camps. Off the living room was a kitchen with a stove and refrigerator from the 1950s. On the walls were plaques with the Morning, Noon, and Evening Grace and other variations like the Camp Siwanoy Vespers:

> Now the Day is nearly over
> And the campfire sheds its glow
> Let us stand and sing together
> To old Siwanoy we know
> Camp Siwanoy, to thee forever
> True and Loyal Scouts will be
> And each Scout to one another
> Holding fast to love and memory

Outside was a horrific latrine, with wooden stalls as dank and foreboding as a dungeon and a hideously soiled apple sitting in the middle of a rusted-out urinal. It wasn't clear whether it was there for some pitifully inadequate hygienic purpose or as a bit of Boy Scout conceptual art.

The best part of the camp was a huge fort in the form of a wooden stockade. It had a guard tower about ten feet tall with a ladder leading to the top, a covered area used for storing lumber or stashing prisoners, and enough space for dozens of kids to stage raids, fight wars, toss grenades, and engage in benign, adolescent mayhem. So while the grown-ups retired to the cabin, the kids took to the fort, where they improvised a war game that consisted of dividing up into two opposing sides, throwing rocks and sticks at one another, trying to take and defend the tower, and committing the sorts of low-level acts of violence that once were routine horseplay and now keep personal injury lawyers in brand-new BMWs.

This outing was, in some ways, like our first two outings. But, for both of us, there was a big difference. Ben clearly didn't worry about being an outsider as much as I worried for him. But for the first time, he didn't seem to me like the new kid. The troop was already sorting itself out by age, by big kids and little kids, and he, by dint of being one of eight sixth graders new to the troop, was already just one of the little kids, not the new kid in town. He trotted off with all the others when they played around on the fort or disappeared into the woods in search of wood. He dutifully listened with the others when Dr. Flank was dispensing wisdom on the perfect tomato sauce or Mr. Toonkel was explaining how to tie a square knot or clove hitch. He was part of the appreciative gallery that hung around when Sam 'n Eric embarked on some riff about Dr. Flank's age, or the infirmities of one teacher or another, or the incredibly awesome qualities of this or that paintball gun.

And, as it turned out, the kids he had the most in common with were the Amigos, sixth graders like him, who on further exposure seemed not so bratty after all. Amigo number 1 was Barrett, a relentlessly energetic computer wonk and midget weatherman who obsessively followed the weather channel and various weather Web sites so he could do his own uncannily accurate daily forecasts every day. Jonah had a quietly assertive manner and short blond hair and seemed the most Todd-like of the kids in Ben's grade. He was the keenest naturalist of the younger kids and considered himself a vegetarian, even though his diet consisted largely of McDonald's fries and pepperoni pizza without tomato sauce—the pepperoni and other pork products apparently deemed too far from anything obviously animal-like to count as meat. The third Amigo was Mark, a tall, dark-haired kid with a wry, sardonic bent and a head stuffed full of information on Trident submarines, Civil War battles, and World War II weaponry gleaned from years of watching the History Channel. He wore a T-shirt reading "What if the hokey-pokey really is what it's all about?" which seemed to sum up his sense of humor.

All the kids returned once it began to get dark, with a few cuts and scrapes, but nothing requiring major surgery. The closest anyone came to real injury was when Mr. Toonkel threw a fit when he found Sam 'n Eric in the bunkroom with a box of matches and a tin can, trying to light Sam's farts by trapping them in the can and thrusting a match inside. There was an absolute ban on kids' having matches or other fire-starting implements inside the cabin, and it didn't take a genius to think that a bunch of boys in a rickety old cabin really didn't need to have any matches. Mr. Toonkel confiscated the contraband and stomped out of the dormitory room, leaving Sam 'n Eric with more ammunition for their sense of grievance and victimhood.

Mr. Toonkel marched through the main room to the kitchen, where Dr. Flank and a small group of campers were preparing dinner.

"What is it?" one of the kids asked.

"It's called Edible Surprise," chimed in Mr. Toonkel. "If it's edible, it's a surprise."

In truth, Dr. Flank's cooking was always at least edible, and this turned out to be a perfectly serviceable stew composed of six pounds of Carolina white rice, four pounds of hamburger meat, onions, green pepper, and sundry seasonings, which was prepared by Dr. Flank and a gaggle of kids. Dr. Flank directed the chopping, cooking, Pamming of the skillet, slicing, and dicing while delivering assorted instructional asides ("Searing means you cook the heck out of it. Sautéing means you pay attention to what you're doing.") to the crew, many of whom were using the occasion to work on their cooking merit badge. There was a long picnic table in the living room, and we had the stew, Dole Classic Iceberg Salad with Kraft Free Zesty Italian dressing, sliced onion bread, and Technicolor pitchers of bug juice followed by chocolate chip and oatmeal cookies for dessert.

After dinner, we threw a bunch of logs on the fire from the stout pile just outside the front door.

"All right, gentlemen," said Mr. Johnson. "It's show time at the Rialto."

Show time, such as it was, began with kids doing a few skits. Then Dr. Flank, Mr. Toonkel, and Mr. Johnson each told a story, a traditional part of the Troop 1 canon. Dr. Flank's was a long, elaborate Lenni-Lenape Indian story, essentially a creation myth of how the Lenni-Lenape came to inhabit the Hudson Valley. Sometimes Dr. Flank's stories took hold and sometimes they were a bit abstruse and airy for the members of the Eminem Generation. But this time the kids listened respectfully and attentively.

Mr. Toonkel specialized in horror stories, which were invariably related to the locale of the camp-out. This time his tale was about the depraved denizens of the nearby psychiatric hospital and what he described as numerous unconfirmed, but ominous, reports of missing boys left in their wake. Mr. Toonkel was a great storyteller with a disarmingly sincere affect. He always delivered his frightful tales in an utterly matter-of-fact voice, occasionally shaking his head as if left totally perplexed by the dark mystery of it all, throwing out scary thoughts and then qualifying them with lame, thoroughly unconvincing assurances that all was probably well. He finally concluded with a resigned shrug and a totally unconvincing expression of lukewarm reassurance. "So no one knows what became of the missing boys," he said in his flat, nasal voice, as if passing on a historical oddity from colonial times. "You hear terrible rumors of beheadings and bodies found in distant caves, but you can't really believe everything you hear. They do their best to catch the inmates who escape, but it's not a perfect world, and sometimes they still get out and are never found. I think I read something about one who got out just the other day. Maybe I'm wrong. The odds are it's nothing to worry about. But you may hear a strange sound tonight. It might sound like an owl or a coyote, but, for your own protection, you might want to listen extra carefully, just in case it's someone you don't want around. Like I said, it's probably nothing. I wouldn't let it bother you."

Mr. Johnson spoke with laconic economy and began his story with a succinct preamble about the creation of legends and myths. "This story is a little bit about how legends begin," he said. "Legends begin by people experiencing real events and then passing stories about them along verbally from one genera-tion to another. Legends actually begin with truth. Sometimes they come to symbolize great, momentous things. Tonight we're going to be the first generation to hear a legend about a great chief, the chief known as the Great Leknoot. The chief went with his tribe to the distant reaches of the north country. And he paddled his kayak through the mountains, the rivers, and the lakes. And when he had to go from one lake to the other, he picked up his kayak and put it on his shoulder and carried it across the land until he reached the next body of water."

Some of the older kids seemed to get a titter of recognition, as if they knew exactly what was going on, but everyone else was listening with rapt attention, not knowing where this story was going.

"The great chief, of course, had his tribe with him, and he was a great provider and wanted to provide for all the people. But after the third day of the journey, they had eaten all their food. Leknoot paddled into the shallows of a great lake, and he cast his line out into the shallows. And out from under a log a huge fish with giant jaws came and took Leknoot's feathered lure and dove back under the water. Leknoot knew that his people were hungry, so he jumped into the water and wrestled with this great beast of a fish. And as he wrestled, his people stood along the shoreline by their canoes. Leknoot stood up to his waist in the water, and then he lifted high into the air this great beast of a fish with the giant hooked jaws and proclaimed, 'This evening we will dine.' Leknoot led the troop paddling the rest of the day until they reached an island. There were eight tribesmen and they were all hungry. So they removed the great beast from the water and that night they ate all the pink flesh until there was nothing left but the skeleton and the great jaws. The tribe knew the fish was the favorite food of the black bear, so they had to dispose of it. So they built a great fire, and into the fire they disposed of all that was left of this great fish, the skeleton, the backbone, the jaw. As the tribe sat around with their leader Leknoot telling tales of past exploits, there arose from the flames a great head with a giant hooked jaw. The great beast of the fish sought revenge upon the tribe in the form of a curse. He said whenever the tribe should camp, at some time in the night the great head with the jaws will rise from the fire and devour them all. So tonight, I want you to look into the fire, think of Leknoot and the tribe alone on the island, waiting for the revenge of the great beast, and be careful to look into the fire and see the shape of the great hooked jaws."

It was truly an artful performance. Leknoot, as I realized midway through the tale, was, of course, Toonkel spelled backward, and the tale was one I had heard in different versions before, of the twenty-six-inch brown trout Mr. Toonkel had caught that summer on the High Adventure trip for the older Scouts in the Adirondacks. He had indeed gone into the water with it, and when they finally filleted it, it made three frying pans full of fish, more fish than any of them had eaten in their life. Mr. Johnson's recitation functioned as a tale, as a bit of troop lore, and as a totally credible lesson in the creation of myth, memory, and community.

The differences in storytelling, I realized, were a microcosm of the different styles of the three men. Take any subject: There was a Flank way, a Toonkel way, and a Johnson way. On the hikes, Dr. Flank favored a carved maple walking stick with the Scout seal on it, Mr. Toonkel used a steel photography monopod, and Mr. Johnson just used whatever he picked up in the woods. Dr. Flank drove that sensible, tidy Volvo; Mr. Toonkel drove a big Suburban with assorted crisp, new baseball caps curled up neatly next to the driver's seat; Mr. Johnson drove a modest beat-up Ford Escort wagon with an Elon College bumper sticker on the back. Dr. Flank had an inexhaustible supply of Scouting attire, the most spectacular being an old red wool jacket with patches going back to the 1960s and '70s. Mr. Toonkel showed up in fancy wet suits or camouflage with eccentric headgear, like an elaborate Russian fur hat or a baseball cap reading "Sing Sing Surf Squad." Mr. Johnson wore old flannel shirts and jeans, as if he had just pulled from the closet whatever was appropriate for the day's weather.

The different roles played by the three struck a chord with me. We keep hearing these days about absent dads and failing dads and uninvolved dads. But I grew up with what felt like three dads. Maybe it was because everyone moved from New York City to the same subdivision at the same time, or because all the men were World War II veterans, or because the freshly minted suburban world of new split-levels selling for $29,999 was equally new to all of them, but we at 39 Tanners Road and the Isaacs next door at 35 Tanners and the Biblowitzes next to them at 31 functioned like an extended family. We walked in and out of each others' houses like they were our own. We took vacations together—usually with just one of the other families, but sometimes with both—the kids piled into the back of station wagons so haphazardly that one summer in Lakeville, Massachusetts, we left my brother behind at a grocery store, assuming he was either with the I's or the B's. Sometimes the parents would gather in our den for pizza and beer, and even as a kid their bond struck me as something special. So much for the soulless anomie of suburbia.

I viewed all six parents as expressions of the infinite, mysterious ways that adults effectively or ineptly exerted their will on or imparted wisdom to the young. But most memorable for me were the three men. My father, Jerome Applebome, combined a warm heart, a cranky mind, and a fatalistic soul. You could take all the ineffably descriptive Yiddish words, from *mensch* to *schlemiel,* and they all held a piece of him. Like me, I'm afraid, he had the quality of a Thurber character never quite settled in the world. He was constantly worried about money, trying to keep fenders on old clunkers in place with Fiberglas tape, endlessly fighting losing battles against crab grass or wily raccoons or squirrels intent on stealing the birdseed or balky commodes likely to spray water in all directions or stocks that went down when you bought them and up when you sold them. But he was (and is) utterly devoted to his kids and taught us to do the right thing. If his friend Sol Budd was in the hospital dying, he'd be there to hold his hand and listen to his fevered ramblings before he passed on. He might not have wanted to visit an elderly relative in a nursing home on a sunny Sunday, but he always showed up, the way others went to church. I know we're not as good at those small gestures as he was, but it wasn't for want of a good example to follow.

Jesse Biblowitz was the sweetest man I knew. He was big and lumbering, slightly stooped, with big ears and thick, dark hair. He never seemed rattled the way my father often was, and I can't ever remember him getting even slightly mad. Jesse had some sort of suburban Zen down pat. A bunch of us—kids and grownups—played tennis every Sunday, and even as I got older and clearly was never going to be as good a player as he thought I might become, he'd still treat every failing as a mild, unexpected aberration in my march toward greatness. He spoiled his kids, and, in a way, he spoiled those of us who weren't his kids too. I never doubted that Jesse cared about us almost as much as my own father did.

And Gilbert Isaacs was the smartest man I knew, a man like no one else. Gilbert had zero interest in baseball, basketball, football, or any of the sports that obsessed the rest of us. He did everything his own way. While the other dads tended their lawns, he built a Japanese pebble garden in his backyard with a ten-foot-tall copy of a famous Isamu Noguchi sculpture—he fabricated it himself in his basement. When a storm knocked it down, he painstakingly built another one. He'd never graduated from college, but he knew about everything—orchids, the paintings of Emil Nolde, astronomy, World War II battles. Once he diagnosed his barber's eye infection and thereafter was always greeted with a respectful "Good afternoon, Doc" by the barber, who assumed he was a physician rather than the owner of a jewelry store he ran with his brother. Gilbert didn't share the fashionable leftist politics of the grownups who were regarded as the local intellectuals, but he was the most genuinely intellectual person I've ever known. As he got older he let his white hair grow long, which gave him a presence that was both austere and distinguished. He looked like some nineteenth-century senator from Kentucky or Tennessee. And that imposing presence and his stern, demanding demeanor could be intimidating in the best way. "DON'T MAKE EXCUSES," he would thunder at his daughters. And we would all get the message that you did your best in life, and you didn't blame others for whatever you failed to accomplish. You just tried to do better next time.

Kids can learn from lots of people, I guess, from coaches and teachers and clergymen as well as from grandfathers and fathers and neighbors. But I don't know any people these days who have that same kind of intimate relationship with their neighbors that my parents did with the I's and B's, or any kid who could claim to have three fathers the way I did when I was growing up. I know Ben doesn't. We had a neighbor in Atlanta—an Eagle Scout, it turned out—named Leon, who had some of Gilbert's quiet *über*-competence. But even if we had stayed there, we would never have vacationed with his family, and Ben would never have wandered in and out of his house the way I did with Gilbert.

In the same way, I did not expect Mr. Toonkel, Mr. Johnson, and Dr. Flank to become as big a part of Ben's life as Jerome, Gilbert, and Jesse were of mine. They couldn't be. But, if in some imperfect way, they could play some of the same role— project qualities and skills and competencies that I didn't have— that seemed a remarkable blessing and gift.

We sat watching the fire for a while. Then Dr. Flank invited everyone to get up for the circle. We all linked arms, the grownups and the kids, and everyone quietly waited for Dr. Flank to speak. Troop 1 was about as determinedly free from religion as a Scout troop can be, but Dr. Flank's campfire closings usually took on the air of a benediction, as if this were Baden-Powell's church of the outdoors and he was, if not the priest, at least the guide.

"We had a terrific hike today," he said. "And I was very impressed with your cooking too. I didn't know you knew so much. And I want you to think about our hike today, about the beauty of the woods and the time we were able to share there together. It's almost ten, and we're all tired, so I want you all to get right into bed, so we can get an early start tomorrow. So," and all the kids and all the adults on hand joined in, "May the Great Master of all Scouts be with us until we meet again."

The kids retired to their sleeping bags on the rock-hard cribs in the bunkroom, while the adults and some of the high school kids stayed up watching the fire for another half hour or so, the older kids and the leaders sharing stories of past High Adventure trips. The kids didn't go to sleep right away, but after much stray talk about farts, the movie *Titanic,* the middle school football team, the band Rage Against the Machine, dirt bikes, body odors, and creative ways to make use of the urine-soaked apple, they began to drop off to sleep one by one.

Just before they all went to asleep, a lone voice piped up.

"Is it true that every time the lights flicker someone just got electrocuted at the insane place?" Sam asked.

"Nahhh," said Todd. "Sometimes they're getting electrocuted. Sometimes, it just means the power went out, the locks don't work, the security system failed, the guards don't have a clue what's happening, they can't even get the searchlights to work, and you've got a bunch of murderous loonies running around like lizards in the dark. Go to sleep, Sam."

7: Gear, God, and the Klondike Derby

It was more Joseph McCarthy's vision of stealth Commies insidiously infiltrating the country's very core than Japanese planes materializing out of the blue to attack Pearl Harbor, but before long Scouting had begun to insinuate itself into every corner of our life. Not that it was an easy fit. Scouting is based on the premise that there's something in boys' DNA primal enough to outlast changing fashions and mores. Cub Scouts put together miniature cars to race in the Pinewood Derby when Dr. Flank was a kid, and they do it now. Boy Scouts learn their square knots and clove hitches, repeat their oaths, and follow the trail from Tenderfoot to Eagle now much as they did when Scouting began. Try to think of something, anything, in boys' lives—clothes? music? academics? sports?—that looks and feels in the era of palm pilots and e-mail the way it did in the era of fountain pens and Underwood manual typewriters. So as we were drawn further into Scouting it felt like traversing two disparate worlds: one, the iconic, timeless world of the Handbook and Dr. Flank's intricately scripted pageant of Scouting activities; the other, the all-enveloping world of pop culture, mass media, and modernity in all its ragged, ever-changing, anti-iconic inconsistency. To the adults, it was at times not entirely clear if we were in the real Scout world or a somewhat loopy modern-day adaptation. But the kids seldom had such qualms. Whatever was encoded in the Scout regimen usually seemed to strike the right chords.

Our immersion into Scouting first manifested itself in the ever-increasing accumulation of gear that began piling up in Ben's room like a version of "The Sorcerer's Apprentice" choreographed by a demented outdoors outfitter. You might think that being a Boy Scout, with its hearty hikes and Spartan summer camp, its ethos of rugged self-reliance, would be a sober counterweight to the heady materialism of our time. You would be wrong. It turns out that for the youth of America, nothing is quite so expensive these days as a simple walk in the woods. Even a hideously expensive activity like skiing, which struck fear into my overextended suburban heart, involved just one equipment outlay for skis, boots, and poles. But hiking and climbing and backpacking is a modern dad's version of the Big Muddy. Once you slog in, there's no way to slog back out without shelling out vast sums of money for things you never knew existed or couldn't imagine mattered.

It was not always thus. The first edition of the Boy Scout Handbook, published in 1911, ends with a catalog of that era's version of Scout Stuff. There's the official Scout axe—"The best axe that money can buy or skill produce"—for 35 cents, a bandana for 10 or 15 cents, $1 breeches, 75-cent knickerbockers, a 10-cent drinking cup, and a 60-cent haversack. For $1.15 you could get a Boy Scout hat. A poncho was $2.50, and mess kits were 50 and 75 cents. The accent was definitely on being simple and utilitarian, so Scouts were advised to make their own tents and find any old footwear for hiking: "Any good shoe that is made up for the purpose of ease and comfort in tromping will serve the Boy Scout's needs. The Boy Scout shoe is convenient, inexpensive and especially designed for scouting." Price $2.50.

This is not quite the way the game is played in the era of Gear Lust as conveyed in the pages of magazines selling hiking gear, climbing gear, adventure gear, camping gear, ab-defining gear, and other accoutrements of today's ruggedly fashionable outdoors lifestyle. You need a tent, of course, like our REI Geomountain three-to-four person, four-season Mountaineering model with dual doors, front and rear vestibules, screen windows, convenient pockets, and enough support, we were told, to stand up under the weight of a blizzard of snow if you happened to be doing particularly out-there winter camping. (That claim, you can be sure, I will never be around to verify.) You need all-weather jackets like Ben's EMS Gore-Tex Downpour shell. You need hiking boots like Ben's Dolomite number, a backpack like his EMS internal-frame Long Trail ST with 4,000-cubic-centimeter capacity, and a sleeping bag like his North Face Thunderhead, guaranteed to keep you comfortable at 20 degrees Fahrenheit. OK, I get that, more or less.

But that's just the start. There's the $12 superabsorbent, lightweight PackTowl ("Soaks up water like a sponge!"), which is apparently needed because plain old towels may have worked well enough for the past century, but only a dolt takes one on a hike now. There's the Guardian Plus Sweetwater portable water purification system, needed to protect us from waterborne viruses such as *E. coli* or cholera and waterborne protozoa like giardia and cryptosporidium. We got a camping stove, a very modest Yellowstone Lite Trail gas stove. Just $28! The cooking set was simple too, a Texsport Stainless Steel, $32.50. There are lots of little things—compass, first-aid kit, carabiners for attaching as many things on your pack as possible, and Nalgene wide-mouth loop-top water bottles. We got a $9.99 tick removal kit, the one extra absolutely invaluable here in Lyme disease country.

There are many midrange things, such as Camelback hiker hydration systems—insulated water bags you strap to your body and sip through a tube to avoid sudden death by dehydration as you're wandering around the A.T. The Outback Oven. Industrial-strength flashlights and tiny high-intensity Mini Maglites and Petzl headlamps suitable for either (a) working in a coal mine or (b) finding a way to the latrine at night. A GCI Outdoors folding chair for short trips or car camping expeditions where you have your gear near at hand, and a lightweight EMS Mountain Chair for those arduous treks into the distant outback somewhere.

To go Dr. Flank one better, in addition to our plain old wool socks, we got two pairs of Trail Runner II outdoor 100-percent super-fine-grade merino wool Smartwool socks. $17.99 a pair! For socks! And I thought Gore-Tex was expensive. To keep our lunch and spare clothes dry on the canoe trips, we got a commodious green rubber SealLine Baja waterproof bag. Tevas! Camping pillows! Mosquito netting! Leatherman multitool set! We got an extra-lightweight tent for hikes when Ben would be alone and our main model would be too heavy to carry. We got an EMS Trekker PL 2600 day pack when the big pack was more than was needed. We got canteens and day packs and canoe pads and stainless steel vacuum-insulated mugs. I say "we," but these were all Ben's purchases. All I bought were my cheapo boots and a copy of Kathleen Meyer's indispensable book *How to Shit in the Woods*. (This is not a joke. Check it out on Amazon.)

I look at the list now and feel faint—*We bought all that??* But built up over time, a purchase made here or there for a birthday or for a trip, it didn't seem like that much. And the other kids were just as bad. Conversation would begin with the ageless query: What would I want to bring if I were hiking to the top of Mount Everest? (This from kids who started whining "Are we almost there?" after the first half-mile or modest incline on every four-mile hike.) And then mumbling stumblebums who heretofore had seemed barely able to string two coherent sentences together would launch into learned disquisitions about North Face Alpenglow Polarguard Delta Sleeping Bags or Patagonia Regulator System shells, the design details of various mummy bags and overbags, goose down versus synthetic insulation, and how much tax you saved by buying at Campmor online instead of getting your dad to take you to the store in New Jersey.

Still, after a while, I got the shakes every time we drove anywhere in the vicinity of Eastern Mountain Sports, Ben's favorite outdoors store, and did my best to rapidly dispose of the Campmor catalogs and EMS flyers and copies of *Backpacker* magazine that arrived in the mail. It was hopeless, of course, and Ben consumed them with religious zeal, sometimes lying in bed with his flashlight after dark, surreptitiously leafing through the Jagged Edge Mountain Gear catalog, sort of J. Crew meets the *Bhagavad Gita*. "The Journey is the Destination," it read. "Follow with Complete sincerity the Path that inspires you most."

While we were accumulating gear, the troop activities were becoming part of our regular schedule. There were the weekly meetings, of course. After the fall hikes, our next event was the annual Christmas tree sale at the Pleasantville First United Methodist Church. So far we had been longer on hiking and camping than on good turns and service. The tree sale was a mixture of service to the church and service to the troop. Each year the church ordered some two thousand trees—balsams and Frazier firs and Douglas firs, which sold for between $14 for tiny desktop models to $75 for the top-of-the-line ten- to twelve-foot-tall balsam premiums perfect for scraping that cathedral ceiling in your brand-new McMansion. The trees were sold by our Scouts, with most kids working a half day each weekend through December. The troop was paid for each hour the kids worked. In the end, it was the church's biggest fundraiser of the year. Half of the troop's proceeds went to our activities, and half went to the council office to support broader Scout activities.

And the kids made tips, which could amount to $10 or $20 a day, not bad for a twelve- or thirteen-year-old.

The trees arrived every year from Canada on the Friday after Thanksgiving, piled fourteen or fifteen high on two huge forty-eight-foot flatbed trucks. Our first job, as we learned when we showed up at eight on a surprisingly balmy November morning, was to unload them all. There were about twenty of us from the troop, plus a handful of men from the church and a dozen or so wrestlers from a nearby high school. The minister of the church soon appeared. He was a big, rugged-looking guy with a full black beard wearing a plain gray sweatshirt and blue jeans. Even the minister was a lumberjack, and he's OK! He gathered us in a circle and led us in a prayer ("Oh, Lord, we thank you for this beautiful day and for this labor we are about to begin. We thank you for giving us this season of peace and love, and we ask that the work goes safely today. May all your blessings be with this group and this church and may this be a joyous season here and around the world. In Christ's name we pray, Amen.").

The troop had more Jewish families—ours included—than Christian ones, but most kids turned out for the sale nonetheless. It struck me that other than the dutiful renderings of the Scout Oath ("On my honor I will do my best to do my duty to God and my country..."), this was the first reference to God in any form we had heard since we joined the troop. The absence of religion was partly a reflection of Dr. Flank's secular, modernist tilt. But just how much religion to inject into Scouting has been a continuing issue. Baden-Powell's version of the Scout Law did not have a single mention of God or religion. He once wrote, "A bad man who believes in a creed is no more religious than the good man who does not." But Scouting in the United States grew out of the tradition of Christian uplift and character-building that gave rise to the Young Men's Christian Association. In fact, when the Boy Scouts of America was getting off the ground, the YMCA did most of the initial organizing. So the B.S.A. stipulated that a Scout is reverent and that a boy cannot become the best sort of man without a grounding in religious faith. But the Scouts were always ambivalent about how much explicit religion needed to be part of the program. The first American version of the Boy Scout Handbook hardly mentions religion. Instead, it precisely mimics Baden-Powell's world view by tying one of its few mentions of God to the duty to do a good turn daily, saying: "It is a practical religion, and a boy honors God best when he helps others most."

Over time, the references to God became much more frequent in the Handbook. The fifth edition of the Handbook, published in 1948 and the best selling of the eleven editions, is expansive in its remarks on God and religion. It notes the importance of worshipping God regularly, and the great religious faith of men like Washington and Lincoln. "Above all you are faithful to Almighty God's Commandments," it advises, and adds: "Sometimes when you look up into the starlit sky on a quiet night, and feel close to Him—thank Him as the Giver of all good things."

The eleventh and latest edition of the Handbook has a broad and somewhat muted sense of religion: "Wonders all around us remind us of our faith in God. We find it in the tiny secrets of creation and in the great mysteries of the universe. It exists in the kindness of people and in the teachings of our families and religious leaders. We show our reverence by living our lives according to the ideals of our beliefs." But while other organizations, the Girl Scouts for example, have explicitly moved away from requiring members to profess their faith in God, the Boy Scouts have chosen to move in the opposite direction, making the requirement an explicit and literal one, leading to controversies in recent years in which Scouts have been expelled for refusing to profess their faith in God.

The tree sale didn't have much to do with faith—especially since it wasn't the faith of most of us anyway—but between the minister's benediction and the air of fraternal comity, it unfolded sort of like a suburban version of a rural barn raising. For our first day's labors, we had all brought sturdy gloves and dispensable old clothes, which were sure to end up caked with pine needles and tree sap. A few of the huskier men and wrestlers climbed a ladder to the top of the trees stacked in the truck bed and began handing them down to the assembled masses below. The men and bigger kids hoisted the trees up on their shoulders, and except for the biggest Douglas firs, lugged them up a wooded slope where signs were set up reading FRAZIER FIR 8-9' $72 or BALSAM PREMIUM 5-6' $29 or BALSAM SELECT 6-8' $41. The kids who couldn't quite manage a tree alone paired off with one another and lugged one between them, eventually heaving it onto the tree pile with a fierce grunt. Then they turned around and marched back for some more. Sam 'n Eric and the bigger kids were in their element, strutting around like construction workers. The church had put out a spread of donuts, bagels, coffee, and hot chocolate, giving the kids the ability to malinger, kibitz, and take long breaks during which they could complain at length about how hard they were working, just like real live grownups did. For a change, none of the three leaders was around. Vince and Robert, the mismatched Italians from the first camp-out, were in charge, giving us the feel of a freelance one-off operation. By noon we were finished and the kids, for the most part, had done the first day of honest remunerative labor in their lives. The next Saturday we showed up again to build wooden bins, put tags on all the trees, and lug about a third of the trees to fill the bins, leaving the rest waiting in reserve on the piles on the hillside. After that, the real selling began. The message on the church sign read IF WE DON'T HAVE CHRISTMAS IN OUR HEARTS, WE WILL NEVER FIND IT UNDER A

TREE, as if to remind one and all that this was supposed to be about moving hearts and not just about moving product. But the kids were there to sell the trees, not to minister to the shoppers, and they took their duties remarkably seriously.

"This is what you need to know to sell a Christmas tree," one of the men from the church began. He was standing by the sale command post, an old clothes dresser that had been modified for the exigencies of tree selling. The two top drawers were intact and loaded with first-aid gear and spare gloves. The other drawers were missing and replaced with a huge rope spool. The top and sides were bristling with box cutters, price tags, spare gloves, and other essentials. "The Fraziers keep their needles the longest," he continued. "That's going to be particularly important to our early shoppers. The balsams smell the best. The Douglas firs are the fullest and last the longest. Some customers pick one right out. Some want to look at five or six or seven. Just be helpful to them, and they'll find one sooner or later. Your job is to help them pick out the tree and carry it back to the curb. Then you ask them if they want a fresh cut on the trunk. It will keep the tree fresh, particularly if they keep it in water with a little sugar mixed in. If they want the cut, do it with one of the hacksaws. Then cut off enough rope to lash the tree to the top of the car and tie it up securely. If you need it, we're there to help, particularly with cars that don't have a luggage rack on top where you need to run a bowline knot through the car."

He reached into a box and pulled out a dozen green baseball caps with a white Christmas tree and the words CHRISTMAS TREE SALE on the crest above the bill. "Oh, and wear these so they know you work here." We put them on, feeling like we'd made it out of Basic Training. As he talked, you could see the kids' minds working in unison: "Let me get this straight. Box cutters. Hacksaws. Knives. Rope. Donuts. Bagels. Tips. This is work?" The lot was festooned with roping and wreaths and bathed in an aural wash of Christmas chestnuts—"I'm Dream-ing of a White Christmas," "Jingle Bells," "I'll Be Home for Christmas," "The Christmas Song." No "Get-Down Hip-Hop Phat Christmas Def Jam Santa Booty Call" or Xmas fantasies with Britney and Christina or anything like that. We might not have been Christians, but we were darn sure going to do Christmas right.

Sam all but pounced on the first couple to show up, sound-ing as eager as one of the commission salesmen at Circuit City. Ben hung back for a while, but after most of the other kids had latched onto customers, he found himself face-to-face with a slim guy of about fifty-five in a blue satin welders' union jacket and his wife, a husky woman about two inches taller than he wearing a Christmas-tree sweatshirt.

"Hi," he said. "I'm Ben Applebome, and I'll be your Christmas-tree salesman for today." This was a swell icebreaker, and I trailed along as they headed toward the trees, which shim-mered in a great green sward.

"Hold this one up, please," the wife said to Ben. He pulled up one of the Fraziers and shook it so its branches, which had been bound tight for shipping, could begin to fall.

"How do you like it?" she asked her husband.

"It's fine. It's nice," he dutifully replied.

"I don't know," she said, circling around it. "I don't quite like the shape. It looks kind of lumpy."

"OK, fine. If it's lumpy, pick out another one that's not lumpy."

"How about this one?" she asked Ben. "That looks nice."

He picked up the new one and held it upright.

"What do you think, Jack?" she asked her husband.

"It's fine. It's nice. It's OK. They're all nice."

"I'm not sure about the color. It looks a little blue to me."

"It's not blue. It's a tree. Trees are green. It's green."

"I don't know. I think it would look funny with the sofa. Ben, put that one down," she said. "It's not right. This one looks nice. Let's try that one."

"It looks like the others. It's good. It's fine," said Jack, before she had a chance to ask him if he liked it. "We don't have all day, Brenda."

"No, it looks a little scrawny when you hold it like that."

And so it went. Too tall. Too short. Too blue. Too green. Too thin. Too full. Bad shape. Bad crest. Looks damaged. Looks dry. A little scrawny. A little puffy. Uneven-looking. Unnatural-looking. Not enough smell. Too much smell. Needles too sharp. Needles too soft. On and on. Finally, after twenty minutes, Brenda reluctantly settled on a seven-to-eight-foot Frazier ("You sure the trunk hasn't been cut on already, and this will last until Christmas? OK, then can you do a nice fresh cut for me, Ben?").

I helped him carry it to the curb. Jack trudged inside the church to pay. Brenda stood over us, looking at the tree suspiciously, as if still looking for the disqualifying feature that was surely there somewhere. Ben sawed off two inches of the trunk, and grabbed a handful of rope. We waited for Jack to pull up in a four-year-old Suburban with a luggage rack on top.

We then came face to face with one of the dirty little secrets of Boy Scouts. You might have the badge, but that doesn't mean you remember how to tie the knots. I, of course, had not forgotten my knots. I had never learned them. But Ben, who should have been our go-to guy in the knot department, having long since made Tenderfoot and nearing Second Class, wasn't much better despite his years of rigorous Scout training. We took to improvising assorted spaghetti-like knots, winding the rope four, five, six times around the luggage rack in various nonsanctioned, unapproved, ad hoc, half-assed maneuvers. The couple looked at our handiwork a bit quizzically but figured their treasure was basically secure. Jack gave Ben two bucks. Ben beamed. They drove off. He went on to customer number 2.

"I'm looking for one that's not too full, has a nice smell, but not an overpowering one, keeps its needles, and won't dry out before Christmas," the woman told Ben. And so it went. Before too long, two things became apparent. The first was that every couple that came in had pretty much the same dynamic. The woman was either mystically or obsessive-compulsively focused on finding the perfect tree with that certain indefinable Yuletide *je ne sais quoi,* and the man was just waiting to get the damn purchase over with so he could go home and watch the Jets or Giants on television. The second was that, in a way that Ben found baffling, I had perfect radar for who was going to tip him. For the most part, it was a simple matter of taking all our social status indicators and turning them upside down. So guys with sweatshirts from Fordham or Long Island University were more likely to tip than guys with shirts from Harvard or Yale. Welders in union jackets driving Chevys were more likely to tip than doctors with MD plates driving a Mercedes wagon. Old cars were better than new, domestic better than foreign. Guys with Noo Yawk accents better than guys with Connecticut lockjaw. Old better than young. Men better than women. Heavy women better than fashionably thin women. You get a fashionably thin doctor's wife with a Yale T-shirt and BMW with a Martha's Vineyard sticker, and she's as likely to tip you as to have Merle Haggard in her CD player. As any parent knows, it is almost impossible to impress your own kids past the age of eleven or twelve, but on this one score, my batting average was so good that finally Ben turned to me and said, "Dad, you're good." My turn to beam. We take our praise where we can get it.

The sale stretched over four weekends. I had periodic panic attacks about the sturdiness of our knots for drivers foolhardy enough to be traveling long distances. In my darker moments I found myself imagining horrid newspaper headlines ("Triborough Bridge Shut for Hours After Christmas Tree Flies Off SUV. Owner Expresses Outrage. Balding Boy Scout Held for Questioning."). But, particularly on the rare days that the temperature dipped below freezing, the whole endeavor became shrouded in the shiny tinsel of seasonal cheer and virtue. Finally, our chance to do a good turn! We'd work for a few hours, take a break for hot chocolate or the big plates of spaghetti and lasagna that the church ladies prepared, talk business with our fellow salesmen, comparing notes on the pace of sales and particularly demanding customers, and then put our gloves and hats back on and wade back into the fray. Bing would be warbling "White Christmas" yet again or we'd be into our fourteenth rendition of "The Christmas Song," but the kids were hustling for business and the dads were pleasantly punch drunk with the seasonal cheer of it all.

It was an unseasonably balmy December for New York, without a trace of snow. On the warmest days, the better-padded kids like Sam 'n Eric showed up in just T-shirts, and the lack of a winter chill gave the undertaking a decidedly off-kilter feel, like the pictures of guys in Santa suits parading down the beach in La Jolla. It was another case of Scouting in the abstract running into the messiness of reality. Instead of the world of Norman Rockwell, it's a half-Jewish bunch of suburban Boy Scouts who've forgotten their knots presiding over a balmy Global Warming Christmas tree sale. Not that we minded; we were all so caught up in the virtuous bonhomie of it all that the warm weather felt as right as anything else. When the sale finally ended the weekend before Christmas with the last scrubby trees marked down and sold cheap, we all wished one another, Christians or not, a Merry Christmas, sorry to see the whole thing end.

The warm weather was just an oddity at the tree sale. But it was an affront to the natural order as our next big activity, the Klondike Derby, beckoned. I really don't know what troops in Florida and Arizona do during January and February. But across the nation's northern tier, Scouts like us were working on building our sleds, practicing our winter skills, and boning up on shelter making, axe management, and first aid in anticipation of the big event. It consisted of two main parts. The first was a series of tests of Scouting skill and fortitude, which were judged by stern and demanding Scouters who were named Mayor of various stations set up around the park. The second was a double-elimination sled race in which Scouts, up to six pulling on a rope in front and one pushing from behind, race across perhaps fifty yards of snow-covered field until one sled team is judged the fastest.

Ben's Falcon patrol convened at Vince's auto repair shop on a Saturday in mid-January to fashion a sturdy-looking sled out of pieces of plywood, a few two-by-fours, and a pair of skis. What a deal! They had the whole cavernous garage to themselves on a Saturday and were able to use Vince's electric drills and detailing paint to cobble together a sled to die for. It had a sleek, aerodynamic design and was painted a fashionable understated gray with blue trim. As the *pièce de résistance,* the kids had cut out the eagles from two Post Office overnight delivery envelopes and pasted them on the sides to serve as fierce-looking surrogate falcons. The result looked like an Alaskan Post Office sled that had taken a wrong turn somewhere around Fairbanks and just kept going, but it still had the aura of a solid, macho sled not to be trifled with—the Derby's version of a Chevy truck. And aside from their construction duties, the kids got to run amok in the garage, riding up and down on the hydraulic lifts and generally having a big old time whether or not the sled was worth a damn.

The other Troop 1 patrols built their own sleds—none, it must be said, quite so imposing as the Post Office Special, but all worthy nonetheless. There were weeks of painting, waxing, replacing perfectly good skis with other indefinably superior skis, designing gallant patrol flags, and making final tinkers to bring the sled to its optimum condition. Finally, at the end of January, the big day dawned clear and bright—too clear and too bright, it turned out. The temperatures had dived into the 20s, giving the day an appropriately Arctic tinge. But when we arrived at Franklin Delano Roosevelt State Park for the Derby, we had everything in place but snow. There had been a minor flurry here or there over the past month, but none of it had amounted to anything and by Derby Day it was all gone. To be sure, a sled race without snow seemed a little like a figure-skating competition without ice. But a Scout is resourceful, and if we had to display our winter skills sans snow, that's what we would do.

When we got there just after 9:00 A.M. a handful of Scouts were pulling sleds of all shapes and sizes out of cars, trucks, SUVs, and vans. Before long the entire lot was filled with more than one hundred Scouts and at least twenty-five sleds, sleds with patrol flags for elks and lions and arrows and antelopes, sleds made from sturdy two-by-fours and sleds that looked like a few pine branches nailed to pieces of wood perched precariously on ancient skis. To be honest, no other sled had the heft, the professional fabrication, the subdued but elegant color scheme, or the fierce faux-heraldic falcons to compare with the Post Office Special. Kids from other troops wandered by admiringly to check it out. But there was not much time for mere milling. The Derby was to begin with inspection and check-in at the Derby starting point, which was designated as Juneau. There the Mayors, equipped with clipboards and scoring sheets, had to make sure that each sled had come equipped with the appropriate patrol equipment. "Before you officially enter the Yukon Territory," our handbook, the Passport, informed us, "you must pass the inspection in order to embark on this extremely hazardous expedition." The list of materials, all of them to be stashed inside the sled, was long and demanding:

Patrol flag
Fire-building materials
1 gallon drinking water
#10 can or pot to boil water in
4 six-foot-long poles
6 ten-foot-long lengths of rope
Tarp
Patrol first-aid kit, including triangular bandages,
     compresses, and splint materials
Blanket or sleeping bag
Backpack stove or equivalent to boil water for lunch
Hot chocolate, Cup-O-Soup, etc. for lunch
Compass
Hand axe
File to sharpen axe
Pencil, paper, and clipboard
Boy Scout Handbook
Garbage bag

I could not tell you what most of that was for and still don't know what a #10 can is, but we had somehow rounded most of it up, scoring eight of a possible ten points. At that point, we began dragging the sled across the frigid grass about two hundred yards away to Station 1, Match Splitting, an exercise in axe handling and fire starting. "The local Indian Tribe has challenged your patrol to a contest," the Passport read. "You must split or light more matches than their braves or lose your scalp." This meant we had to see how many matches we could light by hitting the match head with the hand axe. We ended with a lackluster score of five.

Next was Fire Building. Our Passport informed us that one of the local townspeople needed an operation and we needed to light a fire so the doctor could sterilize his instruments. We had brought plenty of wood, flint, and matches and built one in no time flat. Nine points. Then we went on to Ice Rescue, where a patrol member had fallen through the ice twenty-five feet from the shore. We had to rescue him and treat him for the Scouts' favorite peril, hypothermia. We got nine points again. On to First Aid, where our patrol, we were told, had come upon some injured miners, whom we had to treat for snow blindness, frostbite, and (perhaps you can guess?) hypothermia.

By this point, we had been dragging a bulky sled through the frigid, snowless park for three hours, and most kids were fading into the "When's Lunch?" zone. As luck would have it, lunch, or Ulcer Gap on our Passport, was next. The idea was to demonstrate our cooking skills, but instead of having to build another fire, we were allowed to use our propane stoves to boil water and cook. Thus prepared, we were able to whip up a welcome repast of hot chocolate, Ramen noodles, assorted soups and sandwiches, and more of Elliot's famous homemade beef jerky.

"What do Eskimoes eat in the real Klondike, wherever that is?" Louis asked.

"Whale blubber," answered Jimmy.

"Eskimo pies," answered Mark.

"Italian ices," answered Tom.

"Baked Alaska," answered Les.

"Prime rib of husky," answered Bernie.

Clearly, we could have gone in that direction for a while, but we had to move on to Shelter Building. It entailed building a shelter using natural items plus materials the patrol brought along. Once again we were prepared, not just with the assorted sticks, ropes, and tarps in the sled, but more importantly with a copy of Chapter 8, "Shelters," from the *U.S. Army Survival Manual*. *"You cannot ignore your tactical situation or your safety,"* it warned us, and offered hints on concealment from enemy observation and avoiding flash floods and avalanches. We turned to the section on natural shelters, which seemed more promising than the ones that entailed major construction projects. "Do not overlook natural formations that can give you shelter," it said. "Examples are caves, rocky crevices, clumps of bushes, small depressions, large rocks on leeward sides of hills, large trees with low-hanging limbs, and fallen trees with thick branches." Ah-ha! This was more like it. We ended up hanging a tarp from the front of a granite cave about seven feet high that was surrounded by a scrubby copse of pines and maples. We trudged to a few more destinations after that, but by this point there was just one activity left that could really get everyone's attention—the big race.

The Passport announced the race would begin at 2:15, but, of course, at 2:15 only a handful of thuggish-looking kids and scrawny sleds had arrived at the field where the race was to take place. The kids, various Scoutmasters, Mayors, and dads slowly filtered in, but the time crept from 2:30 to 2:45 to 3:00, with the temperatures sinking from the high 20s to the low 20s. Our feet were getting numb in our boots—wool socks or no wool socks. None of the adults would have been sorry to pack it in, but the race was too big a lure for the kids to miss—that and the orgy of Dunkin' Donuts to follow. Finally, after much mayoral conferring and pacing off the exact configuration of the racecourse, which looked to be about fifty yards altogether, a man with an air gun in one hand and a bullhorn in the other strode toward the assembled masses. "Gentlemen," he announced into the bullhorn. "Listen up. I'm only gonna say this once. We're running a double-elimination race. That means you have to lose two heats to be out. You can have a maximum of six Scouts pulling your sled. You can have one Scout pushing your sled from the rear. You can't lift the sled off the ground. The whole sled and all the patrol members have to cross the line to complete the race. You start when the gun sounds. The Judges' decisions will be final. Good luck, gentlemen."

Left unspoken was the minor problem that there was no snow on the ground. What was most striking was not that we went ahead, but that, as far as I could tell, no one seemed to notice. This made complete sense. Scouting, I had come to realize, was largely about the suspension of disbelief, taking advantage of the way kids now, much like kids in Baden-Powell's day, are still capable of the sort of imaginative play that helps them construct their own reality. How else to explain the vestigial axemanship (when will kids possibly need to strike a match with an axe handle?), the feral shelter building? For all our worries, kids, even in a place like Chappaqua, still seemed to be able to be kids. It was nice to know that in the continuing tug of war between mythic Scout reality and the modern world, the Scout reality could still hold its own.

As we milled around, at least two things were clear. The first was that the Post Office Special was still by far the most solid-looking and artfully decorated sled of them all. The second was that while our kids were mostly sixth and seventh graders—and not particularly imposing ones at that—some of the other patrols were filled with high school jocks. They took off coats to flex bulging biceps, practiced running sprints to warm up, and engaged in all sorts of macho grunting and chest butting to get their juices going.

Before long, the man with the bullhorn called out the names of the patrols in the first heat: "Bears. Arrows. Panthers. Bulldogs. Jackals. To the starting line, gentlemen." (Scoutmasters cannot refer to their charges as "gentlemen" often enough, as if

merely using the word will somehow transform ungainly adolescents into suave James Bond clones.) The pullers took up pieces
of the rope and wrapped it around their wrists. The pusher got
ready to shove off from behind. And at the sound of the horn,
they began sprinting forward. Well, some of them began sprinting forward. The Bears, with a benign Yogi Bear–like figure on
their patrol flag, began by tripping over one another's feet and
pretty much going nowhere. But the rest took off, arms flailing,
legs pumping, occasionally slipping and then scrambling to get
going again. Two of the patrols with the bigger kids raced forward as if the sleds were greased. They raced along neck and
neck until the Bulldog sled pulled away and won easily. It was
the most modest-looking sled out there, two diagonal bars of
pine limbs on a frame over the skis.

Finally we were called, and we headed toward the starting
line. Jimmy, the World's Biggest Scout, was behind. Ben, Mark,
Jack, and Sam were in front, plus Elliot, no doubt as a reward
for bringing along his famous jerky. Our team got into a runner's
half crouch and waited for the horn. HHHOOONNKKKK.
They were off. Sort of. Well, they were off, but they were off in
slow motion. It soon became painfully clear that while the Post
Office Special had the virtue of being the most solid and substantial sled out there, that also made it the heaviest and bulki-
est sled out there. And while the Egrets raced along in their
ratty little bare-bones sled, dragging the Post Office Special
across the grass was like trying to drag the *Queen Mary* across
Franklin D. Roosevelt State Park. And had there actually been
snow, making traction that much harder to come by, it would
have been that much worse. We did our best, but we were about
halfway across the field when the Egrets crossed the finish line.
There was a second heat, but we had no more chance than we
did in the first. We stuck around to watch a bunch of beasts
from one of the tougher towns near New York City compete in

the finals, then lugged the Post Office Special up the hill to the check-in area, where the Mayors were all warming their feet by a hearty fire and twenty or so boxes of Dunkin' Donuts were laid out as a final reward for the Klondikers. We ate our fill of Boston creams, glazed and apple donuts, and petite donut holes, then lugged the grass-stained sled for a final time to Victor's van, its fierce falcon/eagle now looking suspiciously like an albatross. We bid it good riddance until next year, cranked up the heat to high, and got the hell out of the Yukon.

8: The Church of the Woods

The weekly meetings were just one of the places where Troop 1 passed on its values and traditions. Another was the ceremonial Courts of Honor, held three times a year, where merit badges and Eagles were awarded. A third place was camp each summer. But the main transmission came through the camp-outs and hikes. This would have come as a great comfort to Ernest Thompson Seton and Daniel Carter Beard. It seems both utterly remarkable and highly unlikely that a British war hero could have founded a movement that has come to be perceived as so quintessentially American. But Scouting in America has two other fathers, Seton and Beard, who began boy movements even earlier than Baden-Powell. Both formed movements that were grounded in the most fundamental kinds of American images, one the American Indian, the other the American frontiersman. Both, along with Baden-Powell, are reminders that Scouting's origins were diverse and complex, far more interesting than the bland stereotypes Scouting is shrouded in today. And both raise the same question: How much relevance can Scouting have for kids in the twenty-first century if it drew all its inspiration from three eccentric dreamers whose goal was to keep the virtues and values of the nineteenth century alive in the twentieth? Indeed, the more I got involved with the troop, the more Scouting seemed an uncertain jumble of distant past and murky present. Sometimes the disparate parts meshed; sometimes they did not. And even our excursions into the woods almost always ended up being mediations between the two worlds.

Ernest Thompson Seton, born three years after Baden-Powell, created the most compelling and perhaps the most influential alternative universe to the one created by Baden-Powell. Both had similar concerns—what they saw as the moral and physical decline of youth and the threat that that posed to national welfare. But while Baden-Powell's worldview was wildly eclectic, Seton's was so focused as to be almost a manifesto. "This is a time when the whole nation is turning toward the outdoor life, seeking in it the physical regeneration so needful for continued national existence," Seton proclaimed on the first page of his handbook, *The Birch-bark Roll of the Woodcraft Indians,* published in 1906. According to Seton there was an evil afoot in the land, urbanism and the bustle and "grind of the over-busy world." And there was also a cure: the slower, natural world of the woods and the teachings of the American Indians. One of the most affecting pieces of writing in the Boy Scout canon is the introduction Seton wrote for the first Scout Handbook. It revisits a theme he came back to over and over in his writing, but it does it with an urgency and passion that takes your breath away:

There was once a boy who lived in a region of rough farms. He was wild with the love of the great outdoors—the trees, the tree-top singers, the wood-herbs and the live things that left their nightly tracks in the mud by his spring well. He wished so much to know them and learn about them, he would have given almost any price in his gift to know the name of this or that wonderful bird or brilliant flower; he used to tremble with excitement and intensity of interest when some new bird was seen, or when some strange song came from the trees to thrill him with its power or vex him with its mystery, and he had a sad sense of lost opportunity when it flew away leaving him dark as ever.

He continued: "Young Scouts of America, that boy is writing to you now. He thought himself peculiar in those days. He knows now he was simply a normal boy with the interests and desires of all normal boys, some of them a little deeper rooted and more lasting perhaps—and all the things that he loved and wished to learn have now part in the big broad work we call Scouting." In the most narrow sense, Seton was extolling the virtues of the Handbook, "the book that I so longed for in those far-off days when I wandered heart hungry in the woods." But what he was really talking about was his dream for Scouting and what it could offer to boys.

The psychological currents running through Seton were even more complex than the ones that made up Baden-Powell. Seton was an esteemed naturalist and wildlife artist, a celebrated lecturer and a man with aspirations to lead his nation's youth much like Baden-Powell's. But as much as he was animated by his love of the outdoors, he was also animated by his hatred for three people: St. Paul the Apostle, General George Custer, and his own father. He hated St. Paul for the role he played in establishing the doctrine that Woman was created to serve Man—a doctrine, he decided, that forced his mother to submit to the will of his despotic father. He hated Custer as the symbol of the White Man's reign of terror against the Sioux, the Cheyenne, and all of America's Indians. And his father? Seton, the eighth of ten brothers, wrote in his memoirs that his father was "a worthless loafer, a petty swindler, a wife-beater, and a child-murderer...the most selfish person I ever heard of in history or in fiction."

His judgment of his father baffled his brothers, who did not see the monster that Ernest did. But the elder Seton was a rigid fundamentalist, who meted out frequent beatings and wanted his children inside reading religious literature, not playing outside. When Ernest turned twenty-one, his father handed him a bill for $537.50, the money he calculated it took to raise his son, right down to the cost of the midwife's service at his birth. But however much his sense of grievance was based in fact and however much in paranoia, Seton from a young age identified utterly with life's victims, both human, like the Indians, and animal, like the wolves and hares destined to live their lives as man's prey. As a boy, he regularly found refuge in the wild and fantasized about being an Indian brave. The single most revelatory moment of his life happened years later, on a train ride in the middle of a ferocious blizzard. Just outside Winnipeg, he saw outside his window a lone wolf ringed by dogs, successfully fighting them all off. "...chop, chop, chop," he later wrote, "went those fearful jaws, no other sound from the lonely warrior; but a death yelp from more than one of his foes, as those that were able sprang back, and left him statuesque as before, untamed, unmaimed and contemptuous of them all."

Seton came to identify utterly with that wolf. He too, he decided, could be "untamed, unmaimed and contemptuous of them all," and he came to see the wilderness as the ultimate teaching tool. His friends took to calling him "Wolf." He signed his letters with a paw print, and seldom took a bath or cut his hair. For Seton, woodcraft was not the wily, practical military scouting that appealed to Baden-Powell but was akin to religion.

Seton's passion for the outdoors animated a remarkably productive and accomplished life. He all but invented a form of wilderness narrative in which he wrote about animals not as cute anthropomorphic figures, but as heroic, doomed individuals. He was a brilliant illustrator, admired in both popular and professional circles, and an amazingly acute observer of nature. He saw the outdoors as the cure for disease and a balm to the spirit. But, he added, it was not enough to go outdoors. He told the tale of a benevolent rich man who chartered a steamer and sent hundreds of slum boys to the Catskills, where they disappeared and were soon found in groups under the bushes, smoking cigarettes, shooting craps, and playing cards. "Thus," he wrote, "the well-meaning rich man learned that it is not enough to take men out of doors. We must also teach them how to enjoy it. The purpose of this Roll is to show how Outdoor Life may be followed to advantage."

He began promulgating his vision of woodcraft as a national movement in 1902 in, of all places, the *Ladies' Home Journal,* which published seven articles outlining his idea for tribes of Seton Indians. Boys would be grouped in bands of fifteen to thirty, loosely supervised by an adult medicine man. They wore headdresses and won feathers for specific achievements. Each band was identified by a particular totem, and boys won noncompetitive badges for achieving particular goals in the form of wampum medals made from shells engraved with the symbol or deed the boy had accomplished. The organization had a strict code of conduct each boy swore by, and a vow that each boy took upon joining: "I solemnly promise that I will obey the chief and council of my tribe, and if I fail in my duty, I will surrender to them my weapons and submit without murmuring to their decision."

In 1906 when a collection of his work, *The Birch-bark Roll of the Woodcraft Indians,* was finally put in book form, Seton sent a copy to Baden-Powell in England. Baden-Powell, who was struggling to determine precisely how to organize his own movement, read the book with great eagerness. He was particularly taken with the games that Seton used to keep the boys engaged in the wild and the noncompetitive framework for advancement. Seton saw a potential ally for bringing his scheme to England. The two met shortly afterward, and before long Baden-Powell published his *Scouting for Boys* and unveiled his Boy Scout scheme.

Baden-Powell was frank in saying his organization borrowed from many sources, but he never fully conceded how much of his book and movement, its patrols, merit badges, and system of noncompetitive merit-badge advancement, were influenced by Seton. Seton was deeply hurt when Baden-Powell failed to credit some obvious borrowings, including five of Seton's outdoor games, in the first edition of *Scouting for Boys*. Things got worse when Seton decided that Baden-Powell had reneged on an agreement to help promote the Woodcraft Indians in Great Britain. They reconciled somewhat a few years later, and when the Boy Scouts of America was founded in 1910 as the American form of the movement Baden-Powell had started in England, Seton came aboard. He was named Chief Scout and was main author of the original *Handbook of the Boy Scouts of America*. But Seton never really made his peace with Baden-Powell's vision. Seton and the Boy Scouts soon had a falling out, and he went to his grave thinking Baden-Powell had stolen Scouting from him. He was wrong. Baden-Powell borrowed from many people, including Seton, but Seton's idea in the end was doomed by the almost mystical purity of his belief in the outdoors and the narrow focus of being so closely allied to the imagery of the American Indian—particularly at a time people were more likely to think of Indians as drunken savages than as heroic woodsmen. Baden-Powell's was a much richer and more fanciful mix of disparate elements. But Seton remains a true visionary, one of the pioneers of American environmentalism and the source of the passion for the wilderness that is one of the richest threads woven through Scouting in the United States.

Daniel Carter Beard, the founder of the Sons of Daniel Boone, was not quite as complex as Baden-Powell or Seton. But he became more of an icon and role model to the first generations of American Scouts than either of them, a colorful, beloved figure known as "Uncle Dan" who consciously turned himself into the embodiment of the disappearing frontier. Beard, a folksy bear of a man, was in many ways yin to Seton's yang. Outdoorsmen and illustrators, both were attracted to training boys and using the outdoors as their teaching laboratory, but that's where the similarities ended. Raised in Kentucky, Beard saw himself as the last link to the world of Daniel Boone and the personification of American nationalism and the pioneer scout. While Seton evinced an almost spiritual sense of unity with the wilderness and its vulnerable creatures, Beard saw the wild as a laboratory for cultivating rugged frontier virtues that conveyed to him the essence of the American experience. Seton's totem and inspiration was the lonely, untamed wolf; Beard's was the endangered buffalo of the American frontier. In the foreword to his best-known book *The American Boys' Handy Book,* he cites heroes like Daniel Boone, Kit Carson, Davy Crockett, Johnny Appleseed, and Abraham Lincoln. He says:

> Men of this description are not the product of an over-refined civilization. At times they might be and, indeed, are called barbarians. They are essentially boyish; like boys, they have restless minds and are noisy, energetic, fun-loving creatures ... One of the principal purposes in forming and carrying on the Society of the Sons of Daniel Boone was to awaken in the boy of today admiration for the old-fashioned virtues of American Knights in Buckskin and a desire to emulate them.

Beard propounded a sort of hypermasculine, hyper-American brand of Scouting, and he became its folksy image, given to

Crockettlike aphorisms ("This was a good country in the past. It is a good country today. It will be a good country tomorrow unless we fail it."). In his organizational scheme, eight boys made up a stockade and four stockades made a fort. He had his boys dress in homemade pioneer costumes, talked of an organization that would promote "wholesome manliness," environmental awareness, and "admiration for the old-fashioned virtues of American Knights in Buckskin." Beard had the soul of a tinkerer and inventor, and his books, *The American Boys' Handy Book, Shelters, Shacks and Shanties,* and *What to Do and How to Do It,* are an eccentric cavalcade of instruction on how to do almost everything—build a pushmobile, rig a house-wagon, celebrate Johnny Appleseed's Day, handle a gun, decorate and paper the inside of a shack, throw a tomahawk, make a swimming hole, make snowshoes, build a pioneer bob and a cheap bobsled, make an attic gym. So what if we no longer know what half those things are? And so what if he could get carried away with his pedagogical duties, making throwing a tomahawk ("Take aim, as in Fig. 233, bring the tomahawk back over the shoulder, as in Figs. 234 and 235, then bring your hand quickly down, following the line A B, Fig. 233, and swinging the body forward, let fly the tomahawk as in Fig. 236.") sound like AP calculus? For all his frontier machismo, Beard was also an admirer of utopian political movements like the Single Tax Movement, inspired by Henry George's 1879 book *Progress and Poverty,* and a cantankerous radical critic of big business, big money, and industrial plutocrats. He lived to the age of ninety-one and his every utterance and reminiscence made him sound like a character out of Mark Twain, for whom he did the illustrations for the first edition of *A Connecticut Yankee at King Arthur's Court.*

Beard was more a charismatic figure than an organizer, and he promoted his ideas mostly through magazine pieces in periodicals that he inevitably ended up feuding with and/or suing.

Unlike the Woodcraft Indians, the Sons of Daniel Boone never really developed a full program. In fact, for all their celebrity, neither founder knew how to build a real organization, and it is doubtful either group had more than two thousand members. But as Seton and Beard would stress as time went by, both groups were American-born versions of Scouting that existed before Baden-Powell got the English version going. Both were rooted in the romance of the outdoors. And all three were rooted in an alarmism, bordering on panic, about the state of the young.

Indeed, if there's one way that the instincts that drove Baden-Powell, Seton, and Beard seem entirely relevant now, a century later, it's the way boys are seen as imperiled creatures in need of both moral uplift and wholesome activities designed to steer them away from sin. The imminent moral decline of youth—particularly boys—appears to be a constant refrain in modern life. American boys, it seems, have always been on the verge of being swept up by some sinister threat. At the beginning of the century it was smoking, spectator sports, and urban life. They were imperiled by comic books, juvenile delinquency, and rock 'n' roll in the 1950s; then drugs, long hair, and psychedelic rock in the 1960s and '70s; MTV, video games, and heavy-metal, headbanger music in the 1980s; and computer games, the perils of affluence, and gangsta rap since then. Now, depending on which school of pop psychology appeals to you, boyhood itself is under assault from two entirely different directions. One side, in what might be called the neo-Beardian worldview, says that boys are either being feminized or shackled by a culture that is so tame, wussified, and politically correct that it would take Huck Finn and label him a learning-disabled underachiever who needs Ritalin and weekly counseling. A normal, rambunctious boyhood is diagnosed as a disability. The other, with a large dose of Seton in it, says that we demand so much of boys as to turn them by elementary school into competitive fighting machines, unable to tap into the gentler, more eloquent instincts they're so desperate to touch. They don't need to get harder and tougher; they need to have the same kind of transcendent experiences—in the wild or elsewhere—that Seton had as a boy in the woods.

Most of this discussion says more about adults than kids. One comforting thing about Troop 1 was just how normal, in their own ragged ways, the kids seemed. The kids I saw around me did not square with the overheated accounts of the crisis facing America's youth. Yes, these were privileged kids, but the literature of adolescent despair—not to mention the most graphic examples of it, like the shootings at Columbine High School—is often centered around privileged kids. Still, if overblown, there is an element of truth in the two scenarios of boyhood in crisis, and Scouting at its best, I was beginning to think, addresses both of them. It is usually associated with the Neo-Beard school. No wusses here! Toughen 'em up, teach them their knots, let them survive in the woods. But Ben's attraction to Scouting seemed to me all Seton and little Beard. Ben did seem to find something magical in the outdoors. He dreamed of hiking the whole Appalachian Trail, not as a test of physical endurance, but as a wondrous journey. He looked forward to each camp-out or hike the way I used to look forward to the Jets games my father took me to at Shea Stadium when I was a kid. Kids do face unholy pressure these days—I knew we were in trouble when my daughter, Emma, came back from third grade one day and announced that she'd heard that Yale was a good place to go to college. Ben seemed most insulated from those pressures when he was in the woods with his friends in Troop 1.

One Saturday in early April, when we were just about safe from one last freeze, we had our first camp-out of the spring at the Clear Lake Scout Reservation adjacent to Fahnestock State Park. The core of the park was once the estate of Major

Clarence Fahnestock, a Manhattan physician who purchased a rugged swath of abandoned farmland and former iron mine in 1915 as a gentleman's farm and shooting preserve and then died three years later in France during the influenza epidemic.

We parked at the edge of Canopus Lake and got out of our cars. The air was heavy and damp. It had rained overnight and looked like it could drizzle again, but the temperature was already in the high 50s, and it felt like a propitious day to take a hike. "OK, everyone, listen up," Mr. Toonkel barked, as about twenty kids and five dads were gathered around him. Mr. Toonkel, as always, was a sight. He had on his Sing Sing Surf Squad cap and camouflage pants. In his hands was his steel hiking monopod. He handed out topographic maps, with squiggles that brought back vivid, unwelcome memories of my least favorite course of all time, Geology 101. He broke us into groups of seven or eight, pointed out some landmarks we could expect to find, and said the hike would cover only about three miles, so if we were still hiking late in the day we were hopelessly lost.

Next, Mr. Toonkel took out a roll of paper towels and gave two sheets to each kid and adult. Then he tore one into a little shred and held it aloft. "What happens on High Adventure is that if you ask for a paper towel, Dr. Flank gives you a little piece like this. This is your paper towel. Now I'm going to give you each two sheets. Two whole sheets! Put it away. Use it sparingly. Use it for KP to clean your dish and pot, blow your nose, wipe your bottom. It's plenty, believe me."

Various predictably disgusting scenarios immediately began to play across my mind and the dirty little minds of my fellow Scouts. Mr. Toonkel went on as if reading our minds: "What we're trying to teach you is respect for nature and a recognition of how wasteful we are at home. At home you'd use a roll of paper towels in a few days and think nothing of it. Throw it in the trash. Not our problem. But, of course, it has to be someone's problem in someone's landfill. It doesn't just disappear. So here, we want you to be aware that you can get by with so much less if you just think about it a little."

We all strapped on our packs, crossed the two-lane road, and headed for the trail, which was soft and moist after the evening rain. I fell in somewhere in the middle of the pack, right behind Jack, our patrol leader; two Amigos, Mark and Jonah; and a trim dad with a modest mustache and a fly rod poking out of his backpack. Ben and I walked together for a while until he hooked up with the Amigos. I knew enough, by this point, to make sure my pack was snug and my hip belt was carrying the bulk of the weight, rather than having the pack's weight borne by my shoulders. I had on my new Gore-Tex boots, now reasonably broken in, and various layers of plain old clothes, none of them the catalog gear of Ben's dreams, but working fine for me. And while most of the trek was relatively flat, I welcomed the occasional inclines and felt some small macho pride that, despite my advancing years, I was certainly as fit and prepared as most of these little twerps.

We hiked for a half hour or so, took a short break for water and rest, and then resumed. Before long, Mr. Johnson pointed toward a gentle rise to our right. "Anyone know what that is?" he asked. No one did. "Believe it or not, it used to be a railroad," he said. It could have fooled me. "This area used to be full of iron mines, and they built a narrow-gauge railroad to cart out the ore."

Indeed, long before Clarence Fahnestock was around, the area was host to the Sunk Mine and the Canada Mine, part of the Reading Prong formation, which stretched from Pennsylvania to the Berkshires. The formation was rich in magnetite, an iron ore, which was mined as early as the days of the Revolution. First, the ore was smelted and used locally. Later, it was hauled about five miles to the West Point Foundry in Cold Spring, now a spruced-up and tourist-friendly village on the Hudson River, where it was used to make the Parrott gun, a rifled cannon used in the Civil War. The railroad consisted of the track and mule-drawn cars, which carried the ore to horse-drawn wagons for the trip to Cold Spring. But it never became economical to transport the ore for broader commercial purposes, and the mines closed in 1876. Thomas Alva Edison tried to reopen them in 1890, but failed. You can still find old entrances if you root around through the brush.

Our comfortable suburban world was a few light years from the region of rough farms where Seton had stalked the woods. But the kids were hardly immune to the backwoods adventure and romance that captivated Seton, and the story of the abandoned mine struck even me as appealingly spooky, making the place a perfect site for one of the Hardy Boys mysteries (there doesn't seem to be *The Secret of the Lost Mine,* but there should be). You could tell that the kids found something intriguing in this ambitious, low-tech enterprise that flourished fitfully for a time in what were then distant, unforgiving environs that now lay lost and forgotten in this wooded glade a half hour's drive from their own world.

That did not turn out to be the only lesson of the day. The park is laced with old hemlock groves and large areas of second-growth hardwood forest, which have grown up since the rocky farmland was abandoned around the turn of the century. The most conspicuous greenery is vast strands of mountain laurel, which have survived because the deer, which are all over the place, won't eat them. There are swamps and bogs and numerous streams that are small enough to cross on rocks, downed tree limbs, or makeshift tree-stump bridges. Mr. Johnson, it turned out, knew every tree, bird, and rock formation in the park. Without being too didactic about it, he managed to turn the hike into a naturalist's tour of the woods.

"See this," he said at one point, pointing to a tubular plant growing by the side of the trail. "This is called horsetail. The Indians used to use it as a scouring brush. Inside it is a mineral called silica. You take this stuff and break it up, and it works like steel wool. The Indians used it to clean dishes and pots with. This particular one is called *Equisutum hyemale.* You often see it growing around railroad tracks. This was a very valuable commodity back then. Here's another thing. See this little thing on the plants. It's called an insect gall. Who can tell me what a gall is?"

"A seed?" one of the kids guessed.

"Well, sometime it's an egg and sometime it's an insect," Mr. Johnson said. "It doesn't always contain the egg. Sometimes what happens is the insect gets inside the plant and the plant would form this around it. It was kind of like locking him up in jail."

He pointed out Christmas ferns and tulip trees, and what the difference in acidity between Clear Lake and Sperling Pond meant for the fish that could survive there. A little later, we stopped by a mammoth boulder seemingly resting against two modest-sized oak trees. "Gentlemen," Mr. Johnson said. "Aside from the fact that there was a big guy around, how did that get there?"

"A glacier," several kids answered. (That one was easy. It was already a private joke among Ben and the Amigos that anything that was ever moved—earth, boulder, mobile home—was always moved by a glacier.)

"Notice how it's sitting on a smaller rock and how it was pushed there and deposited. What kind of rock?"

"Granite?"

"No, it doesn't look like it. It looks fairly uniform. It's probably a metamorphic rock called gneiss. See the injections in there? What's doing this? It's called frost wedging. The water gets in it, it freezes, and it expands and starts to crack it. See this side? This little flat section? The piece that comes off here? Have you guys talked about exfoliation yet? It heats. It cools. It heats. It cools. And the top layer breaks off. You now know what a glacial erratic looks like. Amaze your friends."

There was a clump of lichen on the rock, and Larry, the dad who had flown in from Georgia for the hike and was wearing a ball cap that read MARKETING MANIAC, asked them what lichen is a combination of. No one knew.

"Fungus and algae," he said. "Freddy Fungus and Alice Algae took a lichen to each other. It's dumb, but you'll never forget it."

We stopped for lunch around 12:30. In the past, Ben and I had found a rock to eat at together. But Barrett, the little weatherman, had pretty much dropped out from the troop, and Ben was spending most of his time with the two remaining Amigos as if he were slipping neatly into Barrett's vacated spot. So they all ate and talked about video games and advanced weapons systems while I sat down with the guy with the fly rod, who put us to shame with a grilled portobello mushroom, roasted pepper, Italian ham, and mozzarella cheese sandwich on a big slab of Italian bread with mustard and crushed jalapeños. He had driven up in a van with a FLY GUY license plate and immediately started talking about his favorite subject.

I had seen *A River Runs Through It,* but other than that I had less than zero interest in the cult of fly fishing. Still, I found Fly Guy's enthusiasm rather charming. Clearly, he was another guy with a thwarted version of the Seton gene. The father of George, who was a year younger than Ben and a blur of adolescent energy, Fly Guy was an attorney for some big investment firm, who worked like a banshee all week. Fly fishing—and the outdoors in general—was his refuge from all that, and he seemed to look forward to the Scout outings more than the kids did. He talked about his law school professor who made the hopelessly boring course in agency and suretyship tolerable by injecting fly-fishing lore and analogies throughout the course, so that any miscreant who committed fraud and fled, for example, would inevitably be found bonefishing in the Bahamas or some such thing. I'm not sure it worked for everyone in the class, but it definitely worked for him. He talked about the days B.C.—before children—when he did a lot of camping and fishing on the Salmon River, where you woke up to the sound of eagles' wings flapping over the water. I had never heard of John Gierach's *Sex, Death and Fly Fishing,* but Fly Guy made it almost sound like it would be worth reading even for a non–Fly Guy like me.

No one was in any great hurry to get going, but after a while Mr. Toonkel passed out his lollipops and then we all saddled up and got back on the trail. After a while it changed from the soft, beaten-down trail we'd been on to a clamber across huge chunks of rock until finally we reached our destination: a rocky hilltop overlooking Clear Lake that is part of the Clear Lake Scout Reservation. Everyone scrambled to lay claim to whatever scarce patches of relatively flat, rock-free territory they could find, with the biggest piece of turf claimed by a group that had carried with them a four-man tent the size of a modest condominium. We had a new tent of our own, an orange REI Mountaineering model that was a gift to Ben from his Uncle Walter, a doctor in Louisiana and an Eagle Scout himself, who actually knew what he was doing. Now, it seemed, Ben did too. Between our first trip and this one, Ben had become completely proficient at putting it up. I looked on or helped pound in stakes. We dragged our packs into the front vestibule, taking care to remove our food, which we then placed in a bear bag, which, as any idiot knows, is a bag that you hang from a tree so bears can't get into any food you've brought along. Then we wandered around to see what our confederates were up to.

From the condominium-sized tent came much merriment over someone's choice of food storage containers—"Look, every-one, Tupperware! We're having a Tupperware party in our tent!" From another came a conversation about the correct way to pre-pare chicken teriyaki. From a third, Allen, the chef and musical expert, was leading a spirited group rendition of "Old Man River"—context unknown.

Doug and Elliot sat on a rock discussing their favorite sub-ject, the computer game Starcraft. Like the Koran or the Bible for the devout, it seemed to them a text of infinite richness. And those who were most versed in its dark mysteries, like Doug and Elliot, could spend hours in the wild discussing the fine points, attack strategies, and metaphysical depths of its infinite permu-tations. Starcraft was based on three species warring with each other somewhere in a dark future following a nuclear war and the rise and fall of one hideous order after another. Terrans are human beings. Zergs are disgusting, alien, buglike monsters. Protoss are telepathic aliens who don't like the Zergs. On and on they went, analyzing the various weapons—Protoss Zealots and Archons; Zerg Hydralisks, Multilisks, and Ultralisks; Terran Wraiths, Vultures, and Arclite Siege Tanks—then parsing strat-egy, like grandmasters playing out chess games in their head. How could they remember all this? It was apparent that Doug in particular, one of the smartest kids in the troop, even dreamed in a different language than I did. On one trip he had relayed a dream about the battle between two groups—one evil humans, the other a benign group of tadpoles, or maybe mudskippers. It was so baroque and layered it left me feeling like a caveman. It was hard enough for adults and adolescents to communicate when they spoke the same language, but their Starcraft talk might as well have been in Urdu. I wanted to ask them what they were doing here in the woods, if their heads were still most at home on their computer screens, the place where today's scouts and explorers apprehend new and strange worlds. But clearly, they were quite used to swinging from one world, one screen, one century, one mindset to another, so it was at least possible for Seton and Beard to coexist with Hydralisks and Wraiths. And really nothing on the trip was neatly situated in either the present or the past; it was all a combination of the two.

When we returned to the campsite, some of the Scouts were clearly ready to practice the manly arts of cooking and camping in the spirit of their primordial ancestors in the woods. As they gathered in little conspiratorial clusters, a red Swiss army knife surfaced here, a Bic lighter there (even for them, eating like a caveman didn't mean rubbing two pieces of wood together). And the more enterprising started to gather firewood, breaking up brittle old oak branches and stray twigs.

"What are you guys doing?" snapped Mr. Toonkel, as he spotted Bernie and Hal comparing knives. They looked up, embarrassed, and mumbled something. It was fairly easy to feel embarrassed by Mr. Toonkel. If Dr. Flank, by dint of his age, experience, and role as Scoutmaster, had a sort of unimpeachable moral authority in the troop, Mr. Toonkel had the no-nonsense air of the keeper of the practical virtues. Dr. Flank could be stern as hell when riled, but he was sort of philosophically tolerant, so he put up with a fair amount. Mr. Johnson was truly affable by nature, and I'm not sure I ever saw him genuinely angry at the kids. Of the triumverate, Mr. T was the easiest to annoy and had the shortest fuse with the kids who got on his nerves.

"Look around you," Mr. Toonkel said, with mild irritation. "There's really not that much usable wood, is there? This place gets used a lot, and each troop that comes through takes away its own little piece. So the days of using the knife as a survival tool or pioneering instrument are pretty much over. That's why people are going more and more to those Leatherman-type tools. They're more appropriate for an industrialized society, when you come down to it. We bring stoves with us and cook on Coleman propane stoves, not on campfires. We bring prefabricated tents, not something we fashion out of the elements. So what do we need a knife for? Rather than having to cut something, we'd get more use of a pair of pliers to bend the metal of a tin back or close a loop or screw something back together. What we mostly want is something to help us cook our meals. So I'm not going to keep you from bringing a knife, although you better not bring it to school. But we really don't need knives. And we certainly don't need axes. An axe is an accident waiting to happen. And we don't need to be tearing up much of the wood you'll be finding here. So, why don't you relax, and get your dinners ready, and we'll get the stoves going."

Indeed, in a few minutes, four propane Coleman stoves were hissing away, their domesticated blue flames boiling water for suppers great and small. Kids and grownups emerged from tents carrying dinners, all of which came from Column A or Column B. Column A, call it the traditionalist fare, consisted of one-pot stews, the foundation of the Scout culinary regimen. They contained various elements, but most of them were built around the following holy quartet: ramen noodles, precooked chicken or beef, rice, and Birds Eye frozen vegetables. There were endless possible variations: a little adobo seasoning, some fresh mushrooms or corn, some Worcestershire sauce, a Cheez Doodle or Pringle thrown in for seasoning or comic effect. But most of the kids played it relatively straight, their ingredients transported in various saggy baggies and soon dumped in pots great and small and boiled till dead.

More common, on this trip at least, was Plan B, the no-work-at-all idiot-proof, buy-it-in-a-bag-add-water-and-eat approach, the outdoors' answer to astronaut's food. There was just-add-water fettucini alfredo and chili, spaghetti with meat sauce, beef stew, and beef stroganoff. Squarely in the Troop 1 mainstream, we had brought along fettucini alfredo, which after our long day on the trail seemed awfully inviting.

We waited for Mr. Johnson to finish his cooking and then sprang into action. First, I whipped out my own red Swiss army knife and cut the bag open, decisively proving that a knife can be a survival tool even in these advanced times. Inside was what appeared to be a mixture of sawdust and stomped-on popcorn. Expertly following directions, we poured water from our Nalgene jar into the two pots we'd brought along that were part of Ben's spiffy Texsport cooking kit. Sure enough, in our capable hands, the water soon reached an insouciant boil. With a chef's intuitive sense of timing, we waited until the most propitious moment, poured the water into the bag with a Gallic flourish, and sealed it shut. We waited the requisite three minutes, like expectant fathers, fighting off the urge to peek too early. Before long, voilà, it was time to dig in. And if our fare was not quite worthy of Le Cirque, it really wasn't bad. It definitely had that ineffable Tang/astronaut/*Rosemary's Baby*/what-the-hell-is-this quality. But somehow it tasted more like food than like faux food, though after a hard day of camping maybe I couldn't tell the difference. We still had our Sprites and some of our sesame sticks. And for dessert, we had brought a four-pack of little tins of peaches and pears that I thought added a healthy grace note to the meal. We tore through the packaging, peeled back the lids, and scooped out the watery fruit swimming in its syrupy ooze.

Mr. Toonkel had been watching us with a vaguely disapproving eye and finally felt moved to speak. "Do you really want to bring that much junk that you'll just have to carry back out with you?" he asked, with a slightly less mild note of irritation in his voice. Indeed, I belatedly realized that no one else had brought anything with the elaborate, environmentally suspect packaging of the tins of peaches and pears. They had all used one pot—or none at all—to the two we'd used just to pour water in the bag. Most had used their cup for both eating and drinking, or eaten their astronaut glop from the bag. We'd used the two plates and two cups. In the land of the one-pot stew and leave-no-trace camping, we were the Ugly Americans. Troop 1 may have been a bunch of comfortable suburbanites, but the troop ethos had a bit of Earth First environmental zealotry in it. None of the adults ever killed a bug if they could help it, and Todd was constantly rescuing caterpillars and ladybugs trapped in someone's tent and releasing them into the wild. The men took "leave-no-trace" incredibly seriously—if they were at a site where they did gather up wood for a fire, they would disperse everything that was left over at the end, flinging it into a facsimile of the natural order they had encountered. And woe unto the kid who kicked at a rotting tree stump or broke a tree limb for no good purpose. Chances are some animals and bugs were safe and warm in the rotting stump, and the Zen of the limb didn't need to be disrupted by some heedless youth with aggression issues.

Still, at least one traditional camp-out accoutrement lived on almost unchanged: After giving the kids a hard time for gathering firewood, Mr. T later dispatched everyone after dinner to gather enough for the night's campfire. The kids, working with respectful quiet and dispatch, built a properly pyramidal Boy Scout campfire, which soon bloomed into a compact blazing pyre. It was almost dark. A luminous band of sunset orange hung over the lake like the day's final exclamation point. Soon everyone gravitated toward the fire. Some kids sat or squatted on the ground. Everyone else got their camping chairs or stools.

Sitting there watching the light slowly fade, I found my thoughts awash in male trios—Seton, Beard, and Baden-Powell; Flank, Toonkel, and Johnson; Zergs, Protoss, and Terrans; Jerome, Jesse, and Gilbert (Father, Son, and Holy Ghost?). Not for nothing were triangles and threesomes constants in rites and reli-

gions around the world since ancient times. Flank, Toonkel, and
Johnson weren't Seton, Beard, and Baden-Powell, but they had
pieces of all three. In a very rough way, you could say that Dr.
Flank had much of Baden-Powell's almost spiritual sensibility
about boys and their possibilities, Mr. Johnson's knowledge of
nature was our answer to Seton, and Mr. Toonkel had a lot of
Dan Beard's practical wisdom and skills. It wasn't that simple,
of course. Dr. Flank, for example, certainly had Seton's fascination with the American Indian and his love of nature, Mr. J was
pretty good on the Beard elements, and Mr. T, in his own gruff
way, had some of B-P's leadership skills and Seton's love for the
outdoors. If Scouting often felt irrelevant in the abstract, sitting
here by the campfire on this night, under these stars, it seemed
entirely rich and alive.

Dr. Flank, who had missed the hike but joined us for the dinner and campfire, loved the ceremonial aspects of Scouting and
his role as Troop 1 paterfamilias. So when he addressed the kids
at a campfire, there was nothing casual about his delivery. He
spoke slowly and deliberately like a minister addressing a con-
gregation, allowing long pauses to punctuate what he had to say.
"Listen up, please," he said, as the crackling of the wood provided the evening's ambient noise. "For those of you who have
not been with us, here are a few rules to understand. The campfire is a sacred thing, an entity unto itself. It goes back to the beginning of man. They gathered around the campfire because
that's how they sustained their lives. But in addition to keeping
them warm, the campfire also brought them together, as a tribe,
a people, a community. We now gather around the campfire in
much the same way, not that we need it to survive, though it
does feel nice and warm and toasty tonight, but as a social gathering, a way to bring us together and to reflect on the things we
did today and what it meant to us. Throughout history, the campfire has been looked on as something almost mystical, a kind of

religious experience, something that touches an important part of us in ways we might not completely understand sometimes. So here are some rules. Turn your flashlights off and put them in your pockets. You don't need them here. The focus should be on the campfire. Second, there is normally one person talking, whoever is telling a story or performing a skit. That should be the only one voice you hear. You need to respect that as part of the way we respect one another. Finally, you need to pay attention. This is an important part of being a member of the troop, and I want your attention here at all times. All that clear? Good. Anyone want to start with a skit?"

Well, there were a few, with the tone set by the first, a ramble through the woods that turned up an unexpected treasure trove of delicious M&Ms. Or were they Skittles? Or Tootsie Rolls? They tasted a tad odd, so it was hard to be certain. Turns out they were rabbit droppings. It wasn't much better in the performance than the précis.

Dr. Flank told one of his Lenni-Lenape tales. "All cultures have myths about the Great Flood," he began. "It's one way very different cultures see the world in similar ways. This is one tale the Lenni-Lenape told. After the Mysterious One made the earth, he put far above it a roof which was sometimes blue and sometimes black. This angered the spirit of the waters, because he was afraid the rain would no longer be able to reach the earth, the earth would become parched and dry, and the people would have no water to drink. So the Mysterious One brought the clouds under the roof. He gathered the dark clouds together and caused the lightning to flash across the sky. Each time the lightning flashed he spoke in deep tones, telling the clouds to shed their water on the earth. The clouds poured out their water until only the highest mountain peaks could be seen above the water. Now the spirit of the water was sorry he had become so angry because he worried the flood would bury all the animals and people. So the Mysterious One caused it to stop raining. He took away the clouds and put a rainbow in their place. Since then the Lenni-Lenape have always been glad to see the rainbow, because it tells them that the great spirits are no longer angry and there will always be life after the waters recede."

Then it was Mr. Johnson's turn. He continued the journey of Chief Leknoot. It seemed the Chief had taken his band of braves to the Mountain of the Great Hunter. Probably by coincidence, the troop just that previous fall had taken a trip to Hunter Mountain. There, he said, they hunted and hunted for what was said to be the great fire that would keep them warm all through the long winter. They had many adventures, at one point scaling the tower of the Eagle to look down over the hills and valleys below. In the end, they returned to the valley and made their campfire, though they never did find the great fire of legend and lore. "They sat around their campfire," he concluded. "And they looked to the left and looked to the right and saw their brothers around them. And all the people realized that there was no need to find the great fire. The great fire burned within them and they were warm."

Finally, Mr. Toonkel stood up. The kids listened respectfully to Dr. Flank's Indian tales, but in truth they could get a little too symphonic for thirteen- and fourteen-year-olds, who were a little old to be into Indians and a little too young to be into myth. Mr. Johnson's Leknoot tales were increasingly popular, but they played out like a nice brisk scherzo, pleasing but fleeting. Mr. Toonkel's dark horror tales, the Grand Guignol of the woods, were clearly the kids' favorites. Everyone sat utterly still as he got up and started pacing around, as if troubled by something and unsure whether he wanted to talk about it. "I don't know if you guys noticed the signs saying 'POSTED. KEEP OUT,' this afternoon," he began in a hesitant voice. "They didn't use to be there, and then they put them up a few years back, not that long ago.

I'll tell you how they got there. Remember when we were walking by the path along the lake? Remember how there was a hollowed-out area just off the trail? It was sheltered and protected. You could sleep there if you wanted to. And that's what happened in the past. Kids would come here and sleep right under there, right where we were today. But in the morning, no one was there. It was quite a mystery. I only bring this up because it became a matter of serious concern, a while back, maybe seven, eight years ago. First, they just chalked it up to inexperience. They figured the kids must have wandered off from the troop. Clear Lake is a large glacial lake, so it's very deep and people figured maybe the kids wandered off, went skinny-dipping, got in too deep on a beautiful warm night, and didn't come out. So they dragged the lake, but they didn't find anything. They had planes fly overhead with searchlights. Still nothing. Back in the old days perhaps parents could dispose of their children more easily than now, but the kids kept disappearing and it was getting very distressing. So they had to close the place down, and the fact that they never found any traces of them made it that much worse. Then a few years ago, Todd Davis can probably remember hearing about this back then, another strange thing happened. A troop was camping on an unnaturally quiet night, a night much like tonight, come to think of it. Everyone had retired to their tents. And when they woke up one of the tents was missing. Father and son and tent, gone. Everyone figured they must have left early and gone to their car, but when everyone got to the parking lot the car was still there, and the father and son were missing. Then about four or five years ago, they were thinking of selling this place and they hired a geologist to come in and do a survey. They found these caves formed over millions of years by glacial action folding layers of earth and rock onto each other. When they went in they could feel a strange, unearthly chill. And what they saw floored them.

There were bags and gear from all different eras, modern stuff like you have and ancient stuff from the '20s and '30s. They went farther into the cave and they found tents. Then they found corpses, not just corpses with regular bones, but corpses that seemed to have been gnawed on and broken apart. This was a rather unsettling experience for these young men. They came out and called the police and the police got the FBI involved and a number of other agencies, but they really came up with nothing. There were theories about a crazy person or a cult of some kind, but no one really knows. It just seems that every four or five years, something like this happens. Anyway, I don't want you to think about it. The last one was four or five years ago, so we might be a little overdue, but it's probably not something to worry about. So when we're through just go back to your tents and go to sleep. And don't think about it. And, if it turns out it is your time to go, just go quietly and don't disturb the rest."

9: Terra Incognita

I'm having a very strange dream.

In my dream, I'm at some corporate training building near Westchester County Airport. On the walls are posters and spreadsheets and corporate exhortations about team building and creativity and thinking outside the box. It's a drab, gray low-slung building, the kind of place that breeds in endless profusion in places like Atlanta and Scottsdale, but this feels like an early incarnation with worn carpeting and water stains on the ceiling tiles. It has the sense of being in some fundamental way behind the times. Still, the place is ordinary enough except for the fact that instead of aspiring junior managers, it's full of men in Boy Scout uniforms. It's winter, and the men—and a handful of large, serious-looking women—come in from the cold in heavy coats and parkas carrying sheafs of paper with the front page reading *Curtis S. Read Scout Reservation Troop Leaders' Guide*. Many of the men are in Scout shirts full of patches and badges and a tooled leather belt with Scout buckles. The rest are in business attire minus the tie or in winter casual dress—old flannel shirts or heavy sweaters. Many of the men seem to know one another. They talk knowingly of Waubeeka and Buckskin, High Cope and Low Cope, Zip Lines and Dragon Wagons—words that mean nothing to me but seem to be fraught with significance for them. One of them, a huge man with cropped hair whose knees barely bend, like Frankenstein, seems very important indeed, because most of the others come by as if to pay their respects. He is there with a smaller, heavy-set man, who seems like his aide-de-camp. I think of him as Igor.

We are in a large room, filled with perhaps sixty of us in plastic chairs. The atmosphere is partly cheery bonhomie and partly dead-serious negotiating for various, only vaguely apparent perks having to do with things like access to tickets for the shotgun range or adequate supplies of bologna and salami at lunch. "Let's make sure we know we're all on the same page here," says the man at the front of the room, who has been identified as the Director of Support Services. "We all want the same thing—the best summer at Camp Read we've ever had." It dawns on me that this is no dream. This is real. My casual descent into Scouting has taken me to a still-more-distant stretch of terra incognita—a meeting of parents prepared to spend a week or two of their summer living in mosquito-infested tents; doing their business in smelly latrines; eating French toast, mashed potatoes, and turkey loaf prepared by thirteen-year-olds; and bringing some semblance of order to adolescent chaos. At forty-nine, I was preparing for my first summer at Scout camp.

I still was not entirely sure how I got to this point. At one of the first meetings of the year, Dr. Flank said that enough boys had expressed an interest in camp that this year we planned to go for two weeks rather than the one we had done in recent years. The only hitch was that we needed enough dads—a minimum of three per week—able to take time off from work to participate. The statement had a buy-this-magazine-or-we'll-shoot-this-dog quality. With Dr. Flank scheduled for the first week, that meant we needed just five dads out of some twenty-five active kids. This hardly sounded like much, but the ranks of volunteers remained meager. Some dads had vacation plans.

They were bug-phobic, too busy, too old, too heavy, or too camping-averse. As it turned out, I was at a Wednesday night meeting where Dr. Flank raised the subject again. My vacation plans remained in flux, and I was too slow to lie, so I told Dr. Flank I'd think about it. I might as well have signed on the dotted line then and there.

The meeting I found myself in now was one of two held by the Westchester–Putnam Council to brief prospective Scoutmasters and their assistants on what to expect this summer at the Curtis S. Read Boy Scout Reservation at Brant Lake in the Adirondacks. We were told about bus schedules and camp orientation, medical forms and swim checks. We were reminded that Camp Buckskin was a mess-hall camp, with all the kids fed three times a day, and Camp Waubeeka was a patrol-cooking camp, meaning the kids prepared food for themselves at their campsites three times a day. There were questions about bringing cell phones (forget it), how to accommodate the number of kids who wanted to do shotgun and rifle shooting, and whether the wilderness survival staff was up to snuff. There were lots of rules delivered with Old Testament sternness. No matches! No lighters! No sheath knifes! No aerosol bug spray! No fireworks! No chainsaws! No blowguns! No computers! No alcohol! No drugs!

For the first time, I realized, I was stepping outside the familiar, comfortable, rather idiosyncratic world of Troop 1 and into the musty maw of the national organization, the Boy Scouts of America. I felt like I was going from Dr. Flank's version of Scouting to Norman Rockwell's. Like all great crusades, the B.S.A. began with a great metaphor. In this case it was The Good Turn in the Fog, which, as a friend and Eagle Scout says, is to Scouting what Saul's conversion on the road to Damascus is to Christianity. In 1909, as Scouting was beginning to spread throughout the British Empire and across Europe, a Chicago publisher named William Boyce was lost one night in a London pea-soup fog. As the tale has been told over the years, a boy materialized like an apparition out of the fog. He saluted smartly and offered to guide Boyce to his destination. When they arrived, Boyce offered the boy a reward of a shilling, but the boy turned him down, saying he was a Scout and Scouts never accept money for doing a good turn. Then the Unknown Scout, as he has come to be known, disappeared into the fog, never to be identified.

Impressed by what he had seen, Boyce decided to start a similar organization back home. It was incorporated on February 8, 1910, in the District of Columbia, but Scouting was becoming such a phenomenon that Boyce soon realized that the idea was bigger than he was. Baden-Powell himself came to the United States to talk up Scouting's virtues, President William Howard Taft was named honorary president of the organization, and Theodore Roosevelt became honorary vice president and chief Scout citizen. The nation's most eminent youth leaders, as well as giants of industry and commerce, signed up to support this wholesome crusade for national renewal. From the start, American Scouting began with audaciously lofty goals. Not only would Scouting restore the moral fiber of the nation's youth, its organizers said; in the process it would create an idealistic movement that would restore the moral fiber of the nation.

Who would head it? Baden-Powell was the image of British Scouting, but he could not serve that function here. YMCA leaders helped get it off the ground, but they were not charismatic figures. So American Scouting began with a delicate and almost certainly doomed balancing act: It needed Seton and Beard to give an inspirational face to the new movement, but instead of designating either as the sole American Baden-Powell, it gave both prominent positions without real authority, naming Seton Chief Scout and Beard National Scout Commissioner.

In the end, though, a third figure was more influential than either Seton or Beard. Executive director James E. West was a lawyer who had grown up lonely in an orphanage and was partially crippled by a deformed foot. He had great energy, flinty will, little charm, much insecurity, and a mania for efficiency. He, more than anyone, made the B.S.A. into the force in American life it would become. And his limitations became the B.S.A.'s limitations as well.

Baden-Powell wanted an organization that was loose knit, decentralized, intuitive, and flexible. West, as things turned out, wanted one that was just the opposite. He wanted Scouting to be orderly, centralized, and run like a business; he soon attracted many of the biggest names in American capitalism as advisors and supporters. He wanted a uniform program so that a troop in Colorado would follow the same program as one in Alabama. Rather than depending on the camp followers and volunteers Baden-Powell had surrounded himself with, West wanted to hire paid staff members ready to provide guidance on everything from the amount of equipment to be taken on outings to the exact ratio of adult supervision.

From the start, an organization dedicated to teaching wholesome, cooperative values to youths developed in an atmosphere of internecine warfare and feuds among adults. Both Seton and Beard never got over their resentment of Baden-Powell, and, though suspicious of the B.S.A., saw it as their vehicle for getting their proper due. Seton almost immediately became convinced that West, like Baden-Powell, had in mind an organization with the covert aim of training soldiers rather than helping boys become honorable men. Seton prepared a first edition of the Scout Handbook, which was two-thirds his own *The Birch-bark Roll* and one-third Baden-Powell's *Scouting for Boys*. Published in 1910 it named Ernest Thompson Seton as its author. You can still go to a Scout shop and buy what's billed as a reprint of the first version of the Scout Handbook, but it's not the one Seton prepared. Seton's attempt to function as the voice of the B.S.A. was immediately overruled—one year later the book was rewritten, newly titled *The Official Handbook for Boys,* and Seton's name was taken off the cover. West and Seton soon were feuding, with Seton demanding more say in running the organization and threatening to resign. West remained firmly in control, but attempted for a time to avoid an ugly public spat that would make the B.S.A. look like it was turning on its best-known public spokesman. Finally, when World War I broke out, the feud went public. Seton, who was still a British citizen even though he had lived in the United States for eighteen years, publicly offered his services to the British crown in any way that might help in the war effort. West made it clear it was inappropriate for the B.S.A. to be headed by someone with allegiances to a foreign power. Then Theodore Roosevelt, West's friend, advisor, and ally, wrote West a public letter, citing "wicked and degrading pacifist agitation" by certain Boy Scout leaders, that all but called Seton a traitor.

Furious, Seton demanded that West accept his resignation and then called a press conference to vent his displeasure. He summed up his version of Scouting's history with epigramatic succinctness: "Seton started it; Baden-Powell boomed it; West killed it." And he dismissed West as someone with "no point of contact with boys, and who, I might almost say, has never seen the blue sky in his life."

With that, Seton was gone. The Scouting magazine *Boys' Life* wrote off his departure as a trifling matter, saying that even his contributions to the handbook were minor and that the "comparatively small number of pages of material" he had written could "be easily replaced in future editions by eminent American citizens"—a cheap-shot reference to Seton's British citizenship.

Beard had watched this with great interest. He and Seton had shared a rivalry with Baden-Powell and a deep suspicion of West, so they were natural allies. As Beard put it, Scouting was being pulled by two factions, the dreamers and the clerks. But even the dreamers had their Machiavellian qualities. Beard had also plotted against Seton, claiming no foreign-born person could head the Scouts and that Seton was insufficiently patriotic. He figured to be the biggest beneficiary when Seton was ousted, and stayed on hoping at last to become Scouting's acknowledged leader. He injected the organization with a solid jolt of patriotism—even some of his peers considered his jingoism a bit excessive. He chafed too at West's power, writing him in one letter that when the Scouts ran off the last of the dreamers, "then the movement will have lost its soul and become a machine which only runs from the momentum of its original impulse." Unlike Seton, Beard never quit. But it soon became clear to him that only one man ran the Boy Scouts—and that man was James E. West.

Seton and Beard's experience carried with it two main lessons. First, Scouting may have been advertised as fun for boys, but it was serious business for the men behind it. Second, within Scouting, one strayed from the most conventional notions of what the organization was about at one's peril. It was hardly the last time that lesson would be taught.

Scouting in the United States developed over the next century with a methodical, relentless sense of manifest destiny. Indeed, it was as if the notion of Scouting—however ill-formed and malleable—had immediately tapped into some primal impulse in American life. West, like any ambitious corporate manager of his era, focused at first on securing his franchise and striving for monopoly. William Randolph Hearst, the publisher and promoter, was trying to create a rival scouting organization, the American Boy Scouts, which dressed its boys in quasi-military garb and trained them in military drill. Using his high-powered business and political connections, West lobbied Congress to designate the B.S.A. as the nation's official scouting organization, succeeding in 1916 when Congress granted a federal charter to the B.S.A. as the rightful owner of the term "Boy Scouts." Congress authorized a Boy Scout uniform, similar to the U.S. Army, Navy, or Marine uniform, and the B.S.A. set about enforcing its copyright. Since 1911, it had already grown from 61,495 Scouts and Scouters to 245,183. Who knows if it was really 245,183 or 245,182—or 230,000 or 240,000, for that matter—but Scouting went about methodically documenting and publicizing its achievements and growth from year to year as if each new membership by itself was testament to the success and worth of the entire organization.

Even now, Boy Scout literature spells out in excruciating detail and quasi exactitude Scouting's long march to greatness. In 1917 Scouting's full resources were placed at the service of the government under the slogan "Help Win the War"; membership was 363,837. In 1918 it adopted a new slogan, "The War Is Over, but Our Work Is Not." Scouts rendered nationwide service in the influenza epidemic, and membership was 418,984. In 1932 Scouting set a goal of enrolling one of every four twelve-year-old boys and keeping them in Scouting for four years. In 1936, the silver jubilee year, membership passed one million for the first time. In 1937 the first national Scout Jamboree was held in Washington, with 27,232 in attendance; membership was 1,129,841. When the second Jamboree was held in Valley Forge, Pennsylvania, in 1950, 47,163 Scouts and leaders ("from every state and territory in the U.S.!") were on hand. Membership was 2,795,222.

From the start, there was something suspect about the accent on numbers, as if the whole enterprise were like a corporation relentlessly focused on getting its profits to meet Wall

Street expectations. And as early as the 1920s, there were minor scandals in which Scout organizations were accused of inflating their numbers. One widely reported case in Cleveland in the 1950s led to the firing of a local Scout executive. For all the bluster, Scouting failed to succeed on its own quasi-corporate terms. The plan in 1932 to recruit one in four twelve-year-old boys was Scouting's first great challenge to itself. But it failed miserably, and the B.S.A. did its best to bury the results rather than face up to its shortcomings.

The numbers game goes on unabated, with local council and district executives knowing that their performance is graded on how many Scouts they can keep moving through the pipeline. In 2000 the B.S.A. celebrated its ninetieth anniversary and the addition of its 100-millionth youth member—said to be twelve-year-old Mario Castro from Brooklyn, New York. According to the 2000 Annual Report, 4.9 million youths participated in B.S.A. programs, both conventional Scouting and an in-school educational program called Learning for Life, over the past year—thanks to the efforts of 1.4 million adult volunteers. More than 40,000 Scouts made Eagle, and 234 Scouts and Scouters earned awards for lifesaving and meritorious actions. The Scouting magazine, *Boys' Life*—which, we're told, has published more than a billion copies—served more than 3.4 million youths. There's a bit of sleight of hand in those numbers. The difference between the 4.9 million youths in B.S.A. programs and the 3.4 million who gets *Boys' Life* is 1.5 million youths who are not Scouts at all, but participants in Learning for Life classroom programs, which began in 1991 as a way for the B.S.A. to contract with school districts to teach values and character development. That program has prospered while membership in Scouting itself has declined. The whole saga of growth and success is delivered in the kind of language West would have understood and Seton and Beard would be baffled by: "Future growth of the Boy Scouts of America is dependent on how we are perceived by our customer groups. The goal of our marketing message is to build awareness and solidify the fact that the Scouting program supports physical, mental, and spiritual development needs of young people and their families."

Much, of course, changes. The original handclasp, in which the little finger was separated from the other three on the right hand, was changed to the normal handclasp—only given with the left hand, the hand closer to your heart. The uniform began with a doughboy look in which the whole thing, including knickers and hat, cost about $4. In 1929 the neckerchief, tied with a square knot and secured with a neckerchief slide, made its debut. By the 1940s, Bermuda shorts had replaced jodhpurs, giving Scout socks an unfortunate prominence that came to define the Scoutmaster as dork. The 1950s saw the broad-brimmed campaign hats of earlier times replaced by a field cap like the ones the GIs wore in *Sergeant Bilko*. In the 1960s the old cotton uniforms gave way to—what else?—polyester, and the whole thing took a lurch toward the disco era in the '80s with epaulets on the shirt, utility pockets on the shorts, and an absurd red beret, which thankfully didn't last long. The epaulets are still around, but the almost intractable problem of finding appropriate headgear has been solved by replacing the ridiculous beret with the same baseball cap that has replaced virtually all other forms of headgear.

And you definitely can't buy the whole uniform for $4. You can't even buy the neckerchief for $4. These days a long-sleeve Scout shirt goes for $28.70. Trousers run from $36.50 to $50.35. A cap is $11.50 or $12.50. Even the little things add up: $4.40 for Scout socks, $4.95 for a neckerchief, $1.65 for a shoulder loop, $1.20 for a flag emblem, $5.15 for a merit badge sash, $7.95 for the handbook, $19.95 for the fieldbook. It can get pretty expensive even before you get to the serious gear.

Merit badges have also changed to fit the times. Since Scouting's beginning there have been 221 different merit badges. There were 57 in the 1911 handbook, and there are 119 now, 27 of which remain from the 1911 list. However, you can no longer get a merit badge in bee farming or blacksmithing, automobiling or mining, nut culture or first aid to animals. Handicapped awareness, phased out in 1984, had the ring of being too un-PC before anyone knew what PC was. World brotherhood sounds nice, but the badge ended in 1972. We're no longer an ag culture, so farewell to badges in cotton farming, legumes and forage crops, and rabbit raising. There's still plenty of cement work and skiing, but the badges died in 1952 and 1999. Given all the sexual innuendo, the Scouts did themselves a huge favor by phasing out their stalking badge in 1952. Now, lots of badges are Boy Scout staples like camping, first aid, swimming, or lifesaving. But you can also get badges in atomic energy, crime prevention, dog care, golf, plumbing, music and bugling, sculpture, and space exploration.

And the Handbook itself, with more than 37 million copies in print—almost certainly more than any English-language book other than the Bible—is a window onto the changes in American life. The first thing the newest version, the eleventh edition, offers is a twenty-one-page pamphlet on avoiding child abuse in the troop and elsewhere. Along with warning them about the perils of the wilderness, it counsels Scouts to "treat all blood as if it were contaminated with blood-borne viruses." It is the first version of the Handbook to deal with dangers lurking on the Internet: "Don't respond to messages or Web sites that make you feel uncomfortable or that you know are meant only for adults." And it warns Scouts not to forsake their map and compass for the false gods of high-tech seductions like the Global Positioning Systems their dads have in their SUVs. It broadens the options for that one-pot stew to include tofu and espouses a brand of no-trace camping that feels like something out of the Green movement.

And yet, as Paul Fussell put it, "The pliability and adaptability of the scout movement explains its remarkable longevity, its capacity to flourish in a world dramatically different from its founders. Like the Roman Catholic Church, the scout movement knows the difference between cosmetic and real change, and it happily embraces the one to avoid any truck with the other."

The comparison with the Catholic Church these days is more unfortunate than Fussell intended. But if one were to leaf through Handbooks published over almost a century, from the presidency of William Howard Taft to the presidency of William Jefferson Clinton, at least as striking as what has changed is what has not. It's not just the practical lessons on knots, splints, tarp tents, camping gear, compass reading, water rescues, ice rescues, and first aid. What's most consistent is the voice—calm, clear, tolerant, sensible, more than a bit square maybe, given to simple words, common wisdom, and a quiet sort of spirituality. Try to pick the years of the following passages:

[A scout] should never look down upon anyone who may be poorer than himself, or envy anyone richer than himself. A scout's self respect will cause him to value his own standing and make him sympathetic toward others who may be, on the one hand, worse off, or, on the other hand, better off as far as wealth is concerned. Scouts know neither a lower nor a higher class, for a scout is one who is a comrade to all and who is ready to share that which he has with others.

A scout is a friend to all. He is a brother to other scouts. He offers his friendship to people of all races and nations, and respects them even if their beliefs and customs are different from his own. Friendship is a mirror. When you have a smile on your face as you greet someone, you will probably receive a smile in return. If you are willing to be a good friend, you will find friendship reflected back to you.

Reverence toward God is a whole lot more than going to church. It is shown in the way you act every day. You take care of your body. You live by the moral code and worship God in the way taught by your own religion. There are many different religious beliefs in the world. Some are like your own. Others are very different. The men who founded the United States of America believed in the right of all men to worship God in their own way. This is a great heritage they have given us. Scouts can strengthen it by their actions.

The passages come from, in order, first edition, 1911; eleventh edition, 1998; eighth edition, 1972. But the passages are virtually indistinguishable in tone and message. All of them could have slipped comfortably into any other year. And the remarkable continuity in terms of programs and philosophy, combined with a selective and often shaky instinct for change, has shaped the balance between the timeless and the ephemeral that has allowed Scouting to keep its core while redefining itself around the edges.

Scouting never reached its most ambitious goals, but it was certainly in synch with the cultural life and values of the nation through the 1950s and early 1960s. The Norman Rockwell paintings of eager Scouts, helpful dads, and kindly Scoutmasters tending the campfire felt like they were channeling the essence of the country. But when the culture changed in the 1960s, Scouting, for the first time, suddenly found itself out of step with much that was going on in American life. In the culture wars of the

Vietnam era, all the vivid iconic imagery built up around Scouting suddenly evoked bad connotations as well as good ones. If Scouts were still trustworthy, loyal, helpful, and friendly, to some they were also militaristic, uptight, sexist, and irrelevant. As racial unrest shook the nation and minorities became an ever-more conspicuous part of American life, Scouting was stuck with the image of being of, by, and for white folks. And finally, West had succeeded in making Scouting run like a business, but it started to feel like one of those corporate dinosaurs about to have its lunch eaten by a more nimble competitor. By the mid-1970s, the B.S.A. was a bureaucratic behemoth that spent more than $100 million a year, owned 453,000 acres of land worth $233 million, and had 4,600 paid employees.

And when the culture changed, Scouting's grand spiral of eternal growth finally petered out and year-to-year membership began falling for the first time. Even by the Scouts' own count, the total number of Scouts and adult volunteers fell from 6.52 million in 1972 to 6.40 million in 1973. The next year it took a real plunge—to 5.80 million. Now it's down to 4.5 million. Some of the falling membership was a function of demographics and the dwindling pool of youths following the baby boom that peaked in the late 1960s and early 1970s. But the B.S.A. knew its problems extended beyond just demographics.

The drop in membership sparked a major fundraising and recruitment drive called Boypower 76, aimed at raising $65 million and recruiting two million new Scouts, a third of them minorities, by 1976. But, once again, the high-pressure push to meet quotas and goals backfired. In 1974, after a four-month investigation, the *Chicago Tribune* reported that the Scouts had padded their membership rolls with nonexistent minority children or troops left on the rolls long after they became defunct—all in the interest of keeping the numbers up and securing charitable funding from groups like the United Way.

Boypower 76 was soon abandoned, but Scouting's problems in recruiting continued. In the mid-1970s, for example, our local council, the Westchester–Putnam Council, put out a piece of recruiting literature with copy reading: "Parents. What do you want for your son?" Below it were two pictures of a cherubic-looking kid with floppy bangs. One was a police mug shot; the other was the kid in his Scout uniform. Even the most socially conservative parent—not the norm in Westchester County—might have been somewhat skeptical of the notion that their choice was a kid in a Scout uniform or a kid in prison overalls. And selling Scouting as a substitute for packing the kid off to some cold military academy didn't make it sound like much fun. At times, Scouting had the look of an organization that was getting a bit desperate and tone deaf. "This tight financial condition will become even more pressing over the next five years unless significantly better progress is made in raising revenues than has been the case during the past five years," wrote Warren B. Coburn, the council president at the time, in a letter sent out in 1978. "In fact, extraordinary efforts will be required just to keep the Council operating at present levels of service, let alone the new higher levels recommended by the Long Range Planning Committee."

The Scouts deserve credit for trying to attract minority youths (though whether that happened out of a sense of mission or one of self-preservation is a more complicated question). The program was altered in the 1970s to put more of an emphasis on urban Scouting and less on swimming and wilderness activities. And Scout publications like the Handbook, once full of white faces, suddenly began to look like brochures for an interracial church advertising its inclusiveness. In fact, it's hard to find a picture of a group of boys in any recent Scout publication that doesn't include black and brown faces. But after three decades of trying to diversify, the results remain spotty at best. And the scandal of inflated rolls keeps recurring. In 2000 Todd Bensman of the *Dallas Morning News* reported on a federal investigation of allegations that the Circle 10 Council, a twelve-county B.S.A. council in the backyard of the national headquarters, had inflated membership rosters by up to 30 percent and treated inactive troops as if they still existed. The chairman of one district was able to verify only fifty-four of ninety-one listed Scout troops. One man listed as a Scoutmaster said his troop had disbanded twelve years before. Three of the six Scouts listed as members of one troop were said to be living at an apartment complex that was bulldozed four years earlier. Scout officials said they were pressured to keep ghost units, particularly inner-city ones, on the rolls to justify funding requests.

Similar incidents were reported in Los Angeles in 1991 and Jackson, Mississippi, in 1994. In 1999 a study by the University of North Florida said the Scouts had exaggerated the growth and success of a Scouting program targeted at inner-city youths in public housing projects. It found that Scouting was almost nonexistent in thirteen of the seventeen apartment complexes where it was said to be flourishing.

Local officials who have blown the whistle on abuses in their own areas say the problem is not a few rogue officials, but something much more systemic. "The name of the game is money," Ardis Russell, a Mississippi accountant who pointed out the fraud there in 1994, told the *Morning News*. "It's always, 'Get the names and get the money.' It's a national problem and the Boy Scouts of America knows it." No one knows just how widespread the problems are, as no one outside the B.S.A. is responsible for checking its membership figures. At the very least, the continuing incidents are an indication that Scouting still has a long way to go in recruiting minorities. At the most, they raise questions about the vitality of Scouting overall.

Back in Scouting's heady beginnings, Dan Beard gave a speech in his distinctive, folksy voice that had summed up his era's view of Scouting as an integral part of the nation's life and the training of its boys and young men:

> There is nothing on God's earth as great as this true training for the boys, and as for we men, we don't amount to shucks, although we pretend we do, but we act as engineers on that train, that is all—engineers and brakemen—and carry this train of boys on toward their future, which is going to be greater and grander than any future we have ever dreamed of.

But by the time he died in 1941, ten days before his ninety-first birthday, even Uncle Dan was disillusioned with Scouting's direction. And as the years have gone by, the notion that Beard's "true training for boys" is the inevitable path for raising boys into men has no longer seemed so certain, not even to the men serving as the engineers and brakemen on the train.

10: Summer Camp 1: The Zen of Scout Socks

The weeks leading up to my departure for camp took on an odd, charged quality—part low-level dread, part expectant glow, as if I were a nervous pilgrim getting ready to embark on a portentous spiritual journey. Ben, of course, used the time to add to his cache of provisions and gear, trooping off to EMS and a Scout supply store to get new mosquito netting, industrial-strength insect repellent, and redundant reinforcements of T-shirts and shorts. I bought nothing, but I prepared nonetheless. First, I went to the doctor for my required camp physical. She was, it turned out, an engaging young woman a few years out of Brown University Medical School.

"Anything you need to tell me about your health?" she asked with an air of solicitous sincerity.

"Well," I said, "I'm going to summer camp in two weeks, and they need to be sure I won't keel over and fall face first into the kids' mashed potatoes."

For some reason, she didn't seem sure what to make of that but replied with the requisite expressions of reassurance.

"Oh, I don't think we need to worry about that, but let's see," she said sweetly. At that point two thoughts occurred to me: First, she was young enough to be my daughter. Second, even if I had been single, I was now too old to date my doctor.

I had my Boy Scouts physical form for her to fill out, a matter of CODE 1 total urgency, I had been repeatedly told, because without it, I wouldn't be able to serve as a Scoutmaster at camp. This warning merited a full five exclamation points in my troop leaders' guide in case anyone had missed its urgency.

"Well," the doctor said pleasantly, as she filled it out, "you seem to be in excellent shape for your age." (See: "too old to date my doctor.")

The deadly kicker—"for your age"—would have stung at any time, but this happened to be the week before I hit the doleful monument of fifty, a number whose import had become an insistent backdrop to daily life. I began casually perusing the obituaries, feeling a sudden urge to check out the various checkout times of the honorably deceased. I hung around the local Borders scanning books on health and nutrition and resolving to eat more garlic, broccoli, green tea, tofu, oatmeal, salmon, and other foods I didn't much like but were allegedly good for me. I took pride in the fact I was in better shape than most of the squirts in Troop 1, but was plagued by the nagging thought that it said more about them than about me.

On the other hand, I took pains to make sure this halfway-to-one-hundred (yikes!) navel gazing didn't get out of hand. I had once written a book with a very famous motivational speaker, who had an uplifting aphorism ("Don't find fault, find a solution," "If you say you can or you say you can't, you're right") for any situation. To my surprise, the turn-lemons-into-lemonade worldview more or less stayed with me. And rather than lament my impending geezerhood or dread my imminent departure into a horrid world of mosquitoes, latrines, and mornings without the *New York Times,* I did my best to put what we in the motivational world call a positive frame around the two unfortunate events. So as geezerhood and camperhood loomed simultaneously, I found myself conflating the two into an opportunity, rather than a burden. At my advanced age, I was preparing for something entirely new. I was not finding fault. I was finding a solution.

Fortified with that patently delusional self-spin, I did the rest of my preparation, such as it was. Ben, who was going for two weeks, took off on the Scout bus a week before I was scheduled to depart. I was counting on him for all flashlights, bug spray, mosquito netting, camping gear, and whatever else we needed from his vast survival arsenal. My packing was more rudimentary. I threw T-shirts, shorts, and underwear, a fleece for cool nights, assorted toiletries, and whatever else seemed vaguely appropriate into a travel bag. I picked out a couple of books and some old Scout handbooks to read. I conferred with my fellow Scoutmasters-to-be on a plan of action, and awaited the big day.

The plan was this: We were to meet with commando-like precision at 6:00 A.M. at Rocky's, a justly famous twenty-four-hour-a-day deli, near the entrance to the Taconic Parkway. Fortified with whatever donuts, bagels, or coffee we deemed appropriate, we would head north in a caravan, communicating via cell phone in the event of enemy attack, geezer bladder, or other problems. We figured to arrive there about ten, in time to get settled and unpack our gear before all heading off for a forty-minute drive to historic Fort Ticonderoga followed by a gala afternoon of doing our laundry and eating dinner we didn't have to cook ourselves.

I got up in the dark, threw my bag plus Ben's discarded sleeping bag and a pillow in the car, and headed toward Rocky's. My watch read 5:49. Sure enough, right there at six were my two compatriots Harry and Dennis, whom I had first met at the Paul Bunyan Camporee. Like Flank and Vanderbilt, they were another odd couple. Harry was the child of Holocaust survivors, organized, businesslike, and totally committed to Scouting. He had his own public relations firm and the orderly, composed personality of the guy at the head of the table at every business meeting. Dennis was a quiet, deferential Southern Baptist from Mississippi with a visceral love for the outdoors. He worked in market research and had an appealingly open, unaffected quality. He was the only person I've ever met whose jaw literally dropped and eyes bugged out when he was surprised by something. Harry was in a spotless new champagne-colored Infinity QX4 SUV. Dennis was in an old Volvo that was even creakier than mine. Harry had a books-on-tape version of Bill Gates's *Business at the Speed of Thought* in his tape deck. Dennis had Eric Hanson's *Stranger in the Forest,* an account of a trek through Borneo. They joked about using semaphore as a backup system in case the cell phones didn't work, a joke I only vaguely shared because I wasn't sure what semaphore was.

We flew past Albany and soon reached the foothills of the Adirondacks. We drove though the village of Brant Lake, whose main features were a tiny beach, Daby's General Store, and the Horicon Free Library, a cobblestone library the size of a phone booth. We passed the main expanse of lake, then came to a dirt road with a sign reading CURTIS S. READ SCOUT RESERVATION, WESTCHESTER–PUTNAM COUNCIL. We turned right and followed the road past the camp garage and the camp ranger's house until we reached a well-worn grassy area with cars parked around its edges. Up a hill was a nondescript brown frame cabin that turned out to be the Camp Waubeeka office, from which one could pick up the sounds of an electric guitar and bass stumbling through the most rudimentary version possible of "Sunshine of Your Love."

On the way up I had realized that the week Ben had been away in camp was the longest time I had been away from him since he'd been born, so I felt a surge of paternal longing as I waited for him to appear. A few minutes after we pulled up, I spotted him walking toward us down the rocky rise in front of the camp office. It was apparent something was not quite right. He appeared to be walking with one shoulder scrunched up, his shoelaces were untied, and from a distance his face looked kind of dirty, even by the standards of Scout camp. But as he got closer it was clear his face wasn't dirty. Instead, there was a vast purple swelling in the general vicinity of his right eye, which was nowhere to be seen but presumably hiding somewhere behind the swollen mass of facial tissue, which was the color of a slab of calf's liver. And his scrunched-up walk, it turned out, was his best Quasimodo imitation, a theatrical effort that was the subject of much merriment within the troop, especially when accompanied by a creaky "Come. There is much to see in the bell tower."

"WHAT HAPPENED TO YOU?" I shouted, thankful only that his mother was not around to witness the sight.

"Hey," he said, as if his feelings were hurt. "What kind of greeting is that?"

"WHAT HAPPENED TO YOU?" I repeated, not at all mollified by his apparent good cheer.

"Well," he began. "There's this game we play called tarp ball..." And he proceeded to describe a game that consisted of two players throwing a hardball back and forth over the steeply pitched tarp that hung over the cooking area. The most enthusiastic player was Jack, the tenth grader who was serving as Senior Patrol Leader during camp. The day before he had unfortunately missed the tarp entirely and sent the ball flying in the precise direction of Ben, who was innocently walking nearby. After his fellow Scouts picked him off the ground, they used their Scout training to realize they'd better have someone take a look at him. At the camp infirmary, the head man, a paramedic named Russ Fleer, decided it was indeed your basic, heavy-duty black eye and gave Ben some ice to put on it. Since then Ben

169

had been something of a camp celebrity, tarp ball had been suspended until further notice (which never came), and life had gone on.

The fact that the guilty party was supposed to be the mature, responsible kid in the troop did not provide great comfort, but Jack seemed genuinely contrite and we could spend only so much time gawking in horror at Ben's hideous shiner. The kids helped us unload our gear and led us past the office and commissary, down a rocky path, across a rudimentary footbridge over a shallow, rocky creek, around a bend, and finally down to the Wolfjaw campsite, Troop 1's home base for as long as anyone could remember.

I'm not quite sure what I expected, but Wolfjaw, unfortunately, came close. It was about two acres of second-growth hemlock, maple, birch, and ash trees that sloped down from the north end to the south. Scattered around were granite outcroppings and boulders. Its most impressive structure was a five-year-old lean-to. It served as Dr. Flank's domicile and office during the first week and was decked out like an officer's barracks, with uniforms neatly hanging from nails and paperwork, flashlights, and lanterns neatly arrayed on a plastic folding table that took up most of the available space. Everyone else bunked in ancient green military surplus tents that were mounted on wooden platforms a few inches off the ground. There were three cooking sites. Each had a wooden picnic table and two wooden benches and a rudimentary pantry called a monster box, stuffed with yellow cooking oil, pink dish soap, breakfast cereal, peanut butter, jelly, napkins, plastic utensils, bread, and whatever else had been saved from previous meals. Cooking was done on sheepherder and half-barrel stoves at each site. In the middle of the site was a bulletin board, which had various announcements, safety messages, a copy of the camp newsletter, "The Waubeeka World News," and the riddle of the day: "How far can a dog run into the forest?" (Answer: Halfway before he starts running out.) Near the upper cooking site was an area for chopping wood, called the axe yard, even though Dr. Flank forbade us from having axes around. At the north end of the site was a long metal basin used for washing, with a pipe above it that dispensed water through four holes that dripped noisily into the basin.

About ten yards from that was my own vision of the heart of darkness, the plywood edifice that housed the Wolfjaw latrine. Sam had already given it the appellation of "the deucer"— meaning the place where one deposited solid waste or, in the gentle lexicon of the troop, dropped a deuce. It had a molded plastic receptacle one urinated into with a pipe underneath it leading into some hellish space underground. There were two toilets with unsteady metal seats above the revolting devil's brew below. Luckily, posted on the wall were explicit instructions about latrine hygiene and information on sweeping the floor, scrubbing the toilets with pine solution, and pouring a chloro solution (½ cup of chloro and water) down the latrine. Unluckily, it still stank like holy hell.

For tonight, at least, I was planning to share a tent with Ben, and we had to move my stuff in before we left for the day's outing. The tent was already a mess, full of gear, dirty towels and T-shirts, Coke cans, and books. The latter were either humor (Dave Barry, Dilbert, The Onion) or macho variations on the Tom Clancy canon, all of them, it seemed, with names using some variation of the words Fear, Steel, Fatal, Phoenix, and Shadow. Was it *The Shadow of the Phoenix* or *Shadows of Steel*? *Fatal Terrain* or *Fatal Phoenix*? *The Sum of All Fears* or *The Shadow of All Steel*? I couldn't keep them straight. But Ben seemed to bridge the gap between the whimsical/ironic and the cold/paramilitary by periodically tossing off stray quotes from the Clancy books ("Gratitude is a disease of dogs") as if he were auditioning for the Sean Connery role in some upcoming thriller. I picked my way through the mess to my cot, which had a mattress that looked like it dated back to the Punic Wars resting on top of a skeletal frame. I put down my sleeping bag and pillow, tied a mosquito net to the post, and figured I'd make the best of it.

The day's activity was a trip to Fort Ticonderoga, a massive stone fortress on a dramatic rise overlooking Lake Champlain, followed by a festive afternoon of doing laundry. The fort, built in 1755 and still a thing of brooding wonder, allowed the kids to drool over ancient weapons—espignoles, halberds, and matchlock muskets—in a reminder that times change but man's lust for mayhem does not. Then we descended, laundry bags on our backs, on the tiny town of Ticonderoga like a parody remake of *The Wild Ones* with Boy Scouts instead of bikers taking over a quiet burg. For most of the kids it was their first time to do their own laundry ("Dude, you pour the white stuff in, turn it on, and it all comes out." "Awesome."). They seemed quite happy to shovel muck-infested shirts, shorts, socks, uniforms, and underwear into the machines, comparing aromas the way the French compare wines. On the way back, the sun was beginning to set and a hint of a chill had crept into the air. We passed a bunch of tepees set up incongruously on a golf course under a pink pillow of puffy stratocumulus clouds. By the side of the road were brilliant patches of orange day lilies. For the first time, I felt that not only were the kids at camp, but I was too, and when we got back, Ben and I and Mark and Jonah sat at the upper picnic table, talking a little and listening to the night sounds of the woods before going to bed.

The next morning we had nowhere to go and no provisions to make breakfast with. Instead, we were supposed to go over to Camp Buckskin, the other camp mentioned at the precamp meeting, where the kids ate their meals cafeteria style, a development Dr. Flank viewed with unveiled contempt. "What we do is real camping," he told the kids. "What they have over there is a hotel."

In fact, Newtown Hall, Buckskin's two-year-old dining and meeting hall, made our dilapidated Waubeeka facilities seem like slums. It had a concrete slab floor and a gleaming laminated pine interior that gave the place the feel of a chapel as much as a cafeteria. On the walls inside were the Scout prayers for the three meals.

We were ushered into a room full of kids in their orange Camp Buckskin T-shirts, and motioned toward a table where we recited the morning grace with the others and waited expectantly for our turn to eat. When one of the counselors finally came by our table and announced, "OK, your turn to go," we filed into the serving area. There, prepared to ladle food onto our plastic trays, was an alarmingly cheerful group of the camp's junior staff and kitchen help. Either they were utterly imbued with the Boy Scout spirit or they had a sense of humor about the cuisine, because in one meal—and a breakfast meal at that— we were about to experience all the major food groups of the average American diet. First came bagels representing the increasingly important food-with-a-hole-in-the-middle group. Then came some colorful sort of hash representing the don't-ask, don't-tell group. Then a little egg, more or less scrambled, from the cholesterol food group. A moist clump of oatmeal representing the Wilfred Brimley/kids-could-care-less group. A sweet roll and a sticky dab of macaroni and cheese representing the dominant carbohydrate group. A touch of quiche for the sophisticates among us. Then over to Old Italia for the traditional breakfast meatball and ziti in breakfast spaghetti sauce. Next up, for the real risk takers in the group, was a little chicken salad. And then finally, for the health conscious among us, a soupy vegetable medley of cooked carrots, peas, and green beans. All were plopped down on the plates in discrete clumps like Balkanized countries sharing a dysfunctional culinary continent. On the table outside were individual servings of various cold cereals, with an accent on the Technicolor varieties like Froot Loops and Lucky Charms. We sat back down and the kids began engaging in a bit of commodity trading—say, a meatball for a sweet roll. Needless to say some objects, particularly the vegetables and oatmeal, were of limited trading value while others, particularly the sweet rolls, consistently traded at the top of their range.

After breakfast Dr. Flank, who planned to leave that day, gave us a brief history tour. First, he showed us a plaque embedded in stone marking a bridge built in the memory of Don Vanderbilt. Then he presided over an impromptu groundbreaking for a new shower building to be built in honor of Todd Frohmann, who had put three kids through the troop and had died of a heart attack the previous year. It wasn't clear how much this meant to the current Troop 1 members, but the observances were incredibly ill timed for Stu Hillman, the camp superintendent. Stu had a problem. Waubeeka, he had realized early Sunday morning, had more troops than space, or at least more than the space that was available. And our troop was down from twenty kids the first week to eleven the second, which left things pretty sparse at a campsite with three cooking sites. Stu, a tall, thin earnest fellow in his early thirties, ambled into Wolfjaw with a modest proposal for Dr. Flank. He hated to do this, he began, but with just eleven kids, Troop 1 didn't have enough kids to make use of the three patrol sites at Wolfjaw. What he'd like to do is move us to a smaller site, so one of the bigger troops could use Wolfjaw. Dr. Flank listened silently, his face stony, his eyes narrowing. Did not young Mr. Hillman realize, he asked, that Troop 1 always camped at Wolfjaw and that we were settled in, having already spent our first week there? Well, yes, Mr. Hillman replied evenly, but the camp policy clearly stated that a troop had to be able to take up a specified percentage of the campsite, and our troop for the second week did not meet the standard. Soon, they were going at it like $500-an-hour litigators, arguing both the letter and the spirit of the camp regulations.

"Bill, I respect where you're coming from, but the policy still says, if I'm reading it right, that a troop must take up 75 percent of the site."

"Yes, but the policy doesn't cover this, a troop that's already settled in a site."

"I understand that, but if you put yourself in their shoes, the other troops, there's a very persuasive case."

"Well, I don't want to move a sitting troop. You don't come to camp and then be told you have to move. That's not right, and I don't think it's something we want to do."

On and on they went, neither budging in a characteristically mulelike male discourse that, to be sure, was better than pistols at ten paces or something else definitive. Finally Harry, in his role as Dr. Flank's heir apparent as top dog for the second week, stepped in to try to mediate.

"We're all trying to be reasonable adults here," he said. "In your opinion, Bill, what are the options?"

They went at it some more, but the obvious fact was that Dr. Flank wasn't budging. Particularly after contemplating Don Vanderbilt's plaque and Todd Frohmann's legacy, this was about something more than a piece of turf or a place to sleep at night. The closest thing we came to a compromise was allowing another troop, which turned out to be Greenwich Troop 35, from the tony town in Connecticut, to expand toward our southern border by taking over the vacant cooking site that was closest to their campsite at neighboring Sunrise.

That battle won, Dr. Flank prepared to take off for home. Dr. Flank's usual drill was to stay the first week only, and he had been packing up since early morning, so the kids knew he was preparing to leave. But it still felt like a big deal, both to the kids who on some level appreciated having him around as an undisputed authority figure and to those who felt that once the boss man was gone they could really run amok. So it was important to send out the right signal that order would be maintained and fully deputized adults would be in charge even if Dr. Flank were not around. For better or worse, that meant Harry, Dennis, and me.

"It is my pleasure to turn this motley crew called Chappaqua Troop 1 over to you, and Mr. Applebome and Mr. Walker," Dr. Flank announced, looking directly at Harry. "I'm sure you will have a great week."

"It is my pleasure," said Harry, "and we'll do our best to maintain your standards."

Both Dennis and I were thrilled to see Harry officially in charge. Not that there was much question. Harry had been active in Scouting in Brooklyn for many years as a young man, even working for a time as a paid Scouting district staff member. He was the only one of us who had shown up in uniform, with neatly pressed khaki shorts and high Scout socks pulled up to his knees. And he had the take-charge personality both of us lacked.

We loaded up Dr. Flank's Volvo, watched him drive off, and then contemplated our first major management issue—a proper Scout hike, or a wild jaunt into Lake George? Harry, responsibly, leaned toward doing what Dr. Flank would have done—the hike. But Dennis and I, the irresponsibility caucus, figured the kids deserved a break before embarking on the rigors of week two. Democracy won out, and before long we were all heading toward Lake George, a teeming menagerie of video-game arcades, ice-cream shops, pizza parlors, hot-dog stands, fast-food franchises, souvenir shops, and wax museums. The kids paraded around like sailors on leave. Sam 'n Eric and Tom took the occasion to flirt with various girls, most of them four years older and at best amused by, at worst utterly indifferent to, these preening little jokers in their Boy Scout uniforms. "There's something about a man in uniform," Sam said, intuiting a far more welcoming response from a passing blond in a tight halter top than was readily apparent. "Yeah," added Mark. "There's something about a man in an ape costume too, but it's not necessarily good." Then it was back to camp for the assembly at the parade grounds, the gala barbecue, and the merit badge sign-up that would begin the second week of camp.

In our brief absence, the camp had become a different place. We had been almost alone in Waubeeka when we arrived, but while we were gone, other troops had streamed in. They were busy setting up camp in Sunrise, Polaris, Cascade, Haystack, and Avalanche, the other campsites at Waubeeka. We could see kids lugging in their gear, throwing a football around the parade grounds, and wandering up and down the rocky road to the office and commissary. When we got back to Wolfjaw, Harry and I took over the two cots in the lean-to, clearly the power position in the campsite. Harry was already established as the week's adult leader, but my status as a lean-to dweller gave me an illusory air of authority as well. I did my best to adopt a stern, don't-mess-with-me demeanor as Harry called all the kids together to prepare for the night's festivities.

The barbecue was our first official gathering of the tribes, and instantly one got a sense of the troops as utterly distinct little pods. Sitting next to us was Troop 4 Bronxville with their purple ball caps and matching neckerchiefs, each kid decked out in matching full uniform. Their hulking leader looked vaguely familiar until I remembered he was the large fellow with the stiff-kneed walk who had been treated with such deference at the precamp meeting the previous winter. Troop 285 Bellmore from Long Island had the rowdy look of an Italian wedding without the bride and bridesmaids, and featured a handful of fierce-looking Mohawks that one of the dads, a barber, fashioned each year for willing victims. Troop 68 from Wappinger Falls in Dutchess County upstate had fringed red neckerchiefs and something of the quality of 4 Bronxville, though without quite the same cocky spit and polish. Other troops were from Rye, Scarsdale, and Greenwich, though I soon found out that it was common for troops to have the name of a ritzy town but really be made up largely of kids from the less high-powered town nearby. We all waited at long picnic tables until called to line up for hot dogs, hamburgers, potato salad, macaroni, and coleslaw, all of them doled out by staff members who were mostly just a few years older than the kids.

Then we all lined up at the parade grounds, where we were addressed by the camp director, Tom Logan. He stood on a rocky outcrop on the hill in front of the office, with his whole staff lined up obediently behind him. In the usual call and response, he made sure we felt real good, that we could always yell louder than the yell before, and that we had a positive mental attitude.

Next was merit badge sign-up, which felt like precomputerized college registration as orchestrated by the Marx Brothers. Most of the kids had come equipped with a list of the four or five merit badges they wanted to earn out of the thirty-five offered at Waubeeka. But, for those still waffling, the staff acted like carnival barkers advertising their wares.

"Come to the econ lodge, where a real man handles snakes and reptiles and learns astronomy, bird study, insect study, and mammal study," announced one teenaged counselor in his finest manly man baritone.

"Come to the econ lodge, if you want to turn into a pathetic sniveling wuss of a girly girl," announced another in the identical voice. "Come to Scoutcraft and learn camping, hiking, orienteering, and pioneering—Scouting the way the Good Lord meant it to be. And Scoutcraft is fun, not school in disguise."

"Scoutcraft is for dorks, and dorks are for Scoutcraft," the first kid yelled back.

Before long a third chimed in—not very credibly—for the manly man-ness of the handicraft shelter, where rugged Scouts could take basketry, leatherwork, and woodcarving, Scout camp's version of rocks for jocks. Before long there was a cacophony of mock baritones improvising together like a Scout camp's version of a free jazz ensemble. The only ones who didn't try to sell their wares were the counselors from the shotgun and rifle range, since it took no prodding to get almost every kid in camp interested in doing both sooner or later. The kids eventually filled up their calendars and lost interest in the show. By now, it was almost dark and time for the evening's final event— the campfire.

We gathered in a little natural amphitheater by the banks of Waubeeka's lake. The amphitheater was ringed by a shimmering crescent of trees and had logs for seats arranged in a semicircle. In the middle of the clearing was an impressive pyramid of logs, branches, kindling twigs, and debris that was set afire as soon as we were all seated, immediately billowing into a flickering orange tongue.

Tom, the camp director, led us in various time-worn Waubeeka cheers, yells, and fight songs—though it was hard to figure out whom we would be fighting against. The prissy hotel dwellers in Buckskin? The girls' camp we had passed along Brant Lake, with dozens of long-limbed girls running around on a perfectly manicured soccer field? The kids against the grownups? No one knew, but the kids got into the spirit nonetheless, urged on by the straight arrows from Bronxville 4, who jumped up, waved their arms wildly, and urged on all the laggards. We were supposed to make up in spirit and voltage what

179

we lacked in eloquence, and the simplest yell was the most effective of all. It went: "Waaaaaahhh-Beeka. Waaaaaahhh-Beeka. Waaaaaahhh-Beeka. Camp. Camp. CAMP." The idea was to shout it out, cut the last word off as if with a knife, and listen to the echo roll over the water. We tried it once and got a modest but unacceptable—at least to Tom—echo. But then we did it a second and third and fourth time, each time a bit louder and producing a clearer and more expansive echo that lingered with a ghostly staying power over the dark waters of the lake.

Finally, the songs and cheers and skits were over, and Tom was standing alone in front of the bonfire.

"We come here to enjoy the true beauty that surrounds us," Tom said, the bonfire crackling and dancing madly around him. "Take only pictures and leave only footsteps. Maybe you've heard that. Maybe you haven't. It's all part of the spirit of Scouting. I want you to think about that as you go back to your cabins. File out quietly, and we'll see you in the morning."

We went back, finding our way along the path by flashlight, visiting the wash basin and the latrine and then crawling into our sleeping bags. In my head, as I drifted off to sleep, I could still hear the echoes of the echoes of the echoes— Waaaaaaahhh-Beeka, Waaaaaaahhh-Beeka, Waaaaaaahhh-Beeka. Camp. Camp. CAMP.

I woke up the next morning in time to see boys trudging into camp with brown plastic garbage cans strapped to their back. It looked like a scene out of a bad Dickens Boy Scout novel.

This, I soon learned, was not a dour form of punishment, but our food delivery system. Each morning at 6:45, one or two kids from each patrol strapped on an empty brown plastic trash can attached to a harness like a backpack and trekked up the trail to the commissary, where a sallow-faced trio of junior staff members loaded it with eggs and cheese, milk and cereal, toast and butter, pancake batter and syrup, and whatever other goodies like bacon or sausage were on the morning menu. They threw in the one mimeographed page of the "Waubeeka World News" plus whatever cups, plates, napkins, or plastic utensils or toilet paper were needed. Then the Scouts trekked back down to Wolfjaw, where the morning psychodrama was already in progress.

A friend who worked at a hospital emergency room once told me that arriving patients were informally, if cruelly, sorted by the staff into two classes of humans. There were citizens—regular folk who chopped off digits with power saws, or fell off ladders, or brought in children who had been bitten by the family dog. And there were dirtballs—essentially denizens of the night who shot, stabbed, stuck, or stomped one another with enough frequency to guarantee business in perpetuity for the ER staff. The level of mayhem at Waubeeka hardly approached the ER level, and "goofball" rather than "dirtball" seemed about the worst label one would care to stick on a thirteen-year-old Scout. But, particularly when there were chores to be done, it was immediately clear that we had our own informal typology at camp—performing and nonperforming assets. And for an enterprising Patrol Leader, the secret to getting meals cooked, latrines cleaned, or litter picked up was to find a way to get some work out of the laggards while not relying overly much on the kids who were willing to work but did not expect to do everyone else's chores as well.

So as our bleary-eyed crew prepared for their first day of activities at seven in the morning, the Scouts were already sorting themselves into tasks like a somewhat dysfunctional ant farm. Clearly of use were the two mules, Tom, now thirteen going on eighteen, and Mark, who had trudged back with the supplies and were now gaily unpacking them and stacking plastic apple juice cups, single-serving boxes of Lucky Charms, Froot Loops, and Apple Jacks, and milk cartons into neat but rickety towers perfectly positioned for someone else to knock over. Ben wouldn't have earned many merit badges for room-cleaning or chore-doing at home, but he and his Amigo Jonah were already up getting wood and helping to make the fire. At the other extreme were Les and Rick, who despite their obvious lack of interest had been talked into giving Scout camp a try. During the first week, Dr. Flank had told us, Les and Rick had tended to huddle together for comfort. They shared a tent. They did the same activities, which usually took place in the relative safety of the handicrafts lodge. And they shared a common distaste for camp chores—and to be honest, for camp altogether. Les was a round-faced twelve-year-old with red hair and a perpetually stricken look in his eyes. He spent most of the day simply pacing, back and forth, back and forth—around the cooking site, around the campsite, toward the latrine and back. Rick was a year older, a good bit taller and heavier, good at math, computers, and drawing nature sketches. But he had no interest in any of the troop activities, particularly those that involved mere chores. So as the others hustled in varying degrees to get breakfast going, Les and Rick wandered dolefully around the campsite and its environs in listless pursuit of firewood, or fire twigs, to be more accurate. They would roam for a few minutes, pick up a desultory twig or two from some distant cover of the site, trudge back to the cooksite, and ostentatiously place their booty on the firewood pile. Then they wandered off again.

In the middle of the performance/nonperformance scale at the upper campsite was Bernie, who had not been particularly active in the troop during the year, but gained a measure of camp-wide acclaim the first week by downing a five-gallon container of fruit punch in one sitting, a feat that won him about the only citation Troop 1 had earned the first week. Bernie specialized in accents and imitations—Fred Flintstone, Homer Simpson, some idiot proclaiming "You can do it," pronounced "you ca do eeet," apparently a particularly memorable phrase from the stupid Adam Sandler movie *The Waterboy*—so he tended toward jobs that involved social interaction more than vigorous initiative. He was quite happy to do his accents, eat, and tend the fire, throwing in kindling wood or discarded packaging with a few of his fellow pyros who were thrilled to keep the fire going. So, by a process of elimination, most of the first day's cooking was really produced and directed by Jack, the Senior Patrol Leader. He did get Bernie to break sixteen eggs and dump the remains in an orange plastic bowl, bidding each a fond farewell in his Homer Simpson voice. But after that, Jonah greased the cooking top with butter, poured messy globs of eggs onto the grill, and mixed them around with a wooden spoon. Then he slathered some more butter onto the grill and went back to work. Within ten minutes he had a dozen pieces of toast, about the same number of strips of bacon, and enough eggs to totally clog the arteries of a previously healthy Olympic marathoner.

The eating was characterized by the same imbalanced effort as the preparation had been. Les and Rick between them ate not much more than the marshmallow pieces they picked out of their Lucky Charms cereal. Les said he was too cold. Upon consideration, Rick decided he was too cold too. Bernie, on the other hand, ate two bowls of Froot Loops, three pieces of toast, three pieces of bacon, and a big clump of eggs that was piled up like a heap of mashed potatoes. The others did their parts in varying degrees. What they didn't finish, Bernie did, which helped the cleanup process immensely. At nine, the kids all fanned out across the camp to go to their activities. For the first time since we'd met at Rocky's, the three adults were alone to compare notes and plot strategy. Harry took the lead. He was decked out in his Scout uniform, shirt, shorts, and socks—no neckerchief—and had with him the troop's schedule for the

week, which he had printed out at home before he left. The activities included a visit to the dry and wet caves, the latter a
spooky cavern in which one had to dip underwater at various
points. One day we had the low COPE course, the kind of
team-building they do these days at corporate retreats, with
teams helping one another across boards or forming human
chains to retrieve a ball. There was a visit to the Zip Line, a trolley on a metal wire that Scouts rode halfway into the lake, hanging on by one or both hands and then letting go and dropping
into the water. And one day we were scheduled to leave camp to
go white-water rafting forty minutes away in Lake Luzerne.

"I thought the transition when Bill left went well," Harry
said. "I think we're in good shape for the week. What issues do
you guys see as needing our attention?"

There were a few. The site was a mess. There were pods of
dissidents, the Sam 'n Eric faction in particular, intent on as-
serting their tribal hegemony in the lower part of the camp,
which I came to see as The Underworld. Les and Rick and one
or two others definitely needed some kind of a jump start. But,
in addition to them, there was the issue of us. Just what did we
do, Dennis asked.

This was a subject that had occurred to me prior to arriving,
and uncharacteristically, I had followed Boy Scout protocol and
was prepared. We, of course, had models from our own troop of
effective leadership—Dr. Flank's patience and wisdom, Mr.
Johnson's wry forbearance and ability to teach, Mr. Toonkel's
cranky air of authority and competence. But I figured I'd scour
some Scout literature for more explicit instruction on just what
it was we were there for.

The Scoutmaster's Handbook was updated over the years
just as the Scout Handbook was, but it spoke in a remarkably
consistent, and, I thought, sensible voice about Scouting and
Scouters. So, for example, the 1972 Handbook seemed not a bit

outdated in its introductory passages on what it took to be a Scoutmaster:

> What qualities should you possess to be a good Scoutmaster? One could make a very long list, but that wouldn't help. Basically, you need to be an open person—one who speaks honestly and listens intently. You need a sense of humor. Not the ability to tell funny stories, but the ability to smile at yourself and at life. You need to understand the place of the outdoor program in Scouting and your part in it. And then—and this is quite important—you ought to like boys.

OK, the last phrase these days is hard to read without a hint of the wink-wink, nudge-nudge of sexual innuendo that has become Scouting's cross to bear. But the rest of the agenda—make it fun, make it educational, there should be a purpose behind each activity, never do for a boy what he can do for himself—was hard to argue with. I had also found two eccentric accounts of the Scoutmaster's lot, one from the 1930s, one from the 1950s. They were a reminder that despite the B.S.A.'s strenuous efforts to mold Scouting into a one-size-fits-all operation, the troops invariably took on the personality of their Scoutmaster.

Take A. Lewis Oswald. Please. Mr. Oswald, author of *Troop One Marches On!* published by the Rotherwood Press of Hutchinson, Kansas, in 1934, peers out from the back cover of his slender little book with a truly maniacal gleam in his dark little eyes. He's wearing a rounded, flat-brim, World War I–era military-style hat strapped tightly around his chin. Across his uniform, which is festooned with medals and patches, is a sash, presumably his Eagle sash, full of badges. If Rosenthal accuses Baden-Powell of putting together a character factory, Ozzie, as the boys call him, was darn proud of it. He writes: "I have no apology for saying to each lad on his twelfth birthday before he takes his oath, 'It is better not to join Troop One than to join and not be an Eagle.'" Yikes. If my friend Dan felt his Scouting experience was a bit harsh, he's lucky he avoided life with the hyena and rattlesnake patrols in Hutchinson Troop 1. Ozzie's obsessive account of life with his boys couldn't be much more creepy. He wrote of a favored class of Eagles:

> They say I gave them Scouting. They are wrong; they taught me the great game. When they outgrew their uniforms, I had a feeling that my heart would never again feel the thrill which was mine when I watched the one and only Charles Grimes Colladay, Eagle Number One of Troop Number One. He and Jerry and Jimmie were the pillars. After all, the test of success is not the make of the family's car; it's the boy, the heir-apparent!

Ozzie's zeal for molding his boys made him, like Machiavelli and Attila the Hun, before him a model for management theory. The Ozzie way of knowledge revolved around two principles, the primacy of the patrol system and the importance of troop ranking—"two of the golden keys, which unlock our secret shrine." So not only were boys organized into patrols, but within the troop Ozzie ranked every boy—Senior Patrol Leader Sidlinger, already an Eagle, at the top, on down to lowly Tenderfeet Leach, Stuckey, and Hamilton at numbers 23, 24, and 25 at the bottom. "Thus the position of every Scout in Troop One is known," he wrote. "By delivering the goods, he moves up. If he falters, others will pass him . . . If he dallies too much with the precious hour in front of him, he is tossed out, on the same principle that the dead wood is removed from the apple tree and for the same purpose, too." As for the older kids, not long after they made Eagle they were told to hit the road to make way for new blood: "It's hard and it's a trifle bitter, but Troop One must March On!" he concludes.

Oh, well. Ozzie was a product of his time and his locale. A more familiar voice is the narrator of *Be Prepared! The Life and*

Illusions of a Scoutmaster, by R. E. Cochran, published in 1952. In a less totalitarian way, Cochran too, sees himself as part of an enterprise dedicated to molding boys back in the days when Scouting was still considered an irony-free zone. "I felt," he says, at the beginning of his tenure, "rather like Toscanini arriving to conduct a rehearsal or Knute Rockne looking over a green squad he would soon mold into a championship team." Ozzie sees himself as a benevolent puppeteer helping to mold the heirs apparent. Cochran wisely sees himself a partner in a mysterious, osmotic process between the boys and their alleged leaders. "A Scout troop," he said, in a phrase he wouldn't dare use these days, "is more effective than a nagging wife in getting a man to do something about his shortcomings."

Cochran's narrative is good-natured and likably earnest. He notes approvingly that during two wars, Scouting never taught military techniques or hatred of the enemy, stressing instead "physical fitness, mental resourcefulness and war service chores." And mostly what he sees in Scouting is a largely respectful community of men and boys. He and his Scouts discuss Walt Whitman, survive pleasant and miserable outings in the woods, navigate the line between chaos and order at their meetings the way we do now, and coexist in a process that benefits both sides. He concludes:

> While it is true that Scouting builds character, it is especially true with reference to the Scoutmaster's character. Almost willy-nilly, he acquires cleanliness, strength, cheerfulness and other virtues listed in the Scout Law. As I slowly became aware, a Scoutmaster's troop is more or less a reflection of himself. The more time he spends with it, the more he finds his own personality mirrored and magnified in it.

Oswald and Cochran hardly covered all the bases of troop management, but they defined its two poles: Robert Duvall in

Apocalypse Now and Ward Cleaver. And in their own ways, their approaches raised at least two of the fundamental questions at the heart of the Scouting enterprise. First, were they training boys (*the heirs apparent!*) for the combat and competition—hopefully in peace, not war—that they'll likely face in life, or were they helping to mold character in a broader, less Darwinian sense? And, second, how much were they ringmasters and how much were they part of the circus?

Cochran had described a Boy Scout summer camp as "a remote, mysterious place to which visitors seldom penetrated and from which campers return speaking in cryptic jargon. Usually, it is entrenched in the farthest shore of some lake or river behind a mountain barrier." This wasn't a bad description of Waubeeka. The Curtis S. Read Scout Reservation, named for an Eagle Scout, assistant Scoutmaster, and naval aviator who died in 1918 in World War I, sprawls over one thousand acres of land not far from the site of the first Boy Scout camp that Seton presided over in 1910. Waubeeka's sliver of the Adirondacks was organized around activity areas that harkened back in a surprisingly literal fashion to Scouting's past. Just before the footbridge, on the way to the lake, was the Scoutcraft compound, surrounded by elaborately lashed-together limbs and planks that gave it the air of a forest fortress. At its heart was the Dan Beard area. There campers learned the basic knots and skills, and counselors laid out the requirements needed to reach Tenderfoot, Second Class, and First Class, the first three ranks on the advancement ladder. Back at the camp office, the walls were covered with quotations from Baden-Powell ("The Patrol is the character school of the individual"), all accompanied by archaic-looking drawings and the simple citation "B-P." It was hard to be sure how many kids even knew who Baden-Powell was, but his presence gave at least the appearance of purpose to the place.

Not surprisingly, there was no formal recognition of Seton, but he too seemed to be there at the Tom and Sonya Hays Memorial Nature Center. The center, a very modest open-air structure built in 1981, was presided over by a fiercely intelligent, bearlike college student named Ted Watson, who had a properly Setonian know-it-all air and a polymath's ability to sound like he knew what he was talking about whether he was spouting off about calculus, astronomy, insect study, geology, or computers. His assistant was Frankie Stanton, the Scout who made the carnival barker's pitch for nature study at the merit-badge sign-up.

I walked down to the shooting area, where kids were happily blasting away with shotguns and rifles. At the handicraft area they were weaving their baskets and carving neckerchief slides out of wood. I walked down to the waterfront, briefly considered taking my swimming test, and then figured it would be too embarrassing if I failed, so I decided to skip it and restrict my aquatic activities to the shower located adjacent to Wolfjaw, where campers and Scoutmasters followed a strict schedule that made sure adults and campers never used the shower at the same time. It occurred to me that, after all the urgent red-alert directives about how crucial it was to get my medical form in, no one had even asked for it. Apparently they did ask for it at the lake, but if you didn't sign up for swimming you could have a medical form saying you had high blood pressure, tuberculosis, or leprosy and were about to drop dead at any second, and no one would ever know.

Before I knew it, it was lunchtime. The commissary had given each patrol two pounds of salami, some American cheese, an industrial-size loaf of white bread, a few heads of iceberg lettuce plus tomatoes, oranges and apples, a big bag of potato chips, and two boxes of chocolate chip cookies. I ate down in The Underworld with Sam 'n Eric and their merry men. They made sandwiches with the salami, cheese, and potato chips; hurled the lettuce, tomatoes, oranges, and apples into the woods; and then downed all the cookies and vast quantities of cherry punch.

After lunch and siesta, during which kids napped, played cards, worked on their merit badges, or read, the kids trekked off again and Dennis and Harry went to the waterfront, where they took and passed their swimming test. I wandered back to the nature shack. It was an inspired blend of Setonian love of nature and contemporary love of wonkdom. The shack consisted of a back room enclosed on three sides full of books; computers; insect, rock, and flora specimens; knives, pins, and other gear. There were books on calculus, butterflies, and chemistry, many versions of the Scout Handbook, nature guides like *The Simon & Schuster Guide to Plants and Animals, The National Audubon Society Field Guide to North American Rocks and Minerals,* and *Birds of North America.* There was also, I was delighted to see, Seton's *Wild Animals I Have Known.* Downloaded on the computer were all sorts of iconic songs and sounds, from Sinatra's "New York, New York" to Weird Al Yankovich's "Barney's on Fire" ("Oh boy, Barney's on fire. It's what we've always desired.").

Ted Watson definitely had a show-off quality, like the camp's version of the Shell Answer Man. He was teaching calculus to a bunch of kids from Scarsdale, answering some kid's question about the likelihood of spontaneous combustion, and extolling the virtues of mica, all at the same time. Some of his schtick was his version of Science Guy stand-up comedy:

KID: "Ted, do you think there are aliens out there?"
TED: "Have you ever met a taxi driver in New York?"

The rest was random displays of knowledge, esoterica, or whimsy. Ted was too intense to keep an assistant for more than a year. But he and Frankie were a perfect pair. One took himself too seriously; the other didn't take anything seriously. One was all full of abstract knowledge; the other was more likely to be out hunting for snakes or talking about *Star Wars* characters than stars when teaching the astronomy merit badge. And the econ lodge—it was officially the ecology lodge, but "ecol" didn't have the right ring—had the feel of a node of Scouting that had evolved the way God intended it—boys teaching boys, techy and fun, respectful of nature and respectful of the boys. Ted had already achieved a top rank nationally in the Order of the Arrow, the national Scouting honorary society. But he was surprisingly unreflective about Scouting—Did it reach enough kids? Did he worry about Scouting being seen as uncool and behind the times? Does the uniform still serve a positive purpose? When I asked, he looked at me as if mildly annoyed. "If you say it's not what the modern Westchester boy does, and it's uncool, you haven't been much of a devil's advocate, because you're not saying anything," he said. "If you say it's uncool, fine. But if you check with the kids who are Scouts, no one really cares about that. Scouting's not much different than it ever was. The goal is to develop character, foster citizenship, and teach fitness. And I think kids get that, without being hit over the head with it."

I headed back toward Wolfjaw. As I approached, I heard the faint strains of a song that sounded a bit like the call of a stricken animal. It was an ancient camp song known to generations of campers hither and yon:

Scout socks.
They never get dirty.
The longer you wear them,
The stronger they get.
Sometimes I think I should launder them.
Something keeps telling me
No no not yet.

For Troop 1, though, the song had taken on a quality that was one part totemic and one part sadistic. During the first week,

191

Sam 'n Eric had made it their personal calling card. They gave it a straight manly Scouts reading, a Whitney Houston soulful reading, a Celine Dionne bombastic reading, and a particularly weaponized *La Traviata* operatic reading. They sang it loud and they sang it louder and loudest. Their rendition had made them instantly famous in camp—over-the-top obnoxiousness always being the quickest route to notoriety for adolescent boys. And their vocal skills had immediately become an enormous sore point for our nearest neighbors, the Scout troop from Greenwich. When I reached camp I learned that Sam 'n Eric had been singing it for perhaps twenty minutes, and every time they resumed their oratorio, screams of pain and anguish could be heard from our friends from Greenwich. One little boy in particular would run to the rise overlooking our site, a stricken look on his face, reminiscent of Munch's *The Scream*. Each time the singing resumed, his eyes would bug out, he'd put his hands over his ears, and he'd yell, "Shut up, shut up" at the top of his lungs. But, of course, the more he complained and hollered, the more Sam 'n Eric were encouraged to sing, often pausing just long enough to lull the Greenwichites into thinking they were finally through, only to crank it up con molto brio once again.

Antagonizing the kids from Greenwich had particular appeal. Greenwich 35 did not have quite the well-drilled hauteur of Bronxville 4, but it soon became apparent that our relationship with them was somewhat like that between the John Belushi frat and the straight-arrow frat in *Animal House*. They stood silently before meals, bowed their heads, and said their vespers, while we didn't do so much as a "Rub a dub dub, thanks for the grub." Their kids showed up in neatly pressed and tended uniforms. Their Scoutmasters were all trim, friendly, and unfailingly polite, except when they were complaining that we weren't pulling our weight in cleaning the latrine we now were sharing. The Greenwich site went dark and quiet right after

"Taps" was played at ten—we pictured them drinking warm milk and kneeling by their cots in their jammies to say their prayers at night. Their one excess was building humongous bon-fires every night that they stoked up to hadeslike intensity, as if allowing all their sublimated energies to play out in each eve-ning's pyre. Still, whether walking to the shower with their monogrammed towels or coming back from the handicrafts shed with that perfect piece of lanyard or the wicker basket done just so, both the Scouts and Scouters of Greenwich 35 had enough of that air of WASPy Connecticut virtue to stir the darker sauces of our guys, particularly the crew down at our lower site, where Louis may have been Patrol Leader but Sam 'n Eric were the true capos.

We made our dinner—chicken patties in marinara sauce, salad, Italian bread, bug juice, oatmeal cookies—and cleaned up quickly. Harry had made it clear he wanted everyone to be on time for all the retreats, which took place at 6:45 each eve-ning, so our guys straggled over to the lean-to by 6:30, and we all trekked up to the parade grounds. We lined up next to Bronxville 4. Each of their kids was in an impeccable uniform right down to a neckerchief perfectly positioned in its slide. Their Senior Patrol Leader inspected their lineup with a cold, unforgiving gaze, like a Marine Corps Drill Instructor, straight-ening a kid's neckerchief or moving the line another six inches to keep it perfectly straight. All our kids had their Scout shirts on, but otherwise we looked like we'd been outfitted at one of those *ropa usada* places in South Texas where people buy mix-and-match clothes by the pound.

Before long, Tom Logan strode out from the camp head-quarters and took his position on the hill above us.

"Camp Waubeeka, attention!" he hollered.

Bronxville 4 turned to ramrods. Greenwich 35 stood erect like perfect toy soldiers. We slouched a bit less than usual.

"Parade rest," he continued. Then he ordered a bugler to sound the retreat. The flag was taken down and folded, we were ordered at ease, and he paced on the rocky rise above us with a sheet of paper in his hands.

"Gentlemen, we had a great day today. I saw a lot of Scout spirit. I saw a lot of hard work. I saw a lot of fun. Gentlemen, if you've been here before, this is something you already know. If you haven't, it's something you need to know. Every week one troop is awarded a special honor."

He held up a large, yellow wooden "W," with names scrawled all over it. "This, gentlemen, is the Waubeeka Award. Each week troops are graded on their daily site inspection, on competitions like the staff hunt, the water carnival, or knot-tying competitions between the SPLs. At the end, the troop with the most points is awarded the Waubeeka Award at the final camp-fire, and every Scout and adult leader gets to sign his name on it. In that context, I have the results of today's inspections. Re-member that nothing counts more than your inspection—how well you keep up your campsite and cooking sites each day. And today, we had three perfect scores—thirty-six of thirty-six. When I call your names, will the SPLs for each troop come for-ward to receive your inspection report. First, the perfect scores. 'Bronxville 4.' (Big surprise.) 'Greenwich 35.' (Ditto.) 'Scarsdale 2.'" Three perfectly outfitted SPLs briskly marched forward, ac-cepted the report, and returned to their troop. I thought I de-tected something of a self-satisfied smirk on the faces of the older Bronxville kids. Then the rest were called: 285 Bellmore, where the SPL looked like a linebacker for the Jets. 313 North Bellmore. 68 Wappinger Falls. 2 Rye. 1 Chappaqua. Jack ac-cepted the report, brought it back, and took a peek.

"How'd we do?" asked Bernie.

"You don't want to know," Jack replied, then relented. "Eighteen."

"D'oh," Bernie replied in his best Homer Simpson. "You bat .500 in baseball, you make the Hall of Fame."

"I don't think that's something we need to worry about," Jack replied.

As soon as the retreat finished up, the kids went to the camp store at the rear of the commissary to get ice creams or Cokes. The big shots in camp were readily apparent. Some were the more conspicuous staff members, like Ted Watson or Frankie Stanton. Others were the most intimidating SPLs, who were figures of unimaginable stature to the smaller kids. And then there were those who just became instant camp characters, a group exemplified by Sam 'n Eric. They strode into the store like Belushi and Ackroyd in *The Blues Brothers,* twice the size of most of the kids and all confidence and bravado. I wasn't quite sure how their fame had spread so quickly, but it was clear that the kids at Waubeeka already knew all about Sam 'n Eric.

There were fraternal "yos" to greet the older kids in Bronxville 4 and Scarsdale 2; informed gossip about who might be interested in dating Rita, a lifeguard who was one of a half dozen female staff members; advice to younger Scouts on which merit badge counselors were least likely to bust your chops, and whispered conversations about Sam 'n Eric's favorite topic—life in Staff City, the collection of tents and huts down the hill from the main office where staff members, it was said, got to stay up all night, play guitars, smoke cigarettes, play Nintendo 64 or Play Station video games, and do cool and scandalous things too fabulous to even contemplate.

Still, there was one personage at Waubeeka who loomed above all the others. If anyone missed the point, there at the flagpole was a plaque with his name: "Dedicated to Lester Allen Rattner. Eagle 1958. Silver Beaver 1990. 27 year Scouter Troop 4, Bronxville. Dedicated July 4, 1994." It was, of course, the big guy from Bronxville 4. Lester Rattner spoke in a deep, raspy growl of a voice, sort of like what Johnny Cash might have sounded like if he'd grown up in Yonkers, New York, instead of Dyess Colony, Arkansas. At Waubeeka, Lester seemed to be everywhere, badgering his kids to straighten their neckerchiefs as they walked to retreat, getting on the commissary about the quantity of salami they were giving out for lunch, or just hanging out on the front porch of the Waubeeka office. Which was where I found him midmorning on the third day. Lester, I soon learned, had a troop philosophy as deeply embedded as anything by Kant and an opinion on all things having anything to do with Scouting. "The slogan of our troop is 'Scouting the way it used to be,' and, parenthetically, we say 'Scouting the way it ought to be.' We wear the full uniform, and we wear it correctly," he said, as he sat on one of the wooden benches that ran around the front porch. He was at least six foot three with a crew cut and had the appearance of a Scouting Zeus dispatched to the Waubeeka porch to check out the mortals. "I joined the troop in 1955 at the age of eleven, and I never left, so by now I should know what I'm doing. At the Scoutmaster meeting the other day, someone said, 'Lester is so rigid, he always wants to do things the same way.' And I said to him, 'I'm not rigid. I'm just not flexible.' There's a rumor that's always going around camp that I'm an ex-Marine. Well, the truth is my entire military training was growing up at a Boy Scout camp."

Like most traditionalists, Lester seemed obsessed with what was no longer so traditional, and the troop motto summed up his view of Scouting as an institution under siege. The assailants came from all corners: the national headquarters in distant Texas, nervous meddling moms, predatory lawyers, feminists intent on turning boys into wusses.

"The biggest problem with Boy Scouts today is that the guys making up the policies sit down in a room in Texas and don't know what the heck is going on in the field," he said. "They don't know how to deal with boys. It's strictly a corporate thing. They're concerned with their careers and with raising money. That's about it. The chief scout executive makes about $400,000 a year. Like a lot of nonprofits, the people there make a hell of a profit. The other big problem is their excessive concern with liability. They've gotten so uptight about everything because they think someone's going to sue them. We used to build signal towers and bridges across streams made out of rope. Now they're all worried someone might fall and cut themselves. Boys aren't supposed to run in camp anymore. They can't climb trees. The raft in the lake used to be twice as far from the dock. You know why? They're afraid of getting sued, so each year kids have to swim less and less to get there. You can't tell ghost stories anymore. Boys might lose sleep. Most of the old songs, if they mention alcohol or gambling or liquor, they're no longer any good. I used to have a guy come to the campfire dressed as a girl with balloons in his blouse. Can't do that. It's sexist. What's the big deal if a couple of guys dress up like girls? It doesn't make them homosexuals. At the water carnival, we used to have a watermelon fight. You greased a watermelon and greased the boys' bodies and you had two teams trying to grab these greased watermelons and push them over to the other team's goal line to score. It's been a tradition at Boy Scout camps since the '40s. But now they think it's too rough, so at the aquatic carnival last week they had an event where they put a watermelon in the water and had the boys get in a line and pass it under their legs to one another. What American boy wants to pass a watermelon under his legs? We've got a girl running our waterfront who plays rugby in college. The girls are playing rugby and the guys are passing watermelons under their legs. Where are we headed in this country?"

The litany of Lester's complaints went on. Kids started too young in the Tiger Cub program, which enrolled boys younger than the Cub Scout minimum age of seven, and left them burned out on Scouting before they finished middle school. Scouting had fouled up the badges in an attempt to save money by using fewer colors in them. There was, he was sure, a slow, relentless move toward integrating girls into Boy Scouts, beginning with what were called Explorer units for older kids. "Sooner or later they're just going to call it Scouting USA and do away with Boy Scouts altogether." Over the past fifteen years, there had been more focus on sports and merit badges for competitive sports like basketball. "If you want to play baseball, you don't join the Boy Scouts. You join Little League."

I was completely respectful of Lester's mastery of the Scouting Way of Knowledge and fully aware of my deficient knowledge base. But Scouting didn't seem quite so bloodless to me. Maybe Troop 1 was so far outside the mainstream that in some ways it was Chappaqua 1, not Bronxville 4, that was Scouting the Way It Used to Be. Troop 1's problem, it seemed to me, was less the kids as docile wimps but the opposite. So when I wandered back down to Wolfjaw after listening to Lester, what I found did not entirely comport with the new dessicated, Politically Correct Scouting environment he seemed to see. Bernie was mincing around the site like a two-bit hooker wearing two big water pitchers inside his shirt, and beckoning to his fellow Scouts with a come-hither voice as he showed off his new Pamela Lee–style chest. "Oh, boys, boys. Over here, boys," he cooed in his best falsetto. Jack, our not-so-strict SPL, was chasing Mark and Jonah around the site carrying two pots full of water as part of an escalating water fight. Running around a rock-strewn site did not seem like the smartest idea to me, but I let it go for a while at least.

While these sideshows were going on, Sam trudged into Wolfjaw holding his head and looking a little dazed.

"You OK?" I asked him.

"I think so, but my head hurts," he replied. Indeed, there was a healthy knot on his forehead.

"What have you been doing?"

"Well, I was over at the shotgun range, and Grissom dared me to break three of the clay pigeons against my head," he said, Grissom being one of the counselors in training, or CITs, at the range—yet another responsible authority figure.

"And?"

"Well, I figured I should at least try. I did three OK. But the second three hurt."

"You mean you broke six clay pigeons against your head?"

"Well, no. I broke four, but the other two just bounced off and didn't break."

Harry and Dennis were returning from their afternoon swim, so I filled them in on what was going on and decided to take Sam to the infirmary for observation. It was a frame house at Buckskin, which had Russ Fleer's Jeep Wagoneer out front and eight empty cots inside. Russ listened to Sam's tale with the mixture of amused familiarity and dutiful disapprobation common to large state prisons and Scout camps. He checked Sam's eyes and the lump on his head and decided the patient would live to sing "Scout Socks" again. He gave him some ice to keep down the swelling and some Tylenol, but said otherwise he was fine.

"I hope you learned a lesson beyond the fact that it's not a good idea to break skeets against your head."

"I guess I did," Sam replied.

"And what might that be?"

"Don't do something stupid because someone tells you to?"

"That's close enough. That and the fact that when you do something that puts you or others at risk, you're all responsible for whatever happens. I don't know who's more to blame, you or Grissom, but you both should know better. In the future, use your head in more productive ways, OK?"

"Yes, sir."

We drove back, Sam temporarily chastened and looking like a twelve-year-old knucklehead rather than an aspiring big shot. We got out of the car and walked down to Wolfjaw. It was quickly apparent it was not a happy scene. Most of the kids were sitting around glumly. It was the middle of the dinner hour, but at least one of the patrols did not seem to have any food prepared. The site was still a mess, with random candy wrappers and bits of foil scattered here and there. Harry was talking with Bernie, whose eyes were downcast and shoulders slumped, like a POW stuck in an interrogation session.

Sam peeled off to huddle with the others. Harry motioned me over. He asked me about Sam's condition and then filled me in on the afternoon's events, which began with the water fight soaking one patrol's monster box and continued through the other patrol forgetting to schedule someone to pick up the food for the evening meal. Harry did not find this funny. He was also not amused when he learned from one of the kids that one reason everyone enjoyed an afternoon rafting outing outside camp so much was that Bernie had entertained the troops on the way back by pulling down his pants and mooning passing cars from the window of the official Curtis S. Read Scout Reservation van. (Only a bunch of fiftyish dads could have thought the kids were so entranced by oldies radio.) Hence the heart-to-heart I'd walked in on.

Like Lester, Harry took Scouting seriously. As a kid growing up on Coney Island with little talent for athletics, the one chosen sixteenth of sixteen, he'd found a home in Scouting. When his troop went to Staten Island to camp, it was his first experience of the outdoors. He got to follow the advancement trail to Life Scout, the step before Eagle, and was elected to the Scouting honorary society, the Order of the Arrow. After college in 1976, he got his first real job as a Scouting professional, working seven days a week for $7,500 a year in a job that was charged with forming units, fundraising, and keeping Scouting alive in an area rapidly going from white to black and Hispanic.

He still has a well-stuffed box at home of his Scouting memorabilia—his 65 ¢ Order of the Arrow Handbook from 1968, old badges and neckerchiefs, the natural fox neckerchief slide he used to wear, his Order of the Arrow sash. Most prized of all are the black-and-white patches, neckerchiefs, and T-shirts reading "Sheepshead Community Scouting Experience Nov. 4–5 1978." The gathering, billed as a tent-o-ral, which is like a camporee only hyphenated, was staged in the area between Brighton Beach and Coney Island. Four blocks from the original Nathan's Famous hot-dog stand, in Asser Levy Seaside Park, close enough to the beach to see the boardwalk and hear the D train rattling by, he organized a jamboree in the heart of Brooklyn that took a half year of planning to pull off. The Army Corps of Engineers supplied water-tank trucks. The Parks Department helped build a midway, and the phone company installed temporary phone booths. The Scouts put up the booths and signs and manned stations exhibiting first aid, map, and compass skills, the Pinewood Derby, and—what else?—knot tying. In the end, six hundred kids camped out in the heart of Coney Island as if it were the Poconos or the Adirondacks. The event got played up on all the local television news shows, and Scouting got more visibility in Brooklyn than it had in years. "Scouting is more alive and viable than ever," Harry told the *Brooklyn Times*. It may have been more a statement of faith than objective reportage. But the event was a big success as something for the kids to enjoy and as a way to fly Scouting's flag and remind people what they were about. It was the coup of his career.

Other moments were not so easy. One troop had a rigorous numerical ranking to choose its Scout of the Year. Its outstanding Scout one year was a hard-working young kid named Evan.

And when the scores were toted up, Evan, to no one's surprise, was the clear winner. The plaque with his name was prepared, and the award ceremony was scheduled. But before it happened, Evan just snapped at home one day. No one really knows why, but the model Scout stabbed his mother to death in her bed. He was sent off to reform school and came back a few years later, showing up at a troop meeting like an unexpected apparition, his plaque still stashed away in a closet at the school where the troop met.

So Harry was acutely aware that Scouting came with no guarantees. It was essentially a volunteer operation. If you had good volunteers you had a good program (unless it got screwed up anyway), and if you had bad ones you probably had a crappy one. And while Harry had complete respect for Dr. Flank, he wasn't in complete accord with the way he ran the troop. He thought the meetings needed more structure and variety; the loosey-goosey, post-'60s ethos of the troop worked fine for Todd Davis but not for a lot of the others. And after half a week at Waubeeka, he was pretty well disgusted with Troop 1's half-assed brand of Zen/*South Park*/Homer Simpson/Scouting Lite. Dennis and I felt if the kids didn't burn down Waubeeka or do irrevocable harm to themselves or each other, we had done our jobs. Harry had much higher expectations. He figured if he could pull off the Brooklyn Jamboree for inner-city kids, he should be able to have a respectable week of camp with a bunch of privileged suburban brats.

"Tonight's the Staff Hunt," Harry said to me, referring to the popular exercise in retribution in which kids got to roam through the woods searching for hiding counselors and staff members and then escort them to the waterfront for a ceremonial dunking. "I'm going to tell them we're missing that, and we're going to have our own meeting instead. They won't like it, but they have to know this is important. I know this is the second week of camp, and they're getting restless. But I don't want to finish the week like this."

Dennis and I nodded and muttered words of support. It was almost time for the evening retreat. Harry called the kids over to the lean-to and told them the plan—that he was not happy with the way things were going, and we were going to have our own meeting and miss the staff hunt. There were assorted groans and whines, but it was clear Harry's mind was made up, so we made the desultory trek up toward the parade grounds. Some-one with a sharp pair of ears could have picked up repeated uses of the word *asshole*. As the other troops got ready for the staff hunt, we marched back down to the campsite. Some of the kids stood. The others sat on the benches by the picnic table.

"Everyone present and accounted for?" Harry said evenly. "Good. Let's begin. First of all, I want you to know this is not punitive. You're not here to be punished. But I thought we should all get together to talk about the week so far, how it's gone, what we can do better."

With that relatively neutral introduction, he began enumer-ating some of the week's greatest hits. The monster boxes no one had bothered to stock with essentials like dish soap, plastic utensils, and paper plates. The trash strewn around the site. The meals barely cooked. The times kids had sat down to eat with-out bothering to wait for the others or the time they were so late the visiting staff members had to leave before they were fed. Louis so frustrated at not being obeyed that he had started cry-ing. Yes, we had a great white-water rafting trip, but Bernie didn't do much for the camp's image by dropping his pants and mooning passing cars from the Camp Read van. (Luckily, none of us knew about one other highlight, a Scout who will remain nameless pissing into an empty water jug as a joke.)

"Can any of you tell me what Scouting is supposed to be about, why we're here?"

There was only a slight pause before various kids came up with answers.

"To learn discipline."

"To have fun."

"To become a team."

"To work together around common goals."

"To develop leadership skills."

Some of it was strained and dutiful, but mostly kids seemed to be taking the question seriously.

"Those are all good answers," Harry continued. "Scouting is not set up as an organization where the adults show up and tell the kids what to do and run the Scout units themselves. Baden-Powell based his idea of Scouting around something called the patrol method, the idea of boys leading boys. And the patrol system was set up as a way for Scouting to foster all those things, discipline, fun, teamwork, leadership, that you just talked about. For now, Louis and Jimmy are the Patrol Leaders and Jack is the Senior Patrol Leader. Tomorrow it might be Sam or Elliot or Tom. But the point is we need to show respect for the leaders and we need to work together as a team to get things done. Because right now we're not working together, we're not exhibiting leadership, we're not completing tasks, we're not having fun. So everything you guys told me before that's part of Scouting doesn't happen when the leadership and the patrol method breaks down. I'm not trying to lecture you, but I really wanted you to be able to sit down and think about what's going on, so we can figure out ways to make this thing work better."

It was hard to tell how much of what ensued was genuine and how much was the kids doing their best Eddie Haskell, but almost everyone had something to say. Eric said the patrol method was fine in theory, but it didn't work when Patrol Leaders issued arbitrary demands and didn't do their share of the work. Sam and Tom seconded the motion. Doug said maybe kids were jealous that they weren't leaders, but there was no excuse not to do the jobs you were supposed to do. One suggestion was to recognize a quartermaster for each patrol to keep the monster box stocked. Someone said it was simple respect to keep the site clean. Someone else said if it wasn't a specific person's job, it would not get done.

My usually brilliant son complained about missing the staff hunt. "No one really wants to sit around and talk about this stuff when other kids are running around yelling, screaming, pushing the staff in the water, finding the counselor you really despise and dunking him in the lake. You could have done it later and still made your point."

Harry heard him out, but said he felt things had gone so far downhill it was important to make the point while the memory was clear rather than having everyone run off and have fun as if nothing had happened. None of the kids seemed convinced.

No fingers were pointed. No edicts were handed down. The kids remained unhappy with the session and with Harry, who had now fully inherited Dr. Flank's status as The Man. But it seemed to make a difference. When we finished, some kids on their own started picking up stray candy wrappers. Singing of "Scout Socks" was curtailed for the evening. The overall tone of the language, at least for a night, improved. Ben and Dennis and I walked up to the parade grounds, where Ted Watson was leading a stargazing class. It was a brilliant, clear night, and Ted was pointing out Mercury and Vega and the North Star, the stars that make up Leo and the Little Dipper, expounding on binary systems with two suns and the death of our solar system. "Scientists disagree on many things, but there's one thing that every scientist on the planet agrees on, which is that eventually our sun will grow cold and die," Ted proclaimed in his best Mr. Wizard voice as we lay on our backs staring mutely into the inky darkness. "When that happens, Einstein and Aristophanes and

Marilyn Monroe and all the rest, all the existence we know of, will be for nothing unless we go to the stars and find a place to begin anew." This seemed an appropriately big thought with which to conclude our evening of introspection.

Maybe it was that cheery thought, or maybe it was the aftermath of Harry's address to the troops, or maybe it was that camp's end was only two days away, but from then on things took a surprisingly benevolent turn. Our performances in the Waubeeka rankings remained dismal, and our absence from the staff hunt guaranteed us yet another last-place finish. But we did keep the site a little cleaner. The meals tended to get done on time, the pantries stayed full, the level of griping and vile language stayed within a reasonable range. With the end nearing, the kids were more focused on piling up merit badges than acting out. And even the adults started to get a little sentimental about the impending end of our Waubeeka experience. So on Thursday morning, while the kids were at their activities, Harry, Dennis, and I decided to embark on our own little adventure, a climb to the top of First Brother, the peak at the Summit Base at the far end of camp. Many of the kids had been there already for their wilderness survival badge, which involved climbing to the top at dusk, building a shelter out of limbs and leaves, and sleeping outdoors without a blanket or sleeping bag while getting bitten to death by mosquitoes. I was perfectly happy not to include that in my Scouting experience.

We set off equipped with water bottles, insect spray, and plastic containers for picking blueberries, said to exist in great profusion at the top of the hill. About ten minutes into our journey, Harry, who was not in the best of shape, found himself totally winded. Opting for discretion rather than valor, he turned around and headed back to camp. But Dennis and I pushed on and with only two stops for water completed the forty-five-minute hike to the top. There we were rewarded with both a majestic view and luxuriant tufts of blue and purple blueberries poking out from rocks and patches of greenery almost everywhere you looked. For a few minutes we sat silently, swatting off mosquitoes and looking out over the lakes, hills, and valleys of Camp Read and the surrounding wilderness. Then we grabbed our berry containers and wandered here and there in a blissful daze. Finally, after we had filled two big containers, we sat on a hard outcrop of exposed rock, eating our berries and talking about our sons. This in itself was something of a wonder. As it turned out, Dennis lived about five houses down the road from me, at the bottom of a steep incline perhaps three hundred yards away. Had we not been in Scouts, we might not ever have met—the lots are long and wooded, and the only people who really get out are the few, like me, who walk their dogs rather than let them roam around and bark neurotically behind their electric Invisible Fences. Plus his son, the famous Eric, and mine were different enough that they were not likely to have become great pals even if they rode the same school bus every day. To the rest of the world, Eric was one of the swaggering *Über*-sized *Über*-Dogs of the troop. But in his dad's forgiving eyes, pretty much like the ones with which I viewed my son, he was a gentle soul who could be a minister, a teacher, a therapist, or certainly an actor if he wanted to go that route. Dennis went on for a while and then segued to a reminiscence of growing up in Mississippi.

"Our big thing when we were kids was swinging from the hickory trees," he said. "That was the Six Flags Over Georgia of its day. It had to be hickory, they're the most flexible; otherwise the branch might break. So what I did in my backyard was we had a whole stand of hickory trees out back in the woods. You would climb about ten to twelve feet up and grab a branch. Then you'd swing back and forth and reach for the next one and do like a Tarzan thing, swinging from hickory tree to hickory tree. It got so I could go through five trees. That was magic. Now it's a lawsuit. The other thing I'd do is I had all these Japanese and Axis toy soldiers, and I'd get out my BB gun and kill them all. Plus I had my individual lady-finger firecrackers. I'd put some of them out there and blow up some of the enemy. I describe this to Eric and he says, 'Dad, you had such a great childhood.' I say, 'Well, my dad beat me with a belt when I disobeyed. I had to take out the garbage, and I didn't get paid anything for it. There were no video games and no computers.' But he still thinks I had a better childhood. I had more freedom. I could go out and risk killing myself without my mom even worrying about it. So he thinks that would be the coolest thing. To be free, which is the way he describes it. To do what you want."

We refilled our containers and headed back down, lightheaded from the exercise and the utter remove from life as we usually knew it. Back when I had time to read books, I was a huge fan of Thomas Pynchon, particularly *Gravity's Rainbow*, his long, twisted masterwork about rocket science, anomie, and World War II. Near its end, Pynchon's schlemiel/hero Tyrone Slothrop, exhausted from his role at the intersection of history, weaponry, and his own libido, finally finds himself peacefully mindless and blissed out, his normal sense of consciousness so overloaded it has shorted out as he watches a thick rainbow after a heavy rain he doesn't even recall: "His chest fills and he stands crying, not a thing in his head, just feeling natural." I hadn't reached quite that point, but I knew what he had in mind.

But it wasn't just Dennis and me. Maybe there was something in the air, maybe all the stars of Waubeeka were somehow aligned for a day with B-P. Not B-P "the Hero of Mafeking," but B-P "the inspired mystic of Scouting." Because the campfire that night seemed to pick up where we had left off on our hike. First Tom Logan got up and asked us to let our eyes sweep over the slumbering lake, black under the gaggle of stars, and the curtain of trees encircling it.

"I remember the first time I ever came to this camp," he said. "It changed my life forever. The appreciation it gave me for nature. The people I've met. I had some of the best times I've ever had in this camp. Can anyone tell me what the outdoors code means to them? Anybody?"

One little kid—he looked about ten or eleven—got up and said, "Nature's given us so much, and what you really need to do is, you need to be aware you just can't take things from the environment. You can't chop down a bunch of trees for no reason or capture animals for no reason. You have to protect nature or one day it will all be gone."

Tom looked beyond pleased.

"'We have to take care of nature or one day it will all be gone.' That was very nice. Thank you. Now all of us are sitting here and we're staring at something which can be amazing. This fire right here. All of this fire is energy. And that's something we need to be very safe with. But tonight I want to draw from that energy. So everyone sitting here tonight is going to go down in Waubeeka history. And the story is going to be passed down to everyone who comes after us. I want us all to put our heads together and create a Camp Waubeeka Outdoor Code. I want us to come up with a sentence, a couple of words, a phrase that will be the outdoor code only for Waubeeka. Who has an idea? Anyone?"

Silence. Then another boy stood up. He was, of course, from Lester's troop. He paused, and then in a surprisingly firm voice for a small kid, announced: "I will do my best to be a guardian of the beauty of Camp Waubeeka."

"Perfect," said Tom. "Perfect. From now on that will be the Outdoor Code for Camp Waubeeka."

We didn't know quite what that entailed, but we were all suitably impressed by the gravity of what we'd just witnessed.

No doubt inspired by the sense of history in the making, the camp commissioner, Lenny Harris, got up next. He was a thin Floridian in his early twenties who wore his blond hair long, in a ponytail. His job was to care for the physical plant at Waubeeka while Tom took charge of the programs. If Tom seemed inspired, Lenny seemed in the throes of mystical revelation. He talked about spending much of the day in the caves, just thinking of Waubeeka and Scouting and what he wanted to say at the night's campfire. Then he started talking about the ideals of Scouting.

"When I was in the caves, I tried to visualize a perfect person," he said. "We all know no one's perfect. But I dreamed of a man who was clean, manly, strong, fearless and kind, gentle with his strength, dignified, silent, and friendly. He was equipped for emergencies and filled with religion that was not only built from creeds or occasional observances but a desire to help those who needed help. This perfect man was athletic, fearless, kind, picturesque, wise in the ways of the woods and without any regret for the way he lived his life. And with this vision, I was led as many before me to choose the life of a Scout. Scouting is my travel guide on the path to being a perfect man. I may never reach being perfect. But I will live my life knowing I'm always striving for the one single goal, to be the best man I can be. And I want all of you to leave here with a vision of how you can be the best you can be. And I know you will never forget what went on here. Thanks for being here with me."

He sat down, and then we all sat in silence for what seemed like an eternity, the fire crackling and snapping in the darkness, the stars dazzling overhead. Who knows what the kids made of it. But I was transfixed by Lenny's intensity and the simple, direct way he had tried to do what most of us, man or boy, almost never do—come to terms with male identity. It was like picking up an "Archie" comic book and getting *War and Peace* instead. After a while, we repeated the new outdoor code and sang "Taps" and filed out, much more quietly than we ever had before.

No one said much about Lenny's oration. Chances are it registered more with the dads than the kids. But when we got back to Wolfjaw, the kids did seem quieter than usual, as if the lofty thoughts of the campfire had stuck with them. They ended up going to bed, for a change, not long after ten. Then Harry and Dennis and I met at the lean-to for our own private observance. In the afternoon, I had gone into town and bought us a bottle of tequila and some margarita mix at the one liquor store in Brant Lake. I barely drink, and didn't have any great need for a beverage more serious than our usual bug juice or Cokes. But we figured we deserved our own little senior management retreat, and this seemed the way to do it. Alcohol is forbidden at Scout camps or activities, but, truth to tell, we weren't exactly the first dads in history to bring a bottle of one kind or another to camp or a camp-out. So we fired up the two Coleman lamps, filled our plastic cups, broke out some peanuts and chips, and sat around talking about the week, about whether Bernie had perhaps learned to curb his instincts to function as class clown as the week went by, about how Louis and Jimmy had struggled as Patrol Leaders but perhaps had learned a bit, about Harry's abilities as a hiker and mine as a swimmer. We didn't talk much about the campfire, but we didn't have to. It was just part of the air that night.

We spent the last day cleaning up the site and turning in our gear. There was a staff barbecue, so the kids didn't have to cook, and then another camp-wide campfire, where, to no one's amazement, Bronxville 4 was declared winner of the Waubeeka Award. During the afternoon, Harry had driven into town and come back with Cokes and Sprites and marshmallows, graham crackers and Hershey's chocolate for s'mores, and various chips and nuts. We piled them on the picnic table at the upper site, and lit the fire.

Harry had come up with his own informal awards for the kids. The meeting that preempted the Staff Hunt had long since been forgotten, and I admired Harry's skill in presiding over the gathering. His awards were the main event, but when we all hung around the campfire afterward telling stories and jokes, my jokes during the open-mike campfire that followed probably came in second. It shouldn't have mattered whether I could entertain a bunch of twelve-year-olds. But just as I admired Harry's skill, I felt some little sliver of pleasure at playing my part too, as if this were my advancement activity for the week. The kids gorged on junk and then straggled back to their tents. By 11:30 all you could hear was a thunderous chorus of snores over the nattering of the crickets and cicadas.

The next morning, we finished our packing. I made a point of paying homage to Lester and saying good-bye to our long-suffering neighbors from Greenwich. Mark and Jonah were coming home with Ben and me, which made our trip back feel like a nice fade-out. We loaded up our gear in my dusty station wagon and headed out. Within thirty minutes, all three boys were sound asleep.

One of Norman Rockwell's most famous works is his 1956 painting *The Scoutmaster.* In the foreground is a Scoutmaster looking like a young John Wayne with his full uniform and yellow neckerchief, tending a campfire under a starry sky as four young Scouts slumber away, their heads poking out of their old-fashioned military surplus tents. I didn't flatter myself by seeing myself quite in that light, but I thought of that painting as I drove along and of how amazingly peaceful and rewarding the whole week had been. I was sorry it had to end.

Year II

11: Peaks and Valleys

Our second year of Scouting began the way the first had, with Dr. Flank's annual exercise in schedule reconciliation where we made up the calendar for the year. The difference, of course, was that rather than something odd and foreign, the troop and its rituals now felt like a central part of our life. So when we loaded up the cars and vans two Saturdays later for the canoe outing, it felt like a welcome return to a thoroughly familiar place. We got a pleasing jolt of déjà vu from the most scenic part of the drive, a serpentine stretch of road winding above the Delaware, and from the lecture on the J stroke and the risks of hypothermia and following the black snake. Then Ben and I shoved off confidently into the water like two of Seton's Indians on our way down the Delaware.

A month or so later we had a new outing scheduled, a hiking trip up Hunter Mountain, about two hours away. We drove up with Fly Guy and got his personal fishing travelogue of upstate New York. He pointed out places like the fishing cemetery, where you park at the end of a roadside graveyard so full of wild oregano that the scent overwhelms you as soon as you open the car doors. When we arrived at Hunter about 10:30 in the morning, there was still a serious chill in the air. It was early October. The week before had felt like Indian summer, but now I felt the first unwelcome tendrils of winter. There was a forecast of a freeze for the night, and we all had been advised to pack for cold weather. We lugged our gear to the campsite and set up our tent. The kids were dispatched to gather firewood, and once that was done, we trekked across a broad trail to the base of a narrower trail heading up a steep slope.

"Gentlemen," began Mr. Johnson. "Well, gentlemen is really exaggerating a tad. Some of you have contour maps. The ones who don't should look at the maps with the ones who do. Where the lines get close together is what? The steepest part of the hike. Basically we're going to follow this up past where it's marked *L* for the lean-to, to the top where there's a state fire tower. That's up to about 4,040 feet. Down here where we are, it's a little over 2,500 feet. So you can see we've got a pretty good stretch to climb."

And with that we started off. The temperature on the thermometer on Mr. Toonkel's backpack read 48 degrees. I walked along in the middle of the pack with Fly Guy. Behind us, I could hear Ben and Mark. "What do you do," Mark asked in his usual deadpan, "if you see an endangered animal eating an endangered plant?" The trail got very wet and sloppy. Before long we saw little patches of snow like a thin glaze over the landscape. It was a bit of a shock. A few days before it had been in the 60s back home, and now we'd suddenly journeyed from one season to another. We passed the lean-to on the contour map and kept going up. The heavier kids, as usual, were groaning and complaining of incipient collapse, dehydration, heart attack, and various forms of ankle, knee, or hip distress. Somehow, they heroically kept going. The snow on the ground became more than a dusting. It was wet and clearly suitable for packing and there was enough to make snowballs—a matter of almost unbearable temptation for the kids. We continued on with a growing sense of excitement. There's always something magical about the first snowfall of the year—especially if you're a kid and you don't have to shovel or drive in it. But this was more than that. Instead of the first snow finding us, we were finding *it,* climbing ever farther into an ever snowier realm, with pristine coatings on limbs and branches and a few inches on the ground.

Finally, the trail widened, and we found ourselves in an open expanse of snow glistening under the mottled blue sky. We had made it to the top. But there was an additional reward in store. Brooding over it, in the most unlikely fashion, was a giant tower—the fire tower Mr. Johnson had mentioned at the beginning. Not only had we reached this startling expanse of untouched snow maybe three or four inches deep, but we had the opportunity to view it from the vantage point of a seventy-foot tower. "Thees ees the promised land," proclaimed Louis in a cartoonish Latin accent that made him sound like a crazed bit player in *The Treasure of the Sierra Madre.*

By this point, Mr. Toonkel's thermometer read 28, and it felt much colder. Some of the dads were perfectly happy to huddle under the eaves of a little ranger station that was the only other structure at the summit and forgo the final trek to the top of the tower. But the rest of us clambered upward, the metal steps slippery with ice and noisy under our clomping boots, the winds snapping like mad the higher we went. The wind was enough to intimidate some of the smaller kids—who seemed in danger of blowing away—into turning back. But most of us kept going, finally bunching up near the top as we waited our turn to linger at the upper level with its spectacular view of the hills and valleys below. Some of the kids scooped the wet snow off the railings as they ascended and had a pretty substantial snowball to hurl down at the ground below. It landed with a triumphant splat. It was not hard to figure out what was coming next. It began with a random snowball Bernie tossed at Allen. Before long snowballs were flying left and right, kids were trying to dump wet piles of snow down one another's backs, and all of them were enjoying the freedom of being rowdy in a mom-free zone. Ben didn't have gloves, a disincentive to snowball-making, so he and I for a while watched at the periphery of the action. But bit by bit almost all the onlookers got sucked in, and before long he was getting his licks in too. After a while, the snowball fights played out. Instead, kids made snow angels, sucked on snow, threw snowballs at trees, and just wandered around, appreciating the unexpected scene. If a huge part of parenthood is vicarious pleasure, being happy because your kid is, this was one of the days you figured to remember for a long time. It just felt magical up there.

We lingered for perhaps a half hour before Mr. Johnson yelled, "Let's go saddle up." In a few minutes we were headed back down, treading slowly and gingerly on the wet trail to avoid slipping. I walked much of the way with Bernie, who drove some of the other dads crazy but struck me as rather endearing. He talked about his Web site, what he programmed onto his Palm Pilot, and his skills with PowerPoint presentations.

By the time we got back, the sky had turned overcast and temperatures were beginning to fall again. Fly Guy boiled some coffee, and the huddled dads broke out some snacks. "Ahhh," said Fly Guy happily. "Donuts, chocolate chip cookies, and Starbucks. The building blocks of life." It was getting cold as hell. I put on an extra fleece for warmth and wandered off to get some more wood for exercise. Suddenly, our epiphany at the top of the mountain seemed a long time ago.

We did our cooking and cleaning and listened to the campfire stories. Dr. Flank had passed on the hike, but he returned for the campfire and a brief benediction. "Troop 1," he said, "has been coming to this place for many years. But this group and this day will come just once. I hope you remember this day for many years and the good friends you shared it with. May the Great Master of all Scouts be with us until we meet again."

When we finally made it back to the tent, Ben was complaining of stomach pains. He attributed this to the chili we had had for dinner and the fact that he had brought only one Sprite for lunch, leaving none as a dinnertime digestive aid. Whatever the cause was, he continued to experience a measure of intestinal distress as he lay reading by flashlight. Chances are it was nothing much. But more dire scenarios also flitted across my brain, like the possibility of a bout of appendicitis here in these too-cold woods, which felt like they were a thousand miles from nowhere. I stayed up half the night listening to him toss and turn and trying to figure out what I'd tell my wife if some major medical emergency was transpiring.

"How was the hike?"

"Well, good and bad."

"How so?"

"Well, we had a wonderful hike to the top of the mountain and experienced an epiphanic bonding moment at the top of a snow-covered peak."

"And what was the bad part?"

"Uh, Ben's appendix burst, and he's at some semipro hospital in Phoenicia being attended by a half-awake guy wearing a baseball cap backward and regularly consulting a medical textbook."

When we woke up the next morning, I was pleased to find that Ben was still alive and apparently recovered. "New rule for hikes," he said. "Two Sprites or we be sure to bring Pepto-Bismol." A thin dusting of snow had fallen overnight on the tents, like the meteorological analogue of a musical theme repeated softly at the end of a symphony.

As soon as breakfast was over we cleaned up, took down our tents, packed up, and headed home. Fly Guy found a '60s rock oldies station that played Fleetwood Mac, the Temptations, Credence Clearwater Revival, Jackson Browne, and the Stones. Fly Guy was in an expansive mood, remembering how he first danced with his wife to "Stairway to Heaven," his experiences with Texas barbecue, his plans to eventually quit the New York rat race of his job as a lawyer for a major financial company and do something like open an outdoors shop. "The End" by the Doors came on.

"This is the Doors, George," he called out to his son in the backseat.

"Sounds like good music," his son replied in an agreeable show of multigenerational musical consensus never heard in my house. From our paternal perch in the front seats, the song's Oedipal Sturm und Drang ("Father," "Yes, son." "I want to kill you. Mother, I want to...") seemed, for some obscure reason, darker and less wonderfully anarchic than it had when I was on the other side of the Oedipal equation as a teenager. But we listened like nostalgic geezer dads while the kids, barely tuned in, remained oblivious to any grand meaning at work. It seemed like a nice way to end the trip, not the transcendent high of the climb, not the chilly hangover of the camp-out, but a comfortable balance point in between.

Whether it was in spite of our epiphany on the mountain or because nothing could come close to it, my enthusiasm for troop life began to wane over the next few months. We did the tree sale, but Ben seemed less thrilled to have his dad around and the seasonal cheer didn't quite get to me. Our second version of the Klondike Derby actually had snow, which was a distinct improvement over the first. But once had been plenty for me, and the highlight was getting our donuts and going home.

We had one event over the winter, a five-mile hike to the cabin at Camp Siwanoy. The Siwanoy trip posed a particularly knotty dilemma. Concomitant with the hike was a critically important event back in Couch-Potatoland, the Duke–Carolina season-ending basketball game, an event that looms on my calendar with the urgency that Christmas mass does for a devout Catholic. I am perfectly aware that there's no rational defense for some middle-aged man planning his schedule around the exploits of a bunch of ectomorphic kids who weren't even born back when he attended the university they were attending now. And this wasn't, say, Duke playing for the NCAA Championship, an event I sure as hell wasn't going to miss for a Scout hike. Still, we all have to have some indulgences, and if this was mine, so be it. I had been perfectly willing to pass up that poetry reading at the White House to make it to Ben's Little League game a few years past, but, the Duke–Carolina game loomed larger than the poetry at the White House. I had said I would go, a promise I planned to honor. But I had not said I planned to stay.

We set off on a gray, windy early-March morning. It felt much more like winter lingering than spring making an appearance. Ben and I drove to Siwanoy with Jeffrey, one of the older kids, a garrulous high school senior who hoped to attend the Air Force Academy and become an astronaut. This was the camp's last year in operation before it was sold, and when we got to Siwanoy it looked even bleaker than I had remembered. We carried our gear to our cabin, a mud-brown building with green trim and a yellow Smoky the Bear fire-prevention sticker outside. All the cabins were named after towns in Westchester County—Pelham, New Rochelle, Port Chester, Larchmont. This one bore a plaque reading "This cabin donated to the Boy Scouts of Harrison by the Lions Club of Harrison. 1981." It looked a heck of a lot older than that. We claimed our bunks, not that there was anything much to choose among, then headed to the Appalachian Trail to begin the hike.

The previous year we had begun at the scenic waterfall in Connecticut. This time we just began by trekking across an open field. There were no surprises as dramatic as the Hunter Mountain snowfall, but the trail twisted agreeably through fields, groves, and swamps. About midway through we came upon headstones from what looked like an old family graveyard. "Dear Brother Max Shenkman," read one, its Hebrew lettering incongruous in the lonely field. "Died Aug. 6, 1946. Age 60 years." Another had a menorah and the words "Sarah Brokaw. Beloved Mother. Died Jan. 18, 1937. Age 48 years. Forever in our hearts."

As the hike went on I found myself increasingly checking my watch, calculating what time we might be back and whether that would be early enough the catch the game, which began at 3:00 P.M. We made it back to the cabin around 2:30. I conferred with Ben, who looked at me indulgently as if counseling someone with an untreated mental disorder. "Why don't you just go watch the game and then come back," he said. This was pretty much what I had in mind. I had mentioned my spiritual crisis to Dr. Flank earlier in the day, as if confessing some dark sin to my parish priest. I assumed that leaving a Scout camp-out to run off to some dark bar to watch a meaningless basketball game must have violated any number of codicils and subclauses of the Scout Oath or Law, but Dr. Flank seemed willing to absolve my sins. "We'll be here when you get back," he said indulgently. "Don't worry about it."

With both Ben's and Dr. Flank's blessings I figured I was OK, so I ran to my car, raced back toward Pawling, the last town we had passed on the way up, and drove frantically around its tiny downtown looking for an appropriate place. Finally, I spotted something called the Pawling Tavern and walked in. There was a television showing not Duke, but some Big Ten game no one seemed to be watching. I sat down, ordered a Bud, and trying to sound as casual as possible, asked the bartender if he minded switching to the Duke game. A refusal would have blown up my whole nutty escapade. But he was happy to change the channel, and voilà! there was the game with Duke up by nine points late in the first half. The tavern, which had a pressed tin ceiling and a regal cavalcade of sports trophies behind the bar, suddenly seemed an amazingly agreeable and comfortable place—much more my world than the drafty cabin and manly cookcraft of Siwanoy. A woman planning to get married was discussing her plans with a guy who had just gotten divorced. Some local firemen had just gotten off from work. I sat alone, watching the game in complete and utter bliss. Duke was in the middle of a 21–8 run, aided by the fact that Carolina's point guard, who apparently needed work on his orienteering merit badge, had run into a teammate and had to leave the game to get five stitches.

I noticed a guy a few stools down who seemed to be following the game too, and out of the blue he looked over at me, as if realizing we were on the same wavelength.

"You really feel good for Carrawell," he said.

Talk about getting it right! Carrawell was Chris Carrawell, who had overcome various injuries to build himself into one of the really reliable Duke players of his era, not the biggest star but a spirited, resilient, likable kid. He was playing his last home game, and had been honored at Duke's version of a Court of Honor before the game. I found myself thinking that, for all its mindless frivolity, sports—my world—at its best could teach values to twenty-first-century kids the way Scouting once did.

"Nice to see him go out on such a good note," I said.

We watched the rest of the game not saying a lot, but musing on Duke's chances in the NCAA tournament. In the interest of not seeming like too much of a freeloader, I ordered another beer and then a bowl of homemade onion soup. We happily watched the game end with Duke winning 90–76.

When it was over I lingered for a while, nursing my onion soup more than my Bud, half watching the next game that came on, perfectly happy to be alone and anonymous in this dark little cocoon. Staying there seemed a heck of a lot more appealing than trekking out into the cold to return to a dank cabin full of flatulent twelve-year-olds. But duty called. So I left a few bucks on the bar, said good-bye to my one fellow fan, and walked outside. It was freezing. My car took a while to heat back up, I drove in discomfort, and I almost missed the turnoff to the camp.

Half the kids didn't know I had been away, and the other half didn't much care. I told the few who were curious—Ben, Dr. Flank, Mr. Toonkel—that the right team had won. It was just about time for dinner. Not that I needed any after my onion soup, but what the heck, there wasn't much to do other than eat. So I had my share of salad, onion bread, and spaghetti with meat sauce. We were all cleaning up when we heard a thunderous knock on the door. It was then flung open to reveal . . . Todd Davis. He had had a swimming meet or choral concert or one of his eight thousand activities in the afternoon but had decided to drive up anyway. It felt like some grand celebrity had appeared.

After dinner Mr. Toonkel broke out some ancient board games, and we played those, played cards, told stories, and told jokes until bedtime. When I crawled into my sleeping bag, which was laid out across one of the hard wooden bunks, it felt like sleeping on cement. Even with the foam mattress underneath, I woke up the next morning—if I ever really went to sleep—cold, sore, and exhausted. Breakfast was pancakes, unless you were Todd. Using his Leatherman tool, he cut up a big hunk of sausage into thin slices and cooked them in a skillet, then added some packaged potatoes and cooked them up too. He had even brought his own kind of hot chocolate. The kids crowded around his sausage like hungry hounds waiting to get a small piece, which he dispensed with his usual magnanimity.

After we cleaned up, I took off by myself for a walk. Siwanoy was even drearier in the early-morning chill. Every building needed repainting. Almost nothing seemed to work. By the camp's lake was an old pavilion—the building had burned, and what was left seemed like it could have been an open-air dance floor in *The Great Gatsby* that had also gone to seed. Around it were old supplies, piles of lumber, old tables, roofing, and shingles, as if someone had wanted to rebuild whatever was there but never got around to it. I circled down toward the water and came to a spillway, where a small calf, much smaller than a Shetland pony, lay entombed in the frigid water, caught in a pile of limbs and brush. One of its hind legs was crossed over the other like a girl primly positioned in the first row of a classroom. Its inky wet skin, glass-eyed stare, and frozen repose gave it an otherworldly appearance, like something out of one of Mr. Toonkel's ghost stories.

I was about ready to get out of there. It was freezing; there was work to be done at home, I wanted to take a shower and change my clothes. We had hiked our hike. Duke had clobbered Carolina. Todd Davis had made sausage. The dead calf was still dead. We had done whatever this trip had called for. It was time to get out of Dodge.

Unfortunately, I saw no sign this was about to transpire anytime soon. To the contrary, Mr. Toonkel was outside, striding across the field with great vigor, stopping purposefully to write something down on a pad. My heart sank. Mr. Toonkel was obviously walking off a compass course, which meant, one assumed, that kids would then be expected to show they could navigate it. I didn't even want to think how long that would take. Sure enough, a few minutes later, I heard Mr. Toonkel's voice: "I want you to get your compasses and line up." For the first time in my brief Scouting career I felt totally alienated from the whole damn thing. I'd gone through life perfectly well without using a compass, and though I could improve on myriad things, I could think of none that would be aided in any way by the knowledge of how to use a compass. It was cold in the stupid cabin and colder in the stupid outdoors. Mr. Toonkel's zeal was, I knew, admirable, but at this moment it struck me as borderline fanatical, like Alec Guiness in *Bridge Over the River Kwai*.

"Who can tell me how a compass works," he barked. "And not you, Todd," he added. We were going to have not just the hands-on course, but the oral exam as well.

"Magnetism," said Louis. "The earth has a magnetic pull that makes one end of the compass point toward the magnetic north."

"Tell me about declination," Mr. Toonkel said.

"Compasses don't point to true north, the North Pole, they point to magnetic north, which is part of Canada one thousand miles away. The angle between them is called declination, and you have to adjust your compass for true north rather than magnetic north."

"OK, we've done this before," Mr. Toonkel barked. "I've mapped out a course. I'm giving you each a sheet with compass directions. Hold the compass in your hand in front of you about waist high and follow the directions, and you should all end up in the same spot."

One by one the kids started off, with Mr. Toonkel checking on their progress and Mr. Johnson hovering around to help. Kids paced off their course, and the ones who got it wrong got to try again. Finally, about 10:30, they all finished up. But we still had plenty to do. All the kids had to pack their bags or backpacks and line them up neatly with the others outside. Then we had to clean the cabin and grounds, sweeping out all the rooms of the cabin, replacing all our wood, cleaning out the fireplace, and scrubbing the kitchen. By the time we were through, you could have performed brain surgery there. Then we had our final lineup, Mr. Johnson told the kids what a swell job they had done, and we were free.

I didn't even think of trying to get to the next camp-out a month later. But I figured I should make a showing at the final event of the year, the overnight canoe trip down the Delaware. This was a big event, a camp-out that often served as a reunion with troop graduates who were off in college. Often it was a two-night camp-out, but this year we were doing just one night. It was probably a good thing. The weather report called for intermittent showers, and if we were going to get a little damp, why not keep it to a minimum? The main group, most of the kids, Dr. Flank and Mr. Johnson, Fly Guy, and two more dads with inexplicably flexible schedules left at 5:00 P.M. I got a ride with Mr. Toonkel and his son Jon, an Eagle who was now in college. There were two kayaks lashed to the top of Mr. Toonkel's van, whose interior bore a little plaque reading "Custom Designed. Marc Toonkel." We drove up listening to a wonderful tribute to Stephen Sondheim, full of snatches of music from *Sweeney Todd,* on NPR, stopped for dinner at a McDonald's, and arrived at the campground at about eleven.

Kids and dads were milling around a picnic table that was shrouded in a soupy fog so thick you could almost see the droplets of water hovering above the Coleman lamps. Still, it wasn't raining, which seemed a good omen. Ben was in the group at the table, and he escorted me to the tent, which was wet on the outside but warm and snug inside. "You think it's gonna rain tomorrow?" he asked. "Nahhh," I said, figuring a show of can-do optimism was part of my dadly duties. "I predict we dodge a bullet, and it's gray but dry while we're on the water and rains all the way home."

We awoke around 7:30 the next morning. I did not hear the sound of raindrops falling. That was good. It was still dry inside the tent. That was good. I looked outside and did not see any evidence of precipitation. That was good too. But the air was still wet and clammy, like a giant sponge. That was not so good. Mr.

Toonkel went down to the water and stuck in a thermometer. The water temperature was 50 degrees. The air temperature must have been about the same or a little cooler, and the sky was a solid wall of misty gray.

"What do you think, professor?" Mr. Johnson asked Dr. Flank.

"Not exactly a perfect day," Dr. Flank replied. "What do you think? Do we take the canoes or do we play it safe and go for the rafts?"

"I can't see how we have much choice," Mr. Toonkel said. "If we're caught in a real downpour, which we probably will be, do we want the kids in the canoes or in the rafts?"

"I'll tell Jerry we want the rafts," Dr. Flank said. "He probably wouldn't let us go out in anything else anyway."

Dr. Flank went from tent to tent, like a captain preparing his regiment for battle, telling everyone to bring their best raingear. Then we proceeded to Jerry's parking lot, where his minions hoisted great, big rubber rafts on top of the battered old buses and tied them on. Unlike the canoes, the rafts, which sat three or four as opposed to the two in a canoe, were almost impossible to sink. They were also fat, slow, bulky things, so you were guaranteed a longer, slower trip, and you had to paddle like a madman to get up any speed at all. We all jumped in Jerry's old vans and buses for the fifteen-minute drive to the place where we would shove off. The drizzle began as we were waiting in the parking lot, ready to leave. It picked up substantially during the ride.

"I feel like we're riding to the top of a roller coaster, and I hate roller coasters," said Doug.

"Nice weather for ducks," said Jonah.

"Or schmucks," said Mark.

By the time we got out, it was pouring. Not raining. Pouring. Pouring like get out the umbrellas or get inside. Pouring like alert the ground crew to roll out the tarpaulin; we're not playing in this. Pouring like no one sane would choose to travel down a river, whether in rafts, canoes, or ocean liners, in this. We stood miserably in a soggy field as Dr. Flank ran through a truncated version of the normal spiel—no worries about downstream gunwales and following the black snake in our bulky, unsinkable rafts. Mr. Toonkel, his respectable belly giving his wet suit something less than a perfect aerodynamic contour, had brought the kayak and seemed, as usual, unfazed by minor issues like being caught in a monsoon. The rest of us felt like laboratory rats being prepared to test the absorption capabilities of our fur. We divided up into groups of three or four for the trip. I was with Rich, an Eagle and a sophomore at Johns Hopkins who had graduated from high school two years ago, and two new kids, Dave and Marty, fifth graders who had just graduated from Webelos and were taking their first trip with the troop. Some introduction.

As usual, I was less than fully prepared. I had on my blue jeans, wool socks, sneakers, teal Charleston River Dogs baseball cap, and a gray Patagonia windbreaker that looked vaguely waterproof. The cap had been soaked with cold rain that spilled down onto my sparsely populated scalp before Dr. Flank was finished with his instructions. My feet got wet shoving off into the water. Within two or three minutes, my jeans were soaked completely through. The jacket turned out not to be even vaguely waterproof. About five minutes into what was supposed to be an all-day canoe trip, I was soaked from head to toe.

Now, it is true, we were not the most afflicted creatures ever to set out on the Delaware or its environs. When George Washington crossed the Delaware near Trenton, New Jersey, on Christmas Eve 1776 with his exhausted, freezing, and ill-equipped men, it was snowing and sleeting like mad and the river was a gauntlet of ice floes. And no one had even invented Gore-Tex. Historical markers nearby commemorated the bloody battle of Minisink between colonial militia and Mohawk Indians and their Tory allies in July 1779. It left a colonial colonel haunted by "the cruel Yellings of these bloody monsters," a sound so awful that "all the fiends in the Confines of the Infernal Regions with one United Cry could not Exceed it."

So, it could have been worse. But that was cold comfort as we began paddling downstream at an excruciatingly turtlelike pace. Dave and Marty looked shell-shocked. Rich, on the other hand, was maddeningly chipper. "I've been in a lot worse," he said. "It's good training. People may talk about the Boy Scouts being in decline, but it's not going to happen. Scouting will be stronger in thirty years than it is now. It's part of Americana. And being an Eagle looks good on your college application." Then he went on at length about how much he loved the *National Review* Web site and William F. Buckley's word of the day, the most recent being *badinage*.

Maybe an Eagle could keep up cheery badinage floating down the Delaware in a chilly gray soup, but not many others could. Instead of the usual intraflotilla horseplay and splashing, there was just the long, slow process of paddling down the river, like slogging through chilled molasses. The rain had slowed to a steady drizzle instead of a downpour, but the temperatures remained in the high 40s. The little kids paddled listlessly. Rich chattered happily. I found myself, for some reason, harkening back to the Sondheim show on NPR and humming "Pretty Women," from *Sweeney Todd*, the duet sung by the demon barber Todd and his prey in his barber's chair whose throat Todd is about to slit. It didn't really take my mind off this soggy debacle, but it helped a little. I don't know how long this went on. Like prisoners of war or victims of dementia, we began to feel like time was a meaningless concept. Finally, the rain stopped, though we were too waterlogged for it to make much of a difference. And soon after that, like sailors spotting land after a transatlantic crossing, we caught a glimpse of a familiar spot on the riverbank. It was a sturdy-looking, two-story frame house with a wide front porch painted white and a sign out front reading ZANE GREY MUSEUM. Zane Grey, famous for his novels of the American West, fishing and baseball, quit his dental practice in New York and moved to Lackawaxen, Pennsylvania, on the Delaware in 1905, where in 1912 he wrote his most famous novel, *Riders of the Purple Sage*. In this watery hell, the notion of a desert landscape of purple sage seemed as foreign as Byzantium, but his home from 1914 to 1918, preserved by the National Park Service, was our midway point. We paddled over to the landing in front of it and clambered out of our rafts.

I was so cold my legs didn't seem to want to bend at the knee, so I hopped straight-legged up toward the front porch. The little kids were huddled together, their teeth chattering, looking vaguely blue. The museum was closed up, and it wasn't any warmer on the porch, but just being out of the raft and off the river seemed a small blessing. Mr. Johnson had a red ice chest full of bologna, turkey, and salami sandwiches. There was Kool-Aid, not precisely what we needed, to drink, and cookies.

I'm not sure why I saw the need to augment all that, but I hobbled off to the Hawk's Nest Café and general store about three hundred yards down the road to get Ben and me Snickers bars and sticks of beef jerky. I lurched in the door shivering and dripping in my wet hat, wet windbreaker, wet jeans, wet wool socks, and wet sneakers. Everyone in the place turned and stared. On the radio, Elvis was singing, "Are You Lonely Tonight?" There were arcane fishing accessories all over the place. It occurred to me that all we lacked was a bunch of nubile coeds in tank tops on their way to a deserted cabin in the woods for me to look like the deranged killer in a slasher movie. I picked up two Snickers bars and two sticks of teriyaki beef jerky—probably what your average slasher dines on—and brought them to the register. "Boy Scout camp-out," I stammered. "Bad day for a canoe trip." It probably sounded more like a threat than a neutral bit of reportage. Good thing I wasn't humming anything from *Sweeney Todd*. I gave the guy a waterlogged $5 bill and waited for my change. "I'm *with* the Boy Scouts," I added. "One of the leaders. Have a nice day." He seemed glad when I left without harming anyone.

I hobbled back to the Zane Grey Museum, gave Ben his Snickers and jerky, and shared some with his friends. By this point Dr. Flank, Mr. Johnson, and Mr. Toonkel were deep in conversation. The question was whether we should abort the mission halfway through and head for home. Finally, Dr. Flank went to the phone, made a call, and came back. "I called Jerry's," he said. "They're coming to get us."

I'm not big on gender absolutism, but those who think that men are inherently irrational could take comfort in my reaction. Because when I heard the words, my first reaction was not relief or elation. Instead, my heart momentarily sank. It had stopped raining, after all. We were all a bit fortified by our sandwiches and snacks. I was beginning to get some feeling back in my lower extremities. Maybe we should have pushed on. This, of course, was pure idiocy. The kids, particularly the little ones, were too cold to keep going. By the time we finished, who knew how cold and nasty it might be? After all that talk about hypothermia, this was the first time it was a potential issue. Even gung-ho types like Fly Guy were ready to pack it in. Still, it left me with the feeling that we'd managed to achieve the worst of all possible outcomes—we were utterly miserable, and we hadn't even managed to complete the trip. We drove back to the parking lot in Jerry's ancient buses and vans, then Ben and I piled into Mr. Toonkel's van. We stopped at a Quik Stop, where I got some French vanilla cappuccino and Ben got some hot chocolate. It helped a little, but our clothes were still soaked, and we were too uncomfortable to fall asleep during the ride home.

"It was an experience," Mr. Toonkel said. "That's what we go for, the experience. Sometimes it's the things that don't turn out so well, that you learn the most from."

Well, that was one way to look at it. I just sat there thinking that it could not get any worse than this.

12: *Boy Scouts of America v. James Dale*

But it did.

On June 28, 2000, a month or so after our disastrous rafting expedition, the U.S. Supreme Court, in the case of *The Boy Scouts of America v. James Dale,* ruled by a 5–4 margin that the Boy Scouts have the constitutional right to exclude gays from Scouting. It was a decisive legal victory for the Scouts that culminated two decades of litigation over whether they could exclude homosexuals. But as public relations, it was madness. It pleased some, enraged others, and put Scouting in the middle of a bitter national debate certain to do it more harm than good. Many people inside and outside Scouting agreed with the decision and applauded the organization for taking the stand it did. Many did not. And for those of us who felt that the B.S.A.'s stance was a betrayal, not a defense, of Scouting's core values, it raised an inescapable question—was this an organization we wanted to keep supporting?

After the past few months of Scout activities, there was some obvious appeal to an excuse—any excuse—to put Scouting behind me. If it involved declaring the moral high ground, so much the better. But, of course, jettisoning Scouting wasn't so easy. By this point Scouting was a huge part of my son's life, and the past few months notwithstanding, an interesting adjunct to mine. That said, how much were we willing to excuse to remain part of it? If Scouting decided to exclude blacks or Hispanics and that was upheld by the Supreme Court, would I stay a part of the organization? The easy answer there was, of course not. So why should it be any different in the case of gays? Could you separate out the values of the troop from the values of the B.S.A.? Could you decide to agree with this part of what Scouting professes but not that part, as if picking and choosing from an ethical smorgasbord? Whatever the case, it soon became clear this was not an issue that would surface and quickly disappear. Instead, the Supreme Court ruling, rather than settling the issue, just magnified it.

James Dale, who had mercifully changed his name from James Dick, was a walking advertisement for Scouting. The son of a lieutenant colonel in the U.S. Army, he joined Cub Scout pack 142 in Middletown, New Jersey, at the age of eight and became a model Scout, earning more than twenty-five merit badges, his Eagle, and membership in the Scouting honorary society, the Order of the Arrow. He was chosen by his council to speak to civic groups about Scouting, recruiting members and seeking donations. When he turned eighteen and had to leave Scouting, he continued on as an assistant Scoutmaster at Troop 73 in Matawan, New Jersey. In July 1990 all that changed. At Rutgers University, Dale, who had attended a military high school and voted for George Bush three months after he turned eighteen, came to accept something else about himself—that he was gay. He came out of the closet as a homosexual in his sophomore year and became active in the Lesbian/Gay Alliance. He kept that world separate from Scouting until July 1990, when his photograph appeared in the *Newark Star-Ledger*, identifying him as copresident of the alliance. Soon afterward, he received letters from the Monmouth Council of the Boy Scouts and from the district council. They said that "avowed homosexuals" are not permitted in Scouting, and he was being expelled. Eagle or not, as far as the B.S.A. was concerned, he was history.

That began a long legal odyssey. Dale filed suit in Monmouth County seeking reinstatement and lost at the trial level in 1995, where the judge's ruling was an antigay screed. "Men who do those criminal and immoral acts," sputtered Judge Patrick J. McGann, "cannot be held out as role models. B.S.A. knows that." In 1998 an appeals court overturned the ruling, saying that the Scouts "are essentially a public accommodation like a hotel or restaurant" and bound by state discrimination laws. And on August 4, 1999, the New Jersey Supreme Court, in a unanimous 7–0 ruling, said Dale's ouster violated the state's antidiscrimination law, and the B.S.A. could not ban gays any more than it could ban blacks, Jews, or Hispanics. His dismissal, Chief Justice Deborah T. Poritz wrote, "was based on little more than prejudice. The sad truth is that excluded groups and individuals have been prevented from full participation in the social, economic and political life of our country. The human price of this bigotry has been enormous."

Similar cases were percolating around the country, with the most closely watched playing out in California, where a gay Eagle Scout named Timothy Curran filed suit in 1981 after being banished from Scouting. It took seventeen years for the California Supreme Court to hear the case and then come to the opposite conclusion that the Supreme Court in New Jersey did: Scouting is a private-member group, not a public accommodation, and thus can bar gays, atheists, agnostics, and others who it feels do not share—or whose conduct goes contrary to—its core values.

The California case did not make it to the U.S. Supreme Court, but the New Jersey one did. In oral arguments in April 2000, the justices focused not on the Boy Scouts or the future of gay rights but on the legal implications of the case. If the Boy Scouts cannot exclude gays, are they allowed to exclude girls? Is a Jewish group obliged to accept non-Jews? If a group says a particular kind of exclusivity is central to its mission, are the courts required to accept that, or can they interpret for themselves the essentials of the group's identity? And if the Scouts can discriminate on the basis of their own sense of their identity, how many other groups could claim the same right? Most observers who heard the questioning felt the justices were more receptive to the B.S.A.'s case than to Dale's. They were right. Two months later, the judges found for the B.S.A., saying the First Amendment's protection for freedom of association meant the Scouts were entitled to set membership standards in accordance with the organization's expressed values. Writing for the majority, Chief Justice William H. Rehnquist argued that the forced inclusion of an unwanted person in a group infringes on the group's freedom of "expressive association" if that person undermines the group's ability to convey a message. "Dale's presence in the Boy Scouts," he wrote, "would, at the very least, force the organization to send a message, both to the youth members and the world, that the Boy Scouts accepts homosexual conduct as a legitimate form of behavior."

In the end, the case centered on two questions. Are the Boy Scouts a public accommodation, or a private group? And is the exclusion of homosexuals central to its "expressive message"? The New Jersey court found that the Scouts, who after all were chartered by Congress, receive money from the United Way, and regularly use public facilities like school buildings, are indeed a public accommodation. And it found that there is virtually nothing in Scout literature that in any way calls for the exclusion of gays. One Justice said he had pored over the group's literature and Web site without finding anything at all that advocated an antigay policy. The four dissenters on the U.S. Supreme Court found the same thing, scoffing at the idea that the phrases "morally straight" and "clean" in the Scout Oath have any bearing on the issue. "It is plain as the light of day that neither one of these principles 'morally straight' and 'clean' says the slightest thing about homosexuality," wrote Justice John Paul Stevens in his dissent. "...B.S.A.'s mission statement and federal charter say nothing on the matter; its official membership policy is silent; its scout oath and law and accompanying definitions are devoid of any view on the topic; its guidance for scouts and scoutmasters on sexuality declare that such matters are not construed to be scouting's proper area, but are the province of a scout's parents and pastor."

The one-vote U.S. Supreme Court majority, looking at the same facts, said the Boy Scouts was not a public accommodation—it was not a restaurant or hotel where anyone had the right to expect service, but a group espousing certain values that admits only those who share those values. And it ruled that if the purpose of the Scouts was to instill values, it had the right to define those values as it saw fit. "Who is better qualified to determine the expressive purpose of the Boy Scouts," Justice Anthony M. Kennedy had asked an attorney for Dale during oral arguments, "the Boy Scouts or the New Jersey courts?" And its ruling was consistent with an earlier unanimous decision in a Massachusetts case that Boston's privately sponsored St. Patrick's Day Parade could exclude gay marchers.

I'm no lawyer, and probably would have voted with the dissenters, but this is one case where a good lawyer could argue it round or argue it flat. Even some generally liberal civil libertarians, like the writer Nat Hentoff, argued forcibly that the right of free association needs to be protected whether the views expressed are popular or not. The Ku Klux Klan should not be forced to accept blacks. The Catholic Church should not be required to accept Jewish priests. If the B.S.A. exists to teach its values to boys, and one of those values is that morally straight means, among other things, heterosexual, it should not be forced to include gays as leaders. On that issue, more than any other, the court based its ruling.

But just because five members of the U.S. Supreme Court found the Scouts' policy legal didn't mean it was admirable or wise or consistent with Scouting's oaths and laws. There is virtually nothing in the Handbook or other Scouting literature specifically about homosexuality, but the handbooks are full of advice about being tolerant and respectful of differences. "Your conscience speaks to you about your relationship to other people," reads the 1959 Handbook, "respecting their rights, treating them justly, giving them a fair chance." The phrase "morally straight," used well before "straight" and "gay" were colloquially used as opposites, is usually invoked in a religious and moral sense—living a moral life that's reverent toward God and respectful and considerate of the rights of others. And Scouting from its start had tried to steer clear of divisive controversies. It embraced such disparate figures as Seton and Beard largely as a way to make it clear that this was a big, rugged tent, open to Indians and to cowboys and to other seemingly opposite constituencies as well.

But that was then. Now, with wearying frequency, Scouting has found itself in the middle of legal scuffles over what it has come to see as the three Gs—God, Girls, and Gays. It has fought to oust and exclude those who don't claim a belief in God, most recently in November 2002, when the Scouts expelled Darrell Lambert, an Eagle Scout from Port Orchard, Washington, because he said he did not believe in God. Lambert, a college freshman, had planned to volunteer as an assistant Scoutmaster. He was told that unless he professed a belief in God he was not welcome. He refused to comply and was told his participation in Scouting was no longer needed. It has gone to court to fight against suits seeking to include girls in Boy Scout activities. And, as we've seen, it has been fighting to keep gays out since 1980. We'll skip over the girls part. Baden-Powell, Seton, Beard, and West would, for once, have been united in their utter bafflement at the notion of girls as Boy Scouts. There does seem to be an awfully high definitional hurdle to the argument that the Boy Scouts have to include girl scouts. And over time, more out of practicality than conversion, Scouting has begun to accept women as troop leaders.

The Gays and God issues were harder to resolve. But they were enormously illuminating about how Scouting has evolved and who controls it today. And those issues reveal two things about Scouting. The first is the way Scouting's identity was forged in the 1950s in an image that's still with us today. The second is that it has come to be dominated by religious groups and the conservative voices of the nation's culture wars. Once the Scouts sat square in the middle of a relatively homogeneous civic culture. Now, if there is a middle, the Scouts don't seem to know how to find it.

We think of Scouting as a consistent, immutable entity, and many of its values are consistent—think of those in the Scout Oath and Scout Law. But on religion, Scouting has veered back and forth between the church of the wilderness—essentially the vision of Baden-Powell, Seton, and Beard—and more conventional expressions of reverence and faith. The early editions of the Handbook have relatively muted references to religion. But as Jay Mechling pointed out in *On My Honor: Boy Scouts and the Making of American Youth,* in the 1950s, both the references to religion and the linkage between religious faith and patriotism became much more explicit. Scouts read about Washington kneeling in the snow to pray at Valley Forge, and Lincoln and Eisenhower praying before making momentous decisions. It was the era when the government added the words "In God We Trust" to coins and paper money and "under God" was added to the Pledge of Allegiance. The sixth edition of the Handbook, published in 1959, reflected the same spirit: "Take a Lincoln penny out of your pocket and look at it. What do you see on it? Just above Lincoln's head are the words 'In God We Trust.' Twelve little letters on our humblest coin. Not only as individuals, but as a nation too, we are committed to live and work in harmony with God and his plan."

It was the same time that Norman Rockwell was giving us the powerful, iconic images of Scouting that still define it in our minds. Even now, Rockwell's reverent, patriotic images still shape our views of Scouting. But what we see is the world Rockwell saw—not that of Baden-Powell or Seton or Beard, but that of America in the 1950s. Of course, the reality of the 1950s was more complicated than the myth. (You can start with Rockwell. He was married three times, was a liberal Democrat, and was an early believer in the civil rights movement and a driven workaholic who worked seven days a week, including holidays.) But in a period of relative political and social consensus, Scouting became a symbol of the nation's shared values and virtues. When the consensus frayed in the 1960s and '70s, Scouting's role became more complicated as well.

And the issue of gays in the organization seemed almost destined to emerge as a flash point for Scouting. As an all-male culture, Scouting has always struggled with the issues of intimacy, homosexuality, and abuse that in recent years have exploded into the devastating scandals that have rocked the Catholic Church. One need only think of Baden-Powell, savoring his pictures of naked boys and swooning over "the Boy," to realize how close sexual issues can cut to the core of Scouting. Baden-Powell often wrote of the male form in a gushing voice ("I see in my mind's eye my friend Jack, a great strapping lumberman...I could watch him by the hour"). He took particular pleasure in watching boys swimming and sunbathing nude at the Scouts' campground at Gilwell Park. He was adamant about rooting out pederasty in Scouting and once said he would have approved of flogging (make of that what you will) as a punishment had the law allowed it. But, as Jeal notes, though many of his early associates saw homosexuality as a huge potential problem for Scouting, Baden-Powell showed very little interest in either discussing or addressing it.

Homosexuality has ebbed and flowed as a concern ever since, but mostly it plays out as a recurring theme for adolescent verbal abuse. Go to almost any troop meeting—or any gathering of adolescent boys, for that matter—and it is soon obvious that few insults are as common as taunts of "queer" or "faggot." Little would be less acceptable, even in a troop in a generally liberal area like ours, than for a kid to be openly gay. It has nothing to do with any policy and everything to do with the insecurities of boys trying to find their way through the adolescent minefield beginning to open up in front of them.

But, if the reflexive name-calling reflects one sort of unease, worries about men preying on boys reflect a far more serious and substantive fear. And Scouting officials have long been aware of pederasty as a concern. In *Scout's Honor: Sexual Abuse in America's Most Trusted Institution*, Patrick Boyle cataloged the long, ugly history of sexual abuse in Scouting, finding that during the 1970s and '80s, more than half of the four thousand people banished by the B.S.A. were accused of sexual abuse. The most sensational case played out in New Orleans, where a group of men had started Scout Troop 137 in a low-income neighborhood. In

August 1976 one of the assistant Scoutmasters took a roll of film to be developed that contained pictures of men having sex with boys. Employees at the store where the film was developed alerted police, who raided the homes of the troop leaders and found caches of pornographic magazines, pictures of men having sex with boys, and evidence of a nationwide network of pedophiles. The Scoutmaster and his two assistant Scoutmasters, it turned out, were regularly having sex with four Scouts as young as nine years old. The New Orleans case gained national attention, but most cases never made the papers, and the Scouts, like the Catholic Church, preferred to handle them quietly, sometimes allowing abusers to go from one troop to another.

Michael Rothschild, an attorney from Sacramento who represented a youth claiming abuse, obtained documents from the B.S.A. in 1992 showing that more than 1,800 Scoutmasters suspected of molesting boys were removed by the B.S.A. between 1971 and 1991.

All in all, the Scouts were forced to hand over 4,000 pages of documents, kept in shocking pink files that around headquarter were known as the "pervert files," on case after case of troop leaders, many of them respected community leaders, suspected of abusing the children in their troops. At least 2,071 Scouts reported being abused by their leaders during that period, though the number is almost certainly several times that. For all the cheap jokes about the dubious motives of Scoutmasters, the truth is the Boy Scouts are very lucky that there wasn't broader news coverage and general awareness of the extent of the abuse within troops.

As litigation became more a part of American life, molestation increasingly became a public issue, and an enormously expensive one for the Scouts. Between 1987 and 1991 alone, the Scouts were ordered to pay at least $15 million in damages in dozens of cases. Throw in the costs of legal fees and increased insurance premiums—not to mention the potential for disastrous public relations for the B.S.A—and it was clear molestation had the ability to do irreparable harm not just to kids who were victimized, but to Scouting itself. What to do about it?

One thing Scouting did, less than a year after the New Orleans verdict was put in writing for the first time a policy that said anyone who declares himself to be a homosexual could not participate in Scouting as a Scout, a volunteer leader, or an employee of the B.S.A. In a March 1978 memo to executive committee members, the President of the Boy Scouts, Downing R. Jenks, and the Chief Scout Executive, Harvey Price, said the policy was aimed at sexual preference, not misconduct, and that the organization knew of no laws that prohibited it.

It was probably a popular and noncontroversial pronouncement within Scouting, and codified the existing practice in which troops routinely kicked out men who were openly or transparently homosexual. But it did very little to deal with pederasts preying on boys. Study after study has shown that pederasty is a twisted sexual preference of its own, engaged in more often by men with female partners than men who are overtly homosexual. More often than not, the abuser is someone who shows no signs of aberrant behavior and gains the trust of a boy, then betrays it. On a practical level, a Scoutmaster who is openly gay and identified as such by other leaders, children, and parents, would probably be far less likely to be able to operate in perverse anonymity and abuse a child without anyone paying attention. And, to its credit, Scouting has since acknowledged that eliminating homosexuals in Scouting and rooting out pederasts are two entirely different things. In 1986 Scouting took a far more effective step, beginning a child abuse prevention program that has since been expanded and given extraordinary visibility within Scouting. Adult leaders are not allowed to sleep in tents with Scouts other than their own sons. They are not allowed to have Scouts over to their own homes. At Waubeeka and other Scout camps there are rigid schedules for use of the showers, mandating that Scouts and adults shower at separate times. The Handbooks now offer extensive information on spotting and reporting abuse, and they quite explicitly say homosexuals are no more likely than hetero-sexuals to abuse boys. And in late 2002, the Scouts for the first time authorized criminal background checks for all new volun-teers applying for leadership positions in Scouting. Whether to protect its Scouts or to protect itself, the B.S.A. has taken enor-mous strides toward rooting out sexual abuse since the period re-flected in the shocking pink files.

But a more realistic approach to the issue of sexual abuse did not resolve the issue of gays. Instead, in the face of lawsuits and public scrutiny, the B.S.A. increasingly took a hard line based on the relatively new argument that the Scout Oath's re-quirement that boys be morally straight and the Scout Law's de-mand that they be "clean" necessitated that gays be barred from participation.

To many in Scouting, this was just common sense. It's often argued that just as an adult male would not be an appropriate guide for a Girl Scout camp-out, a gay man would be problem-atic at a Boy Scout one. When I discussed the issue with Den-nis, my berry-picking pal from summer camp, he was stunned that I might think otherwise. "It all goes back to what I believe is the standard—and I know not everyone does—which is the Bible," he said. He had that wide-eyed, open-faced look he has when saying something that to him seems as obvious as a sun-rise. "When the Bible says that homosexual love is considered an abomination, I don't see too much wiggle room there. It doesn't mean I hate gays. One of my best friends turned out to be gay. Fine, but I don't want him to be a Scoutmaster. I think if I was an Eagle Scout and I was gay, I'd be majorly ticked off if someone told me to leave Scouting. It must be awful. But I also don't think we should say that what this guy is doing is exemplary behavior, which is what Eagle is. The idea that homosexuality is just fine is just not part of the aspirational message of Scouting."

We don't have too many Southern Baptists in Troop 1, but there are plenty of religious conservatives around the county who feel the same way. Most national polls show a majority of people disapprove of homosexual behavior. In a popular election between the Boy Scouts and, let's say, Queer Nation, it's not hard to deduce who would win. And in the culturally divided nation we've become, the gay issue was a particularly charged marker of which side Scouting was on. Scouting had made a big philosophical statement in 1979 when it moved its national headquarters from New Brunswick, New Jersey, to Irving, Texas, just down the road from Texas Stadium. It was more than just a real-estate transaction. At a time when the culture war was becoming an inescapable part of American life, the Scouts were voting with their feet, moving south and west, reflecting both the nation's demographic movement and the increasing influence of Sunbelt cultural conservatives. The increasing ties to conservative culture made sense in other ways as well. Individual troops are chartered by service clubs, or schools, or churches. But service clubs like VFW posts or Kiwanis Clubs are disappearing from American life, so increasingly sponsoring organizations are churches. Methodists, Mormons, and Catholics charter troops that enroll more than 1.2 million Scouts, or about a third of all Scouts. The Mormons in particular are an enormous source of manpower, Scouts, and financial support, chartering 33,272 troops, far more than any other group. The 12,102 troops chartered by Methodist churches enroll slightly more Scouts: 412,864 to 410,805 for the Mormons. But the Mormons almost certainly will take the lead in total Scouts enrolled in a year or two, and it's clear they play a role in the Boy Scouts that is wildly disproportionate to their numbers in the overall population. Scouting is not just something that appeals to many Mormon families; it is the official youth activity of the Mormon church, meaning virtually all Mormon boys are Boy Scouts. And the Mormons have made explicit threats to leave Scouting altogether if gays are admitted. The position of the Catholics is clear as well. Reversing the ban on gays could immediately cost the Scouts almost a quarter of its members.

There's also a financial consideration at stake. In 1993 Jere Ratcliffe, then beginning his tenure as Chief Scout Executive, made a speech to Scout executives around the country. He said that between then and 2006, $6.8 trillion would pass from one generation to the next—"the largest transfer of wealth in the history of our nation." He went on: "The individuals holding this wealth agree with our values and will be passing it to a generation that has demonstrated a lesser charitable attitude." In other words, if Scouting wanted to get its share of the pile of money about to be disbursed, it needed to make clear that its values were those of a generation getting ready to die off. And when he listed some values of particular importance to older Americans, a commitment to keeping homosexuals out of Scouting was a central part of the agenda. In short, Scouting had economic as well as philosophical reasons to stand firm against gay participation.

But if you don't see homosexuality as a sin, you know it's not a predictor of pederasty, and you have gay friends who are pretty much as virtuous and as sinful as you are, it's hard to see the policy as anything other than discrimination. To be honest, gay rights is not a huge part of my political agenda. But just as Harry or Dennis's sex life is none of my business, neither is James Dale's. If he was a model Eagle Scout and an esteemed assistant Scoutmaster before anyone knew he was gay, why should he suddenly be deemed a pariah afterward? If Todd Davis turned

up in his college's gay student association, should we ban him
from being part of Troop 1? And Scouting's formulation of don't
ask, don't tell—the B.S.A. said it had no interest in ferreting out
homosexuals, but was only barring out-of-the-closet ones—
seems only to compound the moral mess. Being an "avowed" homosexual was a crime punishable by expulsion, but if you kept
it secret that was OK? What kind of a lesson for Scouts was
that? The deeper you went, the less sense it made.

The Supreme Court ruling came after we were all but done
with the yearly Scout calendar, so the troop did not have to address it in any way. But it was still impossible to ignore. The
weekend after the ruling, for example, there was the phone call
from a friend who is a lawyer in a nearby town and the father of
three boys.

"Your son is in Scouting, isn't he?" he asked.

I said he was.

"Are you planning to drop out or stay a part of it?" he asked.
It was obvious what the right answer was.

I was taken aback a little by his directness, but said we
planned to stay and that I didn't think one position I don't agree
with should obliterate all that I did.

"I'm planning to pull my son out," he said. "We've talked
about it, and we both agree it's not something we feel comfortable with. You can't teach a kid that discrimination is wrong and
remain a member of a discriminatory organization. If this were
1966 and you were part of an organization that kept out blacks,
would you stay part of it? By remaining a member aren't you
condoning the policy?"

We must have talked for an hour. I said that in the real world,
the policy was more symbolic than functional and that in the
vast, vast majority of troops, no one, leader or Scout, was going
to be openly gay, ruling or no ruling. In the others, in big cities
and on the coasts, if someone would have been accepted before,

he would probably be accepted now, even if it meant ignoring the policy. To compare the Scouts' policy on gays—a policy I disagreed with, but one with minimal real-world implications—with the legalized apartheid of the segregated South that relegated blacks to separate and unequal versions of everything society had to offer was to engage in the kind of overblown moralizing that gives liberals a bad name. I said the only real way to change the policy was from within, not from the outside. And I thought, but didn't say, that Scouting provided one of the only forms of affordable outdoor recreation that's available for middle- and working-class families who can't afford the $5,000 summer camps and exorbitant wilderness outings that well-to-do families in Westchester County send their privileged little princes and princesses off to. Easy for the privileged classes, who seemed to be the most aggrieved, to write off Scouting.

Still, I couldn't dismiss my friend's misgivings, because I shared them. If my son was just starting out in Scouting, as my friend's son was, it might have been a reason not to join or to drop out. But, in the way that the messiness of real life often obliterates abstract judgments, I could not see punishing Ben and Troop 1, which doesn't discriminate against anyone, by pulling out. And I wondered just how much damage should be inflicted on Scouting because of this one policy.

Others I knew were similarly torn. One woman I know called up in distress to try to figure out what to do and then ended up writing about her dilemma in the online magazine *Salon*. She wrote about the Webelos handbook her son was getting as a prized present on his ninth birthday and concluded:

> In commenting on the court's ruling, defenders of the Boy Scouts pointed to an ongoing increase in enrollment as proof that American parents support the organization's condemnation of homosexuals. I thought I heard a dare in

those words: If you want to be around gays, start your own club. So if I allow Jonathan to stay with his pack now, I'm allowing the current Boy Scouts leadership to continue to misrepresent our family as antigay. The alternative is to quit in protest. And break the birthday boy's heart.

(Since enrollment has been dropping in recent years, it's not clear what growth the B.S.A. was talking about. And, on the other hand, when the gaping discrepancy between real enrollment numbers and the officially reported ones first surfaced in the 2000 investigation in Dallas, officials first attributed some of the gap to attrition because of Scouts quitting in response to the gay policy ruling. As a friend in Texas noted, maybe the Scouts need to add a new merit badge for spin.)

Less conflicted was the *New York Times's* "Ethicist," a column in the Sunday magazine that often captures the finger-wagging voice of New York liberalism at its most politically correct:

My son had been a Cub Scout for three years, and I've been a den leader for one, a wonderful experience for us both. But I was appalled by the Supreme Court's decision upholding the Scouts' right to exclude gay people. I cannot feel proud to see my son wearing a uniform that represents bigotry, and we are withdrawing from Scouting. Many of my friends also oppose this discrimination but plan to continue in Scouting anyway. Aren't they wrong to do so?

Resigning as you did is the ethical thing to do. Just as one is honor bound to quit an organization that excludes African Americans, so you should withdraw from Scouting as long as it rejects homosexuals. That Scouting has a legal right of free association does not clear you of this obligation. The right to shun Jews is no less anti-Semitic for all its legality.

Did the Scout uniform now really "represent bigotry"? Ninety years of mostly good works and the uniform was akin to a Klan robe? Maybe I had too much invested in the wrong side, but, though I felt offended by the Neanderthal tendencies of the B.S.A. officials, I also found myself offended by the glib moral hauteur of the antigay side. I know we've got a culture war to fight, but don't the kids fit in here somewhere? Still, these were just the first of the rumblings around the country as people lined up to agree or disagree with the court, to voice their moral outrage against Scouting or their moral outrage against those who would voice moral outrage against Scouting.

Dozens of corporations, local governments, school districts, and United Way chapters withdrew funds or the free use of school facilities for meetings. More than one hundred Eagle Scouts handed in their badges in protest. (To which the B.S.A., always prepared with its numbers, proclaimed in March of 2001 that 47,582 Scouts had made Eagle in 1999 and there were more than a million Eagles overall, so a measly one hundred badges didn't amount to squat.) Steven Spielberg, an Eagle Scout who has been the Scouts' one prominent culturally plugged-in ally, quit his post on Scouting's advisory board, saying, "The last few years in scouting have deeply saddened me to see the Boy Scouts of America actively and publicly participating in discrimination. It's a real shame." The presidents of urban Scout Councils in Chicago, Los Angeles, New York, Philadelphia, Boston, Minneapolis, San Francisco, and Orange County, California, called for the national organization to change its policy. One leader in New York called the Scouts' national board "a bunch of rednecks from Texas." On the other side, the U.S. Senate, by a 51–49 margin, passed a measure proposed by Jesse Helms that would block federal funds for school districts that restrict access to Boy Scouts troops. The American Legion passed a resolution supporting the Scouts' policy. In Cleveland, a ninety-year-old troop lost its sponsoring church because the church had a nondiscrimination policy, and the troop failed to put in writing a pledge not to follow the B.S.A.'s policy on gays.

Sometimes, it just became absurd. In Berkeley, California, a gay member of the city council got the city to cancel a reception for Japanese Girl and Boy Scouts on a goodwill mission to the city, saying it would be an endorsement of the B.S.A.'s discriminatory policies, even though the Japanese Boy Scouts have no such policy, nor do Girl Scouts here or in Japan. But if the most agitated outrage occurred in the usual places (Bay Area gay groups protested an Oakland Raiders charity golf tournament that raised funds for Scouting), the issue cropped up everywhere—in Fort Lauderdale and Boston, Denver and Columbus, Hartford and Kansas City, Sacramento, Raleigh, and Des Moines. Among the United Ways withdrawing support from Scouting was our own, the United Way of Westchester and Putnam, which cost the Westchester–Putnam Boy Scout Council $150,000, or 7 percent of its budget. "There is a recognition that the Boy Scouts have provided a lot of good programs," the local United Way president said. "On the other hand, our organization has always stood for inclusion, and it was extremely important to us to be able to say that all our donor dollars go to programs that are consistent with inclusiveness."

The more the debate raged, the more alienated I felt from both the moral superiority of the Scouting-averse constituency on the left and the moral superiority of the antigay minions on the right. We weren't going to pull out of Troop 1. So the real question wasn't whether I would quit Scouting. It was whether I'd ever be able to reconnect to the whole archaic and now embattled enterprise.

13: Summer Camp 2:
Baden-Powell Meets Bob Dylan

I didn't have much time for abstract reflection on our future in Scouting, because two weeks after the ruling I was headed back to Camp Waubeeka. Whether because of my fond memories of last year, my desire to accumulate Good Dad points, or a taste for masochism (probably a bit of all three), I had volunteered months earlier for a second summer at camp. Even if I had decided that Scouting was America's answer to the Hitler Youth, I was obligated to show up or we wouldn't have enough dads for the second week of camp.

Not surprisingly, given the events of the prior few months, Year Two began with a wary, conflicted sense of duty rather than the last year's buzz of anticipation. And there were other changes right from the start. Unlike that year, there was no dads' caravan. Harry was not coming. His three kids, with the usual perverse logic of adolescence, had declared that they had either no interest in or active contempt for Scouting and had already dropped out. That left Harry, reluctantly, once again out of Scouting. Dennis, thank goodness, was coming, but had gone up a day early, so I headed out on my own, the day a mix of clouds and drizzle.

Under the gray sky, Waubeeka looked somehow smaller than I remembered. But, to my relief, it felt kind of nice to be there, and I found myself remembering the good feelings I had taken from the last year more than the not-so-good ones I was bringing with me this year. The first familiar faces I saw were Fly Guy and Dr. Flank, carrying their fishing poles, returning from the Waubeeka lake where they hoped for bass and were lucky to get perch. A moment later Ben and Mark came up the path, and I was thrilled to see that Ben's face this time bore no swollen purple splotches or other signs of blunt-force trauma. Ben and Mark helped me carry my gear—overnight bag, pillow, sleeping bag—down to Wolfjaw. I stowed my stuff in Ben's tent and surveyed the site.

Ben gave me a quick rundown of the group dynamic so far. Most of the kids from the last year, except for Bernie, were back this time. The only newcomers were Dave and Marty, the little kids who had barely survived our soggy canoe trip. There were, Ben said, three main campsite factions, though factions sounded a bit more nefarious than was appropriate. They were more like the three rings of a circus. There was Sam 'n Eric Enterprises, Inc., in which our two heroes and their cronies huddled in The Underworld, dissing the adult leaders; discoursing on their three favorite topics—music, girls, and dropping a deuce; and resuming their performances of "Scout Socks." There was the Magic Card crowd, led by Doug and Elliot, in which the hard-core computer kids spent hours playing a fantasy card game with wizards and elves and other evil or virtuous creatures who can cast spells or kill off their enemies in a pallid but acceptable real-world substitute for Starcraft, Counterstrike, or their other preferred computer games. This group tended to gather at the cooksite and picnic table I thought of as Middle Earth. And then there were the pyros, mostly younger kids, whose idea of a good time was finding an excuse, any excuse, to make a fire—for cooking, warmth, a troop campfire, or for recreational purposes. Failing in that, they preferred to sit around lighting matches. The groups were not exclusive, and kids went from one to another as they saw fit. And there were some kids, like Ben, Mark, Jonah, Louis, and others, who were more likely to sit around reading or playing cards than joining any of the three factions.

It rained on and off all the next day. The evening was supposed to be the first-night-of-camp barbecue at the handicrafts shed, where the staff prepared hot dogs and hamburgers. The idea was to have a serving line outside, with some troops eating inside the shed and others at picnic tables outside. But by the time the barbecue began, it was pouring in sheets. So everyone was crammed inside the shed, there was not enough room to sit, and the lines of Scouts and Scouters waiting to fill their paper plates moved at a crawl. When I finally got my hamburger, I took one bite and almost coughed it up. It was half cooked, and like everything else it felt cold and soggy. I threw it away and didn't eat anything else until the watermelon for dessert.

After dinner was merit badge sign-up, which also played out amid the chaos of the overcrowded shed. The campfire was canceled by the camp director this year, a dark-haired, loose-limbed, athletic-looking Dartmouth student named Nick Reynolds. He didn't try to recreate all the campfire activities inside, but he did want to put together an appropriate opening-night convocation. So after the merit badge sign-up ended, he climbed onto a bench and hollered for everyone's attention. The room instantly went silent. Nick had short black hair and was wearing green Scout shorts, hiking boots, a T-shirt, and a long red stocking cap with a puff ball on the end that flopped halfway down his back.

He began with the Scout camp call and response:

"Hi, Guys!"

"Hi, Nick!"

When he did the obligatory "I can't hear you," he lifted one leg, put it down like a sumo wrestler preparing to face off, went into an exaggerated crouch, and put his cupped hand over his ear in an artful pantomime, like someone who was either a natural ham or a trained actor.

He then introduced each of the staff members with exaggerated World Wrestling Federation–style bombast, and they improvised various skits with hyperactive bursts of Y-chromosome energy. With the rain pouring down and the kids crammed in, it should have felt miserable in there, but Nick somehow had them mesmerized. I was sorry when the program ended.

By this time we were almost used to the rain. Allen, our ace chef and walking jukebox, broke into a spirited rendition of "Singing in the Rain," and kept singing most of the way down to Wolfjaw. But that was it for the evening's merriment. The muddy, waterlogged camp and everything in it felt like a giant saturated sponge. Ben seemed reasonably content, reading his Tom Clancy novel by flashlight in our tent. But my sleeping bag felt clammy, and the rain pounding on the tent, which was probably Korean War surplus, gave me the sense of being at sea in a leaky dinghy. Worse, there was a puddle on the wooden pallet supporting the tent, and you could hear the dripping water plopping onto the puddle on the floor. I burrowed as deep as I could into my clammy sleeping bag, but the rain outside and the various drips and drabs and puddles and leaks inside were like a noisy, waterlogged Rube Goldberg machine. Our Canoe Trip From Hell, as awful as it was, at least had seemed finite—it had to end that day. But as I lay in bed unable to fall asleep I found myself thinking in horror: What if it rains for days, for the rest of the week even? I'd never make it.

"Hey, Ben," I called.

No answer. At least one of us had fallen asleep.

So I lay alone in the damp darkness, not sure whether to feel depressed or just amused by the masochistic purity of it all. How perfect to be stuck at Waubeeka for a week in the rain, not just suffering, but suffering for an organization now reviled—*its uniform representing bigotry!*—by all right-thinking members of my social class.

This should have felt like the last circle in my Scouting death spiral. But I realized that, rather than scraping bottom, I was feeling a not entirely unpleasant jumble of disparate emotions. Yes, it was uncomfortable as hell, but even in the rain, there was a powerful, primordial appeal to being in this ancient, stupid, leaking tent with my son. I was intrigued by Nick and wanted to know more about him. I had seen Lester and Igor at the festivities earlier in the evening and was eager to catch up on what was new with Bronxville 4 and get their take on the Scouting news of the past year. As the rain continued to pound on the tent, I found myself more discomfited than unhappy or alienated. And after a while I began to feel utterly unhitched from the usual mad rush of daily life with no distractions and no static, nowhere to go, nothing to do. Time seemed to stop. I had those moments all the time as a kid, lying alone in bed thinking about how you crossed the line from consciousness to sleep, too intrigued by stray thoughts to nod off. This didn't have that kind of restless excitement. But the moment did have a solitary, peaceful sort of gravity, disconnected from daily life but reconnected to myself in a way I seldom experienced anymore. If we had background music, it would have been the langorous reverie of "Rainy Night in Georgia." More specifically, it would have been the breathtaking duet Sam Moore, of the soul duo Sam and Dave, and the late country singer Conway Twitty did on a 1994 album of duets between soul and country singers called *Rhythm Country and Blues*. "Lord," sighed Twitty, who died just a few months later, "I believe it's raining all over the world." We weren't in Georgia, but, Lord, it felt to me like it was raining all over the world. I found myself flashing back to a long-forgotten spring afternoon in college. Some friends and I, caught in a powerful soaking downpour, just decided to go, as it were, with the flow. We threw down our umbrellas and shed our rain gear and started doing handstands and somersaults and rolling around on the ground in giddy youthful abandon, cavorting like waterlogged loons on an isolated corner of the campus. I remembered the old folks at a group home across the street watching us all but expressionless as they sat on their front porch, the smell of magnolia and pine, and how conscious I was of being one of the lucky young fools cavorting in the rain and not the tired old folks watching from their rockers and straight-backed chairs from the porch. It seemed a long time ago. It *was* a long time ago. But after a while the memory of that magical rainstorm merged with the reality of this more prosaic one, and without knowing it, I fell into a deep, peaceful sleep, like a pebble dropping into a lake.

I awoke the next morning and poked my head out from the tent. It was gray and foggy, but the rain had stopped. Ben was still dozing, but I pulled on my sneakers and a warm fleece and wandered outside. The familiar ritual of Waubeeka breakfast was getting underway. Kids trekked into camp with those plastic garbage cans strapped to their back. Dr. Flank, who had stayed over for the beginning of Week 2, was preparing coffee for himself and Dennis. The kids were doing their best to get a fire started with the wet wood but had the cereal stacked up just in case.

Before long the sun began to peek out. The kids managed to get a fire started and made some slippery globs of scrambled eggs and mounds of toast slathered with butter. And there I was back with Ben and Mark, Jonah and Doug, Hal and Herb and whoever else came and went, glancing at our copy of the "Waubeeka World News," wondering which of the staff from last year would be back and what Sam 'n Eric had up their sleeves. We finished our breakfast, the kids cleaned up, then they all decamped for their various activities and the adults were left alone.

Dr. Flank, Dennis, and I gathered at the picnic table at the upper cooking site to plot strategy. The last year Harry was the clear heir apparent as soon as Dr. Flank left. Dennis and I, despite our baptism at Waubeeka, still felt clueless. Dr. Flank didn't seem worried—he'd seen dads even less prepared than we were figure out how to get through the week. But we went down the list of kids, determining which ones were homesick, which ones were handfuls, which ones you had to watch, and which ones you could pretty much leave alone. Dr. Flank figured to leave later in the day. But in the meantime he had more important things to do, namely fishing. He headed for the lake with Dennis and his tackle box and fishing poles, while I headed for the camp office to see who was around. Sitting on one of the benches playing his harmonica was Igor, Lester's loyal aide-de-camp. Igor was short and squat to Lester's tall and solid, but like Lester he had an opinion on everything, from the literary quality of Martin Luther King's "I have a dream" speech to Scout camp aquatic training now as opposed to ten years ago. Indeed, often he had so many opinions on the same issue you weren't necessarily sure what his true opinion was. So we chatted idly for a few minutes, and then I asked him about the gay issue. He didn't hesitate.

"The problem is not homosexuals, it is people who are pederasts," he said. "Everyone gets behind an easy victory, and they avoid the hard problems. Really dealing with sexual abuse? That's hard. This is something they could win. They won the Bible Belt. Is it worth it? They think it is. They'll take an easy victory anytime."

I figured this meant he was going to condemn the Scouts' policy. But then as he went on, I wasn't so sure.

"But here's the problem. No one wants to hear about someone's sex life. Don't ask, don't tell. That's fine. The trouble is when someone comes out of the closet. Should a heterosexual swinger be a Scoutmaster? It's the same issue. It's promiscuous sex we're against, and it's a promiscuous lifestyle. Even Allen Ginsberg and Peter Orlovsky, the longest-running gay marriage I know of, broke up a number of years ago and even during their long marriage they had affairs."

This was a reference to the beat poet Allen Ginsberg and his longtime partner, who were immortalized in a nude Richard Avedon portrait, which helped galvanize the gay pride movement back in the 1960s. It wasn't a standard Scout camp reference, but you never know what to expect these days.

"A young man joins the Scouts to learn how to become an adult male. One doesn't push one's own biases; one wants them to discover who they want to be. You want to be—what is the expression? Transparent. Your job is to help them with their problems and keep your own lifestyle out of sight. My father died last Friday. I mourned and buried him and came here Tuesday and did my job. The kids don't know my father died. They're having summer fun. They're only young once. It's not our job to create an unofficial barrier that shouldn't be there. In this case, it was Dale who made it the issue."

The logic was a little threadbare—a gay man is not transparent when he comes out of the closet, but a married man with two kids and a wife who brings three-bean salad to the Court of Honor is? Still, just when I thought that meant he supported the ruling, Igor turned around again. Sort of.

"I know people who after twenty years of marriage, women go off to marry women, men decide they're gay, men become women, women become men. Who can understand it? It's really no one's business what a private life is. It's never been an issue, and we're crazy to make it one. That's why the Scouts can't win in this. Or they win in court but end up with a public relations disaster. Scouts are like Shakers after the Civil War. We're dying off."

By this time, Lester had ambled over. Lester had me pegged as a hopeless liberal and liked starting arguments over almost anything—Vietnam, the war on drugs, school desegregation, the *Times*'s coverage of presidential politics. I figured he'd come out guns blazing on this one, but like Igor, he seemed to want to take the issue all over the map.

"There's not a one-word answer," he said. "First of all one of my all-time best Eagle Scouts and Senior Patrol Leaders turned out to be gay when he went to college. A nicer and more dedicated Scout you never would have found. If he had stayed alive and not died from AIDS, and wanted to help with the troop, I would never have hesitated in having him. Some of my sons' best teachers I'm pretty sure were gay. I never had any problem with that. The council has always had an unofficial policy of ignoring leaders who are gay. They claimed they did not want a lawsuit if they accused someone of being gay. So I don't have a problem with any of those situations and therefore I have no problem with gays as Scout leaders." Somehow I knew a "but" was coming.

"The problem with me and the reason national is justified in their lawsuit is what's going to happen when a Scout leader does molest a kid, and it turns out he was gay. Who are the parents going to sue? The deep-pockets B.S.A. Who's going to pay a multimillion-dollar judgment? The B.S.A. So I'd support the position from a liability standpoint, not a moral standpoint. But having said that, I also don't think the government should be mandating politically correct positions. A private organization should be allowed its right to freedom of association. If you don't want Jews in your country club you should be able to say that. With Scouts now we have some companies and national organizations who no longer contribute to Scouts. Do you hurt all the Boy Scouts by not donating because of one principle and ignore all the good assets? I don't know. But the policy is not going to change, because the biggest sponsoring organization right now is the Mormon church, and the Mormon church is adamantly antigay and would withdraw its support if the Scouts ever allowed gays in. You take a look at *Scouting* magazine and all the honorary awards at the national level and it's this elder in the Mormon church and that elder in the Mormon church. It's the most powerful bloc in national."

After going on a while longer, Lester ended up coming back to his favorite subject, which was the depravity of the idiots at Scouting's national headquarters.

"At that level it's not a youth group, it's just a corporation," he said. "What will get us more money and more new members? That's all it's about. No one knows the name of the Chief Scout. Sure, he's in the handbook like Seton or Beard. But those were personalities who kids looked up to and idolized. These guys are just corporate executives. You see their picture in the Handbook and they go to the national jamboree and give some BS speech, but they have no idea what's going on with youth. They're just stuck in their corridors in Irving, Texas. For them it's just money and numbers. Money and numbers."

Lester and Igor are argumentative enough that you could walk by and say, "Good morning," and two hours later still find yourself arguing about whether global warming is real. But you could draw two lessons from their rambling remarks. The first is that Scouting really has a regional problem. These guys are hardly airy New York liberals. But, like the anonymous leader who called the B.S.A. leadership "a bunch of rednecks from Texas," they inhabit a very different culture from the world of Irving, Texas, and like many other leaders in big cities or on the coasts, they really feel alienated from the Scouting leadership. I don't know much about the Shakers after the Civil War, but it's easy to see why a Scouter on the East Coast would worry about

Scouting dying out. Second, for all the moral absolutism on the left and the right, the gay issue in Scouting really does cut more than just two ways. In a court of law, judges have to rule one way or another. But in the real world, there are plenty of opinions and issues somewhere between the two poles of the uniform as a symbol for bigotry and the blue-nose morality police of the national organization. Because Scouting evokes such strong images—pro and con—that complexity never seems to get reflected in the public argument. It's all about the Scouts as the defenders of morality and virtue or the Scouts as hidebound troglodytes, once again hopelessly behind the times.

I'd had enough of Lester and Igor's amicus briefs for a while and headed back to Wolfjaw. Sure enough, there was Dr. Flank packing up his gear in the lean-to. He called the boys over and said we had a great week during Week 1, and he expected things to go at least as well during Week 2. "I leave you in the capable hands of Mr. Applebome and Mr. Walker," he said. We were probably supposed to think of something appreciative and inspirational to say, but instead just tried to exude some indefinable air of authority. "Do I have some volunteers to carry my gear?" Dr. Flank then asked. Several kids stepped forward to grab it. Dr. Flank directed them toward the gear to be transported. He shook hands with Dennis and me and gave a jaunty wave to the assembled masses. And then Dennis and I were in charge.

Without Harry as the designated grownup, we felt a little outmanned. So, as the week progressed under our too-benign leadership, things at times veered a little off course. The ratio of food consumed to food tossed into the forest veered dangerously in the direction of food tossed. There were a few fights, one of which began with a kid spraying water over the monster box and ended with him being sprayed with mustard and other condiments. The malingerers found it even easier to malinger. Our performance in the Waubeeka competition stayed at last year's abominable level.

On the other hand, the rhythms of Waubeeka don't vary all that much from year to year. And, no matter who's around or who's in charge, a huge part of the week is just spent in hanging around and yapping. So we spent much of our time like geezer spies eavesdropping in the land of the Simpsons Generation. We learned this summer's standard retort: "Thank you, Captain Obvious." We pondered questions without answers ("If a man is in the woods talking, and there's no woman around, is he still wrong?") and questions with answers no one was sure of ("What's the plural of octopus?"). We parsed the fine points of the five-second rule, which held that any piece of food dropped on the ground was still perfectly edible as long as it was picked up within five seconds.

The kids' use of the language was often a lot more sophisticated than mine at thirteen and fourteen ("Is there something wrong with him?" "Do you want the summary or the full essay?" "Do you want the précis or the complete text?"). Except, that is, when it consisted of calling everyone else a "lard butt," this year's insult of choice. There was much talk about extreme soft drinks, with the consensus that nothing could top Jolt Cola, which they said had twelve times the caffeine of Mountain Dew and the most caffeine allowable by law, whatever that meant.

There were constant references to *ur*texts like *Monty Python and the Holy Grail*, Starcraft, and the *ur*-est text of them all, *The Simpsons*, whose every episode seemed engraved in their collective unconscious. The episode where Mr. Burns, the mean old guy who owns the nuclear power plant where Homer works, gets shot after building a device to blot out the sun! The one where Homer cheats on his taxes, undergoes an audit, and is forced to become a spy for the FBI! Homer winning a Pulitzer Prize as Mr. X on a muckraking Web site!

The original Handbook, not the Seton one but the by-committee B.S.A. model, begins with a chapter on Scoutcraft. "In all ages, there have been scouts," it reads, "the place of the scout being on the danger line of the army or at the outposts, protecting those of his company who confide in his care." It talks about stalking animals, about virtues like chivalry, loyalty, and obedience. "When he gets up in the morning, he may tie a knot in his necktie and leave the necktie outside his vest until he has done a good turn," it reads. A Scout should take a cold bath often, rubbing dry with a rough towel. And it continues: "A bright face and a cheery word spread like sunshine from one to another. It is the scout's duty to be a sunshine-maker in the world."

Exactly what that had to do with the world of *The Simpsons* and Starcraft was not entirely clear. It was probably a promising sign that Doug and Elliot seemed somehow at home in both Aiur, the distant green world where the Protoss were bred, and at Waubeeka, the distant green world where Sam 'n Eric held sway. Clearly Scouting's genius has been its ability to adapt, Terran-like, to changing times. Left unclear was whether it could still do it, whether the pace of change had become too fast and Scouting had become too slow and ossified to adapt.

The next day I went out looking for Nick, thinking for some reason that he had some insight on all this. I found him at the Waubeeka office, going over some paperwork with an admirably eclectic pile of CDs on his desk—Chopin, the Doors, Woody Guthrie, Peter Gabriel, U-2, Curtis Mayfield, and an album of Gregorian chants. Nick was, of course, an Eagle, and one with a rather distinguished Scouting lineage. His grandfather had started one of the earliest troops in the country and had even met B-P himself during one of the great man's tours of America in the 1930s. Nick had bounced from the University of Alaska–Fairbanks to the University of New Hampshire to Dartmouth. "I'm a theater geek, but I'm studying astrophysics," he said. "I want to be in a position to help develop the first generation of light spacecraft that could operate on the moon. I figure by 2020 I'll be the first Scoutmaster on the moon."

Nick, as it turned out, was a somewhat indifferent manager, whose underlings felt he didn't attend to camp business as assiduously as he should have. But he radiated a knowing sort of self-confidence—in a different time he could have been a young lieutenant you'd follow into battle. And he came across as a Scouting archetype combining different eras, sort of Todd Davis with more of an edge. He talked about Scouting with a striking blend of passion and disdain, as if the Scouting culture wars were washing back and forth in his head even as he was in charge of running the camp. "My parents were divorced when I was four, and my dad didn't live with us," he said. "Boy Scouts put me in touch with people I could respect and learn from, and I couldn't get that anywhere else. It gave me aspirations and goals. But at the same time, it seemed like Scouting was at war with itself, and it gets more so all the time. It's like the best parts of Scouting are contrary to so much of what the organization seems wedded to. It's not just the gay policy, which I find abhorrent. It's the myopia of the national organization in general. It seems to me that what they want is to develop boys who think and feel in a certain way, rather than to develop boys who think and feel intelligently, who think for themselves. The Scout Oath and Scout Law are such powerful ideas. I like to think they're what Scouting's about, not whatever comes from the national organization. I love Scouting, but when the Supreme Court ruling came out on the gay issue I felt like I wanted to rip my uniform off and set it on fire."

Just then Frankie Stanton showed up. He was not having a good day. Stanty, who had been Ted Watson's assistant at the econ lodge, now was over at the Scoutcraft area. He was a high school senior with thick glasses and thick lips, who like Nick had a gift for theatrics. But his grandmother had died suddenly the night before—healthy one day, gone the next. He had talked to her just two days earlier, and when he got the news from his parents he went quickly from disbelief to rage, leading him to destroy an ancient sofa and chair that had withstood untold indignities over the years at the camp office. On top of that, he had developed a painful ingrown toenail that was glowing an excruciating radioactive red that made each step feel like a stroll barefoot over thumbtacks. He needed Nick to drive him to the medical clinic in nearby Chestertown to have it looked at.

We headed toward Nick's green 1996 Volkswagen Golf parked by the side of the parade ground. Stanty was wearing shorts, a T-shirt reading "MIDDIES SWIMMING," and a black baseball cap reading "FRIENDSHIP THROUGH SCOUTING." Nick was wearing a University of Alaska–Fairbanks T-shirt (much cooler than Dartmouth), green carpenter pants, and flip-flops. He turned to a public radio station playing Vivaldi concertos and lit up a Marlboro as soon as we pulled out of the camp.

"Boy, am I an idiot," Stanty said, as Nick drove—faster than I would have—toward Chestertown. "It says right there in the Handbook that you have to cut your nails straight across, and I don't even do that. What a doof."

Nick was not sympathetic.

"You're really gonna be in for it," he said. "You're screwed, man. You can't handle this. When the doctor lances that thing or whatever he's gonna do, you're gonna puke. You'll pass out from the pain."

"I'm gonna be a hobbler," said Stanty glumly. "You gonna hold my hand if I can't stand the pain?"

"No way," Nick said. "We have our limits. You're gonna be out of commission for a week. It's gonna be ugly."

Stanty just looked pained. They were silent for a moment, and then retreated to the default position of Scout camp— Scouting war stories and lore. Nick started off with a scary tale about a leaking propane stove that exploded when he was stuck in two feet of snow in a little camping hut one winter: "There's a candle on the table and as soon as the gas reaches the table BOOOOOOOOMMMMMMMM! There's a fireball in the cabin. It blew the canister up and out to the other side of the room shooting flames. Set the whole front of my sleeping bag on fire, burned my eyebrows off, all my hair, the hair on my nose, the hair on my arms. We threw the canister out the window, beat the flames out of the sleeping bag and were OK." There's a lot more of a don't-try-this-at-home quality to Scouting than people think.

They went on. About the superiority of the patrol cooking at Waubeeka rather than the fancy—by Scout standards—dining hall at Buckskin. The scandal of the new wussified Scout Handbook. "Man, the only one I read is the '76 edition," said Stanty. "I just hate the new one. They ought to call it the Girl Scout Handbook. No semaphore. No Morse code. There's hardly a skill in it they tell you how to do. I don't think you can find the words *Dutch oven* in the whole thing. Man. It sucks."

Finally, we reached the doctor's office, which was decorated with nature scenes from the Adirondacks and helpful bits of medical wisdom ("An overactive bladder can be an accident waiting to happen."). The nurse called for Stanty, and we sat there listening for the shriek of agony. Five minutes. Ten minutes. Fifteen minutes. Finally, he came out, seemingly intact, a mysterious half smile flitting across his face.

"The doctor says I need to take some antibiotics first," he said, failing miserably in his efforts to act as if he wasn't thrilled to get a reprieve. "I need a frappuccino."

From the doctor we drove to Brooks Pharmacy, in a little strip shopping center a few blocks away. Nick and Stanty hung around waiting for the prescription to be filled, checking out the condoms at the rear of the store, then ventured over to the magazine rack, where Stanty picked up five wrestling magazines to read on his trip home for his grandmother's funeral. This was no mere impulse purchase. Stanty announced that he was in training, more or less, to wrestle professionally and needed the magazines to prepare himself for his chosen life's work.

"It's my dream," he said, gazing intently at Chyna's man hands on the cover of one of the magazines. "To make it in wrestling you need three things. You need mike skills, which I have in abundance. You need the physical stuff. OK, I'm a bit lacking there. And you need a gimmick with a finish. I'm thinking of calling myself The Stud, and my finisher would be a hold I'd call VD. You know, I put him out, and I'd go, "Sorry pal. You've got VD.""

"Maybe you need to rethink that," Nick said clinically, like a doctor delivering a grim prognosis. "Not sure that one will fly."

"What about just being The Boy Scout, a heroic good-guy character?" I asked.

Stanty gagged and almost spat out his root beer.

"You know what you'd be?" he sputtered. "You'd be the chump. You'd be the guy who came out at the very beginning of Wrestlemania and got your butt kicked. Everyone would hate you. 'You Boy Scout. You pansy. With that prissy little uniform. I hope he kicks your ass.' Stone Cold Steve Austin would come out, give you the finger, drink a beer, and drop you with the stunner. The Boy Scout? Who's gonna be for The Boy Scout?"

And this was from someone who loved Scouting. It made you wonder how an institution can be so revered and so disdained at the same time, so much a part of American life and mythology and so utterly marginalized. When we got back to camp, Stanty hobbled back to his tent to pack up to go home for the funeral. I asked Tim if he had an answer. He thought he did.

"I have friends who say, 'How can you be a Boy Scout? You're supporting discrimination and homophobia.' And I just tell them, 'You just don't understand Scouting.' The real Scouting isn't what the Chief Scout Executive says in the Handbook or the uniforms or the badges. The real Scouting is the covert Scouting. The essence of Scouting is the relationships between boys, and between boys and men of differing ages and backgrounds. The national organization provides nothing more than a platform on which those relationships can occur. And what the Boy Scouts say or do has very little bearing on the actuality. You look around this camp. You've got troops of spoiled suburban brats and troops of big macho working-class Italians. You've got troops that do it by the book and are full of great kids, and you've got troops of kids who stand up straight and are good at getting in line but are a bunch of little thugs. But all of Scouting is about an interplay between the ideals of Scouting and the reality of kids, about what the Handbook says and what kids really do. That's why you can only expend so much energy on what national says. That's symbolic. What happens here is real."

He paused for a moment, as if he hadn't quite thought this through and was figuring it out as he went along. "But here's how the symbol affects the reality. If the B.S.A. keeps drifting to the right, you might have more and more parents who'll say, 'That's probably a group with intolerant values. Maybe I don't want to be part of it.' Then you really can get a change in the organization because of the kind of kids who take part."

That night's campfire began with the usual bonfire and skits and cheers and songs. But then Nick wandered off for a moment and came back with a guitar and a harmonica around his neck à la early Bob Dylan. "Here's an old song by an old folkie that makes a little bit more sense every year," he said. And then he started wailing a twangy, primal version of "The Times They Are A' Changing." What was *this* about? His own commentary on the B.S.A.? A universal statement about change and renewal? He never made it clear. He finished singing and said this was a special summer. It wasn't what he'd expected, because some of the friends he was expecting to work with this year didn't make it to camp. But he'd learned that you never know quite what's going to happen in life, so you make plans and you're always prepared to change them. In the meantime, we were all lucky, he said, to be here, watching this bonfire, sharing the moment, being together. Then he started strumming his guitar again, and broke into Neil Young's "Helpless." Then the campfire wound down, the bugler played "Taps," and it was over.

"There is an impalpable, invisible, softly stepping delight in the camp fire, which escapes analysis," the original Handbook had said. "Enumerate all its charms, and still there is something missing in the catalogue. Any one who has witnessed a real camp fire and participated in its fun as well as its seriousness will never forget it."

I guess I'm a sucker for campfire moments, but this one seemed particularly memorable. The message to me wasn't that Scouting wanted to be a bunch of gay-pride leftists singing Dylan songs and reading feminist poetry. But I was willing to buy into Nick's notion that sometimes it could be—that Scouting wasn't some fill-in-the-blanks production of look-alike troops orchestrated out of Texas, but a reflection of the kids and their communities and their times. There's nothing wrong and much right about the Norman Rockwell imagery of Scouting. In recent years we've developed a renewed appreciation for straight arrows. But Seton and Beard and B-P (though not, alas, West) never wanted a movement of cookie-cutter straight arrows. They were men of extraordinarily rough edges and unconventional ideas, and you would like to think they would have applauded Nick's campfire, which was as unexpected in its way as Baden-Powell's thirty thousand Scouts running full tilt toward King George V.

Or maybe, I began to think later, I was still a little obtuse, too much the observer, not enough the Scout. It's possible, maybe likely, that a subversive political thought was implicit in Nick Does Dylan. But, if so, there was almost certainly a universal statement of what was going on under my nose as well. There was, I realized, plenty of subtle change going on in Troop 1 that I'd barely made sense of. There were new expressions of attitude, like George's two-tone peroxide hairdo that made him look like an adolescent skunk, or Sam's new Gorgonlike Italian Afro. Elliot won the camp's Econ Guru award for outstanding work on the wildlife nature badges. The number of kids taller and considerably more buff than the dads was increasing at an alarming rate. And on the last night, when we had our second annual pig-out campfire to celebrate the end of camp, Dennis and I gave the kids congratulatory speeches and high-fived each other when we were done. Even we geezers had grown as pseudo leaders from the rank amateurs we were a year back.

One other inkling of changing times stuck with me. One afternoon, Ben and I went for a run. Without any prodding from me, he'd begun to work out a little, but I still figured that anything he could do physically I could do better. It was a hot day, and we both began with our shirts on but soon took them off. We started off running together at a moderate pace. About ten minutes into the run, he pulled a bit ahead of me, first a few paces, then several yards, then a good bit more. I decided to catch up, but his lead only increased until finally I could barely see him as he ran ahead, kicking up dust, leaving me, for the first time, far, far behind.

Year III

14: Eagles, Ordeals, and Other Transitions

Nick went back to school, and I never saw him again. But I thought of him often as Troop 1 resumed its kabuki-like routine, each event and season, it seemed, coming from some carefully choreographed script. If Scouting at its best is something reinvented by each troop in its own way, I began our third year of Scouting once again struck by the appeal of Troop 1's version of it. My first year of Scouting was all discovery. The second was mostly rejection. The third began with a renewed appreciation of something that I one day realized with a start was probably already beginning to play itself out, like another part of parenthood that ends before you know it.

Our first hike, after the fall canoe trip, was a District-wide camp-out in Sleepy Hollow along the Hudson. We hiked five miles, at one point getting a lecture from Dr. Flank on the aqueduct we were crossing, which was built in 1842 and brought the first water to New York City. We set up camp along with ten or twelve other troops on a grassy field along a glorious stretch of the Hudson. Dr. Flank, Mr. Toonkel, and Mr. Johnson seemed in particularly good spirits. They critiqued Dr. Flank's honey lime chicken with long-grain and wild rice and drank a covert glass of red wine to his health: "It's for medicinal purposes," Mr.

Toonkel said. "We've got to keep him going, because there's no way in hell either of us is going to run this thing."

The next morning there was a worship service. Attendance was voluntary, and just one adult, who led the service, and seven kids showed up. I was the only one from Troop 1 there, drawn more by curiosity than spiritual yearnings. In another time, or maybe in another part of the country, the service would have been a bigger part of the camp-out. Instead, we looked like a lonely fringe of a fringe as our little group gathered under a big oak tree.

"In this place of worship with thy beauty all around us in the sky, in the trees, in the earth, and in all thy creation, we praise thee and come to worship thee," began the leader, a heavy-set man who said he'd been doing this for twenty-four years. "Blessed art thou, O Lord, our God, who gives us each new day. Amen." We sang a hymn and "America the Beautiful." There was a reading from Exodus, and then a reading of the Scout Law, with a bit of commentary for each item ("... A Scout is helpful: The Good Samaritan showed the spirit of doing a good turn. A Scout is friendly: A real friend is one who remains loyal in victory and defeat. A Scout is courteous: Courtesy is the mark of a true gentleman. It is shown in thoughtful acts and kindly respect for everyone..."). After perhaps twenty minutes, the leader said, "May the Lord bless you and keep you. May the Lord make his face to shine upon you and be gracious unto you. May the Lord lift up his countenance upon you and grant you peace. The service is ended." It felt like a perfect version of B-P's church of the woods, at least as worthy and appealing in its traditionalism as Nick's campfire had been in its iconoclasm, and it seemed a shame so few kids had shown up.

Usually the camporees end with a closing ceremony, but this time the troops just attended to their own business and then drifted off to their soccer practices or homework or video games.

We lingered longer than all but one as the kids made breakfast and packed up and had a final review from Dr. Flank. Ben, Mark, and Jonah lugged their gear up a hill to the parking lot where we were parked and were loading it into my station wagon when Mr. Johnson came by. "I was watching the three of you, and I was really pleased with the way you conducted yourselves," he said. "The way you handled the hike, the way you took care of your cooking and cleaning up, the way you dealt with the other kids. It tells me you're ready for High Adventure. You all interested?" They all looked startled by the invitation, did their best to compose themselves and stammer some version of assent, and then chattered nonstop about it on the car ride home.

This was a very big deal. High Adventure was a week-long canoe trip in which the adult leaders and the most trusted older Scouts disappeared into the wilderness, where they might not see another person for a whole week. In our first year, High Adventure had been a distant, exotic experience reserved for high school kids living on some rarefied grown-up plane. In our second, it was a great temptation, still out of reach but something they'd heard enough about to really want to do. This year they could actually go, if chosen. The adult leaders picked three or four kids from Ben's grade—eighth—to join with about the same number of older ones and perhaps four adults for a trip to northern Quebec. Space was limited by the number of cars and the small size of the camping areas. And it was the one troop activity done on a by-invitation basis—the grown-ups figured that if they were going to spend a week in the wilderness with a bunch of fourteen- and fifteen-year-olds, the kids would have to be able to cook, take care of themselves, and avoid any behavior that would fit in a Tom Green or Adam Sandler movie.

Truth to tell, in terms of skills, Ben was not a Scout of Todd Davis-like proficiency. He was lazy about learning his knots and wasn't an inventive cook like Todd or Allen. But if being a good

Scout at its heart was a way to denote a good kid—someone who lived up to all those worthy, admirably behind-the-times values in the Scout Law—he could not have been much better. Ben had his failings. At times, he lapsed into the none-of-your-business, linguistic minimalism of adolescence in which every question about his companions was answered with "Just some kids," every question about what he was watching on TV elicited "Just a program," and the all-purpose answer to anything else was "Just some stuff." But, so far at least, he'd navigated the shoals of adolescence with remarkable equanimity and good humor. In my whole life, I'd never seen him utter an unkind or hurtful word to anyone. He worked as a caddy at a local golf course, volunteered at a local hospital and community center, and made excellent pizzas from scratch. He knew real-world things I did not, like the difference between a truss and a cantilever bridge or the history and design elements of the space shuttle. He was a serious kid who never took himself too seriously and took his cues from Dave Barry, Dilbert, and *Saturday Night Live* as well as from more straightforward texts. I wasn't sure how much Scouting helped mold Ben and how much it was just a good fit for the way he already was, but Scouting played to his best qualities. If I had been choosing kids to venture into the wilderness with, I'd have chosen him too.

Soon other transitions were in store. Ben became a Patrol Leader, a post rendered somewhat less auspicious by his patrol, which consisted of Mark, his assistant Patrol Leader, a few rookies, and lots of kids who were still on the troop roster but seldom showed up anymore. He'd dutifully call them up before every meeting and hike and still end up presiding over a skeleton crew. He reached the rank of Life, the level just below Eagle, and we spent a few Saturdays at merit-badge seminars at a nearby Mormon church, where kids from across the county took courses that helped them earn the badges required for Eagle.

It's a bit of a scam—in an afternoon kids can get credit for badges that could take weeks of work on their own. But just as there's grade inflation at Harvard, there's a measure of Eagle inflation in the B.S.A. And in the spring, Ben was the first one his age nominated by the other kids in the troop to join the Order of the Arrow, the Scouting honorary society, whose Indian iconography is one of the few explicit reminders of Seton's vision for Scouting. The OA was entirely separate from the advancement path from Tenderfoot to Eagle, and being chosen seemed something of a mixed blessing, since his welcome from the OA began with the cheery salutation, "Dear Ordeal Candidate. . . ."

As we soon learned, to join Ben had go through an overnight "Ordeal," or series of tests, so secret that God would strike me dead if I mentioned any of them here. I drove him up to Clear Lake on a chilly Friday night, figuring that liability law being what it is, the ordeal couldn't be too perilous. But it still felt both alarming and momentous to drop him off, like Abraham taking Isaac to be sacrificed to the Scouting Gods. The last thing I wanted to do was spend the night in the woods without a tent, the one thing we did know he'd have to do. But so far we'd done almost everything together in Scouting. I felt a little diminished, being relegated to mere chauffeur rather than participant. We parked in the lot and picked our way in the dark toward the ranger station, where we spotted Lester's sidekick Igor, who was in some supervisory role. He motioned for Ben to come with him, and Ben trotted off eagerly with a quick farewell and not even a glance back. The ride back seemed a lot longer than the drive up. I spent the next day wondering how he was doing, but when I came up to get him Sunday morning, he was beaming and wearing his white OA sash with a red arrow on it. He chattered all the way back, with requisite discretion where state secrets were involved, about the weekend. Highlights, he said, included something having to do with an orange and an egg;

a fair degree of slave labor; and Ted Watson, the too-serious genius from camp, in full Indian regalia offering assorted OA chants, incantations, and other, mostly indecipherable, mumbo jumbo. It sounded like a junior version of the Loyal Order of the Moose, the Knights of Pythias, or the other fraternal organizations going extinct before our eyes, but it allowed Ben to go someplace new and exciting totally on his own and join a group that he, not we, had chosen.

The troop had a transition too—at least one on paper—that was forced by the competing views of the gay controversy. Troop 1 had been chartered over the years by churches, the American Legion, and its own parents' association. For the last several years, it had been chartered by the Roaring Brook School. But since the ban on homosexuals violated the school district's anti-discrimination policy, Dr. Flank quietly changed the chartering back to Chappaqua Troop 1 Parents' Association, at the same time making it clear the troop did not discriminate. In his letter to the local council announcing the change, Dr. Flank added: "It should be noted that Chappaqua Troop 1 has not, and does not, discriminate against any boy or adult on the basis of race, color, creed, national origin, religion, economic status, citizenship or sexual orientation, in accordance with the laws and policies of our State and community." He was taking something of a risk. Seven Cub Scout Packs in Illinois had been disbanded for saying they would accept gays as leaders. But the local council had no interest in losing a venerable, reliable, and generous troop, so the odds were pretty good nothing would happen. In fact, without backing away publicly, the B.S.A. has signaled that it was clearly not in a mood for its own civil war. The giant Greater New York Council had adopted a policy simply saying: "Prejudice, intolerance and discrimination in any form are unacceptable." And indeed, Dr. Flank never heard a word. Unless it was prepared to see its all-important membership numbers fall off a cliff, the national B.S.A. would have to stick to its philosophical statement without going overboard in enforcing it. Dr. Flank orchestrated the move quietly and efficiently. When it looked like there might be discussion at a school board meeting of the Scouts' use of the school, he asked a bunch of us to attend as a show of support. A half dozen dads sat through an interminable meeting. The issue never came up, but we felt as if we'd contributed through our silent witness.

Certification issue aside, the year progressed at its usual leisurely pace. Once a month, the patrol leaders and other boys in leadership positions met at a different Scout's house at what was called the Green Bar meeting to come up with an agenda for the regular weekly meetings held every Wednesday night. It could be a talk and demonstration tied to some upcoming event (canoeing technique, hiking gear, avoiding hypothermia while skiing). It could be a matter of fundamental Scout training and advancement (first aid, knots, avoiding hypothermia while winter camping). Or it could be a thinly disguised way to kill time (Trivial Pursuit, dodge ball, avoiding hypothermia while playing dodge ball).

One weekly meeting, for example, was organized as a cooking free-for-all. The kids all brought their stoves, set up shop in the parking lot outside the school, and made muffins and stews, pizzas and goulash, chicken stir fry and flaming brownies, which they all shared with each other. Todd made a chicken-and-rice concoction with ginger sauce and then prepared some cinnamon rolls with vanilla frosting for dessert. Allen, the heir apparent as troop master chef, made macaroni and rice and lentils in a vodka-marinated tomato sauce. They shared cooking and culinary wisdom ("Yo, dude. The good thing is if there's too much stew or broccoli you just throw it in the woods. It's biodegradable.")

and exchanged greetings heard nowhere else in their peer group ("So Blitz, how fares the quiche?"). We began at dusk and finished well after dark, and everyone went home fat and happy.

The grandest meetings were the three Courts of Honor, meetings of the kids and their families, where merit badges were given out, advancement was noted, and, in the grandest Courts of Honor of all, Eagles were awarded. As with nearly everything Troop 1 did, there was a time-tested model for each of the three Courts of Honor. The first one, in the fall, featured huge hero sandwiches plus salads and covered dishes brought by each family in the troop. Bob Walker, from the Westchester–Putnam Friends of Scouting, gave an impassioned spiel for contributions. The second, in the winter, was just dessert, fewer badges were awarded, and Bob Walker got the night off. The third, in the spring, featured a gala outdoor hot-dog and hamburger barbecue plus salads and covered dishes brought by each family in the troop; Bob Walker gave his impassioned spiel for contributions.

At the spring Court of Honor this year, Jimmy, the World's Biggest Scout, was getting his Eagle. It's not clear just how much making Eagle means in the world at large—almost certainly less than it did when Scouting was more central to community life. Certainly in the enlightened corridors of liberal America, attaining Eagle may be seen more as a sign of retrograde dweebdom than having the right stuff. But within Scouting, and in the less haughty corners of the country, Eagle still has a mythic, almost totemic power as something that people take with them through life. Eagles, as they will be quick to tell you, are Eagles for life (adults aren't former Eagle Scouts, they're Eagle Scouts). The requirements have changed a little over time. Now you have to have been a Life Scout, the rank below Eagle, for six months. You have to earn twenty-one merit badges, including the mandatory badges of first aid, citizenship in the community, citizenship in the nation, citizenship in the world, communications, personal fitness, emergency prepared-ness or lifesaving, environmental science, personal management, swimming or hiking or cycling, camping, and family life. Troop 1 over its eighty-eight years had produced sixty-six Eagles, be-ginning with Andrew W. Maxwell in 1936, so each one was a big deal. After Dr. Flank opened the Eagle part of the evening, the candidate, Jimmy, was escorted to the front by the current Eagles in the troop and by some recent alumni, who were in town or came in for the occasion. "Awarding the Eagle is an im-portant and serious matter," Dr. Flank read in a voice denoting importance and seriousness. "The Eagle is the highest and most coveted award in all of Scouting. If, at this point, Scouting has not achieved its purpose in the building of character—in the training for leadership—in the practice of service—then it probably never shall."

The Eagles at the front of the room then read the obligations that came along with making Eagle. Todd Davis began: "The first responsibility of an Eagle Scout is to live with honor, which to an Eagle is sacred. Honor is the foundation of character—character is what a man really is, down inside, not what some-one else may think he is. An Eagle will live so as to reflect credit upon his home, religious institution, school, friends, upon Scouting and upon himself." Then it was Jack's turn: "The sec-ond obligation of an Eagle Scout is loyalty," read Jack, whose er-rant tarp ball throw had left Ben with the purple eye at camp. "Without loyalty, all character lacks a sense of purpose and di-rection. An Eagle is loyal to his ideals and his values." Rich, my raftmate from the soggy canoe trip, was on hand and read next: "The third obligation of an Eagle Scout is courage. Courage gives character all its force and strength. Trusting in a Supreme Power, and with faith in his fellow beings, the Eagle Scout faces each day unafraid, and seeks his share of the world's work to do." Bob Heller read the last part: "The final obligation of an

Eagle is service. He extends a helping hand to those who toil upward along the Eagle trail he has now completed, just as others helped him in his achievement of the Eagle rank. The habit of the daily Good Turn must take on new meaning and blossom forth into a life of service. The Eagle protects and defends the weak and the helpless. He aids and comforts the oppressed and the unfortunate. He upholds the rights of others while defending his own rights. His code of honor is based upon the belief that real leadership must be founded upon real service."

Then Dr. Flank asked Jimmy to raise his hand in the Scout sign and repeat the Eagle Pledge: "I, Jimmy Francis, believe in the Boy Scouts of America as a movement which has as its aim and purpose character building and citizenship training. I believe it to be a movement that helps a Scout become master of his own powers, helps him get along with other people and helps him find a worthy use for his powers. I, therefore, believe it is my duty to do my best to obey the Scout Oath and Law. I hereby renew my faith in Scouting and promise to do what I can in service to other Scouts who have not come this far along the Eagle trail."

Dr. Flank shook his hand and gave him his Eagle pin, making Jimmy Troop 1's sixty-seventh Eagle, and we all responded with a properly honorable ovation. Most oaths are a little creepy to the modern ear, reeking of lockstep conformity or robotic obedience. When Jimmy was reading his, my mind flashed fleetingly to Michael Corleone at his nephew's christening at the end of *The Godfather* as he piously proclaimed his obedience to the dictates of the Church ("Do you renounce Satan?" "I do renounce him." "And all his works?" "I do renounce them.") while his minions methodically massacred all his enemies. Jimmy didn't seem the massacring kind—though he was big enough to do it himself if the mood struck. And it was hard not to be impressed by the lofty seriousness of it all. When else are kids challenged in quite the same archaically chivalric tones? Paul Fussell once wrote a lovely, admiring essay on the Boy Scout Handbook, calling it, in the end, essentially "a compendium of good sense. . . . Indeed, this handbook is among the very few remaining popular repositories of something like classical ethics, deriving from Aristotle and Cicero." I'm not sure if the ceremony felt quite Aristotelian or Ciceronian, but its choice of values—honor, loyalty, courage, and service—seemed impeccable for a convocation of twelve- to fifteen-year-old boys, and in the end it felt pretty much the way Fussell saw the Handbook—psychologically and ethically on target in a culture woefully short of compendia of good sense.

A few weeks later we returned for a camp-out to Clear Lake, where we had hiked past the old coal-mining railroad the previous year. No one made a big deal of it, but it was a special occasion—Todd Davis's last hike. He was graduating from high school in June and planning to attend Cornell. But he had his prom or some such thing on the date of the overnight canoe trip that always ends the Scouting year, so this figured to be his last outing with the troop. And it wasn't just Todd that was leaving. He was the third of three brothers who had made Eagle. His mother had helped organize every Court of Honor for as long as anyone could remember. It was hard to think back on a time when Troop 1 didn't have one of the amazing Davis brothers in the thick of things. Back in A. Lewis Oswald's heyday in Kansas he could assume an eternal crop of new Scouts, one following another in the Great Game. That was then. As we began the hike, Fly Guy, who had a daughter finishing her junior year in high school, was walking along with Todd, quizzing him on our generation's version of the Great Game, getting into college. Where had he visited? When had he started? Who was his counselor? How involved was she? What did he think of Hopkins or Penn or Dartmouth? Even in the woods, it was hard to avoid the real world kids inhabited. And while there were, no doubt, plenty of kids as remarkable as the Davis brothers out there, it was no longer certain that many of them were headed for the Boy Scouts.

When we reached our campsite, the kids set up their tents and then hiked down to the lake, where Fly Guy was going to give one of his fly-fishing exhibitions. Todd and Mr. Johnson and I stayed in camp. The afternoon sun was just beginning its descent as we sat on a huge slab of granite facing west. I asked Todd where he thought Scouting was headed. He wasn't too optimistic, less because of any gripes with Scouting than because of the dictates of suburban life. "The young ones start at such an early age now," he said. "What do the Tiger Cubs start at? Six? Seven? Maybe the B.S.A. feels like it's got to compete for the kids' attention, but the little kids spend all that time making paper, or whatever they do, they're burned out before they get to camp or do their Wilderness Survival merit badge. We had a peak back in the '70s, I think, and, honestly, I don't see us getting back to it anytime soon, or maybe at all. Kids just do so much. And I include myself. I started private music lessons after the first grade. Kids used to do that in the fourth grade. They start music and sports and everything so early. I do too much too, but I always knew Scouting was going to be part of my life. Most kids aren't that way."

The troop was coming back, and a bunch of them joined us on the rock. We sat in the sun, talking about the hike, Mark's new tent, Todd's ability to cook anything on an outback oven, Leatherman versus Swiss army knife. The day felt long and slow, like the ones I remembered when we played ball all day and hoped no one's mother called him in for dinner so we could keep playing till dark. After a half hour or so, Ben and his friends began drifting off. Todd grabbed his one-man tent and ventured out into the undergrowth, far from everyone else, to set up his tent, alone.

15: Summer Camp 3: Going for the Gold

Maybe it's just paternal pride, but I'd like to think our one brief, dazzling, totally unexpected, semimiraculous eleventh-hour ascent into Scouting Greatness began with Ben's Deucer Improvement and Beautification Project.

There were plenty of reasons not to sign up for a third tour of duty at Camp Waubeeka. I viewed Year One as a mandatory part of my recruitment contract, sort of like a tour of Nam that you couldn't get out of. I signed up for Year Two before I decided I would rather have stayed home, and then enjoyed it anyway. But Year Three was different. I didn't have to go, and I had plenty of time to get out of it if I chose to. And, after two years, I had pretty much done Scout camp. I was a little old to make Eagle. What was the point?

But, in the end, I signed up for a simple reason. I did it because I wanted to—for me, not for Ben. There's no way in the world I could have anticipated that when I ventured into the world of Troop 1 three years earlier. But I did it because the week in the woods with no fax, no e-mail, no phone, no communication with home or office was the most relaxed I got all year. I did it because I treasured the time with Ben and, despite all logic, found the whole ragged lot of kids more likable than not. I did it because I liked arguing with Lester, listening to Igor play his harmonica, seeing the Mohawks on the Bellmore kids, hearing the echoes off the lake during the campfires. I would have felt something missing from my summer if I hadn't been able to check in at Chez Wolfjaw for the week. And I did it because, in the subliminal way we get invested in things without quite knowing it, I liked being a part of the troop and its rhythms, and I was happy to be thought of as part of the reliable corps of Troop 1 Volunteer Regular Irregulars.

As usual, the cast of characters was both old and new. Harry was long since gone from the troop, pining for Scoutdom while his kids sailed blithely through their youth as far from Baden-Powell as they could get. Eric was doing only the first week, so Dennis didn't make it either. Instead, I was to be joined by the all-Italian tag team of Vince Farrentino and Robert Lombardi, the fathers of Sam and Mark, whom I had met back at my first Scout outing at the Paul Bunyan Camporee. This was fine with me. The two were among my favorite dads in the troop and seemed to present an appealing contrast. Vince, I assumed, could play tough guy, and Robert was reputed to be a good cook, no small attribute in the woods. And it meant something else. Since neither of them had been there before, I was, by default, the senior dad, Scouting veteran, and experienced leader. Once Dr. Flank left after completing the first week, the Troop 1 Scoutmaster for the week was—of all people—*moi*.

We met at Vince's house at seven on a cool, clear July morning, gassed up, and took off, Vince and Robert in Robert's pale blue Volvo station wagon and me in my black one. We arrived to find Dr. Flank and the rest of our troop awaiting our arrival.

It soon became apparent the previous week had not been the troop's best week ever. I shrewdly figured this out when everyone gave me the same evasive answer when I asked how the week had gone.

"I'll tell you later," said Fly Guy, so the kids wouldn't hear what he had to say.

"I'll tell you later," said Ben, so as not to be seen consorting with the enemy.

"I'll tell you later," said Dr. Flank, like 007 waiting for the right moment to brief 008.

In truth, I learned, it hadn't been all that atypical a week. Many merit badges were earned. Many vegetables were thrown into the woods rather than cooked. One patrol, in the interest of minimizing KP duties, had set a record for doing the least possible cooking per pound of food meted out. Sam 'n Eric had sung "Scout Socks" at all hours of the night. Dr. Flank and Fly Guy had logged countless hours fishing on the Waubeeka Lake, with the Fisherman of the Week Award going to Fly Guy for his eighteen-inch bass.

That said, the week had not done much to rebut our reputation as Scouting's answer to *Animal House*. Thanks to the helpful and courteous efforts of a Scout from another troop, who was a CIT and thus able to go into town without adults around, six Scouts spent the better part of the first week amassing quite a little weapons cache. This consisted of two blow guns with four-inch-long hypodermic needles that you shot through a foot-long black steel canister, three butane lighters, two butterfly knives, and one lock-back knife, each item capable of keeping squadrons of personal injury lawyers employed for the rest of the decade. Some of the weapons purchasers, wanting to be sure their investments did not go to waste, decided to try out the knives on one of the tarps at the campsite, slicing it neatly like a side of flank steak. This was a very bad idea. It said right in the 2001 Troop Leaders Guide, "Every Scout and every Adult Leader must know that deliberate damage to camp property may result in the person or persons responsible being immediately sent home without return of fee in part or whole." The "may result" left us an out—barely—in terms of expulsion, but Dr. Flank was furious when he found out what had happened, his wrath extending to the innocent as well as the guilty. He confiscated the weapons and made it clear that this offense went way over the line.

There were those at camp, Lester among then, who felt the offenders should have been summarily dismissed, rather than reprimanded and disarmed. But the truth was that if every transgressor were removed from camp, it would turn into a pretty quiet place. So all guilty parties got to stay, but with the knowledge that they had screwed up big time and would sin again at their peril.

Still, despite the fallout from the weapons of mass destruction, it didn't take us long to get into the swing of things. First we drove down to Lake Luzerne, where we dined at our usual eatery, a riverfront restaurant and milk bottle museum, which had mannequin cows in their crisp aprons perched out front to greet us. Then we roamed the streets like a feral band of mall-deprived shoppers, ducking in and out of the Luzerne Market and the local drugstore scooping up junk-food necessities, particularly twelve-packs of Cokes, Sprites, and root beer.

Then we all rendezvoused at the Hudson River Rafting Company for 3.5 miles of rafting on the Sacandaga River. We divided up into three rafts, with eight of us in each raft and Dr. Flank kayaking down behind us wearing a yellow helmet that made him look like some kind of E.T.-like watery alien. Our guide was a young woman with sundry body piercings who was a student at a local college, and the older kids, in particular, clearly liked having this exotic woman, just a few years older than they were, as their guide. The day had stayed cool and the skies had turned overcast. My main goal was to stay dry, something I accomplished just barely by sternly invoking the wallet-and-keys defense ("I can't get in the water. I have my wallet and keys in my pocket"—even though I had left them in Fly Guy's van) while almost everyone jumped or was dragged into the river. It's hard not to enjoy tubing down Class 2 and Class 3 rapids, but I was still half in work mode, my brain stewing over one or another minicrisis from the previous week, so I felt more like observer than participant.

After the trip ended we had nothing to do until dinner, so we just hung out in the parking lot of the outfitter's building. George and Tom threw a tennis ball back and forth. Ben, Mark, and Jonah wandered down by the river. Dr. Flank spent at least a half hour counseling Hal, who was upset because some of the other kids had teased him. Mr. Farrentino and Mr. Lombardi sat on the tailgate of a station wagon talking with some of the kids about the last week's events. It evoked summer at its indolent best, and as I sat there, listening to Doug's analysis of the latest developments in the Starcraft cosmology, I could feel my metabolism reverting to its Waubeeka mean. Finally, we headed out in the general direction of Warrensburg, a motley jumble of roadside commerce, where we got to choose between a generic diner, Gino's Pizzeria, and the Dragon Lee Chinese Restaurant. After dinner, most of the first-week dads and the kids who were returning with them headed south for home, and the rest of us headed back to Waubeeka.

It was eerily quiet. One set of troops leaves Saturday morning and the next arrives Sunday afternoon, so Saturday night is the interregnum between the different weeks of camp. The staff gets the night off. There are no activities. The waterfront and commissary are closed. There's no evening retreat, no blasts from the rifle range, no bugler to play "Taps." Wolfjaw was utterly unchanged. The only unfamiliar item was a letter posted on the bulletin board, red ink on lined notebook paper:

> Dear The Members of Chappaqua Troop 1, We would like to express our sincerest apologies for the embarrassment which was caused by the damage caused to the tarp at one of the patrol cooksites. The responsible parties will gladly pay for the replacement of the tarp and participate gladly in the hanging of a new tarp. We hope you accept our apologies and not hold a grudge. We hope that together we can put this incident behind us.
>
> Regretfully,
>
> Wolfjaw 3 and
>
> other responsible parties.

Dr. Flank was staying overnight, so he still had the lean-to. I ended up, Todd Davis-style, in the most distant tent, situated between Wolfjaw and the nearby Polaris site in what I liked to think of as suburban Wolfjaw. About a half dozen of us, including Ben, Doug, George, Mark, and Jonah, played cards—hearts, spades, an Italian card game called Scopa—for hours on the upstairs picnic table by the light of Dr. Flank's Coleman lantern before we went to bed.

The next morning we had our annual all-foods-known-to-man breakfast at Buckskin and prepared to do our laundry in the small town of Bolton Landing. It was then that deucer lightning struck. All in all, Ben's leadership record thus far had been spotty. He had done his best with his skeleton patrol, but there usually weren't enough kids to make it a real test of leadership. So when he and Jonah were made Patrol Leaders for Week 2 of camp, with Allen, our master chef, as the Senior Patrol Leader, he was determined to take his duties seriously. That very morning he decided to go ahead with his first major management initiative—a fundraising campaign to create an endowment for air fresheners and bug strips for the deucer. He hit up each of the kids for a few dollars, and then went to the adults as well.

"Mr. Farrentino, Mr. Lombardi, have you visited the latrine during your short stay at camp?" he asked.

Indeed they had.

"Did you like what you smelled?"

No, come to think of it, they were less than enchanted by the aromas wafting through the deucer.

"Well, wouldn't you like to replace that horrific stench with a nicer fragrance? Gentlemen, I'm here today to tell you that with a small donation of one or two dollars to the Deucer Beautification Project you can make that dream a reality. Your donation will go toward the purchase of air fresheners and fly traps for the latrine. So, what do you say?"

Needless to say, they were glad to contribute. By the time his fundraising was completed, Ben had $15. He made his purchases at the supermarket in Bolton Landing and installed them immediately upon our return. The change sent shock waves through Wolfjaw. Sam himself was soon seen striding manfully from the latrine, hollering words never before spoken at Camp Read and probably never before spoken on the planet.

"Yo, guys. Have you been in the deucer? It smells awesome."

Campers came up to Ben to congratulate him on his achievement.

"Hey, Ben. Nice job on the crapper."

"Your tax dollars at work," he modestly replied.

At the same time, Allen was hatching plans of his own. Mr. Lombardi, who was never really off duty as a teacher, sat down with him to ask him what his goals were for the week as SPL.

"Well, I'd like to win the Waubeeka Award," he said.

This was a truly novel thought, on the order of a declaration that he'd like to grow a second head or have everyone spend the week speaking Russian and doing campfire skits based on

Dostoyevsky novels. We had finished dead last among the troops in attendance the previous week. Troop 1 was totally absent from the many signed W's that adorned the Scout office in honor of previous Waubeeka Award honorees. No one could remember Troop 1 ever winning the award. Instead, we took pride in our status as The Troop Least Likely to Win the Waubeeka Award.

Still, the idea had some appeal. For leaders Allen, Ben, and Jonah, it seemed the kind of challenge that Scouting, even Troop 1's version of it, was supposed to be about. About half the kids were perfectly happy to go along with whatever the troop agenda was going to be. And even some of the more contrary ones—still smarting from Dr. Flank's weapons confiscation—saw a reason to buy in. Dr. Flank was leaving early Monday, and winning the award when the troop's official authority figure wasn't around would be like getting good grades but managing to piss your parents off at the same time. It was a way to be trustworthy, loyal, helpful, and all that, but something of a wise guy as well. And before long, as if a benign computer virus had wormed its way into every camper's mental hard drive, Troop 1 had achieved a rare degree of unanimity. We had decided to go for the Gold.

Of course, no one knew quite how one went for the Gold, but we started where we could. A big part of the score came from the daily troop inspection report, the document that tallied how well we did at cleaning the site, putting all tools and supplies in their proper place, and showing up more or less respectably attired at the retreat each evening. We bustled around Monday morning cleaning the site in anticipation of the daily inspection, and all the kids showed up at retreat that evening in their Scout shirts and the closest things to khaki shorts they could come up with. Sure enough, after the prior week's daily scores in the mid-to-low 20s (it's hard to get less without incurring fatalities or engendering widespread intestinal distress), we scored an encouraging 34 of 36—not the perfect scores of Bronxville 4 and Scarsdale 2, but pretty damn good. The next day we corrected Monday's shortcomings—saws improperly stowed in the axe yard and water cans for fires improperly placed at the tents instead of a central area—and lo and behold, we scored a perfect 36, which set off a round of high-fives at retreat. In addition, Allen tied the fastest timber hitch knot in the evening Scouting Challenge. The next day we scored 36 again, putting us, according to reliable sources, in the lead after three days.

Having tiptoed toward competence, we felt emboldened to do more. Robert, in a fit of enterprise that deserved a Waubeeka Award on its own, had masterminded a service project that saw the kids construct a majestic WOLFJAW sign out of two long tree limbs and twenty-three beech logs lashed together to spell out the name of the campsite. The kids sawed the logs to size and tied them together with taut square lashing, proving that the knots and lashing can really be used after all. The complete assemblage was hoisted ten feet high above the entrance to the camp, making use of a ladder the kids had made as a side project, and it will no doubt stand for years to come as a monument to Troop 1's enterprise and grit.

While this competition was playing out, a second was also beginning, a new event called the Scoutmaster's Challenge. We Scoutmasters were to undergo a grueling series of challenges designed to test what was described as our mental, physical, and spiritual capabilities as mentors to America's youth. Well, maybe grueling was going a bit far. What we had to do was find the answer to five trivia questions about Camp Waubeeka—things like how many working rifles are there at the rifle range? (10); How many camp staff members have worked at the econ lab? (4); Who is Waubeeka's Waterfront Director? (Nicole Wicks). Then we had to come up with a new camp cheer and compete in a boccilike game using rocks instead of balls to see who could throw the rock closest to a line of rope without going past it. I got most of the answers from Warren, the same CIT who had sold the weapons during Week 1 and was around when the staff came up with the questions. Allen, the SPL, came up with the cheer, which he said was to the tune of the horrid pop song "Lady Marmelade," though you could have fooled me. It went like this:

Hey-beeka, Ho-Beeka. Waubeeka.
Hey-beeka, Ho-Beeka, Probeeka.
Waubeeka. Probeeka.
WAUBEEKA!

It wasn't "The Love Song of J. Alfred Prufrock," but it wasn't any worse than the lyrics to "Lady Marmelade," whatever they were supposed to mean. We had to throw the rocks ourselves. OK, it was neither the Ironman Challenge nor a Mensa exam, but Vince, Robert, and I all competed for the Greater Glory of Troop 1.

Still, we were a mere sideshow. It wasn't as if the Waubeeka Award competition sucked up everyone's attention. Kids continued to pile up merit badges. George and Hal, two kids the same size and age who had turned into a dysfunctional couple, whined and wheedled and fought with each other all week over who had taken out more wood, or made more food pickups, or had started better fires. Sometimes Herb chimed in to add to the cacophony. We took a trip to the Zip Line, the trolley over the water at the Buckskin Lake, where even I got in the water. Upstairs at the campsite Doug was constantly organizing card games, which were augmented by a Scrabble game Mr. Lombardi contributed to the cause. In The Underworld, life was a little quieter because Sam decided it would be sacrilegious to do "Scout Socks" without Eric, so he retired the song for the week.

The deucer continued to serve as an inspiration to latrine management experts around the globe. And Ben and Allen, in a heartwarming tribute to Ben's southern roots, came up with a new camp delicacy: gourmet grits. They got up as early as 6:00 A.M. to have the proper time to do the cooking just so. First they cooked up a pot of grits. Then they added garlic, onions, grated sharp cheddar cheese, and salt and pepper. Voilà! Super Grits strong enough to give your fillings a cheesy radioactive glow. You wouldn't want to start every day that way, but, to be perfectly honest, it was pretty damn good.

Maybe it was because the kids were older and there were fewer discipline issues, but as the week wore on, the dads felt less and less like authority figures and more and more like fellow travelers. Ben would be found sitting in one of the deluxe camp chairs with footrest, backrest, armrest, pillow, and drink holder, directing cleanup by offering Cokes and Sprites as rewards for undesirable tasks. Tom, now fourteen going on twenty-one, was constantly disappearing and hanging out with the staff, particularly the female members. Warren, the weapons dealer from Week 1, joined us every day for lunch in The Underworld, his past sins long since forgotten. Doug prowled around for card partners or soulmates to ponder the mysteries of Starcraft. Kids pored through Campmor catalogs, compiled merit badge notebooks full of leaf or tree drawings, and debated which sleeping bags would be best to have if you found yourself atop Mount Everest. Mark came up with more Seinfeldian questions ("If manatees are the cows of the sea, how come you can't tip them?"). Jonah had developed into an assertive leader with a touch of Todd Davis's cockiness. Even Sam took on the slightly unsettling quality of a respected elder statesman, perhaps humbled by the burdens of leading his faction without Eric. He spent much of his time, like a pilgrim anticipating life in the Promised Land, contemplating a new and loftier existence next year at Staff City. At one point, he shocked the world by expressing interest in attending MIT.

Vince and Robert added their own distinctive touches. Both were born in hill towns in southern Italy, Vince in Muro Lucano,

Robert in Campobasso, and moved to the United States when they were about eight, so they shared not only a similar life story, but the same Italian dialect. And as the week went on, they increasingly found themselves conversing in Italian, which gave our campsite the feel of a commedia dell'arte version of a Boy Scout outing:

ROBERT: Chi è il direttore delle frecce?
VINCE: Non lo so ma penso che si chiama Chris. È l'unico là in ogni caso. È come in Italia—ognuno ha il titolo. Professore, Direttore, Commendatore.
ROBERT: Come gli Italiani, i Boy Socuts amano la burocrazia.

(Who is the archery director?
I don't know. I think it might be Chris. He is the only one there anyway. It's like Italy, everyone has a title: professor, director, commander.
Like Italians, the Boy Scouts like bureaucracy.)

Another morning, they were watching as a new cooking regimen at the upstairs campsite didn't seem to be any more efficient than the old one it replaced:

ROBERT: A che punto stanno con la colazione?
VINCE: Molto meglio. Si sono svegliati più presto stamattina.
ROBERT: Ma ancora non hanno cucinato...
VINCE: Forse era meglio quando era peggio!

(How is breakfast going?
Much better. They woke up earlier today to get things started.
But they still haven't cooked...
Maybe it was better when it was worse.)

By Thursday, the Waubeeka competition was mixing the thrill of victory with the agony of defeat. We suffered a severe setback that day when Steve, the camp commissioner, reported that we had fallen short on inspection. In a fateful twist worthy of Greek tragedy, someone had left the deucer lid up, losing points for cleanliness. It would be just our luck to lose on a deucer technicality after the greatest advances in latrine hygiene in Waubeeka history.

That unexpected setback was particularly worrisome because we'd suffered an even more costly one the day before. We'd had five kids, Sam among them, complete the mile swim—about half the total who completed it in the whole camp—as a way to pile up more Waubeeka points. But as virtuous and impressive as the mile swim no doubt was, we were belatedly informed it did not count toward the Waubeeka Award. Suddenly, fifty points we'd thought were ours had just evaporated. Maybe we just weren't destined to escape our fate.

After retreat that night came the next big event, the staff hunt, where campers had to round up staff members hiding across the vast reaches of Waubeeka. Ben and Mark had prepared for the event by coming up with a precise plan for how to deploy our forces. Unfortunately, they had never got around to actually conveying it to the rest of the troop, so the kids tore off willy-nilly in search of staff members, who were accorded points based on their importance or notoriety and brought once apprehended to the waterfront for summary dunkings. Vince, Robert, and I scurried over to the waterfront to see the warriors return with their spoils.

First came two Bronxville 4 kids with Stanty. Then some little Mohawk kids with Bonnie, the femme fatale from the econ lodge. Some Rye 2 kids showed up with Dolan, one of the lords of Scoutcraft, and then a Scarsdale kid brought grumpy Ted Watson. *Where were we? This was turning into a disaster!* Finally,

Tom showed up with some twit from handicrafts, worth maybe five points, but others, returning to their old desultory form, were wandering back to the waterfront empty-handed before the hunt was even over. *What were they thinking? The hunt was still on! Get back out there, you yo-yos!* Meanwhile, Bronxville had scored an incredible coup—they had bagged Tom Logan, back again as the camp director, which meant fifty points, more than a whole day's worth of deucer cleaning and monster box maintenance.

We felt like we were watching our chances for Waubeeka immortality leech away. Someone clanged the bell at the top of the waterfront watchtower, signaling the end of the hunt, and we glumly headed back toward Wolfjaw.

"Bummer, man," I said.

"Che sfortuna," Vince muttered in Italian.

"Peccato," Robert said in agreement.

And then down the road we saw a sight so startling that at first it seemed an apparition. Sam and Jonah were toddling along next to Steve Silvers, the camp commissioner, like Peter triumphantly bringing home the wolf at the end of *Peter and the Wolf.* Of course! The bell meant the game was over, but it took kids as long as ten minutes to make it back to the waterfront with the staff members they had already caught. *Fifty points. We're still alive!*

Friday, the day that would decide our fate, dawned bright and clear. There were two big events left, the water carnival and the final campfire, and we knew we needed to do well in both. Using my executive powers as acting faux Scoutmaster, I quietly decreed a third event, our now-traditional last-night troop campfire. I mentioned the plan to Robert and Vince (and Ben, who seemed like a quasi adult by this point) and then sneaked out of camp late in the morning to shop for graham crackers, Hershey's chocolate, and marshmallows for s'mores, along with Cokes, Sprites, pretzel rods, and other sources of excess salt and empty calories. I stowed the stuff at the commissary and walked next door to the camp office, where I saw Steve Silvers and asked how we were doing in the competition.

He hesitated for just a moment.

"I can't tell you too much," he said, "but if you kick butt in the water carnival you'll be in great shape."

Yesss!!

"Who else is up there?"

"Bronxville and Scarsdale."

I rushed back to the site, where the kids, of course, had the same information I did only in more detail. At the appointed hour, we all trooped over to the waterfront. There were a few kids from Rye. An enormous gaggle of macho Bellmore Mohawks showed up, which was fine, because they had assumed the mantle of Troop Least Likely to Win the Waubeeka Award and thus posed no threat. Then a contingent showed up from the troop from Glen Cove, Long Island. We waited. And waited some more. It seemed hard to believe our luck could be this good, but Bronxville and Scarsdale had not shown up! Lester sometimes made a point of stressing troop activities over competitions or badges, but whatever the reason for his totally unexpected absence, all we had to do was win a few awards and we were all but in.

Sure enough, like clockwork, we won the first award, the T-Boat Rescue, which consisted of one kid swamping a canoe, two more canoeing out to him and righting his canoe and emptying out its water, and then the first kid rowing back. Next came three challenges: diving and making the biggest splash, diving and making the smallest splash, and best belly flop. We lost the first. We lost the second. We looked to Sam, our obvious candidate for the belly flop.

"I don't know, guys," he said nervously like a rookie paratrooper contemplating his first jump. "I'm worried about hurting my balls."

I stepped forward.

"We need you this time, big guy," I said. "Even if it means a little . . . discomfort, you've got to take one for the troop."

He looked me straight in the eyes, and nodded almost imperceptibly. Then he took off his shirt, flung it behind him, and strode toward the dock, where he proceeded to displace half the lake with a full frontal, zero gainer, zero tuck, classic belly flop. We figured that we were golden until Steve announced, "For the last event we'll need one of your smaller kids."

Last event? Already? The water carnival other years had featured eight or ten events. Just our luck that the one year we were in shape to clean up, the whole thing consisted of only five. Which meant, after the Mohawks had won the previous event, a totally lame exercise that involved blowing a ping-pong ball back and forth the width of the shallow area of the waterfront, we still didn't know who was ahead.

We went into the evening tense but ready. We got a perfect score at our final retreat. We signed up for the maximum two skits. It was now in the hands of the Big Scout in the Sky.

The campfire started late, because we had to wait until it was totally dark to begin. It soon became clear why. As we entered we saw a canoe containing two mock Indians in buckskins and headdresses gliding across the lake, where they lit a big yellow *W* that had been carefully placed for the evening in the shallow water. Two other Indians, faces stern, arms folded, stood on the banks. They lit two enormous bonfires, and the campfire began. First an Order of the Arrow ceremony, the excuse for all the Indian costumes, welcomed six new potential inductees who had been selected to be ordeal candidates. They were applauded by the troops and then led off into the woods, where presumably their skin was cut with rusty kitchen knives for a fraternal blood oath. Then we did the Waubeeka cheer with the "CAMP, CAMP, CAMP," providing a particularly resonant echo off the lake. Gussie, Lester's SPL, who happened to be one of the few black kids at camp, led everyone in the Waubeeka fight song. Many skits were performed and songs sung.

Finally, Steve called for everyone's attention. "I've got two last special announcements," he said. The kids suddenly became absolutely quiet. "First, I want to award the Scoutmaster Challenge to the Scoutmaster who has excelled in the moral, mental, and physical competitions over the past week."

He looked around the amphitheater to drag the moment out. A whisper of breeze blew off the lake. Then he said, "The winner is . . . Peter Applebome of Troop 1 Chappaqua."

If there had been voting booths, they should have been impounded. If there had been punch cards, someone needed to check all the dimpled, pregnant, and hanging chads. Of all the awards in the world I was not qualified to win—a very long list—the Scoutmaster's Challenge would have ranked near the top. Truth to tell, even in our little band, Robert was definitely the best teacher and motivator. But, on the other hand, a challenge is a challenge, and I had not won anything since winning the International Bad Hemingway competition for the worst Hemingway parody perhaps fifteen years ago, so I was delighted to be honored, however comically unworthy I was. I rushed to the front to shake hands with Steve, delivered a properly humble victory speech, crediting my victory entirely to the boys of Troop 1, and returned in triumph to my perch on a log near the back of the semicircle facing the water. The troop responded with high-fives, and expressions of "You go, Mr. Applebome." Ben gave me a look that was part congratulations and part amused recognition of the illogic of it all.

Everyone quieted down in anticipation. The big moment was at hand.

"We have had many tight races for the Waubeeka Award," Steve said, "but I don't know if I've ever seen one as close as this one. Three troops were divided by five points and the fourth was only ten points behind. So we had many troops that worked hard and did a great job here and easily could have been the winner. But the winner of this week's Waubeeka Award is . . . (the pause seemed to last forever) . . . Troop 1 Chappaqua."

I'm not sure who was more excited—the kids or Vince, Robert, and me. We hollered like maniacs in English and Italian. We exchanged high-fives, low-fives, and mid-fives. We did chest butts and butt butts and other suitable expressions of manly enthusiasm. We quieted down for "Taps" and then floated back to Wolfjaw, the kids singing that god-awful "We Are the Champions" song as they marched up the rocky path to the site. It was the Cubs winning the World Series, Gonzaga winning the NCAA basketball tournament, Ball State beating Florida State in football, the Devil Rays beating the Yankees.

We already had the campfire made. I brought the bags of goodies to the upstairs picnic table, opened up the pretzel rods, and gave one to each kid as a victory cigar. Then, with everyone puffing away in contentment, Robert lit the fire, and in a few minutes it was our own small-bore facsimile of the roaring blaze at the lakefront. We hunted for sticks to make s'mores, broke out the chocolate and marshmallows and graham crackers, and relived our moment of triumph.

I had one more duty to perform. I hadn't learned my knots or lashes. I never got around to memorizing the Scout Law. I still didn't know much first aid. Still, there was something exhilarating about being the purported leader of our exultant little band. Like Cochran, the well-meaning Scoutmaster in *Be Prepared*, I felt that something good had rubbed off on me, and I didn't want to blow it. I had never worn the Scout uniform, always feeling a bit of comfortable distance in my familiar old T-shirts and worn-out shorts. But at this moment, for the first time, I found myself wishing I had a Scout shirt (Scout socks and shorts never entered my mind) as a way to erase any vestiges of cool, ironic distance I might have had left. I might have been a temporary, accidental Scoutmaster, but at this moment, it felt really important that I was a good one.

During the afternoon I had taken out my laptop and written an award ceremony, seventy or eighty words on each kid. Not Dr. Flank's Indian tales. Not Mr. Johnson's saga of Great Chief Leknoot. Not Mr. Toonkel's ghost tales. Just Mr. Applebome's Week 2 Award Oration. I figured it was my only chance to be Grand Wizard of the campfire, and I wanted to be certain it was a success. The kids had earned our respect. At this moment, I wanted to be sure I earned theirs.

"OK," I barked in my most authoritative voice. "It turns out we have a few more awards to give out. Listen up. There'll be a test afterward to make sure you were paying attention."

Total quiet. So far so good.

"One Troop 1 Scout has shown a particular affinity for interacting with the females in camp," I began. "He's at the commissary hanging around with Carrie. Joanna always seems to show particular interest when he shows up at the econ lodge. So in recognition of his selfless efforts as an ambassador to the females in camp, his dedication to the worthy cause of furthering intergender relations, and his natural skills as a ladies' man, our honorary Girl Scout Award goes to . . . Mr. Thomas Edwards."

Tom, proving my point, turned out to be the only Scout who wasn't there, which made the award that much better. We toasted him in absentia. Next came the Dream Couple Award: "Throughout history, there have been couples whose undying love for one another changed the course of human events—Romeo and Juliet,

Antony and Cleopatra, Gatsby and Daisy, Bill Clinton and Monica Lewinsky..." It went to Hal and George, the kids who had spent the whole week nagging each other. The two stood up together and beamed as everyone gave them a round of applause. Allen, our peerless master chef, the overlord of onions, the sultan of salt, the greengrocer of garlic, the minister of mustard, one of our first two inductees into the Order of the Arrow and the Royal Order of the Grit, won the Julia Child Award for outstanding cookcraft. Ben, our other inductee into the Order of the Arrow and the Royal Order of the Grit, won the W. Edwards Deming Management Award, for his creative use of Coke and Sprite cans as motivational tools and his groundbreaking innovations in latrine management and maintenance.

By this point all the kids were into the spirit of the event, sucking happily on their pretzel rods, waiting their turn to be recognized, and issuing titters of recognition when it was clear who each lucky recipient would be. Sam deserved and received something of a special citation: "It must be said that in the grand scheme of things, most of us are bit players at Camp Waubeeka. This is not true for our next honoree. Other than Dr. Flank and his absent partner, Mr. Eric Walker, no Troop 1 member is as famous—or infamous—in camp as our next honoree. But we have to ask the question, has this former bad boy gone good? No annoying renditions of 'Scout Socks.' No breaking skeets against his head. No behavior incurring threats by angry Scouts from Greenwich, Bronxville, or Bellmore. Instead, we had a master of cookcraft, an awesome performance in the mile swim, the signal success of finding Steve Silvers in the staff hunt, and his critical victory in the belly-flop competition. Gentlemen, a legend in his own time, the winner of this year's Sam Farrentino Award for Farrentinian behavior is . . . Sam Farrentino."

Sam got a richly deserved standing O, and I felt like a comedian who knew he had his audience. Everyone got his moment of recognition. Jonah got the Todd Davis Award for exemplary patrol leadership, maintaining peace and tranquility in The Underworld. Mark joined former Waubeeka campers Immanuel Kant, René Descartes, Sören Kierkegaard, and Friedrich Nietzsche as the winner of the year's Transcendental, Existential, Aristotelian Award for creative thinking and contributions to world philosophy. I ended with a heartfelt tribute to Doug: "It was hard to know if our final honoree came to us from Las Vegas or whatever planet it is in Starcraft. On the one hand, he was the master dealer of every card game known to man. On the other, he was always one step away from blasting Terrans or Zergs or Protoss. So for outstanding service in two dimensions, the earthly and the extraterrestrial, and for exemplary service to the peanut growers of America, who would be bankrupt without his business, our award for the Scout most likely to be at home in the bar scene from *Star Wars* goes to Mr. Doug Newton."

We hung around until eleven or so, pigging out, telling jokes, toasting our worthy rivals from Bronxville and Bellmore, and evaluating which of us would look best in one of the Bellmore Mohawks. Then we applauded Tom when he sheepishly returned in time for a command repeat performance of his award. Finally, the kids began to look like they were beginning to slow down. A few were clearly ready to nod off. We poured water on the fire, stumbled to our tents, and called it a night.

The next morning we all got to sign the W in our victory lap as Waubeeka Award winners. Then the kids riding the bus home piled in, and the bus pulled out in a billowing pillow of dust. Mr. Farrentino and Mr. Lombardi and their kids pulled out in Robert's Volvo. Ben and Jonah got into my car. I offered a crisp salute to Lester, who was jawing with Steve over something or other, and we pulled away and headed for home. As we lumbered down the dusty road out of camp, I had a fleeting thought: I wondered if I'd ever see this place again.

16: A Final Trip

One spring day about eight months after my last summer at Waubeeka, I took a different kind of Scouting expedition—a visit to the B.S.A.'s National Headquarters, situated in a nondescript brown brick office building in a pod of low-rise office buildings on the featureless prairie between Dallas and Fort Worth. The Boy Scout and American flags flew out front. A famous bronze statue of a Scout from the 1930s stood there too, looking lost and forlorn in this bland corporate landscape. Immediately inside the lobby was a wall of thirty-nine plaques honoring big donors, including the Amoco Foundation, IBM, Burlington Industries, Murphy Oil Corp., Quaker Oats, and McKinsey & Co. On the walls of the reception area were reproductions of four Scout paintings, two by Norman Rockwell, two by his student and successor Joseph Csatari. In a narrow hallway was a large portrait of B-P. It looked totally incongruous, as if there was no place to put it, so they stuck it on a wall and forgot about it.

I had written to Chief Scout Executive Roy L. Williams, who succeeded Jere Ratcliffe, requesting an interview, making the case that I was no mere writer but the distinguished winner of the Camp Waubeeka Scoutmaster Challenge. I guess he wasn't impressed, since I never heard from him. Instead, I met with Gregg Shields, a Senior Account Supervisor with the giant Edelman Public Relations, who handles the Scouts' PR. He met me in the lobby and then took me down to an empty conference room on the lower level. Shields had the rather thankless job of trotting out the Scout line on the gay issue or responding to allegations like the Circle Ten Ghost Troop fiasco. I had heard the Scouts were famously unhelpful to the press, but Shields did his best. He said he wasn't surprised that Williams wasn't available. "He doesn't do interviews," said Shields, a pleasant enough mid-westerner transplanted to suburban Dallas. "I think I can remember maybe one he's done since taking office. It's just not what he does. There's some logic in the Chief Scout Executive for the B.S.A. nationally not taking a public role, but letting the success of the organization speak for itself."

Shields affected a tone that was measured but upbeat. "Gallup did a study five years ago on men who were Boy Scouts," he said. "And men who were Scouts are significantly different, more likely to have leadership roles in the community, more likely to go to church, more likely to espouse values of family, positive values. So we see lots of signs of vitality. Our camp at Philmont is sold out two years in advance. I wish you'd been at the jamboree this year. I don't want to get too schmaltzy, but one of the senior volunteers was a guy who played a saw. Most kids had never seen anyone play a saw, and here he was with forty thousand kids watching him play 'Somewhere Over the Rainbow.' At first I was kind of concerned for the old boy. But he didn't take himself too seriously and he played it and then took a big bow. And then he said, 'For my next piece I'd like to play something we all know,' and he sat down and played 'God Bless America,' and three bars into it, I could hear behind me forty thousand young voices. I could see all these kids, hats off, singing 'God Bless America.' And it was really something. When it was over, we evacuated the site—forty thousand boys—and the only garbage was in the garbage cans."

Other things were not so rosy. Yes, enrollment was steadily dropping, but, he said, there is much more competition for boys' time than there was in the past. I asked Shields how well he thought Scouting had done in reaching out to minority communities, and he said there was no way to be sure. "That's our Scoutreach Program," he said. "We don't know how successful, because we don't have the data. The organization has the belief that you don't need a pedigree to be a Boy Scout. So until just a year or two ago there was no ethnic information on your application. There's still no income information. So it would be hard to say how far we've come because we don't know where we were. But we do know the Boy Scouts are making a very serious effort to reach those populations that have been underrepresented in the past. Today we print literature in thirteen languages." Nor could he say anything about the investigation of the Circle Ten Ghost Troops and other incidents of inflated rolls. "There's currently an open investigation by the Postal Service; that's about all I know," he said in standard flack-speak.

As for the gay controversy, Shields patiently repeated what I'd read elsewhere, that Scouting's essence was its core values and that endorsing homosexuality was inconsistent with them. "There are people who don't agree with it, and we accept that," he said. "But just as we respect their point of view, we ask their tolerance for our values and our ideas. Families who agree with our values embrace Boy Scouting. Those who don't are free to do other things." Then he said something I didn't expect: "One of the biggest growth markets for Boy Scouting has been and will continue to be—and we need to capitalize on it—nondenominational Christian churches who share many of these values—belief in God, belief in family, belief in serving others."

I'm sure it was true, but focusing on the most reliable bastions of the religious right seemed to be a form of niche marketing carrying a pretty clear message of where Scouting thought its future lay. I felt like my friend who had considered pulling her son out of Cub Scouts—being dared to play elsewhere if I didn't like their rules.

"We did a poll in January 2000 asking people if they supported the Boy Scouts policy on gays," Shields continued. "Seventy percent said 'yes'; the other 30 percent either said 'no' or were undecided. This was asked of all parents, both Scouting parents and non-Scouting parents. So we've got a majority, a strong majority. It's certainly a lot stronger than any presidential election we've had recently. You have to separate the essentials from the nonessentials, the mission from the method. The uniform has been changed I don't know how many times. That's not essential. The Scout Oath and Law has not changed. That's essential. The values of Scouting, that's essential."

I asked for a tour, but Shields said there wasn't much to see. Instead, we took the elevator back up, joined by six well-scrubbed young men in white shirts and ties and name tags identifying the towns they were from (workplace casual has not exactly swept through the B.S.A., though there is a Casual Thursday, which means sport coat, no tie). Then we drove five minutes to a nearby strip mall, where we had a buffet lunch at the Veranda Greek Café, with rugs and paintings—*The Last Supper,* flamenco dancers, Dutch still lives, brooding waterfronts—in every genre known to man. Over lunch, Shields mentioned something that I barely took notice of—that there were twice as many Cub Scouts as Boy Scouts. When we came back, he gave me a copy of the B.S.A. annual report. On the cover was a Tiger Cub, a cute black or Hispanic kid who looked like he was just past the age of riding in a car seat. Except for the Learning for Life programs, in which the B.S.A. contracted with schools to teach children about values and character development, all the Scout enrollment totals had dropped for the year, with the total at 3.351 million, down from 3.392 million. (It dropped again to 3.325 million the next year.) But there were 2.1 million kids in the three Cub-age programs and just over a million in Boy Scouts and Varsity Scouts, which enrolled more advanced Scouts ages fourteen to seventeen. This seemed a little shocking. The B.S.A. had resisted the creation of Cub Scouts for two decades, feeling Scouting was meant for older boys. Now, for two-thirds of boys, Scouting ended by the time they were eleven or so. Instead of Scouting's vaunted values and service, the Scouting experience for most kids was doing the Pinewood Derby in elementary school, getting their first camping experience, and then dropping out before the meaningful parts of Scouting could sink in.

We came back and chatted outside in the parking lot for a few minutes, the headquarters no different than any other corporate office except for the Scout posters you could see in the offices. Then I drove off, still thinking about the membership numbers.

Maybe Scouts getting younger was inevitable. Sociologists talk about the compressed lives that kids now lead. Girls who used to play with Barbie dolls until ten might now stop at seven, so maybe Scouting for most boys now ends with Cub Scouts. But the number of kids in the population is exploding because of the baby boomers' "echo boom." If Scouting can't grow now, it never will. If a corporation dropped from 4.9 million customers, the number of boys in Scouting in 1972, to 3.3 million, it would be judged a disaster. But Scouting seems to sail smugly along, secure in its legacy and its mythic, if diminished, place in public life.

Closer to home, recruitment seemed to be looming as a big issue with Troop 1 as well. Dr. Flank professed not to be concerned. The troop's membership had waxed and waned over time, and when we joined, just four years ago, the leaders felt it was getting too many kids, so maybe I was overreacting. But after Ben's first year, new membership fell off a cliff. There were several kids the year ahead of him, and his class of ninth graders so far had retained a solid core of about eight kids from the twelve or so kids who had started out when he did. But there were only five kids left in the eighth-grade group below and none at all in the year after that. Kids like Dave and Marty, the little survivors of our disastrous rafting trip, showed up a few times, maybe spent a summer at camp, and dropped out before I knew their names. We had a great little kid named Sahil, who the big kids identified as his year's star Scout, but he moved to Chicago. So as the next year wore on there were still plenty of Scouts for the meetings and hikes, but they were mostly high school kids, and it was hard to keep them interested in the meetings covering material they'd already learned. We were in danger of becoming a troop with many chiefs and few Indians. A highlight of every year was the last outing before camp, the overnight canoe trip on the Delaware. But this year the trip coincided with the day the high school kids had to take their subject-matter SAT-2 tests. For the first time, the outing had to be cancelled. Getting a dad for the second week of camp was suddenly a huge struggle. For a while we had only Mr. Lombardi until another dad was coaxed into volunteering. And who knew what was going to happen when Dr. Flank finally called it quits? Nearing our ninetieth birthday in 2003, I was beginning to wonder if we'd be around to hit one hundred.

True, the troop had seen similar membership dips in the past. But it felt like Scouting faced a steeper hill all the time, and I wondered if the controversy over the gay issue had, at least in communities like ours, added a glaring new disincentive to joining Scouts. We weren't going to quit Troop 1, but if we had been just beginning, the image of Scouting as harsh and intolerant would have been a reason not to join, as it was for the terrific young son of some friends of ours. In another era, he would have been the archetypal Eagle Scout. In this one, he followed the B.S.A.'s expulsion of James Dale, told his parents that maybe Scouting wasn't his kind of organization, and on his own decided to drop out of Cub Scouts. It wasn't a case of politically correct adults making a political statement. It was an ethically acute fifth grader looking at the B.S.A.'s values and behavior and deciding he did not like what he saw.

The Scouts locally said their research showed their biggest problem in recruiting is not politics but competition for boys' time. But maybe the Boy Scouts needed to learn some lessons from the Girl Scouts. In our two-county Boy Scout council, membership was plummeting, dropping over the past decade from 17,624 in 1992 to 9,450 in 2002. Meanwhile the local Girl Scouts, who quite explicitly mandate no exclusionary standards for religion and sexual preference, had doubled their enrollment since 1984 and grown by 25 percent since 1992. Whatever the cause, as the number of Boy Scouts continues to drop, it reduces the pool of adults likely to be interested in running troops or pushing their kids toward it in the future. It felt like a downward spiral. No wonder national is so solicitous of those eager-beaver Mormons.

Once I was at Harry's house, and he was showing me memorabilia of the Brooklyn camp-out he had put together. One of his sons wandered over to idly poke through the old badges and patches and photographs, amused at his dad's ancient keepsakes. "Dad, if you did that in Chappaqua probably no one would show up," he said dismissively. "Everyone I know hates Scouting. I don't think anyone in the whole middle school does it anymore. They think it's cheesy, uncool, and old-fashioned. Why does anyone need to tie knots and read a compass? If you're in the woods and you need something, you call your dad on your cell phone."

But if Scouting is a harder sell for suburban kids, it's not going away. Membership is down, but 3.3 million scouts is still a lot of kids. Its position in America's collective unconscious and as a recipient of corporate donations remains secure for now. And there are at least three reasons to believe this can be a fairly auspicious time for Scouting. First is what I think of as the North Face Moment—the vogue for hiking and climbing into distant, unpleasant, or inaccessible places in expensive, synthetic outdoors gear. When I was a kid, we played ball. Now, kids still play ball, but they also dream about hiking the A.T. in their Merrell hiking boots, North Face Gore-Tex shell, and Capilene underwear. That's a huge opportunity for Scouting. Second is the breast-beating about endangered boys and absent dads. I'm not sure either is true, but why quibble? The fact is we're at one of those cyclical moments of societal panic about how we're raising boys and the role of dads in the process. Scouting didn't exactly begin as a New Age bonding experience, but there are very few activities in modern life that bring dads and sons together the way Scouting does. You can coach Little League or AYSO soccer, but it's still the kids playing and the adults watching or yelling from the sidelines. In Scouting—at least in Troop 1's version of it—you're all along for the same trips and outings. Third is the world after 9-11. The instant cliché that everything changed after the terror attacks is demonstrably not true. But, if 9-11 put a dent in the primacy of irony as a worldview, if it reminded us of the heroism that can come from men (and it mostly was men) doing tough, unglamorous jobs in fire departments and police stations and the military, that can't hurt Scouting and could help it. A bunch of Boy Scouts carrying the flag in the Memorial Day parade seems a lot more relevant, even to liberal sophisticates, now than it did prior to September 11, 2001.

But whether Scouting can capitalize on any of that is another question. I had asked a few people, like Nick and Dr.

Flank, for their thoughts on how to reinvigorate the B.S.A. Using their ideas and my own, this is what emerged:

1. Stop the discrimination: The B.S.A. defends its exclusionary policies against gays and atheists by saying Scouting is entitled, indeed required, to stand up for its fundamental values. Quite right. But Scouting is undermining its core values—teaching young men to be tolerant, kind, helpful, decent, and friendly—by taking a stand in favor of discrimination. And the real disaster of both policies is that they make Scouting look backward and narrow at a time kids increasingly think of Scouting as something that's already behind the times. The real charm of Scouting has always been its fundamental decency and sense of inclusion. You have never needed a degree in philosophy to understand the Scout Law or the ethic of fairness and tolerance that resonates through Scouting. You don't need one now to see that both policies make the Scouts seem unfair and intolerant. And there's nothing in the writings or the lives of Baden-Powell, Seton, or Beard to think they would have endorsed the B.S.A.'s moral litmus test. Scouting needs to continue to develop and refine rigorous zero-tolerance policies on any kind of sexual abuse or inappropriate behavior. But kicking out gay Eagle Scouts does not help achieve it. Scouting once caught the vast middle of American life. It would be a supreme tragedy if it evolved into a politically laden movement catering to Mormons, Catholics, or the Christian right and writing off everyone else.

2. Find a dynamic leader: Scouting was built by three charismatic, idiosyncratic visionaries—Baden-Powell, Seton, and Beard. Their presence drew generations of kids to Scouting. Now no one knows who they were, and Scouting is led by invisible careerist bureaucrats even the Scouts don't know. If not a new Baden-Powell, Seton, or Beard (though it could use one), Scouting needs its Steve Jobs or Lee Iacocca or Ray Kroc—maybe someone like an astronaut who was a Scout as a kid—a leader who can put a vibrant face on a declining enterprise and make the case for why Scouting still matters.

3. Throw out the uniforms: One of the quotes from B-P on the wall of the office at Waubeeka began: "For the boy, a uniform is a big attraction." Up until the 1950s, a vaguely military uniform was a source of pride. But for middle school and high school kids now, it's just a source of embarrassment, something no one wears in public. Nick suggested doing what, say, the NFL does, licensing its logos and putting them on outdoors clothes. You could have shells and fleeces with the Boy Scout logo, in whatever color a troop wanted, that would give troops uniformity and identity without saddling them with outdated uniforms no one wants to wear.

4. Embrace diversity: They're trying. Scouting makes a good-faith effort at courting minorities, but it can do better. Baden-Powell was a revolutionary. His idea of a movement that joined both tony public-school boys and working-class ones in an organization that spanned class lines struck some as ingenious and others as heretical. There's no longer anything revolutionary in the idea, but no one puts it to work. Scouting has the potential to unite inner-city black kids, rich suburban white kids, and working-class exurban kids in a common movement. The trouble is, it never happens. Scouts, for the most part, interact only through their own troop. Scouting needs a concerted push to get different troops together—something beyond the District Camporee or even the National Jamboree, the huge national gatherings of Scouts held every four years. For instance, a program pairing our troop with a black or Hispanic one from the same county, or one from overwhelmingly white North Atlanta with one from overwhelmingly black South Atlanta, would be a revelation for both groups. It would transform Scouting into what B-P envisioned, a challenge rather than a predictable bromide.

5. Commit to service projects: This is another one where Scouting's values are perfectly aligned with the moment. When I was a kid, public service was a largely obscure notion, left for grown-ups or do-gooders. Now, it's part of the daily vocabulary of youth, a staple on every college campus and college résumé. Scout troops do some of it, but they are perfectly positioned to do a lot more. An obvious area is the environment, which is nonideological and probably has more innate appeal to kids than any other issue. It's also an issue at the heart of Scouting's roots and current culture.

6. Focus on keeping older kids: This has been a problem for Scouting since it began, and it gets harder all the time. It's not easy to keep older kids in Scouting. But make no mistake: Getting first graders involved in Tiger Cubs may keep the B.S.A.'s numbers up, but it won't do much toward realizing the worthy, serious goals that Baden-Powell, Seton, and Beard had for Scouting.

7. Advertise: That's how we spread a message in America. Scouting is saddled with an image so dull and deadly, it's amazing it still has a pulse. Like the U.S. Army did with "Be All That You Can Be" or the Marines with "The Few, The Proud, The Marines," Scouting needs to aggressively put across a positive, contemporary message or it's going to continue to decline.

Maybe a resurgence is impossible. Scouting is a century-old movement that began before there was radio, let alone television or computers. It had peaks of relevance during the World Wars and the Cold War. Now it seems to be becoming a niche product, a movement that is almost aggressively behind the times, where kids get to hear old-timers playing "Somewhere Over the Rainbow" on a saw. And the truth is, for all our egalitarian rhetoric, there's not much interest in a movement that's open to everyone. Our dominant cultural values are all about exclusion and prestige—the fancy Lexus, the Park Avenue address, the Yale sticker on the rear windshield. We're not that interested in something that's as accessible to the kid in Harlem as it is to the kid in Chappaqua. And the biggest hurdle may not be recruiting the kids; it may be finding the adults with the time, energy, and devotion to run a troop and put together a good program for it. It's an enormous commitment few working parents these days are willing to make.

That said, Scouting isn't doomed to continued decline. In my desk at home I have five patches I was awarded for participating in events during my hapless tenure in Scouting. There are two from Camp Read, one from that first Paul Bunyan Camporee, one from a dimly remembered Manitoga Trek 2000, and, my favorite, a lovely pale blue Klondike Derby patch, with whip-wielding driver, dogsled, and huskies from the year we had the Klondike Derby sans snow. They were given to everyone who showed up, but I've come to see them as treasured keepsakes, and sometimes I take them out when I'm working at night and idly ponder them the way I once would have flipped through a stack of baseball cards. This is not a part of dad-dom I ever envisioned or sought, but if Scouting could win me over, it could recruit anyone. Shields, the Scout's PR guy, is right, at least in part. Scouting's core values—as embodied in the Scout Law, not the case law—are wonderful building blocks for a movement and a life. Scouting's genuinely egalitarian goals and instincts are more important now—for poor kids on the bottom and for rich kids on the top—than they've ever been. It's one of the only things that kids do that's genuinely cooperative, not competitive. If my kid starts at quarterback, yours does not. If he finishes first in the class, yours can only hope to finish second. But while the troop is a cooperative venture, kids succeed or don't in Scouting on their own. One kid making Eagle doesn't make it any harder—or any easier—for another to do the same. And at a time when few middle class kids join the military, it's a truly egalitarian activity that's good precisely because it's not exclusive—everyone gets to join, and kids have to get along with each other whether or not they're in the same clique, play on the same team, or exist in the same social niche.

The Harvard sociologist Robert Putnam made a splash a few years ago with the book *Bowling Alone,* which said we're suffering from a loss of social cohesion because institutions that used to knit people together no longer do. We don't join bowling leagues; we bowl alone. But we don't Scout alone. Back in Don Vanderbilt's day, one of his assistant Scoutmasters, John Ripley, gave the same talk to the fathers at the beginning of each year. "This is a golden opportunity that every father here will never have again," he said. "You and your sons do this as equals. You camp, you cook, you hike; everything you do in the woods, you do as equals. You'll never have this opportunity again. You should take advantage of it. If you're planning just to drop him off Wednesday night and not get involved, don't bother. That's not what we're about."

One of the nicest Troop 1 events each year is the spring barbecue and Court of Honor for past and present members and friends of the troop. The Scouts gather in clumps sorted largely by age, the sisters and younger siblings form their own age and gender-appropriate posses, and the parents get to mingle in relative peace. The spring Court of Honor the year after our Waubeeka triumph felt like the flashback at the end of *The Godfather 2,* with Sonny still alive, Fredo still a part of the family, and Michael still young and idealistic. John Ripley was there, serving up hamburgers with Mr. Johnson. Todd Davis came back from college with a scraggly goatee and strolled in with his brother Jeff, also an Eagle, who had his hair in some kind of weird samurai bun. Bob Heller was there too, as was Jack the tarp-ball star. Even the old Scout Hut was sort of there, its image at the center of the huge blue Troop 1 seal that Dr. Flank brings to all the ceremonial occasions. The rest of the cast sauntered in: Sam (minus Eric, who was still active in the troop but a no-show that night) sporting his billowing Italian Afro, Ben's Amigos, Dr. Flank, and Messrs. Toonkel and Johnson. Fly Guy was fretting because he had to miss camp this year, but Mr. Lombardi was planning to be back for a return engagement. There were even a handful of new kids, who looked as impossibly small and young now as the older kids looked impossibly large and old when Ben and I started three years ago. We would have to see how many of them decided to stick around.

The evening went by the familiar Troop 1 script. Dr. Flank gave out the merit badges, talked about camp and High Adventure, and announced the date and time for the planning meeting for next year. Bob Walker made his pitch, passed out pledge cards, and thanked us fulsomely for our support. Mr. Toonkel and Mr. Johnson came up with a tooled leather belt for the outgoing Senior Patrol Leader. Dads and moms who had contributed to the year's events were thanked. Many burgers and hot dogs and plates of pasta salad and chips were consumed.

Before the watermelon and chocolate chip cookies and brownies for dessert, Dr. Flank called all the current and former members forward—from Todd Davis to the tiny sixth graders—to join him in the circle. They linked hands. "I challenge you to be your best and to give Scouting your best personal effort," Dr. Flank said. And they all repeated together: "May the Great Master of all Scouts be with us until we meet again."

Seeing the little kids made things feel a little bittersweet. Just as grownups always think of themselves as younger than they are, we do the same with our kids. And seeing those little kids reminded me how far Ben was from being one. Not that I should have needed the reminder. A few weeks after our triumph at Waubeeka, Ben had gone on High Adventure, his week in the wilds of northern Quebec. I'm not sure I would have been invited, since my cooking and camping skills had stalled around Tenderfoot level, but a week canoeing and hiking through the Canadian wilderness was more outdoors adventure than I had in mind. He went. I stayed. I was glad he had Dr. Flank, Mr. Toonkel, and Mr. Johnson to guide him along. But it felt like we had walked down a road together and had finally reached a point where he kept going, and I turned back.

And, without my quite realizing it, Ben had become a different creature than he was when we started Scouting. One day in eighth grade he had dragged out our old NordicTrack, which we never used, and started working out. Then we got a treadmill, and he started buying hand weights, first fifteen pounds, then twenty, twenty-five, and thirty, which he began using with religious regularity. He bought a book on weight training and drew up intricate tables of the sets and repetitions he did on assorted curls, squats, crunches, lifts, and lunges. Within a few months most of his flab was miraculously gone, and before long he was fit and buff enough to look like the models on the covers of *Men's Health* and *Maxim*. We used to play at a blocking drill where we'd bang into each other like opposing linemen, but hitting him now is like running into a brick wall, so that game has been retired for my protection. So much for worrying he'd be a wuss. One day, Ben picked up one of my Miles Davis CDs and put it into a Sony Discman. He'd never shown much interest in music, but he liked it and asked for other suggestions. Before long, he was listening to Davis's "Kind of Blue," "In a Silent Way," "Jack Johnson," and "Porgy and Bess"; John Coltrane's "My Favorite Things," "A Love Supreme," and "Blue Trane"; Duke Ellington, Herbie Hancock, and other surprisingly sophisticated and unfashionable stuff. He was now bigger than me, so I started wearing his hand-me-downs. I also wore the outdoor watch with the braided leather strap he got me one year for Father's Day, and took to carrying around as a sort of talisman the red Swiss army knife he bought me another year as a birthday gift. It was hard to know how much of Ben was a result of his parents, his genes, his schools, Scouts, happenstance, his horoscope, or dumb luck. But, using the Scout Law as a yardstick, I calculated that by the time he took off for High Adventure, he was very loyal, usually helpful, extremely friendly and courteous, exceptionally kind, reasonably obedient, usually cheerful, fairly thrifty (with the exception of all that camping gear), probably no more or less brave than most, quite clean (if you don't count his room, in which case he's a disaster), and not particularly reverent. Seemed fine to me.

I was almost right about never returning to Waubeeka. I did make one more trip to Camp Read the next winter when the troop took a ski trip to Gore Mountain, about twenty miles away. The temperature was about 10 degrees and everything was covered under a foot of snow with a hard, icy glaze on top. We stayed in one of the fancier (by Scout standards) cabins at Buckskin, and, proving I had learned nothing in three years, I somehow showed up without a sleeping bag. I slept on a bunk bed above Ben's in my clothes and used my coat as a blanket. I woke up cold, stiff, tired, and feeling terminally stupid. If they had ever given me my Scoutmaster Challenge Award (supposedly there was a trophy or plaque, but I never got it), I would have sent it back and told them to give it to Mr. Lombardi or Mr. Farrentino.

But I never made it back to Scout camp. As Ben got older, he didn't lose interest in Scouting. He still appreciated the hikes and camp-outs the way he had when he was younger. In fact, as schoolwork got more stressful with the lethal doses of AP courses that kids take these days, he came to appreciate the outings all the more, signing up for almost every camp-out and hike as natural restoratives. But instead of making it to Waubeeka for a fourth year, Ben moved onto other things his next summer. He spent two weeks on one of those too-expensive wilderness trips, hiking through the Blue Ridge Mountains; took a two-week course in Forensics at the University of Virginia, and then did the troop's High Adventure for the second time. He didn't seem to miss Waubeeka, but I did. It had been a long year working at the *New York Times* post 9-11, and I'd like to have seen if Waubeeka would have had the same restorative powers it did in the past. And Scout camp was something Ben and I shared. I wasn't ready for it to end.

One of Baden-Powell's favorite paintings was a maudlin oil by a London Scoutmaster named Ernest S. Carlos entitled *If I Were a Boy Again*. It shows a wasted man with hollow eyes, sitting slumped in a chair as he watches his son, a radiant young Boy Scout, prepare for an outing. The father sits at a table crowded with books, a teakettle and teacup, staring at the boy. The son jauntily prepares for his adventures oblivious (or indifferent) to the melancholy old coot sitting behind him. I've often wondered why Boy Scouts seems to be invested with so much more cultural significance than Girl Scouts—the one full of powerful metaphorical resonance, the other pretty much identified with cookie sales. In part, of course, it's a reflection of the different opportunities, expectations, and burdens put on boys and girls in the past, and, to some extent, in the present. But I think it's something else as well. Men, as women often remind us, seem fixated on being boys. The most coveted jobs for men are the ones they dreamed about as boys. I'm sure it's fun to play in the WNBA, but it's not as much fun as being Kobe Bryant or Michael Jordan or Barry Bonds or Brett Favre. It's impossible to appreciate the almost spiritual attachment men put on being, say, firefighters or cops without realizing it allows men, in some ways, to always be boys. Baden-Powell's favorite play was—what else?—*Peter Pan*, which he saw twice during the first month it was produced in London. And for this man who never really outgrew being a boy, the Scouts, on whatever level you want to look at it, was always something of an adventure in eternal youth. As long as the boys stayed young, he could too.

Scouting never worked quite on that level for me, and it doesn't work that way in the culture anymore—its symbolism is too out of date. But the melancholy message of Carlos's painting has a tinge of universal truth. You're not a parent for very long, and you do what works for as long as it works before your son takes off to live his own life on his own terms. I feel lucky to have had this unexpected vehicle to share my son's youth, to shape it, and to be shaped by it as well.

We like to think of our kids as extensions of ourselves (*the heirs apparent!*), but that's a parental conceit. Sometimes we lead our kids, sometimes they lead us; sometimes we mix and match, and eventually we just go our separate ways. I hope I led Ben in some good directions, but Scouting turned out to be one rich, revealing, totally unexpected way he has led me, even if he could lead me only so far. It's still his world more than mine.

On spring and summer nights when I get off the train, the field by the station is usually full of other dads' kids playing Little League games in the dwindling sunlight or under the lights at the Rec Department field. I sometimes stop and watch for a few minutes, taking in the busy green pageant and listening to the chatter of the kids, the ping of the balls flying off the aluminum bats, and the familiar thud of ball meeting glove. Invariably, I get a wistful pang of remembrance and regret. How did that end so fast?

I didn't choose Scouting, but I'm glad Ben did, and I'm sure before too long I'll feel a similar shiver of remembrance and regret when it's over too.

Bibliography

I was able to make use of a wide variety of materials in writing this book. Some were especially helpful. The single best source on Baden-Powell is Tim Jeal's *The Boy-Man: The Life of Lord Baden-Powell,* the definitive Baden-Powell biography to date. Less balanced and complete, but also valuable, was Michael Rosenthal's *The Character Factory: Baden-Powell and the Origins of the Boy Scout Movement.* The best source I found on the history of the Boy Scouts of America was Carolyn Ditte Wagner's 1978 doctoral dissertation, *The Boy Scouts of America: A Model and a Mirror of American Society.* Particularly valuable on contemporary Scouting issues and controversies are Jay Mechling's *On My Honor: Boy Scouts and the Making of American Youth* and Chuck Sudetic's "The Struggle for the Soul of the Boy Scouts" in *Rolling Stone.* For Troop 1's history, I was extraordinarily fortunate that Doug Rohde had decided to research the troop's history for his Eagle project in 1989. And Patrick Boyle's *Scout's Honor: Sexual Abuse in America's Most Trusted Institution,* while hard to find, is a powerful, troubling, important look at sexual abuse within Scouting, worthwhile for its insights into pederasty both within and outside Scouting. I did not list every newspaper, magazine, and Internet site I made use of, but the following is the list of the main reference materials I consulted.

Baden-Powell, Lord Robert S. S. *Paddle Your Own Canoe: Or Tips For Boys From the Jungle and Elsewhere.* London: Macmillan and Co. Ltd., 1939.

———. *Scouting for Boys.* Scouts' Edition. London: C. Arthur Pearson, Ltd., 1963.

Beard, Daniel Carter. *The American Boys Handy Book: What to Do and How to Do It.* Rutland, Vt.: C. E. Tuttle, 1966.

———. *Hardly a Man Is Now Alive: The Autobiography of Dan Beard.* New York: Doubleday, Doran & Co., 1939.

Bensman, Todd. "Scouts' controversy similar to '70s flap. Group says it's serious about resolving charges of padded membership rolls." *Dallas Morning News,* 4 June 2000.

———. "Government investigates Scouts' membership figures." *Dallas Morning News,* 14 May 2000.

———. "Boy Scouts' rolls decline by 25%." *Dallas Morning News,* 25 February 2001.

Birkby, Robert C. *Boy Scout Handbook,* 10th ed. Irving, Tex.: Boy Scouts of America, 1990.

Boy Scouts of America. *The Official Handbook for Boys,* 1st ed. Garden City, N.Y.: Doubleday, Page & Co., 1911.

———. *Boy Scout Handbook,* 11th ed. Irving, Tex.: Boy Scouts of America, 1998.

Boyle, Patrick. *Scout's Honor: Sexual Abuse in America's Most Trusted Institution.* Rocklin, Calif.: Prima Publishing, 1994.

Brenna, Susan. "Does My Son Have to Quit the Boy Scouts?" *Salon,* 7 July 2000.

Chappaqua Historical Society. "The Early Quaker Hamlet of Old Chappaqua: its houses, its people, its way of life." Chappaqua Historical Society, 1973.

Cloud, John. "Can a Scout Be Gay? The Boy Scouts' Battle to Stay Straight Goes to the Supreme Court." *Time,* 26 April 2000.

Cochran, R. E. *Be Prepared! The Life and Illusions of a Scoutmaster.* New York: William Sloane Associates, 1952.

Bibliography

Cohen, Randy. "The Ethicist: Demerit Badge." *New York Times Magazine,* 23 July 2000.

France, David. "Scouts Divided." *Newsweek,* 6 August 2001.

Fussell, Paul. *The Boy Scout Handbook and Other Observations.* New York: Oxford University Press, 1982.

Garst, Shannon. *Ernest Thompson Seton, Naturalist.* New York: Messner, 1959.

Gibson, J. *Manual of Drill for Boy Scouts.* Glasgow: James Brown & Son, 1912.

Greenhouse, Linda. "Justices Explore Scouts' Exclusion of Gay Members." *New York Times,* 27 April 2000.

————. "Supreme Court Backs Boy Scouts in Ban of Gays from Membership." *New York Times,* 29 June 2000.

Hanley, Robert. "New Jersey Court Overturns Ouster of Gay Boy Scout." *New York Times,* 5 August 1999.

Jeal, Tim. *The Boy-Man: The Life of Lord Baden-Powell.* New York: Morrow, 1990.

Keller, Betty. *Black Wolf: The Life of Ernest Thompson Seton.* Vancouver: Douglas & McIntyre, 1984.

Letcher, Gary. *Canoeing the Delaware River: A Guide to the River and Shore.* New Brunswick, N.J.: Rutgers University Press, 1985.

MacDonald, Heather. "Why the Boy Scouts Work." *City Journal* (Winter 2000).

Macleod, David I. *Building Character in the American Boy: The Boy Scouts, YMCA, and Their Forerunners, 1870–1920.* Madison: University of Wisconsin Press, 1983.

Mechling, Jay. *On My Honor: Boy Scouts and the Making of American Youth.* Chicago: University of Chicago Press, 2001.

Meyer, Kathleen. *How to Shit in the Woods: An Environmentally Sound Approach to a Lost Art.* Berkeley, Calif.: Ten Speed Press, 1994.

Murphy, Dean E. "Pinning Demerit Badge on Chief Boy Scout S.

Bibliography

Africa: Blacks Seek Amends for Founder Baden-Powell's Alleged Misdeeds a Century Ago." *Los Angeles Times,* 24 July 1999.

New Castle Historical Society. "A Bicentennial History of the Town of New Castle 1791–1991." New Castle Historical Society, 1991.

Oswald, A. Lewis. *Troop One Marches On!* Hutchinson, Kans.: Rotherwood Press, 1934.

Peterson, Robert W. *The Boy Scouts: An American Adventure.* New York: American Heritage, 1984.

Putnam, Robert D. *Bowling Alone: The Collapse and Revival of American Community.* New York: Simon & Schuster, 2000.

Rohde, Doug. "Chappaqua Troop 1 and Scouting in Chappaqua: Seventy-five Years." Unpublished Research Project, 1989.

Rosenthal, Michael. *The Character Factory: Baden-Powell and the Origins of the Boy Scout Movement.* New York: Pantheon, 1986.

Samson, John G., ed. *The Worlds of Ernest Thompson Seton.* New York: Knopf, 1976.

Seton, Ernest Thompson. *The Book of Woodcraft and Indian Lore.* Garden City, N.Y.: Doubleday, Page, 1921.

———. *Wild Animals I Have Known.* New York: Scribner, 1926.

Sudetic, Chuck. "The Struggle for the Soul of the Boy Scouts." *Rolling Stone,* 6–20 July 2000.

Thompson, Tracy. "Scouting and New Terrain." *Washington Post Magazine,* 2 August 1998.

Wade, E. K. *The Piper of Pax: The Life Story of Lord Baden-Powell of Gilwell.* London: C. Arthur Pearson, Ltd., 1924.

Wagner, Carolyn Ditte. *The Boy Scouts of America: A Model and a Mirror of American Society.* Doctoral dissertation. Baltimore: Johns Hopkins University, 1978.

Now and Forever

This Large Print Book carries the
Seal of Approval of N.A.V.H.

NOW AND FOREVER

DANIELLE STEEL

THORNDIKE PRESS
A part of Gale, Cengage Learning

GALE
CENGAGE Learning®

Detroit • New York • San Francisco • New Haven, Conn • Waterville, Maine • London

Copyright © 1978 by Danielle Steel.
"Poem to Danny" first appeared in Cosmopolitan magazine, Copyright © 1974 by Danielle Steel.
Thorndike Press, a part of Gale, Cengage Learning.

LIBRARY OF CONGRESS CATALOGING-IN-PUBLICATION DATA

Steel, Danielle.
  Now and forever / by Danielle Steel.
    p. cm. — (Thorndike Press large print famous authors)
  ISBN-13: 978-1-4104-4451-6 (hardcover)
  ISBN-10: 1-4104-4451-1 (hardcover)
  1. Large type books. I. Title.
PS3569.T33828N6 2012
813'.54—dc23
                                         2011040161

Published in 2012 by arrangement with Dell Books, an imprint of the Random House Publishing Group, a division of Random House, Inc.

Printed in the United States of America
1 2 3 4 5 6 7 16 15 14 13 12

To Beatrix
for being wonderful
and always loving.

D.S.

"There are three kinds of souls,
three kinds of prayers.
One: I am a bow in your hands, Lord.
Draw me lest I rot.
Two: Do not overdraw me, Lord.
I shall break.
Three: Overdraw me, and who cares
if I break!

Choose!"

From "Report to Greco"
by Nicos Kazantzakis

CHAPTER 1

The weather was magnificent. A clear blue sunny day, with sharply etched white clouds in the sky. The perfect Indian summer. And so hot. The heat made everything slow and sensual. And it was so totally unlike San Francisco. That was the best part. Ian sat at a small pink marble table, his usual seat, in a patch of sunlight at Enrico's restaurant on Broadway. The traffic whizzed by while lunch-hour couples strolled. The heat felt delicious.

Under the table, Ian swung one long leg easily over the other. Three daisies bobbed in a glass, and the bread was fresh and soft to the touch. The almost too thin, graceful fingers tore one slice of bread carefully away from the others. Two young girls watched him and giggled. He wasn't "cute," he was sexy. Even they knew it. And beautiful. Handsome. Elegant. He had class. Tall, thin, blond, blue-eyed, with high cheekbones and

9

endless legs, hands that one noticed, a face one hated to stop looking at . . . a body one watched. Ian Clarke was a beautiful man. And he knew it, in an offhand sort of way. He knew it. His wife knew it. So what? She was beautiful too. It wasn't something they really cared about. But other people did. Other people loved to watch them, in that hungry way one stares at exceptionally good-looking people, wanting to know what they're saying, where they're going, who they know, what they eat . . . as though some of it might rub off. It never does. One has to be born with it. Or spend a great deal of money to fake it. Ian didn't fake it. He had it.

The woman in the large natural straw hat and pink dress had noticed it too. She stared at him through the mesh of the straw. She watched his hands with the bread, his mouth as he drank. She could even see the blond hair on his arms as he rolled up his sleeves in the sun. She was several tables away, but she saw. Just as she had seen him there before. But he never saw her. Why would he? She saw everything, and then she stopped watching. Ian didn't know she was alive. He was busy with the rest of the view.

Life was incredibly good. Ripe and golden and easy. His for the plucking. He had worked on the third chapter of his novel all morning, and now the characters were coming to life, just like the people wandering along Broadway . . . strolling, laughing, playing games. His characters were already that real to him. He knew them intimately. He was their father, their creator, their friend. And they were his friends. It was such a good feeling, starting a book. It populated his life. All those new faces, new heads. He could feel them in his hands as he rat-tat-tapped on the typewriter keys. Even the keyboard felt good to his touch.

He had it all, a city he loved, a new novel at last, and a wife he still laughed and played with and loved making love to. Seven years and everything about her still felt good to him: her laughter, her smile, the look in her eyes, the way she sat naked in his studio, perched in the old wicker rocking chair, drinking root beer and reading his work. Everything felt good, and better now, with the novel beginning to blossom. It was a magical day. And Jessie was coming home. It had been a productive three weeks, but he was suddenly lonely and horny as hell . . . Jessie.

Ian closed his eyes and blotted out the sounds of traffic drifting by . . . Jessie . . . of the graceful legs, the blond hair like fine

11

satin, the green eyes with gold specks . . . eating peanut butter and apricot jam on raisin bread at two in the morning, asking him what he thought of the spring line for her shop . . . "I mean honestly, Ian, tell me the truth, do you hate the spring things, or are they okay? From a man's point of view . . . be honest . . ." As though it really mattered, from a man's point of view. Those big green eyes searching his face as though asking him if she were okay, if he loved her, if . . . he did.

Sipping his gin and tonic, he thought of her, and felt indebted to her again. It gave him a tiny pinched feeling somewhere in the pit of his stomach. But that was part of it: he did owe her a lot. She had weathered a lot. Teaching jobs that had paid him a pittance, substitute teaching that had paid less, a job in a bookstore, which she had hated because she felt it demeaned him. So he had quit. He had even had a brief fling with journalism, after his first novel had bombed. And then her inheritance had solved so many of their problems. Theirs, but not necessarily his.

"You know, Mrs. Clarke, one of these days you're going to get sick and tired of being married to a starving writer." He had watched her face intently as she'd shaken

12

her head and smiled in the sunlight of a summer day three years before . . .

"You don't look like you're starving to me." She patted his stomach, and then kissed him gently on the lips. "I love you, Ian."

"You must be crazy. But I love you too." It had been a rough summer for him. He hadn't made a dime in eight months. But Jessie had her money, of course. Dammit.

"Why am I crazy? Because I respect your work? Because I think you're a good husband, even if you're not working on Madison Avenue anymore? So what, Ian? Who gives a damn about Madison Avenue? Do you? Do you miss it so much, or are you just going to use it to torment yourself for the rest of your life?" There was a faint tinge of bitterness in her voice, mixed with anger. "Why can't you just enjoy what you are?"

"And what's that?"

"A writer. And a good one."

"Who says?"

"The critics 'says,' that's who says."

"My royalties don't says."

"Fuck your royalties." She looked so serious that he had to laugh.

"I'd have a tough time trying — they're not big enough to tickle, let alone fuck."

"Oh, shut up . . . creep . . . sometimes

13

you make me so mad." A smile began to warm her face again and he leaned over and kissed her. She ran a finger slowly up the inside of his thigh, watching him with that quiet smile of hers, and he tingled all over . . .

He still remembered it. Perfectly.

"Evil woman, I adore you. Come on, let's go home." They had left the beach hand in hand, like two kids, sharing their own private smile. They hadn't even waited until they'd gotten home. A few miles later, Ian had spotted a narrow creek a little distance from the road, and they had parked there and made love under the trees, near the creek, with the summer sounds all around them. He still remembered lying on the soft earth with her afterward, wearing only their shirts and letting their toes play with the pebbles and grass. He still remembered thinking that he would never quite understand what bound her to him . . . why? And what bound him to her? The questions one never asks of marriage . . . why, for your money, darling, why else? No one in his right mind ever asked those questions. But sometimes he was so tempted to. He sometimes feared that what bound him to her was her faith in his writing. He didn't want to think it was that, but that was certainly

14

part of it.

All those nights of argument and coffee and wine in his studio. She was always so goddam sure. When he needed her to be. That was the best part.

"I know you'll make it, Ian. That's all. I just know you will." So goddam sure. That's why she had made him quit his job on Madison Avenue, because she was so sure. Or was it because she'd wanted to make him dependent on her? Sometimes he wondered about that too.

"But *how* do you know, dammit? How can you possibly know I'll make it? It's a dream, Jessie. A fantasy. The great American novel. Do you know how many absolute zeroes are out there writing crap, thinking 'this is it'?"

"Who gives a damn? That's not you."

"Maybe it is." She had thrown a glass of wine at him once when he'd said that, and it made him laugh. They had wound up making love on the thick fur rug while he dripped wine from his chin to her breasts and they laughed together.

It was all part of why he had to write a good one now. Had to. For her. For himself. He had to this time. Six years of writing had produced one disastrous novel and one beautiful book of fables that the critics had hailed as a classic. It had sold less than

15

seven hundred copies. The novel hadn't even done *that* "well." But this one was going to be different. He knew it. It was his brainchild against hers, Lady J.

Lady J was Jessie's boutique. And Jessie had made it a smash. The right touches, the right flair, the right line at the right time. She was one of those people who casts a spell on whatever they touch. A candle, a scarf, a jewel, a flash of color, a hint of a smile, a glow of warmth, a dash of pizzazz, a dollop of style. A barrel of style. Jessie had been born with it. She oozed it. Stark naked and with her eyes closed, she had style.

Like the way she flew into his studio at lunchtime, her blond mane flying, a smile in her eyes, a kiss on his neck, and suddenly one fabulous salmon rose dropped across his papers. One perfect rose, or one brilliant yellow tulip in a crystal vase next to his coffee cup, a few slices of prosciutto, some cantaloupe, a thin sliver of Brie . . . *The New York Times* . . . or *Le Figaro.* She just had it. A gift for transforming everything she touched into something more, something better.

Thinking of her made Ian smile again as he watched the people at the other tables. If Jessie had been there she would have worn something faintly outrageous, a sundress

16

that exposed her back but covered her arms, or something totally covered up but with a slit that gave passersby just the quickest flash of leg, or an unbearably beautiful hat that would only allow them to catch a glimpse of one striking green eye, while the other flirted, then hid. Thinking of her like that drew his attention to the woman in the straw hat a few tables away. He hadn't seen her before. And he thought she was definitely worth seeing. On a hot, sunny afternoon, with two gin and tonics under his belt. He could barely see her face. Only the point of her chin.

She had slender arms and pretty hands with no rings. He watched her sip something frothy through a straw. He felt a familiar stirring as he thought of his wife and watched the girl in the hat. It was a damn shame Jessie wasn't home. It was a day to go to the beach, and swim, and sweat, and get covered with sand, and rub your hands all over each other, oozing suntan oil. The way the woman in the straw hat moved her mouth on the straw in her drink bothered him. It made him want Jessie. Now.

His cannelloni arrived, but it had been a poor choice. Too creamy, too hot, and too much. He should have ordered a salad. And he was loath to order coffee after his few bites of lunch. It was too easy a day to be hard on yourself. It was so much easier just to let yourself go, or your mind, at least. That was harmless. He was having a good time. He always did at Enrico's. He could relax there, watch strangers, meet writers he knew, and admire the women.

For no reason in particular, he let the waiter bring him a third drink. He rarely drank anything other than white wine, but the gin was cool and pleasant. And a third drink wouldn't kill him. There was something about hot days in a usually cool climate . . . you went a bit mad.

The crowd at Enrico's ebbed and flowed, crowding the sidewalk for tables, shunning the red booths indoors. Businessmen freed their necks of ties, models preened, artists scribbled, street musicians played, poets joked. Even the traffic noises were dimmed by the music and the voices. It reminded him of the last day of school. And the topless bars were silent on either side of the restaurant, their neon doused until nightfall. This was much better than neon. It was real. It was young and alive and had the spice of a game.

The girl in the hat never revealed her face as Ian left, but she watched him, and then silently shrugged, and signaled for the check. She could always come back, or maybe . . . what the hell . . .

Ian was thinking of her on his way to the car, slightly tipsy but not so much that it showed. He was dreaming up verses to "Ode to a Faceless Beauty." He laughed to himself as he slid behind the wheel of Jessie's car, wishing he were sliding into Jessie. He was unbearably horny.

He was driving Jessie's little red Morgan. And thoroughly enjoying it. It had been a damn handsome gift, he reflected, as he pulled out the choke. A damn handsome gift. For a damn handsome woman. He had bought it for her with his advance for the fables. The whole check for the car. Madness. But she had adored it. And he adored her.

He swung back onto Broadway and stopped at a light, passing Enrico's again on his way home, just as a whisper of pink brushed past his right eye. The hat swirled on one finger now as her face looked up toward the sky, her behind undulating freely as she walked in high-heeled white sandals. The pink dress tugged at her hips, but not blatantly, and her red hair framed her face in loose curls. She looked pretty in pink, and so goddam sexy. So round and so ripe and so young . . . twenty-two? . . . twenty-three? He felt the same hunger again in his loins as he watched her. Her copper hair reflected the sun. He wanted to touch it. To tear the hat from her hand and run away, to see if she'd follow him. He wanted to play, and he had no one to play with.

He drove slowly past her, and she looked up, and then her face flushed and she looked away, as though she hadn't expected to see him again and now it changed everything. She turned her head and looked at him again, the surprise replaced by a slow smile and a barely visible shrug. Destiny. Today had been the day after all. She had dressed for it. And now she was glad. She seemed unwilling to go, under the heat of his gaze. He hadn't driven on. He simply sat there, while she stood at the corner and watched him. She was not as young as he'd thought. Twenty-six . . . twenty-seven? But still fresh. Fresh enough, after three gin and tonics and not a great deal of food.

Her eyes searched his face, clawing a little, but carefully, and then, as he watched, she approached, showing the full bosom in sharp contrast to the girlish shape of her arms.

"Do I know you?" She stood holding her hat, one ankle suddenly crossing the other; it made her hipbones jut forward, and Ian's trousers were instantly too tight.

"No. I don't think so."

"You've been staring."

"Yes . . . I'm sorry. I . . . I liked your hat. I noticed it at lunch." Her face eased and he returned her smile, disappointed, though. She was older than Jessie, perhaps even a year or two older than he. Made up to look exquisite at a thirty-foot distance, at twenty feet the illusion was shattered. And the red hair showed a thin line of black roots. But he *had* been staring, she was right.

"I'm really awfully sorry. Do you need a lift?" Why not? She couldn't be headed far off his path; probably to an office a few blocks away.

"Yeah, sure. Thanks. It's too hot to walk." She smiled again, and struggled with the handle on the door. Ian released it for her from within, and she pounced onto the seat, displaying a comforting amount of cleavage. That much was real.

"Where can I take you?"

She paused for a moment and then smiled. "Market and Tenth. Is that out of your way?"

"No, that's fine. I'm not in a hurry." But he was surprised at the address. It was an odd place to work, a bad place to live.

"Did you take the day off?" She was look-

21

ing at him questioningly.

"Sort of. I work at home." He wasn't usually that expansive, but she made him uncomfortable, made him feel as though he should talk. She wore a heavy perfume, and her skirt had slipped well up her thighs. Ian was hungry. But for Jessie. And she was still ten hours away.

"What do you do?" For an odd moment he wanted to say he was a gigolo, kept by his wife. He argued the point in his head as he frowned.

"I'm a writer." The answer was curt.

"Don't you like it?"

"I love it. What made you ask that?" This time he was surprised.

"The way you started to frown. You're a nice-looking guy when you smile."

"Thank you."

"*De nada.* You also drive a nice-looking car." Her eyes had sized up the scene. The well-cut St. Tropez shirt, the Gucci shoes with no socks. She didn't know they were Gucci, but she knew they were expensive. "What is this? An MG?"

"No. A Morgan." *And it's my wife's* . . . the words stuck in his throat. "What do you do?" Tit for tat.

"Right now I wait table at the Condor, but I wanted to see what the neighborhood

22

looks like in the daylight. That's why I came down here for lunch. It's a whole different crowd. And at this time of day they're a lot more sober than they are when we get them later."

The Condor was not known for its decorous clientele. It was the home of the "Original Topless," and Ian assumed that the woman waited on tables half nude. She shrugged and then let her face grow soft in a smile. She looked almost pretty again, but there was a sadness somewhere in her eyes. A kind of regret, haunting and distant. She glanced at him oddly once or twice. And again Ian found that she had made him uncomfortable.

"You live at Market and Tenth?" It was something to say.

"Yeah. In a hotel. You?" That one was a bitch to answer. What could he say? But she filled the pause for him. "Let me guess. Pacific Heights?" The brightness in her eyes was gone now, and the question sounded brittle and accusing.

"What makes you say that?" He tried to sound amused and look mock-hurt, but it didn't come off. He looked at her as they stopped in a snarl of Montgomery Street traffic. She could have been someone's secretary, or a girl doing a bit part in a movie. She didn't look cheap. She looked tired. And sad.

"Sweetheart, you smell of Pacific Heights. It's all over you."

"Don't let fragrances fool you. As in 'all that glitters' . . . ." They laughed lightly together and he played with the choke as the traffic jam eased. He turned the car onto Market.

"Married?"

He nodded.

"Too bad. The good ones always are."

"Is that a deterrent?" It was an insane thing to have said, but he was more curious than serious, and the gin and tonics had taken their toll.

"Sometimes I go for married guys, sometimes I don't. Depends on the guy. In your case . . . who knows? I like you."

"I'm flattered. You're a nice-looking woman, as you put it. What's your name?"

"Margaret. Maggie."

"That's a nice name." She smiled at him again. "Is this it, Maggie?" It was the only hotel on the block, and it was no beauty.

"Yeah, this is it. Home sweet home. Beautiful, ain't it?" She tried to cover her embarrassment with flippancy, and he found himself feeling sorry for her. The hotel looked bleak and depressing.

"Want to come up for a drink?"

He knew from the look in her eyes that she'd be hurt if he didn't. And, hell, he was in no shape to go home and work. And he still had nine and a half hours to kill before driving out to the airport. But he also knew what might happen if he accepted Maggie's invitation. And letting that happen seemed like a rotten thing to do to Jessie the day she was coming home. He had held out for three weeks. Why not one more afternoon? . . .

But this girl looked so lonely, so unloved, and the gin and the sun were spinning in his brain. He knew he didn't want to go back to the house. Nothing in it was his, not really his, except five file drawers of his writing and the new Olivetti typewriter Jessie had given him. The gigolo king. Jessie's consort.

"Sure. I've got time for a drink. As long as you make it coffee. What'll I do with the car?"

"I think you can park it in front of the door. It's a white zone, they won't tow you away."

He parked the car in front of the hotel, and Maggie carefully watched the back of the car as he pulled in to the curb. It was an

25

easy plate to remember. It spelled what she thought was his name. Jessie.

CHAPTER 2

Jessica heard the landing gear grind out of the plane's belly and smiled. Her seat belt was in place, her overhead light was out, and she felt her heart begin to beat faster as the plane circled the runway for the last time. She had a clear view of the lights below.

She looked at her watch. She knew him so well. Right now he would be frantically looking for a parking space in the airport garage, terrified that he was late and might miss her at the gate. He'd find a space then, and run like hell for the terminal, and would be panting and smiling, nerves jangled, when he reached her. But he'd get there in time. He always did. It made coming home something special.

She felt as though she had been away for a year, but she'd bought such good things. The spring line would be lovely. Soft pastels, gentle wools cut on the bias, creamy plaids, silk shirts with full sleeves, and some marvelous suedes. She could never resist the suedes. It would be a great spring at the boutique. The goodies she had ordered wouldn't begin to arrive for another three or four months, but she was already excited thinking about them. She had them all memorized. The spring line was set. She liked to plan ahead like that. Liked knowing what was coming. Liked knowing that she had her life, and her work, all mapped out. Some people might find that boring, but it never bothered Jessie.

She and Ian were planning a trip to Carmel in October. Thanksgiving would be spent with friends. Maybe Christmas skiing at Lake Tahoe, and then a quick hop to Mexico for some sun after the New Year. And then the spring line would start to come in. It was all perfectly planned. Like her trips, like her meals, like her wardrobe. She had what it took to make plans — a business that worked, a husband she loved and could always count on, and reliable people around her. Very little was variable, and she liked it that way. She wondered if that was why she had never wanted a baby: it would be a variable. Something she couldn't totally plan. She didn't know how it would look or act, or exactly when it might be born, or what she would do with it once she had it. The idea of a baby unnerved her. And life was so much simpler like this. Just Jessie and Ian. Alone. And that way there were no rivals for Ian's affection. Jessie didn't like to compete, not for Ian. He was all she had now.

The wheels touched the runway, and she closed her eyes . . . Ian . . . she had longed for him over the past weeks. The days had been full and the nights busy, yet she had usually called him when she'd reached the hotel in the evening. But she hadn't been able to reach out and touch him, or be held. She hadn't been able to laugh into his eyes, or tickle his feet, or stand next to him under the shower, chasing drops of water past the freckles on his back with her tongue. She stretched her long legs ahead of her as she waited for the plane to come to a halt.

It was hard to be patient. She wanted the trip to be over. She wanted to run out and see him. Right now. There had never been other men. It was hard to believe, but there hadn't. She had given it some thought, once or twice, but it had never seemed worth it. Ian was so much better than anyone else, in her eyes. Sexier and smarter and kinder and more loving. Ian understood so well what she needed, and fulfilled so many needs. In the seven years they'd been married, she had lost track of most of her close women friends in New York, and hadn't replaced them with others in San Francisco. She didn't need women friends, a confidante, a "best" friend. She had Ian. He was her best friend, her lover, even her brother, now that Jake was dead. And so what if now and then Ian had a "fling"? It didn't happen often, and he was discreet. It didn't bother her. Men did those things when they had to, when their wives were away. He didn't use it, or flaunt it, or grind it into her heart. She just suspected that he did it. That was all. She understood. As long as she didn't have to know. She assumed, which was different from knowing.

Her parents had had a marriage like that, and they had been happy for years. Watching them, Jessie had understood about the things you didn't talk about, didn't hurt each other with, didn't use. A good marriage relied on consideration, and sometimes keeping your mouth shut and just letting the other guy be was consideration . . . love. Her parents were dead now; they hadn't been young when she'd been born. Her mother had been in her late thirties, her father just past forty-five. And Jessie had been four when Jake was born. But marrying late, they had respected each other more than most couples did. They were not inclined to make changes in each other. It had taught Jessie a lot.

But they were all gone now. It had already been three years. Almost exactly. Her parents had died within months of each other. Jake had died a year before that, in Vietnam, at the crest of his twenties. Gone. Jessica was the only one left. But she had Ian. Thank God there was Ian. It sent little tremors up her spine when she thought of it that way . . . what would she do without Ian? Die . . . the way her father had done without her mother . . . die . . . she couldn't live without Ian. He was her all now. He held her late at night when she was afraid. He made her laugh when something touched too deep and made her sad. He remembered the moments that mattered, knew the things that she loved, understood her private language, laughed at all her worst jokes. He knew. She was his woman, and his little girl. That was what she needed. Ian. So what did it matter if there were occasional indiscretions she didn't really know about? As long as he was there when it counted. And he always was.

She heard the doors slide open; the people began to press into the aisles. The five-hour flight was over. It was time to go home. Jessie brushed the creases from her slacks with one hand and reached for her coat with the other. It was a bright orange suede that she wore over beige suede pants and a print silk shirt in shades of caramel. Her green eyes glowed in her suntanned face, and her blond hair swung thick and free past her shoulders. Ian loved her in orange, and she had bought the coat in New York. She smiled to herself, thinking how he'd love it — almost as much as the Pierre Cardin blazer she'd brought him. It was fun to spoil Ian.

Three businessmen and a gaggle of women pressed out before her, but she was tall enough to see over the chattering women's heads. He was there at the gate, and she waved as he grinned broadly, waving back, and then he moved swiftly toward her, gently weaving his way through the people ahead of her. Then he had reached her and was taking her in his arms.

"It's about time you came home . . . and looking like that, you'll be lucky if I don't rape you right here." He looked so pleased. And then he kissed her. She was home.

"Go ahead. Rape me. I dare you." But they stood where they were, drinking each other in, saying it all with their eyes. Jessie couldn't keep a smile from her lips, or her hands from his face. "You feel so good." She loved the softness and spiced lemon smell of his skin.

"Jessie, if you knew how I missed you . . ." She nodded, knowing. She had missed him at least as much.

"How's the book?"

"Nice." They spoke in the brief banalities of those who know each other better than well. They didn't need many words. "Really nice." He picked up her large brown leather tote from the floor where she'd dropped it to kiss him. "Come on, sexy lady, let's go home." She looped her arm into his, and together they walked in long even strides, her hair brushing his shoulder, her every move a complement to his.

"I brought you a present."

He smiled. She always did.

"Bought yourself one too, I see. That's some coat."

"Do you like it? Or is it awful? I was afraid it was a little too loud." It was a burnt caramel bordering on flame.

"On you it looks good. Everything does."

"Jesus, you're being nice to me! What did you do? Smash up the car?"

"Now, is that a nice thing to say? I ask you. Is that nice?"

"Did you?" But she was laughing and so was he.

"No, I traded it for a Honda motorcycle. I thought you might like that better."

"What a nice thought! Gee, darling, I'm just thrilled. Now come on, tell the truth. How bad is the car?"

"Bad? I'll have you know that it happens to be not only in impeccable condition, but clean, a condition it was *not* in when you left. That poor little car was filthy!"

"Yeah, I know." She hung her head and he grinned.

"You're a disgrace, Mrs. Clarke, but I love you." He kissed the tip of her nose and she slid her arms around his neck.

"Guess what?"

"How many guesses do I get?"

"One."

"You love me?"

"You guessed it!" She giggled and kissed his neck.

"What do I get as a prize for guessing?"

"Me."

"Terrific. I'll take it."

"Boy, I'm glad to be home." She heaved a small sigh and stood in the circle of his arms as they waited for her bags to appear on the turntable. He could see the relief in her eyes. She hated going away, hated flying, was afraid to die, was afraid he'd die in a car wreck while she was gone. Ever since her parents and her brother . . . so many terrors. It wasn't as if they had died violently. Her mother had just been old. Old enough. Sixty-eight. And her father in his seventies. He had died of grief less than a year later. But Jessie hadn't been ready for the double loss and it was incredible to see what it had done to her. She had never fully recovered from her brother's death, but after her parents . . . At times Ian wondered if she'd make it. The terrors, the hysteria, the nightmares. She felt so alone and so frightened. At times she wasn't even someone he knew. She was suddenly so dependent on him, so unlike the old Jessie. And it seemed as though she wanted to be sure he was equally dependent on her . . . That was when he had let her talk him into quitting his job and writing full-time. She could afford it. But in some ways he wasn't sure *he* could. It suited both of them though, most of the time. And supporting him made Jessie feel more secure. He really *was* all she had now.

She looked up at him again and smiled.

"Just wait till I get you home, Mrs. Clarke."

"Lech."

"Yep. And you love it."

"Yes. I do."

People were watching them, but they didn't notice. They gave people something pretty to look at, something to smile at, to feel good about, to wish for. And something to enjoy as well. They were two beautiful people who had it all. That usually aroused an interesting medley of emotions in those who watched them.

They walked to the garage to reclaim the Morgan and Jessie grinned with pride when she saw it.

"Christ, it looks good. What did you do to it?"

"Had it washed. You should try it sometime. You'll love the effect."

"Oh, shut up." She swung at him playfully, and he ducked, catching her arm as she laughed.

"Before you beat me up, Amazon, get in the car." He slapped her on the behind and unlocked the door.

"Don't call me an Amazon, you miserable creep! Masher!"

"Masher? Did I hear you call me a masher?" He looked shocked and walked back to where she stood. "Lady, how dare you call me a name like that?" And with that he swung her off her feet and slid her onto the seat of the car. "There. And let me tell you, with a broad your size, that's no mean feat!"

"Ian, you're a shit." But he knew she wasn't sensitive about her height. They both liked it. "Besides, I think I'm shrinking."

"Oh? Down to six-one now, are you?" He chuckled as he finished strapping her bag to the luggage rack in the back. He still had the top down on the car, and she was watching him with a smile.

"Go to hell. You know perfectly well I'm only five-eleven, but I measured myself the other day and I was only five-ten-and-a-half."

"You must have been sitting down."

He slid in beside her and turned to look into her eyes. "Hello, Mrs. Clarke. Welcome home."

"Hello, my love. It's so good to be back." They shared a long smile as he started the car, and she shrugged out of the new coat and rolled up the sleeves of her blouse. "Was it hot here today? It still feels warm now."

"It was boiling and gorgeous and sunny. And if it's anything like that tomorrow, you can call the boutique and tell them you're snowed in in Chicago. We're going to the beach."

"Snowed in, in September? You're crazy.

And, darling, I really can't." But she liked the idea and he knew it.

"Oh, yes you can. I'll kidnap you if I have to."

"Maybe I could go in late."

"Now you've got the idea." He smiled victoriously as he pulled the choke.

"Was it really that nice today?"

"Nicer. And it would have been better yet if you had been home. I got crocked at lunch at Enrico's, and I didn't know what to do with myself all day."

"I'm sure you found something." But there was no malice in her tone, and no expression on his face.

"Nah. Nothing much."

CHAPTER 3

"Jessie, you are without a doubt the most beautiful woman I know."

"It's entirely mutual." She lay on her stomach, smiling up at him, the scent of their bodies heavy in the air, their hair tousled. They had not been awake very long. Only long enough to make love.

"It can't be mutual, silly. I'm not a beautiful woman."

"No, but you're a magnificent man."

"And you are adorably corny. You must live with a writer." She smiled again and he ran a finger gently up her spine.

"You're going to get into trouble again, darling, if you do that." She accepted a puff on the cigarette they shared, and exhaled over his head before sitting up to kiss him again.

"What time are we going to the beach, Jessie, my love?"

"Who said we were going to the beach?

Jesus, darling, I have to get to the shop. I've been gone for three weeks."

"So be gone for another day. You said you were going to the beach with me today." He looked faintly like a pouting boy.

"I did not."

"You most certainly did. Well, almost. I told you I'd kidnap you, and you seemed to like the idea." She laughed, running a hand through his hair. He was impossible. A great big boy. But such a beautiful boy. She could never resist him.

"You know something?"

"What?" He looked pleased as he gazed down into her face. She was beautiful in the morning.

"You're a pain in the ass, that's what. I have to work. How can I go to the beach?"

"Easy. You call the girls, tell them you can't come in till tomorrow, and off we go. Simple. How can you waste a day like this, for Chrissake?"

"By making a living."

Those were the comments he didn't like. They implied that he didn't make a living.

"How about if I go in this morning and cut the day short?"

"Yeah. And leave the boutique just as the fog comes in. Jessica, you're a party pooper. Yep. Party pooper. A–1." But she was already on her way to make coffee, and answered him over her shoulder as she walked naked into the kitchen.

"I promise I'll leave the shop by one. How's that?"

"Better than nothing. Christ, I love your ass. And you lost weight." She smiled and blew him a kiss.

"One o'clock, I promise. And we can have lunch here."

"Does that mean what I think it does?" He was smiling again and she nodded. "Then I'll pick you up at twelve-thirty."

"That's a deal."

Lady J nestled on the ground floor of a well-tended Victorian house just off Union Street. The house was painted yellow with white trim, and a small brass plaque on the door was engraved with LADY J. Jessie had had a broad picture window put in, and she did the window display herself twice a month. It was simple and effective, and as she pulled the Morgan into the driveway she looked up to see what they'd done with the display while she was gone. A brown tweed skirt, a camel-colored stock shirt, amber beads, a trim knit hat, and a little fox jacket draped over a green velvet chair. It looked pretty damn good, and it was the

41

right look for fall . . . though not for Indian summer. But that didn't matter. No one bought for Indian summer. They bought for fall.

The things she had ordered in New York flashed through her mind as she pulled her briefcase out of the car and ran up the few steps to their door. It was open; the girls had known she'd be in early.

"Well, look who's home! Zina! Jessie's back!" A tiny, fine-featured Oriental girl clapped her hands and jumped to her feet, running toward Jessie with a look of delight. "You look fantastic!" The two were a striking pair. Jessie's fair, lanky beauty was in sharp contrast to the Japanese girl's delicate grace. Her hair was shiny and black and hung in a well-shaped slant from the nape of her neck toward the point of her chin.

"Kat! You cut your hair!" Jessie was momentarily taken aback. Only a month before the girl's hair had hung to her waist — when she hadn't worn it in a tight knot high on her head. Her name was Katsuko, which meant peace.

"I got sick of wearing it up. How do you like it?" She pirouetted swiftly on one foot and let her hair swing around her head as she smiled. She was dressed in black, as she often was, and it accented her litheness. It

42

was her catlike grace that had given her the nickname Jessie used.

"I love it. Very chic." They smiled at each other and were rapidly interrupted by a war cry of glee.

"Hallelujah! You're home!" It was Zina. Auburn-haired, brown-eyed, sensual, and Southern. She was buxom where the other two were elegantly small-breasted, and she had a mouth that said she loved laughter and men. Her hair danced close to her head in a small halo of curls, and she had great, sexy legs. Men dissolved when she moved, and she loved to tease. "Did you see what Kat did to her hair?" She said "hair" as though it would go on forever. "I'd have cried for a year." She smiled, letting her mouth slide over the words. She made each one a caress. "How was New York?"

"Beautiful, wonderful, terrible, ugly, and hot. I had a ball. And wait till you see what I bought!"

"What kind of colors?" For a girl who almost always wore white or black, Kat had a flair for hot colors. She knew how to buy them, mix them, contrast them, blend them. Everything except wear them.

"It's all pastel, and it's so beautiful, you'll die." Jessica strutted the thick beige carpeting of Lady J. It felt good to be back in her

43

domain. "Who did the window? It looks great."

"Zina." Kat was quick to single out her friend for praise. "Isn't that a nice touch with the green chair for contrast?"

"It's terrific. And I see nothing's changed around here. You two are still as tight as Siamese twins. Did we make any money while I was gone?" She sat in her favorite beige leather chair, a deep one that allowed her plenty of room for her legs. It was the chair men usually sat in while they waited.

"We made lots of money. For the first two weeks anyway. This week's been slow; the weather's been too good." Kat was quick with the report, and the last of it reminded Jessie that she had only four hours in which to work before Ian would come to spirit her away to the beach.

Zina handed her a cup of black coffee as she looked around. What she saw was the fall line she had bought, mostly in Europe, five months before, and against the beige and brown wools and leathers of the shop's subtle decor it showed up well. Two walls were mirrored and there was a jungle of plants in each corner. More greenery dripped from the ceiling, highlighted by subtle lighting.

"How's that Danish line doing?" The

Danes had gone heavy on red — skirts, sweaters, three different styles of blazers, and a marvelous wrap-around coat in a deep cherry red that, in its own way, made a woman feel as exotic and sexy as fur would have. It was a great coat. Jessie had ordered one for herself.

"The Danish stuff is doing fine," Zina intervened with her New Orleans drawl. "How's Ian? We haven't seen him in weeks." He had turned up once to cash a check, the day after Jessie had left.

"He's working on the new book." Zina smiled warmly and nodded. She liked him. Kat was never as sure. She helped with the account books, so she knew how much of Jessica's profits he spent. But Zina had been in the shop much longer, and she had come to know Ian and appreciate him. Kat was newer, and still wore the brittle mantle of New York over her heart. She had been a sportswear buyer there until she'd tired of the pressure and decided to move to San Francisco. She had landed the job at Lady J within a week of her arrival, and she felt as lucky to be there as Jessie did having her in the shop. She knew the business. Totally.

The three women spent a half hour chatting over coffee while Katsuko showed Jessie some clippings of articles mentioning the boutique that had appeared in the papers. They had two new customers who had practically bought out the shop. And they talked easily of what Jessie had lined up for the fall. She wanted to set up a fashion show before she left for Carmel in October. Kat could get started on ideas for that.

The shop was alive with her presence, and together they made a powerful threesome. All three had something to offer. It showed in the fact that the boutique hadn't suffered while she'd been gone. She couldn't afford to have it do that, and she wouldn't have tolerated it, either. Both of the girls knew that, and they cherished their jobs. She paid well, they got marvelous clothes at a discount, and she was a reasonable woman to work for, which was rare. Kat had worked for three bitches in a row in New York, and Zina had escaped a long line of horny men who wanted her to type, take shorthand, and screw, not necessarily in that order. Jessica expected long hours and hard work, but she put in the same herself, and often more. She had made Lady J a success, and she expected them to help her maintain it. It wasn't a difficult task. She infused fresh life into it every season, and her clientele loved it. Lady J was as solid as a rock. Just like Jessica herself, and everything around her.

"And now, you two, I'd better dig through my mail. How bad is it?"

"Not too bad. Zina answered the dingy stuff. The letters from Texas from women who were here in March and wonder if the little yellow turtleneck is still on sale. That kind of stuff . . . she answered them all."

"Zina, I love you."

"At your service." She swept a deep curtsy and the bright green halter she wore over white trousers bobbed with the weight of her breasts. But the other two had stopped teasing her long ago. Each was content with herself, and all three had good reason to be.

Jessie wandered into her small office three steps up in the back and looked around, pleased. Her plants were thriving, her mail was neatly divided and stacked, her bills had been paid. She saw at a glance that all was in order. Now all she had to do was sift through it. She was halfway through reading her mail when Zina appeared in the doorway, looking puzzled.

"There's a man here to see you, Jessie. He says it's urgent." She looked almost worried. He was not one of their usual customers, and he hadn't come there to buy.

"To see me? What about?"

47

"He didn't say. But he asked me to give you his card." Zina extended the small rectangle of stiff white paper, and Jessie looked into her eyes.

"Something wrong?" Zina shrugged ignorance and Jessie read the name: "William Houghton. Inspector. San Francisco Police." She didn't understand and looked back at Zina for clues. "Did anything happen while I was gone? Did we get robbed?" And Christ, wouldn't it be like them not to worry her at first, but wait and tell her an hour or two later!

"No, Jessie. Honest. Nothing happened. I don't have any idea what this is about." The drawl sounded childish when Zina was worried.

"Neither do I. Why don't you bring him in here? I'd better talk to him."

William Houghton appeared, following Zina with some interest. The fit of her white slacks over her trim hips was in sharp contrast to the fullness in her halter. The inspector looked hungry.

"Inspector Houghton?" Jessie stood to her full height, and Houghton seemed impressed. The three were an interesting group; Katsuko had not missed his thorough gaze either. "I'm Jessica Clarke."

"I'd like to speak to you alone for a

48

minute, if that'll be all right."

"That's fine. May I offer you a cup of coffee?" The door closed behind Zina, and he shook his head as Jessie indicated a chair near her desk and then sat back down in her own. She swiveled to face him. "What can I do for you, Inspector? Miss Nelson said it was urgent."

"Yes. It is. Is that your Morgan outside?" Jessie nodded, feeling queasy under the sharp look in his eyes. She was wondering if Ian had forgotten to pay his tickets again. She had had to fish him out of jail once before, for a neat little fine of two hundred dollars. In San Francisco, they didn't fool around. You paid your tickets or they took you to jail. Do not pass Go, and do not collect two hundred dollars.

"Yes, that's my car. My name's on the plates." She smiled pleasantly and hoped that her hand didn't shake while she lit another cigarette. It was absurd. She hadn't done anything wrong, but there was something about the man, about the word "Police," that produced instant guilt. Panic. Terror.

"Were you driving it yesterday?"

"No, I was in New York on business. I flew back last night." As though she had to prove that she was out of town, and for a legiti-

49

mate reason. This was crazy. If only Ian were here. He handled things so much better than she did.

"Who else drives your car?" Not "does anyone else?," but "who else?"

"My husband does." Something sank in the pit of her stomach when she mentioned Ian.

"Did he drive it yesterday?" Inspector Houghton lit a cigarette of his own and looked her over, as if assessing her.

"I don't know for certain. He has his own car, but he was driving mine when he picked me up at the airport. I could call him and ask." Houghton nodded and Jessica waited.

"Who else drives the car? A brother? A friend? Boyfriend?" His eyes dug into hers on the last word, and at last she felt anger.

"I'm a married woman, Inspector. And no one else drives the car. Just my husband and I." She had gotten the point across, but something in Houghton's face told her it was not a victory.

"The car is registered to your business? You have commercial plates, and the address on the registration is this store." Store! Boutique, you asshole, boutique! "I assume you own this place?"

"That's correct. Inspector, what is this about?" She exhaled lengthily and watched the smoke as she felt her hand shake slightly. Something was wrong.

"I'd like to speak to your husband. Would you give me the address of his office, please?" He instantly took out a pen and waited, holding it poised over the back of one of his cards.

"Is this about parking tickets? I know my husband . . . well, he's forgetful." She smiled for Houghton's benefit, but it didn't take.

"No, this is not about parking tickets. Your husband's business address?" The eyes were like ice.

"He works at our home. It's only six blocks from here. On Vallejo." She wanted to offer to go with him, but she didn't dare. She scribbled the address on one of her own cards and handed it to him.

"Thank you. I'll be in touch." But what the fuck about, dammit? She wanted to know. But he stood up and reached for the door.

"Inspector, I'd appreciate it very much if you'd tell me what this is about. I —" He looked at her oddly again, with that searching look of his that asked questions but did not answer them.

"Mrs. Clarke, I'm not entirely sure myself. When I am, I'll let you know."

"Thank you." Thank you? Thank you for

what? Shit.

But he was already gone, and as she walked back into the main room of the boutique, she saw him get into an olive green sedan and drive off. There was another man at the wheel. They traveled in pairs. The antenna on the back of the car swung crazily as they drove toward Vallejo.

"What was that all about?" Katsuko's face was serious, and Zina looked upset.

"I wish to hell I knew. He just asked me who drives the car and then said he wanted to talk to Ian. Goddammit, I'll bet he hasn't been paying his parking tickets again." But it didn't feel like that, and Houghton had said it wasn't that — or was it? Jesus. Some welcome home.

She went back to her office and dialed their home number. It was busy. And then Trish Barclay walked into the shop and Jessie got tied up with nonsense like the fur jacket in the window, which Trish bought. She was one of their better customers, and Jessie had to keep up the façade, at least for a while. It was twenty-five minutes later when she got back to the phone to call Ian. This time there was no answer.

It was ridiculous! He had to be there. He had been there when she'd left for the boutique. And the line had been busy when

52

she'd called . . . the police had been on their way over. Christ, maybe it was serious. Maybe he had had an accident with the car and hadn't told her. Maybe someone had been hurt. But he'd have said something. Ian wouldn't just let something like that happen and not tell her. The phone rang endlessly, and no one answered. Maybe he was on his way over. It was a little after eleven.

But Nick Morris needed something "fabulous" for his wife's birthday; he'd forgotten, and he had to have at least four hundred dollars' worth of goodies for her by noon. She was a raving bitch and she wasn't worth it, but Jessie gave him a hand. She liked Nick, and before he left the store weighted down with their shiny brown and yellow boxes, Barbara Fuller had walked in, and Holly Jenkins, and then Joan Wilcox, and . . . it was noon. And she hadn't heard from Ian. She tried the phone again and began to panic. No answer. Maybe this time he *was* on his way over. He had said he'd pick her up at twelve-thirty.

At one o'clock he hadn't shown up and she was near tears. It had been a horrible morning. People, pressures, deliveries, problems. Welcome home. And no Ian. And that asshole Houghton making her nervous

53

with his mysterious inquiries about the car. She took refuge in her office as Zina went out to lunch. She needed to be alone for a minute. To think. To catch her breath. To get up the courage to do what she didn't want to do. But she had to know. It would be an easy way of finding out, after all. Hell, all she had to do was call down there, ask if they had an Ian Powers Clarke, and heave a sigh of relief when they said no. Or grab her checkbook and run down there and get him out if he was in the can for parking violations again. No big deal. But it took another swallow of coffee, and yet another cigarette before she could bring her hand to the phone.

Information gave her the number. Hall of Justice. City Prison. This was ridiculous. She felt foolish, and grinned thinking of what Ian would say if she were calling the jail when he walked in. He'd make fun of her for a week.

A voice barked into her ear at the other end. "City Prison. Palmer here." Jesus. Now what? Okay, you called, so ask the man, dummy.

"I . . . I was wondering if you have a . . . a Mr. Ian Clarke, Ian Powers Clarke, down there, Sergeant. On parking violations."

"What's the spelling?" The desk sergeant

was not amused. Parking violations were serious business.

"Clarke. With an 'E' at the end. Ian. I-A-N C-L-A-R-K-E." She took another drag on her cigarette while she waited, and Katsuko stuck her head in the door with an inquiry about lunch. Jessica shook her head vehemently and motioned to close the door. Her nerves had begun to fray hours ago, with the arrival of Inspector Houghton.

The voice came back on the phone after an interminable pause.

"Clarke. Yeah. We got him." Well, bully for you. Jessica heaved a small sigh of relief. It was disagreeable, but not the end of the world. And at least now she knew, and she could have him out in half an hour. She wondered how many tickets he hadn't paid this time. But this time she was going to let him have a piece of her mind. He had scared the shit out of her. And that was probably what Houghton had wanted to do. He had, too, by not admitting that the problem was parking violations. Bastard.

"We booked him an hour ago. They're talking to him now."

"About parking tickets?" How ridiculous. Enough was enough. And Jessica had had more than enough already.

"No, lady. Not about parking tickets.

About three counts of rape and a charge of assault." Jessie thought she could feel the ceiling pressing down on her head as the walls rushed in to squeeze the breath out of her lungs.

"What?"

"Three counts of rape. And a charge of assault."

"My God. Can I talk to him?" Her hands shook so hard it took both of them to hold the phone, and she felt her breakfast rise in her throat.

"No. He can talk to his lawyer, and you can see him tomorrow. Between eleven and two. Bail hasn't been set. The arraignment's on Thursday." The desk sergeant hung up on her then, and she was holding the dead receiver in her hand, with a blank look in her eyes and tears beginning to stream down her face, when Katsuko opened the door and held out a sandwich. It took her a moment to absorb what she saw.

"My God. What happened?" She stopped in her tracks and stared into the bedlam of Jessica's eyes. Jessica never came apart, never cried, never wavered, never . . . At least they never saw that side of her at the shop.

"I don't know what happened. But there's been this incredible, horrible, most ridicu-

56

lous fucking mistake!" She was shouting and she picked up the sandwich Kat had brought in and threw it across the room. Three counts of rape. And one count of assault. What in hell was going on?

CHAPTER 4

"Jessie? Where are you going?"

She brushed past Zina, returning from lunch, as she rushed out the door.

"Just make believe I never got back from New York. I'm going home. But don't call me." She yanked open the door of her car and got in.

"Are you sick?" Zina was calling from the top of the steps, but Jessica just shook her head, pulled the choke, turned on the ignition, and roared into reverse.

Zina walked into the boutique bewildered, but Katsuko could tell her nothing more than what she had seen. Jessie was upset, but Kat didn't know why. It had something to do with the policeman's visit that morning. The two girls were worried, but she had told them not to call her at home, and the afternoon at the boutique was too busy for them to have time to speculate. Katsuko figured it had something to do with Ian, but she didn't know what. Zina was left in the dark.

When she got home, Jessica grabbed for the phone with one hand and her address book with the other. A cup half filled with coffee sat on the kitchen table. Ian had been in the middle of his breakfast when they'd taken him away, and something in Jessie's heart told her that Houghton had been the one who had taken Ian away. She wondered if the neighbors had seen it.

A stack of pages from the new book lay near the coffee. Nothing else. No note or message to her. He must have been shocked. And obviously it was an insane accusation. They had the wrong man. In a few hours the nightmare would be over, and he would be home. Her sanity had returned. Now all they needed was an attorney. She simply wouldn't allow herself to panic.

Her address book yielded the name she wanted, and she was in luck; he was free when she called, and not out to lunch as she'd feared he would be. He was a man she and Ian respected, an attorney with a good reputation, senior partner of his firm. Philip Wald.

"But Jessica, I don't do criminal work."

"What difference does that make?"

"Quite a lot, I'm afraid. What you want is a good criminal defense attorney."

"But he didn't do it, for Chrissake. We just need someone to straighten things out and get him out of this mess."

"Have you spoken to him?"

"No, they wouldn't let me. Look, Philip, please. Just go down there and talk to them. Talk to Ian. This whole thing is absurd." At the other end of the phone, there was silence.

"I can do that. But I can't take the case. It wouldn't be fair to either of you."

"What case? This is just a matter of misidentification."

"Do you know what it's based on?"

"Something to do with my car."

"Did they have your license plate?"

"Yes."

"Well, yes, then they might have transposed the numbers or letters." She didn't say anything, but it was hard to transpose the spelling of "Jessie" and come up with the wrong name. That was the only thing that bothered her. The tie-in with her car. "I'll tell you what. I'll go down and see him, find out what's going on, and I'll give you some names of defense attorneys. Get in touch with them, and whoever you settle on, tell him I'll give him a call later and fill

60

him in on what I know. And tell them I told you to call."

She sighed deeply. "Thank you, Philip. That helps."

He gave her the names and promised to come by the house as soon as he'd seen Ian. And she settled down with Ian's cold coffee to phone Philip's friends. Criminal defense attorneys all. The calls were not cheering.

The first one was out of town. The second one was in court for at least the next week and could not be disturbed with a new case. The third was too tied up to talk to her. The fourth was out. But the fifth spent some time with her on the phone. Jessie hated his voice.

"Does he have a previous record?"

"No. Of course not. Only parking violations."

"Drugs? Any problems with drugs?"

"None."

"Is he a drinker?"

"No, only wine at social occasions." Christ, the man already thought Ian had done it. That much was clear.

"Did he know this woman before . . . ah . . . was he previously acquainted with her?"

"I don't know anything about the woman. And I assume that this is all a mistake."

61

"What makes you think so?"

Bastard. Jessie already hated him.

"I know my husband."

"Did she identify him?"

"I don't know. Mr. Wald can tell you all that when he comes back from seeing Ian." At the jail . . . oh Jesus . . . Ian was in jail and it was for real, and this goddam lawyer was asking her stupid questions about whether or not Ian knew the woman who was accusing him of rape. Who cared? She just wanted him home, dammit. Now. Didn't anyone understand that? Her chest got tight and it was hard to breathe as she attempted to keep her voice calm to hide the rising panic pumping at her insides.

"Well, young lady, I'll tell you. You and your husband have a pile of trouble on your hands. But it's an interesting case." Oh, for Chrissake. "I'd be willing to handle the matter for you. But there is the question of my fee. Payable in advance."

"In advance?" She was shocked.

"Yes. You'll find that most of my colleagues, if not all, handle matters the same way. I really have to collect before I get into a case, because once I appear in Superior Court for your husband, I then become the attorney of record, and legally I'm locked into the case, whether you pay the fee or not. And if your husband goes to prison, you just may not pay up. Do you have any assets?"

Ian go to prison? Fuck you, mister.

"Yes, we have assets." She could hardly unclench her teeth.

"What kind of assets?"

"I can assure you that I could manage your fee."

"Well, I like to be sure. My fee for this would be fifteen thousand dollars."

"What? In advance?"

"I'd want half of that before the arraignment. I believe you said that's on Thursday. And half immediately after."

"But there's no way I could possibly turn my assets into cash in two days."

"Then I'm afraid there's no way I could possibly handle the case."

"Thank you." She wanted to tell him to get fucked. But by then she was beginning to panic again. Who in God's name would help her?

The sixth person whose name Philip had given her turned out to be human. His name was Martin Schwartz.

"Sounds like you've got yourself one hell of a problem, or at least your husband does. Do you think he did it?" It was an interesting question, and she liked him for even assuming there was some doubt. She hesitated for only a moment. The man deserved a thoughtful answer.

"No, I don't. And not just because I'm his wife. I don't believe he could do something like that. It isn't in him, and he doesn't need to."

"All right, I'll accept that. But people do strange things, Mrs. Clarke. For your own sake, be prepared to accept that. Your husband may have a side to him you don't even know."

It was possible. Anything was possible. But she didn't believe it. She couldn't.

"I'd like to talk to Philip Wald after he sees him," Schwartz went on.

"I'd appreciate it if you would. There's something called an arraignment scheduled for Thursday. We're going to need legal counsel by then, and Philip doesn't feel he's qualified to take the case." The case . . . the case . . . the case . . . she already hated the word.

"Philip's a good man."

"I know. Mr. Schwartz . . . I hate to bring this up, but . . ."

"My fee?"

"Your fee." She heaved a deep sigh and felt a knot tighten in her stomach.

"We can discuss that. I'll try to be reasonable."

"I'll tell you frankly, the man I spoke to before you asked for fifteen thousand dollars by Thursday. I couldn't even begin to swing that."

"Do you have any assets?" Oh Christ, not that again.

"Yes, I have assets." Her tone was suddenly disagreeable. "I have a business, a house, and a car. And my husband also has a car. But we can't just sell the house, or my business, in two days."

It interested him the way she said "my business," not "our." He wondered what "his" business was, if any.

"I wasn't expecting you to liquidate your assets on the spot, Mrs. Clarke." His tone was calm but firm. Something about him soothed her. "But I was thinking that you may need some collateral for the bail — if they make the charges stick, which remains to be seen. Bail can run pretty high. We'll worry about that later. As for my fee, I think two thousand dollars up to trial would be reasonable. And if it goes to trial, an additional five thousand dollars. But that won't be for a couple of months, and if you're a friend of Philip's, I won't worry." It struck her then that people who weren't "friends of Philip's" were in a world of trouble. She felt suddenly grateful. "How does that sound to you?"

She nodded silently to herself, aghast but relieved. It was certainly better than the fee she had heard a few moments before. It would clean out her savings account, but at least she could manage the two thousand. They could worry about the other five later, if it came to that. She'd sell the Morgan if she had to, and without thinking twice. Ian's ass was on the line, and she needed him one hell of a lot more than she needed the Morgan. And there was always her mother's jewelry. But that was sacred. Even for Ian.

"We can manage."

"Fine. When can I see you?"

"Anytime you like."

"Then I'd like to see you tomorrow in my office. I'll talk to Wald this afternoon, and get up to see Mr. Clarke in the morning. Can you be in my office at ten-thirty?"

"Yes."

"Good. I'll get the police reports and see what the score is there. All right?"

"Wonderful. I suddenly feel as though a thousand-pound weight is off my back. I'll tell you, I've been totally frantic. I'm way out of my league. Police, bail, counts of this and counts of that, arraignments . . . I don't know what the hell is going on. I don't even know what the hell happened."

"Well, we're going to find out. So you just relax."

"Thank you, Mr. Schwartz. Thank you very much."

"See you in the morning."

They hung up and Jessica was suddenly in tears again. He had been nice to her. Finally someone had been decent to her in all this. From police inspectors who would tell her nothing, to desk sergeants who announced the charges and hung up in her ear, to attorneys who wanted fifteen thousand dollars in cash on their desks in forty-eight hours, to . . . Martin Schwartz, a human being. And according to Philip Wald, Schwartz was a competent lawyer. It had been an incredible day. And oh God, where was Ian? The tears burned a hot damp path down her face again. It felt as though they had been coming all day. And she had to pull herself together. Wald would be there soon.

Philip Wald arrived at five-thirty. His face wore an expression of grave concern and his eyes were tired.

"Did you see him?" Jessie could feel her

eyes burn again and had to fight back the tears.

"I did."

"How is he?"

"He's all right. Shaken, but all right. He was very concerned about how you are."

"Did you tell him I'm fine?" Her hands were shaking violently again and the coffee she'd been drinking all day had only made matters worse. She looked a far cry from "fine."

"I told him you were very upset, which is certainly natural, under the circumstances. Jessica, let's sit down." She didn't like the way he said it, but maybe he was just tired. They'd all had a long day. An endless day.

"I spoke to Martin Schwartz," she said. "I think he'll take the case. And he said he'd call you this afternoon."

"Good. I think you'll both like him. He's a very fine attorney, and also a very nice man."

Jessica led Philip into the living room, where he took a seat on the long white couch facing the view. Jessica chose a soft beige suede chair next to an old brass table she and Ian had found in Italy on their honeymoon. She took a deep breath, sighed, and let her feet slide into the rug. It was a warm, pleasant room that always gave her solace. A place she could come home to and unwind in . . . except now. Now she felt as though nothing would ever be all right again, and as though it had been years since she had known the comfort of Ian's arms, or seen the light in his eyes.

Almost instinctively, her eyes went to a small portrait of him that she had done years before. It hung over the fireplace and smiled at her gently. It was agonizing. Where was he? She was suddenly and painfully reminded of the feeling she had had looking at Jake's high-school pictures when she'd gone through his things after they'd gotten the telegram from the Navy. That smile after it's all over.

"Jessica?" She glanced up with a shocked expression, and Philip looked pained. She seemed distraught, confused, as though her mind were wandering. He had seen her staring at the small oil portrait, and for a moment she had worn the bereft expression of a grieving widow . . . the face that simply does not understand, the eyes that are drowning in pain. What a ghastly business. He looked at the view for a moment, and then back at her, hoping she might have composed herself. But there was nothing to compose. Her manner was in total control; it was the expression in her eyes that told

69

the rest of the story. He wasn't at all sure how much she was ready to hear now, but he had to tell her. All of it.

"Jessica, you've got trouble." She smiled tiredly and brushed a stray tear away from her cheek.

"That sounds like the understatement of the year. What else is new?" Philip ignored the feeble attempt at humor and went on. He wanted to get it over with.

"I really don't think he did it. But he admits to having slept with the woman yesterday afternoon. That is to say, he . . . he had intercourse with her." He concentrated on his right knee, trying to run the distasteful words into one long unintelligible syllable.

"I see." But she didn't really see. What was there to see? Ian had made love to someone. And the someone was accusing him of rape. Why couldn't she feel something? There was this incredible numbness that just sat on her like a giant hat. No anger, no anything, just numb. And maybe pity for Ian. But why was she numb? Maybe because she had to hear it from Philip, a relative stranger. Her cigarette burned through the filter and went dead in her hand, and still she waited for him to go on.

"He says that he had too much to drink

70

yesterday at lunch, and you were due home last night. Something about your being away for several weeks, and his being a man — I'll spare you that. He noticed this girl in the restaurant, and after a few drinks she didn't look bad."

"He picked her up?" She felt as though someone else were speaking her words for her. She could hear them, but she couldn't feel her mouth move. Nothing seemed to be functioning. Not her mind, not her heart, not her mouth. She almost laughed hysterically, wondering what would happen if she had to go to the bathroom; surely she would pee all over the suede chair and not even know she was doing it. She felt as if she had overdosed on Novocain.

"No, he didn't pick her up. He left the restaurant to go home and work on his book, but he drove past Enrico's again on his way, and she just happened to be standing at the corner when he stopped for a light. And just for the hell of it, he offered her a lift. She didn't look like much when she got in, she was quite a bit older than he had thought. She claims thirty on the police report, but he says she's at least thirty-seven or -eight. She gave him the address of a hotel on Market where she claimed she lived, and Ian says he felt sorry for her when she invited him up for a drink. So he went up with her, had a drink — there was half a bottle of bourbon in her room — and he says it went to his head, and he . . . they had intercourse." Wald cleared his throat, looked away, and went on. Jessica's face showed no expression; the cigarette filter was still in her hand. "And he says that was it. To put it bluntly, he put on his pants and went home. He had a shower, took a nap, made a sandwich, and came out to meet your plane. That's the whole story. Ian's story." But she could hear in his voice that there was more

"It sounds fairly tawdry, Philip. But it does not sound like rape. What are they basing the charges on?"

"Her story. And you've got to remember, Jessica, how sensitive an issue rape is these days. For years women cried rape, and men made damaging statements about those women in court. Private investigators uncovered the supposedly startling fact that the plaintiff was not a virgin, and instantly the men were exonerated, the cases dismissed, and the women disgraced. For many reasons, it doesn't work like that anymore. No matter what really happened. Now the police and the courts are more cautious, more inclined to believe the women, and give the victim a much fairer deal. It's a damn good thing too, and about time . . . except once in a while, some woman comes along with an axe to grind, tells a lie, and some decent guy takes a bad fall. Just like some decent women used to get hurt the way things were before, now some decent guys get it in the . . . ahem . . . where it hurts."

Jessica couldn't suppress a smile. Philip was so utterly, totally proper. She was sure he made love to his wife with his Brooks Brothers boxer shorts on.

"Frankly, Jessica, I think that what happened here is that Ian fell into the hands of a sick, unhappy woman. She slept with him, and then called it rape. Ian says she was seductive in her manner and claimed to be a waitress in a topless bar, which is not the case. But she could have been playing a very sick psychological game with him. And God knows how often she's done this before, in subtle ways, with threats, accusations. Apparently, though, she's never gone to the police before. I think you're going to have a hell of a time proving she's lying. Certainly not without a trial. Rape is hard to prove, but it's also hard to prove that it wasn't rape. If she's insisting it was, then the district attorney has to prosecute. And apparently the inspector on the case believes this woman's story. So we're stuck. If they've decided they want Ian's head, for whatever reasons, it'll have to go to a jury."

They were both silent for a long time, and then Philip sighed and spoke again.

"I read the police reports, and the woman claims that he picked her up and she asked him to take her back to her office. She's a secretary at a hotel on Van Ness. Instead, he took her to this hotel on Market where they . . . where they had that last drink. Given that part of the story, he's damn lucky they didn't hit him with a charge of kidnap as well. In any case, he allegedly forced her into both normal intercourse, and . . . unnatural acts. That's where the second and third counts of rape come in, and the one charge of assault. Though I assume they'll drop the assault — there's no medical proof of it." Somehow Philip sounded horrifyingly matter-of-fact about the details, and Jessica was beginning to feel sick. She felt as though she were swimming in molasses, as though everything around her was slow and thick and unreal. She wanted to scrape the words off her skin with a knife. "Unnatural acts." What unnatural acts?

"For Chrissake, Philip, what do you mean

by 'unnatural'? Ian is perfectly normal in bed." Philip blushed. Jessie didn't. This was no time to be prim.

"Oral copulation, and sodomy. They are felonies, yon know." Jessica pursed her lips and looked fierce. Oral copulation hardly seemed unnatural.

"There was no clear evidence of the sodomy, but I don't think they'll drop it. Again, it's her word against his, and they're listening, and unfortunately, before I got down there, Ian admitted to the inspector on the case that he had had intercourse with the woman. He didn't confess to the oral copulation or the sodomy, but he shouldn't have admitted to intercourse at all. Damn shame that he did."

"Will it hurt the case?"

"Probably not. We can have the tape withheld in court on the grounds that he was distraught at the time. Martin will take care of it."

Jessica sat with her eyes closed for a moment, not believing the weight of it all.

"Why is she doing this to us, Philip? What can she possibly want from him? Money? Hell, if that's what she wants, I'll give it to her, what*ever* she wants. I just can't believe this is really happening." She opened her eyes and looked at him again, feeling the

75

now familiar wave of confusion and unreality sweep over her again.

"I know this is very hard on you, Jessica. But you have an excellent attorney now. Put your faith in him; he'll do a good job for you. One thing you absolutely must not do though, under any circumstances, is offer this woman money. The police won't drop the case now, even if she does, and you'll be compounding a felony and God knows what else if you try to bribe her. And I'm serious — the police seem to be taking a special interest in this. It isn't often that they get their hands on a Pacific Heights rape case, and I get the feeling that some of them think it's about time the upper class got theirs. Sergeant Houghton, the inspector on this case, made some very nasty cracks about 'certain kinds of people who think they can get away with anything they want at the expense of certain other people of lesser means.' It isn't a pretty inference, but if that's how he's thinking, he ought to be treated with kid gloves. I got the feeling that he doesn't like how Ian looks, or what he saw of you. I almost wonder if he doesn't think you're a couple of sickoes doing whatever amuses you for kicks. Who knows what he thinks — I'm just giving you my impression — but I want you to be very careful, Jessica. And whatever you do, don't pay this woman off. You'll be hurting Ian, and yourself, if you try to do that. If she wants money, if she calls you . . . let her talk. You can testify to it later. But don't give her a dime!" He was emphatic on the last point, and then ran a hand through his hair.

"I hate to have to tell you all this, Jessica. Ian was sick about it. But obviously you have to know what went on. It isn't very pretty, though, and I must say you're taking it remarkably well."

But the tears welled up again at that, and she wanted to beg him not to be nice to her, not to congratulate her on how well she was taking it. She could handle the rough stuff, but she knew that if anyone put his arms around her, sympathized, cared . . . or if Ian should walk in the door just then . . . she would sob until she died.

"Thank you, Philip." He thought her voice sounded oddly cold, as though she were warding him off. "At least it's obviously not rape, and that's bound to be made clear in court. If Martin Schwartz is any good."

"Yes, but . . . Jessie, it's going to be ugly. You have to be prepared for that." His eyes sought hers and she nodded.

"I understand that." But she didn't. Not

77

really. It hadn't even begun to sink in yet. How could it? Nothing had sunk in since eleven o'clock that morning. She was in shock. She only knew two things, and she didn't even understand those two things: that Ian was gone, that she couldn't see him, feel him, hear him, touch him; that he had slept with another woman. She had to face that now too. Publicly. The rest would sink in later.

There wasn't much more Philip could do, and he didn't know Jessica well enough to offer her any comfort. Only Ian knew Jessica that well. And Jessie made Philip nervous. She remained so calm. He was grateful that she was subdued, but it made him feel cold toward her, and confused. He found himself wondering what she was really thinking. He thought of his own wife and how she might react to something like this, or his sister, any of the women he knew. Jessie was a different breed of cat entirely. Too poised for his taste — and yet there was something shattering about her eyes. Like two broken windows. They were the only hint that all was not well within.

"Is there any chance he can call me? I thought you had a right to make one phone call from jail." He had before, when they had busted him for his tickets.

78

"Yes. But I gather that he didn't want to call you, Jessica."

"He didn't?" She seemed to recede still further into her own reserve.

"No. He said he wasn't sure how you'd feel. Said something about maybe this would be the last straw."

"Asshole." Philip looked away, and in a few moments took his leave. It had been an excessively unpleasant day. He found himself feeling grateful that he didn't practice criminal law. He couldn't stomach it. He didn't envy Martin Schwartz this case, however much money he made on it.

Jessie sat in the living room long after Philip had left. She was waiting for the sound of the phone . . . or of Ian's key in the door. This couldn't be happening. Not really. He would come home. He always did. She tried to pretend that the house wasn't quiet. She sang little songs and talked to herself. He couldn't leave her alone . . . no! . . . she sometimes heard her mother's voice late in the night . . . and Jake's . . . and Daddy's . . . but never Ian's . . . never Ian . . . never . . . He would call, he had to. He couldn't leave her alone, scared like that, he wouldn't do that to her, he had promised he never would, and Ian never broke his promises . . .

but he had. He had broken a promise now. She remembered it as she sat on the floor in the hall, in the dark, late into the night. That way she would hear his key sooner when he came home. He would come home, but he had broken a promise. He had slept with another woman, and now he was making her face it. She couldn't ignore it anymore. She hated her . . . hated her . . . hated . . . her, but not him. Oh God . . . maybe Ian didn't love her anymore . . . maybe he was in love with the other woman . . . maybe . . . why didn't he call, dammit? Why didn't he . . . why had he . . . the tears ran down her face like hot summer rain as she lay on the smooth wood floor in the hall and waited for Ian. She lay on the floor until morning. The phone never rang.

CHAPTER 5

The offices of Schwartz, Drewes, and Jonas were located in the Bank of America Building on California Street, an excellent address. Jessica rode to the forty-fourth floor looking prim, sleek, and tired. She wore a large pair of dark glasses and a somber navy blue suit. It was an outfit reserved for business meetings and funerals. This was a little bit of both. It was ten-twenty-five. She was five minutes early, but Martin Schwartz was waiting.

A secretary led her down a long carpeted corridor with a sweeping view of the bay. His offices took up one corner on the north side of the building. It was evidently a large, prosperous firm.

Martin Schwartz's office boasted two walls of glass, but the decor was Spartan and chill. He rose from behind his desk, a man of medium height with a full head of gray hair. He wore glasses, and he was

81

frowning.

"Mrs. Clarke?" The secretary had announced her, but he would have known her anyway. She looked the way he had expected her to — wealthy, elegant. But she was younger than he had expected, and more composed than he had dared to hope.

"Yes. How do you do?" She held out a hand, and he took in her full height. She was a striking young woman. He mentally made a pair of her and the unshaven, tired, but still handsome young man he had seen in the city prison that morning. They must look quite something together. They would also look good in court. Maybe too good — too beautiful, too young. He didn't like the looks of this case.

"Won't you sit down?" She nodded, slid into a chair across from his desk, and declined his offer of coffee.

"You've seen Ian?"

"I have. And Sergeant Houghton. And the assistant district attorney assigned to the case. And I spoke to Philip Wald for over an hour last night. Now I want to talk to you, and then we'll see what kind of a case we really have here." He attempted a smile and shuffled some papers on his desk. "Mrs. Clarke, have you ever been into drugs?"

"No. And neither has Ian. Nothing more

than a few joints once in a while. But I don't think we've smoked any grass in over a year. Neither of us ever liked it much. And we don't drink anything more exotic than wine."

"Let's not jump ahead of ourselves. I want to get back to drugs. Are any of your friends in that scene?"

"Not that I know of."

"Would anything of that nature be likely to turn up in an investigation of you or Mr. Clarke?"

"No, I'm sure that nothing would."

"Good." He looked only slightly relieved.

"What makes you ask?"

"Oh, some of the angles that I sense Houghton might be working on. He made some disagreeable remarks about your shop. Some girl in there who looks like a belly dancer, apparently, and an 'exotic' Oriental he mentioned. Also the fact that your husband is a writer, and you know the kind of fantasies people have about that. Houghton is a man with a vivid imagination, a typical lower-middle-class mind, and a strong dislike for anything that comes from your part of town."

"I suspected as much. He came to talk to me at the shop before he arrested Ian. And the 'bellydancer' he's having fantasies about is a young lady who has the misfortune to wear a size 38 bra with a D cup. She happenes to go to church twice a week." Jessica was not smiling. But Martin Schwartz was.

"She sounds delightful." He forced a smile out of her, with some effort.

"And if Sergeant Houghton thinks we look like we have too much money, he happens to be mistaken about that too. But what he does see can be explained by the fact that my parents and my brother died several years ago. I inherited what they had. My brother had no wife and children to leave anything to, and there were no other brothers or sisters."

"I see." And then after a brief pause he looked up at her again. "It must be lonely with no family." She nodded silently and kept her eyes on the view.

"I have Ian."

"Any children?" She shook her head, and he began to understand something. The reason she was not angry, why she so desperately wanted her husband home, without a single word of criticism about the charges. The reason for the almost frightening urgency he had sensed in her voice on the phone, and again now in his office. The "I have Ian" said it all. He suddenly knew that as far as Jessica Clarke was concerned, that was *all* she had.

"I take it there's no chance they might drop the charges?"

"None. Politically, they can't. The victim in this case is making such a stink. She wants his ass, if you'll pardon the expression. And I think it's reasonable to expect that they'll be prying fairly heavily into your lives. Can you weather it?" She nodded, and he didn't tell her that Ian was afraid she couldn't stand the pressure. "Is there anything I should know? Any indiscretions on your part? Problems with the marriage? Sexual . . . well, 'exoticisms,' shall we say, orgies you may have gone to, whatever?"

She shook her head again, looking annoyed.

"I'm sorry I have to ask, but it'll all come out anyway. It's best to be candid now. And of course we'll want our own investigation of the girl. I have a very good man. Mrs. Clarke, we're going to do our damnedest for Ian."

He smiled at her again, and for a moment she felt as though she were living a dream. This man was not real, he wasn't asking her if she'd ever gone to orgies, or been into drugs . . . Ian wasn't really in jail . . . this man was a friend of her father's and it was all a big game. She felt him staring at her then, and she had to return to the pretense that this was reality. Worse yet, to the reality that Ian was in jail.

"Can we get Ian out of jail before the trial?"

"I hope so. But that will most likely depend on you. If the charges were a little less severe, we might have been able to get him released on his own recognizance — in other words, with no bail to pay. But on charges of this nature, I'm almost certain the judge will insist on bail being posted, despite the fact that Ian has no previous record. And his getting out will depend on whether or not you can put up the bail. They're talking about setting it at twenty-five thousand dollars. That's pretty steep, and it means you'd either have to put twenty-five thousand dollars in cash in the keeping of the court until the trial is over, or pay twenty-five hundred to a bailbonds-man and give him collateral to cover his bond. Either way, it's a stiff fee. But we'll see about getting it down to something more reasonable."

Jessica heaved a deep sigh and absent-mindedly took off her dark glasses. What he saw then shocked him. Two deep purple trenches lay beneath her eyes, which were bloodshot and swollen and filled with terror. He was looking at a woman with the eyes of a child. The poise was all a front. He had been so sure she was the balls in the outfit, but maybe not, maybe not. Maybe she was only the bucks, and Ian was her lifeline. It made him feel better, somehow, about Ian. He was in better shape than she was, that was for sure.

Schwartz forced his mind back to the question of bail as Jessica's eyes continued to watch him. She seemed unaware of how much she had just shown him.

"Do you think you'll be able to meet the bail, Mrs. Clarke?" She looked tiredly into his eyes and shrugged slightly.

"I suppose I can put up my business." But she knew that she couldn't pay the bail-bondsman's fee if she handed Schwartz the two-thousand-dollar check in her bag. And she had no choice. They needed a lawyer before they could even begin to worry about a bailbondsman. She'd have to get a loan on the car. Or on . . . something. What the hell. It didn't matter now. Nothing did. She'd even put up the house if she had to. But what if . . . she had to know. "What if we can't quite meet the bail right away?"

"There's no credit there, Mrs. Clarke. You pay the full bailbondsman's fee and put up satisfactory collateral or they simply don't let Ian out of jail."

"Until when?"

"After the trial."

"God. Then I don't have much choice, do I?"

"In what sense?"

"We'll just put up whatever we have to."

He nodded, sorry for her. It was rare that he felt anything stir in his heart for a client, and had she ranted and whined and cried, she would have annoyed him. Instead she had won his respect — and his pity. Neither of them deserved this kind of trouble. It made him wonder again what the real story was with the rape charges. He felt in his gut that it had not been a rape. But the question was, could that be proven?

He spent another ten minutes explaining the arraignment procedures: a simple appearance in court to put the charges on record, establish the bail, and set a date for Ian's next appearance in court, at a preliminary hearing. The victim would not be at the arraignment. Jessica was relieved.

"Is there a number, Mrs. Clarke, where I can reach you today if I need you?" She nodded and scribbled the number of the boutique. It was the first time she'd thought of going in.

"I'll be there after I see Ian. I'm going

over to see him now. And Mr. Schwartz, please call me Jessica, or Jessie. It sounds like we're going to be seeing a lot of each other."

"Yes, we will. And I want you back in my office on Friday. Both of you, if you've managed to get Ian out on bail." The "if" sent a shiver down her spine. "No, actually, make it Monday. In case you do get him out, you two will deserve a little time off. And then we'll get down to work in earnest. We don't have much time."

"How much time?" It was like asking a doctor how long you had to live.

"We'll have a better idea of that after the arraignment. But the trial will probably come up in about two months."

"Before Christmas?" She reminded him again of an overgrown child as she asked.

"Before Christmas. Unless we get a continuance for some reason. But your husband told me this morning that he wants to get this over with as quickly as possible, so you could put it behind you and forget it."

Forget it? she thought. Who would ever forget it?

He stood up and held out a hand, removing his glasses for a moment. "Jessica, try to relax. Leave the worrying to me for a while."

"I'll do my best." She stood up too, shook

his hand, and he was once again taken aback by her height. "Thank you, Martin, for everything. Any message for Ian?" She paused in the doorway.

"Tell him I said he's a lucky man." His eyes warmed her and she smiled at the compliment and slipped out the door.

Martin Schwartz sat down, swiveled his chair to face the view, chewed on his glasses, and shook his head. This was going to be a bitch of a case. He was sure Ian hadn't done it, but they both would be a real problem in court. Young, happy, beautiful, and rich. The jury would resent his screwing around on a woman like Jessie; the women in court would hate Jessie; the men in court would dislike Ian because they wouldn't believe that writing was work. And they looked as if they had too much money, no matter how sensible the explanation of Jessie's inheritance was. He just didn't like the looks of this case. And the victim was obviously a strange woman, maybe a sick one. His only hope was that they'd find out enough on her to destroy her. It was an ugly game to play, but it was Ian's only chance.

CHAPTER 6

Jessica stopped in the lobby to call the boutique. Zina's voice was concerned when she heard her.

"Jessie, are you all right?" They had finally tried her at home at ten-thirty that morning, but she had already gone out.

"I'm fine." But Zina didn't like the sound of her voice. "Everything okay at your end?"

"Sure, we're okay. Are you coming in?"

"After lunch. See ya later." She hung up before Zina could ask more questions and went to reclaim the Morgan from the garage. She was off to the Hall of Justice to see Ian.

She was two thousand dollars poorer, but now she felt better. She had left the check in a blue envelope with the secretary at the front desk. The first part of Martin Schwartz's fee. She had been as good as her word. Now there were a hundred and eighty-one dollars left in their joint savings account, but Ian had an attorney. What a price they were going to pay for one piece of ass!

She tried not to let herself think as she drove across town. She wasn't so much angry as confused. What had happened? Who was this woman? Why was she doing this to them? What did she have against Ian? After speaking to Martin, Jessie was more certain than ever that Ian had done nothing wrong — except pick the wrong woman for an afternoon of delight. Oh Jesus, had he picked the wrong woman!

She found a parking space on Bryant Street, across from a long strip of neon-lit bailbondsmen's offices. She found herself wondering which one she'd be haggling with by the next afternoon. They all looked so sleazy; she wouldn't have wanted to enter any of those places to get in out of the cold, let alone to do business. She walked quickly into the Hall of Justice, where a metal detector checked her out while a guard rifled through her handbag. She had to stop for a pass for the jail, show her driver's license, and identify herself as Ian's wife. There was a crowd of people standing in line, but the line moved forward quickly.

It was a shaggy, disheveled-looking lot of humanity, and she was strikingly out of place. Her height set her apart from the rest of the women and most of the men, and the navy blue suit looked absurd. There were white women in imitation leather pants wearing fake leopard jackets, beehive hairstyles, and floppy white sandals. Black men in puce satin, and black girls in what looked like cheap satin nightgowns or pajamas. It was an interesting crowd, but for a movie, not for a life. She couldn't help wondering if the woman Ian had slept with looked like one of these. She hoped not — not that it mattered at this point. Her knees were already quaking, and she didn't know what she'd say to him. What could she say?

Her hand trembled as she pressed the elevator button for the sixth floor. There was an alternating sensation of sinking and rising in her stomach as she wondered what the jail would be like. She had seen it briefly the one time she had bailed him out, but there had never been time for a visit, thank God. She'd just gone down and gotten him. This time it was all so different.

The elevator let her out on the sixth floor, and all she knew was that she wanted to see Ian. Suddenly she knew she could crawl through any amount of fear and anger, over a thousand puce satin pimps, just to get to Ian.

The visitors waited in single file outside an iron door and a guard let them into the room beyond in groups of five or six. They made their exit through another door at the far side of the room. But it seemed to Jessie that they were being swallowed up, never to be seen again.

A moment later, Jessica was inside. The room was hot and stuffy, windowless and fluorescent-lit. There were long glass panes in the interior walls with little shelves on either side holding telephones. She realized then that she would see him through a window. She hadn't thought about that. What could you say on a phone?

His face appeared in a far window as she wondered which one to go to, and he stood there, watching her as she felt tears burn her eyes. She couldn't let herself cry . . . couldn't . . . couldn't . . . couldn't! She walked slowly toward the phone, feeling a vise tighten around her heart and her legs turn to straw, but she was walking, one foot after the other, and he couldn't see her hands tremble as she waved hesitantly. And then suddenly she was facing him, and she had the phone in her hand. They watched each other briefly in silence. And then he spoke first.

"Are you okay?"

"I'm fine. How are you?"

He was silent again for a moment and then nodded with a small, crooked smile.

"Terrific." But the smile faded quickly. "Oh baby, I'm so sorry to put you through this. It's all so crazy and so goddam . . . I think all I want to tell you, Jess, is that I love you, and I don't know how this whole fucking mess happened. I wasn't sure how you'd take it."

"What did you think? That I'd run away? Have I ever done that?" She looked so hurt he wanted to turn away. It was hard to look at her. Very hard.

"No, but this isn't exactly your run-of-the-mill problem, like a thirty-dollar overdraft at the bank. I mean this is . . . Jesus, what can I say, Jessie?" She gave him a tiny smile in answer.

"You already said it. And I love you too. That's all that matters. We'll get this thing straightened out."

"Yeah . . . but . . . Jess, it doesn't sound like it's going to be easy. That woman is sticking to the accusations, and this cop, Houghton, he acts like he thinks he's got the local hotshot rapist on his hands."

"Adorable, isn't he?"

"He talked to you?" Ian looked surprised.

"Just before he went to the house to see

you." Ian looked pale.

"Did he tell you what it was about?" She shook her head and looked away. "Oh, Jess . . . what an incredible horror show to put you through. I just can't believe it."

"Neither can I. But we'll survive it." She gave him her best brave girl smile. "What do you think of Martin?"

"Schwartz? I like him. But that's going to cost you a pretty penny, isn't it?" Jessie tried to look noncommital and started to say something, but he cut her off. "How much?" There was a look of bitterness in his eyes for a moment.

"That's not important."

"Maybe not to you, Jessie, but it is to me. How much?"

"Two thousand now, and another five if it goes to trial." There was no avoiding that look in his eyes. She had had to tell him.

"Are you kidding?"

Jessie shook her head in reply.

"The man I spoke to before him wanted fifteen thousand, in cash, and by the end of this week."

"Jesus Christ, Jessica . . . that's insanity. But I'll pay you back for Schwartz."

"You're boring me, sweetheart."

"I love you, Jess." They exchanged a long tender look and Jessica felt the hot coals behind her eyes again.

"How come you didn't call me last night?" She didn't tell him that she had lain on the floor all night, waiting, frightened, almost hysterical, but too tired to move. She had felt as though her body were paralyzed while her mind was racing.

"How could I call you, Jess? What could I say?" That you love me . . . "I think I was in shock. I just kept sitting here, stunned. I couldn't understand it."

Then why did you screw her, damn you? But the flash of anger left her eyes again as soon as she looked up at him. He was as unhappy as she was. More so.

"Why do you suppose she accused you of . . . of . . ."

"Rape?" He said it as if it were a death sentence. "I don't know. Maybe she's sick or crazy, or pissed off at someone, or maybe she wanted money. What the hell do I know? I was a fool to do that anyway. Jessie, I —" He looked away and then back into her eyes with tears hovering in the corners of his own. "How are we going to live with this? How are you going to live with it, Jessie? Without hating me? And . . . I just don't see . . ."

"Stop it!" She spat the words into the phone in a whisper. "Stop it right now! We'll see this thing through and it'll be over and straightened out and we'll never have to think about it again."

"But won't you? I mean honestly, Jessie, won't you? Every time you look at me, won't you hate me a little bit for her, and for the money this'll cost you, and . . . fuck." He ran a hand through his hair and reached into his pocket for a cigarette. Jessie watched him and then suddenly noticed his pants. He was wearing white cotton hospital pajama bottoms.

"Good God, what happened to your pants? Didn't they give you time to get dressed?" Her eyes grew wide as she envisioned Sergeant Houghton dragging him out of the house bare-assed and in handcuffs.

"Adorable, aren't they? They took my pants down to the lab to test them for sperm." It was all so goddam tawdry, so ugly, so . . . "I'm going to need some pants for court tomorrow morning, by the way." And then he grew pensive for a moment and took a long drag on his cigarette. "I just don't understand it. You know, if she wanted money, all she had to do was call and blackmail me. I told her I was married." How nice . . . and then for no reason she could fathom, she looked at Ian, at his wrinkled white cotton pajamas, at the boyish face and rumpled blond hair, at the madhouse of people around her, and she started to laugh.

"Are you okay?" He looked suddenly frightened. What if she got hysterical? But she didn't look hysterical, she looked genuinely amused.

"You know something nutty? I'm fine. And I love you, and this is ridiculous, dammit, so will you please come home — and you know what else? You look cute in pajamas." It was the same laughter he had heard a million times at two in the morning when she'd teased him about walking around the house reading his work, stark naked, and with a pencil behind each ear. It was the laughter of splashing water at each other in the shower, of tickling him when he got into bed. It was Jessie, and it suddenly made him smile, as he hadn't smiled since this whole nightmare had begun.

"Lady, you are absolutely screwy, but I adore you. Will you please get me out of this shithouse so I can come home and —" He stopped on the word and looked suddenly pale.

"Rape me? Why not?" And then they grinned again, but quietly. She was okay now. She had Ian right in front of her, she

99

knew she was loved and safe and protected. With Ian suddenly gone and that incredible silence, it had been as though he were dead. But he wasn't dead. He was alive. He would always be alive, and he was all hers. Suddenly she wanted to dance, standing there in the jail in the midst of pimps and thieves, she wanted to dance. She had Ian back.

"Mr. Clarke, how come I love you so much?"

"Because you happen to be mentally retarded, but I love you that way. Hey, lady, could you be serious for a moment?" His face showed that he meant it, but Jessie still had laughter in her tired, bloodshot eyes.

"What?"

"I meant what I said about paying you back. I will."

"Don't worry about it."

"But I will. I think it's time I went back to some kind of job anyway. It doesn't work like this, Jess, and you know it too."

"Yes, it does. What do you mean, 'it doesn't work'?" She looked frightened again.

"I mean I don't like being kept, even if it is for the supposed benefit of my writing career. It's lousy for my ego, and worse for our marriage."

"Bullshit."

"No bullshit. I'm serious. But this isn't the time or the place to talk about it. I just want you to know, though, that whatever money you put out on this, you're getting back. Is that clear?" She looked evasive, and Ian's voice got louder in her ear. "I mean it, Jessie. Don't fuck around with me on this. You're not paying for it."

"Okay." She looked at him pointedly, and at the same moment a guard tapped her on the shoulder. The visit was over. And they had so much left to say.

"Take it easy, sweetheart. I'll see you in court tomorrow." He had seen the stricken look on her face.

"Can you call me tonight?"

He shook his head. "No, they won't let me now."

"Oh." But I need to hear you . . . I need you, Ian . . . I . . .

"Get yourself a good night's sleep before the court thing tomorrow. Promise?" She nodded, looking like a child, and he smiled at her. "I love you so much, Jess. Will you please take care, for me?"

She nodded again. "And you too? Ian . . . I . . . I'd die without you."

"Don't think like that. Now go on, I'll see you tomorrow. And Jess . . . thank you. For everything."

"I love you."

"I love you too."

On the last words, the phones suddenly went dead in their hands, and she waved at him as she followed the flock of visitors into the elevator. She was alone with them again now. Ian was gone. But it was different this time. She felt full of the way he looked and sounded, of the color of his hair, and even the smell of his skin. He was vivid again now. He was still with her.

CHAPTER 7

Zina and Katsuko were both busy with customers when Jessica walked in, and she had a moment to compose herself in her office before joining them. It was crazy, really. Guess where I've been? To visit Ian in jail. From city prison to Lady J in one swift leap. Madness.

The girls were helping a couple of women who wanted dresses for Palm Springs. They were overweight, overdressed, overbearing, and not overly friendly. And Jessica found it nearly impossible to work. She kept thinking of Ian, of the jail, of Martin Schwartz, of Inspector Houghton. The inspector's eyes seemed to haunt her.

"And what does your husband do?" One of the women asked her, while looking over a rack of their new velvet skirts. They were a rich Bordeaux color with black satin trim. Copies of St. Laurent.

"My husband? He rapes . . . I mean,

103

writes!" The women found it hilarious, and even Zina and Kat had to laugh. Jessica laughed through tears in her eyes.

"My husband used to be that way too — before he took up golf." The second woman found the interlude delightful and settled on two skirts and a blouse while the first woman went back to the slacks.

It was a long day, but it saved her from talking to Zina and Kat. It was almost five before they sat down for a round of hot coffee.

"Jess, is everything okay now?"

"Much better. We had a few problems, but everything will be worked out by tomorrow." At least then he'd be home, and they could work it out together. Just so he came home!

"We were worried as hell about you. I'm glad everything's fine." Zina seemed satisfied, but Katsuko continued to search Jessie's eyes. Something didn't sit right.

"You look like shit, Jessica Clarke."

"Flattery, flattery. It's just this grim suit." She looked around, wondering if she should change into something from the shop's fall line just to pick up her sagging spirits. But it was late, and she was tired, and she didn't have the energy to get into or out of anything. It would only be another ten or fifteen minutes before Zina locked the doors for the night.

Jessica stood up, stretched, and was aware of the ache in her back and neck from the long crazy night she'd spent on the floor. Not to mention the tension of the day. She was arching her back gingerly, trying to ease out the kinks, when a woman walked into the boutique. Jessie, Kat, and Zina quickly glanced at each other, deciding who would stand up and be helpful, but it was Jessie who turned toward the woman with a smile. The woman looked pleasant, and it did Jessie good to deal with the clients. It kept her mind off herself.

"May I help you?"

"Do you mind if I browse? I heard about the boutique from a friend, and you have some lovely things in the window."

"Thank you. Let me know if you need any help."

Jessica and the woman exchanged an easy smile, and the customer began to look through the sportswear. She was elegant, somewhere in her mid- to late thirties, maybe even forty, but it was hard to tell. She wore a trim, simple black pantsuit, a cream linen blouse, a small bright scarf at her neck, and a healthy amount of obviously expensive gold jewelry — a handsome bracelet, a nice chain, several very solid looking rings — and a striking pair of onyx-diamond earrings that had caught Jessie's attention when she'd walked into the shop. The woman spelled money. But her face showed warmth, and something else — as though she enjoyed the pretty things she was wearing, but understood that there were other things in her life that mattered more.

Jessie watched her as she moved from rack to rack. She looked content, happy. And she had a kind of grace that made her easy to watch. The face was young, the hair ash blond streaked with gray. In an odd way she reminded Jessie of a Siamese cat, particularly the pale china blue of her eyes. Something about her made you want to know more.

"Did you have anything special in mind? We have some new things in the back." The woman smiled at Jessie and shrugged.

"I should be shot for this, but what about that suede coat over there? Have you got it in an eight?" She looked guilty, like a small child buying more bubble gum than she was supposed to, but she also looked as though she were having a good time. And as though she could afford one hell of a lot of bubble gum, or anything else.

"I'll take a look." Jessica disappeared into

the stockroom, wondering if they did have the coat in a smaller size.

They didn't. But they had a similar one that sold for forty dollars more. Jessica removed the price tag and took the coat out to the woman. It was a warm cinnamon color with a soft clinging shape. It was actually a better-looking coat than the first one, and the woman noticed that instantly.

"Damn. I was hoping I'd hate it."

"It's a hard coat to hate. And it looks well on you."

They watched the woman swirling gracefully in the brown suede coat. It suited her marvelously, and she knew it. It was a pleasure to see clothes on someone like that. But then, she could have worn the rug and looked fabulous.

"How much is it?"

"Three hundred and ten." Zina and Kat exchanged a quizzical glance, but they knew enough not to question the price aloud. Jessie always had a method to her madness, and she was usually right. Maybe this was someone special Jessie had been hoping to lure into the shop. She certainly looked like someone one ought to recognize. And the woman did not look overwhelmed by the price of the coat.

"Does it have matching pants?"

"It did, but they're gone."

"That's too bad." But she managed to casually collect three sweaters, a blouse, and a suede skirt to go with the coat before she decided that she'd done enough damage for one day. It was a beautiful sale for the shop, and an easy one. She pulled out her checkbook, encased in emerald green suede, and looked up at Jessie with a smile. "And if you see me back here in less than a week, throw me out the door."

"Do I have to?" Jessie looked mock-regretful.

"That's an order, not a request!"

"What a pity." The two women laughed and the shopper filled out her check. It was for well over five hundred dollars. But she hardly looked worried. Her name was Astrid Bonner, and her address was on Vallejo, only a block from Jessie's home.

"We're almost neighbors, Mrs. Bonner." Jessie told her her address, and Astrid Bonner looked up with a smile.

"I know that house! It's the little blue and white one, I'll bet, with all those fabulous bright flowers out front!"

"You can see us for miles!"

"Don't apologize; you do wonders for the area! And you have a little red sports car?" Jessie pointed out the window.

"That's me." They laughed together and Zina quietly locked the doors. It was a quarter to six. "Would you like a drink?" They kept a bottle of Johnnie Walker in the back. Some of their customers stayed late to chat. It was another nice touch.

"I'd love to, but I won't. You probably want to get home." Jessie smiled and Katsuko put Mrs. Bonner's purchases in two large shiny brown boxes filled with yellow and orange tissue paper and tied them with plaid ribbons.

"Do you own the shop?"

Jessie nodded.

"You have some beautiful things. And I needed that coat like another hole in my head. But . . . no will power. It's my worst problem."

"Sometimes a splurge is good for the soul."

Astrid Bonner nodded quietly at the remark and the two women exchanged a long glance. Jessie felt very comfortable with her. She was sorry Astrid Bonner wouldn't stay for the drink; Jessie had nothing to rush home for, and she would have liked to talk to her. She wondered which of the houses on the next block was hers. And then she had an idea.

"Can I give you a lift home, by the way?

109

I'm leaving now." It would also spare her the questions that Zina and Kat might have saved to hurl at her after hours. She couldn't face that yet. And Astrid Bonner would give her safe passage. She still hadn't told them she wouldn't be in the following morning, while she went to the arraignment.

"A lift would be terrific. Thank you. I usually walk when I'm this close to home, but with these two boxes . . . delightful." She smiled and looked even younger. Jessie wondered how old she really was.

Jessica picked up her coat, grabbed her bag, and waved at the other two. "Good night, ladies. See you sometime tomorrow. I won't be in in the morning." The four smiled at one another, Jessie unlocked the door for Astrid, Zina locked it again behind them, and they were on their way. No questions, no answers, no lies. Jessie was enormously relieved. She hadn't realized how she had been dreading that all afternoon.

She unlocked the car and Astrid slid in, the boxes tall on her lap, and they headed for home.

"The shop must keep you busy."

"It does, but I love it. And I'm Jessica Clarke, by the way. I just realized that I haven't introduced myself. I'm sorry." They exchanged another smile, and the evening

110

breeze rustled through Astrid Bonner's freshly done hair. "Would you like me to put the top up?"

"Of course not." She laughed suddenly and looked at Jessie. "I'm not that old and stuffy, for God's sake. And I must say, I envy you that shop. I used to work on a magazine in New York. That was ten years ago, and I still miss fashion, in any form."

"We came out from New York too. Six years ago. What brought you here?"

"My husband. Well, no actually it was a business trip. Then I met my husband out here — and never went back." She looked pleased at the memory.

"Never? Are they still expecting you back?" The two women laughed in the soft twilight.

"No, I returned for all of three weeks. Gave them notice and that was that. I was the career-woman sort, never going to marry, all of that . . . and then I met Tom. And bingo, end of the career."

"Did you ever regret it?" It was an outrageously personal thing to ask, but she seemed to invite one to feel at ease with her. And Jessie did.

"No. Never. Tom changed everything." Jessica found herself wanting to say "how awful" and then wondering why. After all,

111

Ian had changed things for her too, but not like that; he hadn't cost her a career, hadn't forced her to leave New York. She had wanted to move to San Francisco, but she couldn't conceive of giving up Lady J.

"No, I never regretted it for a moment. Tom was a remarkable man. He died last year."

"Oh. I'm sorry. Do you have children?"

Astrid laughed and shook her head. "No, Tom was fifty-eight when I married him. We had a splendid ten years — alone. It was like a honeymoon." Jessie was reminded of her life with Ian, and smiled.

"We feel sort of the same way. Children might interfere with so much."

"Not if that's what you want. But we both thought we were too old. I was thirty-two when I married him, and I just wasn't the motherly type. We never regretted it. Except that life is awfully quiet now."

So Astrid was forty-two. Jessie was surprised.

"Why don't you take a job?" she said.

"What could I possibly get a job doing? I worked for *Vogue,* but there's nothing like that out here. And even *Vogue* wouldn't want me anymore, not after ten years. You get rusty, and I've gotten about as rusty as you can get. And besides, I have no intention of moving back to New York. Ever."

"Get something in a field related to fashion."

"Like what?"

"A boutique."

"Which brings us back to where we started, my dear. I'm green with envy over yours."

"Don't be too envious. It has its problems."

"And its rewards, I'll bet. Do you go back to New York often?"

"I came back two days ago." And yesterday my husband got arrested for rape. It was on the tip of her tongue to say it, but Astrid would have been horrified. Anyone would have been. She sighed deeply, forgeting for a moment that she was not alone.

"Was the trip as bad as all that?" Astrid asked, smiling.

"What trip?"

"The trip to New York. You said you just got back from New York two days ago, and then you sighed as though your best friend had died."

"I'm sorry. It's been a long day." She tried to smile, but suddenly everything felt heavy again; the nightmare had rushed back to overwhelm her. There was a moment's pause, and then Astrid looked at her over

113

the brown boxes on her lap.

"Is anything wrong?" It was a deep, searching look, and hard to meet it with a lie.

"Nothing that won't be smoothed out soon."

"Anything I can do to help?" What a nice woman, they were total strangers and she was asking Jessie about her problems. Jessie smiled and slowed at the corner.

"No, everything's okay really. And you already did help. You finished my day with a nice dollop of sunshine. Now, which house is it?"

Astrid smiled and pointed. "That one. And you were an angel to drive me home."

It was a somber brick mansion with black shutters and white trim and politely carved hedges around it. Jessie wanted to whistle. She and Ian had noticed the house often and had wondered who lived there. They had suspected the owners traveled a lot, because the house often looked closed.

"Mrs. Bonner, I'd like to return the compliment on the house. We've envied you this one for years."

"I'm flattered. And call me Astrid. But your house looks like so much more fun, Jessica. This one is awfully . . . well . . ." She giggled. "Grown-up, I suppose is the

114

right word. Tom already had it when we married, and he had some beautiful things. You'll have to come over for coffee sometime. Or a drink."

"I'd love it."

"Then how about right now?"

"I . . . I'd love to, but to tell you the truth, I'm just beat. It's been a very hectic couple of days since I got back, and I ran myself ragged for three weeks in New York. Would a rain check be possible?"

"With pleasure. Thanks again for the ride." She let herself out of the car, and waved as she climbed the steps to her house. Jessie waved back. That was some house! And she was pleased with having met Astrid Bonner. A delightful woman.

Jessica drove into her own driveway, thinking of Astrid and what she had said. It sounded as though she had given up a lot for her husband. And she looked happy about it.

Jessie walked into the dark house, kicked off her shoes, and sat down on the couch without turning on the lights. She was reviewing the day. It had been unbelievable. Everything from the meeting with Martin Schwartz, to emptying her savings into his pockets, to seeing Ian in jail, to the civilized exchanges with Astrid Bonner . . . when would life become real again?

She thought about making herself a drink, but she couldn't get up the energy to move. Her mind raced, but her body had turned to stone. The machinery just wouldn't move anymore. But her mind . . . her mind . . . she kept thinking about the visit to Ian. She was home again now. Alone, where he had always waited for her at night. The house was so unbearably quiet . . . the way Jake's apartment had been when she'd gone back to it . . . after he died . . . why did she keep thinking of Jake now? Why did she keep comparing him to Ian? Ian wasn't dead. And he would be home tomorrow — wouldn't he? He would. But what if . . . she just couldn't stop. The doorbell rang and she didn't even hear it until finally the insistent buzzer yanked her attention off the merry-go-round of her thoughts. It required her last ounce of energy to get up and answer the door.

She stood in her stocking feet in the darkness of the front hall and spoke through the door. She was too tired even to try to guess who it was.

"Who is it?" Her voice barely penetrated through to the opposite side. But he heard her. He looked over his shoulder at his companion and nodded. The second man walked slowly back toward the green car.

"Police."

Jessie's heart flew into trip-hammer action at the sound of the word, and she leaned trembling against the wall. Now what?

"Yes?"

"It's Inspector Houghton. I want to speak to Mrs. Clarke." But he already knew it was she. And on the other side of the door, Jessica was tempted to tell him that Mrs. Clarke was not at home. But her car was plainly visible out front, and he'd just hang around waiting. There was no escaping them anymore. They owned her life, and Ian's.

Jessie slowly unlocked the door and stood silently in the dark hall. Even without shoes, she stood about an inch taller than the inspector. Their eyes held for a long moment. All the hatred she could not feel for Ian's betrayal she lavished on Inspector Houghton. He was easy to hate.

"Good evening. May I come in?" Jessie stood to one side, flicked on the lights, and then preceded him into the living room. She stood in the center of the room, facing him, and did not invite him to sit down.

"Well, Inspector? What now?" Her tone hid nothing.

"I thought we could have a little chat."

"Oh? Is that usual?" she was frightened, but she was even more afraid to show it. What if he wanted to rape her? A real rape this time. What if . . . oh God . . . where was Ian?

"This is perfectly usual, Mrs. Clarke." They seemed to circle each other with their eyes, enemies from birth. A python and his prey. She didn't like her role. She feared him, but would not show it. He found her beautiful, but he didn't let that show either. He hated Ian for a number of reasons. That showed.

"Mind if I sit down?" Yes. Very much.

"Not at all." She waved him to the couch and sat down in her usual chair.

"Lovely house you have, Mrs. Clarke. Have you lived here long?" He glanced around, seeming to take in all the details, while she fantasized about telling him to go fuck himself and scratching his eyes out. But now she knew that wasn't real. You might hate cops, but you didn't let your hostilities show. She was innocent, Ian was innocent, but she was terrified.

"Inspector, is this a formal interrogation or a social call? Our attorney told me today that I don't have to speak to anyone unless he's present." She was watching the brown double-knit leg and the maroon sock, wondering if he was going to try to rape her. He was wearing a shiny mustard-colored tie. She was beginning to feel nauseated, and suddenly panicked, wondering if she had taken the pill that morning. And then suddenly she looked at him and knew she'd kill him if he tried. She'd have to.

"No, you don't have to speak to anyone unless your attorney is present, Mrs. Clarke, but I have a few questions, and I thought it would be more pleasant for you to answer them here." Big favor.

"I think I'd rather answer them in court." But they both knew she didn't have to answer anything in court. She was the defendant's wife. Legally, she didn't have to testify.

"Suit yourself." He stood up to leave and then stopped at the bar. "You a drinker too?" The question infuriated her.

"No, and neither is my husband."

"Yeah, that's what I thought. He claims he was ripped when he took the victim to the hotel. I figured he was lying, though. He doesn't look like a drinker." Jessie's heart sank and her eyes filled with hatred. This sonofabitch was trying to trap her.

"Inspector, I'm asking you to leave. Now."

Houghton turned to her then and searched her eyes with a look of feigned kindness. But his own eyes returned the anger of Jessie's. His voice was barely audible as he stood a foot away from her.

"What are you doing with a weak-kneed punk like him?"

"Get out of my house!" Her voice was as low as his and her whole body was trembling.

"What'll you do when he goes to the joint? Find another gigolo sweetheart like him? Believe me, sister, don't sweat it. They're a dime a dozen."

"Get out!" The words were like two fists in his face, and he turned on his heel and walked to the door. He paused for a moment and looked back at her.

"See ya."

The door closed behind him, and for the first time in her life Jessica wanted to kill.

He was back at ten that night, with two plainclothes-men and a search warrant, to look for weapons and drugs.

This time Houghton was straight-faced and businesslike, and he avoided her eyes for the entire hour they were there, digging into closets and drawers, unfolding her underwear, dumping her handbags on the bed, pouring out soap flakes, and spreading Ian's clothes and papers all over the living room.

They found nothing, and Jessie said nothing about it to Ian. Ever. It took her four and a half hours to get everything put away, and another two hours to stop sobbing. Her fears had been justified. They had raped her. Not in the way she had feared, but in another way. Photographs of her mother lay strewn all over her desk, her birth-control pills lay dumped out in the kitchen, half of them gone, to be tested at the lab. Her whole life was spread all over the house. It was her war now too. And she was ready to fight. That night had changed everything. Now they were *her* enemy too, not just Ian's. And for the first time in seven years, Ian was not there to defend her. Not only that, but it was he who had put her face to face with this enemy. He had brought this down around her ears as well as his own. And she was helpless. It was Ian's fault. Now he was the enemy too.

CHAPTER 8

Jessica waited with Martin Schwartz in the back rows of the courtroom until after ten. The docket was heavily overscheduled, and the court was running late. The procedures Jessie watched looked very dull. Most of the charges were rattled off by number, bails were arbitrarily set, and new faces were brought in. Ian finally arrived through a door leading in from the jail, accompanied by a guard on each side.

Martin walked to the front of the room, and the charges were, mercifully, read off by number, not description. Ian was asked if he understood what he was accused of, and he answered, gravely, in the affirmative.

The bail was set at twenty-five thousand dollars. Martin asked to have it reduced and the judge pondered the question while a female assistant D.A. jumped to her feet and objected. She felt that the matter before the court warranted a heavier bail. But the judge didn't agree. He lowered it to fifteen thousand, smacked his gavel, and had another man brought in. The preliminary hearing had been set for two weeks hence.

"Now what do we do?" Jessica whispered to Martin as he came back to her seat. Ian had already left the court and was back in the jail.

"Now you scare up fifteen hundred bucks to pay to a bailbondsman, and give him something worth fifteen thousand in collateral."

"How do I do that?"

"Come on. I'll take you over myself."

But Jesus . . . fifteen thousand? Now it suddenly hit her. Fifteen thousand. It was enormous. Could anything be worth that much money? Yes. Ian.

They went down to the lobby and across the street to one of a long row of neon-lit bail offices. They didn't look like nice places, and the one they walked into was no better than the rest. It reeked of cigar smoke, the ashtrays were full to overflowing, and two men were asleep on a couch, apparently waiting. A woman with teased yellow hair asked them their business and Martin explained. She called the jail and made a note of the charges while looking lengthily at Jessie. Jessie tried not to flinch.

"You'll have to put up the collateral. Do you own your own home?"

Jessie nodded, and explained the mortgage. "And I own my own business as well." She gave the woman the name and address of the boutique, the address of the house, and the name of the bank where they had their mortgage.

"What do you think your business is worth? What is it, anyway? A dress shop?" Jessie nodded, feeling degraded somehow, though she was not quite sure why. Maybe it was because the woman now knew what the charges were.

"Yes, it's a dress shop. And we have a fairly large inventory." Why did she want to impress this idiot woman? But then she knew that it was because the woman held the key to Ian's bail. Martin Schwartz was standing to one side, watching the proceedings.

"We'll have to call your bank. Come back at four o'clock."

"And then can you bail him?" Oh God, please, can you bail him? The panic was coming back in her throat again, thick and sweet and bitter, like bile.

"We'll bail him depending on what your bank says about the house and the shop," she said flatly. "Do you use the same bank for both?" Jessie nodded, looking gray. "Good. That'll save time. Bring the fifteen hundred with you when you come back. In cash."

"In cash?"

"Cash or a bank check. No personal checks."

"Thank you."

They went back to the street and Jessie took a long breath of fresh air. It felt like years since she'd had any. She breathed again and looked at Martin.

"What happens to people who don't have the money?"

"They don't bail."

"And then what?"

"They stay in custody till after the verdict."

"Even if they're innocent? They stay in jail all that time?"

"You don't know if they're innocent until after the trial."

"What the hell ever happened to 'innocent until proven guilty'?"

He shrugged and looked away, remaining silent. It had depressed him to be in the bail office. He rarely went to bailbondsmen with clients. But Ian had asked him to and he had promised. It seemed odd to treat such a tall, independent-looking woman as though she were frail and helpless. But he suspected that Ian was right: beneath the coat of armor, she hid a terrifying vulnerability. He wondered if that armor would crack before this was over. That was all they needed.

"What do poor people do about lawyers?" Jesus. He had enough headaches without playing social worker.

"They get public defenders, Jessica. And we have plenty to think about ourselves right now, without worrying about poor people, don't you think? Why don't you just get yourself to the bank and get this over with?"

"Okay. I'm sorry."

"Don't be. The system is lousy, and I know it. But it's not set up for the comfort of the poor. Just be grateful that you're not one of them right now, and let it go at that."

"That's hard to do, Martin."

He shook his head and gave her a small smile. "Are you going to the bank?"

"Yes, sir."

"Good. Do you want me to come with you?"

"Of course not. Is baby-sitting service always part of the deal, or did Ian strong-arm you into that?"

"I . . . no . . . oh, for Chrissake. Just go to

the bank. And let me know when you get him out. Or before that, if there's anything I can do."

How about lending us fifteen thousand bucks, baby? She smiled, said good-bye, and walked slowly to her car. She still didn't have any idea of how she'd come up with the money. And what the hell would she tell the bank? The truth. And she'd beg them if she had to. Fifteen thousand . . . it looked like the top of Mount Everest.

After six cigarettes and half an hour of agonizing conversation with the bank manager, Jessica took out a personal loan for fifteen hundred dollars against the car. And they assured her that all would be in order when the bail office called. There was a look of astonishment on the bank manager's face throughout the conversation, and he tried desperately to conceal it. Unsuccessfully. And Jessica had not even told him what the charges were, only that Ian was in jail. She prayed that the bail office wouldn't tell them the charges either, and that if they did he would keep his mouth shut. He had already sworn to her that he would see that everything remained confidential. And at least she had the fifteen hundred dollars . . . she had it . . . she had it! And her house and the business were worth ten times the collateral that she needed. But somehow she still didn't feel that it was enough. What if they still wouldn't let Ian out? And then she thought of it. The safe-deposit box.

"Mrs. Clarke?"

She didn't answer. She just sat there.

"Mrs. Clarke? Was there something else?"

"Sorry. Oh . . . I . . . was just thinking of something. Yes, I . . . I think I'd like to get into my vault today."

"Do you have the key with you?"

She nodded. She kept it on her key chain. She reached into her bag and handed it to him.

"I'll have Miss Lopez open the box for you."

Jessie followed him pensively, and then found herself following Miss Lopez, whom she did not know. And then she was standing in front of her safe-deposit box and Miss Lopez was looking at her, holding the box. It was a large one.

"Would you like to go into a room with this?"

"I . . . I . . . yes. Thank you." She shouldn't have done it. She didn't need it. It was a mistake . . . no . . . but what if the house and Lady J weren't enough? She knew she wasn't making sense now. She was panicking. But it was better to be sure . . . to be . . . for Ian. But it was all so painful. And now she had to face it alone.

Miss Lopez left her in a small, sterile room with a brown Formica desk and a black vinyl chair. On the wall hung an ugly print of Venice that looked as though it had been cut from the top of a candy box. And she was alone with the box. Jessie opened it carefully and took out three large brown leather boxes and two faded red suede jewelry cases. There was another, smaller box at the bottom, in faded blue. The blue box was filled with Jake's few treasures. The studs Father had given him on his twenty-first birthday, his school ring, his Navy ring. Junk, mostly, but very Jake.

The brown leather boxes contained the real treasures. Letters her parents had written to each other over the years. Letters they had exchanged while her father was in the service during the war. Poems her mother had written to her father. Photographs. Locks of her hair and Jake's. Treasures. All the things that had mattered. Now, all the things that hurt most.

She opened the blue box first and smiled through a veil of tears as she saw Jake's trinkets lying helter-skelter on the beige chamois. It still held the faintest hint of

Jake's smell. She remembered teasing him about the high-school ring. She had told him it was hideous, and he had been so damn proud of it. And now there it was. She slipped it on her finger. It was much too big for her. It would have been too big for Ian too. Jake had been almost six foot five.

She turned to the brown boxes then. She knew their touch so well. They were engraved with her parents' initials, tiny gold letters in the lower right-hand corners. Each box identical. They were a family tradition. In the first box she found a picture of the four of them taken one Easter. She had been eleven or twelve; Jake had been seven. It was really more than she could face. She closed the box quietly and turned to what she had come for.

The red suede jewelry cases. It was incredible, really. She was actually going to take her mother's jewelry with her. It was so precious to her, so sacred, so much still her mother's that Jessie had worn none of it in all these years. And now she was willing to leave it in the hands of strangers. For Ian.

She carefully unfolded the cases and looked at the long row of rings. A ruby in an old setting that had been her grandmother's. Two handsome jade rings her father had brought back from the Far East. The emerald ring her mother had wanted so much and had gotten for her fiftieth birthday. The diamond engagement ring . . . and her wedding ring, her "real" one, the worn, thin gold band she had always worn, always preferred to the emerald-and-diamond one Jessie's father had bought to match the emerald ring. There were two simple gold chain bracelets. A gold watch with tiny diamonds carefully set around the face. And a large handsome sapphire brooch with diamonds set around it that had also been Jessie's grandmother's.

The second case held three strands of perfectly matched pearls, pearl earrings, and a small pair of diamond earrings that she and Jake had bought her together the year before she'd died. It was all there. Jessie's stomach turned over as she looked at it. She knew she wouldn't really be able to leave it with the bailbondsmen, but at least she had it if she needed it. Two days before she wouldn't have considered such a thing, but now . . .

She put the rest of the boxes back into the metal vault and left the room almost two hours after she had entered it. The bank was almost ready to close.

When she went back to Bryant Street the

woman was eating a dripping cheeseburger over the afternoon paper. "Got the money?" She looked up and spoke to Jessica with her mouth full.

Jessica nodded. "Did you talk to the bank about the collateral?" She had had enough, and wading through the private agony that safe-deposit box represented had topped it off. She wanted the nightmare to end. Now.

"What bank?" The woman's face wore an unexpectedly blank expression, and Jessie clenched her hands to keep from screaming.

"The California Union *Trust* Bank. I wanted to bail my husband out tonight."

"What were the charges?" For Chrissake, what was this woman trying to *do* to her? She remembered that Jessica was due back with some money — how could she have forgotten the rest? Or was she playing a game? Well, if she was, fuck her.

"The charges were rape and assault." She almost shouted the words.

"Did you own any property?" Oh, shit.

"For God's sake, we went through all that this afternoon, and you were going to call my bank about my business and our mortgage. I was here with our attorney, filled out papers, and . . ."

"Okay. What's your name?"

"Clarke. With an 'E.' "

"Yeah. Here it is." She pulled out the form with two greasy fingers. "Can't bail him now, though."

"Why not?" Jessie's stomach turned over again.

"Too late to call the bank."

"Shit. Now what?"

"Come back in the morning." Sure, while Ian sat in jail for another night. Wonderful. Tears of frustration choked her throat, but there was nothing she could do except go home and come back in the morning.

"You want to talk to the boss?"

Jessie's face lit up.

"Now?"

"Yeah. He's here. In the back."

"Fabulous. Tell him I'm here." Oh God, please . . . please let him be human . . . please . . .

The man emerged from the back room picking his teeth with a dirty finger that boasted a small gold ring with a large pink diamond. He had a beer can in his other hand. He was wearing jeans and a T-shirt, and had a lot of curly black hair on his arms and at the neck of the shirt; his hair was almost an Afro. And he wasn't much older than Jessie. He grinned when he saw her, gave a last stab at his teeth, then removed his hand from his mouth and extended it for her to shake. She shook it, but with difficulty.

"How do you do. I'm Jessica Clarke."

"Barry York. What can I do you for?"

"I'm trying to bail my husband."

"From what? What are the charges? Hey . . . wait a minute. Let's go in my office. You want a beer?" Actually, she did. But not with him. She was hot and tired and thirsty and fed up and scared, but she didn't want to drink anything with Barry York, not even water.

"No thanks."

"Coffee?"

"No, really. I'm fine, but thanks." He was trying to be decent. One had to give him credit for that. He led her into a small, dingy office with pictures of nude women on the walls, sat down in a swivel chair, put a green eyeshade on his head, switched on a stereo, and grinned at her.

"We don't see many people like you, Mrs. Clarke."

"I . . . no . . . thank you."

"So what's with the old man? What's the beef? Drunk driving?"

"No, rape." Barry whistled lengthily while Jessie stared at his stomach. At least he was honest about what he thought. "That's a bitch. What's the bail?"

"Fifteen thousand."

"Bad news."

"Well, that's why I'm here." Good news for you, Barry, baby; maybe you can even buy yourself a gold toothpick after this, with a diamond tip. "I spoke to the young lady out there earlier today, and she was to call my bank, and . . ."

"And?" His face hardened slightly.

"She forgot."

Barry shook his head. "She didn't forget. We don't do bonds that high."

"You don't?"

He shook his head again. "Not usually." Jessica thought she was going to cry. "I guess she just didn't want to tell you."

"So I lost a day, and my husband is still in jail, and my bank is expecting to hear from you, and . . . now what, Mr. York? What the hell do I do now?"

"How about some dinner?" He turned the stereo down and patted her hand. His breath smelled like pastrami and garlic. He stank.

Jessica simply looked at him and stood up. "You know, my attorney must be all wrong about this place, Mr. York. And I have every intention of telling him just that."

"Who's your attorney?"

"Martin Schwartz. He was here with me this morning."

"Look, Mrs. . . . what's your name again?"

"Clarke."

"Mrs. Clarke. Why don't you sit down and we'll talk a little business."

"Now or after dinner? Or after we listen to a few more records?"

He smiled. "You like the records? I thought that was a nice touch."

He turned the stereo up again and Jessie didn't know whether to laugh, cry, or scream. It was obvious that she'd never get Ian out of jail. Not at this rate. "You want to have dinner?"

"Yes, Mr. York. With my husband. What are the chances of your getting my husband out of jail so I can have dinner with him?"

"Tonight? No way. I've got to talk to your bank first."

"That's exactly where I left it at twelve-thirty this afternoon."

"Yeah, well, I'm sorry. And I'll take care of it myself in the morning, but I can't do anything after banking hours, not on a bond the size of the one you're talking about. What are you putting up as collateral?"

"My business and/or my house. That's up to you. I'm willing to put up either one or both. Or I was. But I have another idea." It was crazy, it was stupid, it was immoral, it was wrong, but she was so goddam fed up, she had to. She reached into her bag and pulled out the two cases with her mother's jewelry in them. "What about these?"

Barry York sat down very quietly and didn't say a word for almost ten minutes.

"Nice."

"Better than that. The emerald and the diamond rings are very fine stones. And the sapphire brooch is worth a great deal of money. So are the pearls."

"Yeah. Probably so. But the problem is I don't know nothing until I take them to a jeweler. I still can't get the old man out tonight." The old man . . . asshole. "Very nice jewelry, though. Where'd you get it?"

We stole it. "It's my mother's."

"She know the old man's in the can?"

"Hardly, Mr. York. She's dead."

"Oh. I'm sorry. Listen, I'll take this to the appraiser first thing tomorrow morning. I'll call your bank. We'll get the old man out by noon. Swear, if the stuff is good. I can't do anything before that. But by noon, if everything is in order. Do you have my fee?"

Yes, darling, in pennies. "Yes."

"Okay, then we're all set."

"Mr. York, why can't you just take all the jewelry tonight and let him come home? He

137

won't go anywhere, and we'll get all this financial nonsense straightened out tomorrow. If your assistant had called the bank when she said she would . . ."

He was shaking his head, picking his teeth again and holding up his other hand. "I'd like to. But I can't. That's all. I can't. My business is at stake. I'll take care of it first thing in the morning. I swear. Be here at ten-thirty and we'll get everything done."

"Fine." She rose to her feet, feeling as though the weight of the world were resting on her shoulders. She folded up the two suede cases and put them back in her bag.

"You're not leaving me those?"

"Nope. That was just if I could get him out tonight. I thought you'd recognize their value. Otherwise, I'd much rather put up my house and the business."

"Okay. Yeah." But he didn't look pleased. "That's a hell of a big bond, you know." She nodded tiredly.

"Don't worry. It's a nice house and a good business, and he's a decent man. He won't run away on you. You won't lose a dime."

"You'd be surprised who runs away."

"I'll see you at ten-thirty, Mr. York." She held out a hand and he shook it, smiling again.

"You sure about dinner? You look tired.

Maybe some food would do you good. A little wine, a little dancing . . . hell, enjoy yourself a little before the old man gets home. And look at it this way, if he got busted for rape, you gotta know he wasn't just out with the boys."

"Good night, Mr. York."

She walked quietly out the door, out to her car, and drove home.

She was asleep on the couch half an hour later, and she didn't wake up until nine the next morning. When she did, she felt as though she had died the night before. And she had a terrifying case of the shakes.

It was all beginning to take its toll. The ever deepening circles under her eyes now looked irreparable, the eyes themselves seemed to be shrinking, and she noticed that she was beginning to lose weight. She smoked six cigarettes, drank two cups of coffee, played with a piece of toast, and called the boutique and told them to forget about her again today. She arrived back at Yorktowne Bonding at ten-thirty. On the dot.

There were two new people at the desk — a girl with dyed black hair the color of military boots who was snapping bubble gum, and a bearded young man with a Mexican accent. This time Jessie asked for

Mr. York right away.

"He's expecting me." The two clerks looked up as though they had never heard the words before.

He appeared two minutes later in dirty white shorts and a navy blue T-shirt, carrying a copy of Playboy and a tennis racket.

"You play?" Oh, Jesus.

"Sometimes. Did you talk to the bank?"

He smiled, looking pleased. "Come into my office. Coffee?"

"No, thanks." She was beginning to feel as though the nightmare would never end. She would simply spend the rest of her life ricocheting among the Inspector Houghtons and the Barry Yorks, the courtrooms and jails, the banks and . . . it was endless. Just when it seemed about to end, there would be another false door. There was no way out. She was almost sure of it now. And Ian was only a myth anyway. Someone she had made up and never known. The keeper of the Holy Grail.

"You know, you look tired. Do you eat right?"

"I eat splendidly. But my husband is in jail, Mr. York, and I would very much like to get him out. What are the chances of that, in the immediate future?"

"Excellent." He beamed. "I talked to the

bank and everything's in order. You put up the house and agree to a lien on your earnings at the boutique if he defaults. And we keep the emerald ring and sapphire brooch for you."

"What?" He had made it sound as if he were ordering lunch for her, but he had caught her attention with the mention of her mother's jewelry. "I don't think you understood, Mr. York. The house and the business are all I'm putting up. I told you last night that I was only offering my mother's jewelry if I could get him out then, without your calling the bank and all. Sort of a guarantee."

"Yeah. Well, I'd feel better with that same guarantee now."

"Well, I wouldn't."

"How would your husband feel staying in jail?"

"Mr. York, isn't there a law against bail-bondsmen taking too much as collateral?" Martin had told her about it.

"Are you accusing me of being dishonest?" Oh, God, she was going to blow it . . . oh no . . .

"No. Look, please . . ."

"Look, baby, I'm not gonna do business with some broad who calls me dishonest. I do you a favor and stick my ass out on a limb for your old man on a fifteen-thousand-dollar bond, and you call me a thief. I mean, look, I don't gotta take that shit from no one."

"I'm sorry." The tears were burning her eyes again. She was beginning to wonder if she'd live through this. And then he looked over at her and shrugged.

"All right. I'll tell you what. We'll just keep the ring. You can take the brooch. Does that sound any better?"

"Fine." It sounded stinking, but she didn't care anymore. It didn't matter. It didn't even matter if Ian ran away and they took the house and the business and the car and the emerald ring. Nothing mattered.

York managed to make the forms take twice as long as necessary, and to slide a hand across her breast as he reached for another pen. She looked up into his face and he smiled and told her she'd be beautiful if she ate right, and how he'd had a tall girlfriend in high school. A girl named Mona. Jessica just nodded and went on signing her name. Finally all the paperwork was done. He bit the end off a long thin cigar and picked up the phone to notify the jail.

"I'll have Bernice take you across the street, Jessica." He had decided to call her by her first name. "And listen, if you ever need any help, just call. I'll keep in touch." She prayed that he wouldn't, and shook his hand before leaving his office. She felt as though she would stumble on the way out. She had reached her limit. Days ago.

By the time Barry York had delegated the gum-chewing clerk to take Jessie across the street to bail Ian, it was almost noon. To Jessie it felt like the middle of the night. She was confused and exhausted and everything was beginning to blur. She was living in an unreal world filled with evil, leering people.

The woman he'd called Bernice took charge of the papers, shuffled them for a moment, and then walked across the street with Jessie and into the Hall of Justice. She slipped the sheaf of papers Jessie and Barry York had signed into a slot in a window on the second floor, and then turned to look at Jessica for a moment.

"You going to stick by your old man?"

"I beg your pardon?"

"You going to stay with your husband?"

"Yes . . . of course . . . why?" She was feeling confused again. And why was this woman asking her that?

"That's a hell of a beef, sister. And what's a good-looking chick like you want with a loser like him? He's going to cost you a bundle on this one." She shook her head and snapped her gum twice.

"He's worth it."

The girl shrugged and waved at the bank of elevators. "You can go up to the jail now. We're all through." No, lady, *I'm* all through. That's different. The clerk departed with a last snap of her gum and headed down a stairway.

Jessica reached the jail a few moments later and had to ring a small buzzer to bring a guard to the door.

"Yeah? It's not visiting time yet."

"I'm here to bail out my husband."

"What's his name?"

"Ian Clarke." You know, the famous rapist. "Yorktowne Bonding just called about it."

"I'll check." Check? Check what? With the house, the business, and Mom's emerald ring on the line, you're going to check, mister? Well, screw you. And Yorktowne Bonding . . . and Inspector Houghton . . . and . . . Ian too? She wasn't really sure anymore. She didn't know what she felt. She was angry at him, but not for what he had done, only for not being there when she needed him so badly.

She waited at the door for almost half an

hour, stupefied, dazed, leaning against the wall and hardly knowing why. What if she never saw him again? But suddenly the door opened and he stood there facing her. He was unshaven, bedraggled, filthy, and exhausted. But he was free. Everything she owned was riding on him now. And he was free. She sank slowly toward him with an unfamiliar whimpering sound, and he led her gently into the elevator.

"It's all right, baby . . . it's all right. Everything's going to be all right, Jess . . . sshhhh . . ." It was Ian. Actually, really, honestly Ian. And he held her so gently and almost carried her down to the car. She couldn't take any more and he knew it. He didn't know all the details of what had been happening, but when he saw the bail papers and noticed the mention of her mother's emerald ring, he understood much more than she could tell him.

"It's okay, baby . . . everything's going to be fine."

She clutched him blindly as they stood beside the car, the tears streaming down her cheeks, her face in a rictus of shock and despair, the same little squeaking noises escaping from her between sobs.

"Jessie . . . baby . . . I love you." He held her tightly, and then quietly drove her home.

CHAPTER 9

"What are you doing today, darling?"

Jessie poured Ian a second cup of coffee at breakfast and glanced at the clock. It was almost nine and she hadn't been to the boutique for two days. She felt as though she had been gone for a month, existing in a kind of twilight zone all her own. A never-ending nightmare, but it was over now. Ian was home. She had spent most of the day before asleep in his arms. And he looked like Ian again. Clean, shaven, a little more rested. He was wearing gray slacks and a wine-colored turtleneck. Every time she looked at him she wanted to touch him to make sure he was real.

"Are you going to write today?"

"I don't know yet. I think I might just spend the day feeling good." But he didn't ask her to play hookey with him. He knew she had to work. She had done enough for him in the past few days. He couldn't ask for more.

"I wish I could stay home with you." She looked at him wistfully over her coffee and he patted her hand.

"I'll pick you up for lunch."

"I have an idea. Why don't you hang around the boutique today?"

He watched her eyes and knew what she was thinking. She had been like that for months after Jake had died. That terror that if he left her sight, he'd vanish.

"You wouldn't get any work done, my love. But I'll be around. I'll be right here most of the time." But what about the rest of the time? She reached over and held his hand. Nothing was said. There was nothing to say. "I thought maybe I'd talk to a couple of people about work."

"No!" She pulled back her hand and her eyes darted fire. "No, Ian! Please."

"Jessica, be reasonable. Have you thought of what this disaster is costing us? Costing *you,* to be more exact? And this is as good a time as any to get a job. Nothing exotic, just something to bring a little money in."

"And what happens when you have to start making court appearances? And during the trial? Just how much good do you think you'll be to anyone then?" She held tightly to his hand again and he saw the pain

147

in her eyes. It was going to take months for the desperation to pass.

"Well, what exactly do you expect me to do, Jess?"

"Finish the book."

"And let you pick up the tab for this mess?"

She nodded. "We can straighten it out later, if you want to. But I don't really give a damn, Ian. What does it matter who signs the checks?"

"It matters to me." *It always has mattered, always will matter.* But he knew, too, that he'd never be able to concentrate on anything while this was hanging over his head. The trial . . . the trial . . . it was all he could think of. While she had slept all those hours the previous afternoon, it had kept running through his mind . . . the trial. He was in no frame of mind to get a job. "We'll see."

"I love you." There were tears in her eyes again, and he tweaked the end of her nose.

"If you get dewy-eyed on me once more, Mrs. Clarke, I'm going to drag you back to bed and really give you something to cry about." She laughed in response and poured some more coffee.

"I just can't believe you're home. It was so incredibly awful while you were gone . . . it was . . . it was like . . ." The words caught in her throat.

"It was probably like peace and quiet for a change, and you were too silly to enjoy it. Hell, you didn't think I'd stay down there forever, did you? I mean, even for a writer that kind of living research gets stale after a while."

"Jerk." But she was smiling now; she had nothing to fear.

"Want me to drive you to work?"

"As a matter of fact, I'd love it." She beamed as she put the cups in the sink and grabbed her orange suede coat off the back of a chair. She was wearing it over well-tailored jeans and a beige cashmere sweater. She looked like Jessie again — everywhere except around the eyes. She slid the dark glasses into place and smiled at him. "I think I'd better hang on to these for a couple of days. I still look like I've been on a two-week drunk."

"You look beautiful and I love you." He pinched her behind as they headed out the front door, and she leaned backward to kiss him haphazardly over one shoulder. "You even smell nice."

"Nothing but the best Eau de Mille Pieds." She said it with a broad grin and he groaned.

"Oh, for Chrissake." It was one of their

oldest jokes. Water of a thousand feet.

She pointed out Astrid's house to him on their way to the boutique, and told him about her visit to the shop.

"She seems like a nice woman. Very quiet and pleasant."

"Hell, I'd be quiet and pleasant too, with that kind of money."

"Ian!" But she grinned at him and ran a hand through his hair. It felt so good to be sitting next to him again, to be looking at his profile as he drove, to feel the skin on his neck with her mouth as she kissed him. She had awakened a dozen times during the night to make sure he was still there.

"I'll come by for you around twelve. Okay?"

She looked at him for a moment before nodding. "You'll be here? For sure?"

"Oh, baby . . . I'll be here. Promise." He took her in his arms and she held him so tightly that it hurt. He knew she was thinking of the day he'd been arrested and hadn't shown up for lunch. "Be a big girl." She grinned and hopped out of the car and blew him a last kiss before running up the steps of the shop.

Ian lit a cigarette as he drove away, and glanced over to look at the ships on the bay. It was a beautiful day. Indian summer was passing, and it was not as warm as it had been a few days before, but the sky was a bright blue and there was a gentle breeze. It made him think back to that day five days before. It felt like five years before. He still couldn't understand it.

He paused at a stop sign, and another thought came to mind. The emerald ring Jessie had put up as bail. It still astounded him. He knew how she felt about her mother's things. She wouldn't even wear them. They were sacred, the last relics of a long-demolished shrine. And that ring meant more to her than any of the other pieces. He had watched her slip it on her finger once while her hand trembled out of control. She had put the ring back in the case, and never gone to the vault again. And now she had turned it over to a bailbondsman, for him. It told him something that nothing else ever had. It was crazy, but he felt as though he loved her more than he had before all this had begun, and maybe Jessie had learned something too. Maybe they knew what they had now. Maybe they'd take better care of it. He knew one thing. His days of discreet interludes were over. Forever. All of a sudden he had a wife. More of a wife than he had ever known he had. What more could he want? A child, perhaps, but

151

he had resigned himsef to the absence of children. He was happy enough with just Jessie.

"Morning, ladies." Jessie strolled into the store with a quiet smile on her face. And Katsuko looked up from the desk.

"Well, look who's here. And on a Saturday, yet. We were beginning to think you'd found a better job."

"No such luck."

"Is everything okay?"

"Yes. Everything's okay." Jessica nodded slowly and Katsuko knew that it was. Jessie was herself again.

"I'm glad." Katsuko handed her a cup of coffee and Jessie perched on the corner of the chrome-and-glass desk.

"Where's Zina?"

"In the back, checking the stock. Mrs. Bonner came back looking for you yesterday. She bought one of the new wine velvet skirts."

"It must have looked great on her. Did she try it with the cream satin shirt?"

"Yup. Bought them both, and the new green velvet pantsuit. That lady must have money burning holes in her pockets." Yeah. And loneliness burning holes in her heart. Jessie had had a taste of it now. She knew.

"She'll be back," Katsuko added.

"I hope so. Even if she doesn't buy. I like her. Anything taking shape for the fashion show?"

"I had a few ideas yesterday, Jessie. I made some notes and left them on your desk."

"I'll go take a look." She stretched lazily and wandered toward her office, carrying her coffee. It was a slow morning, and she felt as if she had come back after a very long absence, a long illness maybe. She felt slow and careful and frail. And everything looked suddenly different. The shop looked so sweet, the two girls so pretty . . . Ian so beautiful . . . the sky so blue . . . everything seemed better and more.

She read her mail, paid some bills, changed the window, and discussed the fashion show with Katsuko while Zina waited on customers. The morning sped by, and Ian was there five minutes before noon. With an armload of roses. The delicate salmon ones Jessie loved best.

"Ian! They're fabulous!" There were about three dozen, and she could see an awkward square lump in his jacket pocket. He was spoiling her and she loved it. He smiled at her and headed toward her office.

"Can I see you for a minute, Mrs. Clarke?"

"Yes, sir. For three dozen roses you can

see me for several weeks!" The two girls laughed and Jessie followed Ian into her office. He closed the door gently and grinned at her.

"Have a nice morning?"

"You brought me back to this secluded spot to ask me if I had a nice morning?" He was grinning and she was starting to giggle. "Come on, tell the truth. Is it bigger than a breadbox?"

"What?"

"The surprise you bought me, of course."

"What surprise? I buy you roses and you want more! You greedy spoiled miserable . . ." But he was looking too pleased with himself to convince even Jessie. "Oh . . . here." He pulled the box out of his pocket and grinned from ear to ear. It was a solid chunk of gold bracelet; inside it was engraved ALL MY LOVE, IAN. He had literally stood over the jewelers all morning while they did the engraving. It was no time to spend money, but he'd known that she needed something like that, and it had suddenly come to him as he'd sat down to work. It was a beautiful bracelet, and the proportions were just right for her hand. It had cost him the last of his private savings.

"Oh, darling . . . it's beautiful." She slipped it onto her wrist and it held there.

"Wow. It's just perfect! Oh Ian . . . you're crazy!"

"I happen to be madly in love with you."

"I'm beginning to think you struck oil too. You spent a fortune this morning." But there was no edge to her voice, only pleasure, and Ian shrugged. "Wait till I show the girls!" She planted a kiss on the corner of his mouth, opened the door, and bumped into Zina, who was walking past to the stockroom. "Look at my bracelet!"

"My, my! Does that mean you're engaged to the handsome man with the roses?" She giggled and winked at Ian.

"Oh, shut up. Isn't it super?"

"It's gorgeous. And all I want to know is where you find another one like him."

"Try Central Casting." Ian looked over Jessie's shoulder with a grin.

"I might just do that." Zina disappeared into the stockroom, and, with a look of victory, Jessie showed her new bracelet to Katsuko. A few minutes later, she and Ian were on their way out the door to lunch.

"Boy, I love my bracelet!" She was like a child with a new toy, and held up her arm to look at it in the sunlight. "Darling, it's just gorgeous! And how did you get them to engrave it so fast?"

"At gunpoint, of course. How else?"

"Oh, for Chrissake . . . you know, you really have a lot of class."

"For a rapist." But he was smiling when he said it.

"Ian!"

"Yes, my love?" He kissed her and she laughed as she got into the car. He had more style than any man she knew.

They went to the movies that night, and slept late on Sunday morning. It was another warm blue day, with puffy, pasted-on-looking clouds that rolled along high in the sky, looking like painted scenery.

"Want to go to the beach, Mrs. Clarke?" He stretched lazily on his side of the bed and then reached over and kissed her. She liked the feel of his beard stubble against her cheek. It was rough but it didn't quite hurt.

"I'd love to. What time is it?"

"Almost noon."

"You're lying. It must be nine."

"I am not. Open your eyes and take a look."

"I can't. I'm still asleep."

But he nibbled her neck and made her laugh and her eyes flew open.

"Stop that!"

"I will not. Get up and make me breakfast."

"Slave driver. Haven't you ever heard of women's lib?" She lay on her back sleepily and yawned.

"What's that?"

"Women's lib. It says husbands have to cook breakfast on Sunday . . . but . . . on the other hand." She looked at her bracelet again with a broad smile. "It doesn't say you have to give your wife such gorgeous jewelry. So maybe I'll make you breakfast."

"Beulah Big Heart, don't knock yourself out."

"I won't. Fried eggs okay?" She lit a cigarette and sat up.

"I have a better idea."

"The Fairmont for brunch?" She grinned at him and flashed the bracelet again.

"No. I'll help. You're too busy waving your bracelet at me to make us a decent breakfast anyway. How about a smoked-oyster-and-cheese omelette?" He looked enchanted with the combination and Jessie made a terrible face.

"Yerchk! Can we skip the smoked oysters?"

"Why not skip the cheese?"

"How about skipping the omelette?"

"The Fairmont for breakfast, then?"

"Ian, you're crazy . . . but I love you." She nibbled at his thigh and he ran a hand down the smoothness of her spine.

It was another hour before they got out of bed. Even their lovemaking was different now. There was an odd combination of desperation and gratitude, of "Oh God, I love you" mixed with "Let's pretend everything's better than normal." It wasn't, but the pretense helped. A little. Their motors were still racing a little too fast.

"Are we or are we not going to the beach today?" He sat up in bed, his blond hair tousled like a boy's.

"Sounds fine to me, but I still haven't been fed yet."

"Aww . . . poor baby. You didn't want my smoked-oyster omelette."

She tugged at a lock of his hair. "I prefer what I got instead."

"Shame on you."

She stuck out her tongue at him, got out of bed, and headed for the kitchen.

"Where are you going bare-assed like that?"

"To the kitchen, to make breakfast. Any objection?"

"Nope. Need a voyeur on hand?"

A minute later she heard the garden door slam and then saw him reappear in the kitchen, wearing a blanket around his waist and carrying a mixed bouquet of her petunias.

"For the lady of the house."

"Sorry, she's out. Can I have them instead?" She kissed him gently and took the flowers from his hand and set them down on the drainboard as he took her into his arms and let the blanket fall to the floor.

"Darling, I happen to love you madly, but if you don't stop, the bacon will burn and we'll never get to the beach."

"Do you care?" They were both smiling and the bacon was splattering furiously while the eggs began to bubble.

"No. But we might as well eat while it's ready. Damn." He patted her behind and she turned off the flame and served scrambled eggs, bacon, toast, orange juice and coffee. Still naked, they sat down to breakfast.

They didn't get to the beach until almost three, but it was still a beautiful day and the sun stayed warm until six. They had a fish dinner in Sausalito on the way home, and he bought her a silly little dog made out of seashells.

"I love it. Now I feel like a tourist."

"I thought you should have something really expensive to remember this evening

159

with." They were in high spirits as they crossed the bridge going home, but his words struck her oddly. Suddenly they were buying souvenirs and clutching at memories.

"Hey, sweetheart, how's the book coming?"

"Better than I want to admit. Don't ask me yet."

"For real?"

"For real."

She looked at him, pleased. He looked almost proud of himself and a little bit afraid to be.

"Have you sent any of it to your agent yet?"

"No, I want to wait till I finish a few more chapters before I do that. But I think this one is good. Maybe even very good." He said it with a solemnity that touched her. He hadn't sounded like that about his work in years. Not since the fables, and they had been very good. Not very profitable, but definitely good. The critics had certainly agreed, even if the public hadn't.

On the way home, they stopped outside the yacht club near the bridge and turned off the lights and the motor. It was nice to sit and watch the water lap at a small lip of beach while the foghorns bleated softly in the distance. They were both oddly tired, as though each day were an endless journey. Their few days of trauma had taken a heavy toll. She noticed it in the heavy way he slept now, and she herself felt tired all the time, no matter how happy she was again. There was a new passion too. A new need, a new hunger for each other, as though they must stock up for a long empty winter. They had rough times ahead. This was just the beginning.

"Want to go out for an ice cream cone?" There was a restless look around his eyes.

"Honestly? No. I'm bushed."

"Yeah. Me too. And I want to do some reading tonight. The chapter I just finished."

"Can I read some too?"

"Sure." He looked pleased as he started the car and headed for home. It was funny how neither of them wanted to go home. The stop near the yacht club, the offer of an ice cream cone — what was the lurking demon they feared at home? Jessica wondered; but she knew who her private demon was. Inspector Houghton. She constantly expected him to jump out at her and take Ian back into custody. She had thought about it all day at the beach, wondering if he would spring from behind a dune and try to spirit Ian away. She hadn't said anything to Ian. Neither of them ever spoke of his arrest now. It was all either of them could think of, and the only thing they wouldn't talk about.

He was stretched out in front of the fire reading his manuscript when she decided that she had to remind him. She hated to bring it up, but somebody had to.

"Don't forget about tomorrow, love." She said it softly, regretfully.

"Huh?" He had been deep into his work.

"I said don't forget about tomorrow."

"What's tomorrow?" He looked blank.

"We have a ten o'clock appointment with Martin Schwartz." She tried to make it sound like a double appointment with the hairdresser, but it didn't come off like that. Ian looked up at her and didn't say a word. His eyes said it all.

CHAPTER 10

The meeting with Martin Schwartz was sobering. Sitting there with him, having to discuss the charges, they couldn't hide from it anymore. Jessica felt sick as she sat and listened. It was real now. She even felt sick thinking of the security she had put up. It came home to her now. She had put everything on the line. The house. The shop's profits. Even the emerald ring. Everything . . . Jesus . . . and what if Ian panicked and ran? What if . . . my God . . . she'd lose it all. She looked at him, feeling a lump rise in her throat, and tried to concentrate on what was being said. She almost couldn't hear. She just kept thinking of the fact that she needed one man so desperately that she had given all for him. And now what would happen?

Martin explained the preliminary hearing to them, and they agreed to hire an investigator to see what could be learned of the "victim." Plenty, they hoped, and all of it unsavory. They were not going to be kind to Miss Margaret Burton. Destroying her was Ian's only way out.

"There's got to be a reason for it though, Ian. Think about it. Carefully. Did you rough her up in some way? Sexually? Verbally? Humiliate her? Hurt her?" Martin looked at Ian pointedly, and Jessie looked away. She hated the uncomfortable look on Ian's face. "Ian?" And then Martin looked at her. "Jessie, maybe you ought to let us have this out alone for a few moments."

"Sure." It was a relief to leave the room. Ian didn't look up as she left. They were down to the nitty-gritty now. Of who had done what to whom, where, how, for how long, and how often. He died thinking of what Jessie would hear in court at the trial.

She wandered the carpeted halls, looking at prints on the wall, smoking, alone with her own thoughts, until she found a small love seat placed near a window with the same splendid view as the one from Martin's office. She had a lot to think about.

A secretary came to get her half an hour later and escorted her back to Martin's office. Ian looked harassed and Martin was scowling. Jessie tried to make light of it.

"Did I miss all the good parts?" But her

smile was forced and they didn't try to return it.

"According to Ian, there were no 'good' parts. It must have something to do with a personal grudge."

"Against Ian? Why? Did you know her?" She turned to her husband with a look of surprise. She had understood that the woman was a stranger to him.

"No. I didn't know her. But Martin means that she was out to hurt someone, anyone, maybe just a man, and I came along at the wrong time."

"You can say that again."

"I just hope we can prove it, Ian. Green ought to come up with something on her."

"He'd better, at twenty bucks an hour." Ian frowned again and looked at Jessie, as she nodded almost imperceptibly. This was no time to get tight with money. They'd find it wherever they had to, but they couldn't skimp on this.

Martin explained the preliminary to them once more to make sure it was clear. It was a sort of mini-trial at which the plaintiff/victim and the defendant would state their sides of the story, and the judge would decide if the matter should be dropped, or go on to a higher court for an ultimate decision — in this case, to trial. Martin held out no hope that the matter would be dropped. The opposing stories were equally vehement, the circumstances cloudy. No judge would take it upon himself to decide a case like that at the preliminary stage. It didn't help that the woman had maintained the same job for years and was respected where she worked. And there were certain psychological aspects of the case that made Martin Schwartz exceedingly uncomfortable: the fact that Ian was being virtually supported by his wife and hadn't had a successful book in a number of years, though he'd been writing for almost six, could have produced a certain resentment against women; at least, a good prosecutor could make it look that way. The investigator would be out to talk to Ian that afternoon or the following morning.

Jessie and Ian rode down in the elevator in silence, and Jessie finally spoke as they reached the street.

"Well, babe, what do you think?"

"Nothing good. Sounds like if we don't dig up some dirt on her, she's got me by the balls. And according to Schwartz, the courts frown on that kind of character assassination these days. But in this case, it's our only hope. It's her version against mine, and of course the medical testimony too, but that sounds pretty weak. They can tell that there was intercourse, but no one can tell if it was rape. The assault charge has already been dropped. Now we're just down to the nitty-gritty and my 'sexual aberrations.' " Jessica nodded and said nothing.

It was a quiet drive to the boutique. She was thinking about the hearing with dread. She didn't want to see that woman, but there was no way to escape it. She had to see her, had to listen, had to hold up her end, if only for Ian's sake, no matter how ugly the whole thing got.

"Want me to leave you the car, love? I can walk home." Ian prepared to get out after he drove her to the shop.

"No, darling, I . . . actually, come to think of it, I'm going to need it today. Does that louse you up?" She was trying to sound pleasant, but she had just had a thought. She needed the car today, and there were no maybe's about it, whether it loused him up or not.

"No sweat. I've got the Swedish sex bomb if I need It." He was referring to his Volvo, and she grinned.

"Want to come in for a cup of coffee?" But neither of them felt talkative. The morning's interview had left them feeling pensive and distant from each other.

"No, I'll let you get to work. I want to spend a little time by myself." It was pointless to ask him if he was upset. They both were.

"Okay, love. I'll see you later." At the door to the boutique they parted with a quick kiss.

She rapidly took refuge in her office and made an appointment for one-thirty. It was the only thing she could think of. Ian would be crushed, but what choice did she have? And he was in no position to object.

"Well, what do you think?" She hated the man's looks and resented him already. He was fat and oily and sly.

"Not bad. Pretty slinky little number. How's it look under the hood?"

"Impeccable." He was examining the little red Morgan as if it were a piece of meat in a supermarket or a hooker in a bordello. Jessie's skin crawled; this felt like selling their child into white slavery. To this fat nauseating man.

"You in a hurry to sell her?"

"No. Just curious about the price I might get for it."

"Why do you want to sell her? Need the bread?" He looked Jessie over carefully.

"No. I need a larger car." But it was all very painful. She still remembered her astonishment and delight the day Ian had driven up in the Morgan and handed her the keys, with a broad grin on his face. Victory. And now it would be like selling her heart. Or his.

"Tell you what, I'll make you an offer."

"How much?"

"Four thousand . . . nah . . . maybe, as a favor to you, forty-five hundred." The dealer looked her over and waited.

"That's ridiculous. My husband paid seven for it, and it's in better condition now than when he bought it."

"Best I can do. And I think it's the best you'll get on short notice. It needs a little work." It didn't, and they both knew it, but he was right about the short notice. A Morgan was a beautiful car, but very few people wanted to own one, or could afford to.

"I'll let you know. Thank you for your time." Without further comment she got back in the car and drove off. Damn. What a miserable thing to even consider. But she had the rest of Schwartz's fee to pay, and now the investigator, the business and the house were already tied up by Yorktowne Bonding, and she already had a loan out on the car. She'd be lucky if the bank would even let her sell it. But they knew her well enough. They just might let her. And despite Ian's flourish about going out and getting a job, he had done nothing. He was knee deep in the book and going nowhere except to his studio with a pencil stuck behind his ear. Artistic but hardly lucrative at this point. And even if he did get a job, how much money could he make in the month or two before the trial, waiting on tables or tending bar while he wrote at night? Maybe the book would sell. There was always that to hope for. But Jessie knew from experience that that took time, and too often they had teased themselves with that slim hope. She knew better now. It would have to be the Morgan. Sooner or later.

She kept to herself for the rest of the day, and it was a pleasant surprise when Astrid Bonner walked into the shop shortly before five. She might bring relief from the day's tensions.

"Well, Jessica, you certainly are hard to get hold of!" But she was in high spirits. She had just bought a new topaz ring, a handsome piece of work, thirty-two karats' worth encased in a small fortune in gold, and she "hadn't been able to resist it." On anyone else it would have been vulgar; on Astrid it had style. But it made Jessie's heart ache again over the Morgan. The topaz with the narrow diamond baguettes had probably cost Astrid twice the amount she needed so badly.

"Life has been pretty crazy ever since I got back from New York. And that's some ring, Astrid!"

"If I get tired of it, I can always use it as a doorknob. I can't quite decide if it's gorgeous or ghastly, and I know no one will ever tell me the truth."

"It's gorgeous."

"Truth?" She looked at Jessie teasingly.

"So much so I've been green with envy since you walked in."

"Goody! It really was a shockingly self-indulgent thing to do. Amazing what a little ennui will do to a girl." She laughed coquettishly and Jessie smiled. Such simple problems. Ennui.

"Want a lift home, or did you come to do some shopping?"

"No shopping, and I have the car, thanks. I came by on my way home to invite you and your husband to dinner." The girls had told her that Jessie was married.

"What a sweet thought. We'd love it. When do you want us?"

"How about tomorrow?"

"You're on." They exchanged a smile of

pleasure and Astrid walked comfortably around Jessie's small, cheerful office.

"You know, Jessica, I'm falling in love with this place. I might have to con you out of it one of these days." She laughed mischievously and watched Jessica's eyes.

"Don't waste your energies conning me. I might just give it to you. Right about now, I might even gift wrap it!"

"You're making me drool."

"Spare your saliva. Can I talk you into a drink? I don't know about you, but I could use a stiff one."

"Still those problems you mentioned the other day?"

"More or less."

"Which means mind my own business. Fair enough." She smiled easily; she didn't know that Jessica had spent the day trying to forget that Barry York had a lien on her business. It made Jessica sick to think about it, and all the while Ian was out of touch with the world, working on that bloody book night and day. Jesus. She needed someone to talk to. And why did he have to start tuning out right now? He always got that way when he was into a book. But now?

"I have an idea, Jessica."

Jessie looked up, startled. For a moment she had totally forgotten Astrid.

172

"How about having that drink at my place?"

"You know what? I'd love that. You're sure it's not too much trouble?"

"It's no trouble; it would be fun. Come on, let's get going."

Jessie bid a rapid good night to the girls and found herself relieved to leave the boutique. It hadn't used to be like that. She'd used to feel good just walking in the door in the morning, and pleased with herself and her life as she walked out at night. Now she hated to think of the place. It was shocking how things could change in so little time.

Jessie followed Astrid home in her car. The older woman was driving a two-year-old black Jaguar sedan. It was perfect for her, as sleek and elegant as she was. This woman was surrounded by beautiful things. Including her home.

It was a breathtaking mixture of delicate French and English antiques, Louis XV, Louis XVI, Heppelwhite, Sheraton. But none of it was overwhelming. There was an airy quality to the house. Lots of yellow and white, delicate organdy curtains, eggshell silks, and, upstairs, bright flowered prints and a magnificent collection of paintings. Two Chagalls, a Picasso, a Renoir, and a

Monet that lent a summer night's mood to the dining room.

"Astrid, this is fabulous!"

"I must admit, I love it. Tom had such marvelous things. And they're happy things to live with. We bought a few pieces together, but most of it was already his. I picked out the Monet, though."

"It's a beauty." Astrid looked proud. She had every right to.

Even the glasses she poured the Scotch into were lovely — paper-thin crystal, with a rainbow hue to them as they were held up to the late afternoon light. And there was an overpowering view of the Golden Gate Bridge and the bay from the library upstairs, where they settled down with their drinks.

"God, what a magnificent house. I don't know what to say." It was splendid. The library was wood-paneled and lined with old books. There was a portrait of a serious-looking man on one wall, and a Cezanne over the small brown marble fireplace. The portrait was of Tom. Jessie could easily see them together, despite the broad difference in age. There was a warm light in his eyes; one sensed approaching laughter. As she looked at the portrait, Jessie suddenly realized how lonely Astrid must be now.

"He was a fine-looking man."

"Yes, and we suited each other so well. Losing him has been an awful blow. But we were lucky. Ten years is a lot, when they're ten years like the ones we had." But Jessie could tell that Astrid still hadn't decided what to do with her life. She was floating — into dress shops and jewelers, into furriers, off on trips. She had nothing to anchor her. She had the house, the money, the paintings, the clothes . . . but no longer the man. And he was the key. Without Tom none of it really meant anything. Jessie could imagine what that might be like. It gave her chills thinking of it.

"What's your husband like, Jessica?"

Jessie smiled. "Terrific. He's a writer. And he . . . well, he's my best friend. I think he's crazy and wonderful and brilliant and handsome. He's the only person I can really talk to. He's someone very special."

"That says it all, doesn't it?" There was a gentle light in Astrid's eyes as she spoke, and Jessie suddenly felt guilty. How could she so blatantly rave about Ian to this woman who had lost the man who meant every bit as much to her as Ian meant to Jessie?

"No, don't look like that, Jessica. I know what you're thinking, and you're wrong. You should feel that way. You should say it with just exactly that wonderful victorious look on your face. That's how I felt about Tom. Cherish it, flaunt it, enjoy it, don't ever apologize for it, and certainly not to me."

Jessica nodded pensively over her drink, and then looked up at Astrid.

"We're having some nasty problems right now."

"With each other?" Astrid was surprised. It didn't show in Jessica's face. Something did, but not trouble with her husband — she had looked too happy when she described him. Maybe money problems. Young people had those. There was something, though. It surfaced at unexpected moments. A whisper of fear, almost terror. Sickness, perhaps? The loss of a breast? Astrid wondered, but didn't want to pry.

"I guess you might call this a crisis. Maybe even a big one. But the problem isn't with each other, not in that sense." She looked out at the bay and fell silent.

"I'm sure you'll work it out." Astrid knew Jessie didn't want to talk about it.

"I hope so."

Their talk turned unexpectedly to business then, to how the shop was run and what sort of clients Jessie had. Astrid made her laugh telling her some of the stories from her days at *Vogue* in New York. It was almost seven before Jessie got up to go home. And she hated to leave.

"See you tomorrow. At seven-thirty?"

"We'll be here with bells on. I can't wait to show Ian the house." And then she had a thought. "Astrid, do you like the ballet?"

"I adore it."

"Want to come see the Joffrey with us next week?"

"No . . . I . . ." There was a moment of sadness in her eyes.

"Come on, don't be a drag. Ian would love to take us both. God, what that would do to his ego!" She laughed, and Astrid seemed to hesitate. Then she nodded with a small girl's grin.

"I can't resist. I hate to be the fifth wheel — I went through that after Tom died, and it's the loneliest thing in the world. It's actually much easier to be alone. But I'd love to go with you, if Ian won't mind."

They left each other like two new school friends who have the good fortune to find that they live across the street from each other. And Jessie ran home to tell Ian about the house.

He was going to love it, and Astrid. She reminded Jessie of herself, as she would have liked to be. All the poise in the world, and so gentle, so open and sunny. She might be uncertain about the course her life would take, but she had long since come to terms with herself, and it showed. She radiated loving and peace, no longer grabbing at life like Jessie. But Jessie didn't really envy her. She still had Ian, and Astrid no longer had Tom. And, as she drove home, Jessica found herself speeding the car into the driveway, anxious to see Ian, not just his portrait.

As she approached their front door she saw a man walking away from the house toward an unfamiliar car parked in the driveway. He gave her a long examining glance and then nodded. And Jessie felt terror wash over her. Police . . . the police were back . . . what were they doing now? The terror reached her eyes as she stood there, rooted to the spot. The nightmare was back again. At least he wasn't Inspector Houghton. And where was Ian? She wanted to scream, but she couldn't. The neighbors might hear.

"I'm Harvey Green. Mrs. Clarke?" She nodded and stood there, still eyeing him with horror. "I'm the investigator Martin Schwartz referred to your case."

"Oh. I see. Have you spoken to my husband?" She suddenly felt the cool breeze on her face, but it would take a while for her heart to stop pounding.

"Yes, I've spoken to him."

"Is there anything you want me to add?" Other than money . . .

"No. We have everything under control. I'll be in touch." He made a gesture of mock salute toward his colorless hair and walked on toward his car. It was beige or pale blue, Jessie wasn't even sure in the twilight. Maybe it was white. Or light green. Like him, it was totally nondescript. He had unpleasant eyes and a forgettable face. He would blend well in a crowd. He looked ageless, and his clothes would have been out of style in any decade. He was perfect for his role.

"Darling, I'm home!" But her voice had a nervous lilt to it now, as his did when he spoke. "Darling? . . . We've been invited to dinner tomorrow." Not that either of them cared. Suddenly Harvey Green seemed much more of the present than Astrid.

"Invited? By whom?" Ian was pouring himself a drink in the kitchen. And not the usual white wine either. It was bourbon or Scotch, which he rarely drank, except when they had guests from back east.

"That new customer I met at the shop. Astrid Bonner. She's lovely; I think you'll like her."

"Who?"

"You know. I told you. The widow who lives in the brick palazzo on the corner."

"All right." He tried to muster a smile, but it was rough going. "Did you see Green on your way in?"

She nodded. "I thought he was a cop. I jumped about four feet in the air."

"So did I. Fun, isn't it, living like this?"

She tried to pass over the remark and sat down in her usual chair.

"Could you make me one too?"

"Scotch and water?"

"Why not?" It would be her third.

"Okay. That must be some place the widow's got herself." But he didn't sound as though he really cared. He dropped ice cubes in another glass.

"You'll see it tomorrow. And Ian . . . I invited her to join us at the ballet. Do you mind?" It was a moment and two sips before he looked into her eyes and answered, and when he did, she didn't like what she saw.

"Baby, at this point, I really don't give a damn."

They tried to make love that night after dinner, and for the first time since they'd met, Ian couldn't. He didn't give a damn about that either. It felt like the beginning of the end.

Chapter 11

"Are you dressed yet?" Jessica could hear Ian rattling around in the room where he worked, and she had just finished brushing her hair. She was wearing white silk slacks and a turquoise crocheted sweater, and she still wasn't sure if she looked right. Astrid was liable to be wearing something fabulous, and it sounded as though Ian had stayed submerged in the studio. "Ian! Are you ready?" The rattling stopped and she heard footsteps.

"More or less." He smiled at her from the bedroom doorway, and she looked into his eyes as she walked towards him.

"Mr. Clarke, you look absolutely beautiful."

"So do you." He was wearing the new dark blue Cardin blazer she'd brought him from New York, a cream-colored shirt, and a wine-colored paisley tie with beige gabardine slacks she had found in France. They

181

sculpted his long graceful legs.

"You look terribly proper and terribly handsome, and I think I'm terribly in love with you, darling."

He swept her a neat bow and put his arms around her as she reached him.

"In that case, how about if we stay home instead?" He had a mischievous gleam in his eyes.

"Ian, don't you touch me! Astrid would be so disappointed if we didn't make it. And you'll love her."

"Promises, promises." But he offered her his arm as she picked up the white silk jacket she'd left on the chair in the hall. He was going to the dinner to humor her. He had other things on his mind.

They walked the half block to the brick house on the corner, and it was the first night there had been a chill in the air. Autumn was coming, in its own gentle fashion. San Francisco in the fall was nothing like that season in New York. It was part of the reason they'd both fallen in love with San Francisco in the first place. They loved the easy, temperate weather.

Jessica rang the bell, and they waited. For a moment there was no answer.

"Maybe she's decided she doesn't want us."

"Oh, shut up. You just want to go home and work on your book." But she smiled at him and then they heard footsteps.

The door opened a second later and there was Astrid, resplendent in a floor-length black knit dress and a long rope of pearls. Her hair was loosely swept up in the back and her eyes sparkled as she led them inside. She looked even more beautiful than Jessica had found her before. And Ian was obviously stunned. He had been expecting a middle-aged widow, and had agreed to the evening mostly as a concession to Jessie. He had had no hint of this vision in black with the Dresden-doll waist and long, elegantly arched neck — and that face. He liked the face. And the look in her eyes. This was no dowager. This was a woman.

The two women embraced, and Ian stood back for a moment, watching them, intrigued by the older woman he did not yet know, and by the formidable home he was beginning to glimpse over her shoulder. It was impossible not to stare, whether he looked at her or at the house.

"And this is Ian." He obeyed the summons, feeling like a small boy being introduced by his mother — "Say good evening to the nice lady, darling" — and held out his hand.

"How do you do." He was suddenly glad he had worn the new Cardin jacket and tie. This was not going to be just any old dinner. And she was probably a roaring snob. She had to be, in a setup like that. And widowed, yet. Nouveau riche as all hell . . . but somehow a murmuring suspicion told him that that wasn't the case either. She didn't have the dead-fish eyes of a snob, or the overworked eyebrows. She had nice eyes, in a nice face. She looked like a person.

Astrid laughed gaily as she led them upstairs to the library, and Ian and Jessica exchanged glances as they passed delicate sketches and etchings on the stairs . . . Picasso . . . Renoir . . . Renoir again . . . Manet . . . Klimt . . . Goya . . . Cassatt . . . He wanted to whistle, and Jessie grinned at him like a conspirator who had assisted in getting him into the neighborhood haunted house. He raised both eyebrows and she stuck out her tongue. Astrid was ahead of them and already down the hall. He wanted to whisper, and Jessie wanted to giggle, but they couldn't. Not till they got home. But she was thoroughly enjoying the look on his face; it made her feel suddenly mischievous. She pinched him delicately on the behind as she passed in front of him to enter the library.

Astrid had a plate of hors d'oeuvres waiting for them and a handsome pâté. A fire
roared in the grate. Ian accepted a slice of
pâté on a slim piece of toast and then
laughed into Astrid's eyes.

"Mrs. Bonner, I don't know how to say
this, and I feel about fourteen years old, but
I am overwhelmed by your home." And my
hostess. He smiled the ingenuous smile that
Jessie loved, and Astrid laughed with him.

"I'm delighted, that's a lovely compliment,
but calling me 'Mrs. Bonner' isn't. You may
feel fourteen, but you make me feel about
four hundred. Try 'Astrid' " — she threw
up both hands impishly — "or I may have
to kick you out. And not 'Aunt Astrid'
either, God forbid." All three of them
laughed, and she slid out of her shoes and
tucked her legs under her in a large comfortable chair. "But I really am glad you like
the house. It's embarrassing sometimes,
now that Tom isn't here anymore. I love it
so much, but I occasionally feel that I never
quite grew into it all. I mean, it's so . . .
so . . . well, as though it should be my
mother's and I'm just house-sitting. I mean,
really, me? In all this? How ridiculous!"
Except that it wasn't ridiculous at all. It
suited her perfectly. Ian wondered if she
knew how perfectly, or if she meant what

she had just said. He imagined Tom had built the place around her, right down to the paintings and the view.

"It suits you very well, you know." Ian was watching her eyes, and Jessie was watching the exchange.

"Yes, it does, in some ways, and not in others. It frightens people away sometimes. The lifestyle does. The opulence. The . . . I guess you could call it an aura. A lot of it is Tom, and some of it is just . . . oh . . . things." She waved vaguely around the room, encompassing rapidly a fortune in art objects. Things. "And some of it is me." Ian liked the fact that she conceded the point. "People expect you to be a lot when you live like this. Sometimes they expect me to be something I'm not, or they don't stick around long enough to see what I am. I told you, Jessie, I'd trade you for your jewel of a house any day. But . . ." She grinned like a cat stretching lazily in the sun. ". . . This isn't a bad place to live, either."

"Looks like a damn nice place to live, if you ask me, Mrs. . . . Astrid." They exchanged a quick burst of laughter over the slip. "But I doubt if you'd trade us for our 'jewel,' once you plugged in the hair dryer and the washing machine blew, or when the plumbing fell through to the basement. Our

186

place has a few kinks."

"That does sound like fun." It was clear that nothing like that happened here, and Jessie was grinning broadly, remembering the last time all the fuses had blown, and Ian had refused to deal with it; they had spent the rest of the evening by candlelight — until he wanted to work, and needed the electric typewriter. He looked up sheepishly, knowing what she was thinking.

"Well, children? Do you want a tour of the place?" Astrid interrupted their thoughts. Jessie hadn't seen the whole thing, and Ian nodded quickly.

She tiptoed barefoot along the carpeted hall, flipping switches under brass sconces, opening doors, turning on more lights. There were three bedrooms upstairs. Hers in bright, flowery yellow prints with a large four-poster bed and the same splendid view of the bay. She had a small mirrored boudoir and a white marble bath, which was repeated in pale green across the hall, to go with a quietly elegant bedroom full of small French Provincial antiques.

"My mother sleeps here when she comes to the city, and this suits her perfectly. You'll know what I mean when you see her. She's very lively and little and funny, and she likes lots of flowers everywhere."

"Does she live in the East?" Ian was curious, and remembered only that Jessie had told him Astrid had originally come from New York.

"No, Mother lives on a ranch out here, of all things. She bought it a few years ago, and she's having a great time with it. Much to our astonishment, it actually agrees with her. We thought she'd be bored in six months, but she's not. She's very independent, and she rides a lot and loves to play cowboy. At seventy-two, if you please. She reminds one a bit of Colette."

It made Jessie smile to think of a tiny white-haired woman in cowboy gear ensconced in the delicately appointed room. But if she was anything like Astrid, she could pull it off. With cowboy boots custom-made by Gucci and a hat by Adolfo.

The bedroom next to Astrid's was more somber, and had apparently belonged to her husband. Jessie and Ian exchanged a rapid, casual glance . . . they had had separate bedrooms? But Jessie remembered the difference in age. There was a small, elegant study next to his room, rich in red leathers, with a handsome old desk covered with pictures of Astrid.

Astrid passed quickly through the room and went back out to the hall, closing the door of the green guest room as Jessie and Ian followed.

"It's a magnificent house." Jessie sighed. It was the sort of place that made you want to appear for the next dinner invitation with everything you owned in your arms. You wanted to stay there forever. Now they both understood why she didn't close the house and find something smaller. It told a tale of people who cared — about beauty, about each other, and about living well.

"And you saw the downstairs. It's not very exciting, but it's pretty." Jessie wondered why there was no trace of servants. One expected at least a white-aproned maid, or a butler, but she seemed to live alone.

"Do you both like crab? I really should have called to ask, but I forgot." She looked faintly embarrassed.

"We love crab!" Jessie answered for them both.

"Oh, good! Seems that every time I order it for friends, and forget to ask beforehand, it turns out that someone is allergic to it or something. I love it."

It was an unusual feast. Astrid piled a mountain of dismembered cracked crabs on a vast plate in the center of the dining-room table, set out a huge carafe of white wine, added a salad and hot rolls, and invited her guests to dig in. She rolled up the sleeves of her black knit dress, invited Ian to take off his jacket, and sat there like a child, vying for the claws with whoever saw them first.

"Ian, you're a fiend. I saw that one first, and you know it!" She rapped him gently on the knuckles with the claw as she removed it, giggling and sipping her wine. She was right — she did look like a young girl whose mother was out for the evening and had let her have her friends over for dinner "as long as you're all good." She was delightful, and both Jessie and Ian fell in love with her.

It was an easy-going evening; they looked like three people with no problems at all — just expensive taste, and a liking for pleasure. It was after midnight when Ian stood up and held out a hand to Jessie.

"Astrid, I could stay here till four in the morning, but I have to get up tomorrow and work on the book, and if Jessie doesn't get enough sleep, she turns into a monster." But it was obvious that they all shared regret that the evening was over. "You'll come to the ballet with us next week?"

"With pleasure. And I'll have you know that Jessie said I would love you, and she was absolutely one-hundred-percent right. I can't think of two people I'd rather be a fifth wheel with."

"Good. Because you're not. Fifth wheel, my ass." They all laughed, and Astrid hugged them both as they left, as though she had known them for years. They felt as though she had, as Astrid stood barefoot in the doorway, waving before closing the shiny black door with its brass lion-head knocker.

"Christ, Jess, what a nice evening. And what a marvelous woman. She's amazing."

"Isn't she? But she must be lonely as hell. There's something about the way she invites people into her life, as though she has a lot of leftover loving and no one to give it to most of the time." Jessie yawned on the last words and Ian nodded. Talking over the evening was always the best part. She could no longer remember when Ian hadn't been around to share secrets, and opinions, and questions. He had been with her forever.

"What do you suppose her husband was like, Jess? I suspect he wasn't as much fun as she is."

"What makes you say that?" His comment surprised her; there was nothing to suggest that Tom Bonner had been less amusing than his wife. And then Jessica laughed as she guessed what Ian meant. "The separate bedrooms?" He grinned sheepishly and she pinched him. "You're a creep."

"I am not. And let me tell you, madam, I don't care if I live to be ninety, you'll never get me out of our bedroom . . . or our bed!" He looked adamant and very pleased with himself as he held her closer on the short walk home.

"Is that a promise, Mr. Clarke?"

"In writing, if you'd like, Mrs. Clarke."

"I may just hold you to that." They paused for a moment and kissed before walking the last few steps toward their home. "I'm glad you liked Astrid, love. I really enjoy her. I'd like to get to know her better. She's a good person to talk to. You know, I . . . well, I almost wanted to tell her what's happening to us. We started to talk the other day, and . . ." Jessie shrugged; it was hard to put into words, and Ian was beginning to scowl. "She just kind of makes me want to tell her the truth." Ian stopped walking and looked at her.

"Did you?"

"No."

"Good. Because I think you're kidding yourself, Jess. She's a nice woman, but no one is going to understand what's happening to us right now. No one. How do you tell someone you have a trial pending on charges of rape? Do us both a big favor, babe, and don't talk about it. We've got to hope this whole mess will blow over and we can forget it. If we tell people, it could haunt us for years."

"That's what I decided. And, hey, come on . . . trust me a little, will you please? I'm not stupid. I know it would be hard for most people to handle."

"So don't ask them to."

Jessica didn't answer, and Ian walked ahead of her to open the door to the house. For the first time Jessie could remember, their chosen separateness from the rest of the world, almost like a secret society, now felt like lonely isolation. She couldn't talk to anyone but Ian. He had forbidden it. In the past it had always been a matter of choice.

Jessie followed him inside and left her jacket in the front hall.

"Want a cup of tea before bed, love?" She put a kettle of water on and heard him go into his studio.

"No, thanks."

She stood in the doorway of his studio for a moment and smiled at him as he sat at his desk. He had a snifter of cognac beside him and a small stack of papers on the desk in front of him. He loosened his tie and sat back and looked at his wife.

"Hello, beautiful lady."

"Hi." They exchanged the subtlest of

smiles for a moment and Jessie cocked her head to one side. "You planning to work?"

"Just for a little while."

She nodded and went to take the kettle off the stove; it was whistling fiercely. She made a cup of tea, turned off the rest of the lights, and walked quietly into the bedroom. She knew that Ian wouldn't come to bed for hours. He couldn't. He couldn't try to make love to her tonight. Not after last night. The sour taste of failure had stayed with them. Like the rest of what was happening to them, it was new, and painful, and raw.

Their evening at the ballet with Astrid was as great a success as the dinner at her home. They picked her up just in time to make the curtain, and Jessie had prepared a late supper that was waiting for them at home. Steak tartare, cold asparagus, a variety of cheeses and French bread, and a home-made fudge cake. Off to the side was a large bowl of fresh strawberries and whipped cream, a huge crystal bowl filled with Viennese style *Schlag,* for the berries or the cake. It was a feast, and her audience approved.

"Dear girl, is there anything you can't do?"

"Plenty." But Jessie was pleased at the

194

compliment.

"Don't believe her. She can do anything." Ian seconded the compliment with a kiss as he poured a round of Bordeaux. Chateau Margaux '55. It felt like an occasion, and he had brought out one of his favorite wines.

By now the three were a trio, telling jokes, sharing stories, and feeling at ease. They were well into their second bottle of wine when Astrid stood up and glanced at the clock.

"Good God, children, it's two o'clock. Not that I have anything to do tomorrow, but you do. I feel very guilty keeping you up." Ian and Jessica exchanged a sharp glance: they did have to be up early the next morning. But Astrid did not see the look. She was hunting for her bag.

"Don't be silly. Evenings like this are a gift for us." Jessie smiled at her friend.

"They couldn't be as much so as they are for me. You have no idea how I've loved this. And what are you up to tomorrow, Jessica? Can I tempt you with lunch at the Villa Taverna?"

"I . . . I'm sorry, Astrid, but I can't make lunch tomorrow." Another look flashed its way to Ian. "We have to go to a business meeting in the morning and I don't know what time we'll be through."

"Then why don't all three of us go to lunch?" She had found her handbag and was ready to leave. "You can call me when you're through with your meeting."

"Astrid, we'd better make it another day, much as I hate to." Ian was regretful but firm.

"I think you're both mean." But now she sensed something between them, a tension that hadn't been there before. Something was just a wee bit off balance, but she couldn't tell what, and she found herself remembering the problem Jessica had hinted at when they bad first met. There had never been any mention of it again, and Astrid had gone on assuming that Jessie meant a money problem. It was hard to believe, but it obviously couldn't be anything else. Not health, not problems with the marriage certainly — there was too much hugging, touching, kissing, quick pats on the back, rapid squeezes as they stood side by side — there was much too much of that for anyone to believe the marriage was in trouble.

"Maybe we can all go to a movie this weekend." Ian looked at the two women and tried to make light of the too-quiet moment. "Not as classy as the ballet, but there's a new French thriller on Union. Anyone interested?"

"Oh, let's!" Jessie clapped her hands and looked at Astrid, who grinned and put on a cautious look.

"Only if you absolutely swear to buy me a gallon of popcorn."

"I swear." Ian solemnly held up a hand in a formal oath.

"Cross your heart?"

"Cross my heart." He did, and the three of them started to laugh. "You sure drive a hard bargain."

"I have to. I'm addicted to popcorn. With butter!" She looked at him sternly and he gave her a brotherly hug. Astrid returned the hug and leaned over to give Jessie a kiss on the cheek. "And now I shall bid you both good night. And let you get some sleep. I'm really sorry it got so late."

"Don't be. We aren't."

Jessica followed her to the door, and Astrid left with a curious feeling. Almost an eerie sensation. There was nothing she could see or touch or be absolutely sure of, but something seemed to hang in the air, just over their heads — like a hunk of concrete.

The preliminary hearing was scheduled for the next morning.

CHAPTER 12

Jessica walked into the miniature courtroom with Ian's hand held tightly in hers. She wore the navy blue suit and dark glasses again, and Ian looked tired and pale. He hadn't gotten much sleep, and he had a headache from his share of the wine the night before. The three of them had knocked off both bottles of Margaux.

Martin Schwartz was waiting for them in the courtroom. He was going through a file on a small desk at the side of the room, and he motioned to them to join him outside.

"I'm going to ask for a closed hearing. I thought you should know, so you wouldn't be surprised." He looked terribly professional, and they both felt confused. Ian spoke up first, with a worried frown.

"What's a closed hearing?"

"I think the victim may speak more openly if there are no observers in court. Just you, her, the assistant D.A., the judge, and myself. It's a sensible precaution. If she brings friends, she'll want them to think she's as pure as the proverbial driven snow. And she may react badly to having Jessica there." For no reason she could understand, Jessica flinched involuntarily at the sound of her own name.

"Look, if I can take it, so can she." Jessie was unbearably nervous, and she dreaded seeing the woman. She wanted to be anywhere but there. Every fiber of her being shrieked at the prospect of what lay ahead. The enemy. So much to face in one human being. Ian's infidelity, her own inadequacy, the threat to their future, the memory of the almost unscalable mountain of trying to bail him. All of it wrapped up in that one woman.

Martin could see how tense they both were. He pitied them, and he accurately suspected what was at the root of Jessie's nerves: Margaret Burton.

"Just trust me, Jessie. I think a closed hearing will be best for all concerned. We should be getting under way in a few minutes. Why don't you two go for a walk down the hall? Just stay close enough, and I'll come out and signal when the judge is ready to start." Ian nodded tersely and Martin strode back inside. Ian's arm felt as if it had a lead weight hanging from it. Jessie.

They had nothing to say as they paced the length of the hall, turned at the far end, and came back again. Jessica found her mind drifting to memories of other marble halls . . . City Hall, where she and Ian had gotten their marriage license . . . waiting outside the principal's office in high school . . . the funeral parlor in Boston when Jake had died . . . and then, one by one, her parents.

"Jessie?"

"Huh?" She was frowning oddly as she looked at him, as though she had difficulty coming back to the present.

"Are you okay?" He looked worried; she had been squeezing his arm too tightly and walking faster and faster as they paced the hall. He had had to shake her arm to catch her attention.

"Yeah. I'm okay. Just thinking."

"Well, stop thinking. Everything's going to be fine. Relax." She started to say something, and he could tell from the look in her eyes that it wasn't going to be pleasant. She was much too nervous to be cautious or kind.

"I'm . . . I'm sorry . . . this is just such a weird day. Doesn't it seem weird to you? Or is it just me?" She began to wonder if she were going crazy.

"No, it doesn't seem weird. Shitty, yes, but not weird." He tried to smile, but she wasn't looking at him. She was looking off into the distance, dreamy-eyed again. She was beginning to frighten him. "Look, dammit, if you don't pull yourself together right now, I'm going to send you home."

"Why? So I don't see her?"

"Is that what you're worried about, for Chrissake? Seeing her? Is that all? Jesus. My ass is on the line, and you're worried about seeing her. Who gives a shit about her? What if they revoke my bail?"

"They won't."

"How the hell do you know?"

"I . . . I . . . oh, Ian, I don't know. They just can't, that's all. Why would they?" She hadn't even thought of that. Now it was one more thing to worry about.

"Why *wouldn't* they?"

"Well, maybe if I'd seduced Inspector Houghton, or Barry York, our beloved bail-bondsman, maybe they wouldn't. But since I didn't, maybe they will." Her tone was bitter and scared.

"Go home, Jessica."

"Go to hell."

And then Ian stopped talking and looked past her. Time seemed to stop as Jessica too turned to look. It was Margaret Burton.

She was wearing the same hat. But with a polite little beige suit. She was even wearing white gloves. The clothes were cheap, but they were tidy-looking, and very proper. She looked very dull. Like the stereotype of a schoolteacher or a librarian, somebody terribly serious and asexual. Her hair was pulled back in a tight knot at her neck, scarcely visible under the hat. The black roots were nowhere to be seen. She was wearing no makeup and her shoes were low-heeled and dowdy. It was obvious that a woman like this could only be made love to at gunpoint.

Ian said nothing, but looked for a long moment, then turned away. Jessica was staring, with a look of hatred on her face that Ian had never seen. She was rooted to the spot.

"Jess . . . come on, baby. Please." He took her elbow and tried to propel her back down the hall, but she wouldn't move. Margaret Burton disappeared into the courtroom without ever having shown a sign of having seen them. And Jessica still wouldn't move. Inspector Houghton followed quickly on Miss Burton's heels, and Martin Schwartz came out and beckoned to Ian, while Jessie simply stood and stared.

"Look, Jessie, just sit down on that bench for a few minutes. I'll be back as soon as I can." She was in terrible shape, and he had enough to worry about.

"Ian?" She turned and looked at him with a stricken expression in her eyes, and he felt his guts turn to sand. "I just don't understand anything anymore." There weren't even tears in her eyes. Only pain.

"Neither do I. But I've got to go inside now. Will you be okay out here, or do you want to go home?" He wasn't sure he trusted her alone. The look in her eyes was getting to be all too familiar.

"I'll be here."

That wasn't what he had asked her, but he didn't have time to argue. He disappeared inside the courtroom, and Jessie sat alone on the cold marble bench. She watched people come and go. Ordinary-looking people. Men with attaché cases. Women with tissues clutched in their hands. Small bedraggled children in shoes that were worn through at the heel and pants that were too short for their skinny legs. Bailiffs, lawyers, judges, victims, defendants, witnesses . . . people. They came and went while Jessie sat and thought of Margaret Burton. Who was she? Why had she done it? Why Ian? She had looked so goddamned proud, so self-righteous as she had walked into the courtroom. The courtroom . . .

Suddenly her eyes were riveted to the door. It was of dark, highly polished wood with brass knobs and two tiny glass windows, like eyes, looking out . . . looking out . . . looking in . . . inside . . . she had to be there . . . inside . . . to see her . . . to listen . . . to find out why . . . she had to.

A small sign hung crookedly from one of the doorknobs — CLOSED — and a gray-uniformed bailiff stood slightly off to one side, looking disinterestedly at passersby. Jessica stood to her full height, smoothed her skirt, and suddenly felt very calm. She fixed a small smile in place. There was the tiniest of tremors in the corner of her right eye, the convulsions of a butterfly, but who would notice? She looked very much in command, and smiled curtly at the bailiff as she strode to the door and put a hand on the knob.

"Sorry, ma'am. Courtroom's closed."

"Yes. I know." She looked almost pleased at his news, as though she were responsible and was comforted to learn that her orders had been carried out. "I'm sitting in on the case."

"An attorney?" He started to step aside. The tremor in her eye now felt as though it would tear off the lid.

She nodded quietly. "Yes." Oh, Jesus. No. What if he asked for credentials? Or went inside to talk to the judge? Instead he held open the door for her with a smile, and Jessie walked sedately into the room. The whole scene had been typically Jessica. No one ever questioned her. But what now? What if the judge stopped the proceedings? What if he threw her out? What if . . .

The judge was small and undistinguished, with glasses and blond-gray hair. He looked up momentarily, unimpressed by the new arrival, and directed a raised eyebrow at Martin Schwartz. After a sharp glance at Jessica, Schwartz nodded reluctantly, then threw a rapid look at the assistant district attorney, who shrugged. She was in.

Inspector Houghton was seated near the bench, making some sort of statement. The room was wood-paneled, with leather-covered seats in the front row, and straight-backed chairs behind them. It was hardly larger than Martin Schwartz's office, but there was an aura of tremendous tension in the air. Ian and Martin sat together at a desk, slightly to the left. And only a few feet away sat Miss Burton and the assistant district attorney, who, much to Jessie's chagrin, was a woman. Young, tough-looking, with oversprayed hair and an abundance of powder on too fleshy cheeks. She wore a matronly green dress and a sedate string of pearls, and at the corners of her mouth the hard edges of anger had formed. She exuded righteous indignation for her client.

The young attorney turned to look at Jessica, and Jessie figured her to be about her own age, somewhere in her early thirties. The two women exchanged a look of ice. But Jessica saw contempt in the other woman's face as well, and then she understood what this was going to be. A class war. Big, nasty, college grad, preppie Pacific Heights Ian had raped poor little lower-class, abused, misunderstood secretary, who was going to be defended by clean, tough, pure, devoted middle-class young attorney. Jesus. That was all they needed. Jessica suddenly wondered if she had worn the wrong thing. But even in slacks and a shirt, Jessica had the kind of style those women would hate. How insane even to have to consider what she was wearing.

Miss Burton hadn't seen Jessica come in, or had shown no sign of it, at any rate. Nor had Ian. She slipped quietly into a straight-backed chair behind him, and then suddenly, as though he had been slapped, he raised his head and spun around in his seat, a look of shock on his face when he saw her there behind him. He started to shake his head, and then leaned toward her as though to say something, but Jessica's eyes were steely. She squeezed his shoulder briefly, and he averted his gaze: it was pointless to argue. But as he turned away, his broad shoulders seemed to sag.

Inspector Houghton rose from the seat from which he'd been addressing the judge, thanked the court, and returned to a chair on the other side of Margaret Burton. Now what? Jessica's heart pounded. Suddenly she wasn't so sure she wanted to be there. What would she hear? Could she take it? What if she fell apart? Went crazy . . . screamed . . .

"Miss Burton, take the stand, please."

As Margaret Burton slowly left her seat Jessica's heart seemed hell-bent on freeing itself from her body. A pulse thundered at her temple and she wondered if she'd faint as she stared down at her trembling hands. The oath was administered to Miss Burton, and Jessica looked up, her whole body trembling now. *Why her?* She was so plain, so ugly, so . . . cheap. But no, she wasn't really ugly. There was something about her, a grace to the hands folded over her knees, the vestige of prettiness in a face now grown too hard to be arresting. Something . . . maybe. Jessie wondered how Ian felt, sitting just in front of her. He seemed a thousand miles away. Margaret Burton seemed much, much closer. Jessica felt as though she could see every pore, every hair, the slightly flared nostrils, the weave of the dreary beige suit. She had a wild urge to run up and touch her, slap her maybe, shake her into telling the truth. Tell them what happened, damn you! The truth! Jessica's breath caught and she coughed, trying to clear her head.

"Miss Burton, would you please explain what happened on the day in question, from the moment you first saw Mr. Clarke. Tell us simply, in your own words. This is not a trial. This is merely a preliminary hearing, to determine if this matter deserves further attention from the court."

The judge spoke as though he were reading an orange-juice label — words he had spoken a thousand times before and no longer heard. But it was all the invitation Margaret Burton needed. She cleared her throat with a small look of importance and the tiniest of smiles. Inspector Houghton frowned as he watched her, and the prosecuting attorney seemed to be keeping an eye on the judge.

"Miss Burton?" The judge looked off into

space as he spoke, and everyone waited.

"Yes, sir. Your honor." Jessica felt that the "victim" didn't look sufficiently distraught. Victorious, maybe, but not distraught. Not violated. Pleased? That was crazy. Why should she be pleased? But Jessie could not put aside that impression as she stared at the woman who claimed her husband had raped her. And then the recital began.

"I had lunch at Enrico's, and afterward I started walking up Broadway." She had a flat, unpleasant voice. A little too high. A little too loud. She would have nagged well. And she sounded too loud to be hurt. Hurt inside. Jessica wondered if the judge was listening to more than just the words. He didn't look it.

"I was walking up Broadway," she went on, "and he offered me a ride."

"Did he threaten you, or just offer a ride?"

She shook her head, almost regretfully. "No, he didn't threaten. Not really."

"What do you mean, 'not really'?"

"Well, I think he might have gotten mad if I'd turned down the ride, but it was kind of a hot day, and I couldn't see a bus for blocks, and I was late getting back to the office, and . . ." She looked up at the judge and his face was blank. "Anyway, I told him where I worked." She stopped for a moment, looked down at her hands, and sighed. Jessie wanted to wring her neck. That pathetic little sigh. She dug her hand into Ian's shoulder without thinking, and he jumped, and turned to look at her with a worried face. She forced a tiny smile and he patted her hand before looking back at Margaret Burton.

"Go on." The judge was prodding her. She seemed to have lost the thread of her tale.

"I'm sorry, your honor. He . . . he didn't take me back to my office, and . . . well, I know I was crazy to accept the ride. It was just such a pretty day, and he looked like a nice man. I thought . . . I never realized . . ." Unexpectedly, a small tear glided from one eye and then the other; Jessie's grip on Ian's shoulder became almost unbearable. He reached for her hand and gently held it until she nervously pulled it away.

"Please go on, Miss . . . Miss Burton." He checked the name on the papers on his desk, took a swallow of water, and looked up. Jessie was reminded that this hearing was no more than daily routine to him; he seemed totally separate from the drama that absorbed the rest of them.

"I . . . he took me . . . to a hotel."

"You went with him?" But there was no

judgment in the voice; it was only a question.

"I thought he was taking me back to my office." She sounded strident and angry suddenly. The tears were gone.

"And when you saw that he hadn't taken you back to your office, why didn't you leave then?"

"I . . . I don't know. I just thought it would . . . he only wanted to have a drink, he said, and he wasn't unpleasant, just silly. I thought he was harmless and it would be easier to go along with it — with the drink, I mean — and then . . ."

"Was there a bar in the hotel when you went inside?" She shook her head. "A desk clerk? Did anyone see you go in? Could you have called for help? I don't believe Mr. Clarke held a gun on you, or anything of the sort, did he?"

She flushed and shook her head reluctantly.

"Well, did anyone see you?"

"No." The word was barely audible. "There was no one there. It looked like . . . like sort of an apartment hotel."

"Do you remember where it was?"

She shook her head again, and Jessica felt Ian stir restlessly in front of her, and when she looked there was anger on his face. At last. He looked alive again, instead of buried under grief and disbelief.

"Could you tell us the location of the hotel, Miss Burton?"

Again, the negative shake of the head. "No. I . . . I was so upset I . . . I just didn't look. But he . . . he . . ." Suddenly her face was transformed again. The eyes lit up and almost glowed with such hatred and fury that for an instant Jessie almost believed her, and she saw Ian go suddenly very still. "He took my life and threw it away! He ruined it! He . . ." She sobbed for a moment, and then took a deep breath as the glitter left her eyes. "As we went inside, he just grabbed me, and dragged me into an elevator and up to a room, and . . ." Her silence said it all, as she hung her head in defeat.

"Do you remember what room?"

"No." She didn't look up.

"Would you recognize the room again?"

"No. I don't think so." No? Why not? Jessie couldn't imagine not remembering a room you'd been raped in. It would be engraved on your mind forever.

"Would you recognize the hotel?"

"I'm not sure. I don't think so, though." She still had not looked up, and Jessie doubted her story still further — and then realized what had been happening: if she was doubting the story, then at some point she must have believed it might be true. In that one burst of tears and fury, the woman had convinced them all. Or come damn close to it. Even Jessica. Almost. She turned to look at Ian and saw him watching her, his eyes bright with tears. He knew what was happening too. Jessica reached for his hand again, this time quietly and with strength. She wanted to kiss him, hold him, tell him it would be all right, but now she wasn't so sure. She was sure of only one thing — of how much she hated Margaret Burton.

Martin Schwartz was looking none too happy either. If the Burton woman claimed not to remember where the hotel was, they had lost the last shred of hope of finding a witness who had seen them there. Ian couldn't place the hotel either. He had been just drunk enough that his memory was blurred, and the address he thought he remembered had turned out to be wrong. It was a warehouse. There were plenty of small sleazy residential hotels in the area, and Martin had sent Ian into dozens of lobbies before the preliminary hearing: Nothing looked familiar. So it was going to remain a case of his word against hers, with no one to corroborate either side. Schwartz was liking the looks of the case less and less. She was a damn unpleasant witness. Erratic, emotional, one moment hard as a rock, the next heart-wringing and tearful. The judge would ship them off to trial for sure, if for no other reason than to avoid dealing with the issue himself.

"All right, Miss Burton," the judge said, fingering a pencil and gazing at the opposite wall, "what happened in that room you don't remember?" His tone was dry and uninterested.

"What happened?"

"What did Mr. Clarke do after he dragged you into that room? You did say he dragged you?"

She nodded.

"And he wasn't using a weapon?" She shook her head, and finally looked up at her audience.

"No. Only . . . only his hand. He slapped me several times and told me he'd kill me if I didn't do what he wanted."

"And what was that?"

"I . . . he . . . he forced me to . . . to have . . . oral copulation with him . . . to do . . . to, well . . . to do it to him." My, how painful you make it sound . . . Jessica wanted to slap her again.

214

"And you did?"

"I did."

"And then? Did he . . . did Mr. Clarke have an orgasm?"

She nodded.

"Please answer the question."

"Yes."

"And then?"

"Then he sodomized me." She said it in a dull, flat voice, and Jessie could feel Ian flinch. She herself felt increasingly uncomfortable. She had anticipated drama, not this slow, drawn-out recital. Christ, how humiliating it all was. How dry and ugly and awful. The words, the acts, the thoughts, all so old and dreary.

"Did he climax again?"

"I . . . I don't know." She had the grace to blush.

"Did you?" Her eyes flew open then and Houghton and the young district attorney watched tensely.

"I? But how could I? He . . . I . . . he raped me."

"Some women enjoy that, Miss Burton, in spite of themselves. Did you?"

"Of course not!"

"You did not climax, then?" Jessica was beginning to enjoy the other woman's discomfiture.

"No, of course not! No!" She almost shouted it, looking hot and angry and nervous.

"All right. And then what?" The judge looked terribly bored and unimpressed by Miss Burton's indignation.

"Then he raped me again."

"How?"

"He . . . he just raped me. You know . . . the usual way this time." Jessica almost wanted to laugh. A "usual rape"!

"Did he hurt you?"

"Yes, of course he did."

"Very much?"

But she was looking down again, distant and pensive and sad. It was at those moments that one should feel sorry for her. And for a tiny flash of a second, Jessica wondered about her own reactions. At any other time, the story she was hearing would have touched her. Maybe even very much. But now . . . how could she let it touch her? She didn't believe the woman. But what did the judge think? There had been no answer to his last question.

"Miss Burton, I asked if Mr. Clarke hurt you very much."

"Yes. Very much. I . . . he . . . he didn't care about me. He just . . . he just . . ." The tears flowed slowly down her face and it was

216

as though she were talking about someone else, not Ian, not a total stranger who had raped her. Why would he care about her if he were raping her? "He didn't care if I got pregnant, or . . . or anything. He just . . . just left." And now the tears turned to anger again. "I know this type, they play with poor girls like me! Girls with no money, no fancy family, and then they . . . they do what he did . . . they leave . . ." Her voice sank back to a whisper then as she looked blindly into her lap. "He left, and went back to her."

"Who?" The judge looked confused, and Miss Burton looked up again, with a slightly dazed look on her face. "Who did he go back to?"

"His wife." She said it very plainly, but without looking at Jessica.

"Miss Burton, did you know Mr. Clarke from somewhere, from before this? Had you ever been romantically involved with him before?" So the judge had also picked up on that — a faint suggestion that Ian was not a stranger after all.

"No. Never."

"Then how did you know about his wife?"

"He looked married. And anyway, he told me."

"I see. And he just left you at the hotel afterward?" She nodded again. "What did

217

you do then? Call the police? Go to a doctor? Call a cab?"

"No. I walked for a while. I felt confused.
And then I went home and washed up. I
felt awful." Now she was believable again.

"Did you see a doctor?"

"After I called the police."

"And when did you do that? It wasn't immediately, was it?"

"No."

"Why not?"

"I was scared. I had to think about it."

"And you're sure of your story, now, Miss
Burton? This is the whole truth? The story
you originally told the police was a little
different from this, wasn't it?"

"I don't know what I told them then. I
was confused. But this is the truth now."

"You're under oath now, Miss Burton, so
I hope this is the truth."

"It is." She nodded expressionlessly, her
eyes dead.

"There's nothing you want to change?"

"No."

"And you're certain that this was not a
misunderstanding, an afternoon fling that
went sour?" And then suddenly the hatred
blazed up in her eyes again, and she
squeezed them tightly shut.

"He ruined my life." She hissed the words

218

into the silent room.

"All right, Miss Burton. Thank you. Mr. Schwartz, any questions?"

"Only a few, Your Honor. And I'll be quick. Miss Burton, has anything similar ever happened to you before?"

"What do you mean?"

"I mean, have you ever been raped, even in fun, as a sort of game, by a lover, a boyfriend, a husband?"

"Of course not." She looked incensed.

"Have you ever been married?"

"No."

"Engaged?"

"No." Again there was no hesitation.

"No broken engagements?"

"No."

"Any serious, broken-off loves?"

"None."

"A boyfriend now?"

"No."

"Thank you, Miss Burton. What about romantic interludes? Have you ever picked up a stranger before?"

"No."

"Then you agree that you picked up Mr. Clarke?"

"No! I . . . he offered me a ride, and . . ."

"And you accepted, even though you didn't know him. Does that seem wise to you, in a city like San Francisco?" His tone was politely concerned, and Margaret Burton looked angry and confused.

"No, I . . . it . . . no, I've never picked anyone up before. And I just thought that . . . he looked like he was okay."

"What do you mean by okay, Miss Burton? He was drunk, wasn't he?"

"A little tiddly maybe, but not bombed. And he looked, well . . . like a nice guy."

"You mean rich? Or fancy? Or what? Like a Harvard grad?"

"I don't know. He just looked clean-cut."

"And handsome? Do you think he's handsome?"

"I don't know." She was looking at her lap.

"Did you think he'd get involved with you, maybe? Fall in love? That's a fair assumption. You're a nice-looking woman, why not? A hot summer day, a good-looking guy, a lonely woman . . . how old are you, Miss Burton?"

"Thirty-one." But she'd fumbled.

"You told the police thirty. Isn't it more like thirty-eight? Isn't it just possible that —"

"Objection!" The district attorney was on her feet, her face furious, and the judge nodded.

"Sustained. Mr. Schwartz, this is not a trial, and you might as well save the pressure tactics for later. Miss Burton, you don't have to answer that. Are you almost through, Mr Schwartz?"

"Almost, Your Honor. Miss Burton, what were you wearing on the day of your encounter with Mr. Clarke?"

"What was I wearing?" She looked nervous and confused. He had been pelting her with difficult questions. "I . . . I don't know . . . I . . ."

"Was it something like what you have on now? A suit? Or something lighter, more revealing? Something sexy, maybe?" The prosecuting attorney was frowning fiercely again, and Jessica was beginning to enjoy the situation. She liked Martin's style. Even Ian looked intrigued, almost pleased.

"I . . . I don't know. I guess I must have worn a summer dress."

"Like what? Something low-cut?"

"No. I don't wear things like that."

"Are you sure, Miss Burton? Mr. Clarke says you were wearing a very short, low-cut pink dress, with a hat — were you wearing that same hat? It's a very nice hat." Suddenly she was torn between the compliment and the implication.

"I don't wear pink."

"But the hat is pink, isn't it?"

"It's more a kind of neutral color, more like beige." But there was a pinkish cast to it. That was obvious to all.

"I see. And what about the dress? Did that have a kind of beige cast to it too?"

"I don't know."

"All right. Do you go to Enrico's often?"

"No, I've been just a couple of times. But I've walked by it."

"Had you seen Mr. Clarke there before?"

"No. I don't remember seeing him." She was regaining her composure. These questions were easy.

"Why did you tell him you were a topless waitress on Broadway?"

"I never told him that." Now she was angry again, and Martin nodded, looking almost preoccupied.

"All right, thank you, Miss Burton. Thank you, Your Honor."

The judge looked questioningly at the assistant district attorney, who shook her head. She had nothing to add. He indicated that Margaret Burton could step down, then spoke the words Jessica had dreaded. "Mr. Clarke, please take the stand."

Ian and Margaret Burton passed inches from each other, their faces without expression. Only moments before, she had said that he had ruined her life, yet now she looked right through him. Jessica felt more confused than ever by the woman.

The oath was administered, and the judge looked over his glasses at Ian.

"Mr. Clarke, would you please give us your account of what happened?" The judge looked excessively bored as Ian launched into his version of that day's events. The lunch, the drinks, picking her up, the seductive way she was dressed, her story about being a topless waitress, the drive to Market Street to an address she had given him but which he could no longer remember. And finally her invitation to her room, where they had had a drink and made love.

"Whose room was it?"

"I don't know. I assumed it was hers. But it was kind of empty. I don't know. I'd had a lot to drink at lunch, and I wasn't thinking very clearly."

"But clearly enough to go upstairs with Miss Burton?"

Ian flushed. He felt like an errant schoolboy called to the principal's office . . . *Ian, did you look up Maggie's dress? Tsk, tsk, tsk!* But it wasn't like that at all. The stakes were too high for this to be child's play.

"My wife was away, and had been for three weeks." Jessie's heart was pounding

223

again. Was it supposed to be her fault, then? Was that the implication? Was that what he thought, what he wanted her to feel? She was responsible for his feelings of inadequacy?

"And what happened after it was all over?"

"I left."

"Just like that? Did you intend to see Miss Burton again?" Ian shook his head.

"No. I didn't intend to see her again. I felt guilty as hell for what had already happened." Martin was frowning at his answer and Jessie cringed. The judge had picked up on it too.

"Guilty?"

"I mean, because of my wife. I don't usually do that sort of thing."

"What sort of thing, Mr. Clarke? Rape?"

"No, for God's sake, I didn't rape her!" He had bellowed his denial and small beads of sweat were glistening on his forehead. "I mean, I felt guilty for cheating on my wife."

"But you did force Miss Burton upstairs at the hotel?"

"I did not. She took me upstairs. It was her room, not mine. She invited me up."

"What for?"

"A drink. And probably for exactly what she got."

"Then why do you suppose she claims you

raped her?"

"I don't know." Ian looked blank and exhausted, and the judge shook his head and looked around the room.

"Ladies and gentlemen, neither do I. The purpose of this hearing is to determine if there was a misunderstanding afoot, if the problem is one that can be simply resolved here and now, to determine in effect if a rape did take place, and if the case merits further judicial attention. It is my job to decide to dismiss the action or send it on to a higher court to be tried. In order for me to make the decision to dismiss the action, I have to feel quite certain that this was clearly not a rape.

"In the event that I am unable to decide, that the matter is not clear, then I have no choice but to send it on to a higher court, and possibly to a jury, to decide. And it would appear that this is no simple matter before us now. The stories of the two parties are widely divergent. Miss Burton says rape, Mr. Clarke says not. There is no evidence in either direction. So I am afraid this matter will have to be handled by a higher court, and presumably given a jury trial. We cannot simply dismiss the matter. Serious allegations have been made. I move that the matter be referred to Superior

Court, and that Mr. Clarke be arraigned in Superior Court two weeks from today, in the court of Judge Simon Warberg. Court is dismissed." And without further ado, he got up and walked out of the room. Jessica and Ian rose and looked at each other in confusion as Martin shuffled papers for a moment. Margaret Burton was whisked away by Inspector Houghton.

"Now what?" Jessica spoke to Ian in a whisper.

"You heard the man, Jess — we go to trial."

"Yeah." She looked for a last moment at the retreating back of the Burton woman, fresh hatred filling her soul for this woman who was inexplicably destroying their lives. She knew no more now than she had three hours ago. Why?

"Well, Martin?" Jessica turned to Martin now. He looked very serious. "What do you think?"

"We'll discuss it in my office, but I smell one thing I don't like. I can't be sure, but I had a case like this once years ago. Crazy case with a crazy plaintiff. It had to do with vengeance. Not against the guy she said had raped her, but against someone who actually had raped her in her late teens. She had waited twenty-two years to get revenge against an innocent man. I can't tell you why, it's just a gut feeling, but this reminds me of that case." He had spoken in a barely audible whisper. Jessica leaned toward him to hear, and was intrigued by his idea. She had had a strange feeling about the Burton woman too. Ian still looked too shaken to react to much of anything. He looked at Jessie then with irritation in his eyes.

"I told you to wait outside."

"I couldn't."

"Yeah. I had a feeling you'd wind up in here. Fun, wasn't it?" He sounded bitter and tired. They were the only people left in the courtroom, and he looked around as though he'd just waked up from a bad dream. It had been a grueling session, and even Jessica felt as though she had aged five years in the course of the morning.

"When will the trial be?" she asked Martin. She didn't quite know what to say to Ian: there was so much to say; too much.

"In six weeks. You heard the judge say that the Superior Court arraignment is in two. The trial will be four weeks after that. And we're going to have to do some very fast work." Martin was wearing a look of intense sobriety, and Jessica found herself aching to ask how that other client had come out, the one who had been accused of rape by the woman seeking revenge, but she was afraid to know. Ian hadn't asked the question either, and Martin hadn't volunteered the information. "I want Green on the case night and day, and I want you both available for meetings whenever I call you." His voice was stern.

"We'll be available." Jessie spoke first, trying to keep the tears out of her voice. "We'll win, won't we, Martin?" She was still whispering, but she wasn't sure why. It was no longer necessary.

"I think it'll be a tight one. It's her word against yours, Ian. But yes, we ought to win." He didn't'sound sure enough for Jessie, though, and the full weight of the situation settled on her heart again. How had it all happened? Where had it all started? Was it really just a matter of her having been in New York for too long? Had he just been horny? Was it bad luck? Was the Burton woman some kind of lunatic who'd been gunning for anyone, or had Ian been singled out? Whose fault was it? And when would it all go away?

"Will they revoke Ian's bail?" That had been her constant terror. And Ian's.

"They can, but they won't. There's no reason to, as long as he keeps making his court appearances, and the judge didn't mention it. Just don't either of you go off on any trips just now. No business trips, no disappearing acts, no visits back east to your family. Stick around; I'll be needing you. All right?"

They nodded solemnly and he walked them slowly from the courtroom as Jessie thought of what he'd said. Family? What family? As old and frail as Ian's parents were, they would be the last people to turn to. She and Ian had already agreed on that. His parents were so proper and so gentle, and much too old to understand any of this. He was their only child, and truly it would have killed them. Besides, why tell them? It would all work out. It had to.

Ian and Jessie shook hands with Martin and he left them outside the courtroom. It had been an endless morning.

"Do we have a minute to stop at the john?" Jessica looked at Ian nervously. She felt strange and uncomfortable with him, as though someone had just told them he had cancer. She wasn't sure whether to cry or to offer encouragement, or just to run away and hide. She wasn't even sure what she felt yet.

"Sure. I think it's down the hall. I have to go too." Conversation was awkward between them. It was going to be hard to find the way back. But as they walked along the hall, he stopped her suddenly and turned to face her, holding her arm. "Jessie, I don't know what to say. I didn't do it, but I'm almost beginning to wonder if that even matters. I can't stand seeing what this is doing to you. I was a total ass for a couple of hours, and you're the one who's paying the price."

She smiled tiredly in answer. "And what about you? You're enjoying this maybe? Baby, we're in it now, and we just have to keep on walking till we're through it. That's all. And for Chrissake, don't give up now." She was looking at him with a gentleness he hadn't seen all day. She slid her arms around him as they stood in the long marble hall, and he folded her into his arms without saying a word. He needed her desperately, and she knew it.

"Come on, hot stuff, I have to pee." Her voice was gruff and sexy, and he smiled at her as they walked on down the hall, hand in hand. There was something very special between them. Always had been, always would be — if they could just survive what was happening to them now.

"I'll be back in a second." She pecked a gentle kiss at his neck, squeezed his hand, and disappeared into the ladies' room.

Inside, she let herself into one of the

booths and bolted the door. There were women on either side of her. A pair of red platform shoes and navy slacks on her left, slim ankles and simple black pumps on her right. Jessica straightened her stockings, smoothed down her skirt, and unbolted the door at the same moment that the black pumps emerged to her right. She cast a casual glance in that direction as she headed toward the sink, only to find herself rooted to the floor, staring into Margaret Burton's face — staring down at it, actually, with the difference in their height — the pale pink hat only slightly obscuring her view of the enemy's face.

Margaret Burton stood very still and stared back at her, as Jessica felt her insides turn cold. She was right there in front of her . . . within reach . . . grab her . . . hit her . . . kill her . . . but she couldn't move. There was only the sound of a sharp intake of breath as the Burton woman came to her senses and ran toward the door, the hat flying gently to Jessica's feet. It had taken only a few seconds, but it seemed hours, days, years . . . and she was gone, as Jessie stood there helpless, tears starting down her face. She stooped down very slowly and picked up the hat before walking slowly toward the door. She could hear someone knocking

nervously, frantically. It was Ian. He had
seen Margaret Burton fly through the door
as he'd come out of the men's room across
the hall. And suddenly he was terrified.
What had happened? What had Jessica
done?

She emerged silently, the hat in her hand,
tears on her face.

"What happened?"

Jessica only shook her head, clutching the
hat.

"Did she do anything?"

She shook her head again.

"Did you?"

And again, a silent no.

"Oh, babe." He pulled her into his arms,
and took the hat from her hand, tossing it
onto a nearby bench. "Let's get the hell out
of here and go home." In fact, he was going
to get her out of town. To hell with what
Martin said, they needed to get away. Carmel, maybe. Anywhere. He wondered how
long Jessica could take the pressure. How
long he could. The hat seemed to look at
him accusingly from the bench as he held
his wife in his arms, and he shuddered. It
was the hat she had worn that day at Enrico's. That day . . . the day he'd be paying
for for years, one way or another. He kept
an arm around Jessica's shoulders and

walked her slowly toward the elevator. He wanted to pour his soul into hers, but he wasn't even sure he had enough for himself anymore, let alone for anyone else. He wanted the horror to be over, and it was only beginning.

When the elevator came she walked silently into it. Her eyes were soldered to the doors, and he wanted to shake her. He was watching her slip away again: he had seen this mask before.

The elevator spat them out into the chaos of the lobby. It was filled with police and inspectors, private lawyers and assistant district attorneys, and people waiting in line to get passes to the jail. Ian and Jessica melted into the sea of swarming people. And here and there was an ordinary, untroubled face, someone in the building to pay a parking ticket, or fill out a car-registration form. But they were so few that they blended in with the rest, which was why neither Jessica nor Ian saw Astrid, on her way to get a new sticker for the one that had fallen off her plates at the car wash. They were only a few feet away and never saw her. But she saw them, and was stricken by the expression on their faces. They passed six feet away, and she let them go. It was the same look she had worn when the doctors had told her just how sick Tom really was.

Chapter 13

The following morning, Ian made up his mind. Jessica had to get away. They both did. And when she was making breakfast, he even went to the trouble of clearing it with Martin over the phone. Martin agreed, and Ian announced it to Jessie as a *fait accompli.*

"We're doing what?" She looked at him incredulously as she stood barefoot in her robe in the kitchen.

"We're leaving for Carmel in half an hour." This time he smiled when he said it. "Pack your gear, my love."

"You're crazy. Martin said —"

"— to send him a postcard." Ian smiled victoriously as Jessica chuckled.

"And just when did he say that?"

"Just now."

"You called him?" She still looked dubious, but amused.

"I just hung up. So, my beloved —" he

approached her slowly, with a wisp of a smile — "get your beautiful ass moving before we waste the day."

"You're a nut." He kissed her and she smiled up at him with her eyes closed. "But such a nice nut."

They reached Carmel in two hours with Ian at the wheel of the Morgan. The air was cooler than it had been for weeks, and it was brilliantly sunny all the way down. They put the top down on the Morgan and arrived wind-blown and happier. It was almost as though the constant sweep of wind on the highway had cleared the worry from their minds. The trip hadn't been such a bad idea after all, and after the first fifty miles, Jessie had stopped imagining that Inspector Houghton was following them. She was constantly haunted by him, but maybe now it would stop. It was just that he seemed omnipotent. He would go away and then could come back again, with a search warrant, a gun, a friend, a look in his eye . . . a twist of his mouth . . . he terrified her, and she didn't dare tell Ian how much. She never mentioned him. She had also been worried about the expense of the trip, but Ian had insisted that he had enough left in his account to cover it. She had been ordered to mind her own business and warned that they were going economy all the way, no deluxe accommodations this time. She felt guilty, doubting his assurances, but she was obsessed with their finances now, and the upcoming staggering expense of the trial. And Ian was so strange about money, maybe because he had never had any. He had a way of buying her fabulous presents and creating magnificent moments when they were plainly out of funds. He would take the last of what he had and throw it out the window in style. In the past, this trait had amused her. Right now it did not.

But she was grateful for the trip to Carmel. She knew how much she needed it. Her nerves had been on the raw edge of disaster. And she knew that Ian's had been too, no matter how hard he'd tried to cover up.

Astrid had told them about a little hotel where she had stayed the previous spring that she'd insisted was a bargain. So they forfeited the deluxe delights of the familiar Del Monte for the cozy plaid and pine atmosphere of L'Auberge. It was run by a middle-aged French couple, and among its other pleasures, it boasted "Café Complèt" in bed in the morning. The Café Complèt consisted of home-made croissants and brioches, with bowls of steaming *café au lait.*

They walked to the beach and canvassed the shops, and on Saturday took a picnic out to the edge of a cliff overlooking the sea.

"More wine, love?"

Ian nodded and pushed a long strand of blond hair from her eyes. They were lying side by side, and she was looking up at the sky while he rested on one elbow and looked down at her. He smoothed her face with his hand and kissed her gently on the lips, the eyes, the tip of the nose.

"If you do that, I'll never sit up to get you your wine, my love." He smiled again and she blew him a kiss.

"You know something, Ian?"

"What?"

"You make me very happy." His face clouded as she said it, and she caught his chin in her hand and forced him to look at her. "I mean it. You do."

"How can you say that now?"

"Because now is no different from any other time, Ian. You do beautiful things to me. You give me what I need, and I need a lot. Sometimes you pay a price for that. And okay, so it's hard now, but this'll be over soon. It won't go on forever. All in all I think we're damn lucky." She sat up and faced him, and finally he looked away.

"Lucky, eh? I guess that's one way to look at it." He sounded bitter, and she reached for his hand.

"You don't feel lucky anymore?"

"I do. But do you, Jessie, really? Be honest." He looked back at her with an unfamiliar look in his eyes, a kind of openness that frightened her: as though he were questioning everything. Her. Himself. Them. Life. Everything.

"Yes, I feel lucky." Her voice was a whisper in the brisk wind of the sunny October day.

"Jessica, my love, I was unfaithful to you. I made love to another woman. A neurotic tramp, but still another woman. You've been supporting me for almost six years. I am not a successful writer. And I'm about to go on trial for rape, I may go to prison, and even if I don't, this is going to be the ugliest thing we've ever lived through. And you feel lucky? How do you manage that little feat?"

She looked down at her hands for a long time, and then back up into his face. "Ian, I don't care if you made love to another woman. I don't like it, but it doesn't matter. It doesn't change anything. Not for me. Don't *you* let it change anything. I don't suppose it was the first time, but I don't want to know. That's not the point. The point is, so what? So you made love to someone, so what? So you jacked off, so what? *I don't care.* Does that make any sense to you? I don't care. I care about you, about us, about our marriage, about your career. And I don't 'support' you. Lady J supports us both. We're lucky to have it, and one of these days you're going to sell a book and a movie and another book and a pile of brilliant work, and make a fortune. So what's the problem?"

"Jessica, you're crazy." He was smiling at her, but his eyes still looked serious.

"No, I'm not. And I mean it. You make me happy. You make me glow, you make me care, you make me know I'm loved, you're always there for me. You know who I am and what I am and why I am better than I do even. Ian, that's so rare. I look at other people and they never seem to have what we have." Her eyes were fiery now, and the color of jade.

"I don't know what to say, Jessie . . . I love you. And I need you too. Not just to support me while I write. I need . . . oh, hell —" he smiled, more to himself than to her — "I need you sitting bare-assed and solemn-faced at two in the morning, telling me why my fourth chapter isn't working. I need the way you fly in the door at night with that look of 'Oh, wow!' on your face . . . the way you know, the way you . . . respect me, even when I don't respect myself."

"Oh, Ian." She slid into his arms again and closed her eyes as he held her.

"I need you a lot, babe. But . . . something's going to have to change."

Her eyes opened slowly. He had just said something important. She knew it from the change in the way he held her more than from the words.

"What do you mean?"

"I don't know yet. But something's got to change, after we survive this holocaust we're going to walk through in the next couple of months."

"Like what, dammit? Change what?" Her voice was unexpectedly shrill, and she sat back from him a little so she could read his eyes.

"Take it easy, Jessie. I just think it's about time for an overhaul. I don't know, maybe it's time I shelved my fancy ideas about a writing career. Something. We can't go on exactly like this, though. In some ways it doesn't work."

"Why not?"

"Because I feel kept. You pay the bills, or most of them, and I can't live with that anymore. Do you know what it feels like to have no income? To feel guilty every time you dig into the kitty, the 'joint account,' so-called, to buy a couple of T-shirts? Do you have any idea how it feels to have you footing the bill for this disaster now? To have you pick up the tab on my alleged 'rape'? Jesus, Jessie, it chokes me. It's killing me. Why the hell do you think I've been impotent lately? Because I'm so thrilled with myself for how I'm running my life?"

"You can't really take that seriously. You're under an incredible amount of strain right now." She wanted to brush it aside, but he wasn't going to let her.

"That's right. I am under a lot of strain. But part of that strain is because we haven't got things set up the way they should be. Did you ever wonder what would happen if you didn't have Lady J, or if your parents hadn't left you some money?"

"I'd be working for someone else, and you'd be working in advertising and hating it. Doesn't that sound like fun?"

"No. But what if you weren't working at all, and I were working at something else?"

"Like what?" Her face seemed to freeze on the words.

"I don't know like what. I haven't figured that out yet."

"Ian, you're out of your mind. I've never

seen you work as hard on a book as you are on this one now, I've never heard you sound so sure about anything you've written. And now you want to quit?"

"I didn't say that. Not yet. But maybe. What I'm saying is: What would happen to you, to us, to our marriage, if you didn't support us, Jessie, if *I* did? What if we just kept your money as a nest egg, as an investment?"

"And what would I do all day? Needlepoint? Play bridge?"

"No. I was thinking of something else. Maybe for later." There was something soft and distant in his eyes as he spoke.

"What's the something else?"

"Like . . . well . . . like what if we finally had children — after this whole mess is over, I mean. We haven't talked about that for a long time. Not since before . . ." She knew what he meant by "before." Before things had changed. Before her parents had died. Before she'd inherited their money . . . before. That one word said it all. They both knew. "Jessie . . . baby, I want to take care of you. Besides, you've earned it."

"Why?"

"What do you mean, 'why'?" He looked momentarily confused.

"I mean why should we scramble everything up now? Why should you suddenly take on the whole burden? I love working; it's not a burden for me. It's fun."

"Can't kids be fun too?"

"I didn't say they weren't." Her face was as tight as a drum.

"But?"

"Oh, for Chrissake, Ian, why do we have to get into that now?" That one hadn't come up in years.

"I didn't say now. We're just talking what if's."

"That's ridiculous. It's like playing games." She turned away and suddenly felt Ian's hand on her arm. Hard.

"It's not like playing games. I'm serious, Jessie. I've turned myself into a fucking gigolo in the last six years. I'm a failure as a writer, and I just balled some two-bit tramp and got falsely accused of rape. I'm trying to figure out what means something in my life and what doesn't, and what needs changing. And maybe part of what needs changing is us. Not even maybe. I know it does. Now are you going to listen, and talk to me, or aren't you?"

She sat silent, looking at him. But she knew she had no choice. He let go of her arm and poured two more glasses of wine.

"I'm sorry. But this is important to me, Jess."

"Okay. I'll try." She took the glass of wine and sighed deeply as she looked up at the sky. "All this because I told you that you make me happy? *Oy vey* . . . I should have kept my mouth shut!" She smiled back at him, and he kissed her again.

"I know. I'm a bastard. But Jessie . . . I want to make it work with us. I want to make it better. I don't want to go screwing other women, or hating myself or . . . it matters. It really matters. And I'm glad I make you happy, and you make me happy too. Very happy. But we can do better, I know we can. I've got to feel like your husband, like a man, like I carry the weight, or most of it at least, even if it means selling the house and living someplace where I can pay our rent. But I *need* to do things like that for you. I'm tired of having you 'take care' of me. And I don't mean to sound ungrateful, Jess, but . . . I just need to, dammit."

"Okay. But why? Why now? Because of that idiot woman? Margaret Burton? Because of her, you have to give up writing and move us into some shack in the Mission where you can pay the rent?" She was getting bitchy now and he didn't like it. The comment hadn't missed its mark.

245

"No, sweetheart. Margaret Burton is just a symptom, just like the hundred or two hundred pieces of ass before her. Is that how you want to play this, Jessie? Shitty, or straight? Take your pick. I'm willing to play either way."

She polished off the rest of her wine at a gulp and shrugged. "I just don't get the point."

"Maybe that is the point. Just like when I talk about having a child. You don't get the point of that either, do you? Doesn't that mean anything to you at all, Jessie?"

She shook her head solemnly, looking down, avoiding his eyes.

"I just don't understand that. Why? Look at me, dammit. This is important to me. To both of us." But when she looked up, he was surprised.

"It scares me."

"A baby?" She had never admitted that to him before. Usually she'd gotten nasty about it and closed the subject rapidly. It made him feel tender toward her to hear that. Scared?

"It scares you physically?" He reached for her hand gently and held it.

"No. It . . . I'd have to share you, Ian, and I . . . I can't." Tears swam in her eyes and her chin trembled as she looked at him. "I

246

really can't share you, Ian. I can't, not ever. You're all I have. You're . . ."

"Oh, baby . . ." He took her in his arms and rocked her gently, tears stinging his own eyes. "What a crazy thing to think. A baby's not like that. It would never be. We're special. A baby would be something more, not less."

"Yes, but it would be yours. Real family." And then he understood. He had his parents, of course, but they were so remote and so old. He hardly ever saw them. But a baby would be so present, so real.

"You're my real family, silly. You'll always be my real family." How often had he told her that, after her parents had died? A thousand times? Ten thousand? It was strange to think back to those days. She had been so fiercely independent and sure of herself when he'd married her. But she had loved both her parents and adored her brother; just hearing her speak of them was like hearing reminiscences of very dear friends who had had a marvelous time together. And spending time with them was an extraordinary experience — four exceedingly handsome people, with lightning minds and quick laughter and immeasurable style. They'd been quite something. And when they were gone, part of her went too. Not an obvious part. She still had as much spirit, as much life, as much style, but suddenly in her soul she was an orphan. She had loved Ian before, but she hadn't needed him in the same way. Then she'd become like a frightened child lost in a war zone, stricken, scared, wandering from the burnt shell of one memory to another. Lost and alone. The attempted suicide had come after Jake. And it had left her different. Dependent. It was Ian who had led her to safety again after that. That was when she had started calling him "real family." Where before their closeness had been a loosely woven, sparkling mesh, suddenly there was nothing loose about it, and over the years it had all gotten too goddam tight. And now there wasn't even room in her heart for a child. He had known that for a long time, but he had thought that eventually the panic would ebb. It hadn't, now he was sure of it. Her own needs were still too intense, and probably always would be. It was a bitter thing for him to accept.

"Oh, God, Ian, I love you so much and I'm so scared . . . I'm so fucking scared." He felt her in his arms again, his mind pulled back to her, away from his own thoughts. She took a deep breath and held tightly to him as he slowly stroked her hair, thinking of what he now understood and had to accept. Had to. Nothing was ever going to change. Oh, some things would, and he was going to see about making those changes, but she was never going to stand on her own two feet again, not entirely, not enough for them both to reach out to a child.

"I'm scared too, Jess. But it's going to be okay."

"How can it be okay if you're going to change everything after we get through this? You want me to sell the shop, have a baby, and you're going to stop writing and get a job and make us move and . . . oh, Ian! It sounds horrible!" She sobbed in his arms again and he laughed softly as he held her. Maybe she was all he needed. Maybe it wasn't even normal for a man to want a child as much as he did. Maybe it was just an ego trip. He brushed the thoughts from his mind.

"Jesus, did I say I was going to change all that? It does sound pretty heavy. Maybe we should just pick a couple of things, like I'll have a baby, and you get a job, and . . . I'm sorry, babe, I didn't mean to hit you with ten thousand things at once. I just know that something needs fixing."

"But all that?"

"No, probably not all that. And not unless you agree with me. It wouldn't work otherwise. We've both got to want it."

"But you make it sound like our life will never be the same again."

"Maybe it won't, Jessie. Maybe it shouldn't be. Did you ever think of that?"

"No."

"And you're not going to, either, huh? Look at you, hunched over like an Indian squaw, trying not to hear anything I'm telling you, with an ant crawling up your arm . . ." He waited. It took half a second. She leapt to her feet with a scream.

"A what?"

"Oh . . . tsk . . . how could I forget? That's right, you're afraid of ants." He brushed her sleeve lightly as he stood up next to her and she punched him in the chest.

"Goddam you, Ian Clarke! We're having a serious talk and how can you do that to me! There was no ant on me, was there? *Was there?*"

"Would I lie to you?"

"I hate you!" She was still trembling with a jumble of emotions, terror and fury and fear because of the ant, and the much more real emotions of moments before. He'd invented the ant to lighten the mood.

It was a reprieve. Ian was good at them.

"What do you mean, you hate me? You said I made you happy." He looked all innocence as he put his arms around her.

"Don't touch me!" But she was limp in his arms and trying hard to conceal a smile. "You know —" her voice was soft again now — "sometimes I wonder if you really love me."

"Sometimes everyone wonders stuff like that, Jess. You can't have the kind of ironclad guarantees you want, sweetheart. I love you just as much as your mother and father did, just as much as Jake did, just as much as . . . anyone. But I'm not them. I'm me, your husband, a man, just like you're my wife, not my mother. And maybe one day you'll get sick of me and walk off into the sunset with someone else. Mothers aren't supposed to do that to their kids, but wives do that sometimes. I have to accept that."

"Are you trying to tell me something?" She was suddenly stiff in his arms.

"No, silly, only that I love you. And that I can only be and do so much. I think I'm trying to tell you not to be so insecure and not to worry so much. Sometimes I think that's why you put up with so much shit from me, and pay the bills and all the rest, because that way you know you've got me. But I'll tell you a secret — that way you

251

don't got me. As it so happens you've got me, but for all the other reasons."

"Like what?" She was smiling again.

"Oh . . . like the beautiful way you sew."

"Sew? I can't sew." She looked at him strangely and then started to laugh.

"You can't?"

"Nope."

"I'll teach you."

"You're adorable."

"Come to think of it, lady, so are you. Which reminds me. Reach into my pocket." Her eyebrows lifted with interest and she grinned mischievously at him.

"A surprise for me?"

"No, my laundry bill."

"Creep." But she slipped her hand carefully into his jacket pocket as they talked, her eyes sparkling with excitement. It was easy to find the little square box. She pulled it out with a grin and held it clutched in her hand.

"Aren't you going to open it?"

"This is the best part." She giggled again and he grinned at her.

"It's not the Hope diamond, I promise."

"It's not?"

"Oh, for Chrissake . . ." And then she suddenly snapped open the box. And he watched.

"Oh . . . it's . . . oh, Ian! You nut!" She gave a whoop of laughter and looked at it again. "How in God's name did you get it?"

"I saw it, and I knew you had to have it."

She laughed again and started to put it on. It was a thin gold chain with a gold pendant shaped like a lima bean. The thing she had hated most in the world as a child.

"Good God, I never thought I'd see the day when I'd wear one of the bloody things. And in gold, yet." She laughed again, kissed him, and tucked in her chin to look down at the small gold nugget on its chain.

"Actually, it looks very elegant. If you didn't know what it was, you'd never guess. I had a choice between a kidney bean, a lima bean, and some other kind of bean. They're done by the same very fancy designer, I'll have you know."

"And you just saw it in a window?"

"Yep. And I figured that if you have faith as a mustard seed, you can move mountains and all that stuff. So hell, if you have faith like a lima bean, you can probably move half the world."

"Which half?"

"Any half, sexy lady. Come on, let's go back to the hotel."

"Lima beans . . . sweetheart, you're crazy. May I ask how large a portion of your fortune this sensational lima bean cost you?" She had noticed that it was eighteen-karat gold and that the box was from a very extravagant store.

"You most certainly may not. How can you ask such a thing?"

"Curiosity."

"Well, don't be so curious. And do me a favor. Don't eat it." She laughed again and bit his neck as she reached over for the rest of the wine.

"Sweetheart, there is one thing you can bet on. I ain't never gonna eat lima beans. Not even a gold one." And then they both burst into laughter, because that was exactly what she had told him the first time he had cooked dinner for her at his place eight years before.

He had fixed roast pork, mashed potatoes, and lima beans. She had devoured the meat and potatoes, but he had found her rapidly shoveling lima beans into her handbag when he'd come back from the kitchen with the glass of water she'd requested, and she had looked at him, thrown up her hands, burst into laughter and said, "Ian, I ain't never gonna eat lima beans. Not even if they're solid gold." And this one was indeed solid gold. For the tiniest of moments, her stomach felt queasy at the thought of the expense. But that was Ian. They were going down the tubes in style. With picnics and passion and gold.

The mood for the rest of the weekend was sheer holiday spirit. Jessica flashed her gold lima bean at every possible opportunity, and they teased and hugged and kissed. L'Auberge restored their love life to what it had always been. They had dinner by candlelight in their room — a feast of fried chicken from a nearby take-out place, devoured with a small bottle of champagne they had bought on the way back to the hotel. They giggled like children and played like honeymooners, and the threats of the morning were forgotten. Everything was forgotten except Ian and Jessie. They were the only people who mattered.

The only sorrow, and it was a hidden one, was Ian's hope of a child, now put away. Insanely, desperately, he had wanted to father a child, now, before the trial, before . . . what if . . . who knew what was coming? A year from then he could be in prison or dead. It wasn't a cheerful way to look at things, but the realities were beginning to frighten him. And the possibilities were even more terrifying when he let himself think of them. A baby would be a fresh blade of glass springing from ashes. But now that he understood how panicked Jessie still was, the subject was closed. His books were his children. He would simply work that much harder on the new book.

On Sunday, Jessie bought Ian a Sherlock Holmes hat and a corncob pipe. They shared a banana split for lunch, then rented a tandem bike and rode around near the hotel, laughing at their lack of precision. Jessica collapsed when faced with a hill.

"What do you mean, 'no'? Come on, Jessie, *push!*"

"The hell I will. You push. I'll walk."

"Stinkpot."

"Look at that hill. Who do you think I am? Tarzan?"

"Well, look at your legs, for Chrissake. They're long enough to run up that hill carrying me, let alone bicycling."

"You, sir, are a creep."

"Hey . . . look at the spider on your leg."

"I . . . what? . . . Aaaahh . . . Ian! Where?" But he was laughing at her, and when she looked up she knew. "Ian Clarke, if you do that to me one more time, I'll . . ." She was spluttering and he was laughing harder than ever. "I'll . . ." She hit him a walloping blow on the shoulder, knocking him off the bicycle and into the tall grass next to the path. But he reached out and grabbed her as she stood laughing at him, and pulled her down beside him. "Ian, not here! There are probably snakes in here! Ian! Dammit! Stop that!"

"No snakes. I swear." He was reaching into her blouse with a leer that made her giggle.

"Ian . . . I mean it — no! Ian . . ." She forgot about the snakes almost immediately.

CHAPTER 14

"Well, how did you like my favorite hide-away in Carmel?" With a smile, Astrid poked her head in the door of Jessica's office.

"We adored it. Come on in. How about some coffee?"

Jessie's smile said it all. The two days in Carmel had been a peaceful island in a troubled sea.

"I'll skip the coffee, thanks. I'm on my way downtown to talk to Tom's attorneys. Maybe I'll stop by again on my way home." Jessica showed her the gold lima bean, gave her a brief, expurgated account of the weekend, and blew Astrid a kiss as she left. For the rest of the day, Lady J was a madhouse.

There were deliveries, new clients, old customers who wanted something new but needed it altered "right now," invoices that got misplaced, and two shipments that Jessie needed desperately never showed up at all. And Katsuko couldn't help, because she was swamped with details for the fashion show. So Zina juggled the customers while Jessie tried to untangle the problems. And the bills. The next two weeks were more of the same.

Harvey Green appeared twice at the boutique to discuss minor things with Jessie, things about Ian's habits and her own, but she had little to tell him. Neither did Ian. They led a simple life and had nothing to hide. The two girls in the boutique still didn't know what was happening, and the weeks since Jessie's frantic and erratic disappearances from the shop had been too hectic for questions. They assumed that the problem, whatever it was, had blown over. And Astrid was careful not to pry.

Ian was lost in his new book, and the two subsequent court appearances went smoothly. As Martin had predicted the bail was not revoked: there was never even a suggestion of it. Jessica joined Ian both times in court, but there was nothing to see. He would walk to the front of the courtroom with Martin, they would mumble for a few moments in front of the judge, and then they could all leave. By now it seemed like an ordinary part of their everyday lives; they had other things to think about. Jessie was worried about part of the fall line that hadn't moved, another shipment that had never shown up, and the money that was draining from her bank account. Ian was troubled by chapter nine, and incoherent about anything else. That was what their real life was about, not mechanical appearances before a bored judge.

It was a month later when Harvey Green came up with the first part of his bill. Eighteen hundred dollars. The statement arrived at the boutique, as she had requested, and Jessica gasped when she opened it. She felt almost sick. Eighteen hundred dollars. For nothing. He hadn't unearthed a damn thing, except the name of a man Margaret Burton had gone to dinner with twice and never slept with. Maggie Burton appeared to be clean. Her coworkers thought her a decent woman, not very sociable, but reliable and pleasant to work with. Several mentioned that she was occasionally distant and moody. She had no torrid love affairs in her past, no drug problems, no drinking habits to speak of. She had never returned to any hotel on Market Street in all the time Green had been tailing her, nor had she had any men into her apartment at any time since the surveillance had begun. She went home alone every night after work; had gone to three movies in a month, again alone; and an attempt to pick her up on the bus had totally failed. An assistant of Green's had made eyes at her for several blocks, gotten an encouraging look in response, he said, and had then received a firm "No, thanks, buster" when he'd invited her out for a drink. He had said she'd even looked pissed at him for asking. At worst, she was confused. At best . . . she was the second best thing to the Virgin Mary, and Ian's case would look very flimsy in court. They had to find something. But they hadn't. And now Harvey Green wanted eighteen hundred dollars. And they couldn't even let him go. Martin had said the Burton woman would have to be watched right up until the trial, possibly even during the trial, although both he and Green admitted that the police had probably told her to behave herself. The prosecution didn't want their case shot down by a random piece of ass Miss Margaret Burton might indulge herself with a few weeks before the trial.

Green hadn't even been able to come up with any dirt on her past. She had been married once, at the age of eighteen, and the marriage had been annulled a few months later. But he didn't know why, or who she had married. Nothing. And there was no record of it, which was probably why she hadn't admitted to it at the preliminary hearing. (What he knew he had learned from a woman Margaret Burton worked with.) What Jessie was paying for was a clean bill of health on the woman.

Jessie sat at her desk, staring at Green's bill, and opened the rest of her mail. A statement from Martin for the five thousand they still owed, and nine statements from New York for her purchases for the spring line. Ian's bill for his physical two months before, still due, for two hundred and forty-two dollars, and her own chest X ray for forty, as well as a seventy-four-dollar bill from a record store where she'd splurged before she'd gone to New York. As she sat there, she wondered what had ever made her think that seventy-four dollars for records wasn't so awful. She could still remember saying that to Ian at the time. Yeah . . . not so awful if you haven't found yourself with ten thousand dollars in legal bills in the meantime . . . and the florist . . . and the cleaner's . . . and the drugstore . . . she could feel her stomach constrict as she tried not to add up the amounts. She reached for the phone, looked at the card in her address book, and called.

She phoned the bank before going to the appointment, and she was lucky, more or less. Based on the previous performance of her account, the bank was willing to leave her loan uncovered by collateral. She could sell it. She had been secretly hoping that they wouldn't let her. But now she had no choice.

She sold the Morgan at two in the afternoon. For fifty-two hundred dollars. The guy gave her "a deal." She deposited the check in the bank before closing, and sent a check of her own to Martin Schwartz for five thousand dollars. He was paid. It was taken care of. She could breathe now. For weeks she had had nightmares about something happening to her and nobody being able to help Ian with the bills . . . horrible fantasies of Ian begging Katsuko for the money, and being refused because she wanted the money to buy kimonos for the shop, while Barry York threatened to drag Ian back to jail. Now they were saved. The legal fees were paid. If something happened to her, Ian had his attorney.

She then borrowed eighteen hundred dollars from Lady J's business account to pay Green his fee. She was back at her desk at three-thirty — with a splitting headache.

Astrid showed up at four-thirty.

"You're not looking too happy, Lady J. Anything wrong?" Astrid was the only one who called her that, and it made her smile tiredly.

"Would you believe *everything's* wrong?"

"No, I wouldn't. But — anything special you want to tell me?" Astrid sipped the coffee Zina had poured for her and Jessie sighed and shook her head.

"Nothing much to tell. Not unless you have about six hundred spare hours to listen, and I don't have that much spare time to tell you anyway. How was your day?"

"Better than yours. But I didn't take any chances. I got up at eleven and spent the afternoon having my hair done." Jesus. How could she tell her? How could Astrid possibly understand?

"Maybe that's where I went wrong. I washed my hair myself last night." She grinned lopsidedly at her friend, but Astrid didn't smile. She was worried. Jessie had been looking tired and troubled for weeks, and there was nothing she could say.

"Why don't you call it a day, and go home to your gorgeous young husband? Hell, Jessica, if I had him around, wild horses couldn't keep me here."

"You know something? I think you're

right." It was the first real smile Jessica had produced all day. "Are you heading home? I could use a ride."

"Where's your baby?"

"The Morgan?" She tried to stall. She didn't want to lie, but . . . Astrid nodded, and Jessie felt a pain in her heart.

"I . . . it's in the shop."

"No problem. I'll give you a ride."

Ian watched Astrid drop her off from the window in his studio, and he looked puzzled. It was time to take a break anyway — he'd been working straight through since seven that morning. He opened the door for Jessie before she got out her key.

"What's with the car? Did you leave it at the boutique?"

"Yes . . . I . . ." She looked up and she could almost feel the color draining from her face. She had to tell him. "Ian, I . . . I sold it." She winced at the look on his face. Everything stopped.

You did what?" It was worse than she had feared.

"I sold it. Darling, I had to. Everything else is tied up. And we needed almost seven thousand bucks in the next two weeks for Martin's fee, and the first half of Green's bill, and Green is going to hit us with another one in two weeks. There was nothing else I could do." She reached out to touch him and be brushed her hand away.

"You could have asked me, at least! Asked me, said something — for God's sake, Jessica, don't you consult me on *anything* anymore? I gave you that car as a gift. It meant something to me!" He strode across the room and grabbed for the Scotch. He poured some into a glass while she watched.

"Don't you think it meant something to *me?*" Her voice was trembling, but he didn't hear, and she watched while he swallowed the half glass of Scotch neat. "Darling, I'm so . . . I just couldn't see any other . . ." She fell silent, with tears in her eyes. She remembered so well the day he had driven it home for her. Now . . .

He swallowed the last of his drink and pulled on his jacket.

"Where are you going?"

"Out." His face looked like gray marble.

"Ian, please, don't do anything crazy." She was frightened at the look in his eyes, but he only stood there and shook his head.

"I don't have to do anything crazy. I already did." The door slammed behind him a moment later.

He came back at midnight, silent and

subdued, and Jessica didn't ask him where he'd been. She was afraid to: maybe Inspector Houghton would be paying them another visit. But she hated herself for the thought when she watched Ian take off his shoes. Two small hills of sand poured out of them, and she looked at his face. He looked better. They had always done that together — gone to the beach at night to talk things out, or think, or just walk quietly together. He had taken her there when Jake had died. To their beach. Always together. Now she was afraid even to reach out and touch him, but she wanted to, needed to. He looked at her silently and walked into the bathroom and closed the door. Jessie turned out the lights and wiped two tears from her face. She felt the funny gold lima bean at her throat and tried to make herself smile, but she couldn't. They were past laughing at lima beans now, past laughing at anything, and who knew — one day she might sell the lima bean too. She hated herself as she lay in the dark.

She heard the bathroom door open, then Ian's soft footsteps, and then she felt the bed dip on the far side. He sat there for what seemed like a long time, smoking a cigarette. He leaned against the headboard and stretched his legs. She knew all his movements without looking, and she lay very still, wanting him to think she was sleeping. She didn't know what to say to him.

"I have something for you, Jess." His voice was gruff and low in the stillness of the room.

"Like a punch in the mouth?"

He laughed and put a hand on her hip as she lay on her side with her back to him.

"No, dummy. Turn around." She shook her head like a child, and then peeked over her shoulder.

"You're not mad at me, Ian?"

"No, I'm mad at me. There was nothing else you could do. I know that. I just hate myself for getting us in this spot, and I'd rather have sold a lot of things than the Morgan."

She nodded, still at a loss for words. "I'm so sorry."

"Me too." He leaned over and kissed her gently on the mouth and then put something light and sandy in her hand. "Here. I found it in the dark." It was a perfect sand dollar, a milky white shell with a tiny fossil imprint at its heart.

"Oh, darling, it's beautiful." She smiled up at him, holding it in the flattened palm of her hand.

"I love you." And then with a slow, gentle smile he pulled her into his arms and let his lips follow an exquisite path to her thighs.

The next two weeks spun past them crazily. Hours at the shop, long lunches at home, violent arguments about who wasn't watering the plants, and then passionate making up and making love and making out, and insomnia, and oversleeping, and forgetting to eat and then eating too much, and constant indigestion, and terror about the bills followed by spending huge amounts of money on a Gucci wallet for Ian or a suede skirt from another store for Jessie, when she could have gotten it at cost from her own, and baubles and junk and garbage, and all of it charged, of course, as though the day of reckoning would never come. Utter madness. None of it made any sense. Jessie felt for weeks as though she were ricocheting off walls, never to be stationary again. Ian had the impression he was drowning.

It was the day before the trial when everything finally stopped. Jessie had made arrangements at the shop to take a week off, two if things turned out that way. She left the boutique early and went for a long walk before going home to Ian. She found him sitting pensively in a chair, staring at the view. It was the first time she had seen him not working furiously on the new novel. That was all he seemed to do now, when he wasn't spending money, or silently and urgently taking her body. They talked less than they ever had. Even meals were either silent disasters or frantic and frenzied — never normal.

But that night they lit a fire together, and talked until dark. She felt as though she hadn't seen him in months. At last she was talking to Ian again, the man she loved, her husband, her lover, her friend. She had missed his friendship most of all in these endless lonely weeks. It was the first time they really hadn't been able to reach out to each other and help. Now they shared a quiet dinner, sitting on the floor in front of the fire. Their peacefulness made the trial seem less terrifying. And the reality of it had worn off in the weeks since Ian had been released from jail. Jail had been reality. Fighting her way upstream to bail had been reality. Leaving her mother's emerald ring had been reality. But what was the trial? Merely a formality. A verbal exchange between two paid performers, theirs and the State's, with a black-robed umpire looking on, and somewhere in the background a woman no one knew named Margaret Burton. A week, maybe two weeks, and then it would be over. That was the only reality.

She rolled over on her back on the rug in front of the fire and smiled up at him sleepily as he bent to kiss her. It was a long, haunting kiss that brought back the gentleness they had lost and made her body beg to respond, and in a few minutes they were hungrily making love. It was one of those rare nights when souls and bodies blended and ignited and burned on for hours. They said little, but they made love again and again. It was almost dawn when Ian deposited Jessica sleepily in their bed.

"I love you, Jessie. Get some sleep now. Tomorrow will be a long day." He whispered the words, and she smiled at his voice as she drifted off to sleep. A long day? Oh . . . that's right . . . the fashion show . . . or was it that they were going back to the beach? . . . She couldn't remember . . . a picnic? Was that it?

"I love you too . . ." Her voice drifted off as she fell asleep at his side, her arms wrapped around him like a small child's. He stroked her arm gently as he lay beside her, smoking a cigarette, and then he looked down into her face, but he wasn't smiling. Nor was he sleepy. He loved Jessica more than ever, but there were too many other things crowding his mind.

He spent the rest of the night in a lonely vigil. Watching his wife, thinking his own thoughts, listening to her breathe and murmur, wondering what would come next.

The next morning he was going on trial for rape.

CHAPTER 15

The courtroom at City Hall was a far cry from the small room where the preliminary hearing had been held. This one looked like a courtroom in the movies. Gold leaf, wood paneling, long rows of chairs, the judge's bench set up high on a platform, and the American flag in plain view of all. The room was full of people, and a woman was calling names one by one. She stopped when she had twelve. They were selecting the jury.

Ian sat with Martin at the front of the room, at the desk assigned to the defense. A few feet away sat a different assistant district attorney, with Inspector Houghton at his side. Margaret Burton was nowhere in sight.

The twelve jurors took their seats, and the judge explained the nature of the trial. A few of the women looked surprised and cast glances at Ian, and one man shook his head. Martin made rapid notes and watched the prospective jurors closely. He had the right to excuse ten people from the jury, and the assistant D.A. could do the same. The faces looked innocuous, like those of people you'd see on a bus.

Martin had told Ian and Jessie earlier that morning about the nature of the jury he wanted. No "old maids" who would be shocked at the accusation of rape, or who might identify with the victim; yet perhaps they might try to hang on to some staunch middle-class housewives who might condemn Burton for allowing Ian to pick her up. Young people might be in sympathy with Ian, yet they might resent the way the couple looked, too comfortable for their age. They were walking a delicate line.

Jessie watched the twelve men and women from her seat in the front row, searching their faces and that of the judge. But just as Martin stood up to question the first prospective juror, the judge called a recess for lunch.

It was a slow process; it was the end of the second day before the jury had been picked. They had been interrogated by both attorneys as to their feelings about rape, had been questioned about their jobs and their mates, their habits and the number of children they had. Martin had explained that fathers of women Miss Burton's age would not be a good idea either; they'd feel too protective of the victim. One had to consider so many things, and some base was inevitably left uncovered. There were a couple of people on the jury even now who did not meet with Martin's full approval, but he had used up his challenges, and now they had to hope for the best. Martin had set up an easy bantering style with the jurors, and now and then someone had laughed at a foolish answer or a joke.

Finally the jury was set. Five men, three retired and two young, and seven women, five in their middle years and comfortably married, two young and single. That had been a stroke of good fortune. They hoped it would counterbalance two of the retired men Martin did not like. But on the whole, he was reasonably satisfied, and Ian and Jessie assumed he was right.

As they all left the courtroom at the end of the second day, Jessie felt as though she could have recited the jurors' life stories in her sleep, listed their occupations and those of their mates. She would have known their faces in a crowd of thousands, and would remember them for a lifetime if she never saw them again after that day.

Their first shock came on the third day. The quiet male assistant district attorney who had replaced the irritating female D.A. of the preliminary hearing did not appear in court. He had developed acute appendicitis during the night, it was reported to the court, and had been operated on early that morning for a perforated appendix. He was resting comfortably at Mt. Zion Hospital, which Jessica found to be small consolation. This news was reported to the judge by one of the sick man's colleagues, who happened to be trying a case in the adjoining courtroom. But His Honor was assured that a replacement had been chosen and would arrive at any moment. Jessie's and Ian's hearts sank. The woman from the preliminary hearing would be back on the case. It had seemed immeasurable good luck when she hadn't appeared at the opening of the trial, and now . . .

Martin bent to whisper something in Ian's ear as the judge called a short recess while they waited for the new assistant D.A. to arrive. Everyone stood up, the judge left the courtroom, and there was a stretching and shuffling toward the halls. It was still early, and even a cup of coffee from one of the machines in the hall would taste good. It was something to do. Jessica could feel depression weighing on her shoulders as she held her small Styrofoam cup of steaming, malevolent-looking coffee. All she could think of was that damned D.A. and how badly her presence might hurt their case. She glanced at Ian, but he said nothing. And Martin had vanished somewhere.

He had told them not to discuss the case in the hall during recesses or lunch, and suddenly it was difficult to find banalities with which to break the silence. So they kept silent, standing close together with the look of refugees waiting for a train to arrive, but not really understanding what was happening to them.

"More coffee?"

"Hm?" Her thoughts had been in limbo.

"Coffee. Do you want more coffee?" Ian tried it again. But she only shook her head with a vague attempt at a smile. "Don't worry so much, Jess. It'll be okay."

"I know." Words. All words. With no meaning behind them. Nothing had any meaning anymore. Everything was confusing, impossible to understand. What were they doing there? Why were they standing around like awkward mourners at a funeral? Jessica crushed out a cigarette on the marble floor and looked up at the ceiling. It was ornate and beautiful and she hated it. It was too fancy. Too elaborate. It reminded her of where she was. City Hall. The trial. She lit another cigarette.

"You just put one out, Jess." His voice was soft and sad. He knew what was happening too.

"Huh?" She squinted at him through the flame from her lighter.

"Nothing. Shall we go back?"

"Sure. Why not?" She tried a flip smile as she tossed the empty Styrofoam cup into a large metal ashtray filled with sand.

They walked back into the courtroom side by side, but not touching. Ian walked slowly toward the desk that set him and Martin apart from everyone else. And Jessica followed him with her eyes, watching him, watching Martin rapidly scratch out notes on a long yellow legal pad. The perfect lawyer, the image caught in a pool of sunlight splashed bravely across the inlaid marble floor. She stared at the light for a minute, thinking of nothing, only wishing herself somewhere else, and then absentmindedly she looked across at the desk reserved for the assistant D.A.

There she sat. Matilda Howard-Spencer, tall, lean; everything about her seemed sharp. She had a narrow head with blunt-cut short blond hair, and long thin agile hands that seemed ready to point accusing fingers. She wore a sober gray suit and a pale gray silk shirt, and her eyes almost matched her suit. Slate gray, and just as hard. Long, skinny legs, and the only piece of jewelry she wore was a thin gold band. She was married to Judge Spencer, whose name she had incorporated into hers, and she was the holy terror of the D.A.'s office. Her best cases were rapes. Neither Ian nor Jessie knew any of that, but Martin did, and he had wanted to cry as he'd watched her walk into the courtroom. She had the delicacy and charm of a hatchet delivered bull's-eye to the balls. He had tried another case against her once, and he hadn't won. Nobody had. His client had committed suicide nine days into the trial. He probably would have anyway, but still . . . Matilda, darling Matilda. And all Ian and Jessie knew was what they saw and what they felt.

Ian saw a woman who made him nervous as she seemed to stalk within an invisible cage around her desk. Jessie saw a woman carved in ice, and sensed something that filled her with fear. Now it wasn't a game. It was a full-scale war. Just the way the woman looked at Ian told her that. She glared across at him once, and then through him several times, as though he were not a person to acknowledge, and considerably less than a man. She spoke to Houghton in a rapid flow of words, and he nodded several times, then got up and walked away. It was very clear who was in command. Jessica cursed the man with the appendix. This woman was one piece of luck they didn't need.

"All rise . . ." The judge was back in his seat, and tension filled the air. He showed obvious pleasure at the new addition to the scene, and acknowledged her presence with a respectful greeting. Terrific.

Matilda Howard-Spencer made a few quick, friendly remarks to the jury, all of which they seemed to respond to. She could inspire confidence as well as fear. Her voice and manner exuded authority, and belied her age: she must be no older than forty-two or -three. She was someone you could count on, someone who would take care of business, take care of you, see that things worked. This was a woman who could fight a war, lead an army, and still manage to see that the children took Latin as well as algebra. But she had no children. She had been married for less than two years. The law was her lover. Her husband was only her friend, and he was a man well into his sixties.

The sparring began with one of the least interesting of witnesses. The medical examiner took the stand and said nothing damaging to Ian, nothing helpful to Margaret Burton. He testified only that he had examined her, that there had been intercourse, but that nothing more than that could be ascertained. Despite Matilda Howard-Spencer's best urging, he stuck to his assertion that there was no evidence that force had been used. Martin's objections to her near-badgering were rapidly quelled, but the testimony was too colorless to make much difference. It all seemed very boring to Jessica, and after an hour she settled her attention on the middle red nylon stripe in the flag. It was something to stare at as she tried to float away from where she was . . . those words droning on endlessly . . . "infamous crime against nature" . . . sodomy . . . rape . . . intercourse . . . rectum . . . vagina . . . sperm . . . it was like a child's guide to fantasy. All those terrible words you looked up in the dictionary when you were fourteen, and were titillated by. Now she had a chance to try each one on for size. Vagina. The prosecutor seemed fond of that one. And rape. She said it with a capital letter "R."

The day ended at last, and they went home as silently as they had throughout the week. It was exhausting just being there,

281

keeping up the front for those watchers in the jury box, for anyone who might be paying attention. If you frowned, the jury might think you were mad — mad at Ian — or upset. Upset? No, darling, of course not! If you smiled, it meant you took the proceedings too lightly. If you wore the wrong thing, you looked rich. Something too cheerful, and you looked flip. Sexy in court? At a rape trial? God forbid. Vagina? Where? No, of course I don't have one. It wasn't even frightening anymore, just exhausting. And that damned woman was relentless, squeezing every last thought and word out of the witnesses. And Martin was such a fucking gentleman. But what did it matter anymore? If they could just stay awake and keep turning up in court, soon it would be over. Soon . . . but it seemed as though it had just begun. There were lifetimes to go. They hardly said a word over dinner that night, and Jessica was fast asleep in her bathrobe before Ian came out of the shower. It was just as well; he was too tired to say anything. And what was there to say?

She stretched sleepily in the car the next morning and smiled tiredly at the early morning light on the buildings.

"What are you smiling at, Jess?"

"A crazy thought I was just thinking that

this is like when we used to go to work together in New York." She looked thoughtful, but he didn't smile.

"Not exactly."

"No. Do we have time to stop for a quick cup of coffee on the way?" They hadn't had time for breakfast, and it was already late.

"We'd better just settle for coffee out of the machine up there, Jess. I don't want to be late. They can hold me in contempt for that, and pull my bail." Jesus. And all for a cup of coffee.

"Okay, love." She touched his shoulder gently and lit a fresh cigarette. The only place she didn't smoke now was in court.

She slipped her hand inside his arm as they walked up the steps of City Hall, and everything seemed bright and shiny and new. It was that kind of morning, no matter what horrors were happening to their life. It almost seemed as though God didn't know. He went right on with the sunlight and pretty days.

They reached the hall outside the courtroom with three minutes to spare, and Jessica hurried for the coffee machine.

"Want some?" He started to answer no, but then nodded yes. How much worse could his heartburn get, and what did it matter? He took the cup from her hand; it was so shaky she almost spilled the coffee.

"Baby, it's going to take a year to put us back together after this."

"Yon mean my adorable quivers?" He smiled back into her face.

"Have you seen mine?" He held out a hand and they both laughed.

"Occupational hazard, I guess."

"For a rapist?" She had tried to sound flip, but he didn't.

"Okay, Ian, knock it off." It ended the brief conversation between them, and Jessica noticed a flurry of activity near an unmarked door. There were people coming and going. Four men, a woman, the sound of voices, as though someone of importance were arriving.

The activity caught Jessie's attention, but it was Ian who looked strange, his head cocked to one side, listening intently. She wanted to ask him what was happening, but she wasn't sure she should. He seemed so totally absorbed by the sounds and the voices. Then there was the quick slam of a door, and a woman in a plain white wool dress rounded the corner. Jessica gasped. It was Margaret Burton.

Ian's mouth opened and then closed, but none of them moved. Jessica stood, transfixed, feeling shaken and cold, her eyes driving into Margaret Burton, who had come to a rapid halt, taken one short step backward, and then stopped with an expression of astonishment on her face as the three of them stood there. It seemed as though the entire building had fallen silent, and they were the only three people left in the world. Nothing moved . . . except Margaret Burton's face. Slowly, ever so slowly, like a wax mask melting in the sun, her face molded into an incredible smile. It was a rictus of victory, for only Ian to see. Jessica watched her, horrified, and then, as though her body moved of its own accord, she lurched wildly forward and swung at the Burton woman with the handbag held clenched in her hand.

"Why? Why, dammit, why?" It was a piercing wail of pain from Jessica's heart. The woman fell back a step, looking startled, as though waked from a dream, while at the same moment Ian leaped forward to grab Jessie. Something terrible could have happened. She had murder in her eyes. And that cry of "Why?" was echoed again and again through the halls as Margaret Burton fled, her heels tapping a haunting staccato in the marble corridor as Jessie sobbed in Ian's arms.

A fleet of men rapidly came running, then turned away as they saw only Ian and Jessie standing there. There was no brawl to dispel, nothing more than a husband and wife fighting, and the wife having herself a good cry. But Martin had heard the sounds too, and for some reason, as he had been about to enter the court, something had told him to follow the sounds. And then seeing Margaret Burton hurry into a door near the court, he knew that something had happened. He found Jessie trembling on a bench, with Ian trying to soothe her.

"Is she all right?"

Ian looked grim in response and didn't answer.

"What happened?"

"Nothing. She . . . we just . . . had an unexpected encounter with the illustrious Miss Burton."

"Did she do anything to Jessie?" Martin prayed that she had. It would be the best thing that had happened to their case.

"She smiled." Jessie stopped sobbing long enough to explain.

"She smiled?" Martin was puzzled.

"Yes. Like someone who has just killed someone else, and is glad."

"Now, Jess . . ." Ian tried to pacify her, but he knew she was right. That was exactly how Margaret Burton had looked, but they were the only ones who had seen it.

"You know damn well that's what she looked like." She tried to explain it to Martin, but he made no comment.

"Are you all right now?" She nodded slowly and took a deep breath.

"I'm okay."

"Good. Because we should get into court. We don't want to be late."

Jessica rose unsteadily, with both men watching her worriedly. She took another deep breath and closed her eyes. What a hideous morning.

"Jessie . . ."

"No. Now just let me alone, and I'll be fine." She had known what Ian was going to say. He wanted her to go home.

As they walked into court, she felt a few heads turn, and wondered who had heard her shrieks as the Burton woman had fled down the hall. It rapidly became clear who had. They were less than three feet into the courtroom before Inspector Houghton was standing belligerently in front of them, with an angry look on his face that was directed at Jessie.

"If you ever do that again, I'll have you arrested, and his bail pulled so fast both your heads will swim." Ian looked agonized and Jessica gaped as Martin stepped in front of them.

"Do what, exactly. Inspector?"

"Threaten Miss Burton."

"Jessica, did you threaten Miss Burton?" Martin looked at her as a father would, asking his five-year-old if she had poured Mommy's perfume down the toilet.

"No. I . . . I screamed . . ."

"What did you scream?"

"I don't know."

"She said 'Why?' That's all she said," Ian filled in for her.

"That doesn't sound like a threat to me, Inspector. Does it to you? As a matter of fact, I heard Mrs. Clarke shouting that word all the way down the hall, which was what drew me to the scene."

"I consider that a threat." *I consider you an asshole.* Jessie was dying to say it.

"Where I come from, Inspector, 'why' is a question, not a threat. Unless our asking that kind of question threatens you." And then, without another word, Houghton turned on his heel and returned to the chair next to Matilda Howard-Spencer. But he was looking none too pleased, and neither was Ian. Jessie could feel him shaking next to her.

"I'm going to kill that sonofabitch before this is over." But the look on Martin's face stopped both of them. It was terrifying.

"No, dammit, you're going to sit here and look like Mr. and Mrs. America if it kills *you*. And right now. Is that clear? Both of you? Jessica, that means you too. Smile, beautiful, smile. Bullshit. Better than that. And take her arm, Ian. Jesus, all we need is for the jury to think there's trouble. There isn't. Yet. Just remember that." And with that, he walked toward the desk at the front of the room with a look of solemnity but not of concern. He smiled in the direction of the prosecutor, and took in the room with a benevolent air. Jessie and Ian didn't do quite as well, though they tried. And they still had the Burton woman's testimony to live through. But remarkably, after that demonic smile, hearing her talk wasn't as bad as they had feared.

She told the now-familiar tale as she sat primly on the witness stand. The white dress looked terribly pure, overwhelmingly lady-like. She sat so demurely that her legs might have been soldered together just before she'd come into court, and Jessica noticed that her hair was now tinted more brown than red. If she was wearing makeup, you couldn't see it, and if she had a bosom, she had done remarkable things to make it disappear. She seemed to have no figure at all.

"Ms. Burton, would you care to tell us

what happened?" The assistant district attorney was wearing an extremely somber black dress, a perfect contrast to the witness's white one. It was like something out of a "B" movie.

The recitation that followed sounded very familiar indeed. At the end of her client's story, the prosecutor asked, "Had anything like this ever happened to you before?"

The witness hung her head and barely seemed able to whisper. "No." It was a gentle sound, like a leaf falling to earth, and Jessie felt her nails dig into her palms. It was the first time in her life she had ever hated anyone that much. And sitting there, watching her, having to listen to her, made her want to kill the woman.

"How did you feel after he left you there in that sleazy hotel?" Oh, Jesus.

"Like I wanted to kill myself. I thought about it for a while. That was why it took me so long to call the police." What a performance! It almost required a standing ovation and a chorus of bravos. But it was far from amusing. Jessie knew Margaret Burton was winning over the jury with her demure little airs.

What could Martin do now? If he tore her to shreds, the jury would hate him. Cross-examining her was going to be like roller skating through a mine field.

After more than an hour of testimony, Matilda Howard-Spencer had finished her questioning, and it was Martin's turn to begin. Jessica felt her stomach rise and then rapidly fall. She wanted to hold on to Ian. She couldn't stand it anymore. But she had to. And she wondered what he was feeling as he sat isolated from the world. The accused. The rapist. Jessica shuddered.

"Ms. Burton, why did you smile at Mr. Clarke this morning outside the court?" Martin's first question shocked everyone in the courtroom, even Jessie. The jury looked stunned, while Houghton smoldered and whispered something to the prosecutor.

"Smile? . . . I . . . why . . . I didn't . . . I didn't smile at him!" She was blushing and looked absolutely furious, nothing like the virgin of a moment before.

"Then what did you do?"

"I . . . nothing, dammit . . . I . . . I mean . . . oh, I don't know what I did . . ." Here came the virgin again, and helplessness to boot. "I was just so shocked to see him there, and his wife called me a name. She . . ."

"Did she? What did she call you?" Martin looked vastly amused, and Jessie wondered if he really was. It was hard to tell with him;

she was learning that more each day. "Go on, Miss Burton, don't be shy. Tell us what she called you. But do remember that you are under oath." He smiled at her and assumed an attitude of waiting.

"I don't remember what she called me."

"You don't? Well, if it was such a traumatic encounter, wouldn't you remember what she'd called you?"

"Objection, Your Honor!" Matilda Howard-Spencer was on her feet and looking annoyed. Very.

"Sustained."

"All right. But just one minor point . . . isn't it true that you leered at Mr. Clarke, almost as though . . ."

"*Objection!*" The D.A.'s voice could have shattered concrete, as Martin smiled angelically. He had gotten his point across.

"Sustained."

"Sorry, Your Honor." But it was a good beginning. And the rest of the story droned on after that. How she had been debased, abused, used, humiliated, violated. The words were getting to be almost laughable. "What exactly did you expect from Mr. Clarke?"

"What do you mean?" The witness looked haughty, but confused.

"Well, did you think he'd propose marriage in that hotel room, or whip an engagement ring out of his pocket, or . . . well, what did you expect?"

"I don't know. I . . . he . . . I thought he just wanted to have a drink. He was a little drunk anyway."

"Did you find him attractive?"

"Of course not."

"Then why did you want to have a drink with him?"

"Because . . . oh, I don't know. Because I thought he was a gentleman." She looked delighted with her response, as though that said it all.

"Aha. That was it, eh? A gentleman. Would a gentleman take you to a hotel on Market Street?"

"No."

"Did Mr. Clarke take you to a hotel on Market Street . . . or did you take him?" She flushed furiously, and then hid her face in her hands, muttering something no one could hear, until the judge admonished her to speak up.

"I didn't take him anywhere."

"But you went with him. Even though you did not find him attractive. Did you particularly want to have that drink with him?"

"No."

"Then what did you want to do?" Ouch.

293

The question almost made Jessie smile. Beautiful.

"I wanted . . . I wanted . . . to be friends."

"Friends?" Martin looked even more amused. She was making a fool of herself.

"Not, not friends. Oh, I don't know. I wanted to go back to work."

"Then why would you agree to go and have a drink with him?"

"I don't know."

"Were you horny?"

"Objection!"

"Rephrase your question, Mr. Schwartz."

"How long had it been since you'd had intercourse, Miss Burton?"

"Do I have to answer that, Your Honor?" She looked pleadingly at the judge, but he nodded assent.

"Yes. You do."

"I don't know."

"Give us an idea." Martin was insistent.

"I don't know." Her voice was shrinking.

"Roughly. A long time? Not so long? A month . . . two months . . . a week? A few days?"

"No."

"No? What do you mean by no?" Martin was beginning to look annoyed.

"I mean no, not a few days."

"Then how long? Answer the question."

294

"A while." The judge glared at her, and Martin started moving closer. "All right, a long time," she said finally. "Maybe a year."

"Maybe longer?"

"Maybe."

"Was it with anyone special the last time?"

"I . . . I don't remember . . . I . . . yes!" She almost shouted the last word.

"Someone who hurt you in some way, Miss Burton? Someone who didn't love you as much as he should have, someone who . . ." His voice was so soft it would have lulled a baby to sleep, and then the assistant district attorney jumped to her feet and broke the spell.

"Ojection!"

It took two more hours to finish Martin's questioning, and Jessica felt as though she were going to melt into a small invisible blur by the time it was over. She couldn't even begin to imagine what Margaret Burton felt like as she was led, crying, from the stand. She was assisted by Inspector Houghton while Matilda Howard-Spencer rearranged her papers. Jessica had the impression that the austere prosecutor was interested in the case, not the victim.

The judge called a recess and dismissed them until Monday. For a moment they all stood numbly in the courtroom; it was only lunchtime, but Jessie wanted to climb into bed and sleep for a year. She had never been so tired in her life. Spent. And Ian looked five years older than he had that morning.

When they emerged from the courtroom with Martin behind them, Margaret Burton was nowhere to be seen. She had been escorted out through the judge's chambers, and Martin guessed that she would be taken out some more discreet exit, to avoid another encounter like the one that morning. He had a feeling that Houghton didn't quite trust the woman either, and didn't want any more trouble than he already had.

As they walked out into the sunshine, Jessie felt as though she hadn't seen it for years. Friday. It was Friday. The end of an interminable week, and now two whole days to themselves. Two and a half days. And all she wanted was to go home and forget this rococo hellhole where their lives seemed to be coming to an end at the hands of a madwoman. It was like a Greek play, really . . . the jury could play the chorus.

"What are you thinking?" Ian was still worried about her after the morning's outburst. Now more than ever. The testimony had been grim.

"I don't know. I'm not sure I can think anymore. I was just drifting."

"Well, let's drift on home. Shall we?" He guided her quietly toward the car, and opened the door for her, and she felt two-hundred-years-old as she slid onto the seat of the Volvo. But it was familiar, it was home. She needed that right now more than anything. She wanted to scrub the whole morning out of her soul.

"What do you think, love?" She looked at him through a haze of cigarette smoke as he drove slowly home.

"What do you mean?" He tried to evade her question.

"I mean, how do you think it's going? Did Martin say anything?"

"Not much. He plays it pretty close to the vest."

She nodded again. He hadn't said much as they'd left except that he wanted to see them in his office on Saturday. "But I guess everything's going okay." Sure it was. It had to be.

"It looks okay to me too." Okay? Christ, it looked horrible. But it was supposed to. Wasn't it?

"I like Martin's style."

"So do I."

They both still thought they would win, but now they were beginning to realize the price they'd have to pay. Not in money, not in cars, but in flesh, guts, and souls.

CHAPTER 16

On Saturday morning, Ian went down to Martin's office to discuss his testimony on the stand the following week. Jessica stayed home with a migraine. As a favor, Martin came to see her at the house that evening, to discuss her own testimony.

And on Sunday afternoon, Astrid called, as the pair sat zombielike in chairs, watching old movies on television.

"Hello, children. How about a spaghetti dinner at my place tonight?" For once Jessie was short with her friend.

"I'm sorry, Astrid, we just can't."

"Oh, you two. Busy, busy, busy. I've tried to reach you all week, and you haven't been in the shop." Shit.

"I know. I had some work to do here, and I'm helping Ian . . . edit his book."

"That sounds like fun."

"Yeah. Sort of." But her voice didn't carry the lie well. "I'll give you a call sometime next week. But thanks for the invitation." They blew kisses and hung up, and Jessica marveled at the fact that no one knew what was happening. It seemed remarkable that the newspapers hadn't picked it up, but she had finally realized that what was happening to them was in no way extraordinary. There were a dozen cases like it every day. It was new to them, but not to the news business. And there were far juicier cases than theirs to pick from — except, of course, for the Pacific Heights angle, and Jessie's exclusive boutique. It would destroy her business if it came out. But there didn't seem to be any danger of that. No members of the press had appeared thus far, and there had been no interest shown at all. It was something to be grateful for. And she was. And Martin had promised that if some stray reporter did happen through, he'd call the paper and ask for their discretion. He felt sure that they'd cooperate with him. They had before.

Jessie felt bad about having cut Astrid short. They hadn't seen her in a while, and they hadn't seen their other friends in two months now. It would have been hard to face anyone. It was getting harder even to face Astrid. And it would have been impossible to confront the girls in the shop this week. Jessie had no intention of going near the place. She was afraid they'd read too much in her face. For the same reasons, Ian had been staying away from everyone he knew since the arrest. And he was content to lose himself in his book. The characters he'd invented kept him company.

And meanwhile, the bills continued to mount. Zina dropped off Jessie's mail every day during the trial, and most of it was bills, including Harvey Green's second bill, for another nine hundred dollars. And once again for nothing. It had been "in case" money — in case Margaret Burton had done something she shouldn't have, in case something had turned up, in case . . . but nothing had. He had managed to come up with absolutely nothing. Until Sunday night, right after Jessie talked to Astrid.

The phone rang, and it was Martin. He and Green wanted to come right over. She woke Ian, and they were waiting, tensely, when the two men arrived. They were dying to know what Green had found out.

What he had was a photograph. Of Margaret Burton's husband from the rapidly annulled marriage of almost twenty years before. The photograph could have been of Ian. The man in the picture was tall, blond, blue-eyed, with laughter in his face. He was

301

standing next to an MG; it was of a much earlier vintage than the Morgan, but there was still a great deal of resemblance between the cars as well as the men. If you squinted, even a little, it looked like Ian and the Morgan. The man's hair was shorter than Ian's, his face was a little longer, the car was black instead of red . . . the details were off, but not by much. It was a shock just looking at the photograph. It told the entire story. Now they knew the why. And Martin's first suspicion had been right. It must have been revenge.

The four of them sat in the living room in total silence. Green had gotten the photograph from a cousin of Miss Burton's, a last-minute lead he'd decided to follow, just on a hunch. A damn good hunch, as it had turned out.

Schwartz heaved a sigh of what sounded like relief and leaned back in his chair. "Well, now we know. The cousin will testify?" But Green shook his head.

"Says she'll take the Fifth, or lie. She doesn't want to get involved. She said that Burton would kill her. You know, this woman, the cousin I mean, almost sounds as though she's afraid of the Burton woman. Said she's the most vindictive person she's ever known. You gonna subpoena her?"

"Not if she's going to take the Fifth on us. Did she tell you why the Burton woman annulled the marriage?" Martin was pensively chewing on a pencil as he asked the questions, while Ian and Jessica listened silently. Ian still held the photograph in his hand, and it made him exceedingly nervous. The likeness was startling.

"Maggie Burton didn't annul the marriage. The husband did."

Martin raised his eyebrows quickly. "Oh?"

"The cousin thinks Margaret was pregnant — just a guess," Green went on. "She had just graduated from high school and was working in this guy's father's office, a law firm. Hillman and Knowles, no less." Ian looked up and Martin whistled. "She married Knowles's son. A kid named Jed Knowles. He was only in law school at the time, and was spending the summer working in his father's office. He's the kid in the picture." Green waved vaguely at the snapshot still resting in Ian's hand.

"Anyway, they got married in a big hurry, but very quietly, at the end of the summer. And the father made a real stink that nothing be made public, no announcement of the marriage, no nothing. The Burton girl's parents were both living in the Midwest, so she didn't have any family out here except

303

the cousin, who isn't even sure if they ever lived together. They just got married, and the next thing she remembers is that Margaret was in the hospital for a couple of weeks. She thinks she might have had a complicated abortion, miscarriage, something. Knowles had the marriage annulled right after that, and Margaret was out of a husband, out of a job, and maybe out of a baby. She had kind of a nervous breakdown, it sounds like, and spent three months in a Catholic retreat house. I went back to check out the retreat house, but it was torn down twelve years ago, and the sisters of that order are now located in Kansas, Montreal, Boston, and Dublin. Not very likely we'd find any records on it, and if we did they'd be privileged anyway."

"What about the Knowles boy? Did you check him out?"

"Yeah." Green didn't look pleased. "He married some debutante, with a big splash and a lot of noise, at Thanksgiving of that year. Parties, showers, announcements in all the papers. The clippings at the *Chronicle* said that they'd been engaged for over a year, which was obviously why Papa Knowles didn't want any publicity when sonny boy married the Burton girl."

"Did you talk to Knowles?"

Green nodded unhappily. "He and his bride crashed in a two-engine plane seventeen months later. The father died of a heart attack this summer, and his mother is traveling in Europe, no one seems to know where."

"Terrific." Martin scowled and started to gnaw on his pencil again. "Any brothers and sisters? Friends who might know what happened? Anyone?"

"It's a dead end, Martin. No brothers and sisters. And who'd remember now, among his friends? Jed Knowles has been dead for eighteen years. That's a hell of a long time."

"Yeah. A long time to carry a grudge. Shit. We have it all wrapped up, and we don't have a fucking goddam thing. Nothing."

"What do yon mean, nothing?" It was the first time Ian had spoken since seeing the photograph. He had been listening closely to the other men's exchange. "It sounds like we've got everything."

"Yes." Martin rubbed his eyes slowly with one hand and then opened them again. "And nothing we can use in court. It's all guesswork. That's all it is. What we have here is undoubtedly the truth, and the full psychological explanation of why Margaret Burton has accused you of rape. You look just like some rich man's son who got her pregnant, married her, probably made her have an abortion, and then ditched her and married his high society girlfriend a few weeks later. Miss Burton met the handsome prince and then he shat on her. Back to Cinderella again. And she's been out to get him for twenty years. Which is probably why she hasn't tried to hit you two for money. She doesn't want money. She wants revenge. She probably got a little money out of it the first time. Money is too easy for some people." Jessica rolled her eyes at the remark and Ian gestured to her to keep still.

"The point is, she'd rather see you go to prison than hit you for bucks. In her mind, you're just another Jed Knowles, and you're going to take it for him. You look like him to a frightening degree, your car looks like his, you probably even sound like him, for all we know. And she probably spotted you at Enrico's months ago. You're a regular. She may well have set you up from beginning to end. But the problem is, that we can't prove that in court." He turned back to Green. "You're sure the cousin won't testify willingly?"

"Positive." Green was curt and emphatic. Martin shook his head.

"Wonderful. And that, Ian, is why we can't prove a goddam thing in court. Because a hostile witness who takes the Fifth Amendment would ruin you faster than never having her on the stand at all. And besides, even if she took the stand, we couldn't prove any of this. All we could prove is that Burton married Knowles, and shortly thereafter Knowles had the marriage annulled. The rest is pure conjecture, hearsay, guesswork. That doesn't hold up in court, Ian, not without solid proof. The prosecution would have the whole theory thrown out of court in ten minutes. You and I now know what probably happened, but we could never prove that to the jury, not without someone to testify that she was pregnant when Knowles married her, that she did have an abortion, that she did have a nervous breakdown, that someone heard her swear to take revenge. And how're you going to prove all that, even if the cousin did take the stand? What we have here, I'm afraid, is the truth, and no way to prove it."

Jessica felt tears burning her eyes as she listened, and Ian was paler than she'd ever seen him. He looked almost gray.

"So what do we do now?"

"We give it a try, and we pray. I'll call Burton for redirect and see how much she'll admit to. And how much they'll let us get away with. But it won't be much, Ian. Don't count on anything."

Green left a few moments later with a quiet handshake in the hall for Martin, and a shake of the head: "I'm sorry." Martin nodded, and left a few moments later.

The trial continued on Monday, and Martin recalled Margaret Burton to the stand. Had she been married to Jed Knowles? Yes. For how long? Two and a half months. Ten weeks? Yes. Ten weeks. Was it true that she had to marry him because she was pregnant? Absolutely not. Did she have a nervous breakdown . . . objection! . . . overruled! . . . did she have a nervous breakdown after the marriage was annulled? No. Never. Didn't the defendant bear a striking resemblance to Mr. Knowles? No. Not that she had noticed. Had Mr. Knowles remarried almost immediately after . . . objection! Sustained, with an admonition to the jury to disregard the previous line of questioning. The judge warned Martin about asking irrelevant questions and badgering the witness, and Jessica noticed that Margaret Burton was silent and pale but totally poised. Almost too much so. She found herself praying that the woman would lose control, would disintegrate on the stand and scream and shriek and destroy herself by admitting that she had wanted to destroy Ian because he looked like Jed Knowles. But Margaret Burton did none of those things. She was excused from the stand. And Jessica never saw her again.

Late that afternoon Martin asked Ian to drum up two friends to attest to his character and morals. Like Jessie's testimony it was going to be considered biased, but character witnesses never hurt, Ian agreed to ask a couple of people, but there was a look of despair in his eyes that it killed Jessica to watch. As though Margaret Burton had already won. She had simply slipped away. Dropped her bomb and left, leaving them with a photograph as explanation.

Ian hated having to explain to anyone what was happening, and in recent years he had not been as close to his friends as he once had. His writing seemed to devour more and more of his time, his energy, his devotion. He wanted to finish another book, to sell it, to "make it," before he went back to hanging around bars with old buddies; he needed to do something, be something, build something first. He was tired of explaining about rejections, and agents, and rewrites. So he stopped explaining. He stopped seeing them. And the rest of the time he spent with Jessie. She had a way of making herself an exclusive. She didn't like sharing the time he could spare from the studio.

That night, he called a writer he knew and a classmate from college, a stockbroker who had also moved to the West. They were stunned about the charges, sympathetic, and anxious to help. Neither of them was overly fond of Jessie, but they felt bad for both of them. The writer felt that Jessie wanted too much of Ian, that she was too clinging and didn't leave him enough space to write in. The college friend had always thought Jessie too headstrong. She wasn't their kind of woman.

But the two men made pleasant, clean-cut appearances on the stand. The writer, wearing tweeds, testified that he had recently won an award and published three stories in *The New Yorker* and a hardcover novel. He was respectable, as writers went. And he spoke well on the stand. The college friend made an equally pleasing impression in a different vein. Solid, upper-middle-class, respectable family man, "known Ian for years," hip hip, tut tut, rah rah. They both did what they could, which wasn't much.

On Tuesday afternoon the judge dismissed them all early, and Ian and Jessie came home to relax.

"How are you holding up, babe? I can't say either of us looks like much lately." He smiled ruefully and opened the icebox. "Want a beer?"

"Make it a case." She kicked off her shoes and stretched. "Jesus, I'm sick of that shit. It just goes on and on and on and . . . and I feel like I haven't sat down and talked to you for a year." She took the beer from him and went to lie down on the couch. "Besides which, I'm running out of polite clothes to wear." She was wearing an ugly brown tweed suit that she had had since her college days in the East.

"Fuck it. Go in wearing a bikini tomorrow. By now the jury deserves something to look at."

"You know, I thought the trial would be a lot more dramatic. It's funny that it isn't."

"The case isn't all that dramatic. Her word against mine as to who screwed whom and why, where, and for what. By now, I don't even feel uncomfortable with you there, listening to the testimony." Now that Margaret Burton was no longer in court.

"It doesn't bother me much either, except I want to laugh every time someone says 'an infamous crime against nature.' It seems so overdone." They laughed easily for the first time in a long time. As they relaxed in the familiar charm of their living room, the trial seemed like a bad joke. Somebody else's bad joke.

"Want to go to a movie, Jessie?"

"You know something? I'd love to." The tension was beginning to drain away. They had decided that they had it made, even without solid proof that Margaret Burton was a freak looking for revenge on a man who had been dead for almost twenty years. So what? Ian was innocent. In the end, it was as simple as that. "Want to take Astrid with us, darling?"

"Sure. Why not?" He smiled and leaned over to kiss her. "But don't call her for another half hour." Jessie returned the smile and ran a finger slowly up his arm.

Astrid was delighted with the invitation and the three went to a movie that had them in tears, they all laughed so hard. It was just what Jessie and Ian needed.

"I was beginning to think I'd never see you two again. It's been weeks! What have you been up to? Still working on the book?" They nodded in unison, changed the sub-ject, and went out for coffee.

It was a pleasant evening that did them all good. And Astrid felt better now that she had seen them. Ian looked haggard and Jessica looked tired, but they looked happy again. Maybe whatever problem had been bothering them had been worked out.

Astrid reported having been in the boutique almost every day, and the fashion show had been a smash. Katsuko had done a great job. Astrid had even bought four or five things from the show, which Jessie told her was silly.

"That's ridiculous. Don't buy anymore when I'm not there. I'll give you a discount when I'm in. Wholesale at least. And on some things I can sell to you at cost."

"That's crazy, Jessica. Why should you sell things any cheaper to me? You might as well share the wealth!" She threw her arms wide in a flash of jewelry and the three of them laughed.

They drove her home in the Volvo, and when she asked about the Morgan, Jessica claimed that the engine had needed too much work. They all agreed that it was a shame.

"What a fabulous evening!" Jessica slid into bed with a smile, and Ian yawned, nodding happily. "I'm glad we went out."

"So am I."

She rubbed his back for him and they chatted about nothing in particular; it was the kind of talk they had always shared late at night. Casual mentions of the movie, thoughts about Astrid, Jessie noticed a small bruise on his leg and asked him how he'd gotten it, he told her never to cut her hair. Night talk. As though nothing untoward had ever happened to them. For once they even got some sleep, which was remarkable since Ian was to take the stand the next day.

CHAPTER 17

Ian's testimony under direct examination lasted two hours. The jury looked a little more interested than they had in the previous days, but not much. And it was only during the last half hour that they actually seemed to wake up. It was Matilda Howard-Spencer's turn to question him. She seemed to pace in front of Ian, as though thinking of something else, while all eyes in the courtroom stayed on her, particularly Ian's. And at last she stopped, directly in front of him, crossed her arms, and tilted her head to one side.

"You're from the East?" The question surprised him, as did the friendly look on her face.

"Yes. New York."

"Where did you go to college?"

"Yale."

"Good school." She smiled at him, and he returned the smile. "I tried to get into their law school, but I'm afraid I didn't quite make it." She had gone to Stanford instead, but Ian couldn't know that, and was suddenly baffled as to whether he was supposed to offer sympathy, silence, or a smile. "Did you do any graduate work?" She didn't call him Ian, and she didn't call him Mr. Clarke. She talked to him as though she knew him, or honestly wanted to. An interested dinner partner at a pleasant soirée.

"Yes. I got my master's."

"Where did you do that?" She tilted her head again with an expression of interest. This was not at all the line of questioning Martin had prepared him for. This was lots easier to deal with.

"I went to Columbia. School of journalism."

"And then?"

"I went into advertising."

"With whom?" He named a big firm in New York. "Well, we certainly all know who they are." She smiled at him again, and looked pensively out the window.

"Did you go out with anybody special in college?" Aha, here it came, but she still sounded gently inquiring.

"A few people."

"Like who?"

"Just girls."

316

"From neighboring schools? Who? How about some names?" This was ridiculous. Ian couldn't see the reason for it.

"Viveca Harreford. Maddie Whelan. Fifi Estabrook." She wouldn't know them. Why ask?

"Estabrook? As in Estabrook and Lloyd? They're the biggest stockbrokers on Wall Street, aren't they?" She actually looked pleased for him, as though he had done something wonderful.

"I wouldn't know." Her remark had made him uncomfortable. Of course they were the Estabrooks of Estabrook and Lloyd, but that wasn't why he'd gone out with Fifi, for Chrissake.

"And it seems to me that Maddie Whelan has kind of a familiar ring too. Something tells me she was somebody important. Let's see, Whelan . . . oh, I know, the department store in Phoenix, isn't it?" Ian was actually blushing, but Matilda Howard-Spencer was still smiling angelically, seeming to enjoy the social pleasantries.

"I can't remember."

"Sure you can. Anyone else?"

"Not that I can recall." This was a ridiculous line of questioning, and he couldn't see where she was going, except making him

317

look like a fool. Was it really as simple as that?

"All right. When did you first meet your wife?"

"About eight years ago. In New York."

"And she has a lot of money, doesn't she?" The prosecutor's tone was almost embarrassed, as if she'd asked an indiscreet question.

"Objection!" Martin was livid; he knew exactly where she was going, whether Ian did or not. But Ian was beginning to; he had been led right into her trap.

"Sustained. Rephrase the question."

"Sorry, Your Honor. All right, then, I understand that your wife has a wonderfully successful boutique here in San Francisco. Did she have one in New York too?"

"No. When I met her, she was the fashion coordinator and stylist at the ad agency where I worked."

"She did that for fun?" Now there was an edge to her tone.

"No. For money." Ian was getting annoyed.

"But she didn't have to work, did she?"

"I never asked."

"And she doesn't have to work now, does she?"

"I don't . . ." He looked to Martin for

318

help, but there was none forthcoming.

"Answer the question. Does she have to work now, or is her income sufficient to support her, and you, in a very luxurious style?"

"Not luxurious, no." Christ. Jessie and Martin cringed simultaneously. What an answer. But the questions were coming at him like gumballs from a machine, and there was no time to dodge them.

"But her income is adequate to support you both?"

"Yes." He was very pale now. And very angry.

"Do you work?"

"Yes." But he said it too softly, and she smiled.

"I'm sorry, I didn't hear your answer. Do you work?"

"Yes!"

"At a job?"

"No. At home. But it's work. I'm a writer." Poor, poor Ian. Jessie wanted to run up and hold him. Why did he have to go through all that? The bitch.

"Do you sell much of what you write?"

"Enough."

"Enough for what? Enough to support yourself on?"

"Not at the moment." There was no hiding from her.

"Does that make you angry?" The question was almost a caress. The woman was a viper.

"No, it doesn't make me angry. It's just one of the facts of life, for the moment. Jessica understands."

"But you do cheat on her. Does she understand that?"

"Objection!"

"Overruled!"

"Does she understand that?"

"I don't cheat on her."

"Come, come. You yourself claim that you willingly went to bed with Ms. Burton. Is that a normal occurrence in your life?"

"No."

"This was the first time?"

His eyes were glued to his knees. "I can't remember."

"You're under oath; answer the question." Her voice slithered like a cobra threatening to strike.

"No."

"What?"

"No. This was not the first time."

"Do you cheat on your wife often?"

"No."

"How often?"

"I don't know."

"And what kind of women do you use —

your own kind, or other kinds, 'lesser' women, lower-class women, whores, poor girls, whatever?"

"Objection!"

"Overruled!"

"I don't 'use' anyone."

"I see. Would you cheat on your wife with Fifi Estabrook, or is she a nice girl?"

"I haven't seen her in years. Ten, eleven years. I wasn't married when I went out with her."

"I mean, would you cheat on your wife with someone *like* her, or do you just sleep with 'cheap' women, women you aren't liable to run across in your own social circle? It could be embarrassing, after all. It might be a lot simpler just to keep your playing as far from home as possible."

"I do." Oh, God. No, Ian . . . no . . . Martin was staring at the wall, trying to let nothing show on his face, and Jessie had sensed that disaster was near.

"I see. You do sleep with 'cheap' women, to keep it as far as possible from home? Did you consider Ms. Burton a 'cheap' woman?"

"No." But he had, and his "no" was a weak one.

"She wasn't of your social set, though, was she?"

"I don't know."

"Was she?" The words closed in on him now.

"No."

"Did you think she'd call the police?"

"No." And then as an afterthought, he looked up, panic-stricken, and added "She had no reason to." But it was too late. The damage was done.

She excused Ian from the stand with the proviso that she might want to recall him later. But she had all but killed him as it was.

Ian left the stand quietly and sat down heavily next to Martin. And five minutes later, the judge called a recess for lunch.

They left the courtroom slowly, with Ian shaking his head and looking somber until the threesome reached the street.

"I really blew it." Jessie had never seen him look worse.

"You couldn't help it. That's how she works. The woman is lethal." Martin heaved a sigh and gave them a small, wintry smile. "But the jury sees that too. And the jury's not all that lily pure either." There was no point making Ian feel even worse, but Martin was worried. The cheating didn't bother him nearly as much as the class conflict. "I'm going to put Jessica on the stand this afternoon. At least this way, it'll be over with."

"Yeah, she can massacre us both on the same day." Ian looked tired and beaten, and Jessica looked tense.

"Don't be an ass."

"You consider yourself a match for her?" Ian looked sarcastic and bitter.

"Why not?"

"I'll tell you why not. Because if you pit yourself against her, Ian'll lose," Martin was quick to interject. "You have to be the gentlest, sweetest, calmest wife in the world. You come on like a hellion, and she'll break you in two right on the stand. We went over everything this weekend. You know what you have to do." Jessica nodded somberly, and Ian sighed. Martin had gone over everything with him too, but that damn woman hadn't asked any of the right questions. And God only knew what she'd ask Jessie. "All right?"

"All right." Jessica smiled softly, and they dropped Martin off near City Hall. He had to go back to his office, and they had decided to go home to unwind. Jessica wanted a little time to take care of Ian. He needed it after the morning, and it kept her mind off what she'd have to say that afternoon.

When they got home, she made him lie

down on the couch, took off his shoes, loosened his tie, and ran a soft hand through his hair. He lay there for a few minutes, just looking at her.

"Jess . . ." He didn't even know how to say it, but she knew.

"None of that. Just lie there and relax. I'll go make some lunch." For once he didn't argue; he was too tired to do anything more than just lie there.

When she came back with a covered bowl of steaming soup and a plate piled high with sandwiches, he was asleep. He had the exhausted look of tragedy. The pale rumpled look one got when someone has died, when a child is terribly ill, when one's business had failed. Those times when schedules were disrupted, and one was suddenly at home, in seldom-worn clothes, looking terribly tired and afraid. She stood looking down at him for a moment and felt a wave of pity for him rush up inside her. Why did she feel so protective of him? Why did she feel as though he couldn't cope with it all, but she could? Why wasn't she angry? Why didn't she look like that now? She had when he was in jail, but he was here now, she could touch him and hold him and take care of him. The rest wasn't real. It was awful, but it wouldn't last. It would hurt, and it would rock him and humiliate him and do all sorts of grim things, but it wouldn't kill him. And it wouldn't take him away. As she sat quietly next to him and lifted his hand onto her lap, she knew that nothing would ever take him away from her. No Margaret Burton, no district attorney, no court, not even a jail. Margaret Burton would fade, Matilda Howard-Spencer would go on to some other case, as would Martin and the judge, and it would all be over. It was just a question of keeping themselves afloat until the storm passed. And she needed Ian too desperately to let anything, even her own feelings, jeopardize what they had. She wouldn't let herself get angry. She couldn't afford to.

There was the briefest flash of bitterness as she looked out over the bay and thought of her father. He wouldn't have done something like this, and he wouldn't have let her mother go through it, either. He'd have protected his wife more than Ian was protecting her. But that was her father. And this was Ian. Comparisons served no purpose now. She had Ian. It was as simple as that. She demanded a lot of him, so she had to give a lot too. She was willing. And right now it was her turn to give.

Looking down at him, as he slept there on

her gray skirt, he looked like a very tired little boy. She smoothed his hair off his forehead and took a deep breath, thinking of that afternoon. It was her turn now. And she wasn't going to lose. She had decided that after the disastrous morning. The case was going to be won. And that was that. It was insane that it had gone this far. But it was not going much further. Jessie had had enough.

Ian woke shortly before two and looked up in surprise.

"Did I fall asleep?"

"No. I hit you on the head with my shoe and you fainted."

He smiled at her and yawned into her skirt. "You smell delicious. Did you know that every single item of clothing you own smells of your perfume?"

"Want some soup?" She was smiling at the compliment. He'd gotten them into one hell of a mess, but one thing was certain, and that was how much she loved him. Not just needed him, loved him. How could she be angry? How dare she ask for his left arm when fate had already taken his right? They had suffered enough. Now it was time to finish it.

"Christ, you look determined. What've you been up to?"

"I haven't been up to a thing. Do you want soup?" She eyed him alluringly as she held a Limoges cup in one hand and her mother's best soup ladle in the other.

"My, so fancy." He sat up and kissed her and looked at the tray. "You know something, Jessica, you're the most remarkable woman I know. And the best." She wanted to tease him and ask if she was better than Fifi Estabrook, but she didn't dare. She suspected that the wounds of the morning were still raw.

"For you, milord, nothing but the best." She carefully poured the asparagus soup into the cup and added two neat little roast-beef sandwiches to the plate. There was a fresh salad too.

"You're the only woman I know who can make a sandwich lunch look like a dinner party."

"I just love you." She put her arms around his neck and nibbled his ear, and then stretched and stood up.

"Aren't you going to eat?"

"I already did." She was lying, but she couldn't have eaten a thing before going on the stand in less than an hour. She looked at her watch and headed for the bedroom. "I'll straighten out my face. We have to leave in ten minutes." He waved happily from the midst of his lunch and she disappeared into the bedroom.

"Ready?" He walked into the bedroom five minutes later, tightening his tie and glancing at his ruffled hair in the mirror. "Good lord, I look like I've been sleeping all day."

"As a matter of fact, darling, you do." And she was pleased. The brief hour of sleep had done him good. The time they'd spent at home had done them both good. Jessie felt stronger than she had in weeks. Margaret Burton wasn't going to touch them. How could she? Jessie had decided to ignore her, to rob her of her powers. And it was as though Ian sensed the rebirth in his wife.

"You know something? I feel better. I was really beat after this morning." And he hated to think of what Jessie would have to go through that afternoon, but she seemed ready for it. "You changed?"

"I thought this looked more appropriate." It was a wonderfully ladylike dress, the kind she might wear to a tea. It was a soft gray silk with full feminine sleeves, and a belt of the same fabric. The whole line of the dress was gentle and easy, and without being fancy, it screamed "class." "As long as they're going to bill us as being so upper-class, we might as well look decent. I'm so sick of those fucking tweed skirts, I'm going to burn them all on the front steps the day this is over."

"You look gorgeous."

"Too dressed up?"

"Perfect."

"Good." She slipped on quiet black kid pumps, clipped pearl earrings on her ears, picked up her bag, and headed for the closet to get out her black coat. Ian truly did think she looked gorgeous. He was so damn proud of her. Not just of how she looked, but of how she was taking this.

Martin was not quite as pleased, though, when they walked into the courtroom. He noticed Jessica's black coat and the glimpse of gray silk. It was just what he didn't want. Everything about her looked expensive. It was as though she had set out to prove everything Matilda Howard-Spencer had suggested. Jesus. Where were their heads? Crazy kids, they didn't realize what was happening. They had an unnerving assurance about them as they took their seats, as though they had arranged everything and there was nothing more to worry about. It was a bad time for them to make a show of strength, however subtle. And yet, maybe it was just as well that they felt a little more confident. They had both looked so beaten after the morning.

This new look of confidence underlined the bond between them. One was always aware of that, of them as a pair, not just Ian or Jessie, but both. It was frightening to think what would happen to them both if someone tried to sever that bond. If they lost.

Jessica looked remarkably calm as she walked up to the witness stand. The gray dress moved gracefully with her, the full sleeves gentling her impressive stature. She took the oath and looked at Ian for one tiny instant before turning her attention to Martin.

His questions built up a picture of a devoted couple and of a wife who respected her husband too much to doubt that he was telling the truth. He was pleased with Jessica's quiet, dignified manner, and when he relinquished his witness to the prosecutor, he had to repress a smile. He would have liked to see these two women roll up their sleeves and stalk each other around the room. They were evenly matched. At least he hoped so.

With Jessica, Matilda Howard-Spencer was not going to waste time. "Tell us, Mrs. Clarke, were you aware that your husband had cheated on you before this?"

"Indirectly."

"What do you mean by that?" The attorney looked puzzled.

"I mean that I assumed that was a possibility, but that it was nothing serious."

"I see. Just a little lighthearted fun?" She was back on that track again, but Jessie had seen it coming.

"No. Nothing like that. Ian isn't flip about anything. He's a sensitive man. But I travel quite a bit. And what happens, happens."

"Does it happen to you as well?" Now the attorney's eyes were glittering again. Gotcha!

"No, it does not."

"You're under oath, Mrs. Clarke."

"I'm aware of that. The answer is no."

She looked surprised. "But you don't mind if your husband fools around?"

"Not necessarily. It depends on the circumstances." Jessica looked every inch a lady, and Ian was incredibly proud of her.

"And these particular circumstances, Mrs. Clarke, how do you feel about them?"

"Confident."

"Confident?" Jessica's interrogator looked taken aback, and Martin fidgeted. "How can you be confident, and what about?"

"I'm confident that the truth about this matter will come out, and that my husband will be acquitted." Martin watched the jury. They liked her. But they had to like Ian too. And more than that, they had to believe him.

"I admire your optimism. Are you footing the bill for the expense of this?"

"No, not really." Ian almost cringed. She was lying under oath. "My husband made a very wise investment after he sold his last book. He put the investment in my care, and we decided to sell it to cover the expense of the trial. So I can't say I'm footing the bill." Bravo! The Morgan! And she was telling the truth! He wanted to jump up and hug her.

"Would you say that you have a good marriage?"

"Yes."

"Very good?"

"Extremely good." Jessica smiled.

"But your husband does sleep with other women?"

"Presumably."

"Did he tell you about Margaret Burton?"

"No."

"Did he tell you about any of his women?"

"No. And I don't think there were very many."

"Did you encourage him to sleep around?"

"No."

"But as long as they were little nobodies, you didn't care, is that it?"

"Objection!"

"Sustained. Leading the witness."

"Sorry, Your Honor." She turned back to Jessica. "Has your husband ever been violent with you?"

"No."

"Never?"

"No."

"Does he drink a great deal?"

"No."

"Does he have problems about his manhood, because you pay the bills?" What a question!

"No."

"Do you love him very much?"

"Yes."

"Do you protect him?"

"What do you mean?"

"I mean, do you shield him from unpleasantness?"

"Of course, I'd do anything I had to to shield him from unpleasantness. I'm his wife."

Matilda Howard-Spencer's face settled into a satisfied smile. "Including lie in court to protect him?"

"No!"

"The witness is excused."

The assistant district attorney turned on her heel and went back to her seat as Jessica sat gaping on the witness stand. That damned woman had done it again.

CHAPTER 18

Everyone was back in their seats the next morning for the two attorneys' summations to the jury. Ian and Jessica were pleased by Martin's comments and his style in addressing the jury, and they felt that he created a real wave of sympathy for the defense. Everything was in control. Then Matilda Howard-Spencer stood up, and the assistant district attorney was demonic. She painted a portrait of a wronged, distraught, heartbroken, brutally abused woman — hardworking, clean-living Maggie Burton. She also made a strong case that men like Ian Clarke shouldn't be allowed to dally where they wished, use whom they wanted, rape whom they chose, only to toss the women away and go home to the wives who supported them, who would do "anything to protect them," as Jessie herself had said. Martin objected and was sustained. He explained later that it was rare to have to object to a closing argument, but that this woman breathed fire at the mere mention of Ian's name. And Jessie was still steaming when the court adjourned for lunch.

"Did you hear what that bitch said?" Her voice was loud and strident and Martin and Ian quelled her rapidly with a look.

"Keep your voice down, Jess," Ian pleaded. It wouldn't pay to antagonize anyone now, least of all the jury, who were filtering past them on their way out to lunch. He had seen two of them look at Jess as she'd started to talk.

"I don't give a damn. That woman . . ."

"Shut up." And then he put an arm around her and gave her a squeeze. "Bigmouth. But I love you anyway." She sighed loudly and then smiled.

"Damn, that aggravated me."

"Okay, me too. Now let's forget about this crap for a while, and go get some lunch. Deal? No talk about the case?"

"Okay." But she said it grudgingly as they walked down the hall.

"No 'okay,' I want a solemn promise. I refuse to have my lunch wrecked by this. Just make believe we're on the jury and can't discuss it."

"You really think they stick to that?" He shrugged indifferently and pulled a lock of his wife's hair.

"I don't care what they do. Just tell me if I have that promise from you. No talking about the case. Right?"

"Right. I promise. You nag, you."

"That's me. Your basic nagging husband." He seemed very nervous as they ran down the stairs to the street, yet in surprisingly good spirits.

They went home for lunch and Jessie glanced at the mail while Ian riffled through *Publishers Weekly* and then went on to read the paper over the sandwiches she had made.

"You're terrific company today." She was munching a turkey sandwich and flicked at the center of his paper with a grin.

"Huh?"

"I said your fly is open."

"What?" He looked down and then made a face. "Oh, for Chrissake."

"Well, talk to me, dammit, I'm lonely."

"I read the paper for five minutes and you get lonely?"

"Yup. Want some wine with lunch?"

"No, I'll pass. Do we have any Cokes?"

"I'll go check." She went to look, and he was reading the paper again when she came back with the cold can of Coca-Cola. "Now listen, you . . ."

"Shh . . ." He waved at her impatiently and went on reading. There was something about his face, about the look in his eyes as he read. He looked shocked.

"What is it?" He ignored her, finished the article, and finally looked up with an expression of defeat.

"Read that." He pointed to the first four columns on page two, and Jessie's heart turned over as she read the headline: RAPE — IT'S TIME TO GET TOUGH. The article reported on a criminal justice committee meeting held the day before to discuss current punishment of rapists. There was talk in the article of stiffer sentences, no probation, suggestions for making it easier and less humiliating to report rape. It made anyone accused of rape sound as though he should be hanged without further ado. Jessie put down the paper and stared at Ian. It was bad luck to have that in the paper on the day the jury would be going out to deliberate.

"Do you think it'll have any effect, Ian? The judge told them not to be influenced by . . ."

"Oh, bullshit, Jessica. If I say something to you and someone else tells you to unhear it, will you have heard it or not? Will you remember it or not? They're only human, for Chrissake. Of course they're influenced by what they hear. So are you, so am I, so's the judge." He ran a hand through his hair and pushed his lunch away. Jessica folded the paper and threw it onto the counter.

"Okay, so maybe they read the paper today, maybe not. But there isn't a damn thing we can do about it. So why not just let it pass, darling? Just forget about it. Can we try to do that? You're the one who made me promise not to discuss the case, remember?" She smiled gently at him. His eyes looked like sapphires, dark and bright and troubled.

"Yes, but Jessie . . . for God's . . . all right. You're right. I'm sorry." But it was a tense meal after that, and neither of them finished their sandwiches.

They were silent on the drive down to City Hall, and Jessica heard her heels echo on the marble floors as they walked in. Her heart seemed to be pounding with equal force and in tune to the echo, like a death knell.

The judge addressed the jury for less than half an hour, and they filed out silently to be locked into a room across the hall while a bailiff stood guard outside.

"Now what, gentlemen?" Martin and Ian had joined Jessie at her seat.

"Now we wait. The judge will call a recess if they haven't come to a decision by five. Then they'll come back in the morning."

"And that's it?" Jessie looked surprised.

"Yes, that's it." How strange. It was all over. Almost. All that droning and boredom mixed with tension and sudden drama. And then it's over. The two teams have done their debating, the judge makes a little speech to the jury, they go lock themselves in a room, talk to each other, pick a verdict, everyone goes home, and the trial is over. It was weird somehow. Like a game. Or a dance. All terribly organized and ritualistic. A tribal rite. The thought made her want to laugh, but Ian and Martin were looking so serious. She smiled up at her husband, and their attorney looked at her with worried eyes. She really didn't understand. And he wasn't sure Ian did either. Maybe it was just as well.

"What do you think, Martin?" Ian turned to him with the question, but Martin had the feeling that he was asking more for Jessie's benefit than his own.

"I don't know. Did you see this morning's paper?" Ian's face sobered further.

"Yes. At lunch. That doesn't help, does it?"

The lawyer shook his head.

"Well, at least we put on a good show."

"It would have been a better show if Green could have come up with something solid about Burton and Jed Knowles. I just know that that was the crux of this." Martin shook his head angrily, and Ian patted his shoulder.

"Will she be coming back for the verdict?" Jessie was curious.

"No. She won't be back in court."

"Bitch." It was a small, low word, from the pit of her gut.

"Jessie!" Ian was quick to silence her, but she wouldn't be silenced.

"Well? She fucks up our life, blasts us practically into bankruptcy, not to mention what she's done to our nerves, and then she just walks off into the sunset. What do you expect me to feel toward her? Gratitude?"

"No, but there's no point . . ."

"Why not?" Jessie was getting loud again, and Ian knew how nervous she was. "Martin, can't we sue her after we win the case?"

"Yes, I suppose so, but what would you get out of it? She doesn't have anything."

"Then we'll sue the state." She hadn't thought of that before.

"Look, why don't you two go for a walk down the hall?" He gave Ian a pointed look and Ian nodded. "It may be a while before

341

the jury comes in, probably will be. Just stay close; don't leave the building." Jessie nodded and stood up, reaching for Ian's hand. Martin left them and went back to the desk. It was terrifying the way Jessica would not accept the possibility that they might lose.

"I wish we could go for a drink." She walked slowly into the hall and leaned against the wall while Ian lit their cigarettes. Her legs were shaking and she wondered how long she could keep up the front of Madam Cool. She wanted to sink to the floor and clutch Ian's knees in desperation. It had to go all right. Had to . . . had to . . . she wanted to pound on the door to the jury room . . . to . . .

"It'll all be over soon, Jess. Just hang in there."

"Yeah." She smiled a half-smile and linked her arm in his as they started to walk down the corridor.

They were silent for a long time, and Jessie let her mind travel as it chose, wandering and darting, floating between thoughts as she smoked, and walked, and held on to Ian. It took almost an hour, but her brain finally stopped whirling, probably from exhaustion. She felt lonely and tired and sad, but she no longer felt as if she were going at the wrong speed. It was something, anyway.

She decided to call the boutique, just to see how things were going. It was an odd time to call, but she suddenly wanted to touch base with something familiar, to know that the world hadn't simply shrunk to one endless corridor in which she and Ian were condemned to walk their lives away in terrified silence. She missed the bustle of the boutique. The trivia. The faces.

The girls told her what was happening and she felt better. It was like going to the movies with Astrid. Normalcy. It diminished the proportions of what was happening to them to something she could bear for a while longer.

By four o'clock Ian had relaxed too, and they were playing word games. At four-thirty they started trading old jokes.

"What's gray and has four legs and a trunk?"

"An elephant?" She was already giggling.

"No, dummy, a mouse going on vacation." Ian grinned, pleased with his joke. They were like second-graders sent out to the hall.

"Okay, smartass. How can you tell if your pants have fallen down?" She came back at him quickly and he started to laugh, but then they saw Martin beckon them urgently from the end of the hall. The jokes were suddenly over. Ian stood up first and looked into Jessica's face. She felt pale as terror swept over her. Pale and hollow, as though her frame might break. It was happening now. No more games to make believe it would never happen . . . it was here. Oh God . . . no!

"Jessie, no panicking!" He could see the look on her face, and took her swiftly into his arms and held her as tightly as he could. "I love you. That's all. I love you. Just know that, and that nothing will ever change that, and that you're fine, you're always fine. Got that?" She nodded, but her chin was trembling as he looked at her. "You're fine. And 1 love you."

"You're fine, and you love you . . . I mean me . . ." She laughed a watery laugh and he held her tight again.

"You're fine, silly. Not I'm fine."

"You're not fine?" She was better now. She always was when he held her.

"Oh Jessie . . . I'll tell you one thing. I wish to hell my pants had never fallen down." They both laughed and then he pulled away from her again. "Everything's gonna be okay. Now let's go."

"I love you, darling. I wish you knew how much I love you." Tears blinded her as she walked along at his side, quickly, trying to tell him too much in too little time.

"You're here. That tells me everything. Now stop being so dramatic, and get the mascara off your face." She giggled nervously again and ran her hands over her cheeks. There were black streaks on her palms when she stopped.

"I must look terrific."

"Gorgeous."

And then they were there. The door to the courtroom.

"Okay?" He looked at her long and hard as they stood facing each other. The bailiff watched them and then turned away.

"Okay." She nodded quietly and they smiled into each other's eyes.

They walked into the courtroom and the jury was already seated; the judge was back at his bench. The defendant was asked to rise, and Jessica almost rose from her seat with him and had to remind herself not to. She kept silently repeating to herself. "Okay . . . okay . . . okay . . ." Her fingers dug into the seat of her chair and she closed her eyes, waiting. It would be okay, it was just so horrible waiting. She thought it must be like having a bullet pulled out of your arm. It wouldn't kill you, but God it was so awful getting it out.

The foreman was asked to read off the verdict, and she held her breath, wishing she were standing next to Ian. This was it.

"How does the jury find the defendant on the charge of sodomy, an infamous crime against nature?" They were starting at the least of the charges, and working their way up . . . she waited.

"Guilty, Your Honor." Her eyes flew open and she saw Ian flinch, as though the tip of a whip had struck his face. But he didn't turn around to look at her.

"And on the charge of forcible oral copulation?"

"Guilty, Your Honor."

"And on the charge of forcible rape?"

"Guilty, Your Honor."

Jessica sat there stunned. Ian hadn't moved.

Martin looked toward her, and she felt the tears begin to pour down her face as the jury was dismissed and left the room. Ian sat down now and she went toward him. His eyes were blank when she looked into his face. She couldn't think of anything to say, and two lone tears crept down his face toward his chin.

CHAPTER 19

"I didn't do it, Jessie. I don't care about the rest, but you have to know that. I didn't rape her."

"I know." It was barely a whisper, and she clung to his hand as the assistant district attorney snappily asked that the defendant be taken into custody, pending sentencing.

It was all over in five minutes. They led him away, and Jessica stood alone in the courtroom, clinging to Martin. She was alone in the world, clinging to a man she hardly knew. Ian was gone now. She was gone. Everything was gone. It was as though someone had taken a hammer to her life and shattered it. And she couldn't tell what was mirror and what was glass, what was Ian and what was Jessie.

She couldn't move, she couldn't speak, she could hardly breathe, and Martin led her slowly and carefully from the courtroom. This great, tall, healthy-looking young woman had suddenly become a zombie. It was as though there were no insides left to Jessie, and her whole being was deflating. Her eyes stayed glued to the door Ian had passed through when they'd taken him away, as if by staring hard enough she could make him come back through that door. Martin had no idea how to handle her. He had never been left alone with a client in this kind of condition. He wondered if he should call his secretary, or his wife. The court was deserted now except for the bailiff who was waiting to lock up. The judge had looked at her regretfully when he'd left the bench, but Jessie hadn't noticed. She hadn't even seen Houghton leave, shortly after Ian. It was just as well. And all she could hear was the echo of the word that kept ringing through her head again and again and again. Guilty . . . guilty . . . guilty . . .

"Jessie, I'll take you home." He led her gently by the arm and was grateful that she followed him. He wasn't entirely certain that she knew who he was or where they were going, but he was glad that she didn't fight him. And then she stopped and looked at him vaguely.

"No, I . . . I'll wait for Ian here. I . . . I want . . . need . . . I need Ian." She stood beside the middle-aged attorney and cried like a child, her face hidden in her hands, her shoulders shaking. Martin Schwartz sat her down on a chair in the hall, handed her a handkerchief, and patted her shoulder. She was holding Ian's wallet and watch and car keys in her hand like treasures she had been bequeathed. Ian had left with empty pockets and dry eyes. In handcuffs.

"What . . . what . . . will they do . . . to him now?" She was stammering through her tears. "Can . . . can . . . he come home?" Martin knew she was too close to hysterics now to be told anything even approaching the truth. He just patted her shoulder again and helped her to her feet.

"Let's just get you home first. And then I want to go down and see Ian." He thought it would comfort her, but he had only excited her again.

"Me too. I want to see Ian too."

"Not tonight, Jessica. We're going home." It was the right tone to take. She got to her feet, took his arm, and followed him out of the building. Walking with her was like walking a mechanical rag doll.

"Martin?"

"Yes?" They were out in the fresh air now, and she took a deep breath as he turned to her.

"Can we app— appeal?" She was calmer

again. She seemed to be floating in and out of rationality, but she knew what was happening.

"We'll talk about it."

"Now. I want to talk about it now." Standing on the steps of City Hall, frantic and hysterical, at six o'clock at night. It was hard to believe that this broken women was the confident, sophisticated Jessica Clarke.

"No, Jessica, not now. I want to talk to Ian first. And I want to get you home. Ian will be very upset if I don't get you home." Oh, Jesus. And she was going to make it difficult every inch of the way. Just getting her to the car was taking forever.

"I want to see Ian." She stood at the top of the steps like a pouting child, irrational again. "I . . . I need Ian . . ." And the tears began to flow again. It made it easier to get her into the car. Until she remembered that she had to drive the Volvo home. It was Ian's.

"I'll have it brought to you tomorrow, Jessica. Just give me the garage stub." She handed it to him, and he turned the ignition in the new chocolate brown Mercedes. He kept a close watch on her as he drove her home. She looked frighteningly vague and disheveled, and he wondered if he should call her doctor for her when he got her home. He asked her about it and she objected vehemently. "What about a friend? Is there someone you want me to call?" He hated to leave her alone, but she only shook her head, mute, with an odd look in her eyes. She was thinking of the jury . . . of Margaret Burton . . . of Inspector Houghton . . . she wanted to kill them all . . . they had stolen Ian . . .

"Jessica? *Jessica?*" She turned to look at him blankly. They were in front of the house on Vallejo.

"Oh." She nodded silently again and opened the door carefully on her side. "I . . . will you see Ian now?"

"Yes. Is there anything you want me to tell him?" She nodded quickly and tried to speak normally.

"Just that . . . that . . ." But she couldn't speak through her tears.

"I'll give him your love." She nodded gratefully, and looked into his eyes with an air of being almost herself again. The hysterical vagueness seemed to be fading. What he saw now was shock, and grief. "Jessica, I'm . . . I'm terribly sorry."

"I know." She turned away then, closed the door, and walked slowly toward her house. She moved like a very old woman, and the long brown Mercedes pulled slowly away. It felt wrong to watch her. It seemed kinder to let her grieve in private. But he would never forget the way she looked, walking slowly up the brick walk, her head bent, her hair tangled, with Ian's things cradled in her hands. It was an unbearable sight.

She heard the car pull away and looked at their flower beds blankly as she approached the house. Was this the house where she had come for lunch with Ian that day? Was this the house where they lived? She looked up at it as though she had never seen it before, and stopped as though she couldn't walk any further. She lifted one foot slowly then and mounted the small step. But the other foot was too heavy to lift. She couldn't. She didn't want to. She couldn't go in that house. Not without Ian. Not alone . . . not . . . like this . . .

"Oh God, *no!*" She sank to her knees on the front step and sobbed with her head bowed and her hands full of what had been in Ian's pockets. A voice called her name and she didn't turn. It wasn't Ian. Why bother to answer . . . it wasn't Ian . . . he was gone now. Everyone was gone. She felt as though he had died in the courtroom — or maybe she had. She wasn't quite sure. The voice called her name again, and she felt as if she was sinking through the brick.

The contents of her handbag lay strewn on the step, the knit of her skirt had snagged on the brick, and her hair covered her face like a pale widow's veil.

"Jessie! Jessica?"

She heard the rapid footsteps behind her, but couldn't turn around. She didn't have the strength. It was all over.

"Jessie . . . darling, what's wrong?"

It was Astrid. Jessica turned to look into her face, and the tears continued to flow.

"What happened? Tell me! Everything will be all right. Just take it easy." She smoothed Jessie's hair like a child's, and wiped the tears from her face as they continued to come. "Is it Ian? Tell me, darling, is it Ian?"

Jessie nodded with a distraught look of grief on her face, and Astrid felt her heart stop . . . oh no, not Ian . . . not like Tom. No!

"He was convicted of rape." The words came out as though from someone else's mouth, and Astrid looked as if she'd been slapped. "He's in jail."

"Good lord, Jessica, no!" But it was true. She knew it as Jessica nodded and let her friend gently take her inside and put her to bed. The pills Astrid gave her put her out almost instantly. Astrid still carried them — ever since Tom.

■ ■ ■ ■

It was three-thirty in the morning when Jessie woke up. The house was quiet. She could hear the clock tick. It was dark in the bedroom, but there were lights on in the living room. She listened for Ian's sounds — the typewriter, his chair squeaking back on the studio floor. She sat up in bed, listening, hearing nothing, and her head swam. Then she remembered the pills. And Astrid. And how it had all begun. She sat up in bed and reached for her cigarettes with a trembling hand. She was still wearing her sweater and stockings and slip. Her jacket and skirt were neatly draped over a chair. She couldn't remember getting into bed. All she could remember was the sound of Astrid's voice, cooing gently, saying things she didn't really understand as she drifted off to sleep. But there had been someone there . . . someone . . . now there was no one. She was alone.

She lay there smoking in the darkness of the bedroom, dry-eyed, faintly nauseated and still slowed from the pills, and suddenly she reached for the phone. She got the number from information and called.

"City Prison. Langdorf here."

"I'd like to speak to Ian Clarke, please."

"He work here?" The desk sergeant sounded surprised.

"No. He was taken into custody yesterday. After a trial." She didn't volunteer the nature of the conviction. And she was surprised at the steadiness of her own voice. She didn't feel steady, but she knew that if she could make herself sound calm, they might give her what she wanted. All she had to do was sound terribly calm and put a little authority into her voice and . . .

"He'd be in the county jail, lady, not here. And you can't talk to him anyway."

"I see. Do you have the number there?" She thought of telling them it was an emergency, but decided not to. She was afraid to lie to them. The desk sergeant at the city prison gave her the number of the county jail in the Hall of Justice, and she dialed quickly. But it didn't work. They told her that she could visit her husband the day after tomorrow, and he wasn't allowed to get phone calls. Then they hung up on her.

She shrugged one shoulder and flicked on a lamp. It was cold in the room. Jessie pulled a bathrobe over her sweater and slip and padded out to the living room in stocking feet. She stood in the middle of the room and looked around. The room was faintly

355

messy, but not very, just enough to remind her . . . impressions in the softness of the couch, a mark where the back of a head had pressed into a cushion, the book he'd been reading last weekend . . . his loafers under the chair . . . his . . . she felt a sob rise and stick in her throat and she turned and walked into the kitchen for something to drink . . . tea . . . coffee . . . Coke . . . something . . . her mouth was dry and her head felt fuzzy, but everything else was so clear. She found the plates from lunch in the sink, and the newspaper on the counter where she had thrown it, the article on rape folded out. It was as though he had just been in the room, as though he had taken a walk around the block, as though . . . she sat down at the kitchen table, dropped her head, and cried.

The studio was as bad. Worse. Dark and empty and lonely. It looked as though it expected his presence but had been stood up. It needed him to come alive. Ian was the room's living soul. And hers. Jessie's soul. She needed him more than his studio did. She found herself moving from one foot to the other, like a disturbed child, standing in doorways, smoothing her hand over his books, or his shirts, holding his loafers close to her and jumping when a shadow cast an odd light. She was alone. In the house, in the night, in the world. With no one to help her, or take care of her, or give a damn about her, or . . . she opened her mouth to scream, but no sound came. She simply sank slowly to the floor, with the loafers in her arms, and waited. But no one came. She was alone.

CHAPTER 20

It was nine-thirty in the morning and she was sitting in the bathtub trying to fight a wave of hysteria when the doorbell rang. It was all right. All right. Everything was going to be all right. She'd stay in the bath for a little while and then she'd have a cup of tea, and some breakfast, and get dressed, and go to the boutique. Or maybe she'd stay in bed all day. Or . . . but it was all right. First the hot bath, and then . . . but she couldn't call Ian. She couldn't talk to him. She needed to talk to him. She took another deep breath and then listened. It sounded like the doorbell, or maybe that was just the running water playing games with her ears. But it wasn't. The bell went on ringing. But she didn't have to answer it. All she had to do was keep breathing and stay calm, and let the warm water relax her. Ian had shown her how to stay calm like that, and not get hysterical, when . . . when her mother . . .

and Jake . . . but the doorbell. She jumped out of the tub suddenly, grabbed a towel, and ran for the door. What if it was Ian? She had his keys. What if . . . she ran to the front door, dripping water along the way, a half smile on her mouth, her eyes suddenly bright and large, the towel covering her torso inadequately. She pulled the door open without remembering to ask who was there, and then jumped back, startled. Too surprised to close the door again. She simply stood there, fear pounding in her heart.

"Good morning. I wouldn't make a habit of opening the door like that if I were you." She looked down quickly and tightened the towel. The caller was Inspector Houghton.

"I . . . how do you . . . What can I do for you?" She pulled herself to her full height and stood regally in the doorway in spite of the towel.

"Nothing. I just thought I'd see how you are." He wore the ironical look of victory in his eyes, the look that she had missed the day before. It made her want to scratch his eyes out.

"I'm fine." You filthy bastard. "Was there anything else?"

"Got any coffee ready, Mrs. Clarke?"

From him the formalities were almost abusive.

"As a matter of fact, no, Inspector Houghton, I don't. And I have to get to work shortly. If you have business to discuss with me, I suggest you go buy yourself a cup of coffee on Union Street, and see me in my office in an hour."

"Feisty, aren't you? You must have had a nasty shock yesterday, though."

She closed her eyes, fighting the wave of nausea that rose to her throat. The man was sadistic. But she couldn't faint now. Couldn't. She heard Ian's voice saying "Okay?" with that special way of his, and she nodded imperceptibly and thought "Okay."

"Yes, it was a shock. Do you enjoy that, Inspector? Seeing other people unhappy, I mean."

"I don't see it that way." He pulled out a pack of cigarettes and offered her one. She shook her head. He was enjoying this, all right.

"I guess not. Miss Burton must have been pleased."

"Very." He smiled at her through the cigarette smoke and she had to fight herself not to slap him or flail at him. That took more control than not getting sick.

"And what happens to you now?" So that's what this was all about.

"What do you mean?"

"Any plans?"

"Yes, work. And seeing my husband tomorrow. And dinner with friends next week, and . . ."

He smiled again, but did not look amused.

"If he goes to prison, it could wreak havoc with your marriage, Mrs. Clarke." His voice was almost gentle.

"Possibly. Almost anything can wreak havoc with a marriage, if you let it. Depends on how good your marriage is, and how hard you want to work at keeping it that way."

"And how good is yours?"

"Excellent. And from the bottom of my heart, Inspector Houghton, I thank you for your concern. I'll be sure to mention it to both my husband and our attorney. I know Mr. Clarke will be deeply touched. You know, you're really a very sensitive man, Inspector — or is it just that you have a particular fondness for marriage counseling?"

His eyes blazed back into hers, but it was too late; he had walked right into it. He had come to her house, rung the bell, and made his own mistakes that morning.

"You know, as a matter of fact, I think I might even call your superior to tell him what a marvelously thoughtful man you are. Imagine caring about how my marriage is."

He slipped the cigarette pack back in his pocket and his smile was long since gone.

"All right, I get the point."

"Do you? My, how quick you are, Inspector."

"Bitch." He said it through clenched teeth.

"I beg your pardon?"

"I said 'bitch,' and you can tell *that* to my superior too. But if I were you, baby, I wouldn't bother to call. You've got enough problems, and you ain't gonna see your old man around here for a long time. You'd better get used to it, sister. You and that little literary punk of yours are through. So when you get tired of sitting here by yourself in the dark, start looking around. There's better out there than what you got stuck with."

"Oh, really? And I suppose you're a prime example?" She was trembling with fury now and her voice was rising to match his.

"Pick who you want, but you'll be out looking. I give you two months to be down at Jerry's with the rest of them."

"Get out of here, Inspector. And if you ever set foot near this house again, with or without a search warrant, I'll call the judge, the mayor, and the fire department. Or I may not call a goddam living soul. I may just take aim at you out of my window."

"Have a gun, do you?" He raised an eyebrow with interest.

"Not yet, but I will. Apparently I need one."

He opened his mouth to say something and she took one graceful step backward and slammed the door in his face. Tactically, it was a poor move, but it made her feel better. For a moment. When she walked back into the house, she threw up in the kitchen. It took her two hours to stop shaking.

Astrid arrived at eleven. She had flowers with her, and a roast chicken she'd bought for Jessie to pick on, and a bag full of fruit. And a small vial of yellow pills. But after twenty minutes of persistently ringing the doorbell there was still no answer; Astrid knew Jessie was there because she had called the boutique to make sure. Finally she began to worry seriously and knocked on the kitchen windows with her rings. Jessie peered cautiously between the curtains and then jumped half a foot when she saw Astrid. She had thought it was Houghton again.

"Good Lord, child, I thought something had happened. Why didn't you answer the door? Worried about press?"

"No, there's no problem with that. It's . . . oh . . . I don't know." And then there were tears in her eyes again and she was standing there looking like an overgrown child and telling Astrid about the visit from Houghton. "I just can't take it. He's so . . . so evil, and so happy about what happened. And he said that our . . . our marriage . . ." She was crying too hard to go on and Astrid made her sit down.

"Why don't you come and stay with me for a little while, Jessica? You could have the guest room and get away from here for a few days."

"No!" Jessie sprang to her feet and started pacing the room, touching chairs as she sped past, or picking something up and then putting it down again. It was a series of odd little staccato gestures, but Astrid recognized them. She had reacted the same way when Tom had died.

"No. Thank you, Astrid, but I want to be here. With . . . with . . ." She faltered, not quite sure of what she wanted to say.

"With Ian's things. I know. But maybe that's not such a good idea. And is it worth the price of being heckled by people like that policeman? And what if there are others who show up the same way? Do you want to have to deal with that?"

"I won't open the door."

"You can't live like that, Jessica. Ian won't want you to."

"Yes, he will. Honest. Really . . . I . . . oh, God, Astrid, I'm going crazy, I can't . . . I don't know how without Ian."

"But you're not without Ian. You'll see him. I still don't understand what happened, but maybe you can work it out. He's not gone, Jessica. He's not dead, for God's sake. Stop acting like he is."

"But he's not here." Her voice had a pitiful sound. "I need him here. I'll go crazy without him, I'll . . . I'll . . ."

"No, you won't. Not unless you *want* to go crazy, or make yourself do so. Take yourself in hand, Jessica, and sit down. Right now. Come on, sit down." Jessica had been popping in and out of chairs like a jack-in-the-box for the past five minutes. Her voice was rising to a desperate pitch. "Have you had breakfast?" Jessica shook her head and started to say that she didn't want any, but Astrid held up her hand and vanished into the kitchen. She emerged five minutes later with toast, jelly, the fresh fruit she had brought, and a cup of steaming tea.

"Would you rather have coffee?" Jessie shook her head and closed her eyes for a moment.

"I just don't believe this is happening, Astrid."

"Don't think about it yet. You can't make sense of it, so don't try. When can you see Ian?" Jessie's eyes opened and she sighed at the question.

"Tomorrow."

"All right. Then all you have to do is try and stay calm till tomorrow. You can do that, can't you?"

Jessica nodded, but she wasn't quite sure. That meant a day, and a night, and a morning. And the night would be the worst. Full of ghosts and voices and echoes and terrors. She had twenty-four hours to survive until she saw Ian.

But there was one thing she did want to do. Now. Before she saw Ian. And that was to talk to Martin about an appeal. He was in his office when she called, and he sounded subdued.

"Are you all right, Jessica?"

"I'm okay. How's Ian?" Her voice caught on the words, and at the other end Martin frowned. He was remembering how she had looked the night before when he'd dropped her off.

"He's holding up. He was awfully shocked, though."

"I can imagine." She said it softly, with a distracted smile. Shocked. They both were. "Martin, I called because I wanted to ask you something now, right away, before I see Ian tomorrow."

"What?"

"I want to know what we can do about an appeal, how we do it, do you do it, all of that." And how the hell do we pay for it? That was another thing.

"Well, we can talk about that after the sentencing, Jessica. If he gets probation, then there isn't much point in pressing for an appeal, except as a matter of record, to clear Ian of the felony. He might want to do that. But I think you should wait till after the sentencing to make a decision. There's a limited time in which to file an appeal, but you'll still have plenty of time then."

"How soon is the sentencing?"

"Four weeks from tomorrow."

"But why wait till after that?"

"Because, Jessie, you don't know what's going to happen. If they send him home on probation, Ian may not want to spend his last dime, or yours, on an appeal. It's not as if he's in a delicate position professionally where it can hurt him to have that on his record. All right, it can hurt him," he reconsidered, "but not that badly in his profession. And if he's free, what do you care?"

"What do you mean, *if* he's free?" Jessie was feeling confused again.

"All right, the alternative is, if they don't give him probation, they'll send him to prison. In that case, you may well want to appeal. But all an appeal is going to do for you, Jessica, is get you a new trial. You'll have to go through the whole ordeal again. There isn't a shred of evidence we didn't submit. Nothing would change. So you'd be going through it all again, maybe to no avail. I think right now our push should be for probation. And we can worry about an appeal after we see what happens with that. All right?"

Jessica reluctantly agreed, and hung up. What did he mean, "if" they set Ian free? What was the "if"?

CHAPTER 21

"Okay?"

"Okay." She smiled and instinctively her hand went to the gold lima bean at her throat, and played with it for a moment as she looked at him. She had survived the twenty-four hours, and Houghton had not returned. "I love you, Ian."

"Darling, I love you too. Are you really all right?" He looked so worried about her.

"I'm fine. What about you?"

His eyes told their own tale. He was in county jail this time, and he was wearing the filthy overalls they had given him. They had stuffed his clothes in a shopping bag and returned them to Martin. He had sent them back to Jessie the evening before, along with the Volvo. After that she had taken the two pills Astrid had left her.

"Martin says they might give you probation." But they both remembered the article they had read the day of the trial. It had been in favor of abolishing probation on rape cases. The public mood was not lenient just now.

"We'll see, Jessie, but don't count on it. We'll give it a try." He smiled and Jessie fought back tears. What would happen if he didn't get probation? She hadn't even begun to face that yet. Later. Another "later," like the trial, and the verdict. "Have you been behaving yourself? No panic, no freakies?" He knew her too well.

"I've been fine. And Astrid's been taking care of me like a child." She didn't tell him about Houghton. Or the night of semicraziness that she had had to fill with pills just to survive. She had crawled through that night as if it were a mine field.

"Is she here with you now?" He looked around but didn't see her.

"Yes, but she waited downstairs. She was afraid you'd feel awkward. And she figured we'd want to talk."

"Tell her I love her. And I'm glad you're not here alone. Jessie, I've been worried sick over you. Promise me you won't do anything crazy. Please. Promise." His eyes pleaded with her.

"I promise. Honest, darling. I'm okay." But she didn't look it. They both looked like hell. Ravaged, shocked, exhausted, and in Ian's case two days' growth of beard didn't help.

For half an hour they exchanged the disjointed banalities of people still in shock. Jessie stayed busy trying not to cry, and she managed not to until she rejoined Astrid downstairs. They were tears of anger and pain.

"They have him up there in a goddam cage like an animal!" And that damn woman was probably in her office, doing her job, living her life. She had got her revenge and now she could be happy. While Ian rotted in jail, and Jessie went crazy alone at night.

Astrid took her home, cooked her dinner, and waited until she was half asleep. It was an easier night for Jessie, mostly because she was too exhausted to torture herself thinking, to wander. She simply slept. And Astrid was back early the next morning with fresh strawberries, a copy of *The New York Times* and a brand new *Women's Wear Daily* as though that still mattered.

"Lady, what would I do without you?"

"Sleep later, probably. But I was up so I thought I'd come over." Jessie shook her head and hugged her friend as she poured two cups of tea. It was going to be a long haul, and Astrid was a godsend. It would be another twenty-seven days until the sentencing. And God only knew what would happen after that.

Jessie had the shop to think of too, but she wasn't ready to face that yet. She managed it with increasingly rare phone calls and a great deal of faith in Katsuko. Astrid took her along to her own appointment with the hairdresser, more to keep an eye on her than anything else. Jessie could only see Ian twice a week, and there was a frightening aimlessness about her in the meantime. She'd start to say things and then forget them, take objects out of her handbag and then forget why she'd brought them out; she would listen to Astrid talk and look right through her as though she couldn't see or hear her. She wasn't making a great deal of sense. She looked the way she felt, like a lost child far from home hanging desperately to a new mother. Astrid. But without Ian nothing made any sense. Least of all living. And with no contact, it was hard to remind herself that he still existed. Astrid was just trying to keep her afloat until the next time she could see him.

There had been a small article on the back page of the paper the day after the verdict. But no one had called, only the two friends who had appeared for Ian in court. They were shocked by the news. Astrid took the calls and Jessica dropped them each a note. She didn't want to talk to anyone now.

On Monday she went back to work, and Zina and Katsuko were subdued. Kat had spotted the article, but hadn't mentioned it on the phone; she had wanted to wait until she could say something to Jessie in person. And she had known from the sound of her voice on the phone that Jessie didn't want them to know. It was a painful moment when she and Astrid walked into the shop. She read the knowledge at once in their faces, and Zina instantly had tears in her eyes. Jessie hugged them both.

Now the two girls knew why Houghton had come to the shop, why Jessie had been so frantic, why the Morgan was gone. They finally understood.

"Jessie, is there anything we can do?" Katsuko spoke for both of them.

"Only one thing. Don't talk about it after this. There's nothing I can say right now. Talking doesn't help."

"How's Ian?"

"He's surviving. That's about the best you can say."

"Do you have any idea what'll happen?" She shook her head and sat down quietly in her usual chair.

"Nope. No idea at all. Does that answer everybody's questions?" She looked at the two women's faces, and she already felt tired.

"Do you need any help at home, Jessie?" Zina had finally spoken up. "It must be lonely. And I don't live very far."

"Thanks, love. I'll let you know." She gave the girl a squeeze as she headed toward her office with Astrid at her heels. The last thing she wanted was to spend evenings with Zina commiserating. It would be worse than the terrors of being alone. She turned at the door to her office with a serious look on her face. "One thing, though. I'm not going to be around much for the next few weeks. I have things to do for Ian. People to see about the sentencing, and just a hell of a lot on my mind. I'll be here whenever I can, but you two count on carrying the ball for me. Like you've been doing. Okay?" Katsuko saluted and Jessie smiled. "Couple of nuts. It's nice to be back."

"What if I pitch in and help?" Astrid was looking at her with interest as she sat down at her desk.

"To tell you the truth, I need you more everywhere but the shop. Kat has this place under control. The real problem is me. Mornings, evenings, late nights . . . you know." Astrid did know. She had seen Jessie's face at eight-thirty in the morning, and had heard her voice at two. It told a perfect tale of what the nights were like. The terror that daylight would never come again. That Ian would never come home. That the world would swallow her up and never spit her out. That Houghton would break down the door and rape her. Real fears and unreal fears, demons of her own making and men who weren't worthy of the name — all tangled together in her mind.

"Any idea what time you'll be through work? I'll pick you up. We can have dinner at my place tonight, if you feel up to it."

"You're too good to me." And it was amazing, considering how short a time they'd known each other. But Astrid knew what it was like. She had a healthy respect for what Jessica was going through.

Most of Jessica's efforts went toward Ian's sentencing. Twice she saw the probation officer detailed to the case, and she hounded Martin night and day. What was he doing? What did he have in mind? Had he spoken to the probation officer? What were the man's impressions? Should Martin talk to the man's superiors? She even went to speak to the judge one day at lunchtime. He was sympathetic, but didn't want to be pressured about the sentencing. Jessie had the distinct impression that had she been a little less ladylike the judge might have been a little less kind in his reception. As it was, he was not overly welcoming. She also collected letters from a number of discreet friends, testifying to Ian's good character. She even got a letter from his agent, hoping to show that Ian had to be free to complete the new book, and that going to prison would destroy his career.

Thanksgiving came and went like any other day. Or at least Jessica tried to ensure that it did. She treated it like any day when she wasn't working. She wouldn't allow herself to think of past Thanksgivings. She refused to let it be festive in any way. That would have been too much for her. She spent it with Astrid, and Ian spent it in jail. There was no visiting at the county jail on Thanksgiving Day. He ate stale chicken sandwiches and read a letter from Jessie. She ate steak with Astrid, who went out of her way to ignore the holiday this year, sacrificing a long weekend at the ranch with her mother. But the sacrifice was well worth it. She was worried about Jessie, who always seemed to move about in a haze now, stopping and starting, jangled, at one extreme or the other: fuzzy and full of pills, or wild from too much coffee.

And she worked night and day. Figuring out what to do for the sentencing, and suddenly pouring her energy back into Lady J, as she hadn't in years. She worked on Saturdays again. At home she did anything, everything — cleaned the basement, straightened out the garage, redid her closets, tidied the studio — anything, trying not to think. And maybe, maybe, if she did everything perfectly, maybe at the end of the month, he'd come home. Maybe they'd give him probation, maybe . . . she moved like a whirling dervish, but she had to; the pounding of her mind was deafening her. And constantly there was fear. She never escaped it. Sheer, raw, endless terror. Beyond human proportions. But she wasn't human anymore. She barely ate, she hardly slept. She wouldn't allow herself to feel. She didn't dare to be human. Humans fell apart. And that was what scared her most. Falling apart. Like Humpty-Dumpty. And all the king's horses and all the king's men . . . that was what she was afraid of. Ian knew it, but he couldn't stop her now. He couldn't touch her, hold her, feel her, make her feel. He couldn't do anything except watch her through the window and talk to her on the phone at the jail as she played nervously with the cord and snappd her earring absentmindedly.

And he continued to look steadily worse — unshaven, unwashed, ill fed, and with dark circles under his eyes that seemed to get darker each time she saw him.

"Don't you sleep in here?" There was a raw edge to her voice now. It was higher, shriller, scareder. He pitied her, but he couldn't help her now. They both knew it, and he wondered how long it would take her to hate him for it. For failing her. He was terrified that a day would come when he couldn't keep the boogey man from the door for her, and then she would turn on him. Jessie expected a lot. Because she needed so much.

"I sleep now and then." He tried to smile. Tried not to think. "What about you? Looks like a lot of makeup under your eyes, my love. Am I right?"

"Are you ever wrong?" She smiled back and shrugged, snapping the earring again. She had lost twelve pounds, but she was sleeping a little better. She just didn't look it. But the new red pills helped. They were better than the yellow ones, or even the little blue ones Astrid had let her graduate to after that. They were the same kind, only stronger. The red ones where something else. She didn't discuss it with Ian. He would have been difficult about it. And she was careful. But the pills were the best part of her day. The two bright moments with Ian were the only livable parts of her week, and in between she had to get through the days. The pills did that for her. And Astrid doled them out one by one, refusing to leave the bottle with her.

Ian would have been frantic if he had known. She had promised him solemnly, after Jake had died — no more pills. He had stood at her side all night while they'd pumped her stomach, and afterward she had promised. She thought about that sometimes when she took the pills. But she had to. She really had to. Or she'd die anyway. One way or another. She worried about things like jumping out a window, without wanting to. About little demons seizing her and making her do things she didn't want to do. She couldn't talk to customers in the shop anymore. She stayed in the back office because she was afraid of what she'd say. She was no longer in control. Of anything. Jessica was not in her own driver's seat. No one was.

The four weeks between the verdict and the

sentencing ground by like a permanent nightmare, but the sentencing finally came. The plea for probation was heard by the judge, and this time Jessie stood beside Ian as they waited. It was less frightening now, though, and she kept touching his hand, his face. It was the first time in a month that she had touched him. He smelled terrible and his nails were long. They had given him an electric razor at the jail and it had torn his face apart. But it was Ian. It was, at last the touch of the familiar in a world that had become totally unfamiliar to her. Now she could stand next to him. Be his. She almost forgot the seriousness of the sentencing. But the courtroom formalities brought her back. The bailiff, the court reporter, the flag. It was the same courtroom, the same judge. And it was all very real now.

Ian was not granted probation. The judge felt that the charges were too serious. And Martin explained later that with the political climate what it was, the judge could hardly have done otherwise. Ian was given a sentence of four years to life in state prison, and he would have to serve at least a fourth of his minimum sentence: one year.

The bailiff led him away, and this time Jessie did not cry.

CHAPTER 22

Three days later, Ian was moved from county jail to state prison. He went, like all male prisoners in Northern California, to the California Medical Facility in Vacaville for "evaluation."

Jessica drove there two days later with Astrid, in the black Jaguar, and with two yellow pills under her belt. Astrid said these were the last she would give her, but she always said that. Jessica knew she felt sorry for her.

Except for the gun tower peering over the main gate and the metal detector that searched them for weapons, the prison at Vacaville looked innocuous. Inside, a gift shop sold ugly items made in the prison, and the front desk might have been the entrance to a hospital. Everything was chrome and glass and linoleum. But outside, it looked like a modern garage. For people.

They asked to see Ian, filled out various

forms, and were invited to sit in the waiting room or wander in the lobby. Ten minutes later a guard appeared to unlock a door to an inner courtyard. He instructed them to pass through the courtyard and go through yet another door, which they would find unlocked.

The inmates in the courtyard wore blue jeans, T-shirts, and an assortment of shoes, everything from boots to sneakers, and Astrid raised an eyebrow at Jessie. It didn't look like a prison. Everyone was casually playing with the soda machines or talking to girlfriends. It looked like a high school at recess, with here and there the exception of a sober face or a watery-eyed mother.

What she saw gave Jessie some hope. She could visit Ian somewhere in the courtyard, could touch him again, laugh, hold hands. It was madness to be regressing to that after seven years of marriage, but it would be an improvement over the doggie-in-the-window visits at the county jail.

As it turned out, there was no improvement. Ian was months away from visits in the courtyard, if he stayed in that institution at all. There was always Folsom or San Quentin to worry about now. Anything was possible. And for the time being they were faced once again with more visits through a glass window, talking over a phone. Jessica felt a surging desire to smash the receiver through the window as she tried to smile into his face. She longed for the touch of his face, the feel of his arms, the smell of his hair. And instead all she had in her hands was a blue plastic phone. Next to her there was a pink one, and further down a yellow. Someone with a sense of humor had installed pastel-colored princess-style phones all the way down the line. Like a nursery, with a glass window. And you could talk to the darling babies on the phone. What she needed was her husband, not a phone pal.

But he looked better — thinner, but at least clean. He had even shaved in the hope of a visit. They fell into some of their old jokes, and Astrid shared the phone with Jessica now and then. It was all so strange, sitting there, making conversation with a wall of glass between the two women and Ian. The strain told in his eyes, and the humor they inflicted on each other always had a bitter edge.

"This is quite a harem. For a rapist." He grinned nervously at his own bad joke.

"Maybe they'll think you're a pimp." Their laughter sounded like tinsel rustling.

The reality was that he was there. For at

least a year. Jessie wondered how long she could take it. But maybe she didn't have to. Maybe neither of them did. She wanted to talk to him about an appeal.

"Did you talk to Martin about it?"

"Yes. And there won't be an appeal." He answered her solemnly, but with certainty in his voice.

"What?" Jessie's voice was suddenly shrill.

"You heard me. I know what I'm doing, Jess. Nothing would change next time around. Martin feels the same way. For another five or ten thousand bucks, we'd sink ourselves further into debt, and when the second trial rolled around, we'd have nothing different to say. The suspicions we have about her husband are inadmissible on the flimsy evidence we have. All we've got is an old photograph and a lot of fancy ideas. No one will testify. There's nothing to hang our hats on except blind hope. We did that once, but we didn't have any choice. We're not going through that again. A new trial would come out the same goddam way, and it'll just make these people mad. Martin thinks I'm better off living through this, just being a nice guy, and they'll probably give me an early parole. Anyway, I've made my decision, and I'm right."

"Who says you're right, dammit, and why

didn't anyone ask me?"

"Because we're talking about my time in here, not yours. It's my decision."

"But it affects my life too." Her eyes filled with tears. She wanted an appeal, another chance, something, anything. She couldn't accept just waiting around until he got paroled. There was talk of changing the California laws to bring in a determinate sentence, but who had time to wait for that? And even then, Martin had once said that Ian might have to do a couple of years. Two years? Jesus. How would she survive? She could barely speak as she held the phone in her hand.

"Jessie, trust me. It has to be this way. There's no point."

"We could sell something. The house. Anything."

"And we might lose again. Then what? Let's just grit our teeth and get through this. Please, Jessie — please, please try. I can't do anything for you right now except love you. You've got to be strong. And it won't be for long. It probably won't be more than a year." He tried to sound cheerful about it, for her sake.

"What if it's more than a year?"

"We'll worry about it then." The tears spilled down her face in answer. How could they have decided this without talking to her? And why weren't they willing to try again? Maybe they could win . . . maybe . . . she looked up to see Ian exchanging a look with Astrid and shaking his head. "Baby, you have to pull yourself together."

"What for?"

"For me."

"I'm okay."

He shook his head and looked at her. "I wish to hell you were." Thank God she had Astrid.

They talked on for a while, about the other men there, about some tests they'd put him through, about his hopes of being kept there rather than sent on to another prison. Vacaville at least seemed civilized, and he expected that he could work on his book after he'd been there for a while and had calmed down. Jessie told herself that it made her feel better to know that he was still interested in the book. At least he was still alive mentally, spiritually. But she found that she didn't really care. What about her? After the outburst over the appeal, she felt even lonelier. She tried to pump life into her smile, but it hurt so much not to be able to reach out to him or be held in his arms.

He watched her face for a long moment and wished only that he could touch her.

Even he didn't have enough words anymore, and too often they fell silent.

"How's the shop?"

"Okay. Great, really. Business is booming." But it was a lie. Business was far from booming. It was the worst it had been in all the years since she'd opened Lady J. But what could she tell him, what was there to say without voicing agonizing recriminations, and accusations, and cries of outrage and despair? What was left? There was always the truth that business was lousy and he should have been home working to help pay the bills . . . the truth that he shouldn't be in prison . . . the truth that he looked terrible and his haircut made him look old and tired . . . the truth that she even worried now that he'd become a homosexual in jail — or worse, that someone would kill him . . . the truth that she didn't know how to pay the bills anymore and was afraid that she couldn't survive the nights alone . . . the truth that she wanted to die . . . the truth that he never should have balled Margaret Burton . . . the truth that he was a sonofabitch and she was beginning to hate him because he wasn't there anymore . . . he was gone. But she couldn't tell him the truth. There was too much of it now, and she knew it would kill him.

He was talking again; she had to look up and focus her attention.

"Jess, I want you to do something for me when you get home today. Get the book Xeroxed, put the copy in the bank, and send me the original. I'm getting special permission to work on it, and by the time the manuscript gets here, I'll have the paperwork squared away at this end. Don't forget, though. Try and get it out to me today." There was summer in his eyes again as he spoke, but Astrid wondered at the look on Jessica's face. Jessie was stunned. He had just been sentenced to prison and he was worried about his book?

The visit was called to a close after little more than an hour. There was a frantic flurry of good-byes on the phone, cheery farewells from Astrid, a few last verbal hugs from Ian, and a moment of panic that Jessie thought would close her throat. She couldn't even kiss him good-bye. But what if she needed to hold him? Didn't they understand that all she had in the world was Ian? What if . . .

She watched him walk away slowly, reluctant to leave, but a big boyish smile hung on his face, while she tried to smile too. But she was running on an empty tank now, and secretly she was glad the visit was over. It cost her more each time she saw him now. It was even harder here than it had been in county jail. She wanted to throw a fist through the glass, to scream, to . . . anything, but she gave him a last smile, and numbly followed Astrid back to the car.

"Do you have any more of those magical little pills, fairy godmother?"

"No, I don't. I didn't bring them." Astrid said nothing more, but touched her arm gently and gave her a hug before unlocking the car. There was nothing more she could say. And she left Jessie the dignity of not seeing her tears as they drove home in silence, the radio purring softly between them.

"Want me to drop you off at home, so you can relax for a while?" She smiled as they came to a stop on Broadway where the freeway poured them back into the city traffic. Two blocks later they drove past Enrico's.

"Nope. And that's where it all began."

"What?" Astrid hadn't noticed, and she turned to see Jessie staring at the tables clustered on the sidewalk under the heaters. It was cold now, but a few hardy souls still sat outside.

"Enrico's. That's where he met her. I

wonder what she's doing now." There was a haunted look on Jessica's face, and she spoke almost dreamily.

"Jessie, don't think of that."

"Why not?"

"Because there's no point now. It's over. Now you have to look ahead to the other end. You just have to trot on through the tunnel, and before you know it . . ."

"Oh, bullshit! You make it sound like a fairy tale, for Chrissake. Just what do you think it feels like to look at your husband through a glass window, not to be able to touch him, or . . . oh, God. I'm sorry. I just can't stand it, Astrid. I can't accept it, I don't want this happening to my life, I don't want to be alone. I need him." She ended softly, with tears thick in her throat.

"And you still have him. In all the ways that matter. Okay, so he's behind a window, but he won't be there forever. What do you suppose it felt like when I looked down at Tom in that stinking box? He would never talk to me again, hold me again, need me again, love me again. Ever, Jessie. Ever. With you and Ian, it's only an intermission. The only thing you don't have is his presence in the house every night. You have all the rest."

But that was what she needed. His presence. What "rest" was there? She couldn't remember anymore. Was there a "rest"? Had there ever been?

"And you've got to stop taking those pills, Jessie." Astrid's tone brought her back again. They were a few blocks from her house now.

"Why? They don't do any harm. They just . . . they just help, that's all."

"They won't in a while. They'll just depress you more, if they aren't doing that already. And if you don't watch out you'll get so dependent on them that you'll have a real problem. I did, and it was a bitch to get rid of. I spent weeks down at Mother's ranch trying to 'kick,' as it were. Do yourself a big favor — give 'em up now." Jessie brushed off the suggestion and pulled a comb out of her bag.

"Yeah. Maybe I'll just go straight to the shop."

"Why don't you at least go home for five minutes to unwind first? How would that be?" Lousy. Painful.

"Okay. If you'll come in for coffee." She didn't want to be alone there. "I have to pick up Ian's book and get it Xeroxed for him. He wants to start working again." Astrid noticed the strained tone in her voice. Could she be jealous? It seemed almost impossible. But these days, anything was possible with Jessie.

"At least they'll let him work on the book."

"Apparently." Jessie shrugged as Astrid pulled into the driveway.

"It'll do him good."

Jessie shrugged again and got out.

There was a look of slight disorder in the front hall, of jackets and coats tried on and discarded before her visit to Ian that morning. Astrid noticed Ian's coats crammed to one side of the closet and the now predominantly female clutter here and there. He had only been gone for five weeks, yet it was beginning to look like a woman's house. She wondered if Jessie had noticed the change.

"Coffee or tea?"

"Coffee, thanks." Astrid smiled and settled into a chair to look at the view. "Want any help?" Jessica shook her head and Astrid tried to relax. It was difficult to be with Jessica now. There was obviously so much pain, and so little one could do to help. Except be there. "What are you doing for Christmas?"

Jessica appeared with two flowered cups and laughed hollowly. "Who knows? Maybe I'll hang myself this year instead of a stocking."

"Jessica, that's not funny."

"Is anything anymore?"

Astrid sighed deeply and set down the cup Jessie had given her.

"Jessie, you have to stop feeling so sorry for yourself. Somehow, somewhere, you're going to have to find something to hang on to. For your own sake, not just for his. The shop, a group of people, me, a church, whatever it is you need, but you just have to grab on to something. You can't live like this. Not only will your marriage not survive, but, much worse, *you* won't." That was what had been frightening Ian: Astrid knew that. Once or twice he had looked at her, and she had understood.

"This isn't forever, you know. You'll get back what you had before. It isn't over."

"Isn't it? How do you know that? I don't even know that. I don't even know at this point what the hell we had, or if it's worth wanting back." She was shocked at her own words but she couldn't stop herself now. She gripped her shaking hands together. "What did we have? Me supporting Ian, and him hating me for it, so much that he had to go out and screw a bunch of other women to feel like a man. Pretty portrait of a marriage, isn't it, Astrid? Just what every little girl dreams of."

"Is that how you feel about it now?" Astrid watched the hurt on Jessica's face and her heart went out to her. "From what I've seen, there's a lot more to your marriage than that." They had looked so young and so happy when she'd met them, but she realized now that there was a lot she didn't know. There had to be. She met Jessica's eyes now and ached for her. Jessica had a lot to find out in the next months.

"I don't know, Astrid. I feel as though I did everything wrong before, and I want to make it right now. But it's too late. He's gone. And I don't care what you say, it feels in my gut like he's never coming home again. I play games with myself, I listen for his footsteps, I wander around his studio — and then we go up and see him there, like an ape in a cage. Astrid, he's my husband, and they have him locked up like an animal!" Tears and confusion flooded her eyes.

"Is that what really bothers you, Jessie?"

She looked irate at the question. "Of course it is! What do you think?"

"I think that bothers you, but I think other things bother you just as much. I think you're afraid everything will change. He'll change. He wants his book now, and that frightens you."

"It does not frighten me. It annoys me." At least that was honest. She had admitted it.

"Why does it annoy you?"

"Because I sit here by myself, going crazy, dealing with reality, and what does he want to do? Doodle around on his book, like nothing ever happened. And . . . oh . . . I don't know, Astrid, it's so complicated. I don't understand anything anymore. It's all making me crazy. I can't take it. I *just can't take it.*"

"You can take it, and so can Ian. You've already gone through the worst part. The trial must have been hell." Jessie nodded soberly.

"Yeah, but this is worse. This goes on forever."

"Of course not. And Jessie, you can take a lot more than you think. So can Ian." As she said the words, she hoped she was right.

"How can you be so sure? Remember how he looked today, Astrid? How long do you think he can take all that? He's spoiled, spoiled rotten, and used to a comfortable life with civilized people. Now he's in there. We don't see what it's really like, but what do you think will happen when some guy pulls a knife on him, or some jerk wants to make love to him? Then what? Are you really sure he can handle it, Astrid?" Her voice was rising to an hysterical pitch. "And you know what the real joke of this whole mess is? That he's in there because of me. Not because of Margaret Burton. Because of me. Because I castrated him so completely that he needed her to prove something. I did it. I might as well have put the handcuffs on him myself."

The tragedy of it was that Astrid knew she believed that. She went to her and tried to put her arms around her as Jessica sobbed.

"Jessica, no . . . no, baby. You know . . ."

"I know. It's true! I know it. And he knows it. And the fucking woman even knew it. You should have seen how she looked at me in court. God knows what he told her. But I looked at her with hatred, and she looked at me with . . . pity. Dammit, Astrid, please give me some of those pills." She looked up at Astrid with a ravaged face, but her friend shook her head.

"I can't."

"Why not? I need them."

"You need to think right now. Clearly. Not in a fogged state. What you just told me is totally crazy, and a lot of what you're thinking is probably pretty crazy. You might as well get it all straightened out in your head now, and have done with it. Pills won't help."

"They'll get me through it." She was begging now.

"No they won't. You've lost all perspective about what happened, and they'll only make it worse. And I can tell you one thing for sure. If you don't straighten out your thinking now, it will only get worse, and you won't have a marriage left when Ian comes out. You'll eventually wind up hating him, maybe even as much as you hate yourself right now, if that's possible. You owe yourself some serious thinking, Jessica."

"So you're going to see that I get it, is that it?" Jessica's voice was bitter now.

"No, I can't do that. I can't force you to think. But I won't give you anything to cloud your thinking anymore either. I can't do that, Jessica. I just can't." Jessica felt an almost irresistible urge to stand up and hit her, and then she knew that she must be going crazy. Wanting to hit Astrid was very crazy. But also very real. She wanted those goddam pills.

"You'll have to face it sooner or later anyway." And then suddenly there were tears in Jessie's eyes again.

"But what if I go crazy? I mean really crazy?"

"Why should you?"

"Because I can't handle it. I just can't handle it."

Astrid felt out of her depth and wondered

how her mother had stood her when she had been in similar shape after Tom's death. It gave her an idea.

"Jessie, why don't you come down to the ranch with me at Christmas? Mother would love it, and it would do you good."

Jessica shook her head even before Astrid had finished her sentence.

"I can't."

"Why not?"

"I have to spend Christmas with Ian." She looked mournful at the thought.

"You don't 'have' to."

"All right, I want to." Christmas without Ian? No way.

"Even with the window between you?" Jessica nodded. "Why, for God's sake? As a penance to absolve you of the guilt you're heaping on your own head? Jessica, don't be ridiculous. Ian would probably love to know that you're doing something pleasant, like going down to the ranch." Jessica didn't answer, and after a pause, Astrid said what she had really been thinking. "Or would you rather torture him by letting him see how much you can suffer on Christmas?"

Jessica's eyes flew wide open again on that one.

"Jesus, you make it sound like I'm trying to punch him."

"Maybe you are. I think you just can't decide right now who you hate more — him or yourself. And I think you've both had enough punishment, Ian at the hands of the State, and you at your own. Can't you start to be good to yourself now, Jessica? And maybe then you'll be able to be good to him." There was more truth in Astrid's words than Jessie was ready for.

"You *can* take care of you, Jessie. And Ian will take care of you, even at a distance. Your friends will help. But most of all, you have to see that you're much more capable than you know."

"How do you know?"

"I know. You're scared and you have a right to be. But if you'd just calm down a little, and take stock of yourself, *kindly,* you'd be a lot less scared. But you're going to have to stop running to do that."

"And stop taking pills?"

Astrid nodded, and Jessie remained silent. She wasn't ready to do that yet. She knew it without even trying.

But she did try. Astrid left without giving her any, and Jessica went to the bank with Ian's manuscript — with trembling hands and trembling knees, but without taking another pill. From there she went to the post office, and from there on to the shop.

She lasted at Lady J for less than an hour, and then she came home to pace. She spent the night huddled in a chair in the living room, nauseated, trembling, wide-eyed, and wearing a sweater of Ian's. It still had the smell of his cologne on it, and she could feel him with her. She could sense him watching her as she sat in front of the fireplace. She kept seeing faces in the fire — Ian's, her mother's, Jake's, her father's. They came to her late in the night. And then she thought she heard strange sounds in the garage. She wanted to scream but couldn't. She wanted pills but didn't have any. She never went to bed that night, and at seven in the morning she called the doctor. He gave her everything she wanted.

CHAPTER 23

At Christmas, Astrid spent three weeks at the ranch with her mother. Jessica was swamped at the boutique. She was falling into a routine now with her visits to Ian. She drove up two weekday mornings and on Sundays. She was putting four hundred miles a week on his car, and the Volvo wasn't going to take the wear much longer. She almost wondered if she and the car would die together, simply keel over at the side of the road and die. In the Volvo's case it would be from old age; in Jessie's, from strain and exhaustion. That and too many pills. But she functioned well with them now. Most people still couldn't tell. And Ian hadn't yet confronted her about them. She assumed that he simply didn't want to see what was happening. It was fine with her.

She couldn't send him a Christmas present this year. He was allowed to receive only money, so she sent him a check. And

401

forgot to buy Christmas presents for the two girls in the shop. All she thought about was putting gas in the car, surviving the visits with Ian on the opposite side of the glass window, and getting her prescriptions refilled. Nothing else seemed to matter. And whatever energy she had left she spent figuring out the bills. She was making some headway with them, and she would wake up in the morning figuring out how to cover this, if she borrowed from that, if she didn't pay that until . . . she was hoping that Christmas profits would put her back in the black. But Lady J was having its own problems. Something was off, and she couldn't bring herself to care as much as she'd used to. Lady J was only a vehicle now, not a joy. It was a means of paying bills, and a place to go in the daytime. She could hide in the little office in the back of the shop and juggle those bills. She rarely came out to see customers now. After a few minutes, the now familiar rising wave of panic would seize her throat and she'd have to excuse herself . . . a yellow pill . . . a blue one . . . a quick sip of Scotch . . . something . . . anything to kill the panic. It was easier just to sit in the back and let the girls handle the customers. She was too busy anyway. With the bills. And with trying not to think.

It took a lot of effort not to think, especially late at night or early in the morning. Suddenly, for the first time in years, she had perfect recall of her mother's voice, her father's laughter. She had forgotten them for so long, and now they were back. They said things . . . about each other . . . about her . . . about Ian . . . and they were right. They wanted her to think. Jake even said something once. But she didn't want to think. It wasn't time yet. She didn't have to . . . didn't want to . . . couldn't . . . they couldn't make her . . . they . . .

Christmas did not fall on a visiting day, so she couldn't spend it with Ian after all. She spent it alone, with three red pills and two yellow ones. She didn't wake up until four the next afternoon, and then she could go back to the shop. She wanted to mark some things down for a sale. They had lost money at Christmas and she had to make it up. A good fat sale would really do it. She would send out little cards to their best customers. It would bring them in droves — she hoped.

She worked on the books straight through New Year's, and finally remembered to give Zina and Kat checks instead of the Christmas presents she had overlooked. Jessie had gotten three presents, and a poem from Ian.

Astrid had given her a simple and lovely gold bracelet, and Zina and Kat had given her small, thoughtful things. A homemade potpourri in a pretty French jar from Zina, and a small line drawing in a silver frame from Katsuko. And she had read the poem from Ian over and over on Christmas eve. It was quickly dog-eared as it lay on her night-stand.

She had taken it with her to the office, and now carried it in her bag, to bring out and read during the day. She knew it by heart the day after she'd gotten it.

Katsuko and Zina wondered what she did in her office all the time now. She would emerge for coffee, or to look for something in the stockroom, but she rarely spoke to them, and never joked anymore. Gone were the days of cozy gossip and the easy cama-raderie the three had shared. It was as though Jessie had vanished when Ian did. She would appear at the door of her small office at the end of the day, sometimes with a pencil stuck in her hair, a distracted look, a small packet of bills in one hand, and sometimes with eyes that were bloodshot and swollen. She was quicker to snap at people now, quicker to lose patience over trivial matters. And there was always that dead look in her eyes. The look that said she lay awake at night. The look that said she was more frightened than she wanted them to know. And the unmistakable glaze from the pills.

Only the days when she visited Ian were a little different. She was alive then. Something sparkled behind the wall she had built between herself and the rest of the world. Something different would happen in her eyes then, but she would share it with no one. Not even with Astrid, who was spending more and more time at the shop, and getting to know Zina and Katsuko. In a sense, Astrid had replaced Jessie. She had the kind of easy-going ways that Jessie had had before. She enjoyed the shop, the people, the clothes, the girls. She had time to talk and laugh. She had new ideas. She loved the place, and it showed. The girls had grown fond of her. She even came in on the days when Jessie was with Ian.

"You know, sometimes I think I sit here just so I know when she gets back. I worry about her making that drive."

"So do we." Katsuko shook her head.

"She told me the other day that she just does it on 'automatic pilot.' " Zina's words weren't much comfort. "She says that sometimes she doesn't even remember where she is or what she's doing until she sees that sign."

"Terrific." Astrid took a sip of coffee and shook her head.

"Grim, isn't it? I wonder how long she'll hold up. She can't just keep plodding on like that. She has to go somewhere, see people, smile occasionally, sleep." And sober up. Katsuko didn't say it, but they all thought it. "She doesn't even look like the same woman anymore. I wonder how he's doing."

"A little better than she is, actually. But I haven't seen him for a while. I think he's less afraid."

"Is that what it is with her?" Zina looked stunned. "I thought she was just exhausted."

"That too. But it's fear." Astrid sounded hesitant to discuss it.

"And pressure. Lady J has been giving her a rough time lately."

"Oh? Looks busy enough."

Katsuko shook her head, reluctant to say more. She had taken calls lately from people Jessie owed money to. For the first time the business was in trouble, and there was no money to fall back on. Jessie had bled every last cent of their spare money for Ian. So now Lady J was paying Ian's price too.

Jessie walked into the shop then, and the conversation came to a halt. She looked

haggard and thin but there was something brighter, in her eyes, that indefinable something that Ian poured back into her soul. Life.

"Well, ladies, how has life been treating you all today? Are you spending all your money here again, Astrid?" Jessie sat down and took a sip of someone's cold coffee. The small yellow pill she slipped into her mouth at the same time was barely noticeable. But Astrid noticed.

"Nope. Not spending a dime today. Just dropped by for some coffee and company. How's Ian?"

"Fine, I guess. Full of the book. How was business today?" She didn't seem to want to talk about Ian. She rarely spoke of anything important to her anymore. Even to Astrid.

"It was pretty quiet today." Katsuko filled her in on business while Zina watched the slight trembling of Jessie's hand.

"Terrific. A dead business, and a dead car. The Volvo just breathed its last." She sounded unconcerned, as though it really didn't matter because she had twelve other cars at home.

"On your way home?"

"Naturally. I hitched a ride with two kids in Berkeley. In a 1952 Studebaker truck. It

407

was pink with green trim and they called it the Watermelon. It drove like one too." She tried to make light of it while the three women watched her.

"So where's the car?"

"At a service station in Berkeley. The owner offered me seventy-five bucks for it, and agreed to drop the towing charge."

"Did you sell it?" Even Katsuko looked stunned.

"Nope. I can't. It's Ian's. But I guess I will. That car has had it." And so have I. She didn't say it, but they all heard it in her voice. "Easy come, easy go. I'll pick up something cheap for my trips up to Ian." But with what? Where would the money come from for that?

"I'll drive you." Astrid's voice was quiet and strangely calm. Jessica looked up at her and nodded. There was no point in protesting. She needed help and she knew it, and not just with the drive.

Astrid drove Jessica up to see Ian three times a week from then on. It saved Jessie the trouble of waiting to take the two yellow pills when she got there. This way she could take two in the morning, and another two after she saw him. Sometimes she even threw in a green-and-black one. Every little bit helped.

And Astrid could no longer talk to her. There was no use even trying. All she could do was stand by and be there when the roof finally came down. If it did, when it did, wherever and however. Jessica was heading for a stone wall as fast as she could. Nothing less was going to stop her. And Ian couldn't reach her either. Astrid saw that clearly now. He couldn't face what was happening to Jessie, because he couldn't help. If he couldn't help, he wouldn't see. And each time Jessie appeared, looking more tortured, more exhausted, more brittle, more rooted in pain and draped in bravado, it would only hurt Ian more. He would feel greater guilt, greater indebtedness, greater pain of his own. Their eyes rarely met now. They simply talked. He about the book, she about the boutique. Never about the past or the future or the realities of the present. They never spoke of feelings, but only threw out "I love you" at regular intervals, like punctuation. It was grisly to watch, and Astrid hated the visits. She wanted to shake them both, to speak out, to stop what she was seeing. Instead they just went on dying quietly on opposite sides of the glass wall, in their own private hells, Ian with his guilt and Jessica with hers, and each of them with their blindness about themselves and about each other. While Astrid watched, mute and horrified.

If only they could have held each other, then they might have been real. But they couldn't, and they weren't. Astrid knew that as she watched them. She could see it in Jessie's eyes now. There was constant pain, but there was also the look of a child who does not understand. Her husband was gone, but what was a husband, and where had he gone? The pills had allowed her to submerge herself in a sea of vagueness, and she rarely came to the surface anymore. She was very close to drowning, and Astrid wasn't entirely sure if Ian hadn't already drowned. Astrid could have done without the visits. But they were all locked into their roles now. Husband, wife, and friend.

January bled into February and then limped into March. The boutique had a two-week sale that brought scarcely any business. Everyone was busy or away or feeling poor. The last of their winter line hadn't done well at all; the economy was weak, and luxuries were going with it. Lady J was not a boutique to supply ordinary needs. It catered to a select clientele of the internationally chic. And her clients' husbands were telling them to lay off. The market was bad. They were no longer amused by a "little" sweater and a "nothing" skirt that cost them *in toto* close to two hundred dollars.

"Christ, what are we going to do with all this junk?" Jessie paced the floor, opening a fresh pack of cigarettes. She had seen Ian that morning. Once again through the window. Still through the window. Forever through the window. She had visions of finally getting to touch him again when they were both ninety-seven years old. She didn't even dream of his coming home anymore. Just of being able to touch him.

"We're going to have a real problem, Jessie, when the spring line comes in." Katsuko looked around pensively.

"Yeah, the bastards. It was due in last week and it's late." She swept into the stockroom to see what was there. She was annoyed much of the time now. The pain was showing itself differently. It wasn't enough now to hide: it was taking more to silence her inner voices.

"You know, I've been thinking." Katsuko had followed her into the stockroom and was watching her.

"Was it painful?" Jessie looked up, smiled awkwardly, and then shrugged. "Sorry. What

411

were you thinking, Kat?" That sounded like the old Jessie. But it was rare now.

"About next fall's line. Are you going to New York one of these days?" On what? A broomstick?

"I don't know yet."

"What'll we do for a fall line if you don't?" Katsuko was worried. There was almost no money for a new line, and there were still unpaid bills all over Jessie's desk.

"I don't know, Kat. I'll see."

She walked into her office and slammed the door, her mouth in a small set line. Zina and Kat exchanged a glance. Zina answered the phone when it rang. It was for Jessie. From some record store. She buzzed Jessie's office and watched her pick up the phone. The light on the phone Zina had answered went out only a few moments later.

And in her office Jessie's hands were trembling as she toyed with a pencil on her desk. It had been another one of those calls. They were sure it was an oversight, undoubtedly she had forgotten to send them a check for the amount that was due . . . at least these had been polite. The doctor's office had called yesterday and he had threatened to sue. For fifty dollars? A doctor was going to sue her for fifty dollars? . . . And a dentist for ninety-eight . . . and there was still a liquor store bill for Ian's wine for a hundred and forty-five . . . and she owed the cleaner's twenty-six and the drugstore thirty-three and the phone bill was forty-one . . . and I. Magnin . . . and Ian's old tennis club . . . and new plants for the shop and the electricians' bill when the lights had gotten screwed up over Christmas . . . and a plumbing bill for the house . . . and on and on and on it went, and the Volvo was gone, and Lady J was going down the tubes, and Ian was in prison, and everything just kept getting worse instead of better. There was almost a satisfaction in it, like playing a game of "how bad can things get?" And meanwhile Astrid was buying sweaters from her at cost, and "amusing" gold bracelets at Shreve's, and having her hair done every three days at twenty-five bucks a crack. And now there was the fall line to think about. Three hundred bucks' worth of plane fare, and a hotel bill, not to mention the cost of what she bought. It would sink her further into debt, but she didn't have much choice. Without a fall line, she might as well close up Lady J on Labor Day. But it was getting to the point where she was afraid to walk into the bank to cash a check. She was always sure that she'd be stopped on the way out and ushered to the manager. How long would they put up with the overdrafts, the problems, the bullshit? And how long would she?

As she was trying to figure out how expensive the trip to New York would be, the intercom buzzed to let her know she had a call. She picked up the phone absentmindedly, without finding out from Zina who it was.

"Hi, gorgeous, how's about some tennis?" The voice was jovial and already sounded sweaty.

"Who is this?" She suspected an obscene phone caller and was thinking of hanging up as the man on the other end took a large swallow of something, presumably beer.

"Barry. And how've ya been?"

"Barry who?" She recoiled from the phone as though from a snake. This was no one she knew.

"Barry York. You know. Yorktown Bonding."

"What?" She sat up as though someone had slapped her.

"I said . . ."

"I know what you said. And you're calling me to play tennis?"

"Yeah. You don't play?" He sounded surprised, like a small boy who's just been severely disappointed.

"Mr. York, do I understand you correctly? You want to play tennis with me?"

"Yeah. So?" He belched softly into the phone.

"Are you drunk?"

"Of course not. Are you?"

"No, I'm not. And I don't understand why you called me." Her voice was straight out of the Arctic Circle, long-distance.

"Well, you're a good-looking woman, I was going to play tennis, and I figured maybe you'd want to play. No big deal. You don't dig tennis, we can go have dinner somewhere."

"Are you out of your mind? What in God's name makes you think I have any desire whatsoever to play tennis, play hopscotch, have dinner, or do anything else with you?"

"Well, listen to the red-hot mama. Sing it, sweetheart. What's to get so excited about?"

"I happen to be a married woman." She was shouting and Zina and Kat could hear her tone from the other side of the door. They wondered who had called. Kat raised an eyebrow, and Zina went to help a client. Inside, the conversation continued.

"Yeah, so you happen to be a married woman. And your old man happens to be sitting on his ass in the joint. Which is too bad, but which leaves you out here with the rest of us human beings who like to play tennis, play hopscotch, eat dinner, and get laid." Now she felt genuinely nauseated. She was remembering his thick black hair and the smell of him, and the ugly ring with the pink stone in it. It was incredible. That man, that hideous pig of a man, that absolute total stranger was calling her and talking about "getting laid." She sat there pale and trembling with tears starting to sting her eyelids again. It was funny. She knew that somewhere in all this it was funny. But it didn't make her want to laugh. It made her want to cry, want to go home, want to . . . this was what Ian had left her. The Barry Yorks of the world, and people calling about the checks she had "forgotten" to send and that she would continue to forget for at least another six or seven or nine or ten weeks or maybe even years. To the point that she was afraid to walk into the florist now for so much as a bunch of daisies, because she probably owed him money too. She owed everyone money. And now this animal on the phone wanted to get laid.

"I . . . Mr. . . . I'm . . ." She fought the tears out of her voice and swallowed hard.

"Whatsa matter, sweetheart, married women in Pacific Heights don't get horny, or you already got a boyfriend?"

Jessica sat looking at the phone, her chin trembling, her hand shaking, tears streaming down her face, and her lower lip pouting as if she were a child whose best doll has just been smashed to bits. It had finally all hit her. This was what had happened to her life. She shook her head slowly, and gently hung up the phone.

CHAPTER 24

"See you later, ladies." She picked up her bag, and started out of the shop. It was early April, and a beautiful warm Friday morning. Spring seemed to be everywhere.

"Where are you going, Jessie?" Zina and Kat looked up surprised.

"To see Ian. I have some other things to do tomorrow, so I thought I'd go up today."

"Give him our love." She smiled at the two girls and left the shop quietly. She had been very quiet again lately. Oddly so. The irritability seemed to be passing, ever since the call from Barry York. That had been three weeks ago. She had never told Ian. But the degradation showed in her face.

York, Houghton, people calling for bills, it didn't really matter. It was her own fault. She had done it all to herself. The great Jessica Clarke. The all-powerful, all-knowing, all-paying Mrs. Jessica Clarke, and her wonderful husband Mr. Jessica Clarke. She saw it all now. The sleepless nights were beginning to pay off. She couldn't run away from it anymore. She was beginning to think, to remember, to understand. She heard it now like old tapes played back in the dark of night. She had nothing else to do but remember . . . incidents, moments, trivia, voices. Not her mother's voice now. Not Jake's. But her own, and Ian's. "Fables, darling? Do they sell?" As though that were the only thing that mattered. He had blurted out half a dozen reasons, explanations — as though he owed her any — and the fables had been beautiful. But it didn't matter, she had killed them before they'd been born. With one line. "Do they sell?" Who cared if they sold? It was probably why he had bought her the Morgan with his publisher's advance. It was the loudest way he could think of to answer.

And other times.

"The opera, sweetheart? Why the opera? It's so expensive."

"But we enjoy it. Don't you, Jessie? I thought you did."

"Yeah, but — oh, what the hell. I'll take it out of the house money."

"Oh, is that it?" There had been a long pause. "I already bought the tickets, Jess. With 'my' money." But he had decided not to go in the end. He had decided to work at the last minute. He hadn't gone all that season.

Tiny moments, minute phrases that slashed into hearts with the blow of a machete, leaving scars on a life, on a marriage, on a man. Why? When she needed him so much? Or was that it? That she needed him, and she knew he didn't need her in the same way?

"But he needed me too." Her voice sounded loud in the solitude of the car. She couldn't allow Astrid to chauffeur her three times a week, so she now rented a compact to go up and see him. Another expense she could ill afford. But as she drove along, she wondered. Why the barbs? The small digs over the years? To clip his wings so he never flew away? Because if he had flown away, she couldn't have survived. And the joke of it was that he had flown anyway. For one afternoon, and maybe a thousand afternoons before that, but for one afternoon that had cost them everything. He had needed a woman who didn't shoot off her mouth, didn't cut him down. Someone who didn't need him, didn't love him, didn't hurt him.

It was crazy, really. Whatever she had done, she had done out of the fear of losing him. And now look at where they were. She was so engrossed in her thoughts that she almost missed the turnoff, and she was still pensive as she waited for him to appear at the window.

Even after Ian arrived, she seemed to have her mind more on the past than the present. And he seemed wrapped up in his own thoughts too. She looked up at him and tried to smile. She had a splitting headache and she was tired. She kept seeing her own reflection in the glass window that stood between them. It made her feel as if she were talking to herself.

"You're not very chatty today, Mr. Clarke. Anything wrong?"

"No, just thinking about the book, I guess. I'm getting to the point where it's hard to relate to much else. I'm all wrapped up in it." He noticed an odd flash in her eyes as he finished speaking, and started to tell her about the book. She let him ramble on for a few minutes and then interrupted.

"You know something? You're amazing. I come all the way up here to find out how you are, and to talk to you about what's happening in my life. And you talk to me about the book."

"What's wrong with that?" He looked puzzled as he watched her from the other side of the glass. "You tell me about Lady J."

"That's different, Ian. That's real, for Chrissake." She was sounding shrill, and it irritated him.

"Well, the book is real to me."

"So real that you can't even take an hour of your precious time to talk to me? Hell, you've been sitting there like a zombie for the last hour, telling me about the goddam book. And every time I start to tell you about me, you fade out."

"That's not true, Jess." He looked upset and reached for a cigarette. "The book is just going really well and I wanted to tell you about it. I don't think I've ever hit such a good writing spell, that's all." He knew he'd said the wrong thing as soon as the words were out of his mouth. The look on her face was incredible. "Jessie, what the hell is wrong with you? You look like someone just shoved a hot poker up your ass."

"Yeah, or slapped my face, maybe. Jesus Christ, you sit there and you tell me how brilliantly your writing is going, how you've never 'hit such a good writing spell,' like you're on some kind of fucking vacation in there. Do you know what's happening in *my* life?" She took a deep breath and he felt as if poison were pouring at him through the phone. She had lost control and she wasn't about to stop now.

"You really want to know what's happening to me while you're having such a 'good writing spell'? Well, I'll tell you, darling. Lady J is going broke, people are calling me up day and night telling me to pay our bills and threatening to sue me. Your car fell apart, my nerves have had it, I have nightmares about Inspector Houghton every night, and the bailbondsman called me up for a date three weeks ago. He figured I needed to get laid. And maybe the sonofabitch is right, but not by him. I haven't so much as touched your hand in I don't know how many months, and I'm going goddam crazy. My whole stinking life is on the rocks, and you're having a good writing spell! And you know what else is terrific, *darling* —" she dripped venom in his ear, and others in the room watched as he sat there incredulous. She wasn't keeping any secrets from anyone.

"What's absolutely marvelous, Ian my love, is that I drove all the way up here today blaming myself for the nine-thousandth time for everything I've done wrong in our marriage, about the pressures I've put on you, about the rotten things I've said. Do you realize that by now I've replayed every lousy scene in our marriage, everything I've ever done wrong that made you even want to go to bed with a piece of shit like Margaret Burton? I've been blaming myself ever since it happened. I've even blamed myself for supporting your writing career, thinking that I stole your manhood. And while I'm crucifying myself, you know what you're doing? Having the best writing spell in your life. Well, you know what? You make me sick. While you sit up here in this glorified writers' colony they call a prison, my whole life is coming apart and you're not doing a goddam thing about it, sweetheart. Nothing. And I'll tell you something else, I'm sick to death of that puking window, of having to twist around like a pretzel just to see you and not a reflection of myself. I'm sick of getting sweaty hands and sweaty ears and a sweaty brain just talking to you on the goddam phone here . . . I'm sick to death of the whole goddam mess!" She was shouting so loudly that the whole room was watching now, but neither of them noticed. It had been building for months.

"And I suppose you think I enjoy it here?"

"Yes, I think you enjoy it here. A colony for gigolo writers."

"That's right, sweetheart. That's what this is. And that's all I do here, is write. I never think about my wife, and how I got here, and why, and of that damn woman, or of the trial. I never have to shove my way out of getting laid by some guy with the hots for me.

"Listen, lady, if you think this is my idea of living, you can shove it right up your ass. But I'll tell you something else. If you think our marriage is my idea of living you can put that in the same place. I thought we had a marriage. I thought we had something. Well, guess what, Mrs. Clarke? We didn't have a fucking thing. Nothing. No kids, no honesty, and two half-assed careers. Two half-assed people, the way I see it now. And you've spent most of the last six years trying not to grow up and playing cripple after you lost your parents. Not only that, but making me feel guilty for God knows what, so I'd stick around and hold your hand. And I was dumb enough to swallow all that because I was stupid enough to love you and I wanted to have my writing career too. Well, the combo, such as it was, was a lousy one, Lady Bountiful. And you can have it. I happen to need a wife, not a banker or a neurotic child. Maybe that's why I'm happy right now, believe it or not, as stinking as this place happens to be. I'm writing and you're not supporting me.

How's that for a shocker, baby? You're not picking up the tab and I don't owe you one thing except for the fact that you held my hand every inch of the way during the trial and you were marvelous. But I'm going to pay you back for the bills on that eventually. And if your idea now is to make me suffer as much as possible, to make me feel as guilty as possible over how fucked up you can get, how bad the bills are, and how fast my car can fall apart, then fuck you. I can't do anything about anything in here. All I can do is give a damn about you, be grateful you come to see me, and finish my fucking book. And if you don't dig seeing me, do me a big favor and don't come anymore. I can live without it."

Jessica felt the all-too-familiar surge of panic clutch at her chest as she watched his face. But this time it was worse. They had never said things like this to each other. And she couldn't stop now. She could still feel the bile frothing up in her soul.

"Why don't you want me to come see you, darling? Did you find another sweetheart in here? Is that it, angel? Does the big he-man have another he-man to love?" Ian stood up and looked as if he were going to hit her, right through the glass window, much to the fascination of the now silent crowd on both sides of the glass.

"Is that it, darling? Have you gone gay!"

"You make me sick."

"Oh, that's right, I forgot. You don't like 'infamous crimes against nature.' Or do you?" She looked intolerably sweet as she raised her eyebrows, and her heart pounded violently in her chest. "Maybe you did rape that woman after all."

"Lady, if I weren't in here I'd put my fist right through your face." He towered over her, with the veil of glass between them, the phones still in their hands, and slowly Jessica rose to face him. She knew that the moment had come and she couldn't believe it. She still couldn't stop.

"Put your fist through my face?" Their voices were soft now. He had spoken to her with the measured tone of a man who is almost finished, and she was speaking in the silvery whisper of a viper about to strike the last blow. "Put your fist through my face?" She repeated the words again with a smile. "But why now, darling? You never had the balls to before. Did you, love?"

He answered her in less than a whisper, and her heart almost stopped when she saw the look in his eyes.

"No, Jess, I didn't. But I don't have anything to lose now. I've already lost it.

And that makes everything a lot easier." He smiled a small, strange smile that chilled her, looked at her thoughtfully for a brief moment, put down the phone, and walked out. He never looked back once, and she felt her mouth open in astonishment. What had he just said? She wanted him to come back, so she could ask him again, so that . . . what did he mean, "that makes everything a lot easier"? What did . . . the sonofabitch . . . he was walking out on her, he had no right to, he couldn't, he . . . and what had she done? What had she said? She sank into her seat as though she were in shock, and slowly the babble of voices around her returned to normal. Ian had long since disappeared through the far door, was no longer visible. She had been wrong. He did have the balls. And he had done just what she had always feared most. He had walked out on her.

The front bumper of the rented car brushed the hedges in front of the house as she pulled into the driveway. She put her head down on the wheel and felt the breath catch in her throat. There was a sob lodged there somewhere, but it was stuck, it wouldn't come out. The weight of her head set off the horn, and the sound felt like it was blowing off the top of her head. It felt good.

She wouldn't take her head off the steering wheel. She just stayed there until two men passing by came rushing into the driveway on foot. They knocked on the window and she turned her face slowly to one side, looked at them, and laughed, a high-pitched hysterical giggle. The men looked at each other questioningly, opened the car door, and gently eased Jessie's body back on the seat. She looked from one to the other, laughed hysterically again, and then the laughter snagged on a sob. It wrenched itself from her throat and became a long, sad, lonely wail. She shook her head slowly and said one word over and over between sobs: "Ian."

"Lady, are you drunk?" The older man of the two looked hot and uncomfortable. He had thought she was hurt, or sick, with her head down on the steering wheel like that, and making such a racket with the horn. But here she was, drunk, or crazy, or stoned. He hadn't bargained on that. The younger man looked at her, shrugged his shoulders, and grinned.

Jessie shook her head slowly from side to side and said the only word she could focus on: "Ian."

"Sister, you stoned?" She didn't answer and the younger man shrugged again and grinned. "Must be good stuff."

"Ian."

"Who's Ian? Your boyfriend?"

Another blind shake of the head.

The two men looked at each other again and closed the door of the car. At least the horn wasn't blaring anymore, and she wouldn't sober up for hours. They walked away, the younger one amused, the older one less so.

"You sure she's stoned? She looks kind of mixed up to me. I mean like mixed-up sick. Kinda crazy."

"Stoned crazy." The younger man laughed, slapped his belly, and put his arm around his friend just as Astrid drove by and noticed them walking out of the driveway, laughing and looking pleased with themselves. She stopped the car and frowned as a ripple of fear ran up her spine. They didn't look like police, but . . . they noticed her watching them and the younger man waved while the older one smiled. Astrid couldn't understand what was happening, but they slid into a red sedan and seemed to be taking their time. There was nothing furtive or rapid about their movements, and Astrid noticed Jessie in her rented car now. Everything was all right. Astrid honked. But Jessie didn't turn around. She honked again, and once more, and the two men broke into raucous laughter.

"Not you too, sister. The woman in that car is so loaded we had to peel her off the steering wheel just to get her off the horn." They waved vaguely toward Jessie's driveway, started their car, and pulled out of the parking space as Astrid hopped out of her car and ran into the driveway.

Jessie was still sitting there, crying and sobbing and holding her single word in her mouth. "Ian." Astrid wasn't so sure she was stoned. A little maybe, but not as much as she looked. In shock maybe. Something had snapped.

"Jessica?" She slid an arm around her and spoke gently as Jessie slumped slightly in the seat. "Hi, Jessie, it's me, Astrid." Jessica looked at her and nodded. The two men were gone now. Everyone was gone. Even Ian.

"Ian." She said it more clearly now.

"What about Ian?"

"Ian."

Astrid wiped her face gently with a handkerchief.

"Tell me about Ian." Astrid's heart was pounding and she was trying to keep her mind clear and watch Jessica's eyes. She didn't think it was an overdose of pills.

More like an overdose of trouble. Jessie had finally had enough.

"What about Ian, love? Tell me. Was he sick today?"

Jessica shook her head. At least he wasn't hurt. Astrid had thought of that first, with tales of prison horrors from the newspapers instantly coursing through her head. But Jessica had motioned no.

"Was something wrong?"

Jessica took a deep breath and nodded. She took another deep breath and leaned back against the seat a little.

"We . . . we had . . . a fight." The words were barely intelligible, but Astrid nodded.

"What about?"

Jessica shrugged, looking confused again. "Ian."

"What did you fight about, Jessie?"

"I . . . I don't . . . know."

"Do you remember?"

Jessica shrugged again and closed her eyes. "About . . . everything . . . I think. We both . . . said . . . terrible things. Over."

"Over what?" But she thought she knew.

"Over. All over."

"What's all over, Jessie?" Her voice was so gentle, and the tears poured down Jessica's face with fresh force.

"Our marriage is . . . all . . . over . . ." She

432

shook her head dumbly and closed her eyes again. "Ian . . ."

"It's not all over, Jessie. Just take it easy, now. You two probably just had a lot to get off your chests. You've been through a lot of rough times together lately. A lot of shocks. It had to come out." But Jessica shook her head.

"No, it's over. I . . . I was so awful to him. I've always . . . been awful to him. I . . ." But then she couldn't speak anymore.

"Why don't we go inside so you can lie down for a while." Jessica shook her head and wouldn't move, and Astrid fought to get her attention. "Jessie, listen to me for a minute. I want to take you somewhere." The girl's eyes flew open in terror. "Someplace very nice, you'll like it. We'll go together."

"A hospital?"

Astrid smiled for the first time in five minutes. "No, silly. My mother's ranch. I think it would do you a lot of good, and . . ."

Jessica shook her head stubbornly. "No . . . I . . ."

"What? Why not?"

"Ian."

"Nonsense. I'm going to take you down there, and you'll have a good rest. I think you've really had enough for a while. Don't you?"

Jessica nodded mutely with her eyes closed again.

"Jessie, did you take a lot of pills today?"

She started to shake her head and then stopped and shrugged.

"How many? Tell me."

"I don't know . . . not sure."

"Just give me a rough idea. Two? Four? Six? Ten?" She prayed it wouldn't be that many.

"Eight . . . I don't know . . . seven . . . nine . . ." Jesus.

"Are they in your bag?" Jessica nodded. And Astrid gently took her handbag from the seat. "I'm going to take them, Jessie, okay?" Jessica smiled then for the first time and took a long deep breath. She almost looked like herself again.

"Do I . . . have a choice?" The two women laughed, one fuzzily and the other nervously, and Jessica let her friend help her inside. She wasn't so much stoned as wrung out. She let herself slide slowly into a chair in the living room and didn't even move as she listened to the sounds of Astrid bustling around the bedroom and bathroom. It was going to be so good to be away from it all, even from the sight of Ian behind the glass window. She knew then that she would never see him there again. She'd work the rest out later, but she already knew that. She heaved a deep sigh and went to sleep in the chair until Astrid woke her and led her out to the Jaguar.

Her bags had been packed, the house was locked up, and Jessie felt as though she were a small child again, well taken care of and greatly loved.

"What about the car?"

"The one you rented?" It still sat crookedly in the driveway. Jessica nodded. "I'll have someone pick it up later. Don't worry about it." Jessica didn't. It was part of the bliss of having money. Having "someone pick it up later." Anonymous faces and hands to do menial tasks. "And I called the girls at the shop and told them you were going away with me. You can call them yourself tomorrow and give them instructions."

"Who'll . . . who'll . . . you know, well, run it?" Everything was still jumbled in Jessica's head, and Astrid smiled and patted her cheek gently.

"I will. And I can hardly wait. What a treat, a vacation for you and a job for me." Jessica smiled and looked more like herself again.

"And the fall line?"

Astrid raised an eyebrow in surprise as

she started the car.

"You must be sobering up. I'll send Katsuko, with your permission. I'll take care of the finances of it, and you can pay me back later." Jessica shook her head and looked back at her friend. The brief nap had sobered her.

"I can't pay you back later, Astrid. Lady J is fighting just to survive. That's one of the reasons nobody's gone to New York yet."

"Would Lady J accept a loan from me?"

Jessica smiled. "I don't know, but her mother might. Can I give it some thought?"

"Sure. After Katsuko gets back. I have news for you. You're not allowed to make any decisions for the next two weeks. None. Not even what you eat for breakfast. That's part of the ground rules of this little vacation of yours. I'll advance the money for the fall line, and we'll work it out later. I need a tax write-off anyway."

"I . . . but . . ."

"Shut up."

"You know something?" Jessie looked at her with a small smile and tired, swollen eyes. "Maybe I will. I need the fall line or the shop will fold anyway. What the hell. Was Katsuko happy about going?"

"What do you think?" The two women smiled again and Astrid pulled up in front of her own house. "Can you make it up my stairs?" Jessica nodded, and slowly followed Astrid into the house. "I just need a few things; I'll only be gone overnight. I want to be at work tomorrow." She glowed at the words. And fifteen minutes later they were back in the car and heading for the freeway. Jessie still felt as though a bomb had hit her life, now everything was moving too quickly.

The words with Ian came back to her as they drove along in silence. She had closed her eyes and Astrid thought she was sleeping. But she was wide awake. Too much so. And more awake than she had been in a long time. She needed another pill, and Astrid had flushed them all down the toilet, back at the house. All of them. The red ones, the blue ones, the yellow ones, the black-and-green ones. There was nothing left. Except her own head, pounding with Ian's words . . . and his face . . . and . . . why had they done that to each other? Why the venom, the hatred, the anger? It didn't make sense to her. Nothing did. Maybe they'd always hated each other. Maybe even the good times had been a lie. It was so hard to figure it all out now. And it was too late anyway. Looking for the answers was like searching for your grandmother's silver thimble in the rubble of your home after it had burned to the ground. Together, she and Ian had set fire to their marriage, and from opposite sides of a pane of glass had watched it burn, fanning the flames, refusing to leave until the last beam was gone.

CHAPTER 25

Astrid touched her shoulder again and she woke up, frightened and confused about where she was. The pills had really worn off now and she felt jangled.

"Take it easy, Jessie. You're at the ranch. It's almost midnight, and everything's fine." Jessica stretched and looked around. It was dark but stars shone overhead. There was a fresh smell in the air, and she could hear the whinny of horses somewhere in the distance. And just to their right was a large stone house with bright yellow shutters. The house was well lit and a door stood open.

Astrid had slipped inside for a moment with her mother before waking Jessie. Her mother was not shocked or even surprised. She had been through crises before, with Astrid, with friends, with family years before. Things happened to people, they were shaken for a while, but most of them survived. A few didn't, but most did. And the ranch was a good place to recover.

"Come on, sleepyhead, my mother has some hot chocolate and sandwiches waiting, and I don't know about you, but I'm starved." Astrid stood next to the open car and Jessica ran a comb through her hair with a rueful grin.

"How's she fixed for pills?"

"She's not." Astrid looked searchingly at Jessie. "Is it bad?"

Jessica nodded and then shrugged.

"But I'll live. Hot chocolate, huh? How does that compare to Seconal?" Astrid made a face at her and got her suitcase out of the trunk.

"I went through the same thing after Tom. I arrived here and my mother threw everything out. All the pills. And I was a lot less good-natured about it than you were this afternoon."

"I was just too stoned to react. You were lucky. And here, let me carry that." She reached for the suitcase and Astrid gave it up to her. "Ian always says that an Amazon like me . . ." And then she stopped and let her voice trail off. Astrid watched the bowed head as she quietly walked toward the house. She was glad she had brought her, and only sorry she hadn't done it before. She wondered just how serious the fight with Ian had been. Something told her this was for real, but it was impossible to tell.

Their shoes crunched on the gravel walk that led to the house, and the smell of fresh grass and flowers was everywhere. Jessie noticed that the place looked cheerful even in the dark. There was an array of multi-colored flowers all around the stone building and in great profusion near the door. She smiled as she walked past them and up the single step.

"Watch your head!" Astrid called out as she almost hit it against the doorway, and the two women arrived in the front hall side by side. There was a small upright piano there, painted bright red, a long mirror, a number of bronze spittoons, and a wall of exotic and colorful hats. Just beyond were pine floors and hooked rugs, comfortable couches and a rocking chair by the fire. There were warm-looking oil paintings and a long wall of books. It was an odd combination of good modern, delightful Victorian, simply enjoyable, and pleasantly old, but it worked. Plants and an old Victrola painted red like the piano, some first-edition books, and a very handsome modern couch covered in a pale oatmeal fabric. Old lace granny curtains hung at the windows, and a large tiled stove stood in one corner. The room looked happy and warm, with a surprising element of chic.

"Good evening."

Jessica turned at the sound of a voice and saw a tiny woman standing in the kitchen doorway. She had the same blond-gray hair as her daughter and cornflower blue eyes that sparkled and laughed. The simple words "good evening" sounded as though they amused her. She walked slowly toward Jessica and held out a hand. "It is very nice indeed to have you here, my dear. I take it Astrid has warned you that I'm a querulous old woman and the ranch is dull as dishwater. But I'm delighted you've come down." The light in her eyes danced like flame.

"I warned her of no such thing, Mother. I raved about the place, so you'd better be on your best behavior."

"Good God, how awful. Now I shall have to put away all my pornographic books and cancel the dancing boys, shall I? How distressing." She clasped her hands as though greatly disturbed and then burst forth with a youthful giggle. She gestured comfortably toward the couch and the two women followed her to seats near the fire. The promised hot chocolate was waiting in a Limoges china service patterned with delicate flowers.

"That's pretty, Mother. Is it new?" Astrid poured herself a cup of hot chocolate and looked at the china.

"No, dear. It's very old — 1880, I believe." The two women exchanged a teasing glance. One could easily see that they were not only mother and daughter, but also friends. Jessica felt a pang of envy as she watched, but also the glow of reflected warmth.

"I meant, is it new to you?" Astrid took a sip of the warm chocolate.

"Oh, that's what you meant! Yes, as a matter of fact it is."

"Wretch, and you knew I'd notice and you used it tonight just to show it off." But she looked pleased at the implied compliment, and her mother laughed.

"You're absolutely right! Pretty, isn't it?"

"Very." The two women's eyes danced happily, and Jessica smiled, taking in the scene. She was surprised at the youthful appearance of Astrid's mother. And at the elegance that had stayed with her despite the passing of years and life on the ranch. She was wearing well-cut gray gabardine slacks and a very handsome silk blouse that Jessie knew must have come from Paris. It was in very flattering blues that picked up the color of her eyes. She wore it with pearls and several large and elegant gold rings, one with a rather large diamond set in it. She looked more New York or Connecticut than ranch. Jessie almost laughed aloud remembering the image Astrid had portrayed of her months before, in cowboy gear. That was hardly the picture Jessie was seeing.

"You came at the right time, Jessica. The countryside is so lush and lovely at this time of year. Soft and green and almost furry-looking. I bought the ranch at this time of year, and that's probably why I succumbed. Land is so seductive in the spring."

Jessica laughed. "I didn't exactly plan it this way, Mrs. Williams." But my husband went to prison and I turned into a junkie on sleeping pills and tranquilizers and you see, I tried very hard to have a nervous breakdown and we had this awful fight this morning and . . . she laughed again and shook her head. "I didn't plan it at all. And you're very kind to have me down here on such short notice."

"No problem at all." She smiled, but her eyes took in everything. She noticed that Jessica was eating nothing and only sipping at her hot chocolate. She was smoking her second cigarette in the moments since the two women had arrived. She suspected that Jessica had acquired the same problem

Astrid had had after Tom's death. Pills. "Just make yourself at home, my dear, and stay as long as you like."

"I may stay forever."

"Of course not. You'll be bored in a week." The old woman's eyes twinkled again and Astrid laughed.

"You're not bored here, Mother."

"Oh, yes, I am, but then I go to Paris or New York or Los Angeles, or come up to visit you in that dreadful mausoleum of yours . . ."

"Mother!"

"It is and you know it. A very handsome mausoleum, but nonetheless . . . you know what I think. I told you last year that I thought you ought to sell it and get a new house. Something smaller and younger and more cheerful. I'm not even old enough to live there. I told Tom that when he was alive, and I can't imagine why I shouldn't tell you now."

"Jessica has the sort of place you would adore."

"Oh? A grass hut in Tahiti, no doubt." All three women laughed and Jessica made an attempt at eating a sandwich. Her stomach was doing somersaults, but she hoped that if she ate something her hands might cease trembling. She suspected that she was in for a rough couple of days, but at least the company would be good. She was already in love with Astrid's outspoken mother.

"She lives in that marvelous blue-and-white house in the next block from us. The one with all the flowers out front."

"I do remember it more or less. Pretty, but a bit small, isn't it?"

"Very," Jessica said between bites. The sandwich was cream cheese and ham with fresh watercress and paper-thin slices of tomato.

"I can't bear the city anymore myself. Except for a visit. But after a while, I'm glad to come home. The symphonies bore me, the people overdress, the restaurants are mediocre, the traffic is appalling. Here, I ride in the morning, walk in the woods, and life feels like an adventure every day. I'm too old for the city. Do you ride?" Her manner was so brisk that it was hard to believe she was past fifty-five; Jessica knew she was in fact seventy-two. She smiled at the question.

"I haven't ridden in years, but I'd like to."

"Then you may. Do whatever you want, whenever you want. I make breakfast at seven, but you don't have to get up. Lunch is a free-lance proposition, and dinner's at eight. I don't like country hours. It's embar-

446

rassing to eat dinner at five or six. And I don't get hungry till later anyway. And by the way, my daughter introduced me as Mrs. Williams, but my name is Bethanie. I prefer it." She was peppery as all hell, but the blue eyes were gentle and the mouth always looked close to laughter.

"That's a beautiful name."

"It'll do. And now, ladies, I bid you good night. I want to ride early in the morning." She smiled warmly at her guest, kissed her daughter on the top of her head, and walked briskly up the stairs to her bedroom, having assured Jessica that Astrid would give her a choice of rooms. There were three to choose from, and they were all quite ready for guests. People came to visit Bethanie often, Astrid explained. It was a rare week when no one stayed at the ranch. Friends from Europe included her in their elaborate itineraries, other friends flew out to the Coast from New York and rented cars to drive down to see her, and she had a few friends in Los Angeles. And of course Astrid.

"Astrid, this is simply fabulous." Jessica was still a bit overwhelmed by it all. The house, the mother, the hospitality, the openness of it all, and the peppery warmth of her hostess. "And your mother is remarkable." Astrid smiled, pleased.

"I think Tom married me just so he wouldn't lose track of her. He adored her, and she him." Astrid smiled again, pleased at the look on Jessica's face.

"I can see why he loved her. Ian would fall head over heels for her." Her tone changed as she said it, and she seemed to drift off. It was a moment before her attention returned to Astrid.

"I think it'll do you good to be down here, Jessie."

Jessica nodded slowly. "It sounds corny, but I feel better already. A little shaky —" she held up a hand to show the trembling fingers, and grinned sheepishly — "but better nonetheless. It's such a relief not to have to go through another night alone in that house. You know, it's crazy. I'm a grown woman. I don't know why it gets to me so badly, but it's just awful, Astrid. I almost hope the damn place burns to the ground while I'm gone."

"Don't say that."

"I mean it. I've come to hate that house. As happy as I once was there, I think I detest it twice as much now. And the studio — it's like a reminder of all my worst failings."

"Do you honestly feel that you've failed, Jessica?"

Jessica nodded slowly but firmly.

"Single-handedly?"

"Almost."

"I hope you come to realize how absurd that is."

"You know what hurts the worst? The fact that I thought we had a fantastic marriage. The best. And now . . . it all looks so different. He swallowed his resentments, I did things my way. He cheated on me and didn't tell me; I guessed but didn't want to *know*. It's all so jumbled. I'm going to need time to sort it out."

"You can stay down here as long as you like. Mother will never get tired of you."

"Maybe not, but I wouldn't want to abuse her hospitality. I think if I stay a week, I'll be not only lucky, but eternally grateful." Astrid only smiled over her hot chocolate. People had a way of saying they'd stay for a few days or a week and of still being there five weeks later. Bethanie didn't mind, as long as they didn't get in her hair. She had her own schedule, her friends, her gardening, her books, her projects. She liked to go her own way and let other people go theirs, which was part of her charm and her great success as a hostess. She was exceedingly independent and she had a healthy respect for people's solitude, including her own.

Astrid showed Jessica the choice of available rooms, and Jessie settled on a small, cozy, pink room with an old-fashioned quilt on the bed and copper pots hanging over the fireplace. It had a high slanted ceiling, high enough so she wouldn't bump her head when she got out of bed. There was a lovely bay window with a window seat, and a rocking chair by the fireplace. Jessica heaved a deep sigh and sat on the bed.

"You know, Astrid, I may never go home." It was said between a smile and a yawn.

"Good night, puss. Get some sleep. I'll see you at breakfast." Jessica nodded and yawned again. She waved as Astrid closed the door, and then called a last sleepy "Thanks."

She would have to write to Ian in the morning, to tell him where she was. To tell him something. But she'd worry about that tomorrow. For the moment she was a world and a half away from all her problems. The boutique, Ian, bills, that unbearable window in Vacaville. None of it was real anymore. She was home now. That was how it felt, and she smiled at the thought as she lit the kindling and put a log on the fire before slipping into her nightgown. Ten minutes later she was asleep. For the first time in four months, without any pills.

■ ■ ■ ■

There was a knock on Jessie's door moments after she had closed her eyes. But when she opened them, sunlight was streaming in between the white organdy curtains, and a fat calico cat yawned sleepily in a patch of sunlight on her bed. The clock said ten-fifteen.

"Jessie? Are you up?" Astrid poked her head in the door. She was carrying an enormous white wicker tray laden with goodies.

"Oh no! Breakfast in bed! Astrid, you'll spoil me forever!" The two women laughed and Jessie sat up in bed, her blond hair falling over her shoulders in a tumult of loose curls. She looked like a young girl, and surprisingly rested now.

"You're looking awfully healthy this morning, madam."

"And hungry as hell. I slept like a log. Wow!" She was faced with waffles, bacon, two fried eggs and a steaming mug of hot coffee, all of it served on delicate flowered china. There was a vase in the corner of the tray with one yellow rose in it. "I feel like it's my birthday or something."

"So do I! I can hardly wait to get to the

shop!" Astrid giggled and slid into the rocking chair while Jessie went to town on the breakfast. "I should have let you sleep a while longer, but I wanted to get back to the city. And Mother decided you needed breakfast in bed on your first day."

"I'm embarrassed. But not too embarrassed to eat all this." She chuckled and dove into the waffles. "I'm starving."

"You should be. You didn't have any dinner."

"What's your mother up to this morning?"

"God knows. She went riding at eight, came back to change, and just drove off a few minutes ago. She goes her own way, and doesn't invite questions."

Jessica smiled and sat back in the bed with a mouthful of waffle. "You know, I should feel guilty as hell, sitting here like this with Ian where he is, but for the first time in five months, I don't. I just feel good. Fabulous, as a matter of fact." And relieved. It was such a relief not to *have* to do anything. Not to have to be at the shop, or on the way to see Ian, or opening bills, or taking phone calls. She was in another world now. She was free. "I feel so super, Astrid." She grinned, stretched, and yawned, with a splendid breakfast under her belt, and the sun streaming across her bed.

"Then just enjoy it. You needed something like this. I wanted to bring you down here over Christmas. Remember?" Jessica nodded regretfully, remembering what she had done instead. She had blotted out Christmas with a handful of pills.

"If I'd only known."

She stroked the calico cat and it licked her finger as Astrid sat in the rocking chair, quietly rocking and watching her friend. With one good night of sleep she already looked better. But there was still a lot to resolve. She didn't envy Jessica the task ahead of her.

"Why don't you stay down for a couple of days, Astrid?"

Astrid let out a whoop and shook her head. "And miss all the fun of running the boutique? You're crazy. You couldn't keep me down here if you tied me to a gatepost. This'll be the most fun I've had in years!"

"Astrid, you're nutty, but I love you. If it weren't for you, I couldn't sit around down here like a lady of leisure. So go have a good old time with Lady J. She's all yours!" And then Jessie looked wistful. "I almost wish I really never had to go back."

"Do you want to sell me Lady J?" Something in Astrid's voice made Jessica look up.

"Are you serious?"

"Very. Maybe even a partnership, if you don't want to sell out completely. But I've given it a lot of thought. I just never knew how to broach it to you."

"Like you just did, I guess. But I've never thought of it. It might be an idea. Let me mull it over. And see how you enjoy it while I'm gone. You may hate the place by next weekend."

But Astrid could tell from the sound of her voice that Jessica had no intention of giving up Lady J. There was still that pride of ownership in her voice. Lady J was hers, no matter how out of sorts with it she was at the moment.

"Were you really serious about sending Katsuko to New York, by the way?" Jessie was still stunned by all that had happened in a mere twenty-four hours.

"I was. I told her to plan on leaving tomorrow. That way you can give her any instructions you want. We can square the finances of it later. Much later. So don't go adding that to your pile of worries. What about the fall line? Any thoughts, orders, requests, caveats, whatever?"

"None. I trust her implicitly. She has a better buying sense than I do, and she's been in retailing for long enough to know what she's doing. After the season we just had, I'm not sure I'm fit to buy for the place anymore."

"Everyone can have an off season."

"Yeah. All the way around." Jessie smiled and Astrid looked back at her friend with warmth in her eyes.

"Well, I'd best be getting my fanny in gear. I have a long drive ahead. Any messages for the home front?"

"Yeah. One." Jessica grinned, then threw back her head and laughed. "Good-bye."

"Jerk. Have a good time down here. This place put me back together once."

"And you look damn good to me." Jessie climbed lazily out of bed, stretched again, and gave Astrid a last hug. "Have a safe trip and give the girls my love."

She watched her leave and waved from the bedroom window. Jessie was alone in the house now except for the cat, which was parading slowly across the window seat. There were country sounds from outside, and a delicious silence all around her in the airy, sun-filled house. She wandered barefoot down the long upstairs hall, peeking into rooms, opening books, pirouetting here and there, looking at paintings, chasing the cat, and then went downstairs to do more of the same. She was free! Free! For the first time in seven years, ten years, fifty years, forever, she was free. Of burdens, responsibilities, and terrors. The day before she had hit rock bottom. The last support of her decaying foundation had come tumbling, roaring down . . . and she hadn't fallen with it. Astrid had held her up, and taken her away.

But the best part of all was that she hadn't cracked. She would remember all her life that moment when two strangers had pulled her back from the steering wheel where she was pressing on the horn. She had decided to let herself go crazy then, just slide into a pool of oblivion, never to return to the land of the ugly and dying and evil, the land of the "living." But she hadn't gone crazy at all. She had hurt. More than she had ever hurt in her life. But she hadn't gone crazy. And here she was, wandering around a delightful house in the country, barefoot, in her nightgown, with a huge breakfast in her stomach and a smile on her face.

And the amazing thing was that she didn't need Ian. Without him, the roof hadn't fallen in. It was a new idea to Jessie, and she didn't quite know what to do with it yet. It changed everything.

CHAPTER 26

It was late in the afternoon of her first day on the ranch that Jessica decided to sit down and write to Ian. She wanted to let him know where she was. She still felt she had to check in. But it was hard to explain to him why she was there. Having kept up the front for so long, it was difficult to tell him just what kind of shape she'd been in behind the façade. She had blown it the day before, but now she had to sit down and tell him quietly. It turned every "fine" she had ever told him into a lie. And most of them had been lies. She hadn't been willing to admit to herself how far from fine she was, and now she had to do both — admit it to herself and to him. She had no more accusations to level at him, but no explanations she wanted to give either.

Words didn't come easily. What could you say? I love you, darling, but I also hate you . . . I've always been afraid to lose you, but now I'm not sure anymore . . . get lost . . . she grinned at the thought, but then tried to get serious. Where to begin? And there were questions. So many questions. Suddenly she wondered how many other women there had been. And why. Because she was inadequate, or because he was hungry, or because he needed to prove something, or . . . why? Her parents had never asked each other questions, but they had been wrong, or at least, wrong for her. She had followed their example, but now she wanted answers, or thought she did. But she recognized the possibility that the answers she sought were her own. Did she love Ian? Or only need him? Did she need him, or only someone? And how do you ask seven years of questions in half a page of letter . . . do you respect me? Why? How can you? She wasn't sure if she loved or respected him or herself at this point.

She wanted to take the easy way out and simply tell him about Mrs. Williams and the ranch, but that seemed dishonest. And so it took her two hours to write the letter. It was one page long. She told him that yesterday had shown her she needed a rest. Astrid had come up with a marvelous suggestion, her mother's ranch.

It is precisely the kind of place where I can finally relax, come to my senses, breathe again, and be myself. Myself being, these days, an odd combination of who I used to be, who I have been catapulted into being during the past six months, and who I am becoming. It all frightens me more than a little. But even that is changing somewhat, Ian. I am tired of always being so frightened. It must have been a great burden on you all this time, my constant fears. But I am growing now. Perhaps "up"; I don't know yet. Keep at the book, you're right, and I'm sorry for yesterday. I will regret all our lives that we have borne all of this with such dignity and self-control. Perhaps if we had screamed, shrieked, kicked, yelled, and tore at our hair on the courtroom floor instead — perhaps we'd both be in better shape now. It has to come out sooner or later. I'm working on that now. Right? Well, darling. I love you. J.

She hesitated lengthily with the letter in her hands, and then folded it carefully and put it into an envelope. There was much she had not said. She just didn't want to say it yet. And she carefully inscribed his name on the envelope. But not her own. She wondered if he would think the lack of a return address was an oversight. It wasn't.

Jessica joined Astrid's mother in the living room for an after-dinner drink.

"You have no idea how happy you've made Astrid, my dear. She needs something to do. Lately all she's done is spend money. That's not healthy. The constant acquisition of meaningless possessions, just to pass the time. She doesn't enjoy it, she just does it to fill a void. But your boutique will fill that void in a far better way."

"I met her through the boutique, as a matter of fact. She just walked in one day, and we liked each other. And she's been so good to me. I hope she really enjoys the shop this week. I'm relieved to be away from it."

"Astrid mentioned that you'd had a hard time of late."

Jessie nodded, subdued.

"You'll grow from it in the end. But how disagreeable life can be while one grows!" She laughed over her Campari, and Jessie smiled. "I've always had a passionate dislike for character-building situations. But in the end, they turn out to be worthwhile, I suppose."

"I'm not sure I'd call my situation worthwhile. I suspect it's going to be the end of my marriage." There was a look of over-whelming sorrow in Jessica's eyes, but she was almost certain that she knew her mind now. She simply hadn't wanted to admit it to herself before this.

"Is that what you want now, child? Free-dom from your marriage?" She was sitting quietly by the fire, watching Jessica's face intently.

"No, not my freedom, really. I've never had problems about my 'freedom.' I love being married. But I think we've reached a time when we're simply destroying each other, and it will only get worse. In looking back now, I wonder if we didn't always destroy each other. But it's different now. I see it. And there's no excuse for letting it continue once you see."

"I suppose you'll have to take the matter in hand, then. How does your husband feel about it?" Jessie paused for a moment.

"I don't know. He's . . . he's in prison right now." She couldn't think of anyone else she would have told, and she didn't know that Astrid had already told her mother, only that Bethanie appeared to take the news in stride. "And we've had to visit each other under such strained conditions that it's been difficult to talk. It's even hard to think. You feel obliged to be so staunch and brave and noble, that you don't dare admit even to yourself, let alone each other, that you've just plain had it."

"Have you 'had it'?" She smiled gently, but Jessie did not return the smile as she nodded. "It must be very hard for you, Jessica. Considering the guilt attached to leaving someone who's in a difficult situation."

"I think that's why I haven't allowed myself to think. Not past a certain point. Because I didn't dare 'betray' him, even in my thoughts. And because I wanted to think of myself as noble and long-suffering. And because I was . . . scared to. I was afraid that if I let go, I'd never find my way back again."

"The funny thing is that one always does. We are all so much tougher than we think."

"I guess I'm beginning to understand now. It's taken me a terribly long time. But yesterday everything fell apart. Ian and I had an all-out fight where we both went for the jugular with everything we said, and I just let myself go afterward. I almost tempted the fates to break me. And . . ." She raised her hands palm up with a philosophical shrug. "Here I am. Still in one piece."

"That surprises you?" The old woman was

amused.

"Very much."

"You've never been through crises before?"

"Yes. My parents died. And my brother was killed in Vietnam. But . . . I had Ian. Ian buffered everything, Ian played ten thousand roles and wore a million different hats for me."

"That's a lot to ask of anyone."

"Not a lot. It's too much. Which is probably why he's in prison."

"I see. You blame yourself?"

"In a way."

"Jessica, why can't you let Ian have the right to his own mistakes? Whatever got him into prison, no matter how closely it relates to you — doesn't he have a right to own that mistake, whatever it was?"

"It was rape."

"I see. And you committed the rape for him." Jessica giggled nervously.

"No, of course not. I . . ."

"You what?"

"Well, I made him unhappy. Put a lot of pressure on him, paid the bills, robbed him of his manhood . . ."

"You did all that for him?" The older woman smiled and Jessica smiled too. "Don't you suppose he could have said no?"

Jessica thought about it and then nodded.

"Maybe he couldn't say no, though. Maybe he was afraid to."

"Ah, but then it's not your responsibility, is it? Why must you wear so much guilt? Do you like it?" The younger woman shook her head and looked away.

"No. And the absurd thing is that he didn't commit the rape. I know that. But the key to the whole thing is why he was in a position even to be accused of rape. And I can't absolve myself."

"Can you absolve the woman, whoever she was?"

"Of course, I . . ." And then Jessica looked up, stunned. She had forgiven Margaret Burton. Somewhere along the line, she had forgiven her. The war with Margaret Burton was over. It was one less weight on her heart. "I'd never thought of that before, not lately."

"I see. I'm intrigued to know how you robbed him of his manhood, by the way."

"I supported him."

"He didn't work?" There was no judgment in Bethanie's voice, only a question.

"He worked very hard. He's a writer."

"Published?"

"Several times. A novel, a book of fables, several articles, poems."

"Is he any good?"

"Very — he's just not very successful financially. Yet. But he will be." The pride in her voice surprised her, but not Bethanie.

"Then how dreadful of you to encourage him. What a shocking thing to do." Bethanie smiled as she sipped her Campari.

"No, I . . . it's just that I think he hates me for having 'kept' him."

"He probably does. But he probably loves you for it too. There are two sides to every medal, you know, Jessica. I'm sure he knows that too. But I'm still not quite clear about why you want to get out of the marriage."

"I didn't say that. I just said that I thought the marriage would end."

"All by itself? With no one to help it along? My dear, how extraordinary!" The two women laughed and then Bethanie waited. She was adept with her questions. Astrid had known she would be, and had purposely not warned Jessica. Bethanie made one think.

Jessica looked up after a long pause and found the core of Bethanie's eyes. She looked right into them. "I think the marriage already has ended. All by itself. No one killed it. We just let it die. Neither of us was brave enough to kill it, or save it. We just used it for our own purposes, and then

465

let it expire. Like a library card in a town you no longer live in."

"Was it a good library?"

"Excellent. At the time."

"Then don't throw the card away. You might want to go back, and you can have the card renewed."

"I don't think I'd want to."

"He makes you unhappy, then?"

"Worse. I'd destroy him."

"Oh, for God's sake, child. How incredibly boring of you — you're being noble. Do stop thinking of him, and think of yourself. I'm sure that's all he's doing. At least I hope so."

"But what if I'm not good for him and never was good for him, and . . . what if I hate the life I lead now, waiting for him?" Now they were getting to the root of it. "What if I'm afraid that I only used him, and I'm not even sure if I love him anymore? Maybe I just need someone, and not specifically Ian."

"Then you have some things to think out. Have you seen other men since he's been gone?"

"No, of course not."

"Why not?" Jessica looked shocked and Bethanie laughed. "Don't look at me like that, my dear. I may be ancient, but I'm not dead yet. I tell Astrid the same thing. I don't know what's wrong with your generation. You're all supposed to be so liberated, but you're all terribly prim and proper. It could just be that you need to be loved. You don't have to sell yourself on a street corner, but you might find a pleasant friend."

"I don't think I could do that, and stay with Ian."

"Then maybe you ought to leave him for a while, and see what you want. Perhaps he *is* a part of your past. The main thing is not to waste your present. I never have, and that's why I'm a happy old woman."

"And not an 'old' woman."

Bethanie made a face at the compliment. "Flattery won't do at all! I seem extremely old to me, each time I look in the mirror, but at least I've enjoyed myself on the way. And I'm not saying that I've been a libertine. I haven't. I'm merely saying that I didn't lock myself in a closet and then find myself hating someone for what I chose to do to myself. That's what you're doing right now. You're punishing your husband for something he can't help, and it sounds to me as though he's been punished enough, and unjustly at that. What you have to think about, and with great seriousness, is whether or not you can accept what happened. If you can, then perhaps it'll all work itself out. But if you're going to try to get restitution from him for the rest of your lives, then you might as well give up now. You can only make someone feel guilty for so long. A man won't take much of that, and the backlash from him will be rather nasty."

"It already has been." Jessica was thinking back to the argument in Vacaville as she looked dreamily into the fire.

"No man can take that for very long. Nor any woman. Who wants to feel guilty eternally? You make mistakes, you say you're sorry, you pay a price, and that's about it. You can't ask him to pay and pay and pay again. He'll end up hating you for it, Jessica. And maybe you're not just making him suffer for the present. Maybe you're just using this as an opportunity to collect an old debt. I may be wrong, but we all do that at times."

Jessica nodded soberly. It was exactly what she had been doing. Making him pay for the past, for his weaknesses and her own. For her insecurities and uncertainty. She was thinking it out when Bethanie's voice gentry prodded into her thoughts again.

"Maybe you should tell me to mind by own business."

Jessica smiled and sat back in her chair

again. "No, I think you're probably right. I haven't been looking at any of this with much perspective. And you make a great deal of sense. More than I want to admit, but still . . ."

"You're a good sport to listen, child." The two women smiled at each other again and the older woman rose to her feet and stretched delicately, her diamond rings sparkling in the firelight. She was wearing black slacks and a blue cashmere sweater the color of her eyes, and as Jessica watched her, she found herself thinking again what a beauty the woman must have been in her youth. She was still remarkably pretty in a womanly way, with a gentle veil of femininity softening whatever she did or said. She was actually even lovelier than her daughter. Softer, warmer, prettier — or perhaps it was just that she was more alive.

"You know, if you'll forgive me, Jessica, I think I'll go up to bed. I want to ride early in the morning and I won't ask you to join me. I rise at such uncivilized hours." Laughter danced in her eyes as she bent to kiss Jessica's forehead, and Jessie quickly lifted her arms to hug her.

"Mrs. Williams, I love you. And you're the first person who's made sense to me in a very long time."

"In that case, my dear, do me the honor of not calling me 'Mrs. Williams.' I abhor it. Couldn't you possibly settle for 'Bethanie,' or 'Aunt Beth' if you prefer? My friends' children still call me that, and some of Astrid's friends."

"Aunt Beth. It sounds lovely." And suddenly Jessica felt as though she had a new mother. Family. It had been so long since she'd had any, other than Ian. Aunt Beth. She smiled and felt a warm glow in her soul.

"Good night, dear. Sleep well. I'll see you in the morning."

They exchanged another hug, and Jessica went upstairs half an hour later, still thinking about some of the things Bethanie had said. About punishing Ian . . . it made her wonder. Just how angry at Ian was she? And why? Because he had cheated on her? Or because he was in prison now and no longer around to protect her? Because he had gotten 'caught' sleeping with Margaret Burton? Would it have mattered as much if she hadn't been forced to confront it? Or was it other things? The books that didn't sell, the money that only she made, his passion for his writing? She just wasn't sure.

Breakfast was waiting for Jessica when she came down the next morning. A happy little note signed "Aunt Beth" told her there were brioches being kept warm in the oven, crisp slices of bacon, and a beautiful bowl of fresh strawberries. The note suggested that they drive over the hills in the Jeep that afternoon.

They did, and they had a marvelous time. Aunt Beth told her stories about the "ghastly" people who had lived at the ranch before and had left the main house in "barbarous condition."

"I daresay the man was a first cousin of Attila the Hun, and their children were simply frightful!"

Jessica hadn't laughed as easily or as simply in years, and as they tooled over the hills in the Jeep, it dawned on her how well she was doing without pills. No tranquilizers, no sleeping pills, nothing. She was surviving with Aunt Beth's company, a lot of sunshine, and much laughter. They cooked dinner together that night, burned the hollandaise for the asparagus, underdid the roast, and laughed together at each new mistake. It was more like having a roommate her own age than being the guest of a friend's mother.

"You know, my first husband always said I'd poison him one day if he wasn't careful. I was a terrible cook then — not that I'm much better now. I'm not at all sure these asparagus are cooked." She crunched carefully on one of the stems, but seemed satisfied with what she found.

"Were you married twice?"

"No. Three times. My first husband died when I was in my early twenties, which was a great shame. He was a lovely boy. Died in a hunting accident two years after we were married. And then I had a rather enjoyable time for a while —" she sparkled a bit and then went on — "and married Astrid's father when I was thirty. I had Astrid when I was thirty-two. And her father died when she was fourteen. And my third husband was sweet, but dreadfully boring. I divorced him five years ago, and life has been far more interesting since." She examined another asparagus stalk and ate it as Jessica laughed.

"Aunt Beth, you're a riot. What was the last one like?"

"Dead, mostly, except no one had told him yet. Old people can be so painfully dull. It was really quite embarrassing to divorce him. The poor man was dreadfully shocked. But he got over it. I visit him when I'm in New York. He's still just as boring, poor thing." She smiled angelically and Jessica dissolved in another fit of laughter. Aunt

Beth wasn't nearly as flighty as she liked to make herself sound, but she certainly hadn't led a dull life either.

"And now? No more husbands?" They were friends now. She could ask.

"At my age? Don't be ridiculous. Who would want an old woman? I'm perfectly content as I am, because I enjoyed my life when I was younger. There's nothing worse than an old woman pretending that she isn't. Or a young woman pretending she's old. You and Astrid do a fine job of that."

"I didn't used to do it."

"Neither did she, when Tom was alive. It's time she found herself someone else and burned down that tomb of a mansion. I think it's appalling."

"But it's so pretty, Aunt Beth. More than pretty."

"Cemeteries are pretty too, but I wouldn't dream of living in one — until I had no other option. As long as one has the option, one ought to use it. But she's getting there. I think your shop might do her some good. Why don't you sell it to her?"

"And then what would *I* do?"

"Something different. How long have you had the shop?"

"Six years this summer."

"That's long enough for anything. Why

not try something else?" Long enough for a marriage too?

"Ian wanted me to stay home and have a child. At least that's what he was saying recently. A few years ago he was perfectly happy with things as they were."

"Maybe you've just found one of the answers you've been looking for."

"Such as?" Jessica didn't understand.

"That a few years ago he was 'perfectly happy with things as they were.' How much has changed in those few years? Maybe you forgot to make changes Jessica. To grow."

"We grew . . ." But how? She wasn't really sure they had.

"I take it you didn't want children."

"No, it's not that I didn't want any, it's that it wasn't time yet. It was too soon and we were happy alone."

"There's nothing wrong with not having children." Aunt Beth looked at her very directly. A little too directly. "Astrid has never wanted any either. Said it wasn't for her, and I think she was quite right. I don't think she's ever regretted it. Besides, Tom was really a bit past that when they married. Your husband is a young man, isn't he, Jessica?"

She nodded.

"And he wants children. Well, my dear,

you can always stay on the pill and tell him you're trying, can't you?" The older woman's eyes hunted Jessie's. Jessica averted her gaze slightly and looked thoughtful.

"I wouldn't do that."

"Oh, you wouldn't, would you? That's good." And then Jessica's eyes snapped back to Aunt Beth's.

"But I've thought of it."

"Of course you have. I'm sure a lot of women have. A lot of them have probably done more than thought of it. Sensible in some cases, I imagine. It seems a pity to have to be that dishonest. You know, I was never that sure I wanted children. And Astrid was a little bit of a surprise." Aunt Beth almost blushed, but not quite. It was more a softening of her eyes as she looked backward in time and seemed to forget Jessica for a moment. "But I really grew quite fond of her. She was very sweet when she was small. And simply horrid for a few years after that. But still sweet in an endearing sort of way. I actually enjoyed her very much." She made Astrid sound more like an adventure than a person, and Jessica smiled, watching her face. "She was very good to me when her father died. I thought the world had come to an end, except for Astrid." Jessie almost envied her as she listened. She made it sound as though life were less lonely because of Astrid, instead of more so.

"I've always been, well, afraid, I guess. Afraid of having children, because I thought it would put an obstacle between me and Ian. I thought it would make me lonely." Bethanie smiled and shook her head.

"No, Jessica. Not if your husband loves you. Then he'll only love you that much more because of the child. It's an additional bond between you, an extension of both of you, a blending of what you love most and hate most and need most and laugh at most, of the two of you. It's a very lovely thing. I can think of a good many reasons to fear having children, but that shouldn't be one of them. Can't you love more than one person?"

It was a good question, and Jessica decided to be honest.

"I don't think so, Aunt Beth. Not anymore. I haven't loved anyone but Ian in a long time. So I guess I can't imagine him loving someone besides me — even a child. I know it must sound selfish, but it's how I feel."

"It doesn't sound selfish. It sounds frightened, but not really selfish."

"Maybe one day I'll change my mind."

"Why? Because you think you ought to? Or because you want to? Or so you can punish your husband some more?" Aunt Beth didn't pull any punches. "Take my advice, Jessica. Unless you really want a child, don't bother. They're a terrible nuisance, and even harder on the furniture than cats." She said it with a straight face as she stroked the calico cat sitting on her lap. Jessica laughed in surprise at the remark. "As pets go, I much prefer horses. You can leave them outside without feeling guilty." She looked up with another of her saintly smiles, and Jessica grinned. "Don't always take me seriously. And having children is really a matter of one's own choice. Whatever you do, don't be pressured by what other people think or say — except your husband. And my, my, aren't you lucky to have me stomping about where angels fear to tread?"

The two women laughed then and moved on to other subjects. But it amazed Jessica to realize the depth of the topics they discussed. She was finding herself revealing secrets and feelings to Aunt Beth that before she would have shared only with Ian. She seemed to be constantly showing Aunt Beth one piece or another of her soul, pulling it out to exhibit, dusting it off, questioning; but she was beginning to feel whole again.

The days were delightful and relaxing on the ranch, filled with fresh air and pleasant mornings spent on horseback in solitary canters over the hills or in idle walks. And the evenings flew by with Aunt Beth to laugh with. Jessica found herself taking naps in the afternoon, reading Jane Austen for the first time since high school, and making small idle sketches in a notebook. She had even made a few secret sketches that could be worked into an informal portrait of Aunt Beth. She was feeling shy about asking her new friend to sit for a portrait. But it was the first one she had wanted to paint since Ian's, years before. Aunt Beth's face would lend itself well to that sort of thing, and it would make a nice gift for Astrid — who appeared, much to Jessica's chagrin, two weeks later.

"You mean I have to come home now?" Astrid looked tired but happy, and Jessica had the sinking feeling she'd had as a child when her mother had arrived too early to fetch her home from a birthday party.

"Don't you dare come home, Jessica Clarke! I came down to see how Mother was doing."

"We're having a great time."

"Good. Then don't stop now. I'll be miserable when you come back to the city and take away my toy." She filled Jessie in on Katsuko's trip to New York, and the spring line was doing better than Jessie had dared to hope. It seemed years since she had bought those pastels, years since she'd come home and Ian had been arrested, centuries since the trial. The shock of it all was finally beginning to fade. The scars barely showed. She had gained five pounds and looked rested. Astrid brought her a letter from Ian, which she didn't open until later.

... I can't believe it, Jess. Can't believe I'd say those things to you. Maybe this disaster is finally taking its toll. Are you all right? Your silence is strange now, your absence stranger. And I find that I don't really know what I want: you to reappear, or for that damn window between us to disappear. I know how you hate it, darling. I hate it as much. But we can overcome it. And how is the vacation? Doing wonders, I'm sure. You've really earned it. I suppose that's why I'm not hearing from you. You're "busy resting." Just as well, probably. As usual, I'm all wrapped up in the book. It's going unbelievably well, and I'm hoping that ...

The rest was all about the book. She tore the letter in half and threw it into the fire.

Aunt Beth quizzed her about the letter later, after Astrid had gone to bed. There was a kind of conspiracy between them now that excluded even Astrid.

"Oh, he says that he loves me and the book is going well, all in the same breath." She tried to sound blithe and only succeeded in sounding a trifle less bitter.

"Aha! So you're jealous of his work!" Aunt Beth's eyes sparkled. Now she saw something she had not seen before, not clearly, anyway. It was all coming into focus.

"I am not jealous of his work. How ridiculous!"

"I quite agree. But why do you begrudge him his writing? What would happen, Jessica, if you no longer had to support him? You'd have no control over him then, would you? What if he actually did get successful? Then what would you do?"

"I'd be delighted for him." But it didn't sound convincing, even to Jessica.

"Would you? Do you think you could handle it? Or are you much too jealous even to try?"

"How absurd." She didn't like the sound of Beth's theory.

"Yes, it is absurd. But I don't think you

know that yet, Jessica. The fact is that he either loves you or he doesn't. If he doesn't you couldn't keep him. And if he does, you probably can't lose him. And if you insist on supporting him forever, my dear, he'll wind up finding someone he can support, who lets him feel like a man. Someone who might even give him children. Mark my words."

Jessica fell silent and they went up to bed. But Aunt Beth's words had hit home. Ian had said the same thing to her himself, in his own way. In Carmel, he had told her that things would have to change. Well, they were going to. But not the way Ian had in mind.

Chapter 27

"Good morning, Aunt Beth . . . Astrid."
There was a look of determination on Jessica's face as she sat down to breakfast with them. That expression was new to her friends.

"Good heavens, child, what are you doing up at this hour?" She had rarely risen before ten since she'd been on the ranch, and Aunt Beth was surprised.

"Well." She looked carefully at Astrid, knowing how disappointed she would be. "I want to enjoy my last day. I've decided to go home with you tonight, Astrid." Her friend's face fell at the words.

"Oh no, Jessie! Why?"

"Because I have things to do in town, and I've been lazy for long enough, love. Besides, if I don't go back now, I probably never will." She tried to make her tone light as she helped herself to some cinnamon toast, but she knew that the words were a blow to

Astrid. And she felt bad about leaving the ranch too. Only Aunt Beth looked unruffled by the news.

"Did you tell Mother before you told me, Jessie?" Astrid had noticed the look on her mother's face.

"She did not." Aunt Beth was quick to answer. "But I felt it coming last night. And Jessica, I think you're probably right to go back now. Don't look like that, Astrid, it will give you wrinkles. What did you think? That she'd never go back to her own shop? Don't be foolish. Are either of you going to ride with me this morning?" She buttered her toast matter-of-factly, and Astrid cleared the frown from her brow the way a child smoothes messages out of the sand. Her mother was right about Jessie going back, of course. But she had enjoyed Lady J even more than she had thought she would.

Jessie had been watching her face and now looked almost remorseful. "I'm really sorry, love. I hate to do it to you." The two younger women fell silent and Aunt Beth shook her head.

"How tedious you both are. I'm going riding. You're quite welcome to mope here. One feeling ridiculously guilty, the other feeling childishly deprived, and both of you making fools of yourselves. I'm surprised either of you has time for such nonsense." Jessica and Astrid laughed then, and decided to ride with their more sensible elder.

It was a pleasant ride and an enjoyable day, and Jessie left Aunt Beth with regret. She vowed to come back as soon as she could, and struggled for the words to tell her how much the two weeks had meant.

"They restored me."

"You restored yourself. Now don't waste it by going back to the city and doing something foolish."

So she knew. It was astonishing. There was nothing you could hide from her.

"I won't approve if you do something stupid, child. And I'm not at all sure I like the look in your eye."

"Now, Mother." Astrid saw Jessie's discomfort, and Bethanie did not pursue the matter after the interruption. She simply gave them a bag of apples, a tin of homemade cookies, and some sandwiches.

"That ought to keep you two well fed till you get home." Her expression softened again and she put a gentle arm around Jessica's waist. "Come back soon. I shall miss you, you know." There was a soft hug about the waist, a warmth in the eyes, and Jessica bent her head to kiss her on the cheek.

"I'll be back soon."

"Good. And Astrid, dear, drive safely."

She waved at them from the doorway, until the sleek black Jaguar had turned a corner and sped out of sight.

"You know, I really hate to leave here. The last two weeks have been the best I've had in years."

"I always feel like that when I leave."

"How come you don't just move down here, Astrid? I would if she were my mother, and it's such beautiful country." Jessie settled back in her seat for the long drive, musing over the two precious weeks, and the last few moments of conversation with Aunt Beth.

"Good Lord, Jessica, I'd die of boredom down here. Wouldn't you, after a while?"

Jessica shook her head slowly, a small, thoughtful frown between her eyes. "No, I don't think I'd be bored. I never even thought of that."

"Well, I have. In spite of my mother. There's nothing to do here except ride, read, take walks. I still need the insanity of the city."

"I don't. I almost hate to go back."

"Then you should've stayed." For the tiniest moment, the spoiled child was back in Astrid's voice.

"I couldn't stay, Astrid. I have to get back.

But I feel like a rat taking the shop back, if you can call it that. You really gave me the most marvelous vacation." Astrid smiled back at Jessie's words.

"Don't feel bad. The two weeks were a lovely gift." Astrid sighed gently and followed the serene country road. The sun had just set over the hills, and there was a smell of flowers in the air. In a distant field they could see horses in the twilight.

Jessie took a long look around the now familiar countryside, and sank back in her seat with a small private smile. She'd be back. She had to come back. She was leaving a piece of her soul here, and a new friend.

"You know something, Mrs. Bonner?"

Astrid grinned in response. "What, Mrs. Clarke?"

"I adore your mother."

"So do I." The two women smiled, and Astrid stole a glance at Jessie. "Was she good to you? Or did she give you a hard time? She can be very tough, and I was a little bit afraid she'd indulge herself with you. Did she?"

"Not really. Honest, but not tough. And never mean. Just straightforward. Sometimes painfully so. But she was generally right. And she made me think a lot. She saved my life. Hell, I'm not even a junkie anymore!" Jessica laughed and bit into one of the apples. "Want an apple?"

"No, thanks. And I'm glad it worked out. How did Ian sound in the letter I brought you, by the way? I meant to ask, and I forgot." Jessica's face set at the question, but Astrid had her eyes on the road and didn't see.

"That's why I'm going back."

"Something wrong?" Astrid stole a quick look at Jessica.

"No. He's fine." But her voice was strangely cold.

"You're going back to see him, Jessie?" Astrid was a trifle confused.

"No. To see Martin."

"Martin? Ian's lawyer? Then something is wrong!"

"No, not . . . not like that." And then she turned her face away and watched the hills drift past the window. "I'm going back to get a divorce."

"You're what?" She slowed down the car and turned to face Jessie, stunned. "Jessica, no! You don't want that! Do you?"

Jessica nodded, holding the apple core in her trembling hand. "Yes. I do." They did not speak for the next hundred miles. Astrid couldn't think of anything to say.

Martin was free to see her when Jessie called him the next morning. She went right down to his office and was shown down the painfully familiar corridor. It seemed that she was never there for anything except the high points of drama in her life.

As usual, he was sitting at his desk with his glasses pushed up on his head and the standard frown on his face. She hadn't seen him since December.

"Well, Jessica, how have you been?" He looked her over as he stood up and held out his hand. It still gave her a sinking feeling to see him. In his own way, he was as painful a reminder to her as Inspector Houghton was. He was part of an era. But the era was finally coming to a close.

"I've been fine, thank you."

"You look very well." So much so it surprised him. "Have a seat. And tell me, what brings you here? I had a letter from Ian last week. He sounds like he's weathering it." A flash of something passed through Martin's eyes. Regret? Sorrow? Guilt? Or maybe Jessie only wished it. Why hadn't he been able to keep Ian free? Why hadn't he talked him into an appeal and then won? If he had, she wouldn't be in his office now. Or maybe she would.

"Yes, I think he's surviving."

"He mentioned that he thinks he might be selling his book. Said he was waiting to hear more from his agent."

"Oh." That was news. "I hope he does sell it. That would do a lot for him." Especially now. But that was all Ian wanted anyway. Another book, and this time a big one, a hot seller. He wouldn't need her if he had a book. Wouldn't even miss her.

"So? You still haven't told me what brings you here." The amenities were now officially over. Jessica took a small breath and looked him in the eyes.

"What brings me here, Martin, is a divorce." But nothing registered on his face.

"A divorce?"

"Yes. I want to divorce Ian." Something inside her trembled at the words, turned over and gasped, and tried to clutch at the old familiar branch. But she wouldn't let it. It didn't matter if she fell into a bottomless pit now; she had to do this. And she knew now that she would survive the bottomless pit. She had already been there.

"Jessica, are you tired of waiting for him? Or is there someone else?" The questions seemed indiscreet, but perhaps he had to know.

"No. Neither, really. Well, maybe a little tired of waiting. But only because I don't think we'll have a marriage left when he gets out. So what is there to wait for?"

"Did you have a marriage before?" He had always wondered, had never been quite sure. It had looked as if they had a strong bond and a firm commitment, but you never knew from the outside.

Jessica nodded at his question, and then looked away, her hands clenched in her lap.

"I thought we had a marriage. But . . . I told myself a lot of fairy tales then."

"Such as?" She wondered why they had to get into all of this now.

"Such as I thought we were happy. That was a lie, among other lies. Ian was never really happy with me. Too many things got in the way. My shop, his work, other things. He'd never have gone off with that woman if he'd been happy."

"Do you really believe that?"

"I don't know. I didn't at first. But now I begin to see what I didn't give him. Self-respect, for starters. And my time . . . my faith, maybe. I mean real faith that he could make a big success of another book."

"You didn't respect him?"

"I'm not absolutely sure. I needed him, but I don't know if I respected him. And I never wanted him to know how much I needed him. I always wanted him to think he was the one who needed me. Pretty, isn't it?"

"No. But it's not unusual either. So why the divorce? Why not just clean up the picture and stick to what you've got? It's still better than most, and you're lucky — you see the mistakes; most don't. Does Ian see it as clearly as you do?"

"I have no idea."

"You haven't spoken to him about this?" He looked shocked as she shook her head. "He doesn't know you want a divorce?" She shook her head again and then looked up at him squarely.

"No, he doesn't. And . . . Martin, this is just the way I want it. It's too late to 'clean up the picture.' I've given it a lot of thought, and I know this is the right way. We have no children, and, well . . . this is as good a time as any."

He nodded, chewing on the stem of his glasses.

"I can understand your thinking, Jessica, and you're a young woman. It may prove to be quite a burden to be married to a man who was sent to prison for rape. Maybe you should be free now to start another life."

"I think so." But why did it feel like such a betrayal of Ian? Such a rotten thing to do . . . but she had to. Had to. She wanted this for herself. She had decided. But she kept hearing Aunt Beth's words, just before she'd left the ranch the night before: "I won't approve if you do something stupid." But this wasn't stupid. It was right. But what was Ian going to say? . . . And why should she care now? Except that she did. She did, dammit.

"Would it affect your decision in any way if he sold this new book, Jessica?" She thought about it for a moment and then shook her head.

"No, it wouldn't. Because nothing would change. He'd come home, bitter about the time he's spent in prison, and even more bitter against me, because I'd just be supporting him all over again eventually, and nothing would have changed. Book advances don't last long, unless the book is a success."

"You don't think he's capable of writing a success?" The tone of Martin's voice filled her with shame, and she lowered her eyes again.

"I didn't mean that. And that's not the point anyway. Everything would still be the same. I'd still have the shop, the bank account . . . no, Martin. This is what I want. I'm absolutely sure."

"Well, Jessica, you're old enough to make your own decisions. When are you going to tell Ian?"

"I thought I'd write to him tonight. And —" she hesitated, but she had to ask him — "I was hoping you'd go up to see him."

"To break the news?" Martin looked very tired as he asked. She nodded slowly. "Frankly, Jessica, I don't normally handle domestic affairs. Marital law, as you know, is not my specialty." And this was going to be a mess. But Ian was his client. And his client's wife was sitting opposite him, looking at him as though it were his fault that she was getting the divorce, as though he had cost her her marriage. And why the hell did he always feel guilty if things didn't work out just right?

"Oh well, I suppose I could handle this for you. Will it be a complicated sort of affair?"

"No. Terribly simple. The shop is mine. The house belongs to both of us, and I'll sell it if he wants, and put his share of the money in an account for him. That's all there is. I get custody of the plants, and he gets his file cabinets in his studio. End of a marriage." The only thing she had left out was the furniture, and neither of them cared, except for the few pieces that were her parents', which were obviously hers. So simple. So miserably simple after seven years.

"You make it sound very quick and easy." But he was dubious, and sad for them both.

"Maybe quick, but no, not very easy. Will you go up and see him soon?"

"By the end of the week. Will you be going up to see him yourself?" She shook her head carefully. She had seen Ian for the last time . . . on that godawful day when he had gotten up and walked away and she had watched him from behind a window, holding a dead phone in her hands. Her eyes filled with tears at the memory, and Martin Schwartz looked away. He hated this kind of thing. It seemed so wasteful.

Jessica looked up at Martin, holding back the tears. Her voice was barely a whisper. "No, Martin, I won't see him anymore."

He told her that she would be divorced in six months. In September. A year after he had been arrested, a year after the end of their marriage had begun.

There was a letter from Ian waiting when she stopped by the house for her mail on her way to the boutique. It was only a brief note. And a poem. She read it with wide, sad eyes, and then tore it carefully in half and threw it away. But it had stuck in her mind somehow. Like a satin thorn. It was the last letter from Ian she opened. The poem decided her.

You are the explosive celebration
  of my sunbursts
    every morning,
You are the whisper
  in my late
    late nights,
You are the symphony in my sunsets,
You are the splendor and the glory
  of the dawning
    of my life.

The dawning of his life was past, with her, at least. But she felt as though she had singlehandedly killed the sunrise. Canceled it. Sent it away. Made it cry. Broken something sacred. Him, and herself, and the thing that was both of them. The thing she now believed had never been at all. But she knew she had to do what she was doing.

CHAPTER 28

The boutique was in beautiful shape. There were new displays all over the main room, and the window looked like a vision of spring. Astrid had done it herself. And the pastels and creams and delicate shades Jessie had bought in New York more than six months before looked good on display. There were two new plants in her office, with bright yellow flowers in full bloom, and there was a neat, crisp air to the shop that she had almost forgotten. She had been gone for only two weeks, but Lady J had been reborn, just as she had been. It looked the way it had when Jessie had first opened it, in the days when she'd been madly in love with it and had put her heart and soul into its birth. Now it showed the signs of Astrid's fresh enthusiasm and love. She hadn't changed anything radically, she had just pulled it together. Even Katsuko and Zina looked happier.

"How was the vacation?" Katsuko looked up, delighted to see her, but she didn't need to ask. Jessie looked like Jessie again, only better.

"It was exactly what I needed. And look at this place! It looks like you painted it or something. So cheerful and pretty."

"That's just the new line. It looks pretty damn good."

"How's it selling?"

"Like hotcakes. And wait till you see what I picked up for fall. Everything's orange or red. Lots of black, and some marvelous silver knits for the opera." The browns of the winter before were already forgotten. Next year it would be red. Bright, busy, alive, maybe that was a good sign for her new life . . . new life. Jesus. She didn't want to think about it yet. And there would be so many people to tell . . . to explain to . . . to . . .

Jessica settled down in her office, looked around with pleasure, and enjoyed the feeling of having come home. It softened the burden of the morning, the meeting with Martin. She tried to keep it out of her mind. She would write to Ian tonight. For the last time. She didn't want to get into a long exchange of letters with him. He was too good at it. The letters would be . . . too much. They could work everything out through their lawyer. The less they said to each other, even by letter, the better. She had made up her mind. It was done now, and it was for the best. Now she had to look ahead and steel herself not to look back at the years with Ian. They were over now. A part of her past, like out-of-date fashions. Jessica and Ian were "passé."

"Jessie? Got a minute?" Zina's curly head poked in the door, and Jessie looked up and smiled. She felt older, quieter, but no longer tired. And she felt strong. For the first time in months, the nights alone did not terrify her. The house was no longer haunted. Her life was no longer infested by ghosts. Her first night back in the house had actually been peaceful. Finally.

She forced her attention back to Zina, still hovering in the doorway. "Sure, Zina. I've got lots of time." The slower pace of the country was still with her. She didn't feel harried yet, and she loved it.

"You're lookin' good." Zina sat in the chair next to Jessie's desk and looked slightly uncomfortable. She asked a few questions about Jessie's vacation, and seemed to hesitate each time there was a pause. Finally, Jessie had had enough.

"Okay, lady, what's on your mind?"

"I don't know what to say, Jessie, but . . ." She looked up and suddenly Jessie sensed it. The hard months had taken their toll on everyone, not only on her. And she was almost surprised that neither of them had done it before. They probably hadn't because they were too loyal. She took a long breath and looked into Zina's eyes.

"You're quitting?"

Zina nodded. "I'm getting married." She said it almost apologetically.

"You are?" Jessie hadn't even known that Zina had a boyfriend. She hadn't had one the last time they'd talked . . . but when had that been? Last month? Two months ago? More like six. Since then she'd been too busy with her own problems to inquire or to care.

"I'm getting married in three weeks."

"Zina, that's lovely news! What are you looking so sorry about, dummy?" Jessie smiled broadly and Zina looked overwhelmingly relieved.

"I just feel bad about leaving you. We're moving to Memphis."

Jessica laughed. It sounded like a horrible fate, but she knew Zina didn't think so, and now that the news was out, Zina looked ecstatic.

"I met him at a Christmas Eve party, and

oh . . . Jessie! He's the most beautiful man, in all possible ways! And I love him! And we're going to have lots of babies!" She grinned contentedly and Jessica jumped up and gave her a hug. "And look at my ring!" She was pure Southern belle as she flashed the tiniest of diamonds.

"Were you wearing that before I went on vacation?" Jessica was beginning to wonder just how much she'd been missing.

"No. He gave it to me last week. But I didn't want to write and tell you, so I waited till you got back." And Astrid had forbidden all potentially disturbing communications to Jessie. Like news of the creditors who kept calling about the bills she still hadn't paid. "It's such a pretty little ring, isn't it?"

"It's gorgeous. And you're crazy, but I love you, and I'm so happy for you!" And then a flash of pain struck through to her core. Zina was getting married, she was getting divorced. You come, you go, you start, you end, you try, you lose, and maybe later you get another try, a fresh start, and this time win. Maybe. Or maybe it didn't really matter. She hoped Zina would win on the first try.

"I feel so bad giving you such short notice, Jess. But we just decided. Honest." She almost hung her head, but the smile was too big to hide.

"Stop apologizing, for heaven's sake! I'm just glad I came home. Where's the wedding?"

"In New Orleans, or my mother would kill me. I'm flying home in two weeks, and she's already going crazy over the wedding. We didn't give her much notice either. She called me four times last night, and you should have heard Daddy!" They both giggled, and Jessica started to think.

"Do you need a dress?"

"I'm going to wear my great-grandmother's."

"But you need a trousseau. Right? And a going-away dress, and . . ."

"Oh, Jessie, yes, but . . . no . . . I can't let you do that . . ."

"Mind your own business, or I'll fire you!" She waggled a finger at Zina and they both started to laugh again. Jessie flung open her office door and marched Zina into the main room of the shop and stopped in front of a startled Katsuko.

"Kat, we have a new customer. VIP. This is Miss Nelson, and she needs a trousseau." Katsuko looked up in astonishment, then understood and joined in their giggles and smiles. She was relieved that it had gone well. She had been worried for Zina. For

501

the last couple of months it had been frightening to tangle with Jessie. But she was all right now. They could all tell. And now she was bubbling on about Zina's trousseau.

"It's going to be perfect with all the spring colors. Kat, give her anything she wants at ten percent under cost, and I'll give her her going-away suit as a wedding present. And as a matter of fact . . . don't I know just the one!" A gleam had come into her eyes, and she walked into the stockroom and came out with a creamy beige silk suit from Paris. It had a mid-calf skirt and a jacket that would subtly conceal Zina's oversized chest. She pulled out a mint green silk blouse to go with it, and Zina practically drooled.

"With dressy beige sandals, and a hat . . . Zina, you're going to look unbelievable!" Even Katsuko's eyes glowed at the outfit Jessie held up in her hand. Zina looked shocked.

"Jessie, no! You can't! Not that one!" She spoke in a whisper. The suit sold for over four hundred dollars.

"Yes, that one." Her voice was gentle now. "Unless there's another one you like better." Zina shook her head solemnly and Jessica gave her a warm hug, and with a smile and a last wink at Zina she walked back into her office. It had been a startling morning, and now she had another startling idea.

She reached Astrid at the hairdresser.

"Is something wrong?" Maybe Jessie had hated the window display, or didn't like what she'd done with the stock. She was worried as she stood there dripping hair-setting lotion on her new suede Gucci shoes.

"No, silly, nothing's wrong. Want a job?"

"Are you kidding?"

"No. Zina just quit. She's getting married. And I may be crazy, because with you in the shop there'd be three of us capable of running this joint, but if you don't mind being the overqualified low man on the totem pole for a while, the job's all yours."

"Jessie! I'll take it!" She grinned broadly and forgot about what she was doing to her shoes.

"Then you're hired. Want to go to lunch?"

"I'll be right over. No, I can't, dammit, my hair is still wet . . . oh . . . shit." They both laughed and Astrid's smile seemed to broaden by the minute. "I'll be there in an hour. And Jessie . . . thanks. I love you." They both hung up with happy smiles and Jessica was glad she had called.

The four of them closed the doors to Lady J promptly at five instead of at five-thirty, and Jessica brought out a bottle of champagne she had ordered that afternoon. Zina had decided to leave a week earlier than planned now that Jessie had Astrid to take her place. They finished the bottle in half an hour, and Astrid drove Jessica home.

"Want to come home with me for a drink? I still haven't celebrated my new job."

Jessie smiled, but shook her head. She was beginning to feel the effects of the day . . . which had begun with seeing Martin about the divorce. It was odd how she kept forgetting that. The morning seemed light years behind her. She wished the divorce were already behind her too.

"No thanks, love. Not tonight."

"Afraid to fraternize with the help?" Jessie laughed at the thought.

"No, silly, I'm pooped and I'm already half crocked from the champagne, and . . . I've got a letter to write." Astrid's face sobered as she listened.

"To Ian?" Jessica nodded gravely, the laughter totally gone from her eyes now.

"Yes. To Ian."

Astrid patted her hand and Jessie slid quietly out of the car with a wave. She unlocked the door and stood in the sunlit front hall for a moment. It was so quiet. So unbearably quiet. Not frightening anymore. Only empty. Who would take care of her now? It was odd to realize that no one knew what time she came home or went out, or where she was. No one knew and no one cared. Well, there was Astrid, but no one to report to, explain to, rush home for, do errands for, wake up for, set the alarm for, buy food for . . . an overwhelming sensation of emptiness engulfed her. Tears slid down her face as she looked around the house that had once been their home. It was a shell now. A hall of memories. Someplace to come back to at night after work. Like everything else, it had suddenly been catapulted into the past. It was all moving so quickly. People were going and changing and moving away, new people were taking their places . . . Zina getting married . . . Astrid in the shop . . . Ian gone . . . and in six months she'd be divorced. Jessica sat down on the chair in the front hall, her coat still on, her handbag slung on her shoulder, as she tasted the word aloud. Divorced.

It was almost midnight before she licked the stamp on the letter. She felt a hundred years old. She had forced Ian out of her life, and she would stand by her decision. But now she had no one except herself.

CHAPTER 29

"Well, look at you! What are you up to tonight?"

Astrid looked embarrassed as she buttoned the mink coat. It was May, but still chilly at night, and the fur coat looked good on her.

Jessie had just locked the doors to the shop. The arrangement was working out well. She, Katsuko, and Astrid got along like sisters. They made a powerful team, almost too much so, but they liked it, and the boutique was doing much better. Calls from creditors were getting rare. You could see the relief in Jessica's face.

"All right, nosey-body —" Astrid looked at Jessica watching her with amusement — "I happen to have a date." She said it like a sixteen-year-old, with a faint blush on her cheeks, and Jessica burst out laughing.

"And you already look guilty as hell. Who's the guy?"

"Some idiot I met through a friend." She looked almost pained.

"How old is he?" Jessie was suspicious of Astrid's passion for men over sixty. She was still looking for Tom.

"He's forty-five." With a virginal expression, she finished buttoning the coat.

"At least he's a decent age. For a change."

"Thank you, Aunt Jessie." The two women laughed and Jessica pulled a comb out of her handbag.

"As a matter of fact, I have a date too." She looked up with a small smile.

"Oh? With whom?" The tables were turned now, and Astrid looked as though she enjoyed it. But Jessie had been going out a good deal in the past weeks. With young men, with old ones, with a photographer, a banker, even with a law student once. But never with writers. And she never talked about Ian anymore. The subject was forbidden and mention of Ian met with silence or black looks.

"I'm going out with a friend of a friend from New York. He's just in San Francisco for a week. But what the hell, why not? He sounded decent on the phone. A little bit of a Mr. New York Smoothie, but at least he seemed halfway intelligent. He had a nice quick sense of humor on the phone. I just hope he behaves himself." Jessica sighed softly as she put her comb back in her bag. Her hair hung well past her shoulders in a sheet of satiny blond.

"*You* should worry about how he behaves? Big as you are, you can always beat him up."

"I gave that up when I was nine."

"How come?"

"I met a kid who was bigger than I was, and it hurt." She grinned and propped her feet up on the desk.

"Want a ride home, Jessie?"

"No thanks, love. He's picking me up here. I thought I'd show him the action at Jerry's." Astrid nodded, but Jerry's wasn't her style. It was a local "in" bar, full of secretaries and ad men looking to get laid. It made her feel lonely. She was having dinner at L'Etoile. That was much more her style. It would have been Jessie's style too, if she'd let it. But she was still seeking her own level. A new level. Any level. Jessie knew Jerry's wasn't for her, but the action gave her something to watch as she listened to the hustles being carried on at the bar.

"See you tomorrow."

Jessie waved good night, and Astrid passed a young man on the steps. He was slightly taller than Jessie and had dark bushy hair. He was wearing a gray turtleneck sweater and jeans. Nice-looking, but too "fuzzy," Astrid decided, as she smiled and walked past. She wondered how Jessie stood them; they all looked the same, no matter what color their hair, or how they dressed, they looked hungry and horny and bored. Astrid was suddenly glad she was no longer thirty. Thirty-year-old men had so far to go. With a sigh, she slipped into the Jaguar and turned on the ignition. She wondered how Ian was doing. She had wanted to write to him for a month, but she hadn't dared. Jessica might have considered it treason. Astrid saw the letters torn in half before they were opened when she emptied the wastebasket in the office they now shared. Jessie could be unyielding when she decided to be. And she had decided to be. The door to the shop opened and Astrid saw the young man go inside.

"Hi, Mario. I'm Jessie." She assumed he was the young man she was waiting for, and offered him her hand. He ignored it with a casual smile.

"I take it you work here." No greeting, no introduction, no handshake, no hello. He was just looking the place over. And her with it. Okay, sweetheart, if that's how it is.

"Yes. I work here." She decided not to tell him she owned it.

"Yeah. I think I just passed your boss on the stairs. An old chick in a fur coat. Ready to go?" Jessie was already bristling. Astrid was not an "old chick," and she was her friend.

He seemed bored with the action at Jerry's, but he had four glasses of red wine anyway. He explained that he was a playwright, or was trying to be, and he tutored English, math, and Italian on the side. He had grown up in New York, in a tough neighborhood on the West Side. At least that's how he put it. But Jessie wondered. He looked more like middle-class West Side than tough anything. Or maybe even the suburbs. And now he had grown up to be unwashed, unfriendly, and rude. It made her wonder about the friends who'd given him her name. People she knew through business, but still . . . how could they send her this?

"Well, how's New York? I haven't been back in a while."

"Yeah? How long?"

"Almost eight months."

"It's still there. I went to a great cocaine party last week in St. Mark's Place. How's the action out here?"

"Cocaine? I wouldn't know." She sipped her wine.

"Not your thing?" He continued to look bored while working hard at looking cynical. Big-city kid in the provinces. Jessie was wishing he would drop dead on the spot. Or disappear, at least.

"You don't dig cocaine?" He pursued the point.

"No. But this is a nice city. It's a good place to live."

"It looks dull as shit." She looked up and smiled brightly, hoping to disappoint him. Mario the playwright was turning out to be an A-1 pain in the ass.

"Well, Mario, it's not as exciting as West Side New York, but we do have our fun spots."

"I hear it's an intellectual wasteland." So are you, darling.

"Depends on who you talk to. There are some writers out here. Good ones. Very good ones." She was thinking of Ian and wanted to cram him down this jerk's throat. Ian was quality. Ian was charming. Ian was brilliant. Ian was beautiful. What was she doing out with this pig? This boor? This . . .

"Yeah? Like who?"

"What?" Her mind had wandered away from Mario to Ian.

"You said there are some good writers out here. And I said like who. You mean science-fiction writers?" He said it with utter distaste and that cynical smile that made Jessica want to plant the wineglass in his teeth.

"No, not just science-fiction writers. I mean like fiction, straight fiction, nonfiction." She started reeling off names, and realized that they were all friends of Ian's. Mario listened, but offered no comment. Jessica was fuming.

"You know what knocks me out?" No. But tell me quick, I'll find one.

"What?"

"That a bright woman like you sells dresses in some shop. I don't know, I figured you were doing something creative."

"Like writing?"

"Writing, painting, sculpture, something meaningful. What kind of existence is that, selling dresses for old broads in fur coats?"

"Well, you know how it is. One does what one can." Jessie tried to keep her lip from curling as she smiled. "What sort of play are you writing?"

"New theater. An all-female cast, in the nude. There's a really great scene taking shape now for the second act. A homosexual love scene after a woman gives birth."

"Sounds like fun." Her tone went over his head. "Hungry yet?" And she still had dinner to look forward to with him. She was considering pleading a violent attack of bubonic plague. Anything to get away from him. But she'd live through it. She'd been through it before. More often than she wanted to admit.

"Yeah. I could dig a good meal." She made several suggestions and he settled on Mexican, because good Mexican food was rare in New York. At least he had that much sense. She took him to a small restaurant on Lombard Street. The company stank, but at least the food was good.

After dinner she yawned loudly several times and hoped he'd take the hint, but he didn't. He wanted to see some "night life," if there was any. There was, but she wasn't going for it. Not tonight and not with him. She suggested a coffeehouse on Union Street, close to home. She'd have a quick cappuccino and ditch him. She needed the coffee anyway. She had drunk three or four glasses of wine at dinner. But Mario had had at least twice that, after his earlier consumption at Jerry's. He was beginning to slur his words.

They settled down in the coffeehouse, he with an Irish coffee and she with a frothy cappuccino, and he eyed her squintingly over the top of his glass.

"You're not a bad-looking chick." He

made it sound like a chemical analysis. Your blood type is O positive.

"Thank you."

"Where do you live, anyway?"

"Just up a hill or two from here." She drank the sweet milk foam on the top of her coffee and busied herself looking evasive. One thing she was not planning to share with Mario was her address. She'd had more than enough already.

"Big hills?"

"Medium. Why?"

" 'Cause I don't want to walk any big motherfucking hills, sister, that's why. I'm piss-eyed tired. And just a wee bit drunk." He made a pinch with his fingers and smiled leeringly. It almost made Jessie sick to look at him.

"No problem, Mario. We can take a cab and I'll be happy to drop you off wherever you're staying."

"What do you mean 'wherever I'm staying'?" There was a small spark of anger in his eyes, smoldering in confusion.

"You're a smart boy. What did it sound like?"

"It sounded for a minute there like you were being a prissy pain in the ass. I assume that I'm staying with you." For a moment she wanted to tell him she was married, but she wouldn't solve it that way. Besides, then how could she explain going out to dinner with him?

"Mario —" she smiled sweetly at him — "you assumed wrong. We don't do things that way out in the provinces. Or I don't, anyway."

"What's that supposed to mean?" He sat slumped in his chair now, with a disagreeable expression on his face.

"It means thank you for a lovely evening." She started buttoning her jacket and stood up with a wistful look in her eyes. But he leaned across the table and grabbed her arm. His grip on her wrist was surprisingly painful.

"Listen, bitch, we had dinner, didn't we? I mean what the fuck do you think . . ." There was a look on his face that she never wanted to see again, and suddenly the earlier conversation with Astrid flashed into her mind . . . "If he misbehaves, you can hit him" . . . and she wrenched her arm free, and something in the set of her face told him not to press the point.

"I don't know what you think, mister. But I know what I think. And I think you'll be extremely sorry if you touch me again. Good night." She was gone before he could react again, and it was the waiters who bore the brunt of his anger as he swept his arm across the table, knocking the cups and glasses to the floor. It took two waiters to convince him that what he wanted was some air.

Jessica was almost home by then. As she walked quietly up the last hill to the house, the night air was soft on her face, and she felt surprisingly peaceful. It had been a rotten evening, but she was rid of him. And she would never have to see him again. Men like that made her flesh crawl, but at least she knew how to handle them. And herself. At first, such evenings had terrified her. But she had dated all types by now — all the creeps in creepdom. The good ones were either married or off hiding somewhere. And what was left were all the same. They drank too much, they laughed too hard or not at all, they were pompous or neurotic or borderline gay, they were into drugs or group sex, or wanted to talk about how they hadn't had an erection in four years because of what their ex-wives had done to them. She was beginning to wonder if she wouldn't be happier staying home by herself. The libertine life wasn't much fun.

"How was last night?" Jessie asked Astrid first, as she came into the shop the next morning. She was hoping to quell Astrid's questions that way. She had no desire to talk about Mario.

"It was a nice evening, actually. I sort of liked it." She looked happy and relaxed and almost surprised. Unlike Jessie, she didn't really expect to have a good time on a date. It made her easier to please.

"How was your evening? I think I passed your young man on the steps on my way out."

"I think you did too. Damn shame you didn't trip him up on your way."

"That bad, huh?" Astrid looked sympathetic, which hurt more.

"Actually, considerably worse. He was the pits." In Astrid's opinion, he had looked it. "Well, back to the drawing board."

Jessie managed a thin smile as she sifted quickly through the mail, sorting out the letters from the bills. She paused only for a moment to look at a long plain white envelope before tearing it in half and dropping the pieces in the wastebasket. Another letter from Ian. It hurt Astrid every time she saw Jessie do that. It seemed so unkind, such a waste. She wondered if Ian knew, or suspected, that Jessie wasn't reading his letters. She wondered what he was saying in the letters.

"Don't look like that, Astrid." Jessica's voice broke into her thoughts.

"Like what?"

"Like I tear your heart out every time I throw out his letters." She had continued sorting the mail, looking almost indifferent. But not quite. Astrid saw her hands tremble just a trifle.

"But why do you do that?"

"Because we have nothing to say to each other anymore. I don't want to hear it, read it, or open any doors. It would be misleading. I don't want to get suckered into any kind of dialogue with him."

"But shouldn't you give him a chance to say what he thinks? This way seems so unfair." Astrid's eyes were almost pleading, and Jessica looked back at the mail as she answered.

"It doesn't matter. I don't give a damn what he says. I've made up my mind. He could only make things harder now. He couldn't change anything."

"You're that sure you want the divorce?"

Jessica looked up before she answered and fixed Astrid's eyes with her own. "Yes. I'm that sure." In spite of the Marios, in spite of the loneliness and the emptiness, she was still sure divorce was the right thing. But that didn't mean it didn't hurt.

Two customers walked into the shop at that moment and spared Jessica any further discussion. Katsuko was out, and Astrid had to offer to help. Jessica walked into her office and gently closed the door. Astrid knew what that meant. The subject was closed. It always was.

It was a busy day after that, a busy week, a busy month. The shop was in fine shape now, and people were buying for summer.

They had occasional postcards from Zina, who was already pregnant, and Katsuko had decided to grow her hair long again. Life had returned to trivial details: who was going to Europe, what the new hemline would be, whether or not to paint the front of the shop, planting new geraniums in Katsuko's tiny garden apartment. Jessie never ceased to feel gratitude for the trivia. The orchestration in her life had been so somber for so long; now it was Mozart and Vivaldi again. Simple and easy and light. And having made the decision to get the divorce, there were no big decisions left.

It was almost as if the horror story had never happened. Her mother's emerald ring was safely back in the bank. The ownership on the house and the shop were free and clear again. The shop was back on its feet. But there had been changes. A lot more than she wanted to admit. And she had changed. She was more independent, less frightened, more mature. Life was moving along.

They were all having coffee in the boutique one morning when Jessie got to her feet and started going through some of the racks.

"Planning to knock five or ten inches off your height?" Astrid smiled as she watched Jessie go through the size eights.

"Oh, shut up." She looked over her shoulder with a grin, and then knit her brow. "Kat, what size does Zina usually wear?"

"Oh, Jesus. That's a tough one. A size four on the hips, and about a fourteen up top."

"Terrific. So in a smock shape, what size would you say?"

"An eight."

"That's what I was looking at." She cast a victorious glance at Astrid. "I thought maybe we should send her a present. That kid she married doesn't have much money, and she's going to be hard to fit now that she's pregnant. What do you think of these?" She pulled out three tent-shaped dresses from the spring line, in ice cream colors and easy shapes.

"Super!" Kat instantly approved, and Astrid looked touched.

"What a sweet thing to do."

Jessie looked almost embarrassed as she smiled and handed them to Katsuko.

"Ahh . . . bullshit." All three of them laughed and Jessie sat back down to her coffee. "Send those out to her today, okay, Kat? Do you suppose we ought to send her something for the baby?" She didn't know why, but she wanted to celebrate Zina's baby. As though he, or she, were someone special.

"Not yet. It isn't due for months. Besides, that's bad luck." Astrid looked slightly uncomfortable. "What's with all the interest in maternity goodies?"

"I've decided that if I'm never going to be a mother, I might as well enjoy being an aunt. Besides, I figured that if I started buttering her up early, she might make me godmother." Astrid laughed, and Katsuko carefully folded the dresses into a box full of yellow tissue paper. She glanced quickly at Jessie, but Jessie got up and walked away. She felt lonely suddenly. Lonely for a child for the first time in her life. And why now? She decided that it was just because she was ready to love somebody again.

"She's going to adore them, Jessie. And who says you're never going to be a mother?" Katsuko was intrigued. It was the first time Jessie had talked openly about children. Katsuko had always suspected that Jessie must have come to some decision about children, but it was rare for her to open up about anything personal. She was not one of those women who discussed her sex life and her dearest dreams in the office. But Jessie seemed to be in an unusually chatty mood. And she didn't have Ian to confide in anymore. She often seemed hungry for someone to talk to these days. She sat down once more before she replied.

"*I* say I'm never going to be a mother. I mean, Jesus, have you seen what's out there these days? If I've been seeing any kind of standard sampling, I wouldn't think of propagating the breed. They ought to be considering how to stamp it out!" The other two women laughed and Jessie finished her coffee. "Halfwits, no wits, nitwits, and dimwits. Not to mention the ones who've blitzed out their brains on acid, the sonsof-bitches cheating on their wives, and the ones with no sense of humor. You expect me to marry one of those darlings and have a kid, maybe?" And then her face grew serious. "Besides, I'm too old."

"Don't be ridiculous." Astrid spoke up first.

"I'm not. I'm being honest. By the time I

got around to having a child, I'd be thirty-four, thirty-five maybe. That's too old. You should do it at Zina's age. How old is she? Twenty-six? Twenty-seven?" Katsuko nodded pensively and then asked Jessie a question that hit hard.

"Jessie . . . are you sorry now that you didn't have children with Ian?" There was a long pause before she answered, and Astrid was afraid she'd lose her temper, or her cool, but she didn't.

"I don't know. Maybe I am. Maybe I can only say that because I've never been within miles of a kid. But it seems sad — worse than sad, wasted, empty — to live so many years with a man and have nothing. Some books, some plants, a few pieces of furniture, a burnt-out car. But nothing real, nothing lasting, nothing that says 'We were,' even if we aren't anymore, that says 'I loved you,' even if I don't love you anymore." There were tears in her eyes as she shrugged gently and stood up. She avoided their eyes and looked busy as she headed back to her little office. "Anyway, so it goes. Back to work, ladies. And don't forget to send the dresses to Zina right away, Kat." They didn't see her again until lunchtime, and neither Astrid nor Katsuko dared comment on the conversation.

But they were all basically happy. Jessie was restless and sick of the men she was going out with, but she wasn't unhappy. There were no traumas, no crises in her life anymore. And Astrid was still seeing the same man she had been seeing earlier that spring. And enjoying it more than she wanted to admit. He took her to the theater a lot, collected the work of unknown young sculptors, and had a small house in Mendocino that Astrid finally admitted she'd been to. She was spending weekends there, which was why Jessie never heard from her anymore between Friday and Monday.

Jessica was busy too; she was working Saturdays at Lady J, and there were always new men. The trouble was that there were never "old" men, men she had known long enough to feel comfortable with. It was always a birthday party, never old galoshes. She got bored with the constant explanations. Yes, I ski. Yes, I play tennis. No, I don't like to hike. Yes, I drive a car. No, I'm not allergic to shellfish. I prefer hard mattresses, wear a size eight narrow shoe, a size ten dress, am five feet ten and a half, like rings, love earrings, hate rubies, love emeralds . . . all of the above, none of the above. It was like constantly applying for a new job.

She was having trouble sleeping again, but

she had stayed away from pills ever since her stay at the ranch. She knew they weren't the solution, and someday . . . someday . . . someone would come along, and she'd want him to stay. Maybe. Or maybe not. She had even considered the possibility that no one would come along again. No one she could love. It was a horrible thought, but she did admit it as a possibility. It was what had made her suddenly and almost cruelly regret never having had children. She had always thought she had the option. Now her options were gone.

But maybe it didn't matter if she never had children, or loved another man, or . . . maybe it didn't matter at all. She wondered if she had already fulfilled her destiny. Seven years with Ian, an explosion at the end, a boutique, and a few friends. Maybe that was it. There was a sameness to her life now, a blandness and lack of purpose that made her wonder. All she had to do was get up, go to work, stay at the shop all day, close it at five-thirty, go home and change, go out to dinner, say good night, go to bed. And the next day it would all start all over again. She was tired, but she wasn't depressed. She wasn't happy, but at least she wasn't frightened or lonely. She wasn't anything. She was numb.

Ian had sent a message, via Martin, not to sell the house; he'd buy her half eventually if he had to, but he didn't want the house to go. So she went on living there, but now it was just a house. She kept it tidy, it suited her needs, it was comfortable, and it was familiar. But she had put all of Ian's things in the studio and locked it. And the house had lost half its personality when she'd done that. It was just a house now. Lady J was just a shop. She was just another soon-to-be divorcee on the market.

"Morning, madam. Want a date?" Astrid was carrying lily of the valley as she walked into the shop, and she dropped a clump of it next to Jessie's coffee cup.

"Jesus, don't you look happy for this time of the morning." Jessica attempted a smile and winced, regretting the last half bottle of white wine the night before. But it pleased even Jessie to see Astrid like that, wearing her hair down much of the time now, and with a happy light in her eyes.

"Okay, Miss Sunshine. What kind of date?" She tried another smile and meant it. It was impossible not to smile at Astrid.

"A date with a man." She looked almost girlish.

"I should hope so. You mean a blind date?"

"No, I don't think he's blind, Jessica. He's only thirty-nine." The two women laughed and Jessica shrugged.

"Okay, why not? What's he like?"

"Very sweet, and a little bit 'not too tall.' " Astrid looked cautiously at Jess. "Does that matter?"

"Will I have to stoop over to talk to him?"

Astrid giggled and shook her head. "No. And he's really very nice. He's divorced."

"Isn't everyone?" It constantly amazed Jessie to realize how many marriages failed. She hadn't been that aware of it before she'd filed for divorce herself. It had always seemed that everyone she knew was married. And now everyone she knew was divorced.

They had dinner as a foursome that Thursday night, and Astrid's beau was delightful. He was elegant, amusing, and good-looking. In fact, he was the first man Jessie had met in a long time who actually appealed to her. He had the same kind of graceful looks as Ian, but with silver hair and a well-trimmed narrow rim of beard. He had traveled extensively, was knowledgeable in art and music, was very funny as he told of some of his exploits, and he was wonderful with Astrid. Jessica wholeheartedly approved, but what pleased her most about the evening was seeing Astrid's happiness. She had really found the perfect man for her.

Jessie's date for the evening was pleasant, kind, and unbearably boring. Divorced with three children, he worked in the trust department of a bank. He was also five feet seven, and Jessie had worn heels. She stood almost a head taller than he. But when Astrid suggested dancing, Jessie didn't have the heart to argue. At least this one didn't wrestle her at the door. He shook her hand, told her he'd call her while she made a mental note not to hold her breath waiting, and he went home alone. She was sure that by the next morning she wouldn't even remember his name. Why bother?

She took off her clothes and went to bed, but it was two hours later when she finally fell asleep. She felt as if she had just closed her eyes when the phone rang the next morning. It was Martin Schwartz.

"Jessie?"

"No. Veronica Lake." Her voice was husky and she was still half asleep.

"I'm sorry, I woke you."

"That's okay, I have to get to work anyway."

"I have something for you."

"My divorce?" She sat up in bed and

reached for her cigarettes. She wasn't sure she was prepared for that kind of news.

"No. That won't be for another four months. I have something else. A check."

"What in hell for?" It was all very confusing.

"Ten thousand dollars."

"Jesus. But why? And from whom?"

"From your husband's publisher, Jessica. He sold the book."

"Oh." She exhaled carefully and frowned. "Well, put it in his account, Martin. It's not mine, for Chrissake."

"Yes, it is. He endorsed it to you."

"Well, unendorse it, dammit. I don't want it." Her hands were shaking now, and so was her voice.

"He says it's to reimburse you for my trial fee, and Green's fee, and a number of other things."

"That's ridiculous. Just tell him I don't want it. I paid those bills, and he doesn't owe me anything."

"Jessica . . . he signed it over to you."

"I don't give a damn. Cross it out. Tear it up. Do whatever you want with it, but *I don't want it!*" Her voice was rising nervously.

"Can't you do it for him? It seems to mean so much to him. I think it's a question of integrity with him. He really seems to feel that he owes this to you."

"Well, he's wrong."

"Maybe I'm wrong." Martin could feel a thin film of sweat veiling his brow. "Maybe he just wants to give it to you as a gift."

"Maybe so. But whatever the case, Martin, I will not accept the check." Martin's voice had been pleading and she shook her head vehemently as she stubbed out her cigarette. "Look. It's simple. He doesn't owe me anything. I don't want anything. I won't accept anything. I'm glad he sold the book, and I think that's just wonderful for him. Now he should keep the money and leave me alone. He's going to need money when he gets out anyway. Now that's it, Martin. I don't want it. Period. Okay?"

"Okay." He sounded defeated and they hung up. At her end, she was trembling; at his he sat looking out at the view, wondering how to tell Ian. His eyes had been so alive when he'd talked about paying Jessie back. And now Martin had to tell him this.

Jessie's day was off to a bad start. She burned her coffee, and her shower ran cold. She stubbed her foot on the bed, and the newspaper boy forgot to leave her the morning paper. She looked fierce by the time she got to the shop. Astrid looked at her sheepishly.

"All right, all right. I know. You hated him."

"Hated who?" Jessica looked suddenly blank.

"The guy we introduced you to at dinner last night. I never realized he was that dull."

"Well, he is, but that's not what I'm mad about, so forget it." And then she looked up and saw Astrid's face, hurt and confused, like a child's. "Oh, hell, Astrid, I'm sorry. I'm just in a stinking lousy mood. Everything has already gone wrong today. Schwartz called this morning."

"What about?" Astrid's face instantly turned worried.

"Ian sold his book."

"What's wrong with that?" The worry turned to confusion again.

"Nothing. Except he's trying to give me the money, and I don't want it, and it's a pain in the ass, that's all." She poured herself a cup of coffee and sat down. But Astrid's face was grave now.

"Now you know how he used to feel. Taking your money."

"What does that mean?"

"Just what it sounded like. Sometimes it's easier to give than it is to take."

"You sound like your mother."

"I could do worse."

531

Jessie nodded and walked into her office. She stayed there until lunchtime.

Astrid knocked on the closed door at twelve-thirty. A smile was struggling to escape her serious face . . . wait till Jessie saw it! She forced her features back into an expression of official business and looked almost somber when Jessie opened the door.

"What's up?"

"We have a problem, Jessica."

"Can't you take care of it? I'm just checking the invoices."

"I'm sorry, Jessica, but I simply can't handle this."

"Terrific." Jessie threw her pen on the desk behind her and walked into the main room. Astrid watched her nervously. She had signed for it. Maybe Jessie would kill her, but she didn't care. She owed that much to Ian.

Jessie looked around. There was no one in the shop but Katsuko, busy on the phone. "So? Who's here? What's the problem?" She was beginning to look extremely annoyed.

"It's a delivery, Jessie. Outside. They made a big fuss about not unloading inside. Said something about not having to do anything more than make sidewalk deliveries, muttered about the waybill, and drove off."

"Damn them! We hassled that out with

them last month, and I told them that if . . ." She yanked open the door and stalked outside, her eyes blazing, checking the sidewalk for their delivery. And then she saw it. Parked in the driveway where Astrid's Jaguar had been a little while earlier.

It was a sleek little racing green Morgan with black trim and red leather seats. The top was down. It was a beauty, and in even better condition than her old Morgan had been. Jessica looked stunned for a moment, and then looked at Astrid and started to cry. She knew it was from Ian.

Chapter 30

With Astrid badgering her day and night, she decided to keep it. "As a favor to him." She wouldn't admit how much she loved it, and she still wouldn't open his letters.

In June she decided to take a five-day vacation and go down to visit Aunt Beth at the ranch.

"Hell, Astrid, I've earned it. It'll do me good." She was vaguely embarrassed about going but she wasn't sure why.

"Don't make excuses to me. I'm taking three weeks off in July." Astrid was flying to Europe with her beau, but she was loath to discuss it. She kept her affairs very private, even from Jessie. Jessie wondered if maybe she was afraid things would fall through.

Jessica left early on a Wednesday afternoon in the Morgan, in high spirits, her hair flying out behind her. Aunt Beth had been delighted to hear she was coming.

■ ■ ■ ■

"Well, well, you have a new car, I see. Very pretty." She had heard Jessica drive up on the gravel, and had come out to meet her. The sun was setting over the hills.

"It was a present from Ian. He sold his book."

"Very handsome present. And how are you, dear?" She hugged Jessica fondly, and the younger woman bent to kiss her cheek. Their hands found each other and held tightly. They were equally pleased to see each other.

"I couldn't be better, Aunt Beth. And you look wonderful!"

"Older by the hour. And meaner too, I've been told." They chuckled happily and walked into the house arm in arm.

The house looked the same as it had two months before, and Jessica let a sigh escape her as she looked around.

"I feel like I'm home." She looked at Aunt Beth from across the room, and found her own face being carefully searched by the other woman's piercing blue eyes.

"How have you really been, Jessica? Astrid says very little, and your letters tell me even less. I've wondered how things worked out.

Cup of tea?" Jessica nodded and Aunt Beth poured her a cup of Earl Grey.

"I've been fine. I filed for a divorce when I went back, but I told you that in my first letter."

Aunt Beth nodded expressionlessly, waiting for more. "Do you regret it?"

Jessica hesitated for only a split second before answering and then shook her head. "No, I don't. But I regret the past a great deal of the time, more than I like to admit. I seem to find myself hashing it over, reliving it, thinking back to 'if only' this and 'if only' that. It seems so pointless." She looked sad as she set down the cup of tea and looked up at Aunt Beth.

"It is pointless, my dear. And there is nothing more painful than looking back at happy times that no longer are. Or just simply old times. Do you hear from him?"

"Yes, in a way." Jessica tried to look vague.

"What does that mean?"

"It means he writes to me and I tear his letters up and throw them away." Aunt Beth raised an eyebrow.

"Before or after you read them?"

"Before. I don't open them." She felt foolish and averted her eyes from the old woman's.

"Are you afraid of his letters, Jessica?"

To Aunt Beth she could tell the truth. She nodded slowly.

"Yes. I'm afraid of recriminations and pleas and poems and words that are perfectly designed to sound the way he knows I want to hear them. It's too late for that. It's over. Done with. I did the right thing, and I won't hash it over with him. I've seen other people do that, and there's no point. He'd only make me feel guilty."

"You do that to yourself. But you know, you make me wonder. If he weren't in prison, would you still be pressing for this divorce?"

"I don't know. Maybe eventually it would have come to this anyway."

"But aren't you rather taking advantage of his situation, Jessica? If he were free, he could force you to discuss it with him. Now all he can do is write, and you won't give him the courtesy of reading his letters. I'm not sure if that's rude, or cowardly, or simply unkind." They were harsh words, but her eyes said she meant them. "And I also don't understand about the car. You said he gave you the new car. You accepted that . . . but not his letters?" Jessica flinched at the inference.

"That's Astrid's fault. She said that I owed it to him to keep it. He wanted to pay me back the money I put out for the trial, and I wouldn't accept the check from our attorney. So Ian had him buy me the car. And I assume he kept the rest of the money."

"And you didn't thank him for the car?" She sounded every bit a mother. What? No thank-you note to your hostess? Jessica almost laughed.

"No, I didn't."

"I see. And what now?"

"Nothing. The divorce will be final in three months. And that'll be that."

"And you'll never see him again?" Aunt Beth looked doubtful, but Jessica shook her head firmly. "I think you'll regret it, Jessica. One needs to say good-bye. If you don't, in a satisfactory way, you never quite get all the splinters out of your soul. It might trouble you more like this. You can't really wash seven years out of your life without saying good-bye. Or can you? Well, you seem to have made up your mind, in any event." She sat watching Jessica's bent head as the younger woman played with the calico cat. "You have made up your mind, haven't you?" She was determined to get at the truth, if only for Jessie's sake.

"I . . . yes, well . . . oh, damn. I don't know, Aunt Beth. Sometimes I just don't know. I've made up my mind, and I'll go through with it, but now and then, I . . . oh, I suppose it's just regret."

"Maybe not, child. Maybe it's doubt. Maybe you don't really want to divorce him."

"I do . . . but . . . but I miss him so awfully. I miss the way we know each other. He's the only person in the whole world who really knows me. And I know him just as well. I miss that. And I miss what we used to dream, what I thought we once were, what I wanted him to be. Maybe I didn't even know him, though. Maybe I only think I did. Maybe he cheated on me all the time. Maybe that woman was his girlfriend, and she accused him of rape because she was mad about something else. Maybe he hated me for paying the bills, or maybe that's why he stayed married to me. I just don't know anything anymore. Except that I miss him. But it could just be that what I'm missing never even existed."

"Why don't you ask him? Don't you think he'd tell you the truth now? Or is it that you're afraid he might indeed tell you the truth?"

"Maybe that. Maybe the truth is something I'd never want to hear."

"So you'll keep tearing up letters and make sure you never do. And what'll you do when he gets out? Move to another town and change your name?" Jessica laughed at the preposterous suggestion.

"Maybe by then he won't want to talk to me either." But she didn't sound as though she believed it.

"Don't count on it. But more important, Jessica, do you realize what you're saying? You're saying that the man probably never loved you, that there was nothing about you he loved except your ability to pay his bills. Isn't that it?"

"Maybe." But her eyes grew sullen. She had had enough of the painful probing. "What difference does it make now?"

"All the difference in the world. It means the difference between knowing you were loved, and thinking you were used. And what if he did use you, if he loved you too? Didn't you use him too, Jessica? Most people who love each other do, and not necessarily in a bad way. It's part of the arrangement, to fulfill each other's needs — financial, emotional, whatever."

"I never thought of it that way. And the funny thing is that I always thought I was using him. Ian's not afraid to be alone. I always was. I felt so lost without my family after they all died. I had no one except Ian. I could make all the decisions in the world, do anything I wanted, be proud of my-self . . . as long as I had Ian. He kept me propped up so I could go on fooling the world, and myself, that I was such tough stuff. I used him for that, but I never thought he knew it." She looked almost ashamed to admit it.

"And what if he did know it? So what? It's no sin to have weaknesses, or to use the strength of the person you love. As long as you don't use it unkindly. And what about now? Are you stronger?"

"Stronger than I thought."

"And happy?" That was the crux of it.

She hesitated and then shook her head. "No. I'm not. My life is so . . . so empty, Aunt Beth. So dead. Sometimes I feel as if I have nothing to live for. For what? For myself? To get dressed up every morning and changed at six o'clock at night? To go out with some idiot stranger with bad breath and no soul? To water my plants? What am I living for? A boutique I don't give a damn about anymore? . . . What?" Aunt Beth waved a hand and she stopped.

"I can't bear it, Jessica. You sound just the way Astrid used to. And it's all nonsense. You have everything to live for, with or without young men with bad breath. But at your age, above all you have *yourself* to live for. You have it all ahead of you. You have youth. And look at me, I still find things to live for, many things, and not just begrudgingly. I thoroughly enjoy my life, even at my age."

"Then I envy you. I wake up in the morning and I honestly wonder why sometimes. The rest of the time I just keep moving like a robot. But what in hell do I have?"

"You have what you are."

"And what's that? A thirty-one-year-old divorced woman who owns a boutique, half a house, several plants, and a sports car. I have no children, no husband, no family, no one who loves me and no one to love. Jesus, why bother?" There were hot tears filling her eyes as she continued.

"Then find someone to love, Jessica. Haven't you tried? Other than the soulless ones with bad breath." Aunt Beth's eyes twinkled and Jessica laughed tearily and then shrugged.

"You should see what's around. They're awful." The tears started to creep down her cheeks now. "They're really just awful. And . . . no one knows me." She closed her eyes tightly on the last words, and bent her head.

"That's what Astrid used to say, Jessica, and now look at her." Aunt Beth walked around the back of Jessica's chair and gently stroked her hair. "She's flapping around like a schoolgirl, pretending to be 'discreet,' and having a marvelous time. She's about as discreet as the sunrise. But I'm glad for her. She's finally happy. She's found someone, and so will you, my dear. It takes time."

"How much time?" Jessie felt twelve years old again, asking the impossible of an all-knowing parent.

"That's up to you."

"But *how? How?*" Jessie turned in her seat to look up at Aunt Beth. "They're all so awful. Young men who think they're terrific and want to go to bed with you and every other woman on the street, who want to leave their track shoes on the dining-room table, and their drug stash in your house. They make you feel like a parking meter. They put a dime in and come around later . . . maybe . . . if they remember where they parked you. They make me feel like a nameless nothing. And the older men aren't much better; they're all out proving they're macho and pretending to love women's lib because it's expected . . . but Ian never was . . . oh, hell. It all bores me to tears. Everything does. The people I know bore me, and the people I don't know bore me. And . . ." She knew she was whining, but she didn't sound bored as much as she sounded frantic.

"Jessie, darling, *you* bore *me.* With garbage like that. All right, you need a change. Let's agree on that much. Then why not leave San Francisco for a while? Have you thought of that?" Jessie nodded sorrowfully, and Aunt Beth gave her the look she reserved only for very spoiled children. "Are you thinking of going back to New York?"

"No . . . I don't know. That would be worse. Maybe the mountains or the beach, or the country. Something like that. Aunt Beth, I'm so tired of people." She sat back with a sigh, dried her face, and stretched her legs. Aunt Beth was looking annoyed.

"Oh, shut up. Do you know what your problem is, Jessica? You're spoiled rotten. You had a husband who adored you and made you feel like a woman, and a very loved woman at that, and you had a boutique you enjoyed, and a home that you both shared and seemed to have enjoyed too. Well, by your own choice, you no longer have the husband, and you've squeezed all you can from that shop, and maybe the house has served its usefulness too. So get rid of it. All of it. And start fresh. I did when I got my divorce, and I was sixty-seven. Jessica, if I can do it, so can you. I came out from the East, bought this ranch, met new people, and I've had a wonderful time since. And if in five years it begins to bore me, then I'll close up shop, sell, and do something else, if I'm still alive. But if I *am* alive, then I'll *be* alive. Not living here half dead and no longer interested in what I'm doing. So, what are you going to do now? It's time you did *something!*" The old woman's eyes blazed.

"I've been thinking of getting rid of the shop, but I can't sell the house. It's half Ian's."

"Then why not rent it?"

It was a thought. The idea had never occurred to her before. And she was a little bit shocked at what she had just said. Sell the shop? When had she thought of that? Or had she been thinking of it all along? The words had just slipped out.

"I'll have to think it all out."

"This is a good place to do it, Jessica. I'm glad you came down."

"So am I. I'd be lost without you." She went to her side and gave her a hug. Aunt Beth was becoming a mainstay to her.

"Are you hungry yet?"

"I'm getting that way."

"Good. We can burn dinner together."

They made hamburgers and artichokes

with hollandaise sauce, a favorite of Aunt Beth's, and this time they neither burned nor curdled the sauce. It was a delightful meal and they sat up until almost midnight, speaking of easier subjects than those they had covered before dinner.

Jessica stretched out on the bed in her now familiar pink room and watched the fire glow and flicker as the old calico cat settled down next to her. It was good to be back. It really did feel like home. This was one place she was not tired of.

Aunt Beth was out riding when Jessie arose the next morning, and there was a note in the kitchen explaining which horse she could ride if she chose to. She had learned the terrain well enough the time before to handle a ride in the hills on her own now.

Shortly after eleven, she set off on a pleasant chestnut mare. She wore a wide-brimmed straw hat and had tucked a book and an apple into a small saddlebag. She felt like being alone for a while, and this was a perfect way to do it. After a half hour's ride, she found a small stream and tied the horse to the limb of a tree. The mare didn't seem to object, and Jessie took off her boots and went wading. She laughed as she sang songs to herself and unbuttoned her cuffs to roll up her sleeves. She felt freer than she had in as long as she could remember. It was then that she saw the man watching her.

She looked up with a start and he smiled an apology. It was frightening to suddenly see someone in what she thought was her own private wilderness, but he was tall and very well dressed in a fawn-colored riding habit. He spoke gently, and with a British accent.

"I'm sorry. I meant to say something earlier, but you looked so happy, I hated to spoil your fun." She was suddenly glad she hadn't taken off her shirt, which she had been considering.

"Am I trespassing?" She stood barefoot in the stream, one sleeve rolled up, and her hair loosely tied in a knot on top of her head. To him, she looked like a vision. A golden-haired Greek goddess in modern riding dress. One didn't see many women like that — not here in the "provinces." Lost on a hillside, barefoot in a stream. It was like a scene in an eighteenth-century paint-ing, and it made him want to walk down and touch her. Kiss her perhaps. The thought made him smile again as she watched him.

"No, I fear I'm the trespasser. I came out for a ride this morning, and I'm not very familiar with the territory, property boundaries and the like. I daresay I'm intruding." The accent was pure public-school English. Eton, perhaps. The alleged "intruder" was every inch a gentleman. And as she looked at him, it struck her how much he resembled Ian. He was taller, a little broader, but the face . . . the eyes . . . the tilt of the head . . . his hair was very blond, blonder than Jessie's. But still there was something of Ian about him, enough to haunt her. She looked away from him and sat down to put on her boots, carefully rolling her sleeves down first. While the unknown man continued to watch her with a small smile.

"You needn't leave because of me. I have to get home now in any case. But tell me, do you live here?" She shook her head slowly, unpinned her hair, and looked up at him. He was very good-looking.

"No, I'm a houseguest."

"Really? So am I." He mentioned the name of the people he was staying with, but she didn't recall having heard Aunt Beth mention them. "Will you be down here long?"

"A few days. Then I'll have to get back."

"To?" He was very inquisitive. Almost annoyingly so, except that he was so damned good-looking.

"San Francisco. I live there." She had avoided the next question, and now it was her turn. Why not? "And you?" The idea of questioning him amused her.

"I live in Los Angeles. But I'll be moving to San Francisco within the month, actually." She almost giggled as she listened to him. He sounded like all the imitations she'd ever heard of stuffy Englishmen. He was *sooo* British, standing there on a hilltop in his impeccable riding habit and flicking a riding crop across his palm. He was really quite something.

"Did I say something funny?"

"No, sir." With a half smile, she started up the hill toward him. Her horse was tied quite close to where he stood.

"My firm is transferring me to San Francisco. I came out from London three years ago, and I've had enough of L.A."

"You'll like San Francisco; it's a wonderful town." It was a totally mad conversation between two strangers in the middle of nowhere; they were behaving as though they were on Fifth Avenue, or Union Street, or the Faubourg St. Honoré. She burst into laughter as she found herself standing next to him.

"I seem to have a way of amusing you without intending to."

She smiled again and shrugged gently. "Lots of things do that."

"I see." He held out a hand to her then and looked rather solemn, but the smile still danced in his eyes. "How do you do? I'm Geoffrey Bates."

"Hello. I'm Jessica Clarke." Standing under the tree, they shook hands and she smiled at him again. At close range, he didn't look quite so much like Ian. But he was very pretty in his own right, Mr. Geoffrey Bates from London. And he was thinking how much he liked the way she looked when she smiled. And she seemed as though she did that a lot.

He hesitated for a moment before asking her the next question, but he finally gave in. He wanted to know.

"Where are you staying, by the way?" By the way? It made Jessica smile again and then laugh.

"With the mother of a friend." She was vague, and he smiled as he raised an eyebrow.

"And you won't tell me who? I promise not to disgrace you and appear uninvited to dinner."

She laughed back and felt silly, but the Englishman's face had grown serious. He had just realized that she might well be traveling with a man. That would be awkward. He had looked at her left hand almost instantly and been relieved to see it bare of rings, especially plain gold ones. But he hadn't look closely enough to see the little worn ridge or the slightly paler strip where she had worn her wedding band for seven years before removing it a few months before.

"I'm staying with Mrs. Bethanie Williams."

"I believe I've heard someone mention her name." He looked enormously relieved. "Leg up?" She was standing next to her horse as he asked, and she turned to him with a look of amusement.

"Hardly. But should I say yes?" She thought she saw him blush as she swung easily into the saddle. It was a foolish question to ask someone as tall as she was, but then she noticed his height. He was at least four or five inches taller than Ian . . . six five? Six six? Not even Ian was that tall . . . "not even" . . . why did she still think of him that way? As though he were the ultimate man. The paragon of perfection to which all other men would always be compared, in her mind.

"May I call you at Mrs. Williams'?" Jessica nodded, cautious again. This was certainly an unusual way to meet a man, and she really had no idea who or what he was.

"I won't be here for very long."

"Then I'll have to call you soon, won't I?" Persistent bastard, aren't you? She smiled again, wondering. But he didn't look like a bastard. He looked like a nice man. Somewhere in his mid-thirties, with gentle gray eyes and soft silky hair. And the clothes he wore looked expensive. He was also wearing a small gold ring on the smallest finger of his right hand; she thought she could see a crest etched into the gold, but she didn't want to stare. Everything about him looked formal and elegant. With his jodhpurs he was wearing polished black boots and a soft blue shirt with a stock. His fawn-colored tweed jacket hung from a branch and he looked a bit odd in the rugged setting, but at the same time incredibly beautiful. Better and better as she watched him. Which was precisely how he felt about her, although Jessica had begun to wonder how disheveled her hair looked.

"Nice to meet you." She prepared to ride off with a smile and a wave.

"You didn't answer my question." He held her horse's bridle as he watched Jessica's eyes. She knew what he meant. And she liked his style.

"Yes. You can call me." He stepped back in silence and, with a dazzling smile, swept her a bow. She liked that about him too. His smile. And she laughed to herself as she rode off toward the ranch.

CHAPTER 31

"Have a nice ride, dear?"

"Very. And I met a very strange man."

"Really? Who?" Aunt Beth looked intrigued. Strange men were few and far between around the ranch, except an odd foreman here and there.

"He's someone's houseguest, and terribly British. But he's also very nice-looking."

Aunt Beth smiled at the look on her face. "Well, well. A tall, dark, handsome stranger on my ranch? Good heavens! Where is he? And how old?"

Jessica giggled. "I saw him first. And besides, he's not dark. He's blond, and a lot taller than I am."

"Then he's yours, my dear. I never did like tall men."

"I adore them."

Aunt Beth looked over the top of her reading glasses with careful solemnity. "You haven't much choice." They both laughed again and enjoyed a blazing sunset over the hills.

It was another peaceful evening, and Jessica was up at seven the next day. She had a craving to wander, but this time not on the chestnut mare. She made herself a cup of coffee — for once up before Aunt Beth was — and took off as quietly as she could in the Morgan. She had never driven much around there, and she had been itching to explore.

The sun was high in the sky when she found it. And it was in very sad shape. But it was a beauty. It looked as though someone had lost it in the tall grass and then tired of looking for it, decades before. And now there it sat, alone and unloved, with a FOR RENT sign listing badly to one side just beyond the front steps. It was a small but perfectly proportioned Victorian house. She tried the front door, but it was locked. And Jessica found herself sitting on the front steps, fanning her face with her large-brimmed straw hat, smiling. She wasn't sure why, but she felt good. And incredibly happy.

She drove home at fifty on the dusty country road and strode into the house with a grin. Aunt Beth was checking her mail and looked up, surprised.

"Well, where have you been? You left aw-fully early." There was mischief in the old woman's blue eyes, and delighted suspicion.

"Wait till you hear what I've found!"

"Another man on my land? And this time a Frenchman! I knew it. Dear girl, you're having delusions from the sun." Aunt Beth clucked sympathetically and Jessica burst into laughter and tossed her hat high in the air.

"No, not a man! Aunt Beth, it's a house! An incredible, beautiful, marvelous, Victo-rian house! And I'm madly in love with it."

"Oh God, Jessie, not the one I think it is? The old Wheeling house out the North Road?" She knew exactly which one.

"I haven't the vaguest idea, I just know that I love it."

"And you've bought it, and your decora-tor is due in from New York first thing tomorrow morning." Aunt Beth refused to be serious.

"No. I mean it. It's lovely. Did you ever stand back and look at it? I did, for an hour this morning, and I sat on the front steps for almost as long. What's it like inside? It was locked, dammit. I even tried all the windows."

"God only knows what it looks like inside. No one's lived in it for almost fifteen years.

Actually, it used to be very lovely, but it hasn't much land, so no one will buy it. You could probably get more land with it now, though, because the Parkers behind there just decided that they want to sell off a very nice parcel. Almost forty acres, if I remember correctly. But as far as I know, the Wheeling place just sits there empty. Year after year. The realty people showed it to me when I came down to buy the ranch, but I had no interest in the place. Too much house, too little land, and I wanted something more modern. Why on earth would you want a Victorian house out in the middle of nowhere?"

"But Aunt Beth, it's so beautiful!" Jessica looked young and romantic as she smiled at her friend.

"Ah, the illusions of youth. Maybe you have to be young and in love to want a house like that. I wanted something more practical-looking. But I can see why you liked it." She was noticing the brightness in her young friend's green eyes. "Jessica, what exactly do you have in mind?" Her voice was quiet and serious now.

"I don't know yet. But I'm thinking. About a lot of different things. Maybe they're all crazy ideas, but something's brewing." Jessica looked decidedly pleased with herself. It had been a marvelous morning, and something wonderful had happened in her head or her heart, she wasn't sure which, but she felt alive and excited and brand new again. It was crazy, really. A Bible passage that she had once learned in Sunday school had come to mind as she sat looking at the house. "Behold, old things are passed away. All things are become new." She had kept thinking of that, and she knew it was true. All the old things were drifting out of her life . . . even the horror of the trial . . . even Ian . . .

"Well, Jessie, let me know what you come up with when everything's 'brewed.' Or before that, if I can help."

"Not just yet. But maybe later." Aunt Beth nodded and went back to her mail and Jessie headed up the stairs, humming to herself. And then she stopped and looked back at Aunt Beth. "How would I go about seeing the inside of that house?"

"Call the realtors. They'll be thrilled. I don't suppose they get to show the place more than once every five years. Just look them up in the book. Hoover County Realty. Terribly original name." Aunt Beth was beginning to wonder . . . but she couldn't take Jessie seriously. This must be a passing fancy, a mood. But it would keep Jessie amused. Just thinking of something other than her own boredom would do her good. One thing was certain — she hadn't looked bored when she'd come in. Not that morning. And certainly not the evening before.

Geoffrey Bates telephoned that afternoon while Jessie was out, and he called again around five, just when she got back. He politely inquired if he could "come around" for a drink, or bring her over to meet the people where he was staying. Jessie opted to have him for drinks at Aunt Beth's. And she was in high spirits.

He was terribly charming, very amusing, very proper, and quite taken with Aunt Beth, which pleased Jessie. But he was even more taken with Jessie, which pleased Beth. He looked even more splendid than Jessie had warned, in a blazer and ivory gabardine slacks, a Wedgewood blue shirt, and a navy ascot at his neck. Terribly elegant, but also very appealing. And they made a spectacular couple, both tall and blond, with a natural grace. They would have turned heads anywhere, just as they looked sitting easily in the living room at the ranch.

"I rode the hills in search of you today, Jessica, and all in vain. Where were you hiding?"

"In a house with a bathtub four feet deep

and a kitchen straight out of a museum."

"Playing Goldilocks, I presume. Did the three bears come home before you left, and how was the porridge?"

"Delightful." She laughed at him and blushed slightly when he reached for her hand. But he held it for only a second.

"I thought you were an apparition yesterday on the hills. You looked like a goddess."

"Aunt Beth accused me of delusions from the sun."

"Yes, but she didn't think she'd seen a god, at least." Aunt Beth cut him down to size just to see how he'd take it, but he took it well. He was very gracious, and left them shortly before dinner, having invited them both to join him at his hosts' for lunch the next day. Aunt Beth excused herself on the grounds that she would have business to attend to on the ranch, but Jessica accepted with pleasure. He drove off in a chocolate brown Porsche, and Jessica looked up with a girlish gleam in her eyes.

"Well, what do you think?"

"Too tall by far." Aunt Beth tried to look stern, but instantly failed as her face broke into a grin. "But otherwise, I heartily approve. He's perfectly lovely, Jessica! Simply lovely." Aunt Beth sounded almost as excited as Jessie herself felt. She was trying to fight it, but with difficulty.

"He is nice, isn't he?" She looked dreamy for a moment and then pirouetted on one foot. "But he's not as nice as my house."

"Jessica, you confuse me! I'm too old for such games! What house? And how dare you compare a man like that to a house?"

"Easily, because I'm mean. And I'm talking about *my* house. The one I rented today, for the whole summer!"

Aunt Beth's face grew serious at the news. "You rented the Wheeling house for the summer, Jessica?"

"Yes. And if I like it, I'll stay longer. Aunt Beth, I'm happy down here, and you were right, it is time for a change."

"Yes, child. But to something like this? This is a life for an old woman, not for you. You can't lock yourself up in the country. Who will you talk to? What will you do?"

"I'll talk to you, and I'll start to paint again. I haven't done that in years, and I love it. I might even paint you."

"Jessica, Jessica! Always so flighty! You worry me at times. Last time you leapt to your feet and ran home to get a divorce, and now what are you doing? Please, dear, think this over with care."

"I have, and I am, and I will. I only rented it for the summer. And we'll see after that.

It's not a permanent move. I'll try it. The only permanent decision I've come to is to sell the shop."

"Good God, you have been busy. Are you sure about all this?" Aunt Beth was more than slightly taken aback. She'd suggested selling the shop, but she hadn't thought Jessica would take her seriously. What had she done?

"I'm absolutely sure. I'm going to sell Lady J to Astrid, or offer it to her, anyway, when I go back."

"And she'll buy it. You can be sure of that, Jessica. I can't say I'm sorry. I think it would be good for her. But won't you be sorry? The boutique seems to mean a lot to you, dear."

"It did, but it's a part of the past now. A part I have to get rid of. I don't think I'll regret it."

"I hope not." There was a change in the air again; they both sensed it. But for the first time in a long time, Jessie felt alive, and not in the least bored.

"Is the house livable?"

"More or less, with a good scrub. A very good scrub."

"What will you do about furniture?"

"Live in a sleeping bag." She didn't look at all perturbed.

"Don't be ridiculous. I have some spare furniture out in the shed, and more in the attic. Help yourself. At least you'll be comfortable."

"And happy."

"Jessie . . . I hope so. And please try not to do anything major too quickly. Take your time. Think. Weigh your decisions."

"Is that what you do?"

Aunt Beth couldn't stifle her mirth at the question. "No. But it's the sort of advice old women are supposed to give young girls. I always rush in and do what I want, and mend fences later. And to tell you the truth, I'll love having you down here for the summer." The older woman smiled gently and Jessica grew pensive.

"And what if I stay after the summer?"

"Oh, I'll close my doors to you and shoot at you from the kitchen windows. What do you suppose I'd do? Be delighted, of course. But I won't encourage you to move down here for my sake. I don't even do that to Astrid." But she didn't really think Jessie would move down; by the end of the summer she'd be tired of the lack of excitement . . . and the Englishman who was moving to San Francisco looked very promising.

He came to take Jessie to lunch the next

day, and she returned to Aunt Beth's in high spirits. She had liked his friends, and they had been delighted at the prospect of her moving down for the summer, and had extended an invitation to drop in on them anytime she liked. They were a couple in their fifties who invited friends up often from L.A. Geoffrey was among them . . .

"I see I'm going to be spending a lot of time here this summer," he'd said.

"Oh?"

"Yes, and it's a damn long drive down from San Francisco. You could have picked someplace closer for your summer haunt, Jessica." She had not yet mentioned to him that she was thinking of moving down for good. She'd laughed up into his eyes as he'd handed her out of his car at Aunt Beth's. "Speaking of which, Miss Clarke, when are you going back to the city?"

"Tomorrow." But the "Miss" Clarke had unnerved her . . . Miss? It had sounded so strange. So . . . so empty.

"I'm going back to L.A. tomorrow too. But as a matter of fact —" he'd looked down at her almost slyly, and definitely pleased with himself — "I'm planning to be in San Francisco on Wednesday. How about dinner?"

"I'd love it."

"So would I." He'd looked surprisingly serious as they'd walked toward the house, and he'd quietly slipped his hand around hers.

Chapter 32

Astrid was stunned by Jessica's offer, but she leapt at the idea. She had wanted to buy the boutique since the first time she'd seen it.

"But are you sure?"

"Positive. Take it. I'll give you an idea of what the inventory's worth, talk to my attorney, and we'll come up with a price." She spoke to Philip Wald and two days later they set a price. Astrid didn't hesitate.

She asked her own attorneys to have the papers drawn up. Lady J would become hers for the sum of eighty-five thousand dollars. Both she and Jessie were pleased with the price. The only twinge Jessica felt was at the mention of Astrid's changing the name of the boutique to Lady A. At least it would sound almost the same to their clients. But it wouldn't be the same anymore. It would be Astrid's. The end of an era had finally come.

They were sitting in the back office discussing plans for the sale when Katsuko appeared in the doorway with a smile on her face.

"There's someone here to see you, Jessie. Someone very pretty to look at, I might add."

"Oh?" She poked her head out the door and saw Geoffrey. "Oh! Hello." She beckoned him into the office, and introduced him to Astrid, explaining that Mrs. Williams was her mother.

"You know my mother?" Astrid was surprised. Her mother didn't know anyone like Geoffrey.

"I had the pleasure of meeting her this weekend, at the ranch." Astrid's eyebrows shot up as she cast a look of surprise at Jessica, and Geoffrey added quickly, "I was down there visiting friends." And suddenly Astrid's face said that she understood why Jessica was planning to spend the summer down there, in her creaking rented Victorian house. Astrid almost wondered if that was why she was selling the shop. But she felt as though she had missed a piece of the story somehow. Had Jessica been keeping secrets? She looked over to see Geoffrey looking at Jessica warmly. And Astrid restrained the questions on the tip of her lips. How? When?

What next? Did he . . . was he . . . would he . . . He broke into her thoughts with another blistering smile.

"May I invite you two lovely ladies to lunch?" He even managed gently to encompass Katsuko with a look of regret; he knew someone would have to stay home, to mind the store. His manners were impeccable. And Astrid liked that. She was almost tempted into lunch, out of curiosity, but she didn't want to do that to Jessie. But Jessica was quick to shake her head about lunch.

"Don't even tempt us, Geoffrey. We were just discussing some business matters, about the sale of the shop, and . . ."

"Oh, for heaven's sake, Jessica!" Astrid broke in on Jessie's conscientious protests. "Don't be silly — we can talk business later. I have some errands to do anyway. I have to go downtown —" she looked sorrowfully at Geoffrey — "but you two go ahead and have a nice lunch. I'll meet you back here around two or two-thirty."

"Make it two-thirty, Mrs. Bonner." Geoffrey was quick to step in. And Jessica sat back and watched. She liked the way he dealt with things. He was used to wielding power and it showed. It made her feel safe, but not threatened. Now that she didn't need to be taken care of, his attentions were a luxury, not a life-giving plasma. She was enjoying the difference, and found herself wondering what it would have been like with Ian, had her needs not been so desperate, had she been more sure of herself. But she brushed the thought from her mind.

They had lunch nearby, in a garden restaurant on Union Street, and it was a very pleasant meal. He had a passion for horses, and flew his own plane, was planning a trip to Africa the following winter, and had gone to Cambridge, after Eton. And it was clear that he was very taken with Jessie. And every time he smiled that magnificent smile of his, she melted.

"I must say, Jessica, you look very different up here, in town."

"It's amazing what a difference it makes when I comb my hair." They both smiled at the memory of their first meeting. "I even wear shoes around here."

"Do you? How refreshing. Let me take a look." He teasingly swept aside the table-cloth to glance at her feet, and saw a very handsome pair of cinnamon suede Gucci shoes. They were almost exactly the color of the suede skirt she had on with a salmon silk blouse. The salmon shade was Ian's favorite color, and she had had to force herself to put it on this morning. So what if it was Ian's favorite? That was no reason to give it up. She hadn't worn the blouse in months, as though by not doing so she were somehow renouncing him. Now it seemed foolish.

"I approve of your shoes. And by the way, that's a very handsome blouse." She blushed at the compliment, mostly because it reminded her of Ian. There was something about Geoffrey . . .

"What were you just thinking?" He had glimpsed a shadow passing rapidly across her eyes.

"Nothing."

"Shame on you, telling lies. Something serious crossed your mind. Something sad?" It had looked that way.

"Of course not." She was embarrassed that he had seen so much. Too much. He was very observant.

"Have you never been married, Jessie? It seemed remarkable to have the good fortune to find a woman like you, free and unattached. Or am I making assumptions?" But he had wanted to know ever since he'd met her.

"You're making the right assumptions. I'm free and unattached. And yes, I was married." His timing was amazing, as though he had read her mind.

"Any children?" He raised an eyebrow with a curious air.

"No. None."

"Good."

"Good?" It was an odd thing to say. "You don't like children, Geoffrey?"

"Very much. Other people's." He smiled without embarrassment. "In fact, I'm a perfectly marvelous uncle. But I'd make a perfectly terrible father."

"What makes you say that?"

"I move about too much. I'm too selfish. When I love a woman, I detest sharing her in any major way, and if you're going to be a proper mother, you've got to spread yourself pretty thin between husband and offspring. Perhaps I'm too much a child myself, but I want to enjoy long romantic evenings, unexpected trips to Paris, skiing in Switzerland without three little runny-noses crying in the car . . . I can give you a thousand dreadful, horribly selfish reasons. But all of them honest. Does that shock you?" He didn't apologize for what he was saying, but he was willing to accept that she might not approve. He had long since stopped making excuses. In fact, he had seen to it that there was no longer a possibility of a "slip." He had made up his mind, and now there was no question of it.

"No, it doesn't shock me. I've always felt that way myself. In fact, exactly that way."

"But?"

"What do you mean?"

"There was a 'but' in your voice." He said it very softly, and she smiled. "Was there? I'm not sure. I used to have very definite ideas on the subject. But I don't know . . . I've changed a lot."

"Changing is natural if you've gotten divorced. But suddenly you find you want children? I should think you'd want permanent freedom."

"Not necessarily. And I haven't made any grandiose policy changes about children either. I've just started asking myself a lot of questions."

"Actually, Jessie —" he held her hand gently as he said it — "I rather think you'd be happier without children. You seem very much like me. Determined, free; you enjoy what you do; I somehow can't imagine you chucking all that for a little squally person in diapers." She grinned at the thought.

"God."

"Quite." They laughed for a moment, and took a sip of their wine as the second batch of lunch customers began to arrive. They had already been sitting there for almost two hours. It was odd to be talking to him about children all of a sudden. She got the feeling that the subject was important to him, and he wanted to get it out of the way early. And he certainly shared all the views she'd held dear for a decade.

Jessica stretched her legs and finished her wine, wondering if she should get back to the shop, and then suddenly thinking that she must be keeping him from appointments too. But the time together was so pleasant, it was hard to bring it to an end.

"I'm going to Paris on business next week, Jessica. Is there anything I can bring you?"

"What a lovely thought. Paris." Her eyes danced at the idea. Paris.

"Let's see . . . you could bring me . . . the Louvre . . . Sacre-Coeur . . . the Café Flore . . . the Brasserie Lipp . . . the Champs Elysées . . . oh, and the entire Faubourg St. Honoré." She giggled at the thought of it.

"That's what I like. A woman who knows what she wants. As a matter of fact, how about coming with me?"

"Are you kidding?"

"I certainly am not. I'll only be gone for three or four days. You could get away for that long, couldn't you?" Yes, but with a total stranger? God only knew who he was.

"I've been meaning to go to New York for

the shop, but now I don't need to, and . . . Paris . . . ?" She didn't know what to say. After all those jerks who had crawled all over her, here was a perfectly heavenly man, and he wanted to take her to Paris.

"We don't . . ." He looked awkward but sweet. "We don't have to share the same room. If you'd be more comfortable . . ."

"Geoffrey! You're an angel. And stop it, or I'll wind up doing it and neglecting all the things I ought to do here. I'm very touched that you'd ask, but I really can't."

"Well, let's wait and see. You might change your mind."

Wow. Geoffrey was really quite amazing. Paris? She almost wanted to say yes, but . . . why not? Why the hell not? Paris? . . . God, it would be gorgeous, but . . . dammit, why did she feel as if she'd be cheating on Ian? What difference did it make now? She was free. He wouldn't even know. She never saw him anymore anyway. But . . . somehow . . . he was there . . . with a look of pain in his eyes, as though he didn't want her to go. She tried to shake his face from her mind, and smiled at Geoffrey.

"Thank you for the offer."

"I do wish you'd come. See what I mean about enjoying impromptu trips? I love that sort of thing! Not much fun if you have to drag along a nanny and four brats, or leave them at home and feel guilty. Being an uncle is really much simpler. Have you any nieces or nephews?" She shook her head quietly. "Brothers or sisters?"

"No. I had a brother, but he died in the war."

Geoffrey looked puzzled for a moment. "The second one, or Korea? In either case, he must have been quite a bit older."

"No. Vietnam."

"Of course. How stupid of me. How awful. Were you very close?" His pressure on her hand grew a trifle stronger, as though to support her. His thoughtfulness pleased her a great deal.

"Yes. We were very close. It did awful things to me when he died." It was the first time she had ever been able to say that. The last few months had freed her in more ways than she knew.

"I'm sorry."

She nodded and smiled. "And how many brothers and sisters do you have?"

"Two sisters, and a very stuffy brother. My sisters are quite mad. But very amusing."

"Do you still spend much time in Europe?"

"Quite a bit. A few days here, a few days

there. I enjoy it very much that way. By the way, Jessica, shouldn't I be taking you back to the shop for your meeting with Astrid?"

"Christ. I forgot all about it. You're right!" She looked at her watch regretfully, and smiled at him again. It had been a lovely few hours.

"I've been keeping you from your appointments too, I suspect."

"Yes, I . . ." But laughter took the place of seriousness and he looked at her with a mischievous smile. "No, I didn't have a single appointment. I came up here entirely to see you." He sat back in his chair and laughed at himself, as though very pleased.

"You did?" Jessica looked astonished.

"I most certainly did. I hope you don't mind."

"No. I'm just surprised." Very surprised, and a little taken aback. What did that mean? He had come up to see her . . . and the suggestion of the trip to Paris . . . dammit. Was he going to be like everyone else and expect to exchange a meal for her body?

"Oh, the look on your face, Jessica!"

"What look?" There was laughter and embarrassment in her voice. What if he really had known what she'd been thinking? He seemed to do that a lot.

"Would you like to know what look?"

"Okay. See if you can guess." She might as well brazen it out.

"Well, if I tell you that I have a room at the Huntington, will you feel any better?"

"Oh! You!" She swatted him with her napkin. "I was not . . . !"

"You were too!"

"I was too!"

They both laughed, and he slipped a large bill onto the waiter's plate and got up to help Jessica into her jacket.

"I apologize for my thoughts." Jessica hung her head with a grin.

"You certainly ought to." But he gave her a friendly hug on their way out and they laughed and teased all the way back to the shop. Astrid was waiting for them with a relaxed smile when they got in. It pleased her to see Jessie happy again, and with a man.

"I'll leave you now to your meetings and your business and your whatever-it-is-you-do. And Jessica, what time shall I fetch you?"

"From here?" She looked surprised. It was strange to be taken care of again, escorted and assisted, picked up and brought back. She had missed it for so long, and now she didn't quite know how to handle it again. It was like coming back to shoes after months of barefeet.

577

"Would you rather I meet you after work?"

"Either way." She looked at him happily, and for a moment neither of them spoke. She had been about to offer him her car, but she couldn't quite do that. Not . . . not the Morgan. She felt rotten for not offering it, but she couldn't.

"Why don't I give you time to go home and relax? May I pick you up there?" Since he already knew that she was a little bit skittish, they both laughed, but she nodded.

"That'll be fine."

"Say at seven? Dinner at eight."

"Super." And then suddenly she had a thought. He was almost at the door of the shop, and she quickly walked toward him. "You don't know San Francisco very well, do you?"

"Not very. But I expect I can find my way around." He looked amused at her concern.

"How would you like a tour at the end of the day?"

"With you?"

"Of course."

"That's a splendid idea."

"Great. Where will you be around five?"

"Anywhere you say."

"All right. I'll pick you up outside the St. Francis Hotel at five. Okay?"

"Very much so."

He gave her a quick salute and ran quickly down the steps of the shop as Jessica turned back to Astrid.

Somehow she had a hard time keeping her mind on what they were saying as they discussed the sale of Lady J.

"Right, Jessie?"

"Huh?" Astrid was grinning at her when she looked up. "Oh, shit."

"Don't tell me you're falling in love."

"Nothing like it. But he's a very nice man. Isn't he?" She wanted Astrid's approval.

"He looks like it, Jessie."

Jessica looked up at her friend and giggled like a schoolgirl. It seemed hours before they had their business settled, although both women were pleased with the results. Jessica got up jubilantly from her desk, pirouetted on one heel of the pretty Gucci shoes, and looked at her watch.

"And now, I have to go." She picked up her bag, blew Astrid a kiss, and paused happily at the door for a moment. "In fifteen minutes I have to pick up Ian." With a rapid wave she was out the door and down the steps — without ever realizing what she had said. Astrid shook her head and wondered if she'd ever get over him. More than that, she wondered how Ian was doing. She missed him. And thinking of him threw a damper on her excitement about Jessie's new friend.

Jessie was already backing out of the drive and on her way to meet Geoffrey.

CHAPTER 33

"Am I late?" She looked worried as she pulled up in front of the St. Francis. She had run into unexpected traffic on the way downtown. But he looked happy and relaxed, like a man who is looking forward to seeing someone, not like a man who has been kept waiting.

"Oh, I've been here for hours."

"Liar."

"Heavens! What an outrageous thing to call a man!" But he looked delighted to see her, and allowed himself to lean over and give her a peck on the cheek. She liked the friendliness of it. The hugs before passion ever became an issue. The little touches of the hand, the quick kiss on the cheek. It made things less awesome that way. They were becoming friends. She was falling in like.

"Where are you taking me?"

"Everywhere." She eyed him with pleasure

as she drove up to Nob Hill.

"What a promise. Well, I know where we are now, anyway. That's my hotel." She ignored him, and he grinned.

"This is Nob Hill." And she pointed out Grace Cathedral, the Pacific Union Club, and three of the city's poshest hotels. From there they swooped down California Street to the Embarcadero, the Ferry Building, and a quick view of the docks. Up toward Ghirardelli Square and the Cannery, where she pointed out the honeycomb of boutiques right after they passed Fisherman's Wharf (where she had stopped and bought him a well-filled cup of fresh shrimp and a huge hunk of sourdough bread).

"What a tour. My dear, I'm overwhelmed." And she was having a marvelous time as well.

From there, they went on to watch the old men playing boccie on the rim of the bay, and then up to the yacht basin and the St. Francis Yacht Club. This was followed by a sedate tour past blocks and blocks and blocks of elaborate mansions. After which they took refuge in Golden Gate Park. And her timing was perfect. It was just nearing sunset, and the light on the flowers and lawns was gold and pink and very lovely. It was Jessica's favorite time of day.

They walked past endless flower beds, and along curved walks, past little waterfalls, and around a small lake, until at last they reached the Japanese tea garden.

"Jessica, you give an extraordinarily good tour."

"At your service, sir." She swept him a formal curtsy, and he put a quick arm around her shoulders. It had been a beautiful day and she was beginning to feel as though she really knew him.

She liked his reactions, his way of thinking, his sense of humor, and the gentle way he seemed to care about how she felt. And he seemed so much like her. He had the same kind of free and easy ways, the same craving for independence. He seemed to like his work, and he certainly didn't appear to be suffering financially. He really seemed the perfect companion. For a while, anyway. And he was nice to her. She had learned to be grateful for that, without leaning on him too heavily.

"What do you like to do more than anything in this world, Jessica?" They were sipping green tea and munching little Japanese cookies in the tea garden.

"More than anything else? Paint, I guess."

"Really?" He seemed surprised. "Are you good? Stupid question, but one always feels compelled to ask that, useless though it is. People who are any good insist that they're awful. And of course the bad ones tell you they're the best."

"Now what do I say?" They both laughed and she shared the last cookie with him. "I don't know if I'm any good or not, but I love it."

"What sort of things do you paint?"

"It depends. People. Landscapes. Whatever. I work in watercolor or oils."

"You'll have to show me sometime." But he sounded indulgent and not as though he took her very seriously. He had a kind of placating, fatherly way about him sometimes, which made her feel like a little girl. It was odd that now that she had gotten used to being a grown-up, someone had appeared who would have let her go on being a child. But she wasn't sure she still wanted to be one.

When the tea garden closed, they walked slowly back to the car, and Geoffrey seemed to see it for the first time.

"You know, Jessica, it's really a beauty. These are almost collectors' items now. Where did you get it?"

"I'm not sure one should admit that sort of thing, but it was a gift." She looked proud as she said it.

"Good lord, and a handsome one." She nodded in silence and he cast her a glance without asking the question. But whoever had given her the car, he knew it was someone important in her life, and most likely her husband. Jessica was not the sort of woman to accept large gifts from just anyone. He already knew that much about her. She was a woman of breeding, and considerable style.

"Have you ever flown? I mean flown a plane yourself." She laughed at the idea and shook her head. "Want to try?"

"Are you serious?"

"Why not? We'll go up in my plane sometime. It's not hard flying at all. You could learn in no time."

"What a funny idea."

He was full of funny ideas, but she liked them. And she liked him.

They shared a wonderful evening. The food at L'Etoile was superb, the piano in the bar was gentle, and Geoffrey was delightful to be with. They shared a chateaubriand with truffles and béarnaise, white asparagus, hearts of palm with endive salad in a delicate mustard dressing, and a bottle of Mouton-Rothschild wine, 1952, "a very good year," he assured her in his clipped English way, but warmed by a smile produced just for her. He always managed to create an atmosphere of intimacy without making her feel uncomfortable.

And after dinner they danced at Alexis'. It was a far cry from the evening she'd spent there with the blind date Astrid had provided. Geoffrey danced beautifully. It was a thoroughly different evening from any she had spent in years. There was luxury and romance and excitement. She hated to go home and see it end. They both did.

They drove to her house in silence, and he kissed her gently at the door. It was the first time he had really kissed her, and it didn't send rockets off in her head, but it pulled threads all the way up her thighs. Geoffrey was a totally magnetic man. He pulled away from her slowly, with the tiniest of smiles tugging at one side of his mouth. "You're an exquisite woman, Jessica."

"Would you like to come in for a drink?" She wasn't sure if she wanted him to, and the way she said it told him so. She almost hoped he'd refuse. She didn't want to . . . not yet. But he was so appealing, and it had been such a long time.

"Are you sure you're not too tired? It's awfully late, young lady." He looked so gentle, so thoughtful, so much like . . . like Geoffrey. She forced her thoughts back to the present and smiled into his eyes.

"I'm not too tired." But she stiffened a little and he sensed it. He smiled at her back as she opened the door with her key. She had nothing to fear from him. He wanted much more than she could give in a night. He wasn't going to rush her. He already knew what he wanted, and what he wanted was for keeps.

She opened the door and turned on some lights, and he lit the candles as she poured cognac into two handsome shifters.

"Is cognac all right?"

"Perfect. And so is the view. This is quite a house." But he wasn't surprised. He had expected something like this. "And what a beautiful woman you are . . . taste . . . style . . . elegance . . . beauty . . . intelligence . . . a woman of a thousand virtues."

"And a fat head, if you don't stop soon." She handed him the snifter of cognac and sat down in her favorite chair. "It's a nice view from here."

"It is. I'll be looking for something like this in a few weeks."

"Will you?" She couldn't resist a burst of laughter. "Or did you make up that story about moving to San Francisco too?"

He smiled boyishly. "No, that was true. Are houses like this hard to find?"

"You mean you want to buy?" She had assumed that he would rent.

"That depends." He looked into her eyes and then into his cognac while she watched him.

"Maybe I'll rent you this place for the summer." She was teasing, and he raised an eyebrow.

"Are you serious?"

"No." Her eyes grew sad as she looked into the candle and spoke. "You wouldn't be happy here, Geoffrey." And she didn't want him in "their" house. It would have made her uncomfortable.

"Are *you* happy here, Jessica?"

"I don't think of it that way." She looked back into his eyes, and he was surprised at the pain he saw lurking there. It made her seem suddenly years older. "To me, it's just a house now. A roof, a clump of rooms, an address. The rest is gone."

"Then you should move out. Maybe we'll find a . . . I'll find . . . a larger place. Would you consider selling this?"

"No, just renting. It's not mine to sell."

"I see." He took another sip of his cognac and then smiled at her again. "I should be going soon, Jessica, or you'll be terribly tired tomorrow. Are you busy for breakfast?"

"Not usually." She laughed at the thought.

"Good. Then why don't we have breakfast somewhere amusing before I fly back to L.A. I can pick you up in a cab." She loved the idea of breakfast with him. She would have preferred to cook it for him and sit naked at the kitchen table with him, or juggle strawberries and fresh cream on a tray in bed. But she almost wondered if one did that sort of thing with Geoffrey. He looked as if he might wear a dressing gown and silk pajamas. But there was a definite sensuality about him too.

"What do you eat for breakfast?" It was a crazy question, but she wanted to know. It suddenly mattered to her. Everything did.

"What do I eat?" He seemed amused. "Generally something light. Poached eggs, rye toast, tea."

"That's all? Not even bacon? No waffles? No French toast? No papaya? Just poached eggs and rye toast? Yerghk." He roared with laughter at her reaction and began to enjoy the game.

"And what do you eat for breakfast that's so much more exotic, my love?"

"Peanut butter and apricot jam on English muffins. Or cream cheese and guava jelly on bagels. Orange juice, bacon, omelettes, apple butter, banana fritters . . ." She let her imagination run wild.

"Every day?"

"Absolutely." She tried to look solemn but had a hard time.

"I don't believe you."

"Well, you're right . . . about most of it. But the peanut butter and cream cheese part was true. Do you like peanut butter?"

"Hardly. It tastes like wet cement."

"Have you eaten a lot of that?" She looked across at him with interest.

"What?"

"Wet cement."

"Certainly. Marvelous on thin wheat toast. Now, are you serious about joining me for breakfast tomorrow? I'm sure we can get you some peanut butter on croissants. Will that do?"

"Perfect." She was starting to be Jessie now, and it amused him. He liked everything about her. She kicked off her shoes and curled her legs up in her chair. "Geoffrey —" she tried to sound solemn — "do you read comic books?"

"Constantly. Particularly Superman."

"What? No Batman comic books?"

"Oh yes, of course, but Superman has always been my favorite." He stopped playing for a minute then and looked into his glass. "Jessica . . . I like you. I like you very much." He surprised her with the directness of his words, and she was touched by the way he said them. His style was an odd mixture of formality and warmth. She hadn't thought the combination was possible, but apparently it was.

"I like you too."

They sat across from each other and he made no move to approach her. He didn't want to rush her. She was a woman you got close to gradually, after much thought.

"You haven't said much about it, nothing in fact, but I somehow have the feeling that you've suffered a lot. A very great deal, even."

"What makes you think that?"

"The things you don't say. The times you back off. The wall you run behind now and then. I won't hurt you, Jessica. I promise I'll try very hard not to."

She didn't say anything, but only looked at him and wondered how often promises turned to lies. But she wanted him to prove her wrong, and he wanted to try.

CHAPTER 34

"Well, how was your evening?" Astrid was already at the shop when Jessie got there the next day. Jessie wasn't getting in as early anymore. She didn't have to. Or want to.

"Delightful." She beamed, even more enchanted with their breakfast at the Top of the Mark that morning, but she didn't feel like telling Astrid about it. "Very, very nice." She looked cryptic and pleased with herself.

"I'd say he's 'very, very nice' too."

"Now, Mother. Don't push." The two women laughed, and Astrid held up a hand innocently in protest.

"Who needs to push? He sells himself all by himself. Are you in love with him, Jessie?" Astrid looked serious and so did Jessica.

"Honestly? No. But I like him. He's the nicest man I've met in a long time."

"Then maybe the rest will come later. Give him a chance." Jessica nodded and looked at the mail that was hers. She didn't like sharing the shop anymore. It was different now. And it was like prolonging the end. She wanted to say good-bye to Lady J and get out of town. This was just like one more divorce. And there was another letter from Ian with the rest of her mail. She took it and set it apart from the rest. Astrid noticed, but she didn't say anything. This was the first time Jessie hadn't torn up one of his letters. She saw Astrid's look and shrugged as she poured herself a fresh cup of coffee.

"You know, I keep thinking that maybe I should drop him a note and thank him for the car. Seems like the least I could do. Your mother and I talked about it last weekend."

"What did she say?"

"Nothing much." Which only meant that Jessie wasn't telling.

In the end, she threw out the letter he had sent her.

They met with the lawyers for the next two afternoons, and everything was settled. On Saturday morning, Jessie went to three real-estate agents and listed the house as a summer rental. But she wanted careful screening of the tenants; she was leaving all her furniture there. And Ian's studio would be locked. She felt she owed him that.

It was almost midnight on Sunday when she sat down to write him a note about the car. In the end, she jotted down five or six lines, telling him how pleased she had been, how lovely it was, and that he hadn't had to do that. She wanted to cancel the debt between them. He didn't owe her anything. But it took her almost four hours to compose the short note.

Five days later the house had been rented from the fifteenth of July till the first of September, and she was almost ready to leave town. She hoped to be gone in a week. Geoffrey wanted to come up and see her again, and even invited her down to L.A. for a weekend, but she was too busy. She had found leads to two houses and an apartment for him, but she was tied up with her own affairs. There didn't seem to be room for Geoffrey just then, and she wanted him to stay away until she had closed the house, given up the shop, put away the past. She wanted to come to him "clean" and new, if he would just give her the time. She had to do it that way. Be alone to sever the last cords by herself. It was harder this way, but he didn't belong in her life yet. She would see him in the country once she was settled.

She seldom went to the shop now, except to answer questions for Astrid. But now

Astrid knew fairly well how everything worked, and Katsuko was a great help. She was staying on at Lady J. And Jessie just didn't want to be there anymore. Workmen were busy changing the sign, and cards were being sent to all their customers announcing the small change in the name. It still hurt, but Jessica told herself that all changes did, perhaps especially those for the better. She wouldn't regret it once she left town. But then what would she do? Yes, paint . . . but for how long? She wasn't ready to become another Grandma Moses. But something would turn up . . . something better. Geoffrey? Maybe he was the answer.

Jessica stopped in at the shop for the last time on a Friday afternoon. She was leaving two days later, on Sunday. She had put away all the small treasures she didn't want to share with her new tenants. And photographs of Ian. She had unearthed so much as she'd packed. Everything hurt now. It seemed as though every moment were filled with painful reminders of the past.

She slid the car into the driveway behind Astrid's car and walked quietly into the shop. It already looked different. Astrid had added a few things, and a lovely painting in what was now her office. It was all Astrid's now. And the money from the sale was all

Jessie's. It was funny how little that meant to her now. Nine months before, seven months, six . . . she would have begged for one-tenth of that money . . . and now . . . it didn't matter. The bills were paid, Ian was gone, and what did she need? Nothing. She didn't know what to do with the money, and she didn't really care. It hadn't dawned on her yet that she had made a great deal of money selling the shop. Later she would be pleased, but not yet. And she still felt as though she had sold her only child. To a good friend, but still . . . she had abandoned the only thing she had ever nurtured and helped to grow.

"Mail for you, madam." Astrid handed it to her with a smile. She looked happy these days, and even younger than she had when Jessie had met her. It was difficult to believe that she had just had a birthday and turned forty-three. And in July, Jessie would be thirty-two. Time was moving. Quickly.

"Thanks." Jessie slid the letters into a pocket. She could look at them later. "Well, I'm all packed and ready to go."

"And already homesick." Astrid had guessed. She took her out to lunch and they drank too much white wine, but Jessie felt better. It helped. She went home in a much better mood.

She opened the windows and sat in a patch of sunlight on the floor, looking around the living room she had sat in so often with Ian. She could see him sprawled out on the couch, listening to her talk about the shop, or telling her about something brilliant he'd said in a new chapter. That was what was missing — that excitement of sharing the things they loved doing. Of laughing and being two kids on a warm sunny day, or a cold winter afternoon while he lit the fire. A man like Geoffrey would spoil her, and take her to the best restaurants and hotels all over the world, but he wouldn't take a splinter out of her heel, or scratch her back just right where it itched . . . he wouldn't burp over a beer watching a horror movie in bed, or look like a boy when he woke up in the morning. He would look very handsome, and smell of the cologne he had worn to dinner that time . . . and he hadn't been there when Jake had died . . . or her parents . . . but Ian had. You couldn't replace that. Maybe you shouldn't even try.

She wondered as she stared out at the bay, and remembered the letters Astrid had handed her before lunch. She went back to them now, digging into her jacket pocket . . . she hoped . . . she didn't . . . and she did . . .

and there was . . . a letter from Ian. Her eyes swept quickly across the lines. He had gotten her note about the car.

. . . I write these to myself now, wondering only for a moment if you read them. And then suddenly, a few quick nervous lines from you, but you kept the car. That's all that mattered. I wanted you to have that more than you can know, Jess. Thanks for keeping it.

I assume that you don't open my letters . . . I know you. Rip, snap, gone.

She smiled at the image. And he was, of course, right.

But I seem to need to write them anyway, like whistling in the dark, or talking to myself. Who do you talk to now, Jessie? Who holds your hand? Who makes you laugh? Or holds you when you cry? You look such a mess when you cry, and God, how I miss that. I imagine you now, driving the new Morgan, and that note the other day . . . it sounded like something you'd write to your grandmother's best friend. "Thank you, dear Mr. Clarke, for the perfectly lovely car. I needed one just that color to go with my best skirt and my favorite gloves and hat." Darling, I love you. I only hope that you'll be happier now. With whomever, whenever. You have a right to that. And I know you must need someone. Or do you have a right to that? My heart aches so at the thought, yet I can't see myself stamping my feet and raising hell. How could I possibly say anything after all this? Nothing except good luck . . . and I love you.

It does make me sad that now that the book has sold, and I have sat back and taken a look at my life, you're not here to enjoy the changes. I've grown up here. It's a tough school to learn in, but I've learned a lot about you, and myself. It isn't enough just to make money, Jessie. And I don't give a damn who pays the bills. I want to pay them, but I don't think I'd get an ulcer anymore every time you signed a check. Life is so much fuller and simpler than that, or it can be. In an odd way, my life is full now, yet so empty without you. Darling, impossible Jessie, I still love you. Go away, leave my mind, let me go in peace, or come back. Oh God, how I wish you'd do that. But you won't. I understand. I'm not angry. I only wonder if it would have been different if I hadn't walked out that day, leaving you there with the phone in your hand. I still see your face on that day . . . but no, it's not all because of that one stinking day. We're both paying for old, old sins now — because I still believe that we are both suffering this loss. Or are you free of it now? Maybe you don't care anymore. I can't tell you the empty feeling that gives me, but that's what will happen in time, I suppose. Neither of us will give a damn. Not something I look forward to. A lot of good years "from dust to dust." Gone. And I still see you and see you and see you. I touch your hair and smile into your eyes. Perhaps you can feel that now — my smile into your eyes as you go your own way. Go in peace, Jessie dearest, and watch out for lizards and ants. They won't bite you, I promise, but the neighbors might call the cops when you scream. Just keep the hair spray handy, and take it easy on yourself. Always, Ian.

She laughed through her tears as she read it . . . lizards and ants. The two things she had always feared most. Other than loneliness. But she had lived with that now, so maybe she could even get used to lizards and ants . . . but to life without Ian? That would be so much harder. She hadn't realized how much she had missed the sound of his voice until she read the letter. It was there. His words, his tone, his laughter, his hand rumpling her hair as he talked. The look he gave her that made her feel safe.

Without thinking, she got to her feet and went to the desk. There was still some paper there. She reached for a pen and wrote to him, telling him that she had sold the shop, and about the house near Aunt Bethanie's ranch. She described the house down to its tiniest detail as he had taught her to do when she had thought she wanted to write. She didn't have a knack for it, but she had learned how to write careful descriptions so that her reader could see all that she did. She wanted him to see the fading Victorian in all its possible splendor, now nestled in weeds. She was going to clean it up and make it pretty. That would keep her busy for a while. She gave him the address and mentioned that she had rented the house, but to a pleasant couple without children or pets. They'd keep it in good shape, and she was sure to tell him that the studio was locked. His file cabinets were safe. And she would try to stay safe from lizards and ants.

It all flowed into the letter. It was like writing to a long-lost best friend. He had always been that. She put a stamp on the envelope and walked out to the mailbox on the corner, slipped it in, and then noticed Astrid driving home. She waved, and Astrid drove into the block and stopped at the corner.

"What are you up to tonight, Jessie? Want to have dinner?"

"You mean you're not busy for a change, Mrs. Bonner? I'm stunned." Jessica laughed, feeling happier than she had in ages. She was actually looking forward to leaving. For the past weeks, she had almost wondered if she'd done the wrong thing. It was all so brutal, so final. But now she knew that she'd been right, and she was glad. She felt relieved, and as though she had just touched base with her soul. Ian still lived there. In her soul. Even now. Jessica tried to pry her thoughts from Ian as she smiled at Astrid.

"No, smartass, I'm not busy. And I have a wild craving for spaghetti. How's the packing going?"

"All done. And spaghetti sounds great."

They dined in the noise and chaos of Vanessi's, and moved on to a sidewalk café, for cappuccino, after that. They watched the tourists beginning to appear, the first wave of the summer, and the air was surprisingly warm.

"Well, love, how do you feel? Scared, miserable, or glad?"

"About leaving? All three. It's a little bit like leaving home forever . . ." Like leaving Ian — again. Packing up their private treasures and odds and ends had revived so many feelings. Feelings that were better left buried now. She would not unpack those boxes again, and she had separated her things from Ian's. It would be very easy now, if they ever sold the house. Their worldly goods were no longer in one heap.

"Well, that house of yours will keep you busy. Mother says it's a mess."

"It is. But it won't be for long." Jessica looked proud as she said the words. She already loved the place. It was like a new friend.

"I'll try to get down to see it before we go away in July."

"I'd love that." Jessica smiled, feeling lighthearted and happy. A burden she couldn't quite identify had been lifted from her shoulders. She had felt its absence all evening. It was like no longer having a toothache or a cramp that she had lived with for months, not really aware of it yet subtly crippled by its presence.

"Jessica, you look happy now. You know, I felt terribly guilty for a while, for taking the shop away from you. I was afraid you'd hate me for it." Astrid looked young and unsure as she looked into Jessie's face. But Jessica only smiled and shook her blond mane.

"No. You don't need to worry about that." She patted her friend's hand. "You didn't take it away from me, Astrid. I sold it to you. I had to. To you, or to someone else, even if it hurt a little. And better to you. I'm glad it's yours now. I had outgrown it, I guess. I've changed a lot."

Astrid nodded assent. "I know you have. I hope it all works out."

"Yeah, me too." Her smile was almost rueful, and the two women finished their coffee. They were like two soldiers who have weathered the war together and now have nothing left to talk about except to make occasional guesses about the peace. Would it work? Jessie hoped so. Astrid wondered. They had both come a long way in the past months. And Astrid knew she had what she wanted now. Jessica wasn't yet quite as sure.

"Any news of Geoffrey this week, Jessie?"

"Yes. He called and said he'd come up to the country to see me next week." He had been sensitive enough to know she needed to be left alone in the city.

"That'll do you good."

Jessica nodded, but she didn't say more.

The doorbell rang at nine-fifteen the next morning. Her bags were packed and Jessica was washing the breakfast dishes for the last time, keeping one eye on the view. She wanted to remember it all, hang on for one last hour, and then leave. Quickly. She felt almost the way she had the morning she had left for college, old times packed away in mothballs and a new life ahead. She planned to come back, at least that was what she said, but would she? She wasn't really sure. She had the odd sensation that she was leaving for longer than a summer. Maybe forever.

The bell rang again and she dried her hands on her jeans and ran to the front door, throwing her hair back from her face, barefoot, her shirt buttoned but not quite far enough. She looked precisely the way she did when Ian loved her best. Pure Jessie.

"Who is it?" She stood beside the front door with a small smile on her face. She knew it was probably Astrid or Katsuko. One last good-bye. But this time she would laugh, not cry as they all had at the shop.

"It's Inspector Houghton." Everything inside her turned to stone. With trembling hands, she unbolted the door and opened it. The party mood was suddenly gone, and for the first time in months, there was terror in her eyes again. It was amazing how quickly it could all come flooding back. Months of slowly rebuilding the foundations, and in as long as it took to ring a doorbell her life was a shambles again. Or that was how she felt.

"Yes?" Her eyes looked like greenish-gray slate and her face was set like a mask.

"Good morning. I . . . uh . . . this isn't an official call exactly. I . . . I found your husband's pants in the property room the other day and I thought I'd drop them off and see how you were doing."

"I see. Thank you." He handed her a brown bag with an awkward smile. Jessie did not return the smile.

"Going on a trip?" His eyes glanced over the bags and boxes in the hall, and she looked over her shoulder and then quickly back into his eyes. Bastard. What right did he have to be there now? Jessica nodded in answer to his question and looked down at her feet. It was a good time to end the war, to hold out a hand in peace, to go quietly. But she couldn't. He made her want to scream again, to pummel him, to scratch his face. She couldn't bear the sight of him.

Terror and hatred swept over her like a tidal wave and she had the sudden urge to slither down the wall and crumple into a heap and cry. She felt as though she had been swept up in a hurricane and then cast aside by her own emotions. She looked up at him suddenly, with open pain in her eyes.

"Why did you come here today?" There was the look of a child who does not understand in her face, and he looked away and down at his hands.

"I thought you'd want your husband's . . ." His voice trailed off and his face grew hard. Coming to see her had been a dumb thing to do, and now he was sure of it. But he had just had that feeling for days now. Of wanting to see her. "Your husband's pants were just lying around the property room. I thought . . ."

"Why? Why did you think? Is he liable to be coming home and needing them in the immediate future? Or aren't they wearing denims in prison anymore? I'm a little out of touch. I haven't been up there in a while." She instantly regretted the words. His eyes showed interest and warmed again slightly.

"Oh?"

"I've been busy." She looked away.

"Problems?" Vulture. And then she found

his eyes again.

"Do you really give a damn?" She wouldn't let go of his eyes. She wanted to scratch them out.

"Maybe I do give a damn. Maybe . . . I'm sorry. You know, I always felt sorry for you through the whole case. You seemed to believe in him so much. You were wrong, though. You know that now, don't you?" She hated the tone of his voice.

"No. I wasn't wrong."

"The jury said you were." He looked so smug, the bastard, so sure of "the system." So sure of everything, including Ian's guilt. She wanted to hit him. The urge was almost overpowering now.

"The jury didn't make me wrong, Inspector Houghton." She held tightly to the brown bag he had given her and clenched her fists.

"Are you . . . are you free now, Mrs. Clarke?"

"Does that mean, have I left my husband?" He nodded and pulled a pack of cigarettes out of his coat pocket. "Why?"

"Curious." Horny.

"Is that why you came back here? Out of curiosity? To see if I'd left my husband? Would that make you happy?" She was boiling now. "And why didn't you bring this to the shop?" She held out the brown bag with Ian's pants in it.

"I did. I was there yesterday. They told me that you don't work there anymore. True?" She nodded.

"I don't. So now what?" She looked him in the eye again and suddenly almost a year of fear vanished. He could try to do anything he wanted and she'd kill him. With pleasure. It was a relief to confront him. She looked at him again and six months of pain passed from her eyes to his. It was a naked vision he saw there, of a human being badly scarred, and he took a long drag on his cigarette and looked away.

"What time are you leaving on your trip? Have you got time for lunch?" Oh, Jesus. It was almost laughable, except that it still made her want to cry.

She shook her head slowly, looking down, and then slowly she looked up again as tears filled her eyes and slid down her cheeks. It was over now. The last of the anger and the horror and the terror and the pain slid slowly down her cheeks; the trial and the jury and the verdict and the arrest and Inspector Houghton all melted into silent tears, pouring slowly down her face. He couldn't bear to look at her. It was much worse than a slap in the face. He was sorry he had come. Very sorry.

She took a deep breath, but she did nothing about the tears. She needed them to wash all the filth away. "I'm leaving this town to get away from a nightmare, Inspector. Not to celebrate it. Why would we possibly want to have lunch together? To talk about old times? To reminisce about the trial? To talk about my husband? To . . ." A sob caught in her throat and she leaned against the wall with her eyes closed, the paper bag still clutched in her hand. It was all rushing in on her again. He had brought it all back in a brown paper bag. She put a hand to her forehead, squeezed her eyes tightly shut, took a slow breath, and then opened her eyes again. He was gone. She heard the door to his car slam shut at that precise moment, and a moment later the green sedan pulled away. Inspector Houghton never looked back. She closed the front door slowly and sat down in the living room.

The trousers she pulled out of the bag had large holes carefully cut out of them at the crotch, where the police lab had tested the fabric for sperm. As she looked at them she remembered that first time she had seen Ian in jail, in the white pajama bottoms. The pants were a great good-bye present.

But now she knew once again why she was

leaving town. And she was glad. As long as she stayed it would all have stayed with her. In some form or other. She would always have wondered if Houghton might appear again. Sometime. Somewhere. Somehow. He was gone now. Forever. As was the nightmare. And the trial. All of it. Even Ian. But she had had to leave it all. There was no carving the good from the bad anymore. It was all bad, corrupt, venomous, cancerous. And suddenly she wasn't even angry at Ian anymore. Or at Inspector Houghton. She dried her face and looked around the room and realized something. It wasn't hers anymore. None of it was. Not the pants, not the problems, not the inspector, not even the bad memories. They no longer belonged to her. They belonged in the garbage with the trousers she held in her hand. She was leaving. She had left.

It was all behind her now. His papers in the studio. Her old check stubs filed in boxes in the basement. She was leaving all of that forever. What she was taking with her were the beautiful moments, the tender memories from long before, the portrait of Ian that she had painted when they were first married — she couldn't leave that with the new tenants — favorite books, cherished treasures. Only the good stuff. She had decided that was all she had room for anymore. To hell with Inspector Houghton. She was almost glad he had come. Now she knew she was free. Not wanting to be free, or trying to be free, or working at being free. But free.

CHAPTER 35

Leaving San Francisco was easier than she had thought it would be. She wouldn't let herself think. She just got on the highway and kept driving. No one had come to wave handkerchiefs or cry bitter tears and she was glad.

After Inspector Houghton's visit, she had had a cup of tea, finished the dishes, put on her shoes, checked the house and the windows one last time, and left.

The drive south was lovely, and she felt young and adventurous when she reached her decaying house on the old North Road. And she was touched when she went inside and saw what Aunt Beth had done. The house was spotlessly clean, and the sleeping bag she had left there earlier was unnecessary. There was a narrow bed in the bedroom with a bright patchwork quilt carefully folded at the foot. It was the one from her bedroom at Aunt Beth's. A young girl's

Victorian desk stood in a corner, and two lamps made the room bright. The kitchen was stocked, and there were two rocking chairs and a large table in the living room, and a large easy chair by the fire. There were candles all around, and logs near the fire. She had everything she needed.

And dinner with Aunt Beth the next day was a jovial affair. She had spent the first night alone in the new house. She had wanted it that way, and had wandered from room to room like a child, not feeling lonely, only excited. It was like the beginning of an adventure. She felt reborn.

"Well, how do you like it? Are you ready to go home yet?" Aunt Beth chuckled with her over tea.

"Not on your life. I'm ready to stay here forever. And thanks to you, the house is as cozy as can be."

"It'll take more than that to make it cozy, my dear."

But what Jessica had sent in the two crates helped a bit. Photographs, planters, a little marble owl, a collection of treasured books, two bright paintings, and the portrait of Ian. There were also blankets and brass candlesticks, and odds and ends that she loved. And she filled the house with plants and bright flowers. At the end of the week, she added to her old treasures with a few new ones she acquired at auction. Two low roughhewn tables, and an oval hooked rug. She put them in the living room and stood back, looking pleased. It looked more like home every day. She had sent books in the trunks, and her painting things were set up in a corner, but she hadn't had time to paint anything yet. She was too busy with the house.

The foreman's son from Aunt Beth's spent the weekend pulling weeds and mowing the lawn, and they had even discovered a crumbling gazebo far out in the back. And now she wanted a swing. Two of them. One to hang from a tall tree near the gazebo, where she could swing high and watch the sunset on the hills, and another to sit in front of the house, the kind on which young couples sat and whispered "I love you's" on warm summer nights, creaking slowly back and forth, sure that they were unique in the world.

The letter from Ian came on Saturday morning. She had been in her new house for six days.

And there you are, funny girl, with dust in your hair and a smudge on your nose, grinning with pride at the order you're making from chaos. I can see you now, barefoot and happy, with a cornstalk in your teeth. Or wearing your Guccis and hating it? What's it like? I can see the house perfectly now, though I can't imagine you happy in a sleeping bag on the floor. Don't tell me you've gotten that rugged! But it sounds lovely, Jessie, and it will do you good. Though I was shocked to hear about the shop. Won't you miss it? Sounds like a hell of a good price, though. What'll you do with that pile of bucks? At this end, I'm hearing news about the making of a movie from the book. Don't hold your breath; I'm not. Those things never happen. They just get talked about. Though on the other hand, I never thought you'd sell the shop. How does that feel? Painful, I'll bet, but maybe a relief? Time to do other things. Travel, paint, clean up that palace you've saddled yourself with for the summer — or longer? I heard something in the tone of your last letter. It sounds like love for the house, and the country around it, and Aunt Beth. She must be a remarkable woman. And how are the ants and the lizards so far? Staying away? Or all wearing your best hair spray and loving it?

She chuckled as she read; once she had tried to kill a lizard in their hotel room in Florida with her hair spray. They had asphyxiated themselves out of the room, but the lizard had loved it.

She finished reading the letter and went to sit at the large table Aunt Beth had provided. She wanted to tell him about the things Aunt Beth had put in the house, and the goodies she'd found at auction. It didn't seem fair to let him think she was sleeping on the floor.

The correspondence got under way as simply as that, and without the determination of their halt in communication. She didn't think about it, she just wrote to him to give him the news. It was harmless, and she was pleased for him about the movie. Maybe this time it would happen. She hoped so, for him.

She was surprised at the length of her response. It covered six tightly written pages, and it was almost dark when she sealed the envelope and put on the stamp. She cooked dinner on the old stove, went to bed early, and got up very early the next morning. She drove into town, mailed the letter, and stopped at Aunt Beth's for a cup of coffee. But Aunt Beth was out riding.

The afternoon was quiet and pretty. Jessie

did some sketches while sitting dangling her feet on her front porch. She felt like Huck Finn's older sister, in overalls and a red T-shirt and bare feet. The sun was bright on her face and it was a beautiful day, and her hair looked like spun gold looped up in loose curls at the top of her head.

"Good afternoon, mademoiselle." Jessica jumped, the sketch pad flying from her hands. She had thought there was no one anywhere near the house. But when she looked up, she laughed. It was Geoffrey.

"My God, you scared me to death!" But she hopped lightly from the porch as he picked up her pad and looked at it with surprise.

"Great Scott, you *can* draw! But much more interesting than that, you're exquisite and I adore you!" He folded her into a great warm hug, and she smiled up at him from her bare feet in the tall grass around the house. They hadn't quite gotten up all the weeds yet. "Jessica, you look perfectly beautiful!"

"Like this?" She laughed at him, but she was slow to leave his embrace. She was just beginning to realize how much she'd missed him.

"Yes, I adore you like that. The first time I saw you, you were barefoot and had your hair looped up like that. I told you, you looked just like a Greek goddess."

"Heavens!"

"Well, aren't you going to give me the grand tour, after you've kept me at arm's length all this time?"

"Of course, of course!" She laughed delightedly, and pointed majestically toward the house. "Won't you come in?"

"In a moment." But first he drew her into his arms for a long tender kiss. "Now I'm ready to see the house." She laughed at him, and then stopped and took a long look at him.

"No, you're not."

"I'm not?" He looked confused. "Why not?"

"First take off your tie."

"Now?"

"Absolutely."

"Before we go inside?" She nodded insistently, and, smiling at her, he took off the navy blue tie dotted with white, which she correctly guessed was from Dior.

"It's a lovely tie, but you don't need it here. And I promise, I won't tell a soul you took it off."

"Promise?"

"Solemnly." She held up a hand and he kissed it. The feeling in the center of her palm was delicious.

"Oh, that was nice."

"You're a tease. All right, then, will this do?" She looked him over again but shook her head. "What?"

"Take your jacket off."

"You're impossible." But he slipped out of it, dropped it over his arm, and swept her a bow. "Satisfied, milady?"

"Quite." She imitated his accent and he laughed as, at last, he followed her inside.

She took him around room by room, holding her breath a little, afraid he might hate it. And she wanted him to love it. It was important to her. The house meant so much to her. It was symbolic of so much in her that had changed. And it was still a little bare, but she liked it that way. She had room to grow in, and to collect new things. She felt freer here than she had in San Francisco. Here, it was all new and fresh.

"Well, what do you think?"

"Not exactly overdecorated, is it?" She smiled as he chuckled, but she wanted him to like it, not make fun of it. "All right, Jessica, don't look so sensitive. It's lovely, and it ought to be great fun for a summer." But what about for a life? She hadn't said anything to him yet about staying there, but she wasn't quite sure yet either, so there was no point. And it didn't really matter. If he fell in love with her, he could fly down to see her in his plane. It would give her the weeks alone to paint and walk and think and spend time with Aunt Beth, and the weekends with him.

"What on earth are you thinking about?" She jumped as he broke into her thoughts. "You had the most outrageous little smile on your face."

"Did I?" But she couldn't tell him what she had in mind. It had to grow slowly, she couldn't sketch it all out for him ahead of time.

"You did, and I love your little house. It's sweet." But he made it sound silly, and she was disappointed. He meant well, but he just didn't understand.

"Would you like a cup of tea?" It was a hot day, but he seemed to like hot tea whatever the weather. That or Scotch. Or martinis. She already knew.

"Love some. And then, Jessica my love, I have a surprise for you."

"Do you? I love surprises! Give it to me now." She looked like a little kid again as she plonked down on the couch and waited.

"Not now. But I thought we'd do something special tonight."

"Like what?" She wanted to do something

special too, and it showed in her smile, but he let it pass.

"I want to take you down to Los Angeles; there's a party at the consulate. I thought you might rather enjoy it."

"In Los Angeles?" But why Los Angeles? She wanted to stay in the country.

"It's going to be quite a nice party. Of course, if you'd rather not . . ." But the way he said it didn't leave her much choice.

"No, no . . . I'd love to . . . but I just thought . . ."

"Well, what would we do here? I thought it would be much nicer to run down to the city for a bit. And I want to introduce you to some of my friends." He said it so nicely that she felt badly about her reluctance. It was just that she had wanted to share a quiet evening with him in the new house. But there would be other times. Lots of them.

"All right. It sounds terrific." She was going to get into the spirit of it. "What sort of party is it?"

"White tie. Late dinner. And there ought to be quite a lot of important people there."

"*White* tie? But that means tails!"

"As a rule, yes!"

"But Geoffrey, what in hell can I wear? I don't have anything here. Just a lot of country stuff."

"I thought that might be the case."

"So what'll I do?" She looked horrified. White tie? Christ. She hadn't even seen white tie since all those ridiculous deb balls her mother had made her go to fifteen years ago. And she had nothing even remotely possible to wear. Everything dressy was still in San Francisco.

"Jessica, if you won't be too cross at me, I took the liberty of . . ." He looked more nervous than she had ever seen him. He knew she had exquisite taste and he was terrified of what he had done. "I hope you won't be angry, but I just thought that under the circumstances . . . admittedly, I . . ."

"What on earth is going on?" She was half amused, half frightened.

"I bought you a dress."

"You did what?" She was dumbfounded.

"I know, it was a ridiculous thing to do, but I just assumed that you probably didn't have anything here and . . ." But she was laughing at him. She wasn't angry. "You're not cross?"

"How could I be cross? No one's ever done that for me before." Certainly not a man she barely knew. What an amazing man he was turning out to be! "That was a lovely

623

thing to do." She hugged him and laughed again. "Can I see it?"

"Of course." He bolted toward the door and returned five minutes later, as he had parked a little distance away. He had wanted to surprise her when he arrived, and the Porsche didn't lend itself well to surprises. But he was back with an enormous box in his arms, and a large bag that seemed to hold several smaller boxes.

"What on earth did you do?"

"I went shopping." He looked pleased with himself now. He dumped all of it on the couch and stood back with a breathless look of pleasure.

Jessica slowly pulled open the large box and gasped. The fabric was the most delicate she'd ever seen. It was a silk crepe, the lightest imaginable. It seemed to float through her fingers, and it was a warm ivory, which would set off her dark tan to perfection. When she took the dress out of the box, it seemed to clasp at one shoulder and leave the other bare. And when she saw the label it explained the design and the fabric. Geoffrey had bought her a couture dress, which must have cost him at least two thousand dollars.

"My God, Geoffrey!" She was speechless.

"You hate it."

"Are you kidding? It's magnificent. But how could you buy me that?"

"Do you like it, dammit?" He couldn't make head or tail out of what she was saying, and it made him nervous, waiting to find out.

"Of course I like it. I love it. But I can't accept it. That's a terribly expensive dress."

"So? You need it for tonight." She laughed at the logic.

"Not exactly. That's like wearing a new car." And a Rolls, yet.

"If you like it, I want you to wear it. Will it fit?" She considered not even trying it, but she was dying to know how it looked, how it felt. Just for a moment.

"I'll try it. But I won't keep it. Absolutely not."

"Nonsense."

But she went to try it on, and when she came back she was smiling. And the vision he saw made him smile too.

"Good heavens, you're beautiful, Jessica. I've never seen anyone look like that in a dress." It looked as though it had been made for her. "Wait, you have to try it with these." He dove into the bag of goodies and came out with a shoebox. Little ivory satin strands of sandals on delicate heels. Again, a perfect fit. Geoffrey certainly knew how to shop. A little silver and white beaded bag. All put together, it was dazzling. And they were equally overwhelmed. He with looking at her, and she to be wearing it all. She was used to good clothes, but these were extravagantly beautiful. And outrageously expensive.

"Well, it's settled, then." He looked decisive, and pleased. "Where's my tea?"

"You don't expect me to serve tea in this, do you?"

"No. Take it off."

"Yes, love, and I'm going to keep it off. It's so pretty, but I just can't."

"You can and you will, and I won't discuss it. That's all."

"Geoffrey, I . . ."

"Quiet." He silenced her with a kiss, and she had the feeling that the entire matter had been taken out of her hands. When he wanted to be, he was very forceful. "Now get me my tea."

"You're impossible." She took off the dress and got him the tea, but in the end he won. At six o'clock she got out of the tub, did her makeup and her hair, and slipped into the dress. She felt faintly as though she were prostituting herself. A two-thousand-dollar dress was no small gift. Somehow he made it seem like a scarf or a hankie, but this was no hankie. As she slipped the dress over her head, she practically drooled.

And so did he when he saw her twenty minutes later in her new bedroom doorway. The house certainly wasn't used to this sort of grandiose coming and going in its halls. Geoffrey had gone to his friends' house to change, and had come back looking impeccable in white tie and tails. His shirt front was perfectly starched. Nothing on him appeared to move. He looked like someone in a 1932 movie. And Jessica smiled when she saw him.

"You look beautiful, sir."

"Madam, you have no idea how extraordinary you look."

"I must say, this all feels pretty super. But I feel like Cinderella. Are you sure I won't turn into a pumpkin at midnight?" She was still more than a little embarrassed by the extravagance of it all, but for some reason she had let herself be swept away on the tide of his insistence. And she had to admit, it was fun.

"Are you ready to go, darling?" The "darling" was new, but she didn't mind it. She could get used to it. She supposed that she could get used to a lot of things if she tried.

"Yes, sir." She looked down at her bare hands then and wished she had both jewelry and gloves. At any event as formal as this one obviously was going to be, it seemed as though long white kid opera gloves were in order, and jewelry . . . jewelry . . . she thought of something as they started to leave. "Wait a second, Geoffrey." She had brought it with her, and she had totally forgotten it. She had hidden it, for safety's sake. But it would be perfect.

"Something wrong?"

"No, no." She smiled mysteriously and ran back into the bedroom, where she bent down carefully to look for a tiny package tied in the underside of the bed. It had been the only place she could think of. But she had wanted to bring it with her. She didn't know why, but she had wanted to. She quickly took the box from its hiding place and then opened it, pulling the soft suede jewel case out of the box, and then spilling the gem into her hand. It was more beautiful than ever, and for a moment her heart stopped as she saw it. It brought back so many painful memories, but so many nice ones as well. She could remember seeing it on her mother's hand . . . and then taking it out for Ian . . . putting it back when the trial was all over. It was her mother's emerald ring. She had never brought herself to wear it, just as a piece of jewelry, a thing, a bauble. But tonight was a night to wear it, as a thing of beauty and pride, as something special that had been given to her. Tonight it signified a new beginning to her life. It was perfect. And tears came to her eyes as she slipped it on. She felt her mother approve.

"Jessica, what are you doing? We've got quite a drive to L.A. — do hurry up."

She smiled to herself as she slipped it on her hand. It was exactly what was needed. She also had on a pair of pearl earrings that Ian had given her years ago. They were the only jewelry she had brought, except for the ring, which she really hadn't planned to wear. She caught a last glimpse in the mirror, and smiled to herself as she rushed out to join Geoffrey. "Coming!"

"Everything all right?"

"Wonderful."

"Ready?"

"Yes, sir."

"Oh, and by the way, I forgot to give you these."

"These" were two more boxes, a long thin flat one and a small cube.

"More? Geoffrey, you're crazy! What are you doing?" It was like Christmas. And why was he doing this? She didn't even want presents, but he looked so hurt when she balked that she started to open the packages. No man had ever done this to her before.

As she began with the long thin box, Geoffrey suddenly exclaimed.

"Jessica, how lovely. What an extraordinarily fine piece of jewelry." He was admiring her mother's ring, and with a trembling hand, she held it up for him to see. "It means a great deal to you, doesn't it?" She nodded, and then, after a pause, his voice softened. "Was it your engagement ring for when you were married?"

"No." She looked at him solemnly. "It was my mother's."

"Was? . . . Is she . . ." So that was why she never spoke of her family. She had told him about the brother, but she had never mentioned her parents. Now he understood.

"Yes, she and my father died only a few months apart. It's a long time ago now, I suppose, though it doesn't really feel like it. But I've never . . . I've never worn the ring, like tonight."

"I'm honored that you'd wear it with me." He pulled her face gently toward him with the tip of one finger, and kissed her ever so carefully. It made her whole body tingle. And then he stood back and smiled. "Go on. Finish opening your things." She had forgotten the boxes, and she went back to them now.

The long thin box yielded the gloves she had thought of as she was dressing. It was as though he read her mind. Again.

"You think of everything!" They made her laugh, but she was delighted as she slid one into place. "How did you know all my sizes?"

"A lady should never ask a question like that, Jessica. It implies I have too much knowledge of women."

"Aha!" The idea amused her. And she went on to the next box. This one was small enough to fit into the palm of her hand. Geoffrey was watching her with interest as she tore off the paper and got to the small navy blue leather box. It had a snap holding it closed and she flicked it open and gasped. "Jesus. Geoffrey! No!" He couldn't tell if she was angry or pleased, but he quietly took the box from her and took them out, holding the diamond teardrops to her ears.

"They're just what you need. Put them on." It was a quiet order, but Jessica took one step backward and looked at him.

"Geoffrey, I can't. I really can't." Diamonds? She hardly knew him. And the earrings were not terribly small. They were heavenly, but not at all something she could accept. "Geoffrey, I'm sorry."

"Don't be silly. Just try them for tonight. If you don't like them, you can give them back."

"But imagine if I lost one."

"Jessica, they're yours." But silently she shook her head and stood firm.

"Please." He looked so woebegone that she felt sorry for him, but she couldn't take diamonds from this man . . . she had already accepted the outfit she was wearing, which was far too expensive a gift as it was. But diamonds? Who in heaven's name was he? No matter who, she knew who *she* was, and what she could and could not do. This she could not. No. But he was looking at her so sadly that she finally wavered for an instant. "Just try them on."

"All right, Geoffrey, but I won't wear them tonight and I won't keep them. You save them. And maybe someday . . ." She tried to make him feel better about them as she reached up to take off one of her own earrings, and then she remembered that she was wearing Ian's pearls.

The pearls were much less grandiose than the diamonds, but she loved them. She tried on one of Geoffrey's sparkling teardrops and it looked dazzling on her left ear . . . but on the right ear sat the pretty little pearl

632

from the man who had loved her . . . from Ian . . .

"You don't like them." He sounded crushed.

"I love them. But not for right now."

"You looked just now as though something had made you terribly sad."

"Don't be ridiculous." She smiled, and handed him back the earring, and then leaned up to kiss him chastely on the cheek. "No man has ever been as good to me, Geoffrey. I don't quite know what to do with it all."

"Sit back and enjoy it. Now. We're off." He didn't press the point about the earrings, and they left them carefully hidden in her desk drawer. She felt relieved not to be wearing them. Geoffrey had been right. Taking off Ian's pearls would have made her sad. She wasn't quite ready to yet. It would come in time. She still clung to some of their souvenirs. Like his portrait, which now hung over the fireplace.

The party was like something in a multimillion-dollar movie. Gallons of champagne, platoons of liveried butlers, and armies of black-uniformed maids. Every two feet of inlaid marble floor space seemed to be covered by the looming shadow of an immense crystal chandelier. And pillars and columns and Aubusson rugs and Louis XV furniture, and a fortune in diamonds and emeralds and sapphires, and hundreds of minks. It was the kind of party you read about but couldn't even faintly imagine going to. And there she was, with Geoffrey. Almost everyone there was either British or famous or both. And Geoffrey seemed to know everyone. Movie stars whom Jessie had only read of in the papers ran up to greet him, promised to call him, or left lipstick on his cheeks. Ambassadors cornered him over the pâté, or urged Jessie to dance. Businessmen and diplomats, socialites and politicians, movie stars and celebrities of dubious fame. Everyone was there. It was the kind of party people worked years to get invited to. And there she was, with Geoffrey, who turned out to be not "Mr.," but "Sir."

"Why didn't you tell me?"

"Why? It's silly. Don't you think so?"

"No. And it's part of your name."

"So now you know. Does it matter?" He looked amused, and she shook her head. "All right, then. Now how about dancing with me, Lady Jessica?"

"Yes, sir. Your Majesty. Your Grace. Your Lordship."

"Oh, shut up."

The party went on until two and they stayed till the end. It was almost four when they got back to the little Victorian house tucked into the hills.

"Now I know I'm Cinderella."

"But did you have fun?"

"I had a fabulous evening." She had felt a tiny bit as though he had put her on display, like a pretty new doll, but he had introduced her to everyone, and how could she complain? How many dates give you two-thousand-dollar evening dresses and diamond earrings? What an evening. She looked down at her mother's ring again as they got out of the car. She was glad she had worn it. Not just because it was an emerald, but because it had been her mother's.

"You looked radiant tonight, Jessica. I was so proud of you."

"It was just the dress."

"Bullshit."

"What?" She gave a tired little crow of laughter and looked at him with amusement. "*Sir* Geoffrey said 'bullshit'? I didn't think you said things like that!"

"I do, and I say lots of things you don't know about, my dear."

"That sounds intriguing." They exchanged

a glance of mutual interest in front of her house. "I don't know whether to offer you brandy, coffee, tea, or aspirin. Which'll it be?"

"We can figure that out inside." She glided up the steps with the grace of a butterfly in the magnificent white dress. Even at the end of the evening, she looked like a vision, and seemed scarcely tired. She pleased him enormously. In fact, he had decided not to wait a great deal longer. She was everything he wanted, and it was time for him. He had been waiting for Jessie for a long, long time. He knew that she wasn't quite ready, but she would be very quickly. He would help her sweep the cobwebs from her present. Now and then he saw old ghosts haunting her eyes, but it was time she left them. He needed her. And she had done beautifully at the party. Everyone said so.

"Do you go to things like that often?" She stifled a yawn as she slipped out of the sandals he had given her.

"Fairly. Did you really enjoy it?"

"What woman wouldn't, for heaven's sake? Geoffrey . . . excuse me, *Sir* Geoffrey —" she grinned — "that's like being queen for a day. And everyone in the whole world was there. I must say, I was very impressed."

"So were they."

"About what?"

"About you. You were the most beautiful woman there." But she knew that wasn't true, and more than half the attention she'd gotten had been over the dress. He had equipped her well for her debut, even down to the virginal white dress. But some of the great beauties of the world had been at that party. She was hardly stiff competition. She just wasn't that kind of woman. Not the sort who drips diamonds ear to ear while dragging chinchilla behind her, in the latest Givenchy dress. Those women were in the big leagues.

"Thank you." It seemed simpler not to argue. "Tea?"

"Not really." He was looking at her pensively, a little distracted.

"Would you like me to light a fire?" She felt like sitting with him and talking, as she'd used to do with . . . no! She couldn't let herself do that.

"Who's that?" He waved to the boyish face over the fireplace, and Jessica smiled. "Your brother?"

"No. Someone else."

"Mr. Clarke?" She nodded, sober-faced now. "You still keep his portrait up?"

"I painted it."

"That's not much of a reason. Do you still

see him?" Somehow he had thought she didn't, though they had never discussed it.

"No. Not anymore."

"That's for the best." And then he did something that made Jessica's heart stop. Very quietly, without asking, without saying a word, he lifted the portrait from where it hung and set it gently down on the floor near her desk, facing the wall. "I think this is a good time to put that away, darling, don't you?" But there was no question in his voice and for a moment she was too stunned to speak. She wanted it up. She liked it. She had brought it specially from San Francisco. Or was he right? Was there no place for that anymore? There shouldn't have been, and they both knew it.

"Don't you want tea?" She couldn't think of anything else to say, and her voice was only a croak.

"No." With a gentle smile he shook his head and walked slowly toward her. He stopped in front of her and kissed her longingly. It stirred the very tip of her soul. She needed him now. He was stripping her of something she had needed to survive. And now she was beginning to need him. He couldn't take Ian from her, but he was going to, and she was letting him. They stood together, their mouths hungrily discovering each other, and ever so gently he unclasped the hook at the shoulder of her dress. As it gave, the dress fell loosely to her waist, and he lowered his mouth slowly to her breasts, as her whole body seemed to reach out to him — but something inside her said no.

"Geoffrey . . . Geoffrey . . ." He went on kissing her, and the dress fell slowly away from her. All that exquisite silk crepe lying heaped at her feet as carefully, relentlessly he undressed her. She fumbled at the hard white starched shirt front, and got nowhere. All she could reach of him was the bulge in his trousers, but even his zipper seemed to resist her. And in a moment she stood there, naked before him, and he was still fully dressed in white tie and tails.

"My God, Jessica, how beautiful you are, my love . . . beautiful, beautiful, elegant little bird . . ." He led her slowly into her bedroom, speaking loving words to her all the way, and she followed him, as though in a trance, until he laid her carefully on her bed and slowly slipped off his jacket as she waited. He seemed to purr at her, and she felt she was under his spell. He had the jacket off now, but the starched white front was still in place. It made him look like a surgeon, and as she turned her head on the pillow, something pinched her ear. She was still wearing her earrings, and she reached up to take them off and felt the pearls fall into her hand. The pearls . . . Ian's pearls . . . and here was this man undressing in front of her. He had undressed her. She was naked and he was going to be, and he had taken Ian's portrait off the wall . . .

"No!" She sat bolt upright on the bed and stared at him as though he had just thrown cold water in her face.

"Jessica?"

"No!"

He sat down next to her and folded her into his arms, but she fought free of them, still clutching the pearl earrings in her hand. "Don't be afraid, darling. I'll be gentle, I promise."

"No, no!" There were tears welling up in her throat now and she jumped past him, pulling at Aunt Beth's quilt at the foot of the bed and covering herself with it. What was wrong with her, though? For a moment she thought she was crazy. Only a few minutes before she had wanted him so desperately, or had thought she did. And now she knew that she didn't. She couldn't. Now she knew everything.

"Jessica, what in hell is going on?" She was cowering near the window, with tears running down on her face.

"I can't go to bed with you. I'm sorry . . . I . . ."

"But what happened? A moment ago . . ." For once, he looked totally baffled. This had never happened to him. Not like this.

"I know. I'm sorry. It must seem crazy, it's just that . . ."

"That what, dammit?" He stood in front of her, and he was looking very unnerved by the experience. His jacket lay strangely on the floor, as though it had been thrown there. "What happened to you?"

"I just can't."

"But, darling, I love you." He walked to her again and tried to put his arms around her, but she wouldn't let him.

"You don't love me." It was something she could sense, not something she could explain. And more importantly, she didn't love him. She wanted to love him. She knew she *should* love him. She knew that he was the kind of man women are supposed to love, and beg to marry. But she didn't, and she couldn't, and she knew she never would.

"What do you mean I don't love you? Goddammit, Jessica, I want to marry you. What sort of game do you think I've been playing? You're not the sort of woman one makes a mistress of. Do you think I'd have taken you to that party tonight if I weren't serious? Don't be absurd."

"But you don't know me." It was a plaintive wail from the corner.

"I know enough."

"No, you don't. You don't know anything."

"Breeding shows." Oh, Jesus.

"But what about my soul? What I think, what I feel, what I am, what I need?"

"We'll learn that about each other."

"Afterward?" She looked horrified.

"Some people do it that way."

"But I don't."

"You don't know what the devil you do. And if you have a brain at all, you'll marry a man who tells you what to do and when to do it. You'll be much happier that way."

"No, that's just it. I used to want that, Geoffrey, but I don't anymore. I want to give as well as take, I want to be the grown-up as well as the child. I don't want to be pushed around and shown off and dressed up. That's what you did tonight. I know you meant well, but I was nothing more than a Barbie doll, and that's all I ever would be. No! How could you!"

"I'm sorry if I offended you." He stooped down and picked up his jacket. He was beginning to wonder about her; it was almost as though she were a bit mad.

But suddenly she didn't feel mad at all.

She felt good, and she knew she was doing the right thing. Maybe no one else would think so, but she knew it.

"You don't even want children." It was a ridiculous accusation to be making at five o'clock in the morning, standing wrapped in a quilt, talking to a man in white tie and tails.

"And you do want children?"

"Maybe."

"Nonsense. The whole thing is nonsense, Jessica. But I'm not going to stand here and argue with you. You know where I stand. I love you and I want to marry you. When you come to your senses in the morning, give me a call." He looked at her pointedly, shook his head, walked to the corner, kissed the top of her head, and patted her shoulder. "Good night, darling. You'll feel better in the morning."

She didn't say a word as he left, but when he was gone she packed all of his gifts into the large white box he had brought; in the morning she would send it all over to the house where he was staying. Maybe it was an insane thing to do, but she was so sure of it. She had never been so sure of anything in her life. She had put the pearl earrings down on her night table, and now she wasn't even sleepy. She stood happy and naked in her living room, drinking steaming black coffee, as the sun rose over the hills. The portrait was back on the wall.

CHAPTER 36

"And how's your young man?" She and Aunt Beth were drinking iced tea after a long ride, and Jessica had been unusually quiet.

"What young man?" But she wasn't fooling anyone.

"I see. Are we going to play cat and mouse, or has he fallen out of the running?" Aunt Beth's eyes searched hers and Jessie ventured a smile. Cat and mouse, indeed.

"Your point. Fallen out of the running."

"Any special reason?" For once she was surprised. "I saw a rather spectacular photograph of you two, at some very posh party in L.A."

"Where in hell did you see that?" Jessica was not pleased.

"My, my. He must have fallen into considerable disfavor! I saw the photograph in the L.A. paper. Something about a consulate party, wasn't it? Quite a number of illustrious people seemed to be hovering around you too."

"I didn't notice." Jessie sounded gloomy.

"I'm impressed." And so was Jessie. But not pleasantly so. She was wondering who else had seen the picture. There was no point in being linked with Geoffrey now. Oh, well — like everything else, the gossip would die down eventually. And it was probably much harder on Geoffrey. He had to live with all those people. She didn't. "Did he do something dastardly, or was he simply a bore, or should I mind my own business?"

"Of course not. No, I just couldn't, that's the only way to put it. I wanted to make myself love him. But I couldn't. He was perfect. He had everything. He did everything. He was everything. But . . . I . . . I can't explain it, Aunt Beth. I had the feeling he was going to try to make me into what he wanted."

"That's a disagreeable feeling."

"I kept feeling that he was checking me out, like a quarterhorse. I felt so . . . so lonely with him. Isn't that crazy? And there was no reason to." She told her about the dress and the diamond earrings. "I should have been thrilled. But I wasn't. It frightened me. It was too much . . . I don't know. We were such strangers."

"Anyone will be a stranger at first." Jessica nodded pensively and finished her iced tea. "He seemed nice enough, but if that special ingredient isn't there, that special magic . . . there's really no point." It made Jessica think back to that night.

"I'm afraid I didn't back off very elegantly. I went bananas." She smiled at the memory, and the older woman laughed.

"Probably did him good. He was awfully proper."

"He certainly was. And he was wearing white tie and tails while I freaked out and practically started throwing things. I sent back all his goodies the next day."

"Did you hurl them through the window?" Beth looked greatly amused, and almost hoped that she had. Men needed excitement.

"No." She blushed for a moment. "I had one of your ranch hands take them over."

"So that's what they do with their afternoons."

"I'm sorry."

"Don't be. I'm sure whoever it was enjoyed the whole thing immensely."

They sat quietly for a moment with their iced teas, and Jessica was frowning.

"You know what bothered me too?"

"I'm anxious to hear."

647

"Stop teasing — I'm serious." But she enjoyed the banter with her friend. "He didn't want children."

"Neither do you. What bothered you about that?"

"That's a good question, but something's been happening. I don't think the idea of children frightens me so much anymore. I keep thinking that . . . I don't know, I'm too old anyway, but I keep thinking that . . ." She knew she wasn't too old, but she wanted someone to tell her so.

"You want a baby?" Beth was stunned. "Do you mean that?"

"I don't know."

"Well, it's certainly not too late at your age. You're not even thirty-two yet. But I must say, I'm surprised."

"Why?"

"Because your fear of it ran so deep. I didn't think you'd ever be sure enough of yourself to weather the competitition. What if you had a beautiful daughter? Could you bear that? Think about it. That can be very painful for a mother."

"And probably very rewarding. Doesn't that sound corny? I feel like an ass. It's been bothering me for a while, but I haven't had the courage to tell anyone. Everyone is so sure that I am what I am. Career woman, city slicker, child hater, now gay divorcee. Even when you stop being the same person, it seems as though no one will let you take the old labels off."

"Then burn them. You certainly have, though. You got rid of your husband, the shop, the city. There's not much left to change." She said it ruefully, but with affection. "And to hell with other people's labels. There's plenty we can't change, but if there are things you want to change and can, go ahead and enjoy it."

"Imagine having a baby . . ." She sat there, smiling, enjoying the thought.

"You imagine it. I can't even remember it, and I'm not sure I'd want to. I never felt very romantic on the subject, but I love Astrid very much."

"You know, it's as though I've lived several chapters of my life one way, and now I'm ready to move on. Not to throw the past out the window, but just to go on. Like a journey. We've been long enough in the same country; after a while you have to move on. I think that's what's happened. I've just moved on to different places, different needs. I feel new again, Aunt Beth. The only sad thing is that I have no one to share it with."

"You could have had Geoffrey. Just think

what you missed!" But Aunt Beth didn't think she'd missed anything either. There hadn't been enough fire in the man, enough daring and wild dreams. He was traveling a well-charted course. If nothing else, it would have been very boring. She knew Jessie had done the right thing. She wondered only at the violence of Jessie's reaction. "Something else has been bothering you lately too, hasn't it?"

"I'm not sure what you mean."

"Yes, you are. Quite sure. You're not only quite sure of what I mean, but you're quite sure of the rest. In fact, I daresay that was the problem with Geoffrey, wasn't it? It had damned little to do with him after all." Jessica was laughing, but she wouldn't say anything.

"You know me too well."

"Yes, and you're finally beginning to know yourself too. And I'm glad. But now what are you going to do about it?"

"I was thinking of going away for a couple of days."

"You don't want permission from me, do you?" Aunt Beth was laughing, and Jessica shook her head.

She began the drive at six the next morning as the sun peeked its nose over Aunt Beth's hill. She had a long way to go. Six hours, maybe seven, and she wanted to be there in time. She had worn a light shirt for the ride, and a skirt, which was cooler than pants. She had a Thermos full of iced coffee, a sandwich, a bag full of apples, and some nuts and cookies in a tin that the foreman's boy had brought her a few days before. She was fully equipped. And determined. And also afraid. They had exchanged letters two and three times a week for two months now. But letters were very different. It had been four months since she'd seen his face. Four months since he'd turned his back and walked out on her after they had both thrown rocks they should never have picked up. And so much had changed now. They were both cautious in their letters. Careful, afraid, and yet joyful. Bursts of fun would turn up on every page, silly remarks, casual references, foolishness, and then caution again, as though each was afraid to show too much to the other. They kept to safe subjects. Her house, and his book. There was still no news on the movie contract, but the book was due out in the fall. She was excited for him. As excited as he was about her house. He was careful always to call it "hers," and it was. For the moment.

They were separate people now, no longer

woven together of a single cloth. They had been blasted apart by what had happened to them, by what they had done to each other, by what neither could any longer pretend. She wondered if there was a way to come back after something like that. Maybe not, but she had to know. Now, before they waited any longer. What if he expected never to see her again? He sounded as though he had almost accepted it. He never asked for a visit. But he was going to get one. She wanted to see him, to look into his face and see what was there, not just hear the echo of his voice in the letters.

She drove up to the familiar building at one-thirty that afternoon. They checked her through, searched her handbag, and she went inside and wrote her name on a form at the desk. She took a seat and waited an endless half hour, her eyes restlessly darting between the wall clock and the door. Her heart was pounding now. She was here. And she was terrified. Why had she come? What would she say? Maybe he didn't even want to see her, maybe that was why he hadn't mentioned her coming for a visit. It was madness to have come here . . . insanity . . . stupid . . .

"Visit for Clarke . . . visit for Ian Clarke."

The guard's voice droned his name and Jessica jumped from her seat, fighting to keep her pace normal as she walked toward the uniformed man who stood sentry at the door to the visiting area. It was a different door than the one she had passed through before, and as she looked beyond she realized that Ian was in a different section now. Maybe there would be no glass window between them.

The guard unlocked the door, checked her wrist for the stamp they'd impressed on the back of her hand at the main gate, and stood aside to let her through. The door led out to a lawn dotted with benches and framed with flower beds, and there were no apparent boundaries, only a long strip of healthy-looking lawn beyond. She crossed the threshold slowly and saw couples wandering down walks on either side of the lawn. And then she saw Ian, at the far end, standing there, watching her, stunned. It was like a scene in a movie, and her feet felt like lead.

She just stood there and so did he, until a broad smile began to take over his face. He looked like a tall, gangly boy, watching her and grinning, his eyes damp, but no more so than her own. It was crazy — half a block of lawn between them and neither of them moved . . . she had to . . . she had come here to see him, to talk to him, not just to stand there and gape at him with a smile on her face. She walked slowly along the walk, and he began to walk toward her too, the smile on his face spreading further, and then suddenly, finally, at last, she was in his arms. It was Ian. The Ian she knew. It smelled like Ian, it felt like Ian, her chin fit in the same place on his shoulder. She was home.

"What happened? You run out of hair spray, or did the lizards get to be too much for you?"

"Both. I came up so you could save me." She was having a hard time fighting back tears, but so was he, and still their smiles were like bright sunshine in a summer shower.

"Jessie, you're crazy." He held her tightly and she laughed.

"I think I must be." She was clinging to him tightly. He felt so damn good. She put a hand on his head and felt the silk of his hair. She would have known it blindfolded in a room full of men. It was Ian. "Jesus, you feel good." She pulled away from him just to look at him. He looked fabulous. Skinny, a little tired, a little suntanned, and totally overwhelmed. Fabulous. He pulled her close again and nestled her head on his shoulder.

"Oh, baby, I couldn't believe it when you started writing. I'd given up hope."

"I know. I'm a shit." She felt bad suddenly for the long months of silence; now, looking right into his face, she could see how much they must have hurt him. But she had had to. "I'm a super-shit."

"Yeah, but such a beautiful super-shit. You look wonderful, Jessie. You've even gained a little weight." He held her at arm's length again and looked her over. He didn't want to let go. He was afraid she'd vanish again. He wanted to hold on to her, to make sure she was real. And back. And his. But maybe . . . maybe she had only come back to visit . . . to say hello . . . or good-bye. His eyes suddenly showed the pain of what he was thinking, and Jessica wondered what was on his mind. But she didn't know what to say. Not yet.

"Country life is making me fat."

"And happy, from the sound of your letters." He pulled her close to him again, and then pinched her nose. "Let's go sit down. My knees are shaking so bad, I can hardly stand up." She laughed at him and wiped the tears from her cheeks.

"*You're* shaking! I was afraid you wouldn't see me!"

"And pass up the chance to make the other guys drool? Don't be ridiculous." He noticed then that she was wearing the gold lima bean, and he quietly took her hand in his.

They found a bench to one side of the lawn and sat down, still holding hands. He had one arm around her, and her hand was trembling in his. And then the words began to rush out. She couldn't hold back anymore. The dam had finally given way.

"Ian, I love you. It's all so lousy without you." It sounded so corny, but that was what she had come to tell him. She was sure of it now. She knew what she wanted. And now it was a question of want more than need. She still needed him, but differently. Now she knew how much she wanted him.

"Your life doesn't sound lousy, baby. It sounds good. The country, the house . . . but . . ." He looked at her with gratitude rushing over his face. ". . . I'm glad if it's lousy, even if it's only a little bit lousy. Oh Jess . . . I'm so glad." He pulled her back into his arms.

"Do you still love me a little?" She was wearing her little-girl voice. It was so long since anyone had heard that, so long since he had. But what if he didn't want her anymore? Then what would she do? Go back to the Geoffreys of the world and the fuzzy-haired idiot playwrights from New York? And the emptiness of a house and a gazebo and a swing and a world made for Ian . . . but without him? What was there to go back to? Staring at his portrait? Thinking of his voice? Wearing the pearl earrings he'd given her?

"Hey, lady, you're drifting. What were you thinking?"

"About you." She looked him square in the eyes. She needed to know. "Ian, do you still love me?"

"More than I can ever tell you, babe. What do you think? Jessie, I love you more than I ever did. But you wanted the divorce, and it seemed fair. I couldn't ask you to live through all this." He gestured vaguely to the prison behind him. It brought worry to her eyes.

"What about you? Are you surviving it?" She pulled away to look at him again. He looked a lot thinner. Healthy, but much thinner.

"I'm making it a lot better than I thought I would. Ever since I finished the book. They're letting me teach in the school now, and I'm due . . ." He seemed to hesitate, looked at something over her head, and took a deep breath. "I'm due for an early hearing

657

in September. They might let me go. In fact, it's almost certain they will. Through some kind of miracle, they've knocked out the famous California indeterminate sentence since I've been here, and as a first-time offender my time could be pretty much up, if they're amenable. So it looks like I could be coming home pretty soon."

"How soon could it be?"

"Maybe six weeks. Maybe three or four months. Six months at worst. But that's not the point, Jess. What about all the rest of it? What about us? My being in prison wasn't our only problem."

"But so much has changed." He knew it was true. He had heard it in her letters, knew it from what she'd done, and now he could see it in her face. She was more woman than she had ever been before. But something magical also told him that she was still his. Part of her was. Part of her belonged only to Jessie now, but he liked it that way. She had been that way long, long ago. But she was better now. Richer, fuller, stronger. She was whole. And if she still wanted him now, they would really have something. And he had grown a lot too.

"I think a lot has changed, Jess, but some of it hasn't and some of it won't. And maybe it's more than you want to mess with. You could do a lot better." He looked at her, wondering about the photograph he'd seen in the paper. He had seen the same article Beth had. And if she could have Sir Geoffrey Whatnot, why the hell did she still want him?

"Ian, I like what I've got. If I've still got it. And I couldn't do better. I don't want to do better. You're everything I want."

"I don't have any money."

"So?"

"Look, I got a ten-thousand-dollar advance for the book, and half of that went for your new car. And the other five thousand won't go very far when I get out. You'll be stuck supporting me again. And baby, I have to write. I really know that. It's something I have to do, even if I have to wait table in some dive to support myself in the meantime. There's no way I'll give up writing, though, to be 'respectable.' " He looked rueful but firm. And Jessie looked impatient.

"Who gives a damn about 'respectable'? I made a fortune selling the shop to Astrid. What the hell difference does it make now who earns what doing what, for what . . . so what, dummy? What do you think I'll do with that money now? Wear it? We could do such nice things with it." She was thinking of the house. And other things.

"Like what?" He smiled at the sound of her voice and held her closer.

"All kinds of things. Buy the house in the country, fix it up a little. Go to Europe . . . have a baby . . ." She turned her face and smiled at him, nose to nose.

"What did you say?"

"You heard me."

"I'm not so sure I did. Are you serious?"

"I think so." She smiled mysteriously and kissed him.

"What brought that on?"

"A simple process, darling. I've grown up since I saw you last. And it's just something I've been thinking about lately. And I realized something else. I don't just want 'a baby.' I want *your* baby. Our baby. Ian . . . I just want you, with kids, without kids, with money, without . . . I don't know how else to tell you. I love you." Two huge tears slid down her face and she looked at him so intensely that he wanted to hold her forever.

He threw his arms around her and held her to him with a huge smile on his face. "You know what's going to happen, Jess? Any minute, some asshole with a flashlight is going to walk up to me, it's going to be two in the morning, and I'm going to wake up, holding my pillow. Because this can't be real. I've dreamed it too often. It's not happening. I want it to be, but . . . tell me it's for real."

"It's for real . . . but you're breaking my left arm."

"Sorry." He pulled away from her for a moment and they both laughed. "Sweetheart, I love you. I don't even care if you want a baby anymore. I love you, in that ramshackle empty house you got yourself, or in a palace, or wherever. And aside from that, I happen to think you're nuts. I don't know what made you come back, but I'm so damn glad you did."

"So am I." She threw her arms around him again, nibbled his ear, and then bit him. "I love you," she whispered it in his ear, and he pinched her. It had been so long since he'd even touched her, held her, felt her. Even pinching and biting felt good. It was all such a luxury now. "Christ, Ian, what's the matter with you?"

"What do you mean?" He looked suddenly worried.

"You didn't even yell when I pinched you. You always yell when I pinch you. Don't you love me anymore?" But her eyes were dancing as they hadn't in years. Maybe as they never had before, Ian thought.

"You came up here for me to yell at you?"

"Sure. And so I could yell at you. And hug

you and kiss you, and beg you to get the hell out of here and come home, for Chrissake. So will you please, dammit? Will you!" Jesus. Twelve hours ago, she hadn't even been sure he still wanted her. But he did! Thank God he did!

"I will, I will. What's your hurry? What do you have, snakes in that place? Spiders? That's why you want me, right? The exterminator — I know your type."

"Bullshit. No spiders, no snakes, but . . ." She grinned.

"Aha!"

"Ants. I walked into the kitchen the other night to make a peanut-butter sandwich, and I screamed so loud, I . . . what are you laughing at? Goddam you, what are you laughing at?" And then suddenly she was laughing too, and he had his arms around her and he was kissing her again, and they were both laughing through their tears. The war was over.

And eight weeks later, he was home.

The employees of Thorndike Press hope you have enjoyed this Large Print book. All our Thorndike, Wheeler, and Kennebec Large Print titles are designed for easy reading, and all our books are made to last. Other Thorndike Press Large Print books are available at your library, through selected bookstores, or directly from us.

For information about titles, please call:
  (800) 223-1244

or visit our Web site at:
  http://gale.cengage.com/thorndike

To share your comments, please write:
  Publisher
  Thorndike Press
  10 Water St., Suite 310
  Waterville, ME 04901

663